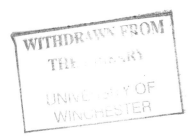

WOMEN
AND SPORT

INTERDISCIPLINARY
PERSPECTIVES

D. Margaret Costa, PhD
Sharon R. Guthrie, PhD
California State University–Long Beach

Editors

Human Kinetics

Library of Congress Cataloging-in-Publication Data

Women and sport : interdisciplinary perspectives / D. Margaret Costa,
editor, Sharon R. Guthrie, editor.
    p.   cm.
    Includes index.
    ISBN 0-87322-686-0
    1. Sports for women.   2. Sports for women--Social aspects.
3. Sports for women--Physiological aspects.   4. Sports for women-
-Psychological aspects.   I. Costa, D. Margaret, date.
II. Guthrie, Sharon Ruth, date.
GV709.W56   1994
796'.0194--dc20   93-50167
                                          CIP

ISBN: 0-87322-686-0

Acquisitions Editor: Richard D. Frey, PhD; **Developmental Editor:** Marni Basic; **Assistant Editors:** Julie Lancaster, Julie Marx, Dawn Roselund, Hank Woolsey; **Copyeditor:** Elisabeth Boone; **Proofreaders:** Sue Fetters and Anne Meyer Byler; **Indexer:** Theresa J. Schaefer; **Production Manager:** Kris Ding; **Typesetter:** Sandra Meier; **Text Designer:** Keith Blomberg; **Layout Artist:** Tara Welsch; **Photo Editor:** Karen Maier; **Cover Designer:** Keith Blomberg; **Photographer (cover):** © ALLSPORT USA/Dan Smith; **Illustrator:** Thomas E. Janowski; **Printer:** Braun-Brumfield

Printed in the United States of America

10 9 8 7 6 5 4 3 2 1

Human Kinetics
P.O. Box 5076, Champaign, IL 61825-5076
1-800-747-4457

Canada: Human Kinetics, Box 24040, Windsor, ON N8Y 4Y9
1-800-465-7301 (in Canada only)

Europe: Human Kinetics, P.O. Box IW14, Leeds LS16 6TR, England
(44) 532 781708

Australia: Human Kinetics, Unit 5, 32 Raglan Avenue, Edwardstown 5039, South Australia
(08) 371 3755

New Zealand: Human Kinetics, P.O. Box 105-231, Auckland 1
(09) 309 2259

This book is dedicated to my husband Joe, my children Robyn and Dean, and their spouses David and Sandi, all of whom continue to enrich my life through support of and participation in my many intellectual and physical pursuits.

D.M.C.

This book is dedicated to my parents, Ruth and Keith Guthrie, who taught me the importance of mind-body excellence and committing my energies to humanitarian concerns.

S.R.G.

Contents

Preface

As we approach the 21st century, we are experiencing an exciting time for women. Throughout the world there have been dramatic changes in the roles of women, in attitudes toward women, and most importantly, in women's perceptions of themselves. In many circles, women are gaining political, economic, and social power, and feminist spirit is on the rise. Rapidly expanding opportunities for women in sport are an important part of this context, as is the growing body of scholarship about women's sporting experiences.

Although women have made incredible progress, the road forward has been paved with numerous setbacks and disappointments. If equality with men is to become a reality, there is still much to be accomplished. Although the body of knowledge about women has grown exponentially, there is far more to be learned that is presently unknown and much to be corrected in previous historical accounts. This book reflects our desire to advance these processes.

Women and Sport: Interdisciplinary Perspectives has evolved from more than a decade of teaching courses on women in sport for both women's studies and physical education departments, athletes and nonathletes, physical education majors and nonmajors, and women and men.

Although the courses have been taught at the undergraduate level for general education credit, they also have stimulated graduate student research on topics ranging from homophobia to corporate sponsorship. As a result, thousands of students have helped inspire and create a need for this text.

We designed this book as a scholarly text for those studying women's sporting experiences from a variety of perspectives. We examine three major subdisciplinary areas in sport and exercise science: historical and cultural foundations, biomedical considerations, and psychological and social dimensions. All of the authors were selected for their expertise and prior contributions to the body of knowledge about women in sport. They also were selected because of their willingness to take scholarly yet provocative approaches to the subject matter.

Women and Sport is envisioned as a benchmark book for students, as well as scholars and researchers in the field. We hope the information presented, the questions raised, and the implications for future research and practice suggested will serve as catalysts for further discussion and research and thereby facilitate the progress of sporting women in the 21st century.

Acknowledgments

We would like to acknowledge the early and ongoing support of our colleagues whose feminist scholarship and leadership continues to inspire us: Betty Brooks, Shirley Castelnuovo, Norma Chinchilla, Betty Edmondson, Consuelo Nieto, Patricia Rozée, and Sharon Sievers.

Special thanks is also given to Bonita Hester, Shirley Ito, Carmen Rivera, Michael Salmon, and Wayne Wilson of the Paul Ziffren Sports Resource Center at the Amateur Athletic Foundation of Los Angeles. Without their tireless assistance with research and referencing, this book would not have been possible.

Many of the rare pictures in the historical section were procured with the diligent assistance of Sally Fox. We are extremely grateful for the generous time and effort that she put into that procurement.

Significant developmental and editing support was given by Human Kinetics staff Rick Frey, Marni Basic, Julie Lancaster, Julie Marx, Dawn Roselund, Hank Woolsey, and Karen Maier, and by freelancers Elisabeth Boone, Anne Meyer Byler, and Sue Fetters. Thanks for a job well done.

Credits

Figure 2.1 from *The Partnership Way* by R. Eisler and D. Loye. Copyright © 1990 by Riane Eisler and David Loye. Reprinted by permission of HarperCollins Publishers, Inc.

Figure 2.2 © D + I Mathioulakis, Andromedas Street, Vyrouas 16231 Athens, Greece. Tel. 7661351.

Figure 2.3 is from *Women in Antiquity* by C. Seltman, 1955, New York: St. Martin's Press.

Figure 2.4 is from the collection of the Cleveland Museum of Art, purchased from the J.H. Wade Fund.

Figure 3.3 is from *Men, Maidens and Manners a Hundred Years Ago* by J. Ashton, 1888, London: Field and Tuer.

Figure 8.1 is from the Paula Welch Collection, courtesy of Phillip Dunne.

Figure 12.1 is from "Alterations in Strength, Body Composition, and Anthropometric Measurements Consequent to a 10 Week Weight Training Program" by J.H. Wilmore, 1974, *Medicine and Science in Sports*, **6**, 133-138. Adapted by permission.

Figure 13.1 is from "Effects of Exercise Training on Sex Steroids: Endocrine Profile and Clinical Implications" by M.J. De Souza, J.C. Arce, and J.C. Nulsen, 1992, *Infertility and Reproductive Medicine Clinics of North America*, **3**, 131. Reprinted by permission.

Figure 13.2 is from *Clinical Endocrinology* (p. 12.12) by G.M. Besser and A.G. Cudworth,

1987, London: Gower Medical Publishing Ltd. Reprinted by permission.

Figure 13.3 is from *Clinical Gynecologic Endocrinology & Infertility* (p. 81) by L. Speroff, R.H. Glass, and N.G. Kase, 1983, Baltimore: Williams & Wilkins. © 1983 the Williams & Wilkins Co., Baltimore. Reprinted by permission.

Figure 13.4 is from *Lecture Notes on Gynaecology* (p. 242) by J. Barnes, 1980, London: Blackwell Scientific Publications. Reprinted by permission.

Figure 13.5 is from "Effects of Exercise Training on Sex Steroids: Endocrine Profile and Clinical Implications" by M.J. De Souza, J.C. Arce, and J.C. Nulsen, 1992, *Infertility and Reproductive Medicine Clinics of North America*, **3**, 131. Reprinted by permission.

Figure 13.6 is from "Alterations in the Hypothalamic-Pituitary-Ovarian and the Hypothalamic-Pituitary-Adrenal Axes in Athletic Women" by A.B. Loucks, J.F. Mortola, L. Girton, and S.S.C. Yen, 1989, *Journal of Clinical Endocrinology and Metabolism*, **68**, 408. Copyright 1989 by The Endocrine Society. Reprinted by permission.

Figure 13.7 is from "Alterations in the Hypothalamic-Pituitary-Ovarian and the Hypothalamic-Pituitary-Adrenal Axes in Athletic Women" by A.B. Loucks, J.F. Mortola, L. Girton, and S.S.C. Yen, 1989, *Journal of Clinical Endocrinology and*

Metabolism, **68**, 408. Copyright 1989 by The Endocrine Society. Reprinted by permission.

Figure 14.1 is from *A Colour Atlas of Bone Disease* (p. 35) by V. Parsons, 1980, London: Wolfe Medical. Adapted by permission.

Figure 14.2 is from ''Local and Systemic Factors in the Pathogenesis of Osteoporosis'' by L.G. Raisz, 1988, *New England Journal of Medicine,* **318**, 820. Copyright 1988 by the Massachusetts Medical Society. Reprinted, by permission of the New England Journal of Medicine.

Figure 14.3 is from *Osteoporosis: A Clinical Guide* (p. 41) by A.D. Woolf and A.S. Dixon, 1988, Philadelphia: J.B. Lippincott Co. Reprinted by permission.

Figure 14.4 is from ''Humeral Hypertrophy in Response to Exercise'' by H.H. Jones, J.D. Priest, and W.C. Hayes, 1977, *Journal of Bone and Joint Surgery*, **59**, 204-208. Reprinted by permission.

Figure 14.5 is reproduced from ''Differential Changes in Bone Mineral Density of the Apendicular and Axial Skeleton'' by B.L. Riggs, H.W. Wahner, W.L. Dann, R.B. Mazees, K.P. Offord, and L.J. Melton, 1981, *Journal of Clinical Investigation*, **67**, 328-335. Reprinted by permission.

Figure 14.6 is from ''Bone Mineral Content of the Lumbar Spine in Normal and Osteoporotic Women: Cross-Sectional and Longitudinal Studies'' by B. Krølner and S. Pors Nielsen, 1982, *Clinical Science*, **62**, 331. Copyright 1982 by the Medical Research Society and the Biochemical Society. Reprinted by permission.

Table 10.1 is from *Evaluation and Regulation of Body Build and Composition* by A.R. Behnke and J.H. Wilmore, 1974, Englewood Cliffs, NJ: Prentice Hall. Adapted by permission.

Table 11.2 is adapted from *Exercise Testing and Training of Apparently Healthy Individuals:*

A Handbook for Physicians by the American Heart Association, 1972, Dallas: American Heart Association.

Table 12.1 and Figure 12.2 data are from *Changes in Strength, Power, and Anthropometry Following Universal Gym and Hydra-Fitness Training in Women* by L. Smurl, 1987, unpublished master's thesis, University of Massachusetts, Amherst.

Table 16.1 is from ''Beyond Androgyny: Some Presumptuous Prescriptions for a Liberated Sexual Identity'' by S.L. Bem. In *Psychology of Women: Future Directions for Research* (pp. 1-23) by J. Sherman and F. Denmark (Eds.), 1978, New York: Psychological Dimensions.

Table 16.2 is from ''Sex Roles and Achievement'' by R.L. Helmreich and J.T. Spence, 1977, *Psychology of Motor Behavior and Sport*, **2**, 33-46. Reprinted by permission.

Photo Credits

Figure 14.7a x-rays are courtesy of Barbara A. Kammer, MD, Department of Radiology, Carle Clinic Association, Urbana, IL.

Figure 14.7b x-rays are courtesy of Barbara A. Kammer, MD, Department of Radiology, Carle Clinic Association, Urbana, IL.

Figure 15.1 is courtesy of Esther Fujimoto, photo by Yoshitaro Sakai.

Figure 18.2 is courtesy of Sharon R. Guthrie.

Figure 19.1 is courtesy of Keith Ian Polakoff.

Figure 21.2 is courtesy of Louisiana Tech University Sports Information Office.

Figure 22.1 © Tim McKinney. Courtesy of Cornell University Sports Information Office/ Athletics and Physical Education.

Figure 22.2 is from Indianapolis Motor Speedway Corporation.

Part I

Historical and Cultural Foundations of Women's Sport

W omen's sport history has three sources: history in all of its forms, the tradition of sport, and the feminist movement. Until the 1960s, historians rarely paid attention to sport and almost never to women's sport. The notable exceptions to this disregard were works by early 20th-century historians: John Allen Krout's *Annals of American Sport* (1929), Herbert Manchester's *Four Centuries of Sport in America*, and Foster Rhea Dulles' *America Learns to Play* (1940). Into these histories were woven intriguing narratives that were directed at a male audience and emphasized the excitement, competitiveness, and drama of sport. Other early works that could be characterized as sport history were written by journalists and officials who were mainly concerned with the tradition of sport, that is, record-breaking performances and stories of heroism as well as the accumulation of statistics for purposes of debate.

Works by, about, and for women have existed since Abigail Adams's 1776 "Remember the Ladies" letter to her husband, John Adams, which suggested that the "ladies" would rebel if they were overlooked by the Second Continental Congress.[1] Ever since that time, those in power have been nudged to "remember the ladies" by such writers as Judith Murray (1751-1820), Mary Wollstonecraft (1759-1797), Frances Wright (1795-1852), Lucretia Mott (1793-1880), Harriet Martineau (1802-1876), Margaret Fuller (1810-1850), John Stuart Mill (1806-1873), Elizabeth Blackwell (1821-1910), Susan B. Anthony (1820-1906), Elizabeth Cady Stanton (1815-1902), Jane Addams (1860-1935), Margaret Sanger (1883-1960), Virginia Woolf (1882-1941), Margaret

Mead (1901-1969), and Simone de Beauvoir (1908-1982), as well as contemporaries Gerda Lerner, Carol Dubois, Vicki Ruiz, Rochelle Gatlin, and Patricia Williams.[2]

Before the 1970s, material about women's sport was found in such popular magazines as *Godey's Lady's Book* (a fashion and advice magazine published throughout the 19th century) and *Atlantic Monthly*, which included "opinion" essays on appropriate behavior; in biographies of famous women athletes written by journalists as commentary on record-breaking performances (often identifying the woman athlete as being atypical); and in medical journals in the form of admonitions to women and girls about the dangers of sport participation.

Inspired by de Beauvoir's *The Second Sex* (1957)[3] and empowered by their own sporting experiences, women were already writing their own sport histories at the time of the first North American history of sport conference at The Ohio State University in 1972. At that conference Virginia Evans' "Women's Sport in the 1920 Era" and Ellen Gerber's "The Controlled Development of Collegiate Sport for Women" were eagerly received by the women in attendance. In that same year Gerber, a noted feminist sport historian, offered the first women and sport course (University of Massachusetts) and published the first article on women's sport history in the first edition of the *Journal of Sport History*.[4]

Over the past two decades, research on women's sport history has developed from important descriptive studies of the participation of middle- and upper-class women to the current offerings, which use a variety of methodologies. The most recent suggest that since its inception, sport has been a source of social, racial, and sexual tension. As more sources become available, themes will continue to broaden and the history of all sporting women will be told in accordance with the periodization of women, which was not necessarily the same for men.

The eight papers that comprise this section represent a number of important themes, the most

central of which emphasizes maintenance of the patriarchal social order to the virtual exclusion of women and sport. Other themes are the dominant influences of class, race, and gender that have shaped public perceptions of women's sport experience; the use of women's sport participation to promote political ideology, such as occurred during the "cold war" Olympic Games; and the co-optation of women's recreational practices to encourage socially desirable but medically dangerous body images. This section therefore stands as a necessary corrective to the conceptual and content inadequacy of general sport history texts, which omit or diminish the rich variety of women's sport experiences.

In chapter 1, Catriona Parratt opens with a discussion of male-defined sport history scholarship, then proceeds to acquaint the reader with the terrain of women's sport history by presenting the theoretical models that have been used to correct the historical record on women and sport. Parratt further familiarizes the reader with the tenets of feminist scholarship, namely those that focus on gender as a central category of historical research. Finally, Parratt pleads for a critical analysis of the literature on women and sport.

June Kennard and John Marshall Carter in chapter 2 provide a revisionist examination of the belief that sport began with the Greeks and continued unabated in its male-dominated form through the Renaissance. They introduce the reader to the splendid women's sporting heritage of the partnership societies of the Goddesses and acquaint us with letters, court documents, legal records, birth announcements, obituaries, and poems, all of which provide information about the medieval sporting woman.

With a compelling description and analysis of the setting—17th- and 18th-century Europe—Roberta Park in chapter 3 introduces the initial ideology of the early 17th century, illuminates the changes that occurred through the 18th century, and analyzes the ways these developments affected women's sport participants. Class, gender, cultural context, and educational offerings all are examined for their influence on women's lives and consequently their sport participation.

Nancy Struna in chapter 4 presents a mosaic of the lifestyles of our colonial forebearers. She also explores the connections among recreational activities, work tasks, social practices, behaviors, and the changes that occurred in America through the 18th century. In addition, Struna's discussion of regional differences, gender concepts, and the historical underpinnings of the sports that were adopted in the colonies, provides bases from which the reader can evaluate the lifestyle of the colonial woman.

Chapter 5 focuses on women's health and exercise and on efforts to portray exercise as unnatural and therefore not in the best interests of 19th-century America. Patricia Vertinsky clearly demonstrates how the idealism of the time period had little grounding in reality. Biological and medical thought was used to "prove" that a desirable social condition, the inherent weakness of women, was the norm for middle- and upper-class women. At the same time, women of the working and agricultural classes toiled daily in the fields and factories of Victorian-era America.

In chapter 6 Joan Hult explores gender constructs, the continuing influence of the medical profession, the birth of public vocations for women in physical education, assumptions about appropriate female behavior, changing concepts of health and beauty, the separatist practices of women physical educators as they tried to "protect the ladies" from the evils of competition, and the power relations in athletic governance that developed in reaction to the passage of Title IX.

Catapulted into the work force by economic necessity in the early 1800s, by the end of the century working women throughout America were organizing, practicing, and competing in sports leagues. In chapter 7 Lynne Emery examines the industries that provided the jobs as well as the companies that sponsored sports teams to improve the morale and health of their women workers. Emery also analyzes the reasons for this altruism and examines the equalitarian nature of

the competition as well as the organizational structure of the industries and the competition.

The modern Olympic Games were reconstituted in 1896, but it was not until 1900 that women participated. In chapter 8 Paula Welch and D. Margaret Costa trace a century of women's Olympic competition, from the chance participation of the first women Olympians to the struggles spurred by racism, classism, and gender constructs of subsequent eras. The authors also examine the influence of organizational structures on the Olympic experience and introduce the reader to the achievements and battles of renowned women Olympians. Nowhere in sports are social convention, biomedical determinism, and political influence more obvious than in the saga of women's Olympic competition.

Throughout this section's historical introduction to women in sport there is an emphasis on the gender, class, and social constructs that permeated the sporting experiences of women. Political and social mores are examined to demonstrate their influence on the discord and harmony, the continuity and instability, the achievements and the failures of women on the playing fields and in the gymnasiums of America. Presenting the saga of women's sporting experiences from a gender-centered point of view realigns sport history to the center of the gender divide.

Notes

[1]*The Adams Papers, Series II, Adams Family Correspondence*, ed. L.H. Butterfield (Cambridge: Harvard University Press, 1963), 76-402.

[2]See *The Feminist Papers*, ed. Alice S. Rossi (Boston: Northeastern University Press, 1988), xv; Gerder Lerner, *Teaching Women's History* (New York: American Historical Society, 1981); *Unequal Sisters: A Multicultural Reader in U.S. Women's History*, ed. Carol DuBois and Vicki L. Ruiz (New York:

Routledge, 1990); Rochelle Gatlin, *American Women Since 1945* (Jackson, MS: University Press of Mississippi, 1987); Patricia Williams, *The Alchemy of Race and Rights* (Cambridge: Harvard University Press, 1991).

[3]Simone de Beauvoir, *The Second Sex* (New York: Alfred A. Knopf, 1957).

[4]Ellen Gerber, ''The Controlled Development of Collegiate Sport for Women, 1923-1936,'' *Journal of Sport History*, **2**(1): 1-28.

Chapter 1

From the History of Women in Sport to Women's Sport History: A Research Agenda

Catriona M. Parratt

Has our literature moved beyond the parochial to the universal questions which historians ask; has it begun to suggest what "ultimate difference" women's sporting experience makes in our "total understanding of the human experience"? Is it contributing to theoretical debate and methodological innovation?

NANCY L. STRUNA
"Beyond Mapping Experience:
The Need for Understanding in the History of American Sporting Women"

Struna posed the questions I have quoted in a 1984 commentary on the state of scholarship in American women's sport history. Although research in the field has begun to move in the directions outlined by Struna, I maintain it still has some way to go before her questions can be answered yes.

Over the past decade or so, historians have begun to devote more attention to women and their sport experiences. Yet despite signs of development, there are problems with the current scholarship that must be addressed if the field is to continue to flourish. With few exceptions, historians of women's sport have not tackled critical conceptual and methodological issues; rather, their tendency has been to accept the assumptions and use the constructs of a male-defined and male-dominated scholarship. Research grounded in such a framework provides only limited insights into women's experiences of sport and, more serious, distorts our understanding of the significance of those experiences. The central question I examine in this chapter is, How might these limitations be overcome?

Feminist history provides a powerful model for reshaping women's sport history. Forging a link between the two not only will help contextualize research on women's sport but, more important, will help place women at the center of that research. Ultimately, the goal should be to incorporate both women and men fully and to examine sport's role in shaping their social relationships. For now, the most pressing task is to remake women's sport history into "a women-centred history—a history seen through the eyes of women and validated by women's values."[1]

To achieve this end, several steps need to be taken:

- Move away from compensatory and contribution history.
- Reexamine traditional models of periodization.
- Redefine and expand basic concepts such as sport.
- Make gender a central category of research.
- Recognize the importance of feminist theory.

I will consider each of these matters in turn, look at feminist historians' approaches to them, and suggest how feminist history might inform scholarship in women's sport history.

Beyond Compensatory and Contribution History

During the late 1960s and early 1970s, feminists embarked on a sustained critique of historians' traditional ways of researching and writing about women. Lerner, a pioneer of feminist scholarship, described two common approaches to women's history as *compensatory* and *contribution* history.

Compensatory history seeks to answer, Who are the women missing from history? and focuses on women of achievement, rather than the mass of women. Contribution history describes "women's contribution to, their status in, and their oppression by male-defined society." Both approaches help disclose women's role in history, and they are therefore an important starting point. But the defining conceptual framework of both compensatory and contribution history is still male. "Herstory" is told, but women are fitted into "categories and values which consider *man* the measure of significance."[2]

Most literature on women's sport has been written in the tradition of compensatory and contribution history, as Hult suggested in her assessment of the work on American women. Hult noted several studies of women's institutions and organizations as well as some biographies of pioneers in women's physical education and sport.[3] Many of these and other works were based on source materials that only provided evidence about the cultural prescriptions for women's roles and behavior. Given that sport has been defined as a male preserve, it is understandable that historians began with this kind of history, uncovering women's past athletic endeavors and documenting their struggles to gain entry into the world of sport. As a result, for each of the major periods, there have been studies designed to show that women had a place in the history of sport.[4]

This work has provided an important foundation for the scholarship, and there is a great deal more to do in the way of simply describing women's experiences. But we must go further. The underlying assumptions and biases that shape so much of the scholarship must be questioned, and methodologies and tools of research must be made appropriate for studying women. Feminist historians tackled this issue from the beginning of their critique of orthodox scholarship. Proceeding from one of the central tenets of feminist history, "that the relation between the sexes is a social and not a natural one," feminist scholars have questioned traditional ideas about several conceptual and methodological issues: periodization, the definition of basic concepts, research categories, and the importance of theory.[5]

The Shortcomings of Periodization

One of the ways in which historians attempt to make sense of the past is by dividing it into distinctive periods such as the Renaissance or the Middle Ages. Feminist scholars have argued that traditional models of periodization that revolve around politico-economic events, such as wars and revolutions, are not appropriate for women's history. Some Marxist scholars envision a model in which the pivotal elements are women's sexuality and reproduction, as well as the relationship between the two. Others have asserted that such radical restructuring is neither necessary nor desirable because it tends to isolate women's history from the main flow of events. As an alternative, Kelly suggested that the traditional periodization should be adapted for the project of women's history simply by recognizing that the major turning points for men were not necessarily those for women—or at least not for the same reasons.[6]

Working from this basic premise, several scholars have revised earlier standard interpretations of various periods. Challenging the notion that women's history follows precisely the same contours as men's history, they have questioned particularly the liberal progressive view that women's lot improved during such periods as the Renaissance and the Enlightenment. For example, Kelly argued in one essay that "There was no renaissance for women, at least not during the Renaissance." The major contribution of this feminist challenge to traditional periodization is that it has shown that women's history cannot be forced into a model that is based on men's experiences.[7] This has clear implications for sport history, where the traditional male model is firmly entrenched.

A challenge to male periodization in sport history might begin by questioning the validity of seeing ancient Greece as the starting point for the history of women's sport in Western cultures. Spears has documented the inappropriateness of this periodization for women, concluding that, with the exception of a few outstanding persons, women's sport in this period was insignificant. This, of course, begs the question: Where are the origins of organized female sport? One possibility is the city-state of Sparta where physical training for females was evidently mandated, albeit for eugenic purposes. The later Hellenistic and Roman periods are other possibilities, because in these eras there is more concrete evidence of women's competitive sport. It is significant that some scholars have viewed negatively the appearance of females at later athletic festivals. Both Gardiner and Harris saw this development as a further sign of the corruption and decline of an earlier, more pristine form of sport, an interpretation that reveals a great deal about their own assumptions about women and sport.[8]

It also would be useful to consider why the ancient period has been seen as so significant in the history of sport. Many mainstream scholars have celebrated ancient Greece as the cradle of Western athletics and have viewed ancient Greek philosophies and practices as exemplars for modern sport. Feminist sport historians might be more interested in this period as a source of ideas and beliefs that have made women's participation in sport highly problematic. Several scholars have discussed the negative attitudes toward women expressed in the writings of such classical philosophers as Plato and Aristotle. (See box on page 8 for quotation.) For example, Spelman has argued that Plato's misogyny, when linked with the tradition of dualism that is at the core of much Western (including feminist) thought, has contributed to a philosophical tradition in which women and their bodies are devalued. Given this cultural heritage, it is not surprising to find that although men often have celebrated their physicality and defined their sexuality through sport, women have had to battle

Plato's Misogyny

"He who lived well during his appointed time was to return and dwell in his native star, and there he would have a blessed and congenial existence. But if he failed in attaining this, at the second birth he would pass into a woman, and if, when in that state of being, he did not desist from evil, he would continually be changed into some brute who resembled him in the evil nature which he had acquired."
   Timaeus 42b-c, *The Collected Dialogues of Plato*, ed. Edith Hamilton and Huntington Cairns (New York: Pantheon Books, n.d.), 1171.

"Of the men who came into the world, those who were cowards or led unrighteous lives may with reason be supposed to have changed into the nature of women in the second generation."
   Timaeus 91a, ibid., 1210.

against cultural, pseudoscientific, and religious ideologies that identify being female with frailty and associate female athleticism with sexual "deviance."[9]

The persistence of such beliefs is worthy of investigation. Even in such periods as the Renaissance, when the classical ideal of the harmonious development of mind and body once again provided a rationale for physical education, men and not women were the beneficiaries. As Maclean has noted, the flowering of learning in the Renaissance did very little to change long-established beliefs about women's nature and their inherent inferiority. In fact, Baldassar Castiglione's *The Courtier*, one of the classic statements on physical education, was an early contribution to the process of defining sport as a male preserve. Among Castiglione's prescriptions for the woman of the court is a call for her "to give up unbecoming physical activities such as riding and handling weapons."[10]

There is considerable debate in feminist history as to the exact nature and direction of change in women's status over time; and, as Park's work on Enlightenment educators has shown, women were not always excluded from the agenda for change. But even with these caveats, we must seriously question the validity of the standard model of periodization in sport history and attempt to devise schemas that are more consonant with women's experiences. Reassessing periods in this way should not isolate women's history from men's; in fact, the two can and should be related. Struna has attempted this task, pointing out that there was a time lag of some hundred years between the emergence of certain female and male sporting practices in early America. However, traditional periodization remains largely unchallenged in sport history.[11]

Redefining and Expanding Concepts

The inclusion of women has enriched the scholarship in several fields of history, not only by making traditional models of periodization problematic, but also by expanding the meaning of key concepts such as work, power, resistance, and activism. For example, feminist scholars in labor history have shown that the generally accepted notion of work as productive endeavor in the public sphere that is remunerated with wages is too narrow and inflexible to encompass the diversity of women's work.

Historians of women's sport also must be prepared to expand their conception of certain critical constructs. The first step is to question the utility of the most common contemporary understanding of sport as "male, modern, and athletic." Most sport historians have worked with this notion of sport, and they have been preoccupied with charting its development from earlier "premodern" or "traditional" forms. This practice has contributed to the neglect and trivialization of those activities that do not conform to the dominant pattern. More significant, it has contributed to the marginalization of women and female sport forms, consigning the former to the sidelines as spectators and belittling the latter. Several feminist scholars have argued both academic and political cases for redefining such concepts as sport and competition. For example, Birrell and Richter have focused on a women's recreational softball league to show how feminists can shape sport around such values as care, collectivity, and inclusiveness.[12]

Although few sport historians have reconceptualized in this way, Struna is an exception. She has offered a perceptive and insightful commentary on one particular "feminine-defined sport form," the spinning contest. Struna has interpreted these matches as capturing the contradictions of the late 18th-century townswoman's life: "More than either a task of labour or even a simple utilitarian pastime or diversion . . . the spinning contest was an act of autonomy carved out of domestic endeavour and facilitated by corporate life in the towns." There were surely many other uniquely female sporting practices in the past that historians have overlooked in their eagerness to document women's entry into formal, organized, "modern" sport.[13]

Beyond the need to expand the meaning of the concepts employed and to encompass a more diverse range of activities, there is also the need to eliminate the hierarchical approach to particular subjects. This is manifested in the common tendency to pay more attention and attribute greater importance to certain roles—for example, playing, organizing, and leading rather than spectating. The consequence of such a ranking of roles

is the positioning of the vast majority of women outside the scope of investigation because, generally, they have been excluded from participating.

Viewing sport involvement in a more expansive way than the term *participation* implies is also important because it allows us to include in the scope of our research the facilitating, supporting, and servicing roles that women have played. In no sense should these forms of involvement be perceived as peripheral or secondary: In fact, they are central to the maintenance of the institution of sport and consequently merit scholar's serious attention.

In broadening our conception of sport in this way, we are compelled to address issues that otherwise might remain obscure, such as the interrelatedness of various roles. For example, the participation of men, as well as upper- and middle-class women, actually depended on the nonparticipation of working-class women who washed and repaired team uniforms, who prepared picnic lunches for fishing trips and teas for cricket matches, and who stitched riding habits, boots, and golfing outfits. An analysis of this hidden and devalued aspect of women's involvement in sport is long overdue.

For many American historians, exploring the female experience has involved a search for a unique and distinctive community of women, a "universal sisterhood." The women's culture construct is one of the most influential ideas to have emerged from feminist history in the United States. It refers to a constellation of shared values, institutions, and networks that historians argue middle-class women created during the late 18th and 19th centuries. The thesis is that women who were excluded from or subordinated in male-dominated cultures established enclaves in which they afforded each other support, solidarity, and sisterhood.[14]

This notion of a separatist community or culture of women is useful for examining the history of women's sport and physical education. Twin, among others, has argued that there was a dialectical interplay of conservatism with forces of change shaping developments in the early part of the 20th century. Feminists turned "antifeminist arguments inside out by describing women's limitations as virtues . . . postwar female physical educators did the same thing, first declaring women incapable of competition and then calling 'play for play's sake' superior." In casting women as agents, in acknowledging their role in shaping themselves and their world, the construct of women's culture allows us to see female physical educators' insistence on controlled and circumscribed competition not simply as capitulation to the dominant culture's view of women, but also as an effort to assert "some degree of psychic autonomy." The notion of women's culture is a means both of empowering women in history and of developing more nuanced accounts of their past.[15]

The complexities and contradictions of late 19th- and early 20th-century developments in women's sport and physical education have been thoughtfully handled by several scholars. Their work, informed by and informing the scholarship in women's history, represents some of the most insightful research in the field. But this exchange of ideas and information should not flow in only one direction. There are ways in which women's sport history can inform women's history. For example, in an essay on the American women's movement, Freedman argued that a primary reason for its collapse in the 1920s was the disintegration of the separate, self-nurturing communities that women had established during the latter part of the 19th century. These female enclaves were eroded as women attempted to assimilate into male-dominated spheres and professions. In particular, Freedman has noted that many women in academe severed their ties with other women, but found no alternative support system in the generally hostile, masculine world of the university. Yet this was the very period in which female physical educators forged and tempered powerful links with one another, rejecting male overtures for assimilation. This fact suggests that sport, physical education, and leisure are domains that

feminist historians generally, and not just sport historians, should examine more fully.[16]

Gender as a Research Category

All of this questioning of traditional approaches to history stems directly from feminist scholars' insistence that gender must be used as a central category of historical research. Gender, in the sense that feminist scholars have used the term, draws attention to the nature of the social relationship between women and men and implies that women's particular status and position in society at any given time are culturally constructed. Scott has pointed out that historians employ gender as a research category in two different ways: as a descriptive tool to refer to "the existence of phenomena or realities without interpreting, explaining or attributing causality," and as a tool of analysis to theorize about those phenomena or realities.[17]

The Need for Theory

As Scott also has noted, historians are generally more comfortable with description rather than theory, but feminist historians have recognized the importance of attempting to explain rather than simply document gender. This is because their objective is not merely to point out that women have been and continue to be oppressed, but to do something to end that oppression. In challenging any system of oppression, it is essential to understand and explain how it works; and that necessitates the development of theoretical frameworks.

There are many forms of feminist theory, and they can be categorized in various ways.[18] For the purposes of this chapter, the most significant division is between radical theories, such as Marxist feminism, which call for a fundamental restructuring of the social system, and liberal feminism, which focuses on reform. With its emphasis on simply finding a place for women in the existing social order, liberal feminism shares many of the underlying assumptions of compensatory and contribution history.

It is not surprising, then, that most of the historical research on women's sport has been set in a liberal feminist framework. From this perspective, the history of women's sport has been seen as a gradual, progressive unfolding of increased opportunities for participation. Industrialization and modernization have been presented implicitly as the moving forces that created the material, ideological, and political conditions for women's emergence as a sporting constituency during the 19th century. The result has been a body of scholarship that, as Adelman noted, "has remained mainly descriptive, meliorative and too frequently repeats the same theme—that sport mirrors women's societal status." Because it has been largely descriptive and uncritical, the scholarship in women's sport history has left unasked an extremely important question: How has sport been implicated in the social construction and maintenance of gender relations?[19]

Theory and Women's Sport History

Some of the most recent historical studies of women's sport address the question of sport's role in shaping gender relations and are clearly informed by critical feminist theories. These works have pointed the way for future research in their examination of such fundamental issues as sexuality and reproduction. For example, Vertinsky's work on 19th-century prescriptions for women and exercise builds on theories of patriarchy that explain the gender system as a consequence of the male need to dominate women. This domination is exercised in various ways, one of which is the institutionalization of certain practices and ideas about reproduction. Vertinsky examined the role 19th-century male physicians played in attempting to "control the life choices of middle class women and set limits upon their activities." Assuming the role of "expert," members of the medical establishment prescribed the nature and extent of women's activity with reference to its effect on their reproductive capacities. So complete was the Victorian identification of "woman" with "mother" that the menopause was frequently interpreted in medical literature of the period as "the death of the woman in woman."[20]

Another important attempt at incorporating feminist theory is found in Lenskyj's work. Lenskyj explored the issue of male control of female sexuality in a study of the United States and Canada that covers the period from the late 19th century to the present. Lenskyj uses the concept of hegemony to explain how the "ideas of male 'experts' in medicine, science, and religion" were taken up and used by conservatives, including women in the physical education profession, to rationalize the restriction of women's physical activity.[21]

At present we lack an understanding of how women have defined and expressed their sexuality through sport; and, concomitantly, how sport has presented a particular model of sexuality as more legitimate than others. Cahn opened up the debate on some of these issues with her study of homophobia and women's physical education. Cahn argued that during the 1930s and 1940s, leaders in the profession developed policies and philosophies that institutionalized heterosexism as the "privileged sexual mode." The 1930s were the crucial period during which several forces converged to create a climate in which "femininity" was increasingly identified with heterosexual attractiveness, "and the positive image of the P.E. major as modern athlete receded before a negative portrait of physical educators as mannish, social misfits." This kind of theoretically informed research is important not only because it improves our understanding of the relationship between women, sport, and society but also because it underlines the fact that gender and sexuality are not immutable. Rather, they are cultural constructs that have changed in the past and can be changed in the future.[22]

Beyond Gender

It is also important to consider the inequalities and conflicts that arise from differences in class, race, and ethnicity. These critical issues have not been adequately examined in the scholarship, although they are acknowledged as variables that have had some bearing on the nature and extent of women's participation. Sport historians must be sensitive to sport's role in the construction and maintenance of a constellation of social inequalities, not simply those between women and men. For example, materialist feminist theory, which focuses on the economic and class bases of social inequality, could enrich our understanding of developments in women's physical education and sport during the late 19th and early 20th centuries: In both the United States and England, pioneering physical educators' desire to improve women's lot mixed with a desire to control, shape, and "uplift" workers and immigrants.

Peiss's study of working women's leisure in turn-of-the-century New York underlines the importance of class, ethnic, and generational dynamics, as well as gender. Peiss has documented the tensions between middle-class reformers who attempted to direct working women toward "wholesome" and "rational" activities and the latter's spirited assertion of their right to determine these matters for themselves. Todd's research on professional strongwomen also examines alternatives to middle-class ideas about appropriate activities, "femininity," and women's physicality and beauty. Whether these ideas were any less confining or controlling is a matter for further research.[23]

An exploration of such alternative ideas and practices is essential, not only because the current neglect of women of color, working-class women, and ethnic women should be redressed, but also because we have at present an extremely limited understanding of sport's role in the construction of various power relationships. Our current interpretation of women's sport history could be said to be hegemonic, because it implies that all women have shared a common experience of, understanding of, and desire for "sport." We must challenge this notion by asking critical questions about the diversities, complexities, and tensions engendered by differences in race, class, and ethnicity.

Summary and Conclusions

In this chapter I have argued that changes should be made in the way researchers approach women's sport history. These changes are patterned on recent feminist scholarship in women's history and include moving beyond compensatory and contribution history, questioning traditional models of periodization, redefining and expanding basic concepts, using gender as a central research category, and incorporating feminist theory. If these changes are implemented, in a few years it may be possible to assess the work in women's sport history in much the same way that Birrell has recently appraised feminist scholarship in sport sociology: "The field has transformed itself from . . . generally atheoretical investigations of the patterns of women's involvement . . . to a theoretically informed, critical analysis."[24] Given the nature and quality of the most recent work in women's sport history, there is every reason to believe that the scholarship in this field will be similarly transformed.

Notes

[1]Judith L. Newton, Mary P. Ryan, and Judith R. Walkowitz, eds. *Sex and Class in Women's History* (London: Routledge & Kegan Paul, 1983), 4.

[2]The quotations are from Gerda Lerner, "Placing Women in History: Definitions and Challenges," *Feminist Studies*, **3** (1975): 5,7; idem, *The Majority Finds Its Past: Placing Women in History* (New York: Oxford University Press, 1979; Berenice A. Carroll, ed. *Liberating Women's History: Theoretical and Critical Essays* (Urbana, IL: University of Illinois Press, 1976), 369-84; Joan Kelly, "The Doubled Vision of Feminist Theory," *Feminist Studies*, **5** (1979): 216-27.

[3]Joan Hult, "Women to the Mainstream of Sport History." Paper presented at the AAPHERD preconvention conference, Las Vegas, 13 April 1987.

[4]For examples of work on the ancient, medieval, and Renaissance periods, see Manfred Laemmer, "Women and Sport in Ancient Greece," in *Medicine and Sport*, **14**, ed. E. Jokl (Basel: Karger, 1981), 16-23; Reet Howell and Maxwell Howell, "Women in the Medieval and Renaissance Periods: Spectators Only," *Journal of Sport History*, **17** (1986): 11-30.

[5]Joan Kelly, "The Social Relations of the Sexes: Methodological Implications of Women's History," *Signs: Journal of Women in Culture and Society*, **1** (1976): 809. For a good introduction to feminist history, see *Becoming Visible: Women in European History*, ed. Renate Bridenthal and Claudia Koonz (Boston: Houghton Mifflin, 1977) or Linda K. Kerber and Jane DeHart Mathews, *Women's America* (New York: Oxford University Press, 1982).

[6]Kelly, "Social Relations of the Sexes," 810-12.

[7]Kelly, "Did Women Have a Renaissance?," in *Women, History and Theory: The Essays of Joan Kelly* (Chicago: University of Chicago Press, 1984), 19.

[8]Betty Spears, "A Perspective of the History of Women's Sport in Ancient Greece," *Journal of Sport History*, **11** (1984): 32-47; E.N. Gardiner, *Athletics of the Ancient World* (Oxford: Clarendon Press, 1930), 41-42; H.A. Harris, *Sport in Greece and Rome* (London: Thames & Hudson, 1972), 41.

[9]Dualism is a theoretical philosophy of being and knowing that sees the mind and/or soul as separate from and superior to the body. Elizabeth V. Spelman, "Woman as Body: Ancient and Contemporary Views," *Feminist Studies*, **8** (1982): 108-31; Nicholas D. Smith, "Plato and Aristotle on the Nature of Women," *Journal of the History of Philosophy*, **21** (1983): 467-78.

[10]Kelly, "Did Women Have a Renaissance?," 33; Ian Maclean, *The Renaissance Notion of Woman: A Study in the Fortunes of Scholasticism and Medical Science in European Intellectual Life* (Cambridge: Cambridge University Press, 1980).

[11]Roberta J. Park, "Concern for the Physical Education of the Female Sex From 1675 to 1800 in France, England, and Spain," *Research Quarterly for Exercise and Sport*, **12** (1974): 104-19; Nancy L. Struna, "'Good Wives' and 'Gardeners', Spinners and 'Fearless Riders': Middle- and Upper-Rank Women in the Early American Sporting Culture," in *From 'Fair Sex' to Feminism: Sport and the Socialization of Women in the Industrial and Post-Industrial Eras*, ed. J.A. Mangan and Roberta J. Park (London: Frank Cass, 1988), 244.

[12]Susan Birrell and Diana Richter, "Is a Diamond Forever? Feminist Transformations of Sport," *Women's Studies International Forum*, **10** (1987): 395-409. The expression "male, modern, and athletic" is taken from Nancy L. Struna, "Beyond Mapping Experience: The Need for Understanding in the History of American Sporting Women," *Journal of Sport History*, **11** (1984): 131.

[13]Struna, "'Good Wives,'" 245.

[14]Nancy F. Cott, *The Bonds of Womanhood: "Women's Sphere" in New England, 1780-1835* (New Haven, CT: Yale University Press, 1977).

[15]Stephanie Lee Twin, ed. *Out of Bounds: Writings on Women and Sport* (Old Westbury, NY: Feminist Press, 1979), xxii.

[16]For an early essay on women's physical education, see Paul Atkinson, ''Fitness, Feminism and Schooling,'' in *The Nineteenth-Century Woman: Her Cultural and Physical World*, ed. Sarah Delamont and Lorna Duffin (London: Croom Helm, 1978). Estelle Freedman, ''Separatism as Strategy: Female Institution Building and American Feminism, 1870-1930,'' *Feminist Studies*, **5** (1979): 519-29.

[17]Joan W. Scott, ''Gender: A Useful Category of Historical Analysis,'' *American Historical Review*, **91** (1986): 1056.

[18]Susan Birrell, ''Separatism as an Issue in Women's Sport,'' *Arena Review*, **8** (1978): 21-29. For a discussion of historians' use of feminist theory, see Joan W. Scott, *Gender and the Politics of History* (New York: Columbia University Press, 1988), 31-41.

[19]Melvin L. Adelman, ''Academicians and American Athletics: A Decade of Progress,'' *Journal of Sport History*, **10** (1983): 96. See also Struna, ''Beyond Mapping,'' 128-33.

[20]The first quotation is from Patricia Vertinsky, ''Exercise, Physical Capacity, and the Eternally Wounded Woman in Late Nineteenth Century North American,'' *Journal of Sport History*, **14** (1987): 7; the second quotation is from idem., ''Final Prescriptions: Menopause, Old Age and Exercise for Nineteenth Century Women'' (paper presented at the 17th North American Society for Sport History convention, Clemson University, Clemson, SC, 26-29 May 1989).

[21]John Hargreaves defines hegemony as ''the achievement by a class, or by a class fraction or alliance, of leadership over the rest of society. . . . It is a power relation in which the balance between the use of force and coercion . . . and voluntary compliance with the exercise of power . . . is shifted so that power relations function largely in terms of the latter mode.'' John Hargreaves, *Sport, Power and Culture: A Social and Historical Analysis of Popular Sports in Britain* (New York: St. Martin's Press, 1986), 7; Helen Lenskyj, *Out of Bounds: Women, Sport and Sexuality* (Toronto: Women's Press, 1986): 12.

[22]Susan Cahn, ''Crushes, Competition, and Closets: The Emergence of Homophobia in Women's Physical Education,'' in *Women, Sport and Culture*, ed. Susan Birrell and Cheryl Cole (Champaign, IL: Human Kinetics, forthcoming).

[23]Nancy Hewitt, ''Beyond the Search for Sisterhood: Women's History in the 1980s,'' *Social History*, **10** (1985): 299-321; Kathy Peiss, *Cheap Amusements: Working Women and Leisure in Turn-of-the-Century New York* (Philadelphia: Temple University Press, 1986); Jan Todd, ''The Strong Lady in America: Professional Athletes and the *Police Gazette*'' (paper presented at the 17th North American Society for Sport History convention, Clemson University, Clemson, SC, 26-29 May 1989).

[24]Susan Birrell, ''Discourses on the Gender/Sport Relationship: From Women in Sport to Gender Relations,'' *Exercise and Sport Sciences Reviews*, **16** (1988): 492.

Chapter 2

In the Beginning: The Ancient and Medieval Worlds

June Kennard
John Marshall Carter

"So what I did attempt to argue," Nzingha said . . . "there in the Sorbonne, in one of the foremost bastions of Western civilization: that the reason Athena had sprung 'full blown' from the mind of Zeus was because she was an idea, given by Greek men to their God: and that 'idea' was the destruction of the African Goddess Isis and the metamorphosis of Isis into the Greek Goddess Athena. But since no one at the Sorbonne had been taught anything about Isis, it was impossible for them to connect her with Athena. I must have appeared to be simply another raving African."

ALICE WALKER
The Temple of My Familiar

As Walker suggests, women in both the ancient and modern worlds have been viewed through a white male Eurocentric perspective, a perspective defined by those in power. Consider, for example, that the interpretation of paleolithic artifacts has been based on an image of man the hunter and warrior as the key to human evolution and behavior. Throughout Europe, however, female figurines and cave drawings suggest quite a different image: woman as giver of life and Goddess worship. In this regard, Eisler has written:

One assumption of scholars was—and is— that paleolithic art was done by men in spite

15

of evidence to the contrary. . . . Paleolithic wall paintings were interpreted as relating to hunting even when they showed women dancing.[1]

The stick and line drawings found in European paleolithic caves were interpreted to be weapons such as spears, harpoons, and arrows. These drawings most likely were stylized depictions of plant life, which would have meaning for people who were so reliant on vegetation for survival.[2]

Much historical literature is written in the guise of a "generic" history of man when it is in fact a history of males. The ideological hegemony of sport as a male institution invalidates the athletic experience as a worthwhile human pursuit for females. As a result, one is inclined to perceive

women *in* men's sports. Women who play team sports are especially denigrated because powerful women in groups often are perceived to be threatening.

Although Western scholarship has largely ignored women's sport participation in ancient times, it is known that females ran foot races, played ballgames, wrestled[3], hunted, swam, drove chariots, danced, and sang, as well as spectated and participated in athletic events and festivals. This chapter begins by reexamining prehistoric and ancient "partnership" societies of Old Europe[4] and their subsequent alteration into "dominator" societies beginning some 6,000 years ago.

"Partnership" and "dominator" societies are models used by Eisler in *The Chalice and the*

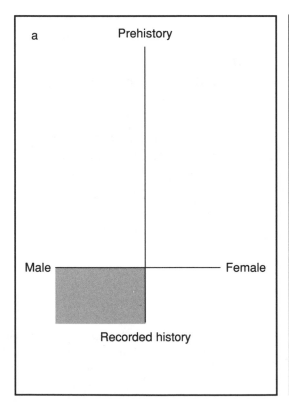
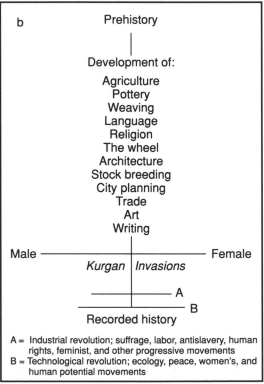

Figure 2.1 Comparison between (a) history as we learn it (shaded area), and (b) who really did what—and when. Reprinted from Eisler and Loye (1990).

Blade. Partnership societies, represented by the chalice, were generally nurturing, peaceful, and equalitarian. Matrilineal in social organization, the people worshipped female deities. It should be noted that the cultures were not matriarchal, that is, the inverse of patriarchal. They actually were "partnership" societies. In contrast to partnership societies, dominator societies, represented by Eisler as the blade, worshipped fierce Gods of the sky and the lethal power of the blade. They existed in a rigid hierarchy, which was supported by force or by the threat of force.

The basis for Eisler's construction of partnership and dominator models is that male and female form the basic human social organization, and from it, all other power/social arrangements emanate. Overall, Eisler's dominator model is more useful than a patriarchal construct because many women, especially those of privilege with respect to race and class, are dominators and/or co-opt into a patriarchal social system. Eisler's partnership model is useful because it broadly defines matrifocal societies without implying that they were matriarchal.

The Coming of the Indo-European Gods

The process by which societies became male dominated occurred in different places and at different times, sometime between about 4300 and 600 BC. Destruction of the Goddess religions was a murderous assault on clans, which were the principal units of tribal organization, in which descent was usually recognized maternally. These dominator peoples, called by scholars Indo-Europeans (Aryans), or Kurgans,[5] were from the Russian steppes. Their culture, which dates back to the seventh and sixth millennia BC, was characterized by "patriarchy; patriliny in which descent was reckoned paternally; and small-scale agriculture and animal husbandry, including the domestication of the horse."[6] The Kurgans brought their male divinities with them as they swept through Greece, Mesopotamia, Canaan, and Egypt. These pastoral, seminomadic peoples brought a revolution by altering the very structure and values of the societies they conquered. They worshipped fierce Gods of the sky and mountaintops. They were rigidly hierarchic; they subscribed to the belief that might makes right; and their technology was designed for means of destruction. They plundered, looted, raped, and murdered.

One group of such peoples, the Hebrews, left an indelible imprint on the Western world with their religion. Theologian Pagels wrote:

> The God of Israel shared his power with no female divinity . . . Indeed, the absence of feminine symbolism for God marks Judaism, Christianity, and Islam in striking contrast to the world's other religious traditions, whether in . . . Greece, . . . Rome, . . . Africa, India, and North America, which abound in feminine symbolism.[7]

Attack on the Goddess religions was continued by the followers of Christianity and Islam, both of which evolved from Judaism.

One of the primary sources of Western patriarchy is the biblical Book of Genesis. In the Garden of Eden story, Eve was seduced by the serpent into eating from the tree of knowledge against God's will. Eve's sin forever consigned her to pain in childbirth and to the rule of man. In Genesis, the Goddess was denied her role as creator, having been replaced by God, the father. Male authority was further consolidated, symbolized by Abraham's seed and the circumcised male who represented God's chosen people.[8] God was male, and his authority on earth would necessarily have to be enforced by men.

Like the God of the Hebrews, the Olympian Gods were also creators and procreators. Zeus births Athena himself. Aphrodite is born from the semen-foam of her father's severed genitals. In the *Oresteia*, the patriarchal Goddess Athena casts the deciding vote to acquit Orestes of matricide on the grounds that mothers are not real parents.

In ancient times, the symbols of the Goddess religions were transformed to demolish the power and popularity of the Goddesses. The serpent, identified with the Goddess as guardian and representative of wisdom, regeneration, and immortality, now becomes evil. The tree of knowledge was associated with the wisdom of the Goddess. In the Old Testament, Jehovah killed Leviathan. Hercules killed Ladon, guardian of the sacred fruit tree of Hera, said to be given to her by the Goddess Gaia at the time of her marriage to Zeus. The Olympian God Apollo murdered Python, the serpent of the oracle at Delphi. The Pythian games, one of the four pan-Hellenic games, were held in honor of Apollo's deed. The bull horns[9] of consecration, found throughout the world in the Goddess religions, became satanic in the Occidental world.

The Goddess Athena's changing image over time mirrors the transition from partnership to dominator societies:

> The historical process that changed Athena, . . . "lady," of the Myceneans . . . into Athena the virgin-warrior deity of the Homeric and later periods culminated in a liminal figure very like the Amazon. The Amazon myth explained Athena as a warrior-virgin who was not threatening; . . . that the daughter would use her own productivity, . . . her own military might, to found her own household and city—had been excised in the death of her surrogates, the Amazons.[10]

In addition to Athena, the changing status of Hera exemplifies the gradual diminishing of the Goddess. Hera (originally Gaia) once ruled alone; later she had a young son/lover; eventually she lost her powerful status and became the jealous wife of Zeus.

In the preancient and ancient worlds, partnership societies were clan societies in which one's loyalty was to the clan, not the individual household. In the clan society, women had political and economic power. A Goddess was the supreme deity; women, and sometimes men, served as priests to the Goddess.

Ancient festivals often included sacrifice, purification, sacred rituals (usually executed by women), and initiation rites that were accompanied by foot races, games, dancing, singing, and music. Among such festivals that survived patriarchy were Attica festivals to Demeter in classical times. At the Eleusinian festival, the central event "was the games in which the prizes were grain from the Rarian field at Panathenaia."[11] Included in the games were gymnastics, musical competition, a horse race, and a mock battle.[12] In some of the festivals to Demeter, only women participated.

The Genesis of Sport

To find women and men in sport, one must look to prehistory and the genesis of sport itself. Most writers cite the main wellsprings of sport as originating in the rituals of religion and hunting. Religious and secular life were not separate, certainly in prehistory and well into the historical era.[13] Because Goddess-centered cultures predate God-centered cultures, it is inconceivable to write about the genesis of sport without women. Although it seems obvious that certain sport forms evolved from hunting skills, there has been an exaggerated emphasis on man and hunter. Aside from the fact that women have been hunters, the big hunt theory is problematic in other respects. We have already seen that Paleolithic cave drawings have been misinterpreted in their depictions of man the hunter. In addition, large-animal hunting was a group activity involving women, men, and children who banded together to drive animals over cliffs or into traps to be left to die.

If both women and men were involved in sport's origins, what was sport like? At this time, it is not known. What one can do is examine matrifocal societies[14] and, further, explore the vestiges of sport that survived into patriarchal times. In the partnership societies that predate patriarchal societies, people appear to have lived harmoniously. War was not glorified, nor was technology employed as weaponry for destruction. Let us examine the Minoan civilization (named by Evans, who uncovered the civilization, after King Minos of later Greek mythology) on Crete, which was a partnership society.

Crete

There is much to be admired in the Minoan civilization, which began about 6000 BC and ended abruptly about 1450 BC. Most scholars believe that earthquakes severely damaged the civilization, followed by the invading Mycenaeans. According to Eisler, Crete was the last partnership society in the Western world; she believes that Atlantis may well be a garbled version of Cretan civilization. The Cretans had four writing systems and advanced technologies that included flush toilets. Their magnificent art bespeaks a love of life and a harmonious blending of all living things. Minoan art shows a remarkable absence of war or glorification of violence and domination. Minoan architecture demonstrates an openness designed for ease and pleasure of living. Women had high status, and it is certain that the dominant figure was the Goddess.[15] Relations between women and men appear to have been appreciative and equal. Although there was a degree of social stratification, it appears that wealth was equally shared. Such public works as roads, drainage, and plumbing seem to have been constructed for the benefit of all.[16]

In the first palace period (2000-1700 BC), bull vaulting (see Figure 2.2) was popular among aristocratic young men and women. One infers from the frescoes that the participant grabbed a charging bull's horn and performed a front handspring off its back. It is difficult to imagine how the participants accomplished such a dangerous feat, and there is much disagreement about how it was done. In Figure 2.2 note the male vaulter, the female who appears to be holding the bull's horns, and the female who appears to be ready to assist the vaulter with his landing. All interpretations of bull vaulting point to its religious significance.

Figure 2.2 Bull vaulting in Crete. © D + I Mathioulakis.

Many articles about bull vaulting do not mention women at all, whereas some say that women "also" participated. Not only were women participants, they were prominent in the rituals as well as spectating. The bull was sacred, its horns of consecration always associated with a female divinity. One explanation has been offered by Gimbutas:

> The identity of the bull with uterus and regenerative waters accounts for its role as the principal sacrificial animal in the drama of creation. . . . The prominence of the bull in this symbolic system comes not from that animal's strength and masculinity, as in Indo-European symbolism, but rather from the accidental similarity between its head and the female reproductive organs. The bull is not a god but essentially a symbol of becoming. Its intimacy with the uterus further explains the bull's association with symbols of regeneration and becoming such as life, water, moon, eggs, and plants.[17]

Women's Sport in Ancient Greece

Historians have tended to assume that civilization began with the ancient Greeks, but grand civilizations existed 25 centuries before the Greeks; and, further, the Greeks borrowed much from these earlier civilizations. What has usually been written about Greek women is that they were excluded from the political arena, had little or no economic power, were married as adolescents, endured numerous births, and died at a young age. Their lives, especially after marriage, were not conducive to participation in sport.

All writings about the Greeks tend to begin with Homer, who leaves no doubts about his patriarchal bias: Zeus is the all-powerful God. It thus is not unexpected that Homer provides us with a rich account of men's sports. Male athletic contests were held with prizes such as a horse, tripod,

and a woman skilled in handiwork. Fathers held contests to select husbands for their daughters and in honor of fallen heroes.

In Homer's *Iliad* and *Odyssey*, it comes as no surprise that there is a dearth of females in sport. Still, Goddesses hunted and drove chariots, and there was a simple ballgame involving Nausisca and her maidens. Particularly interesting in Homer's work is his changing of myths so that they conformed to a patriarchal society. Butterworth wrote: "The Olympic movement was a revolution, and like all important revolutions was accompanied by a great deal of propaganda. An aspect of this zeal was the obscuration or denigration of the past."[18]

Sparta

Plutarch's remark that Spartan women were "bold and masculine, overbearing to their husbands" was typical of what one usually reads about Spartan women: In antiquity they were admired or maligned for their independence. Historians have erroneously assumed that women had more independence in Sparta than in other Greek states by default—that is, they had to take care of their absent husbands' affairs. Men lived in military barracks until age 30 and made only occasional visits to wives by stealth. Even after age 30, men spent much of their time with other men.

In terms of sport, Spartan girls developed skills in racing, wrestling, and throwing the discus and javelin. They also took part in orgiastic, or ecstatic, dances at festivals. It has been assumed falsely that vigorous activity for girls was for eugenic purposes—only for the sake of birthing strong sons.

In contrast to the popular impression of Sparta as a male-dominated war machine, Kunstler offers a fresh perspective about what was in fact a gender-equal society. Misogyny and homophobia were absent; in addition, adultery was not a class of behavior.[19] Nonetheless, Sparta had an enormous helot (slave) population; thus it was a dominator society.

Unlike women in other Greek poleis (city-states), Spartan women had a great deal of physical, emotional, and intellectual freedom, even during Sparta's time of greatest power, 700-371 BC. Kunstler contends that this was because of women's prerogatives emanating from pre-poleis society.[20]

The basis for women's power was their traditional control over produce, medicine, and woven wealth, and their central role in the clan. As landowners, overseers of food storage and distribution, and possessors of movable wealth such as jewelry, textiles, olive oil, etc., they asserted a strong political influence within the community.[21]

Spartan girls, in marked contrast to Athenian girls, were well-nourished; additionally, they were empowered to a degree that their brothers never were. They had the attention of both their parents, and they were encouraged to be independent and to participate in vigorous sports and numerous festivals (see Figure 2.3).

Herean Games at Olympia

In many histories, one finds that the Herean games were auxiliary to the games of Zeus. The main source of information about the games is Pausanias, writing about 175 AD. According to Pausanias, foot races, shortened by one sixth of those of men and boys, were run for maidens who were divided into different age brackets. The contestants wore tunics that reached to just above the knee; the right shoulder was bare as far as the breast. Prizes included a crown of olive branches and a portion of cow that had been sacrificed to Hera. The participants could erect statues with their names inscribed. Pausanias traced the founding of the games to Hippodameia (Hera's old name), who initiated the games honoring Hera, giving thanks for her marriage to Pelops. After a period of strife between Elis and Pisa, the Eleans chose a wise, elderly woman from each of 16

Figure 2.3 "Olympic Girl Runner." Marble reconstruction of lost bronze statue, circa 430 B.C. Reprinted from Seltman (1955).

city-states to settle their disputes. The women's duties included weaving a robe for Hera every 4 years and conducting games in her honor.[22]

Ordinarily we read only this description, but Kunstler has illuminated the significance of the Herean games. ''Usually we have only the fragments of myth or heroic genealogies as remnants of kinship and exchange systems. But here, among the Eleans there survived the practice and the memory of important socio-political prerogatives that were held by women.''[23] He wrote that the foot races conducted by age groups ''suggests a social organization in which the ephebic roles of maidens and their future roles as clanswomen central to the community's economic life have not been entirely lost.''[24]

The 16 Elean women, Pausanias' ''oldest and most worthy in judgement, the best among them,'' were appointed, one from each of the 16 cities, to settle disputes between Pisa and Elis. All married women, they oversaw the games; further, it was their duty to weave a robe for Hera every 4 years. As matrons of the matrilineal clans chosen for their status, they:

> oversaw the initiatory rites of the community, in which the foot races frequently play a major role. They were in charge too of the choral dances in which maidens were initiated into the secrets of their femaleness and their functions within the tribe. . . . Phuskoa's dance was . . . probably part of a female initiation rite which was . . . associated with women's control over the techniques and distributory functions of medicine, agriculture, wine making, weaving, and other productive tasks, as well as the important role played by women within their clans.[25]

Olympia

Long before the arrival of the Greeks, Olympia, like Delphi, was a sacred place. Gaia or the Great Goddess was worshipped there before Hercules

and Zeus, as revealed by archaeological and literary evidence.[26] Mouratidis has written:

> It is possible that the Olympic Games had some roots in prehistoric fertility cults which can be detected through not only the presence of the priestess of Demeter Chamyne . . . but also by the very fact that the victorious athletes were crowned with wreaths of wild olive. . . . The vegetation elements [arose from] . . . traditions of the original inhabitants, who worshipped their Goddess of nature with dances and games.[27]

With the coming of Heracles, women were excluded from the games, but vestiges of the Goddess remained with the priestess of Demeter Chamyne who took over most of Artemis' functions.[28]

The Middle Ages

Public spectacle for men and women alike became a private affair in the early Middle Ages (for this chapter about 300-800 AD). Pastimes and diversions thrived in the Early, High, and Later Middle Ages and into the period of the so-called Italian Renaissance.

One of the most illuminating sources of information about sport and recreation in the Early Middle Ages is the work of the fifth-century bishop, poet, and epistolarian Sidonius Apollinaris. Born at Lyon about 430, into a family of some distinction, Sidonius was trained in the manner of the late imperial period: grammar, literature, rhetoric, philosophy, geometry, astronomy—what amounts to a close approximation of the seven liberal arts. By 469 or 470, Sidonius had become Bishop of Clermont.

We have in Sidonius' work the insights of the insider, at both the ecclesiastical and lay courts of Gaul. Sidonius, in several vignettes from his poems and letters, allows us to see the sports and recreations of Roman emperors, Germanic chieftains, and several other classes of people, including women. His description of the Gothic chief Theodoric II (reigned 453-466 AD) includes several insights into sport and recreation of the Germanic royalty and nobility. Women as well as men apparently played chess and other board games in the Early Middle Ages (see Figure 2.4).

Sidonius suggests that women as well as men engaged in several varieties of ballgames. In a letter to his friend Eriphius, son-in-law of Philomathius, the writer relates how a large group of people worshipping at the tomb of St. Justus were moved, after a ceremonial, to engage in a game of ball (Sidonius used the words *pila* and *sphaerae* synonymously to describe the ball). Although we do not possess a great number of documents that illuminate sport and recreation in the Early Middle Ages, we are fortunate to have those such as Sidonius' letters and poems to help us

Figure 2.4 A man playing chess with a woman, Early Middle Ages. Scene carved on the back of a mirror. Mirror in the collection of the Cleveland Museum of Art.

dispel the myth that women did not engage in recreation, sport, and pastimes.[29]

We are on much firmer ground when searching for women's recreation in the High Middle Ages (about 1000-1300 AD). By the 12th century, feudalism and chivalry had evolved into a medieval worldview. Women had very important roles in that world order. Women of the nobility, as Power remarked, were expected to be educated, not only in reading and writing, but in other areas of life: hawking, playing chess, telling stories, responding with great wit, singing and playing on various instruments, and dancing. Indeed, women of the nobility were expected to know most of the things that the male courtier was supposed to know![30]

The Medieval Tournament

The medieval tournament in its many phases provides us a microcosm of medieval society in the High Middle Ages, as well as a useful view of women's recreation. By the 12th century, the tournament was a military/social/chivalric festival for warriors of feudal Europe. Women played a significant part in this spectacle. Admittedly, writers were notorious in their omissions of women in the great chivalric tales; however, even in these verse histories, such as *Raoul de Cambrai* and the *History of William the Marshal*, women are present, albeit in small numbers.

Generally speaking, women of the nobility exhorted their champions on to victory. As many medieval writers attest, the real prize of the tournament for the jouster was the lady. A liaison with a lady of noble birth could enhance the reputation of a knight. As Harvey has said: "Only a woman of noble character and sentiments, selected by the knight as a fitting object of his service, could confer the reward in such a way as to enhance the honor of both." Von Liechtenstein also emphasized this point:

When I found them jousting where
I knew how I might win the fair?
and charming one whose love I sought

If I'm to serve her, so I thought
I'll do it as an errant knight
With sword and lance I'll boldly fight
for her each day and never waver
God grant that I may win her forever[31]

If the knight won, or if he demonstrated all the traits of a true chevalier (a noble warrior with chivalric traits), he would win his most sought-after prize, that is, the lady. Harvey has illustrated clearly the contractual agreement between knight and lady:

A compact of service and reward was not, of course, confined to the tournament. . . . But the tournament was clearly the most satisfying way in which it might be put into effect. To the ladies it offered, in addition to the pageantry, the spectacle of a number of men fighting, at least ostensibly, on their behalf, and the flattering thought that they had by their presence inspired feats of which they were witnesses.[32]

The role of women in medieval tournaments, as well as in other areas of sport and pastimes, has been a controversial theme for all scholars who have looked at that aspect of the tournament. Recently Barker and Ruehl have sharpened the focus of the debate: The former has argued for a more active role for women, suggesting that women sometimes kept score at tournaments and frequently made presentations of awards to the tournament champions; the latter has demonstrated that in later medieval English tournaments, women were little more than cheerleaders for chivalry.

Legal Evidence

Legal evidence found in such sources as the English eyre and coroners' records and in the French letters of remission is a useful addition to information from other sources. Eyre rolls offer some indirect information about women's sport and recreation in later medieval England.

The Yorkshire Eyre of 1218-19 reveals that in 1218, Beatrice of Pontegract was boating on the River Ouse with a male friend when the boat capsized and they were both drowned; in 1244, an unnamed female was swimming alone and drowned; in 1249, in Wiltshire, Alice of Eston was killed while watching two men engaged in archery; in 1249, Wiltshire, Gunnilda, daughter of Agnes of Marisco, was killed accidentally by Roger, son of Gilbert le Cat, who while sporting with her fell on her and stabbed her with his knife; in London in 1276, Alice of Enefeud drowned while swimming alone; in London in 1276, Juliana, wife of Richard Le Cordwaner, was killed as the result of an argument over a chess match; also in London in 1276, Agnes, wife of Robert, was killed as the result of an argument that arose during a period of drinking and gaming with other men and women.[33] The list goes on. It appears that women were where recreations were, as both spectators and participants.

What We Can Learn From Art

Although William Fitzstephen's famous *Description of London* would have us believe that only males engaged in various forms of recreation, it can be concluded from works of art such as Peter Brueghel the Elder's ''Children's Games'' that women (or girls in this case) were heavily involved in sport and recreation. Although there is a period of approximately 350 years between Fitzstephen's time and Brueghel's time, there is little reason to doubt that women participated in the games and recreations mentioned by Fitzstephen in the late 12th century and depicted by Brueghel in the 16th century. In fact, the legal, literary, and artistic evidence from the High and Later Middle Ages makes it apparent that women participated in archery, attending fairs, bathing, boating, chess, drinking, hawking, hunting, ice skating, riding, and other recreations.[34]

Summary and Conclusions

The revolution that brought Yahweh and Zeus to power did not entirely eliminate the Goddess cults and their festivals. Goddess religions today can be found all over the world. For example, in spite of official denunciations by the Roman Catholic church, Mary is worshipped as a Goddess by millions every day. Rituals commonly found today, such as the wearing of consecrated robes, the use of holy water, and the lighting of candles, were and are prominent features of the Goddess religions. In sport, processions such as those found in the Olympic Games, the crowning of winners with olives wreaths or other vegetation, and awarding winners' cups (chalices) all evolved from the sacred Goddess religions.

The sports of Homer, especially noted in the funeral games of Patroclus, and the Olympic Games, as well as other pan-Hellenic festivals, have much appeal to us because we *recognize* them. They are the masculine model by which we define sport. As a result, it is easy to understand why the image of the woman athlete, like that of the Amazon, is autonomous, strong, and threatening to male authority. In addition, the Eurocentric bias of history would have us believe that civilization began with the ancient Greeks. Writing did not begin with the ancient Greeks; historical literature existed 2,000 years before them, yet it remains virtually untouched. More is written about Greece than any other ancient culture; yet many scholars exclude women altogether, whereas others report that evidence is too scanty to construct a history. Specialists of ancient Greece know that there is a women's history; however, they have chosen to ignore it. For example, there was a feminist movement in classical Athens, but all we read about is its rampant misogyny.

In both the millennia preceding patriarchal takeover and the millennia of the medieval-Renaissance period, sport may well have been different from that which we know as sport today. By piecing together the available primary sources (historical, legal, literary, artistic, and other), the interested investigator may become educated about women's recreation in ancient, medieval, and Renaissance times. It is in this realm of study that we may find the true history of human sport.

Notes

[1] Riane Eisler, *The Chalice and the Blade* (San Francisco: Harper & Row, 1988), 3-4.

[2] Ibid., 4-5.

[3] We know that girls wrestled in Sparta and Africa. "Among the Ibo in Nigeria, women of one village would challenge those of a neighboring one at a particular annual festival. Occasionally women also wrestled men, for instance, at harvest time." Sigrid Paul, "The Wrestling Tradition and Its Social Functions," in *Sport in Africa*, ed. William J. Baker and James A. Mangan (New York: Africana, 1987), 36.

[4] Characterized by archaeologist Gimbutas, "The term *Old Europe* is applied to a pre-Indo-European culture of Europe, a culture matrifocal and probably matrilinear, agricultural and sedentary, egalitarian and peaceful. It contrasted sharply with the ensuing proto-Indo-European culture which was patriarchal, stratified, pastoral, mobile, and war-oriented, superimposed on all Europe." Preface to new edition. Marija Gimbutas, *The Goddesses and Gods of Old Europe: 6500-3500 BC: Myths and Cult Images* (Berkeley: University of California Press, 1982).

[5] Gimbutas calls these peoples, *Kurgan*, which means barrow in Russian: Their "dead were buried in round barrows that covered the mortuary houses of important males." Marija Gimbutas, *The Language of the Goddess* (London: Thames & Hudson, 1989).

[6] Gimbutas, *Language of the Goddess*.

[7] Elaine Pagels, *The Gnostic Gospels* (Hammondsworth: Penguin Books, 1979), 71.

[8] Gerda Lerner, *The Creation of Patriarchy* (New York: Oxford University Press, 1986), 187-98.

[9] *Black Women in Antiquity: Journal of African Civilizations*, ed. Ivan Van Sertima. Rev. ed., **6**(1) Sept, 1987, 110.

[10] William Blake Tyrrell, *Amazons: A Study in Athenian Mythmaking* (Baltimore: Johns Hopkins University Press, 1984), 125-26.

[11]Allaire Chandor Brumfield, *The Attic Festivals of Demeter and Their Relation to the Agricultural Year* (New York: Arno Press, 1981), 183.

[12]Brumfield, 183.

[13]Eisler, 23.

[14]See the writings of Jean Auel.

[15]Anne G. Ward, et al. *The Quest for Theseus* (New York: Praeger, 1970), 79.

[16]Eisler, 29-41.

[17]Gimbutas, *Language of the Goddess*, 265-66.

[18]E.A.S. Butterworth, *Some Traces of the Pre-Olympian World in Greek Literature and Myth* (Berlin: Walter De Gruyer & Co., 1966), 5.

[19]Barton Lee Kunstler, ''Women and the Development of the Spartan Poleis: A Study of Sex Roles in Classical Antiquity,'' doctoral dissertation. Boston University Graduate School, 1983, iv. Kunstler writes that gender status is a function of a variety of socio-economic factors, not a single determinant, e.g., who controls the means of production. Factors in certain combinations are likely to lead to high or low status.

[20]Kunstler, 424.

[21]Kunstler, 282-83.

[22]*Pausanias*, Vol. 16. Trans. Peter Levi (Penguin Books, 1971), 2-8.

[23]Kunstler, 307.

[24]Kunstler, 303.

[25]Kunstler, 305-6.

[26]John Mouratidis, ''Heracles at Olympia and the Exclusion of Women From the Ancient Olympic Games, *Journal of Sport History*, **11**, 3 (Winter, 1984): 51.

[27]Mouratidis, 52.

[28]Mouratidis, 55.

[29]W.B. Anderson, trans. *Sidonius Apollinaris: Poems and Letters* (Cambridge, MA, 1936).

[30]Eileen Power, ''The Position of Women,'' in *The Legacy of the Middle Ages*, ed. C.G. Crump and E.F. Jacobs (Oxford, 1926). More recently, Power's seminal essays have been edited by her husband, M.M. Postan, and published as *Medieval Women* (Cambridge, 1975).

[31]Ulrich von Liechenstein, *Service of Ladies*. Ed. and trans. J.W. Thomas (Chapel Hill, NC, 1969), 131.

[32]Ruth Harvey, *Moriz von Craûn and the Chivalric World* (Oxford: Clarendon Press, 1961), 89.

[33]Martin Weinbaum, *The London Eyre of 1276* (London, 1976); Doris M. Stenton, ed. *Rolls of the Justices in Eyre: Being in the Rolls of Pleas and Assizes for Yorkshire in 3 Henry III (1218-1219)* (London, 1937); C.A.F. Meekings, *Crown Pleas of the Wiltshire Eyre 1249* (Trowbridge, 1961).

[34]William Fitzstephen, *Descriptio Londoniae*, in *Materials for the History of Thomas Becket*, ed. J.C. Robertson and J.B. Sheppard (Roll Series, 67) (London, 18, 85) 3: 4-5; see also Joseph Strutt, *The Sports and Pastimes of the English People* (London, 1801). See also: John Marshall Carter, *Medieval Games: Sport and Recreation in Feudal Society* (Westport, CT, 1992); John Marshall Carter and Arnd Krüger, *Ritual and Record: Sports Records and Quantification in Pre-Modern Societies* (Westport, CT, 1990).

Chapter 3

From ''Genteel Diversions'' to ''Bruising Peg'': Active Pastimes, Exercise, and Sports for Females in Late 17th- and 18th-Century Europe

Roberta J. Park

I wish to persuade women to endeavor to acquire strength of both mind and body . . . a character as a human being.

MARY WOLLSTONECRAFT
A Vindication of the Rights of Woman

We cannot say what the woman might be physically, if the girl were allowed all the freedom of the boy in romping, swimming, climbing, and playing.

ELIZABETH CADY STANTON
The Lily

Bred by the women's movement, and fed by the torrents of social change in the '60s, the women's athletic revolution now touches all phases of American life.

''Revolution in Women's Sports''
WomenSports, September 1974

Nearly two hundred years separate the English feminist Mary Wollstonecraft's declaration of the inalienable rights of women and the 1974 article "Revolution in Women's Sports." During this period—indeed throughout history—females did not have the same political, economic, or social advantages that males enjoyed. Opportunities to engage in games and sports also were few. By contrast, the changes that have occurred since 1974 have been remarkable, even though full equality has not been achieved. When at the end of the 18th century Mary Wollstonecraft declared that girls should be "allowed to take the same exercises as boys," she pointed out that only then could there be a fair test of the assertion that males were "naturally superior." Writing for *The Lily* six decades later, American women's rights advocate Elizabeth Cady Stanton expressed the same view. When girls were allowed the same freedoms as boys in "romping, swimming, climbing, and playing," they would demonstrate that they were as capable as boys.[1] These are opportunities that Title IX of the Education Amendments of 1972 hoped to ensure.[2]

This chapter examines games, sports, and active pastimes during a short period of Western history, from 1660 to 1810. Although the focus is on girls and women, some attention is given to the larger structures of society as these influenced patterns of participation.

Contemporary sport sociologists have noted how difficult it has been to arrive at a universally accepted definition of "sport."[3] This challenge becomes even greater when dealing with earlier centuries.

Highly structured, rule-laden games did not emerge until the 19th century. Earlier the term *sport* (from Middle English *sporte*) might describe a variety of activities that gave enjoyment or recreation.[4] There were "blood sports" like bull baiting and bear baiting.[5] Hunting was referred to as sport; bowles and cricket were called games. These were governed by conventions rather than written rules; their organization was relatively simple. The title of British antiquarian Joseph Strutt's 1801 treatise aptly conveys the breadth of activities earlier peoples recognized as sports and pastimes: *The Sports and Pastimes of the People of England, Including the Rural and Domestic Recreations, May-Games, Mummeries, Pageants, Processions, and Pompous Spectacles, From the Earliest Period to the Present Time.*[6]

A glance at the organization of Strutt's massive work sheds further light on 17th- and 18th-century perspectives. Book I is titled "Rural Exercises Practiced by Persons of Rank" (nobility and gentry); Book II discusses "Rural Exercises Generally Practiced"; Book III is devoted to "Pastimes Usually Exercised in Towns and Cities"; Book IV takes up "Pastimes Appropriate to Particular Seasons." These designations indicate that social class, rural or urban location, and the seasons (natural and religious) were important defining characteristics.

Popular recreations in the 17th and 18th centuries, as Robert Malcomson, Dennis Brailsford, and others have shown, were associated with fairs, wakes (Anglican festivals held annually to commemorate dedication of the parish church), and holiday seasons such as Christmas and Easter.[7] Seasonal rhythms exerted an especially powerful influence on recreational patterns, particularly among the laboring classes. Many, perhaps most, individuals never traveled more than 20 or 30 miles from their homes. The village provided life's necessities, small comforts, and pleasures. The village was the focus of communal experience. During spring planting and autumn harvest farmers (women as well as men) worked from dawn to dusk, sometimes as many as 16 hours a day.[8] The completion of the harvest (Harvest Home) was celebrated with feasting, drinking, dancing, and revelries. Following a tradition handed down from the Middle Ages, Shrove Tuesday and Easter Monday were occasions for rough and tumble football games.[9]

Matters of religion also influenced participation in sport. On the Continent, where the Roman Catholic Church maintained a powerful presence, there were not the same prohibitions against Sunday diversions that arose in Britain. In 1618, James I rebuked Lancashire Puritans "for prohibiting and unlawfully punishing his good people for using their lawful recreations and honest exercises upon Sundays and other Holy Days after the afternoon sermon." Charles I reissued the Declaration of Lawful Sports in 1633.[10] Puritans continued to press their objections, however; and the legacy of the Puritan Sunday persisted with considerable force well into the 20th century.

The aristocracy and landed gentry, in contrast to the laboring classes, enjoyed a great deal of leisure. They hunted, arranged cockfights and horse races, and otherwise diverted themselves on their country estates. In the 17th century horse racing began to draw large crowds. Charles II, who ascended the throne in 1660, made Newmarket the headquarters of the Turf; by 1800, the Epsom Derby, Ascot, and other great annual races had been established. Cricket attained popularity in the southeastern part of England in the 1700s, where it was played by both gentry and commoners; and pugilism (prizefighting) was reestablished as a popular spectator event with all classes in the same century.[11]

In 1751 English novelist Henry Fielding described the divisions of society as royalty, gentry, and commoners. Actual distinctions, however, were probably closer to those identified by Daniel Defoe a half century earlier: rich, middle sort, working trades, country and farmers, poor, and miserable.[12] A certain mingling of the classes in sports like bull baiting and cricket, it has been suggested, helped diffuse social tensions. (Local squires often provided the bulls for "baitings.") Historian George Trevelyan has gone so far as to suggest that if the French *noblesse* had had the tradition of "playing cricket with their peasants," as the English gentry did, their chateaux might not have been burned by angry mobs during the French Revolution.[13]

Across *La Manche* (English Channel) a hierarchical order also prevailed. Before the Revolution (1789–1792), the French population was divided into three *estates* (legal categories). These defined a man's rights and obligations. Clergy comprised the First Estate. *La noblesse*, divided between those who spent their time at Court and *les gentils-hommes campagnards* (rural aristocracy), formed the Second Estate. As their finances declined in the mid-1700s, many *campagnards* had difficulty maintaining their hunting, dancing, and social life. The Third Estate, composed of commoners, accounted for more than 90% of the population. The *bourgeoisie* included merchants, artisans, and urban workers; at the bottom of the social order were the peasants. A major contributing cause of the French Revolution was the growing discontent of the Third Estate, heavily taxed to enable the monarchy to keep up expensive wars and a lavish lifestyle.[14]

In Germany, the decline of the Holy Roman Empire and the Thirty Years' War (1618–1648) had left numerous independent states of various sizes. Their rulers enjoyed what amounted to absolute power. Heavy taxes were imposed on subjects to finance extravagant hunts and balls. In the early 1700s, the province of Prussia began its rise to prominence. Aided by the military and administrative skills of Frederick the Great (1712–1786), Prussia became a major European power. A rigid social system stressed duty, obedience, austerity, and work. The *Junkers* (noble landowning families) consolidated their power by serving as administrators of the civil government and in the higher ranks of the military. Between the aristocracy and the *Burghers* (middle-class townsmen) and peasants there was an immense gulf that was exacerbated by the nobility's preference for French over indigenous German culture.[15]

Where Were Women in This Hierarchical Order?

Although there were differences from country to country, the place of women everywhere in Europe was inferior to that of men. Moreover, it had declined in the late 17th century. In southern

Germany in the 1600s, women worked in occupations like retail selling, bell making, flax production, and toll collection. As guilds (craft unions of artisans) began to see them as competing labor, women were increasingly excluded from the workforce.[16] Clark has found a similar reduction in the range of occupations available to women in England. Davis records the same situation in early modern France, where the subjection of wives to husbands increased "from the 16th to the 18th centuries as the patriarchal family streamlined itself for more efficient property acquisition, social mobility, and preservation of the line."[17] Although the French Revolution proclaimed *Liberté, Fraternité, Egalité*, (liberty, brotherhood, equality), these lofty ideals did not extend to females. In 1793 the National Convention outlawed all women's clubs, alleging that the active participation of females in politics would lead to hysteria and disorder.[18]

Doubtless Mary Wollstonecraft, who lived in Paris during much of the Revolution, witnessed such inconsistencies. It was in rejection of such prejudices that she wrote in *A Vindication of the Rights of Woman* (1792) that it was time to restore to women "their lost dignity and make them part of the human species."[19] Social and political injustices were scarcely fewer in her own country, however. British women had no voice in Parliament; they could not make or abolish laws. The law subsumed a married woman within her husband's identity; hence she ceased to exist as a person! Neither her money nor her children were hers by right. A married woman could not leave her husband unless he continually beat her; and divorce was virtually impossible. Single women were subject to the control of male relatives; and women from the lowest classes fared even worse.[20]

Women, Sports, and Active Pastimes: 1660–Early 1800s

Given the prevailing laws, customs, and attitudes, one might think that females were wholly excluded from sports and active pastimes. This was not the case, although the extent of their participation was far less than that of males. Unfortunately, little was written about their recreations. For this reason, as a leading historian of sport has observed, to study sport and women in the centuries prior to the late 1800s, one must be willing to search through a great many obscure sources.[21]

When in 1702 Anne became Queen of England, Scotland, and Ireland, Britain already had a considerable male sporting tradition. Throughout the 18th century, opportunities expanded and leisure became more commercialized. A modicum of systemization was brought to yacht racing, prizefighting, and horse racing. However, the only team game that could be considered to have attained such hallmarks of modern sport as rules and umpires was cricket. As cricket moved from the southeastern counties to London, important matches began to attract several thousand spectators. The Marylebone Cricket Club was founded in 1787.[22]

Early in the 18th century the ancient sport of prizefighting (pugilism) was revived with the aid of royal patronage. James Figg, the first British champion (1719–1730), opened an amphitheater in London where staged fights drew spectators from all classes of society. A "sporting" young gentleman in the late 1700s and early 1800s might drive his female companion to boxing matches, horse races at Epsom or Ascot, rowing matches, or many other events. It was also in this period, contemporary Pierce Egan claimed, that young gentlemen began exhibiting "a mild taste for physical exercise."[23] It would not be until the 1850s, however, that the intense athleticism that characterizes modern sport emerged.[24]

Among the popular sports, cockfighting was a male-oriented activity typically associated with inns and alehouses, gambling, and bowling at ninepins. Cockfights also were held on private premises where, according to a few reminiscences, females occasionally were spectators. Bowling (skittles) was popular both in Britain and on the Continent. There were several versions of the game. Although it tended to be a male-oriented

Figure 3.1   Bowling (skittles), mid 17th-century France. Courtesy Sally Fox Collection.

activity, women also participated.[25] Samuel Pepys (1633–1703), author of what has been called the greatest diary in the English language, records playing bowles, billiards, and shuffleboard[26] with his wife. When he visited Whitehall Gardens in the 1660s Pepys watched "lords and ladies" at bowles. There are records of ladies playing ninepins at Epsom and other English "watering places" in the early 1700s. In France, both peasant women and young demoiselles bowled at *quilles* (ninepins).[27]

Elizabeth I (1593–1603) and her court enjoyed hunting and bear baiting. During the 18th century, bear baiting, bull baiting, and fights between animals continued to attract the interest of both sexes and all levels of society. Queen Anne (1665–1714) is said to have "delighted in bear and bull baiting."[28] There are reports of ladies who attended baitings having dogs thrown into their laps by the enraged bull.[29]

There are also several records of prizefights between women. Many, perhaps most, of these were "staged" to attract the largest crowds possible. Female boxers had their seconds and "shouted odds," as did male fighters. Brailsford records a match between Mrs. Ruff and Moll Glass in 1799; another fight in 1813 attracted 400 female spectators. In 1722 a match was held between Elizabeth Wilkinson and Hannan Highfield for 3 guineas at Hockley-in-the-Hole. Arranged matches among such notables as Mrs. Stokes (the City Championess) and the Hibernian Heroine were held at Figg's Amphitheater. A favorite costume seems to have been a tight-fitting jacket, short petticoat, Holland drawers, and white stockings and pumps. In 1768, "Bruising Peg" claimed victory over her outclassed opponent. With their husbands, women also engaged in staged fights against other couples, using swords or quarterstaffs (long, stout staffs formerly used as weapons). Victors might earn £40 or more.[30]

Wrestling, a popular sport among laboring men, also had occasional female combatants. In North Wales, Margaret Evans is said to have enjoyed a reputation as "such a powerful wrestler that, even at 70, few young men dared to try a fall with her."[31] Women also were rowing for cash prizes

Figure 3.2 Billiards, late 17th century. Engraving by N. Amoult. Courtesy Sally Fox Collection. Photo by Jean-Loup Charmet.

in the 1790s, the decade that the Doggett's Coat and Badge Race for professional watermen began to keep cumulative records. Eighteenth-century French tapestries depict peasant women propelling small boats of holidaymakers. A 1751 painting of *joutes nautiques* (water jousting contests held at Paris and Lyon to celebrate the patron saint's day of watermen) features a female contestant in the center foreground holding a jousting pole. The northern Italian city of Venice held an annual regatta for women beginning in the late 1600s.[32]

In England, women and children as well as men engaged in the annual Stamford bull running.[33] In the parish of Inverness (Scotland) there was an annual "standing match at foot-ball" between the married and unmarried women. The Marrieds

always won.[34] Although contemporary sources are silent on the involvement of women in the rough and tumble local versions of "football" that were played at Christmas or Easter, they surely had ample opportunities to witness these wild melees, much as women in the French countryside might watch a game of *soule*.[35]

Women also occasionally played cricket. Ashton writes of women playing "prettily" at cricket in the late 1700s. A 1779 painting of the Countess of Derby's match at Surrey depicts such a group. The batswoman holds the curved cricket bat used in the 18th century, while another (possibly the

Figure 3.3 Female cricket player, circa 1779. Reprinted from Ashton (1888).

wicket keeper) is pointing to the stumps. All are dressed in skirts that extend to the top of the foot, peplumed jackets, and large hats.[36] The *Sporting Magazine* for 1793 reports that women of Burry Common in Sussex were "famous at the game of cricket." The Married ladies played the Maidens in a match reported in 1796. A women's match was played before 3,000 spectators in Sussex during the early 1800s. Teams were attired in white cricket dresses decorated with distinguishing colors. The Blues won over the Pinks by a score of 108 to 97.[37] The October 1811 *Monthly Magazine* reported a women's match between Surrey and Hampshire for the sizable sum of 500 guineas. The players' ages ranged from 14 to more than 50. An etching by Thomas Rowlandson, which may be a caricature of the event, was published by Tegg.[38]

Trapball (a ball and stick team game that may be a distant predecessor of baseball) was associated with the Easter season. Dyer recounts that on Shrove Tuesday, Easter Monday, and Whitsuntide, 12 old women at Bury St. Edmunds played trapball "with the greatest spirit and vigor until sunset."[39] A woman reputed to be some 60 years of age was celebrated as "the mistress of the sport." After playing strenuously all day, one writer stated, these "hearty old sportswomen spent the rest of the evening in feasting, singing, and merriment."[40]

Stoolball, which had several local variations, was a particularly popular women's game. In one version, the bowler sought to strike a player's milking stool with a thrown ball. In another, the ball was driven from stool to stool.[41] The most widespread athletic contest for women was foot racing, often referred to as "smock racing" (the winner's prize being a linen smock decorated with ribbons). When men raced they generally wore little clothing. Women runners also might be scantily attired. An advertisement for a cricket match in 1744 promised the additional attraction of a race between two women who were to "run in drawers only." Such contests were taken seriously enough to be run in heats; in certain instances competitors were congratulated on their

speed. In 1797, "Folkstone Bess" won the race at Kent. A women's three-heat race was held near Canterbury in the 1790s; at Brighton the "charms of the fair sex" were displayed in a foot race. Hone reports "blushing damsels" racing in the western counties.[42]

There were also female pedestrians who engaged in competitive walking and running contests. In 1765 a young woman completed 72 miles from Blencogo (Scotland) to Newcastle in 2 days. Three decades later, a woman wagered £2 that she could run a mile in 5-1/2 minutes. The *Sporting Magazine* in 1806 announced that a woman pedestrian of some 40 years of age was victorious over a younger man. Peter Radford recently reported that women's foot racing achieved somewhat of a Golden Age in the 18th century, and that women's races were "significantly *more* frequent than those for men." Radford further categorized events as: regular races associated with such things as local fairs and horserace meetings; "occasional races" held in connection with cricket matches and weddings; and races expressly for wages, which involved the lowest class women.[43]

Foot races for women also were held in Germany, the best known of which is said to have taken place on St. Bartholomew's Day at Marktgröningen in the principality of Wurtemburg. The contestants were dressed in short skirts and bodices. Apparently no holds were barred in gaining victory.[44]

German women also skated in winter—a pastime that had been popular since at least the 1400s. Young ladies were pushed across the ice while sitting in sleds and sleighs. When the Venice lagoon froze in 1708, these pastimes were enjoyed. Racing on skates, between women as well as between men, became especially popular in the Low Countries where frozen canals served both for sport and as highways for the transport of goods. In Friesland in the north of Holland, "almost every village established a skating rink." A depiction of two female competitors crossing the finish line at Leeuwarden in 1805 shows several hundred spectators.[45] Ter Gouw records groups of female and male skaters and sledders engaged in *ijs-en-Sneeuwvernaken* (ice and snow amusements) much as if they had been subjects of the famous Flemish painter Peter Brueghel the Elder (ca. 1525–1569) in the 16th century.[46] Prints and paintings from the 18th century France likewise show both peasant women and city ladies skating, ice sledding, and sleighing.[47]

Contemporaries would have included as diversions events like "blindman's bluff" and "barley break." In the latter, a man and a woman stood in the middle ("Hell") of a portion of ground divided into three parts and tried to catch other couples as they advanced from the outer sections.[48] In Staffordshire, Lancashire, and the north of England, the custom of "heaving and lifting" was practiced at Eastertide (a custom thought to represent the resurrection of Christ). On Easter Monday the men lifted the women three times by holding them horizontally by their arms and legs. On Easter Tuesday the women lifted the men. In another version the person to be lifted sat in a chair. The *Gentleman's Magazine* for February 1784 declared "lifting" to be an indecent and dangerous diversion practiced chiefly by lower class people.[49]

In England, dancing was widely popular among all classes, with cotillions and balls for the gentry and country dancing in the servants' hall.[50] There were also Maypole dances, the Milkmaid's Dance (traditionally performed on the first day of May), and dances at Harvest Home.[51] Dancing was also popular among the French—from grand balls for the nobility to *la danse de village*. Dancing, Babeau asserts, was "the first of pleasures" of the French peasantry. More lively forms predominated in the north, while around Paris country balls became popular.[52] Extravagant balls were also popular among the German-speaking nobility; the *Volk* (common people) danced *Reigen* (round dances) on May Day and at other festivals.[53]

In France, *l'escarpolette* (the swing) provided both genteel demoiselles and peasant girls with mild exercise. Contemporary prints and paintings depict ladies and gentlemen balancing on seesaws and playing *volant* (battledore)[54] and other simple games. An 1808 drawing features a young, smartly dressed couple executing overhand racquet exchanges of a rather modern-looking shuttlecock.[55] It is said that Christina, queen of Sweden, so loved *volant* that she frequently insisted that her nobles take off their coats and play it with her. Durivier's *La gymnastique de la jeunesse* (1803) recommends the game as excellent hygienic exercise for girls.[56] Battledore was also played by girls and women in England.[57] Fashionable English, French, and German ladies played billiards in drawing rooms.[58] *Tric Trac* (backgammon) was a popular diversion for both sexes. Simple games like *colin-mallard* (blindman's bluff) occupied some of the extensive free time forced on upper-class French girls; *loup* (a children's game) appears to have been played by both rustics and young ladies.[59]

The European aristocracy had long been attracted to riding and hunting. It is claimed that Louis XVI recorded 1,562 hunting days between 1755 and 1789. Although others may not have been quite as devoted to *la chase* as was the French monarch, hunting was a popular upper-class diversion in many countries. Pietro Longhi's 18th-century painting "The Rabbit Hunt" features a young Italian lady holding her firearm.[60] At the beginning of the 18th century, English ladies hunted and no social stigma was attached to their participation. To the extent that her health permitted, Queen Anne joined in hunting parties. George II's daughter Princess Amelia hunted with staghounds, as did Lady Mary Wortley Montague and others. Paintings and drawings indicate that in many countries women also fished for pleasure.[61]

When Louis XVI reintroduced horse racing from across the Channel in the 1700s, Marie Antoinette (1755–1793) is said to have taken an interest in this *anglomanie*. The French queen rode astride, adorned in elegant attire. She was not the only woman to do so at a time when the two-pommel sidesaddle was preferred by most. The countess of Derby was an accomplished rider who

Figure 3.4 *The Ladies Shooting Poney* by John Collet. English, 1780. Courtesy Yale Center for British Art, Paul Mellon Collection.

jumped fences that many men were reluctant to try, and a good shooter as well.[62] Maria Teresa, empress of Austria, and various aristocratic German ladies were portrayed in riding attire and in hunting costumes holding guns.[63]

Women were spectators at horse races—and occasionally contestants. The *Newcastle Courant* for August 28, 1725, announced a forthcoming Lady's Plate race in the amount of £15 for the winning woman rider. In 1758, a young woman wagered that she could ride 1,000 miles in as many hours and won in considerably less time.[64] Pierce Egan's *Book of Sports* records a race in 1804 between the late Colonel Thornton's lady and Mr. Flint for over £500. Mrs. Thornton led for the first 3 miles and lost only because her saddle girth slipped. The several thousand spectators who watched applauded her fine horseman-

ship. Flint declined her challenge for a race the next year.[65]

Archery enjoyed renewed interest in the 18th century. Numerous competent women shooters won prizes. The Royal British Bowmen, composed mainly of ''gentlemen and ladies of North Wales,'' met every 2 weeks. By the end of the century there were at least 90 such clubs. One of the reasons for the sport's growth is that it provided an opportunity for both sexes to enjoy respectable sport together.[66] Certain other diversions, however, were likely criticized for the moral laxness they fostered. One was the gaming table. In 1797, three ladies of position were fined for gambling at Lady Buckinghamshire's house. On the Continent ladies also gambled. It is said that Mme de Montespan, mistress of Louis XVI, lost 700,000 *écus* in one evening.[67]

Gambling was enjoyed at the mineral springs that became increasingly popular as health resorts in the late 1600s. By the early 1700s the more affluent were spending time at Bath, Tunbridge Wells, Epsom, and other English ''watering places.'' Mixed bathing led to accusations of scandalous behavior. To entertain clients, proprietors opened eating, drinking, and gaming establishments. John Toland's 1711 *Description of Epsom* reports that its two rival bowling greens were not to be missed. Here the ladies might play ninepins and attend fancy balls in the evening.[68] ''Taking the waters'' was also popular on the Continent. In 1764 J.P. DeLimbourg, Fellow of the Royal Academy of Sciences at Montpellier, described the buildings, springs, coffee houses, and amusements offered at the town of Spa on the road from Liege to Aix-la-Chapelle (Aachen). Among its diversions were walks in formal gardens and local woods, riding excursions, concerts, and evening balls.[69]

Education for Females

No account of women, sport, and active physical pastimes in the late 17th and 18th centuries would be complete without some attention to the education of females and to those educational treatises that devoted at least a modicum of attention to physical education. Modest as these were by our standards, the ideas of a Mme de Genlis or Ambroise Riballier were innovative—if not revolutionary—at the time they were written. At the highest ranks of society, boys had tutors and girls had governesses. The typical education of the latter was at best perfunctory. In France genteel young ladies received their education in *pensionnats* (private boarding-schools) and *petites écoles* where the curriculum emphasized religion, preparation for ''motherhood, and home management.''[70]

In England, girls were sent to small boarding schools that dotted the landscape. One that opened in 1711 was typical. It taught English, French, dancing, music, and needlework. Days were carefully planned; no time was given to recreation. In 1786, German sightseer Sophie von la Roche compared a boarding school in London's Queen Square to Paris' St. Cyr, concluding that the ''French girls were livelier and more easily amused than the English girls.''[71]

Mme de Maintenon, morganatic wife[72] of Louis XIV, had opened St. Cyr in 1686 as a school for daughters of the minor French aristocracy. Although extremely conservative by 20th-century standards, it was rather liberal for the 17th century. Simple games like shuttlecock and blindman's bluff were used for dexterity and relaxation. Apparently Madame was often present during the girls' recreations. By 1692, however, St. Cyr had become more conservative, a reflection of general tendencies in female education. In the 1700s, English mathematician Mary Somerville recalled that her schooldays had been ''utterly wretched.'' Enclosed in corsets with steel stays and wearing a rod to keep her back straight, she said her lessons consisted of such tasks as committing to memory an entire page of Johnson's *Dictionary*.[73]

Nonetheless, in the 18th century some women found opportunities to engage in serious intellectual endeavors. After several years of married life devoted to card parties, dinners, and visits to Bath and Tunbridge Wells, Elizabeth Montague began to invite to her home cultured men and women. Literary subjects dominated the conversation. It was at such a gathering, organized in the 1750s by Montague's friend Elizabeth Veysey, that the derisive term ''bluestocking'' (a woman of pedantic literary tastes) was first used. In France, the *salon* offered similar opportunities for literary, philosophical, and political discussions. Gifted individuals such as Mlle de Lespinasse and Mme du Chatelet attracted luminaries like Montesquieu, Helvetius, and Voltaire. At some salons, parties and amusements like blindman's bluff entertained the guests.[74]

Women also gained influence as confidantes of royalty. Such was the case of Stéphanie Félicité du Crest, la Comtesse de Genlis. In the 1780s she became mistress of the Duc D'Orléans, second in line to the throne of France. Before long she was named governess to all his children and began to establish a reputation as a writer on educational subjects.[75]

The tradition that la Comtesse de Genlis drew on for her somewhat progressive educational ideas had its roots in the previous century. Beginning in the late 1600s, a small group of writers had begun to mildly question the limited educational opportunities open to females. François de Salignac de la Mothe Fénelon, Archbishop of Cambrai, (1651–1715) wrote *De l'éducation des filles* (1678) at the request of the Duc and Duchesse de Beauvillier for the education of their many daughters. Although a woman's role in society differed markedly from that of a man, Fénelon wrote, she should not be regarded as inferior. As had Czech educator Jan Comenius three decades earlier, Fénelon recommended mingling games and diversions with intellectual studies and exercising children with suitable activities.[76]

Across the Channel, the English philosopher John Locke was composing *Some Thoughts Concerning Education* (1693), a book that would have an enormous impact on subsequent educational thought. Locke rejected the then popular belief that we are born with "innate ideas." Quite the contrary, he wrote, we are born knowing nothing. The mind is a *tabula rasa* (blank tablet). Everything we know comes through the senses: seeing, hearing, touching, etc. Not surprisingly for someone who placed such an emphasis on the body, Locke considered exercise and recreation to be important. His treatise opens with the famous dictum *mens sana in corpore sano* (a "sound mind in a sound body").[77]

Written for the son of Edward Clarke, Esq., *Some Thoughts Concerning Education* is not concerned with girls. However, Locke had already spoken on this subject in a letter to Clarke's wife. Because he acknowledged no difference of sex that related to "truth, virtue and obedience," Locke saw no need to alter the basic ideas he proposed for boys: "I think the meat, drink and lodging and clothing should be ordered after the same manner for girls as for boys."[78] Their daughter Elizabeth would not engage in fencing or wrestling; but her clothing, like that of her brother, should allow ample freedom of movement. She was to walk a mile or two and play outside before the sun was hot and begin dancing lessons early (as should boys) to develop physical and social skills.[79]

In *Émile* (1762), the Swiss-born philosopher and political theorist Jean Jacques Rousseau referred to "the wise Locke." La Comtesse de Genlis and Gabriel Françoise Coyer also greeted Locke's ideas with approbation. Coyer's *Plan d'é-ducation publique* (1770) contained an entire section, comprehensive for its time, devoted to physical education, exercise, and games. He discussed tennis, archery, pall-mall, running, dancing, gymnastics, wrestling, and fencing. Although he was writing about boys, Coyer explicitly stated that the education of girls was important and that games should be proportioned to the age and *sex* of the child.[80] Coyer's contemporary Louis Philipon de le Madelaine (1783), writing 6 years before the outbreak of the French Revolution, outlined a program of education for the children of manual laborers. The state must teach children of "the

people" enough reading, writing, and arithmetic to enable them to carry out simple tasks. What he has to say about the administration of schools for boys he also advocates for girls: the same food, the same health practices, and the same, but lighter, exercises.[81]

His contemporary Jean Verdier, a trained doctor and lawyer, opened a *maison d'éducation* in which he attempted to carry out his own ideas regarding the education of boys and girls. Because the health of women operates on the same principles as the health of men (an argument that would be advanced repeatedly by advocates of women's rights),[82] they should have the same exercises: jumping, running, playing ball, quoits, shuttlecock, tennis, archery, dancing, and "particular gymnastics" (specific exercises for different parts of the body). In the case of girls, emphasis was to be given to agility rather than strength.[83]

More emphatic in his advocation of improved education and social status for females was Ambroise Riballier. Writing in collaboration with Charlotte-Catherine Casson de la Cressoniere, Riballier opened *De l'éducation physique et morale des femmes* (1779) with the statement that it was his intent to bring about a better existence for women. Having examined various societies, he concluded that an "absurd system of male superiority" had created most of the world's problems. Women, he maintained, were as capable as men of devoting themselves to science, art, and philosophy. Physical education should render girls' bodies strong and supple. "In all that concerns the education of the mind and the body," Riballier wrote, "there should be no difference between the [education] of girls and that of boys."[84]

La Comtesse de Genlis attempted to put similar ideas to practice. When she became governess to the princes in 1781, it was unheard of for a woman to hold such a post. The boys' tutors resigned in protest, leaving her in full control of the child who one day would become King of France. La Comtesse was critical of both the traditional curriculum and Rousseau's advocation of leaving children to their own devices. Girls, no less than boys, she insisted, should learn to run, jump over obstacles, carry weights, balance on narrow edges, play battledore, and shoot archery. She devised exercise programs and equipment, distinguished between speed and endurance running, and commented on proper mechanics in running. Her observations regarding exercise dosage and prescription anticipate, in outline, modern ideas.[85]

In Germany, Johan Bernhard Basedow opened his Philanthropinum in 1774. Influenced by ideas similar to those Rousseau had set down in *Émile*, Basedow provided time in the morning and the afternoon for games and exercises. Girls and boys played ball and battledore in the school's garden.[86] Even conservative Spain experienced the impact of educational ideas that spread throughout Europe in the late 1700s. Doña Josepha Amar y Borbon wrote in *El discuso sobre la educación física de la mujeres* (1790): "Among the riches of nature, there is none which compares with health and robustness of the body." Proper attention therefore should be given to the diet and exercise of girls.[87] In England, Erasmus Darwin (1731–1802) proposed teaching girls botany, chemistry, physics, languages, geography, and history in addition to the customary drawing, music, and dancing. Because exercise was needed to ensure good health and a happy disposition, girls should play ball and shuttlecock, and exercise with pulley weights. It was unfortunate, he said, that social fashion denied girls opportunities to engage in activities like skating and swimming.[88]

All these proposals were eclipsed by the visions of Mary Wollstonecraft. Dedicated to both co-education and a rational education for females, she maintained that civilized women had been made weak by false notions of refinement. Social conventions that denied females opportunities to develop physical strength were contrary to nature and a violation of civil justice. She recommended the establishment of elementary day schools "where boys and girls, the rich and poor, should meet together." Botany, mechanics, astronomy, reading, writing, arithmetic, and experiments in natural philosophy (i.e., physical and biological

sciences) should be taught. Playgrounds were needed so that both sexes could engage in "gymnastic plays in the open air." Although education should prepare girls to become fit wives and mothers, it was imperative that they be recognized as "rational creatures and free citizens."[89]

These same demands have been made repeatedly since Wollstonecraft's premature death in 1797. They run through recent documents like the *AAUW Report: How Schools Shortchange Girls*. Summarizing this 1992 publication, the A.A.U.W. *Outlook* pointed out that the first study undertaken by the American Association of University Women (founded in 1882) had been "to dispel the commonly accepted myth that higher education was harmful to women's health." A substantial section of that early study, *Health Statistics of Women College Graduates* (1885), was devoted to health and the exercise habits of the graduates of 12 colleges. Not surprisingly, those whose custom it had been to exercise 6 or more hours a week reported that their health was "excellent or good" more often than did respondents who had exercised less often.[90] Although we cannot know for certain what "Bruising Peg," Mary Wollstonecraft, or their contemporaries might think of current sports opportunities for girls and women, we might reasonably assume that they would have been quite pleased.

Acknowledgments

Deepest gratitude is owed to Dr. Dennis Brailsford for sharing with me a portion of the manuscript pages for his *Sport, Time, and Society: The British at Play* (1991) and providing a chronological listing of excerpts from the *Sporting Magazine* (1792-1806). One of the many pleasures of historical research is the opportunity to meet and correspond with such kind and generous individuals.

Notes

1"Man Superior—Intellectually, Morally and Physically," *The Lily*, 2:4 (1 April 1850),

31. Stanton is questioning this assertion. See Roberta J. Park, ''Embodied Selves: The Rise and Development of Concern for Physical Education, Active Games and Recreation for American Women, 1776-1865,'' *Journal of Sport History*, **5** (1978): 5-41; Lionel S. Sobel, ed. *Conference of Women, Sports and the Law* (University of California, 1976). See also Elizabeth Flexner, *Century of Struggle: The Woman's Rights Movement in the United States* (Cambridge, MA: Harvard University Press, 1975), 82-84; passim.

[2]See, for example, Joan S. Hult, ''The Philosophical Conflicts in Men's and Women's Collegiate Athletics,'' *Quest*, **32** (1980): 77-94.

[3]The taxonomy presented in chapter 1 of John W. Loy, Barry D. McPherson, and Gerald Kenyon, *Sport and Social Systems: A Guide to the Analysis, Problems, and Literature* (Reading, MA: Addison-Wesley, 1978), and the references for that chapter provide a useful orientation.

[4]See definition 1 of *sport* in *Webster's New World Dictionary of the English Language* (Second College Edition).

[5]The range of ''blood sports'' was extensive. It included bears, bulls, badgers, monkeys, cats, and other animals. *Baiting* refers to setting attacking dogs against a chained animal. See, for example, Carl B. Cone, ed. *Hounds in the Morning: Sundry Sports of Merry England* (Lexington: University Press of Kentucky, 1981), especially Part III.

[6]Joseph Strutt, *Sports and Pastimes of the People of England: Rural and Domestic Recreations, May-Games, Mummeries, Pageants, Processions, and Pompous Spectacles, From the Earliest Period to the Present Time: Illustrated by Engravings Selected from Ancient Paintings; in Which Are Represented Most of the Popular Diversions*, 2d ed. (London: T. Bensley, 1810).

[7]Robert W. Malcomson, *Popular Recreations in English Society, 1700-1850* (Cambridge: Cambridge University Press, 1973); Dennis Brailsford, *Sport and Society: Elizabeth to Anne* (London: Routledge & Kegan Paul, 1969); idem., *Sport, Time and Society: The British at Play* (London: Routledge & Kegan Paul, 1991); Hugh Cunningham, *Leisure in the Industrial Revolution* (New York: St. Martin's Press, 1980). Brailsford's *Sport, Time and Society* is almost certainly the most useful single source available for information concerning women and sport in 18th- and early 19th-century Britain.

[8]Barbara A. Hanawalt, *The Ties That Bound: Peasant Families in Medieval England* (New York: Oxford University Press, 1986) gives an excellent overview. See also Roberta J. Park, ''Human Energy Expenditure From Australopithecus Afarensis to the 4-Minute Mile: Exemplars and Case Studies,'' in *Exercise and Sport Sciences Review*, ed. John O. Holloszy, vol. 20 (Baltimore: Williams & Wilkins, 1992), 185-220.

[9]The description given in Strutt's *Sports and Pastimes* (92-94), although for an earlier period, probably holds true for the 18th century as well. Kicking others in the shins and knocking them down seem to have been both acceptable and enjoyable parts of the game.

[10]Peter McIntosh, *Sport in Society* (London: C.A. Watts, 1963), 35-45.

[11]The beginnings of such sports are discussed briefly in John Arlott, ed. *The Oxford Companion to World Sports and Games* (London: Oxford University Press, 1975), passim; and in many instances much more fully in Brailsford, *Sport, Time and Society*.

[12]Asa Briggs, *How They Lived: An Anthology of Original Documents Written Between 1700 and 1815* (Oxford, UK: Blackwell, 1969), 113-20.

[13]Malcomson, *Popular Recreations*; George M. Trevelyan, *Illustrated English Social History: The Eighteenth Century*, vol. 3 (London: Longmans, Green, 1942), 211.

[14]Albert Babeau, *La vie rurale dans l'ancienne France* (Paris: Didier,1885), 187-202;

William H. Lewis, *The Splendid Century: Life in the France of Louis XIV* (Morrow, 1971).

[15]A. Menhennet, *Order and Freedom: Literature and Society in Germany from 1720 to 1805* (New York: Basic Books, 1973), 12; O. Zierer, *History of Germany* (New York: Leon Amiel, 1977), 88; James J. Sheehan, *German History, 1770-1866* (Oxford, UK: Clarendon Press, 1989), ch. 3.

[16]Merry E. Wiesner, *Working Women in Renaissance Germany* (New Brunswick, NJ: Rutgers University Press, 1986), 187.

[17]Alice Clark, *Working Life of Women in the Seventeenth Century* (London: Routledge & Kegan Paul, 1919); Natalie Davis, *Society and Culture in Early Modern France* (Stanford, CA: Stanford University Press, 1975), 126.

[18]Lynn Hunt, *Politics, Culture, and Class in the French Revolution* (Berkeley: University of California Press, 1984), 104.

[19]Mary Wollstonecraft, *A Vindication of the Rights of Woman With Strictures on Political and Moral Subjects* (London: J. Johnson, 1792), 73-78; 294-308.

[20]Moira Ferguson, Introduction. In Mary Wollstonecraft, *Maria or the Wrongs of Woman* (New York: Norton, 1975), 5-6.

[21]For a detailed account of one year see Dennis Brailsford, "1787: An 18th Century Sporting Year," *Research Quarterly for Exercise and Sport*, **55** (1984): 217-30.

[22]Ibid.; John H. Plumb, *The Commercialism of Leisure in 18th Century England* (Reading, England: University of Reading, 1973); Arlott, *Oxford Companion to World Sports and Games*, 200; 645-46.

[23][Pierce Egan], *Real Life in London: Or, the Rambles and Adventures of Bob Tallyho, Esq., and His Cousin, the Hon. Tom Dashall Through the Metropolis: Exhibiting a Living Picture of Fashionable Characters, Manners, and Amusements in High and Low Life*, vol. 1 (London: Methuen, 1905), 41; 44; 71;

passim. (original ed., 1829.) See also John Ford, *Prizefighting: The Age of Regency Boximania* (Newton Abbot: David & Charles, 1971), 83-90.

[24]Roberta J. Park, "Athletes and Their Training in Britain and America, 1800-1914," in *Sport and Exercise Science: Essays in the History of Sports Medicine*, ed. Jack W. Berryman and Roberta J. Park. (Urbana: University of Illinois Press, 1992), 57-108.

[25]Peter Burke, *Popular Culture in Early Modern Europe* (New York: Harper & Row, 1978), 109-10; Longueville Thomas, *Pryings Among Private Papers: Chiefly of the Seventeenth and Eighteenth Centuries* (New York: Longmans, Green, 1905), 93.

[26]"Shuffleboard" (or "shovel-board") refers to a game played on smooth tables (often beautifully inlaid) several feet long. The object was to slide each of four flat metal disks into the scoring area. Strutt, *Sports and Pastimes of the People of England*, records that "in former times residences of the nobility, or mansions of the opulent, were not thought to be complete without a shovel-board table" (p. 263).

[27]Samuel Pepys, *The Diary of Samuel Pepys*, vol. 1 (New York: Random House, 1893); 267-68; idem., vol. 2, 446-48. William Hone, *The Year Book of Daily Recreation and Information; Concerning Remarkable Men and Manners, Times and Seasons, Antiquities and Novelties, On the Plan of the Everyday Book and Table Book* (London: William Tegg, 1832), 888-890. See also Bartlett Burleigh James, *Women of England*, vol. 9 of *Woman: In All Ages and in All Countries* (Philadelphia: George Barrie & Sons, 1908), 302-303; 323-27; Rene Alleau, *Dictionnaire des jeux* (Paris: Realités de l'Imaginaire, 1964), 28; Henry R. D'Allemagne, *Sports et jeux d'adresse* (Paris: Libraire Hachette, 1903), 283-88.

[28]Christina Hole, *English Sports and Pastimes* (London: B.T. Batsford, 1949), 28; William

Howitt, *The Rural Life of London*, vol. 2 (London: Longman, Orm, Bronson, Green & Longmans, 1838), 268.

[29]William B. Boulton, *The Amusements of Old London, Being a Survey of the Sports and Pastimes, Tea Gardens and Parks, Playhouses and Other Diversions of the People of London from the 17th to the Beginning of the 19th Century*, vol. 1 (London: John C. Nimmo, 1901), 8.

[30]Boulton, *Amusements of Old London*, ibid., vol. 1, 30-31; idem., vol. 2, 234-35; Brailsford, *Sport, Time and Society*, 134.

[31]Brailsford, *Sport, Time and Society*, 133.

[32]Marie-Madeline Rabecq-Maillard, "Jeux, fêtes, spectacles," in *La vie populaire en France du moyen âge a nos jours*, vol. 2 (Paris: Editions Diderot, 1964-66), 14-16; Alfonso V. Giardini and Elena Biaggio, *Italy's Book of Days* (Rome: Ente Nazionale Industrie Turistiche, 1960), 148-49.

[33]R. Chambers ed. *The Book of Days: A Miscellany of Popular Antiquities in Connection With the Calendar*, vol. 1 (London: W.R. Chambers, 1869), 574-76; T.F. Thiselton Dyer, *British Popular Customs, Present and Past; Illustrating the Social and Domestic Manners of the People* (London: George Bell & Sons, 1876), 421.

[34]William Hone, *The Every-Day Book; or Everlasting Calendar of Popular Amusements, Sports, Pastimes, Ceremonies, Manners, Customs, and Events, Incident to Each of the Three Hundred and Sixty-Five Days, in Past and Present Times* (London: Hunt & Clarke, 1826), 260.

[35]Rabecq-Maillard, *Jeux, fêtes, spectacles*, 14-16. *Soule* is described as an ancestor of European-style handball and football. Played with a leather ball filled with straw, moss, or like material, it is said to have appeared in the Middle Ages. The most popular form of this rough and tumble contest was "handball." Rabecq-Maillard reports that *soule* was played in Brittany until 1887. Its demise

seems to have been caused by both the extreme brutality that sometimes occurred and the rise of modern forms of soccer football (p. 14).

[36]John Ashton, *Men, Maidens and Manners a Hundred Years Ago* (London: Field & Tuer, 1888), 85-86; Hole, *English Sports and Pastimes*, 61 facing.

[37]Pierce Egan, *Pierce Egan's Book of Sports and Mirror of Life: Embracing the Turf, the Chase, the Ring, and the Stage Interspersed with Original Memoirs of Sporting Men, etc.* (London: T.T. & J. Tegg, 1832), 346-47.

[38]Hole, *English Sports and Pastimes*, 61-62. The etching is reproduced in James Laver, *English Sporting Prints* (London: Ward Lock Ltd., 1970), 70.

[39]Dyer, *British Popular Customs*, 86.

[40]Hole, *English Sports and Pastimes*, 61-62.

[41]Arlott, *Oxford Companion to World Sports and Games*, 996-98; John Brand, *Observations on Popular Antiquities of Great Britain: Chiefly Illustrating the Origin of Our Vulgar and Provincial Customs, Ceremonies, and Superstitions*, vol. 2 (London: Henry G. Bohn, 1854), 442.

[42]Dyer, *British Popular Customs*, 214; William Hone, *The Year Book of Daily Recreation*, 1525; Cone, *Hounds in the Morning*, 100.

[43]Brailsford, *Sport, Time and Society*, 134-35; Peter F. Radford, "Women's Foot-Races in the 18th and 19th Centuries: A Popular and Widespread Practice." Paper presented at the 1993 International Congress on the History of Sport, 30 June - 4 July, Berlin, Germany.

[44]Guillaume Depping, *Merveilles de la force et de l'adresse—Agilité, souplesse, dextérité: Les exercices du corps chez les anciens et chez les modernes* (Paris: Librairie de L. Hachette, 1869), 133-38.

[45]Ibid., 240-45; Jan Feith, *Het Boek der Sporten* (Amsterdam: van Holkema & Warendorf, n.d.), 263.

[46]J. Ter Gouw, *De Volksvermaken* (Haarlem: Erven F. Bohn, 1871), 583-602.

[47]Camille Piton, *Le costume civil en France du XIIIᵉ au XIXᵉ siècle* (Paris: Ernest Flammarion, 1913), 277; 310; Rabecq-Maillard, *Jeux, fêtes, spectacles*, 239; Wolfgang Eichel, *Illustrierte Geschichte der Körperkultur*, vol. 1 (Berlin: Sportverlag Berlin, 1983), 105; 111; G.A.E. Bogeng, *Geschichte des sports aller völken und zeiten*, vol. 1 (Leipzig: Verlag von G.V. Geemann, 1926), 529-56.

[48]Hole, *English Sports and Pastimes*, 36; Alice B. Gomme, *The Traditional Games of England, Scotland and Ireland*, vol. 1 (New York: Dover Publications, 1964), 21-23. (Originally published in 1894.)

[49]John Brand, *Observations on Popular Antiquities, Chiefly Illustrating the Origin of Our Vulgar Customs, Ceremonies, and Superstitions* (London: Chatto & Windus, 1877), 97-98.

[50]Trevelyan, *English Social History*, 207.

[51]Brand, *Observations on Popular Antiquities* [1877], 121; Dyer, *British Popular Customs*, 231-32.

[52]Babeau, *La vie rurale*, 209-13.

[53]Gustav Freytag, *Bilder aus der Deutschen Vergangenheit*, vol. 5 (Leipzig: Verlag Paul List, 1924), 335; F. Bohme, ed. *Geschichte des Tanzes in Deutschland. Beitrag zur Deutschen Sitten—Litteratur—und Musikgeschichte* (Leipzig: Breitkopf & Härtel, 1886); Agnes Fyfe, *Dances of Germany* (New York: Chanticleer, 1951).

[54]*Battledore* is a game rather like modern badminton in which a flat bat or racket is used to propel a rounded piece of cork in which feathers have been inserted (a shuttlecock).

[55]"Federballspiel um 1808" adorns the posters announcing the 1st International Congress for the History of Physical Education and Sports (ISHPES), Berlin, 30 June - 4 July 1993.

[56]J.A. [Amar] Durivier, *La gymnastique de la jeunesse; ou, traité élèmentaire de jeux d'exercise* (Paris: A.G. Debray, 1803).

[57]D. Hartley and M.M. Elliott, *Life and Work of the People of England: A Pictorial Record from Contemporary Sources* (London: B.T. Batsford, 1931), 59.

[58]Freytag, *Bilder aus der Deutschen Vergangenheit*, 291; Piton, *Le costume civil en France*, 217.

[59]Alleau, *Dictionnaire des jeux*, 127; Babeau, *La vie rurale*, 208; D'Allemagne, *Sports et jeux d'adresse*.

[60]Giardini and Biaggio, *Italy's Book of Days*, 156.

[61]Meriel Buxton, *Ladies of the Chase* (London: The Sportsman's Press, 1987), 28.

[62]Piton, *Le costume civil en France*, 318; Nesta H. Webster, *Louis XVI and Marie Antoinette Before the Revolution* (London: Constable, 1936), 155.

[63]Moriz Bermann, *Maria Theresia und Kaiser Josef II* (Vienna: Hartleben's Verlag, 1881), 216-17; 528; Bogeng, *Geschichte des Sports*, 613; 697-99.

[64]Hone, *The Every-Day Book*, 1061; Hone, *The Year Book of Daily Recreation*, 538.

[65]Egan, *Pierce Egan's Book of Sports*, 129.

[66]Brailsford, *Sport, Time and Society*, 133.

[67]Boulton, *Amusements of Old London*, vol. 1, 153; Webster, *Louis XVI*, 155.

[68]Reginald Lennard, ed. *Englishmen at Rest and Play: Some Phases in English Leisure, 1558-1714* (Oxford, UK: Clarendon Press, 1931), 61-66; see also Phyllis Hembry, *The English Spa, 1560-1815: A Social History* (London: Athlone Press, 1990).

[69]J.P. De Limbourg, *New Amusements of the German Spa* (London: L. Davis & R. Reymers, 1764).

[70]Elizabeth Rapley, "Fénelon Revisited: A Review of Girls' Education in Seventeenth Century France" *Histoire Sociale—Social History*, **20** (1987): 299-318.

[71]Mary C. Borer, *Willingly to School: A History of Women's Education* (London: Lutterworth Press, 1975), 184-88.

[72]Morganatic refers to a marriage in which a man of nobility marries a woman of lower social status with the provision that any children that issue from the marriage, although legitimate, may not claim his rank or his property.

[73]Borer, *Willingly to School*, 240.

[74]H.P. Thieme, *Women of Modern France*, vol. 7 of *Women: In All Ages and in All Countries* (Philadelphia: George Barrie & Sons, 1907), 272.

[75]Roberta J. Park, "Stéphanie–Félicité du Crest la Comtesse de Genlis (1746-1831): Early Female Proponent of Physical Education" *Research Quarterly*, **44** (March 1973): 34-45.

[76]Roberta J. Park, "Concern for the Physical Education of the Female Sex From 1675 to 1800 in France, England, and Spain," *Research Quarterly*, **45** (May 1974): 104-119; Theophile Lavalée, *Entretiens su l'education des filles* (Paris: Charpentier, 1854), xvi-xviii; Henry Barnard *Fénelon on Education* (Cambridge: Cambridge University Press, 1966).

[77]John Locke, *Some Thoughts Concerning Education* (London: A. & J. Churchill, 1693), 1.

[78]James L. Axtell, *The Educational Writings of John Locke* (Cambridge: Cambridge University Press, 1968), 344-46.

[79]Roberta J. Park, "Concern for Health and Exercise as Expressed in the Writings of 18th Century Physicians and Informed Laymen (England, France, Switzerland), *Research Quarterly*, **47** (December 1976): 56-767.

[80]Gabriel F. Coyer, *Plan d'éducation publique* (Paris: Duchesne, 1770).

[81]Louis Philipon de la Madelaine, *Vues patriotiques sur l'éducation du peuple* (Lyon, France: Bruyset-Ponthus, 1783), 5-15.

[82]See Park, "Embodied Selves"; Berenice A. Carroll, ed. *Liberating Women's History: Theoretical and Critical Essays* (Urbana: University of Illinois Press, 1976). Also Dorothy V. Harris, ed. *DGWS Research Reports: Women in Sports*, vol. 2 (Washington,

DC: American Association for Health, Physical Education and Recreation, 1973).

[83]Jean Verdier, *Cours d'éducation à l'usage des élèves* (Paris: L'auteur, 1777), 60-67; idem., *Discours sur l'éducation nationale, physique et morale des deux sexes* (Paris: L'auteur, 1792), 3-7.

[84]Ambroise Riballier, *De l'éducation physique et morale des femmes* (Paris: Freres Estienne, 1779), 3-6; 62-73; idem., *De l'éducation physique et morale des enfants des deux sexes* (Paris: Nyon, 1785), 378-400.

[85]Stéphanie Félicité Genlis, *Discours sur la suppression des couvents des religieuses et sur d'éducation publique des femmes* (Paris: Onfroy, 1790), 40-44; idem., *Leçons d'une gouvernante à ses élèves* (Paris: Onfroy, 1791), 516-31.

[86]See Fred Eugene Leonard, *A Guide to the History of Physical Education* (Philadelphia: Lea & Febiger, 1923), 67-70; Ellen W. Gerber, *Innovators and Institutions in Physical Education* (Philadelphia: Lea & Febiger, 1971), 83-86.

[87]See Roberta J. Park, "The 'Enlightenment' in Spain: Expressed Concern for Physical Education in Spanish Educational Thought, 1765-1810," *Canadian Journal of History of Sport and Physical Education*, **9** (1978), 1-19; Josepha Amar y Borbon, *Discurso sobre la educación física y moral de las mujeres* (Madrid: Imprenta de D. Benito Cano, 1790), 1; 313-40.

[88]Erasmus Darwin, *A Plan for the Conduct of Female Education in Boarding Schools* (Derby: J. Dewry, 1797), 10; 68-85; 100-112.

[89]Mary Wollstonecraft, *A Vindication of the Rights of Woman*, 73-81; 251; 294-304.

[90]"The AAUW Report, How Schools Shortchange Girls: Executive Summary," *Outlook*, **86:1** (1992): 1-8; Association of Collegiate Alumnae, *Health Statistics of Women College Graduates*. Anne G. Howes, Chairman of Special Committee (Boston: Wright & Potter, 1885), 19-78.

Chapter 4

The Recreational Experiences of Early American Women

Nancy L. Struna

I cannot say that I think you very generous to the ladies, for whilst you are proclaiming peace and good will to men, emancipating all nations, you insist upon retaining an absolute power over wives . . . [but] we have it in our power not only to free ourselves but to subdue our masters.

ABIGAIL ADAMS
to her husband John, *Adams Family Correspondence*

Until the mid-1980s, women were all but invisible on the canvas of early American sport. There appeared to be little evidence to suggest that they competed in horse races and hunts, the signal events of the era, or in fistfighting matches and sport clubs. Of course, historians occasionally did discuss the gambling experiences of native American women, the fishing and sailing forays of white New Englanders, and the penchant for dancing among many women, including African-Americans. Still, such descriptions did little to alter the sense that historians had typically made of sport in the 17th and 18th centuries. It was a man's domain, and women were little more than "good wives" or at most ornamented spectators who existed on the periphery.[1]

How are we to reconcile this conclusion with an important fact about gender experiences in early America: that women were omnipresent? Even where there were no white women, as was the case in the early European plantations of Jamestown and New Amsterdam, their specter loomed large. Moreover, as the Euro-American and African-American female population increased throughout the 18th century, its members affected every aspect of early American life, including work, religion, race relations, popular consumption, and even political ideology.[2]

There is probably no way to reconcile historians' treatment of early American sport with the demographic and social history of the period. Only a fresh start will do. Consequently, and with the advantage of recent scholarship on early American society and a broader body of historical sources, this chapter portrays women as active agents in the construction of early American recreations.[3] It also maintains that recreations were significant social practices in a complex and complicated scheme of life.

This chapter draws on some of the many schemes of life that early American women experienced. There *were* many women, and their experiences as "producers" and "consumers" of recreations—rather than as mere participants and spectators—defy neat generalizations. They lived in times and places and under conditions that were as different from our own as day is from night. Their experiences even differed considerably from one generation to the next, from one region to another, from one race or rank to another. Thus we need to appreciate the historically specific lifestyles and social contexts—the tasks and rhythms of labor, the rituals of community life, and the negotiations that underlay gender relations, among other things—in which colonial women's sporting practices were rooted.

Scenes From the Early 17th Century

As the 17th century began, there were no white women along the Atlantic seaboard of what eventually would become the United States. There were, however, many women, and in some places they outnumbered and outworked men. In Virginia, as Captain John Smith recorded, they made pots and baskets, sowed and reaped corn, and bore burdens and children. They also managed the family economies, even to the extent of placing and holding the wagers in gambling contests, and they played central roles in religious rituals and community celebrations. According to Smith, many of these women appeared "very strong, of an able body and full of agilitie."[4] Later Euro-American observers would comment as well on the strength and endurance of native women.

These were the true Native Americans, the people whom Europeans, seeking the Indies, called Indians. We understand all too little of the recreations practiced by native women, though we perhaps know enough to sketch in some context and conditions. Perhaps foremost, their recreations were embedded in the rhythms and relations of Native American life. Religious ceremonies, for example, called on women (and men) to dance for hours at a time; and rites of passage from maidenhood to womanhood included physical displays and tests. Ballgames occurred in the context of women's daily tasks, and the outcomes could affect one's place in the family or the village. Even the equipment and the items for wagering came from the material stores of wood, corn, shells, and animal hides that were used and valued in everyday life.[5]

The sexual division of labor, and gender relations more generally, also affected the context and structure of recreations among early 17th-century Native Americans. Rarely if ever did women compete against men, but the large-scale and often intertribal contests of men, such as lacrosse, invariably required the cooperation of village women. They prepared the food that the contestants consumed, and they determined what was to be wagered on the men's prowess. Aside from their performances in village rituals, however, women's own recreations generally occurred in the context of other women, a context complicated by the fact that their societies practiced polygamy and slavery. Performance in a foot race or a good showing in a dance thus could be meaningful in different ways to a free tribeswoman than it was to a slave or a concubine, who had to make her place in a family and clan that could either be cruel to or accepting of all challengers.[6]

The arrival of Europeans did little to alter the recreational experiences of Native Americans, either women or men, at least at first. For about a decade after 1607, the transactions between the British and Dutch newcomers and the tribes were limited primarily to trading ventures of native furs and food stocks and land for European goods. Drawing on the traditions of both peoples, many of these meetings combined business and pleasure. Displays of prowess, drinking, dancing, and food, much of which was produced by native women, accompanied the exchange of goods.[7] In the 1620s, however, relations between the races became strained and eventually quite hostile as white settlements encroached on Native American lands. During and after the middle of the 17th century, as the European dispossession of Native Americans proceeded, peaceful exchange among the races became the domain of a few white traders and an occasional surveyor and declining numbers of native people.

The flow of Europeans to the Atlantic coast of North America began in earnest in the 1630s, and it continued throughout the century. By 1700 nearly 155,000 people from England, Ireland, and Scotland—and an unknown but certainly smaller number from the Netherlands—had made the arduous journey across the ocean.[8] Of this number, women were a minority, and they remained so until natural increase nearly leveled the sex ratio in the 18th century. Like the male majority, however, the women came for and with a variety of interests and largely from the ranks of free and tenant farm families, craftspeople, small merchants and shopkeepers, and servants. Some women arrived with their families and began the difficult and often deadly process of settlement. Many others came as indentured servants and worked in households and fields, often for as long as 7 years before they earned their freedom.[9]

The societies that white women helped create on the North American mainland were both similar to and different from the ones they had left behind. On the one hand, like the communities of Britain and the Netherlands, the American settlements were patriarchies. Few women could expect the rights accorded to free men: to own or inherit land, to vote, or even to preach. They did, however, participate more equitably in some experiences, especially work and death. Labor often mitigated traditional European gender divisions, in part because there was so much to do and so few to do it. So, even as women carried out their age-old responsibilities of bearing children and caring for households, they also worked in the fields, ran taverns, and in a few instances managed plantations. Moreover, for both sexes, death, and particularly death at young ages, was a fact of life until native-born colonists no longer succumbed to the "seasoning," the debilitating illness brought on by the voyage, the climate, and the work in America.

The demands of labor and the rhythms and relations of work also contributed to a less vibrant social life, including recreations, than many of the colonists had known or seen in Europe. Work was hard, and women labored for relatively long periods of time either in isolation or with just one or two other people. Especially for servants, who were a majority of all white immigrants in the 17th century, the fairly full European calendar of festivals and fairs gave way to "sorrow, grief and woe" and few respites in the new world.[10] One contemporary ballad recounted the life of a servant girl sent to Virginia:

So soon as it is day, to work I must away,
I have play'd my part both at Plow and Cart,
. . .
Billets from the Wood upon my back they load.[11]

As other portions of this servant's story also suggest, however, work discipline was not the only factor that led to a constricted popular culture among the colonists. Compared to Europe, the range of social relations in America was narrower, both because the population was smaller and because not all of the old-world ranks were represented. Further, the store of material goods was smaller, which meant that many animals and much of the equipment used in European recreations were not available in America. Finally, some festivals and community celebrations and recreational practices were "lost in transit" across the ocean. Some European celebrations and recreational practices either were not a part of the customs of the people or they were not reproduced in the colonies.[12]

The Expansion of Popular Culture: 1670s–1720s

This relative dearth of recreations was not to last, however. During and after the middle of the 17th century, as the first and second native-born generations came of age, the townspeople, farmers, and traders of New England, Virginia and Maryland, and New Netherlands (Dutch New York) had begun to construct a distinctive cycle of communal and colonial events. Militia trainings, elections, court days, weddings, and even funerals brought together colonists from all ranks to celebrate and to complete the business at hand. For women, these gatherings were opportunities to chat with relatives and friends whom one did not see regularly, to acquire information, to sing and dance, and to watch the menfolk and children, including daughters, compete in games and races.[13]

Events such as these emerged as one aspect of an important cultural process that took place in the late 17th- and early 18th-century colonies: the invigoration of popular culture. In simple terms this means that the system of behaviors and values evident in the course of daily life among ordinary people became more vibrant and diverse. Compared to what the earlier immigrants and their immediate offspring had known, these now native-born colonists created multiple forms of social and economic exchange, and both women

and recreations were important in this process.[14] Recreations, of course, were both consequences and causes of the revitalized popular culture; they were cultural performances in which ordinary people displayed and communicated behaviors and values. Moreover, women were actively involved in the construction of recreations, both as producers and as consumers.

Women figured in the expansion of colonial popular culture in several ways. First, their presence encouraged changes in public celebrations. The earliest colonists, most of whom had been men, had gathered to celebrate a particular event, such as a military victory or a royal anniversary, by drinking a "health," or a toast. By the third quarter of the century, as the number of women increased and family formation gained in importance, a new mode of celebration emerged, especially among the emerging merchant and planter upper rank. Some of the men who gathered in public to drink healths and to observe cannon salutes also began to arrange balls so "that the Ladies might also partake of the Rejoicings on this extraordinary Occasion."[15] Thereafter, elaborate dances became one of the most common recreations of genteel men and women; and throughout the 18th century, the presence of women became one of the distinguishing marks of genteel culture.[16]

Late 17th- and early 18th-century women affected colonial popular culture and recreations in more direct ways as well. Some of them owned the equipment with which settlers played games, especially card games. In rural areas where harvest festivals came to be fairly common, women prepared the food that the grain-cutters would consume during the post-harvest celebration.[17] Then, too, villages and the emerging towns became the settings for diverse social practices. On warm summer days in New England, where village life was the norm, husbands and wives abandoned their work "to drink cydor & recreate our Selves" with outings on the numerous waterways.[18] An even greater variety of recreations—ranging from dances to races to fistfights—

Figure 4.1   Dancing, late 18th century. Courtesy Enoch Pratt Free Library, Baltimore, MD.

emerged in the urban centers along the Atlantic coast, especially New York, with 4,700 people in 1700, and the more recent settlement at Philadelphia, with some 2,100 inhabitants.[19] Some of these practices were even public, commercial physical displays, such as "slack rope and tight rope dancing by men and women" that the Philadelphia *Gazette* announced in 1724.[20]

Women also were more visible in one of the most common popular culture settings, the taverns. Known in many places in the colonies as "ordinaries," in part because they provided "ordinary" fare (food and drink), taverns proliferated as the population expanded and became more mobile. Before 1660, for example, Boston had had only 14 licensed tavernkeepers, or 1 taverner for approximately 500 people. By 1690, however, 51 people had obtained licenses, and the ratio diminished to 1:99. Moreover, none of the mid-century innkeepers was a woman, whereas in 1690, 23, or 45% of the total, were women. In places like New York and Philadelphia as well,

women tavernkeepers were a fact of life as the 17th century drew to a close.[21]

The increasing numbers of taverns affected the women proprietors in several ways. First, they earned needed, though not always stable, incomes. Second, these women, many of whom were widows, acquired a degree of social status they otherwise might not have enjoyed. Tavernkeepers in general were often respected members of the commercial and social communities. Third, tavernkeeping enabled women to negotiate the male-dominated culture, both inside and outside of the taverns, and to shape the economic affairs and social relations of their customers. As did male tavern proprietors, women extended credit, both for drinking and gaming; they provided equipment and space for games and contests; and they could admit or eject whom they wished.[22]

Tavernkeeping thus afforded women some degrees of independence and control over the affairs of ordinary life, and it would continue to do so throughout the 18th century. This is not to suggest,

Figure 4.2 Corn husking festival, late 17th century. Courtesy Library of Congress.

however, that tavern life encouraged gender equality. As tavernkeepers, women obtained tavern licenses for shorter periods of time than did men; and as customers, women rarely engaged either as regularly or as frequently as did men in the broad range of tavern recreational activities. In short, tavern culture may have stretched but it did not undermine the widely held conception of gender differences predicated primarily, though not only, on the basis of biological ones.

Seventeenth- and 18th-century colonists generally subscribed to sex-based roles and expectations, and childbearing and home tending were women's primary duties. Robert "King" Carter, one of the wealthiest and most powerful turn-of-the-century Virginians, clearly identified his era's expectations for the right-acting woman in a 1720 letter to his agents in London:

I greatly want a suitable woman for the care and education of my younger children. A grave person of about 40 years of age, that hath been well bred and is of good reputation and hath been used to breed up children, I would willingly entertain.[23]

Carter wanted, in effect, a surrogate mother who could do what her "sex" prepared her to do.

Of course, not all late 17th- and early 18th-century women fulfilled Carter's expectations. Some women found themselves either indicted or convicted by the courts when they violated legal statutes and local moral codes that forbade drunkenness, adultery, and gambling.[24] For other women, agriculture and the tasks of clearing the land, rather than the sex-based gender distinctions that were especially meaningful to polite society,

Figure 4.3   Women watching a boxing match, late 1800s. Courtesy Spalding Archives, Chicopee, MA.

defined what women could and should do. A case in point was a Mrs. Francis Jones, who lived on the Virginia-North Carolina border, as described by Philip Ludwell, the royal auditor in Virginia, in 1710. The Joneses were carving a plantation out of the wilds in this newly settled area, and Ludwell found Mrs. Jones at work in the fields with their slaves. His comments revealed both his own conceptions of appropriate female behavior and some of the physically demanding tasks that a woman on the frontier expected to perform. In the language of genteel society, Ludwell saw Mrs. Jones as a proper woman: She "shews nothing of ruggedness or Immodesty in her carriage." Her work, however, was anything but that which men like Ludwell and Carter expected of women. Not only did she work in the fields, but she also "will carry a gunn in the woods and kill dear . . ., catch and tye hoggs, knock down beeves with an ax and perform the most manfull Exercises."[25] Ludwell apparently had never met anyone like her, and he struggled with the reality of her endeavors as well as the image he had of her gender.

Labor and Leisure in the 18th Century

In subsequent years this perception of women as the "inferior sex," which was predicated on biological and cultural differences, persisted among many Americans, both male and female. In fact, at no point in the 18th century did women effectively challenge what must be understood as a culturally constructed tradition. In the wake of the war for independence against Britain, of course, some relatively well-educated and prominent women such as Abigail Adams, Mercy Otis Warren, and Judith Sargent Murray called on men to grant women more rights, especially legal and property rights. Even these women did not argue for equality with men. Such a modern position was beyond the realm of colonial experience and ideology.[26]

Still, this persisting perception was not the sole conditioner of women's experiences, especially in the years after 1730. The simple fact is that few 18th-century women lived the kinds of lives that men like Carter and Ludwell had envisioned as the ideal: bound to home, hearth, and family. Instead their experiences became even more varied as the population expanded numerically, geographically, and ethnically; as the economy diversified; and as the popular culture became more complex and elaborate.[27] Race, for example, figured prominently in the work and recreational practices of southern women, both African-American and European-American. There, as slavery became more pervasive, African-American women not only supplied much of the labor that underlay white women's leisure but also constructed their own recreations. In the brief respites from work—on Sundays, in the evenings, or in the days of celebrating made possible by the observance of holidays—slave women danced, played simple games, and ran races. Agricultural fairs, initiated by white farmers, planters, and traders, also included contests, especially foot races, for black women who competed for articles of clothing. Finally, there were times when African-American women simply left their labors behind, occasions sometimes interpreted by whites as escape attempts, in search of companionship and the joy of drinking and dancing in taverns with other Africans.[28]

African-Americans were not the only women who found their recreations conditioned by work and relatively spartan styles of life. After 1730 many women became part of the movement to stake out new farms and towns in the western backcountries, and these tasks meant hours of clearing trees and planting fields and few neighbors. In such places, which were not unlike the original colonies a century earlier, planting and harvest festivals punctuated the hours of labor and loneliness. Weddings and funerals also drew scattered families together for food, drink, games, and dancing. Once again, women were the primary producers of what were clearly kin- and neighborhood-created recreations.[29]

Some of these women, as well as their more affluent contemporaries, were also visible consumers in what became the most common public sport of the 18th century, horse racing. Most historians traditionally have viewed horse racing as a male creation, even a passion, and many men arranged competitions among themselves. What is also clear, however, is that some women did race, especially those who grew up with horses and who learned to ride at early ages. Contemporary diaries and travel accounts suggest that women raced most often among themselves, and they were ''fearless'' in such matches.[30] However, they also raced against men, as a German visitor, Gottlieb Mittleberger, observed in his travels from Philadelphia to Reading, Pennsylvania, in 1750. What he saw was women not just riding or even racing; rather, they were competing ''with the best male riders for a wager.''[31]

We shall probably never be able to gauge the full extent of women's involvement in 18th-century horse racing. Few men commented on such practices, and few women left literary records of personal experiences. What is a less uncertain prospect, however, is that women were interested in racing, and racing men were interested in women. Clearly this was the case in eastern Maryland and Virginia, where the thoroughbred form of racing—blooded horses pitted against one another in several heats of 3 and 4 miles each—became the dominant form.[32] At least by the 1760s, the genteel jockey clubs that organized the races, which had become major local and even colony-wide events, had established specific ''ladies purses,'' apparently as a means of generating the support of women as spectators. They also assigned specific seats in the stands for women, and they built ''a commodious House'' on the grounds of tracks for the comfort and protection of their female patrons.[33]

Precisely why these planters in the Chesapeake appealed to and accommodated their wives and daughters in such ways remains unknown. Given that they were among the most visible proponents of the belief that women were the ''weaker sex,'' it seems reasonable to suggest that they built stands to protect women, both from the elements and from the rest of the crowd, which could be

Figure 4.4 Women were both participants in and spectators of horse races in the 1700s. Courtesy Harvard Theatre Collection.

rowdy. The race men also may have recognized women's commercial interests in the sport and expected to gain from them. Some women did wager on races, and others might have been willing to have their own horses bred, for a fee, by the winners of matches. It is also possible, however, that the initiative for such practices came from the women. As one chronicler of plantation life remarked, women were "passionately fond of Riding."[34]

Racing and riding were not, however, the only recreations enjoyed by southern women. They also played cards and gambled; they paddled canoes and raced on river-going boats propelled by slaves at the oars below deck; and on many occasions they danced.[35] Made possible in part by the labor of slaves and a variety of clothing and equipment, these practices were meaningful in particular ways to the women who themselves worked long hours and were often isolated from the company of other whites for days at a time.

A case in point was Eliza Pinckney, who lived as a child and later as a married adult on rice plantations in South Carolina. One of the few mid-18th-century women who left a record of her affairs, Pinckney has provided us with a glimpse of daily life on a large plantation. As a young girl, she would rise at five o'clock, "read till Seven, then take a walk in the garden or field, see that the Servants are at their respective business, then to breakfast." Afterwards she practiced music and French, taught slave girls to read, and attended to much of the "writing, either of the business of the plantations, or letters to my friends."[36] This young girl also rationalized the benefits and limits of recreations, particularly card play and dancing, that loomed so large in her social engagements:

That there is any real hurt in a pack of Cards or going a suet [sweet] figure round the room, etc., no body I believe are obsurd [sic] enough to think, but tis the use we make of them. The danger arises from the too frequent indulgin[g] ourselves in them.[37]

In the religious tradition usually associated with New Englanders, Pinckney concluded that the "immoderate love of them [cards] is sinful."[38]

As an adult, Pinckney's affairs became even more varied and complicated. After she married, she spent much of her time managing a plantation upriver from Charleston, from which her husband was often absent on business. In this role she not only supervised the planting, harvesting, and other work, but she also dealt with the innumerable crises that intruded in the course of daily life. In 1760, for example, the problems were twofold: "Indians on our back settlements, and a violent kind of small pox." Instead of going to Charleston, she stayed at Belmont, "to keep my people out of the way of the violent distemper" and to await British troops to "manage these savage Enemies."[39]

Given the demands on Pinckney there is little wonder that she avidly pursued recreations with company or journeyed to Charleston for the "season." In moderation, certainly, Pinckney enjoyed the array of recreations and the relations with other women and men that they enlivened. Moreover, over time members of the colonial upper rank had both the means for and access to a wider variety of manufactured and handcrafted items for sport, as well as to rules and conventions for games and events. As members of British society in the provinces, all along the Atlantic coast families like the Pinckneys participated in an early consumer revolution.[40] Hunting clothes, riding whips, backgammon and billiard tables, fishing lines, sulkeys, skates, stopwatches, books, battledores and shuttlecocks (for a version of badminton) were theirs to purchase.[41]

To be sure, not all hardworking women possessed the material goods or the range of social relations that underlay Pinckney's recreations. Within the growing population one group in particular struggled with insufficient incomes and seasonal work: These were women of laboring families in the large cities, such as New York, Philadelphia, and Boston. Some of them were ill treated both by their family men and their social superiors. They found relief in but a few recreations, often considered illicit by the dominant culture. Some women took out tavern licenses and made a few shillings selling beer and grog to working men. A few women resorted to prostitution, which was becoming important in the recreational life of the emergent working class on the eve of the Revolution.[42]

Probably the largest segment of women by and after midcentury were those who existed on the social scale between the extremes of gentlewomen like Pinckney and the slaves, servants, and urban laborers. Middling-rank artisanal, craft, and small-merchant mothers and daughters with stable but not substantial incomes relied on locally made articles for sports and took advantage of the increasing number and variety of public entertainments in their towns and cities. In New England, fishing parties, frolics, country dances, and sailing involved many townswomen, sometimes with their husbands. In the middle colonies, women also participated in sleigh rides, skating, and walks in the countryside. At the time of the Revolution, when Americans refused to import cloth and clothing from Britain, groups of middling-rank women also arranged spinning contests. Dividing themselves either by neighborhood or by skill, these women essentially raced to see which group could produce more yarn and which group would earn the prize.[43]

Postwar Experiences

Before we conclude this story in the decades after the Revolution, we need to clarify some of the important themes that have emerged thus far. First is the fact that recreations drew from the rhythms and rituals of life and the lifestyles of early American women. Second, because they were embedded in the affairs of ordinary life, the recreations of women were as diverse as were the women who constructed them. Third, women's recreations expressed race and class distinctions. Like so many other elements of colonial life—houses, horses, clothing, and manner of speaking, for instance—recreations both bore the imprint of and translated socioeconomic conditions and race relations. They were both badges and conditioners of one's place of society.

All of these themes suggest one final conclusion: Recreations were significant in the negotiations of relations among women and between women and men. We "moderns" may struggle to understand this concept, in part because we tend to view sports and other forms of recreations just as things we do, often in our spare time when we do not have to attend to more "serious" matters. Such a passive view of sports, however, ignores an important point: that people create and perform sports. In other words, human beings construct all the forms of sport, like races, games, and exercises, in which we engage. We write the rules, and we break the rules. We decide where and how games are to be played and even whether a game is the appropriate form for a particular social gathering or context. We decide with whom we shall play and, of course, why we play. We decide how and why sports are meaningful.

The construction of sports also involves relationships among people, or social relations. In simple terms, people deal with other people in a variety of ways in sport contexts, such as passing a ball to someone who is closer to the basket, recruiting minority athletes, boycotting sporting events, or any of the innumerable ways in which we as producers and consumers interact with other players, fans, or officials. Each situation requires that we either maintain or change relations, sometimes by exerting our influence, sometimes by yelling, sometimes by refusing to buy a product. Because there are always at least two people involved, however, what we really are doing can be captured in a single word: negotiating. Colonial women engaged in precisely this process of nego-

tiation in constructing their recreations. Thus recreations were forms of social discourse.[44]

Negotiations occurred at various levels in the recreational practices of 17th- and 18th-century women. At a simple level there is the example of a woman in Salem, Massachusetts, who wanted to go sailing. To do so, she had to deal with the owner of the boat, her husband and a neighboring couple who accompanied her, and perhaps even a servant who would take charge of the house and whose labor freed the women to go. At another level, women horse racers had to dicker with local craftsmen or a London-connected merchant to purchase saddles. They also had to persuade their brothers or male friends to agree on the race time and wager. Finally, they had to bargain with the local culture's perceptions of what women as the "weaker sex" could and could not do.

There were many other kinds of negotiations, some of which had great cultural significance, that women as both consumers and producers of recreations had to make. One may recall the provisions that the jockey club members made for their female contemporaries, a practice that changed the face of thoroughbred racing. One also may consider that the recreations of a genteel woman like Eliza Pinckney were at least in part the consequences of negotiations with her slaves. Their labor made possible her recreations, and her freely chosen attendance at balls, card games, and races reinforced the gulf between white mistress and black slave.

The point of this discussion is that colonial recreations were the products of negotiation—of choices, decisions, and deals with other people made in the context of particular conditions. In turn, recreations were social practices in which colonial women negotiated with other women and with men for culturally meaningful things like power, status, and economic gain. Thus, for 17th- and 18th-century women who lived within the bounds of a culture that defined women as inferior to men, recreations were no small matters.

Recreations remained important matters for women in the decades after the Revolution. The transformation of colonies to independent nation clearly affected the political, social, religious, and economic contexts in which women lived, worked, and played. This is not to suggest, however, that the change from colonies to nation revolutionized all aspects of women's lives, especially their standards and styles of daily living. In fact, many recreations actually persisted through the end of the century and into the next. Rural frolics and harvest festivals, genteel assemblies for dancing and cards, tavern events, and the various kinds of races all continued in much the same form as they existed prior to 1776.[45]

Changes in some aspects of women's recreational experiences did, however, occur in the decades after the Revolution; and they were changes affected by two primary processes. One of these processes, the transition to a capitalist economy, had begun long before the war; and the aftermath of the war primarily quickened the pace and broadened the dimensions of economic change. The second process was a direct political consequence of the Revolution. This was the emergence of republican ideology, or the set of beliefs that people held about themselves, their independent and relatively democratic nation, and their elected representatives. This belief system also embraced and affected not only relations between men but also relations between men and women.

The emergent capitalist economy affected the recreational experiences of women, especially those who lived in urbanizing areas, in two ways. First, the manufacture and marketing of goods and services provided women of means with a broader array of sporting equipment for both home use and public consumption. There were more backgammon and card tables, sleighs and fishing equipment, horses and packs of cards, and specialized guns and saddles. By 1810 the estate of a woman in Boston also registered a set of barbells.[46]

The transition to capitalism also resulted in the expansion of commercial entertainments. There were, for example, numerous public exhibitions by equestrian experts, acrobats and tumblers, and the owners of exotic animals. There were also "bathing machines" for swimming and "pleasure gardens," or early urban resorts with concerts, beautiful gardens for walking, and dancing.[47] In fact, if she could afford the price of admission, a woman in New York, Philadelphia, Baltimore, or Boston could find something to do almost every night of the week.

Some of the entrepreneurs who arranged these entertainments were cognizant of the female population. To entice customers to his tavern in Philadelphia, Charles Quinan constructed "flying coaches" for women and "horse[s]" for men, both of which whirled about and gave his patrons exciting rides.[48] Farther north in New York, where the competition for the public entertainment audience was relatively stiff and where pleasure gardens were quite numerous, Joseph Delacroix added a "grand Amphitheatre" to the grounds of his Vauxhall Garden and refused to admit male patrons without women. Both efforts suggest that Delacroix actively cultivated a female audience.[49]

Precisely why he did so remains something of a mystery, but it seems reasonable to suggest that Delacroix realized, as did other entrepreneurs, that women exerted considerable influence on decisions involving money and expenditures. He also may have accepted what had come to be a prevailing pattern of thought about the moral influence of women: They could temper, if not tame, the behavior of men. As a member of the generation that had embraced republican ideology, Delacroix also may have subscribed to the role for women that this belief system laid out, that of the republican mother.[50]

Republican ideology defined women's place in the new nation as mothers and moral guardians. As such, women acquired particular significance as the managers of behavior. Morality derived from women, so the argument held; and women, far more than men, were able to cultivate morality and to act morally. Such a position, of course, was the ideological ground in which was rooted the later 19th-century notion that women were morally superior, even as they remained physically inferior, to men. For the particular and immediate practice of recreations, however, this belief also was significant. Because it distinguished women from men, the ideology supported and may have encouraged the social construction of two realms of activity, whose differences would be captured in the phrase ''separate spheres.'' Men were to operate in public as breadwinners and decision makers, while women reared children and managed the household, all in private. Moreover, the ideology, as well as the notion of ''separate spheres'' that clearly stated ideal gender roles and relations, resulted from negotiations between men and women.[51]

It is not, then, coincidental that some women's recreational practices of the early 19th century would draw from their domestic labors and responsibilities or that someone like Catharine Beecher would advocate sweeping, walking, and light calisthenics as appropriate recreations for women. Beecher and her peers were literally the daughters of America's first ''republican mothers.''[52] We must keep in mind, however, that both republican motherhood and the subsequent ''cult of domesticity'' drew from and described the experiences of only particular women: the women whom the transition to capitalism had redefined as an emergent urban Anglo-American middle class. For working-class women, rural farm women, African-American slave and free women, and native American women, the ideology of domesticity, which stressed that women's place was in the home doing light work and engaging in relatively passive recreations, was less meaningful.

Summary and Conclusions

There are at least two ways to interpret the post-Revolutionary experiences of early American middle-class women. The first posits the emergence of the cult of domesticity, with its relatively inactive recreations and games, as an historical step backwards. After all, many early and mid-18th-century women had raced horses, gambled, and exerted considerable influence on the events participated in by men. Compared to Eliza Pinckney, in short, Catharine Beecher lived a far more sheltered, even circumscribed, life.

The second interpretation maintains that the recreations and the lifestyles of late colonial and early national middle-class women were clearly changed by capitalism and republicanism, but they nonetheless remained embedded in these women's ordinary lives. The women's lives had changed, and so had their recreations. They worked in their houses and cared for their children in settled towns and cities rather than in the woods and fields. They attended well-regulated and commercial exhibitions and events with husbands and families rather than rollicking harvest festivals, taverns, and sporadically occurring weddings and funerals. Few of them owned or learned to ride horses, let alone race. Even card play and gambling had acquired a taint, and polite women stayed aloof from the tavern and street culture of the working classes.

Over the longer span of colonial and early national life, this second interpretation, and the view of history on which it rests, seem to have more merit than does the first. It makes sense of any one generation's experiences in the context of that generation's life, and it sees recreations as historically specific and meaningful practices. Without doubt, these two concepts—making sense of the past in terms of the past and viewing recreations as meaningful and context-specific social practices—have shaped the story I have tried to relate in this chapter. Women's recreations varied over the course of the 17th and 18th centuries, and what they did or did not do depended on what they owned, where they existed on the social scale, what they did, and what they believed. Their styles of recreations in turn tell us a good deal about who they were.

Notes

[1]The conclusion that women were nonplayers on the early American sporting scene is evident

in the textbooks used in undergraduate sport history courses. See, for example, Benjamin Rader, *American Sports. From the Age of Folk Games to the Age of Televised Sport* (Englewood Cliffs, NJ: Prentice Hall, 2d ed., 1990); John A. Lucas and Ronald A. Smith, *Saga of American Sport* (Philadelphia: Lea & Febiger, 1978). A not very successful effort to revise this story appears in my " 'Good Wives' and 'Gardeners,' Spinners and 'Fearless Riders': Middle- and Upper-Rank Women in the Early American Sporting Culture," in *From "Fair Sex" to Feminism. Sport and the Socialization of Women in the Industrial and Post-Industrial Eras*, ed. J.A. Mangan and Roberta J. Park (London: Frank Cass, 1987), 235-55.

[2]Exemplary revisionist works include Laurel T. Ulrich, *A Midwife's Tale. The Life of Martha Ballard, Based on Her Diary, 1785-1812* (New York: Knopf, 1990); Jeanne Boydston, *Home and Work. Housework, Wages and the Ideology of Labor in the Early Republic* (New York: Oxford University Press, 1990); Elizabeth Fox-Genovese, *Within the Plantation Household. Black and White Women of the Old South* (Chapel Hill: University of North Carolina Press, 1988).

[3]On Women's agency and the gendering of early American sporting practice, see Nancy L. Struna, "Gender and Sporting Practice in Early America, 1750-1810," *Journal of Sport History*, **19** (Spring 1991): 10-30.

[4]Cited in Karen O. Kupperman, ed. *Captain John Smith. A Select Edition of His Writings* (Chapel Hill: University of North Carolina Press, 1988). On native American societies and native American–white relations, see James H. Merrell, *The Indians' New World* (Chapel Hill: University of North Carolina Press, 1989); Peter H. Wood, Gregory A. Waselkov, and M. Thomas Hatley, eds. *Powhatan's Mantle. Indians in the Colonial Southeast* (Lincoln: University of Nebraska Press, 1989).

[5]John Lawson, *A New Voyage to Carolina* (1709), ed. Hugh T. Lefler (Chapel Hill: University of North Carolina Press, 1967), 34; William Byrd, *The Prose Works of William Byrd of Westover*, ed. Louis B. Wright (Cambridge, MA: Harvard University Press, 1966), 219.

[6]Kupperman, ed. *Captain John Smith*, 142-45; Lawson, *A New Voyage*, 34, 39, 45.

[7]Edward Winslow, *A Relation or Journall of the Beginnings and Proceedings of the English Plantation Setled at Plimouth in New England* (1622), ed. Dwight B. Heath (New York: Corinth Books, 1963), 82; Sydney V. James, ed. *Three Visitors to Early Plymouth* (Plymouth, MA: Plymouth Plantation, 1963), 29.

[8]Stephen Innes, ed. *Work and Labor in Early America* (Chapel Hill: University of North Carolina Press, 1988), 7.

[9]Ibid.; Isaac N.P. Stokes, *The Iconography of Manhattan Island, 1498–1909*, 6 vols. (New York: Arno Press, reprint ed., 1967), **4**: 148-49; David Cressy, *Coming Over. Migration and Communication Between England and New England in the Seventeenth Century* (Cambridge, England: Cambridge University Press, 1987), 43-57; Russell R. Menard, "Economy and Society in Early Colonial Maryland" (PhD diss., University of Iowa, 1975).

[10]Nancy F. Cott, ed. *Root of Bitterness* (New York: Dutton, 1972), 31.

[11]Ibid.

[12]Nancy L. Struna, "Sport and Society in Early America," *International Journal of the History of Sport*, **5** (December 1988): 292-311; Richard L. Bushman, "American High-Style and Vernacular Cultures," in *Colonial British America. Essays in the New History of Early America*, ed. Jack P. Greene and J.R. Pole (Baltimore: Johns Hopkins University Press, 1984), 372.

[13]Struna, "Sport and Society," 295-97; Lorena S. Walsh, "Community Networks in the Early

Chesapeake," in *Colonial Chesapeake Society*, ed. Lois Green Carr, Philip D. Morgan, and Jean B. Russo (Chapel Hill: University of North Carolina Press, 1988), 222-33.

[14]Struna, "Sport and Society," 296-98.

[15]Cited in Edmund S. Morgan, *Virginians at Home* (Williamsburg, VA: Colonial Williamsburg, 1952), 88-89. On the demographic changes, see John J. McCusker and Russell R. Menard, *The Economy of British America 1607-1789* (Chapel Hill: University of North Carolina Press, 1985), 134-35; Jim Potter, "Demographic Development and Family Structure," in *Colonial British America*, ed. Greene and Pole, 123-57; Lorena S. Walsh, " 'Till Death Us Do Part': Marriage and the Family in Seventeenth-Century Maryland," in *The Chesapeake in the Seventeenth Century*, ed. Thad W. Tate and David Ammerman (Chapel Hill: University of North Carolina Press, 1979), 126-52.

[16]Nancy L. Struna, "Sport and the Awareness of Leisure," in *Of Consuming Interests: The Style of Life in the Eighteenth Century*, ed. Ronald Hoffman, Peter J. Albert, and Cary Carson (Charlottesville: University Press of Virginia, 1994) 406-43.

[17]Inventories and Accounts, Vol. I, pt. 1, 1674-1704, Maryland Hall of Records, Annapolis; Joseph H. Smith, ed. *Colonial Justice in Western Massachusetts, 1639-1702* (Cambridge, MA: Harvard University Press, 1961), 257; Morgan, *Virginians at Home*, 86; "Narrative of a Voyage to Maryland, 1705-06," *American Historical Review*, **12** (January 1902): 334-35.

[18]Joshua Hempstead, "Diary of Joshua Hempstead 1711-1758," New London County Historical Society *Collections*, **1** (1901):24.

[19]Gary B. Nash, *The Urban Crucible. Social Change, Political Consciousness, and the Origins of the American Revolution* (Cambridge, MA: Harvard University Press, 1979), 19.

[20]John F. Watson, *Annals of Philadelphia* (Philadelphia: Carey and Hart, 1830), 239.

[21]Lyle Koehler, *A Search for Power. The 'Weaker Sex' in Seventeenth-Century New England* (Urbana: University of Illinois Press, 1980), 339-40, 433.

[22]Kym S. Rice, *Early American Taverns: For the Entertainment of Friends and Strangers* (Chicago: Gateway, 1983); Francis M. Manges, "Women Shopkeepers, Tavernkeepers, and Artisans in Colonial Philadelphia" (PhD diss., University of Pennsylvania, 1958); Struna, "Gender and Sporting Practice."

[23]Robert Carter, *Letters of Robert Carter 1720-1727. The Commercial Interests of a Virginia Gentleman*, ed. Louis B. Wright (San Marino, CA: The Huntington Library, 1940), 22-23.

[24]Koehler, *Search for Power*, 193, 205; Carol F. Karlsen, *The Devil in the Shape of a Woman. Witchcraft in Colonial New England* (New York: Norton, 1987).

[25]Philip Ludwell, "Boundary Line Proceedings, 1710," *Virginia Magazine of History and Biography*, **5** (July 1897):10.

[26]Elizabeth Evans, *Weathering the Storm. Women of the American Revolution* (New York: Paragon House, 1989), 1, 5; Judith Sargent Murray, *The Gleaner* (Boston, 1798), **3**:189. See also Toby L. Ditz, "Ownership and Obligation: Inheritance and Patriarchal Households in Connecticut, 1750-1821," *William and Mary Quarterly*, **47** (April 1990): 235-65; idem, *Property and Kinship. Inheritance in Early Connecticut 1750-1820* (Princeton, NJ: Princeton University Press, 1986); Marylynn Salmon, *Women and the Law of Property in Early America* (Chapel Hill: University of North Carolina Press, 1986); Carole Shammas, Marylynn Salmon, and Michel Dahlin, *Inheritance in America: Colonial Times to the Present* (New Brunswick, NJ: Rutgers University Press, 1987).

[27]Struna, "Sport and Society," 299-302; Daniel Blake Smith, *Inside the Great House. Planter Life in the Eighteenth-Century Chesapeake Society* (Ithaca, NY: Cornell University Press, 1980), 80-124; McCusker and Menard, *Economy of Early America*, 295-330; Potter, "Demographic Development and Family Structure," 123-57.

[28]*Boston Evening-Post*, 14 January 1740; *Maryland Gazette*, 8 September 1747; Josiah Quincy, "Journal of Josiah Quincy," Massachusetts Historical Society *Proceedings*, **49** (1915-16): 455; Philip V. Fithian, *Journal and Letters of Philip Vickers Fithian, 1773-1774: A Plantation Tutor of the Old Dominion*, ed. H.D. Farish (Williamsburg, VA: Colonial Williamsburg, 1943), 180-81; Nicholas Cresswell, *The Journal of Nicholas Cresswell 1774-1777* (New York: Dial Press, 1924), 18-19.

[29]Peter Gordon, *The Journal of Peter Gordon, 1732-1735*, ed. E. Merton Coulter (Athens: University of Georgia Press, 1963), 30; William Stephens, *The Journal of William Stephens 1741-1745*, ed. E. Merton Coulter, 2 vols. (Athens: University of Georgia Press, 1958), **1**: 81, **2**: 183; John Brickell, *The Natural History of North-Carolina* (Dublin, 1737), 32-34, 40; Jonathan Green, Diary 1738-1752, in Linscott Papers 1653-1922, ms, Massachusetts Historical Society, Boston, 27 February 1740, 1 March 1741; Anne Grant, *Memoirs of an American Lady: With Sketches of Manners and Scenery in America, as They Existed Previous to the Revolution* (New York: Printed for Samuell Campbell, C.K. and G. Bruce, 1809), 51-53; Charles Woodmason, *The Carolina Backcountry on the Eve of the Revolution. The Journal and Other Writings of Charles Woodmason, Anglican Itinerant*, ed. Richard J. Hooker (Chapel Hill: University of North Carolina Press, 1953), 129.

[30]Ferdinand Bayard, *Travels of a Frenchman in Maryland and Virginia With a Description of Philadelphia and Baltimore in 1791*, ed. Ben C. McCary (Williamsburg, VA: Author, 1950), 40. About a woman renowned for her riding, see Herman Mann, *The Female Review: Life of Deborah Sampson* (New York: Arno Press, reprint ed., 1972), 167. Estate inventories also establish ownership of women's saddles.

[31]Gottlieb Mittleberger, *Journey to Pennsylvania*, ed. and trans. Oscar Handlin and John Clive (Cambridge, MA: Harvard University Press, 1960), 89.

[32]Struna, "Sport and Society," 299-300.

[33]*Maryland Journal and Baltimore Advertiser*, 30 April 1782; *Virginia Gazette and Alexandria Advertiser*, 7 October 1790.

[34]Fithian, *Journal and Letters*, 266.

[35]*Virginia Gazette* Day Book, 1764-1766, Colonial Williamsburg Research Library, Williamsburg, VA, 98, 124, 168; Eliza Pinckney, *The Letterbook of Eliza Lucas Pinckney 1739-1762*, ed. Elise Pinckney (Chapel Hill: University of North Carolina Press, 1972), 57; William Black, "Journal, 1744," ed. R. Alonzo Brock, *Pennsylvania Magazine of History and Biography*, **1** (1877): 130-31; Fithian, *Journal and Letters*, 57-58, 101-102, 201-202, 248; Landon Carter, *The Diary of Colonel Landon Carter of Sabine Hall, 1752-1778*, ed. Jack P. Greene, 2 vols. (Charlottesville: University Press of Virginia, 1965), **1**: 320; Julia Spruill, *Women's Life and Work in the Southern Colonies* (Chapel Hill: University of North Carolina Press, 1938), 1081.

[36]Pinckney, *Letterbook*, 34-35.

[37]Ibid., 48-49.

[38]Ibid.

[39]Ibid., 147-48.

[40]Carole Shammas, *The Pre-Industrial Consumer in England and America* (Oxford: Oxford University Press, 1990); Lois Green Carr and Lorena S. Walsh, "Changing Lifestyles and Consumer Behavior in the Colonial Chesapeake," in *Of Consuming Interests*, ed. Hoffman, et al.; Lorena S. Walsh, Gloria L. Main,

and Lois Green Carr, "Toward a History of the Standard of Living in British North America," *William and Mary Quarterly*, **45** (January 1988): 116-69; Gloria L. Main and Jackson Turner Main, "Standards and Styles of Living in Southern New England, 1640-1774," *Journal of Economic History*, **48** (1988): 27-46; T.H. Breen, "An Empire of Goods: The Anglicization of Colonial America, 1690-1776," *Journal of British Studies*, **25** (1986): 467-99.

[41]Struna, "Sport and the Awareness of Leisure"; idem, "Gender and Sporting Practice."

[42]Stokes, *Iconography*, **4**: 640; Baltimore County Court Minutes, 1762, 1763, 1772, 1775, Maryland Hall of Records, Annapolis; John Adams, *Diary and Autobiography of John Adams*, ed. L.H. Butterfield, 4 vols. (Cambridge, MA: Harvard University Press, 1961), **1**: 172-73; Christine Stansell, *City of Women. Sex and Class in New York, 1789-1860* (Urbana: University of Illinois Press, 1987).

[43]John Gibson to Mrs. John Ross, Letter, 14 July 1741, Gibson Maynadier Papers, ms, Maryland Historical Society, Baltimore; *Virginia Gazette*, 28 November 1745, 25 July 1766, 26 October 1769, 8 November 1770, 22 October 1772; Anna Green Winslow, *Diary of Anna Green Winslow*, ed. Alice M. Earle (Boston: Houghton Miffin, 1894), 28; Watson, *Annals of Philadelphia*, 242; Mays Dramatic History of Baltimore, ms 995, Part 6 (1747-1819), 26 July 1764, Maryland Historical Society, Baltimore; James Parker, "Diary," *New England Historical and Genealogical Register*, **69** (January 1915): 14, 121; *Maryland Gazette*, 14 June 1753; *Essex Gazette*, 2 August 1768; *Boston Gazette and Country Journal*, 16 October 1769.

[44]Struna, "Gender and Sporting Practice." The argument also draws from Raymond Williams, *The Sociology of Culture* (New York: Schocken Books, 1982); Kathy Peiss, "Commercial Leisure and the 'Woman Question,' " in *For Fun and Profit. The Transformation of Leisure into Consumption*, ed. Richard Butsch (Philadelphia: Temple University Press, 1990), 105-17; idem, "Gender Relations and Working-Class Leisure: New York City, 1880-1920," in *"To Toil the Livelong Day." America's Women at Work, 1780-1980*, ed. Carol Groneman and Mary Beth Norton (Ithaca, NY: Cornell University Press, 1987), 98-111.

[45]Moreau de St. Mery, *Moreau de St. Mery's American Journey (1793–1798)*, trans. and ed. Kenneth and Anna M. Roberts (Garden City, NY: Doubleday, 1947), 59-60, 154, 156, 336-37; Johann David Schoepf, *Travels in the Confederation (1783-1784)*, trans. and ed. Alfred J. Morrison, 2 vols. (New York: Franklin, 1968), **1**: 173-74; John F.D. Smyth, *A Tour in the United States of America* (1784), 2 vols. (New York: Arno Press, reprint ed., 1968), **1**: 98-99; Stokes, *Iconography*, **5**: 1311.

[46]Probate Records of Baltimore, Anne Arundel, Worcester, Frederick, Queen Anne, and St. Mary's counties, Estate Inventories, 1770, 1790, 1810, Maryland Hall of Records, Annapolis; Suffolk County Probate Records, Inventories, 1769, 1790, 1810, Suffolk County Courthouse, Boston; Struna, "Sport and the Awareness of Leisure"; idem, "Gender and Sporting Practice."

[47]Henry Wansey, *Henry Wansey and His American Journal, 1794*, ed. David John Jeremy (Philadelphia: American Philosophical Society, 1970), 112, 218-19; *Columbia Mirror and Alexandria Gazette*, 22 October 1795; *New York Daily Advertiser*, 25 June 1805.

[48]Cited in Watson, *Annals of Philadelphia*, 239.

[49]*New York Daily Advertiser*, 4 July 1801.

[50]Linda K. Kerber, " 'History Can Do It No Justice.' Women and the Reinterpretation of the American Revolution," in *Women in the Age*

of the American Revolution, ed. Ronald Hoffman and Peter J. Albert (Charlottesville: University Press of Virginia, 1989), 3-42; idem, "The Republican Ideology of the Revolutionary Generation," *American Quarterly*, **37** (1985):474-95; Linda K. Kerber, Nancy F. Cott, Robert Gross, Lynn Hunt, Carroll Smith-Rosenberg, and Christine M. Stansell, "Beyond Roles, Beyond Spheres: Thinking About Gender in the Early Republic," *William and Mary Quarterly*, **46** (July 1989): 565-85; Mary Beth Norton, *Liberty's Daughters: The Revolutionary Experiences of American Women, 1750-1800* (Boston: Little, Brown, 1980); Carroll Smith-Rosenberg, "Domesticating 'Virtue': Coquettes and Revolutionaries in Young America," in *Literature and the Body: Essays on Populations and Persons*, ed. Elaine Scarry (Baltimore: Johns Hopkins University Press, 1988), 160-84.

[51]Struna, " 'Good Wives' and 'Gardeners'," 247-50; Mary Kelley, *Private Woman, Public Stage: Literary Domesticity in Nineteenth Century America* (New York: Oxford University Press, 1984); Nancy F. Cott, *The Bonds of Womanhood. Woman's Sphere in New England 1780-1835* (New Haven, CT: Yale University Press, 1977); Kathryn Kish Sklar, *Catharine Beecher. A Study in American Domesticity* (New Haven, CT: Yale University Press, 1973).

[52]Struna, " 'Good Wives' and 'Gardeners'," 247-50; Roberta J. Park, " 'Embodied Selves': The Rise and Development of Concern for Physical Education, Active Games and Recreation for American Women, 1776-1865," *Journal of Sport History*, **5** (Summer 1978): 5-41.

Chapter 5

Women, Sport, and Exercise in the 19th Century

Patricia Vertinsky

It is hoped that by understanding women's sporting heritage and by becoming alert to the ways in which sport has been and continues to be co-opted for the purpose of male control over female sexuality and the female reproductive function, women will be strengthened in the struggle for autonomy in sport.

HELEN LENSKYJ
Out of Bounds: Women, Sport and Sexuality

Revisiting the story of women, sport, and exercise in the 19th century evokes the heady anticipation felt by late 20th-century women seeking to hone and test their physical powers in fitness and sporting endeavors. It also underlines the reality that women of all ages and talents continue to be denied equal access to many of the benefits that participation and success in sport can bring. Much of the rhetoric about the sporting gains of women during the 19th century has couched those gains as a victory of feminism and scientific rationality over the tyranny of male dominance, restrictive female fashion, and ignorance about health matters.

To be sure, the seeds of change were sown in many quarters: by the female health reformers of the first half of the 19th century and then through the leadership of pioneering women physicians and professional physical educators. Opportunities for women to be sportive began to flourish in voluntary organizations and athletic clubs and at exclusive women's colleges, as well as through participation in agricultural fairs, Western rodeos, and popular amusements such as commercial dance halls frequented by working-class women at the turn of the 20th century. By the end of the 19th century, women were engaged in a more varied and strenuous sports life than could have been envisioned a century earlier. They lived longer and had fewer children. They had better health and better medicine, and some had greater access to higher education and professional opportunities. In both image and fact, says Verbrugge, "a new model of able-bodied womanhood had emerged."[1]

In this chapter we will examine some of the main strands of evidence that historians have uncovered about women's health, exercise, and sporting activities in the 19th century. Much of the story is not widely known, for traditional histories of sport and physical education tend to focus on the male experience, often rendering women invisible. Until recently historians had paid more attention to the development of sport in female educational institutions and the well-reported sporting activities of the wealthier and more leisured classes. Our comprehension of the nature and extent of sporting activities beyond these boundaries is quite limited, and Struna has suggested that if we are to push back the boundaries of our knowledge we must seek out fresh source material.[2]

Consequently, sport historians are beginning to explore diverse source materials to reconstruct a broad range of images of women in sport. They are asking new questions about the differences between groups of women, the influence of the interaction of class and race with gender on women's sport and leisure, and the effect of specific localities on sporting activity. Studies such as Guttmann's recent history of women's sports are enriching our historical knowledge of women's sporting experience and helping to enlarge our understanding of the complex forces that affect the development of women's sport and exercise.[3]

The Antebellum Years— A Growing Concern for Female Health and Exercise (1820–1860)

America at the beginning of the 19th century was a pioneer country in which women generally were relegated to a dependent and subordinate role. Wifehood and motherhood were twin goals to which women were expected to aspire. Their place was at home, and few were fortunate enough to obtain educational opportunities.[4] American women were bound to their husbands, in most states having no legal rights to their own property or children, as well as being isolated from and generally denied participation in public life.

Life in a rural environment placed strenuous physical demands on women, and where puritan sentiment discouraging recreational pastimes did not prevail, leisure time allowed attention to be paid to a number of sporting diversions such as dancing, horseback riding, and ice skating.[5] Indeed, the sport that became most acceptable for women was horseback riding, so long as they retained their grace and femininity.[6] Bulger has pointed out that women rode more in the South than in the North, and that by the 1850s it was fairly common to see women attending horse races and riding at agricultural fairs.[7] Pioneer farm and ranch women joined their menfolk at work, running farms, riding the range, and overseeing herds of cattle. On the frontier, independent women fished, hunted, hiked, and camped.

Among urban dwellers, girls had few opportunities for sport at home or in seminaries, normal schools, and high schools. Those private schools that accepted women offered a "trifling, narrow, contracted education" consisting of courses such as needlework, music, drawing, and French.[8] There was no systematic provision for the physical culture of women, and when Oberlin College in Ohio first opened its doors to women in 1833 there was no evidence of attention to the physical in the curriculum.

By this time, however, voices were being raised concerning the poor physical condition of American women. Women's fragility and lack of health and energy was a recurrent theme in the early years of the 19th century, in spite of the fact that available life expectancy and mortality rates suggested that women were not necessarily less hardy than males.[9] Concern arose that women's lifestyles were an important contribution to "a terrible decay of female health all over the land."[10] There were lamentations in the popular and medical literature of antebellum society that women were being corrupted by fashion, wearing restrictive clothes, and feigning chronic invalidism as a sign of female delicacy. Physiologists were particularly worried that women who were living "unphysiologically" might produce weak and degenerate offspring. Girls, they insisted, needed more exercise at a critical developmental period to become robust mothers.[11]

Concern about exercise focused on the schools. Confined to their desks for long periods of time and restrained from exercising at recess, girls inevitably suffered stunted development.[12] "It seemed," noted William Bentley Fowle, "as if the sex had been thought unworthy of an effort to improve their physical powers."[13] An article in the *American Annals of Education* complained that "There is something radically wrong in the present system of education among young ladies, [for] their physical condition does not receive from parents or teachers that consideration which it deserves."[14]

In response to growing concern about the perceived poor physical development of women, health reformers called for physical exercise to play a larger role in female education. Indeed, the decades between 1820 and 1860 were characterized by a wave of health reformers and feminists advocating the increase of physical vigor and health of women through exercise and hygienic living habits.[15] Catharine Beecher (daughter of the Congregational minister, Lyman Beecher, and sister of Harriett Beecher Stowe, author of *Uncle Tom's Cabin*) was one of the earliest and most influential leaders to stress the value of female exercise. She lectured on the physical needs of women and founded two female seminaries that emphasized daily exercise.[16] Emma Hart Willard, who founded the Troy Female Seminary in 1821, prescribed a daily program of physical education including calisthenics, dancing, riding, and walking. Her helper, Almira Phelps, elaborated on

exercises for health and beauty in her *Lectures to Young Ladies*. "Calisthenics, or female gymnastics," she said, "is very properly becoming a branch of education."[17]

Catharine Beecher, founder of the Hartford Female Seminary in Connecticut in 1824, considered herself to be the inventor of a system of calisthenics that was widely used for several decades. Her book *Physiology and Calisthenics for Schools and Families* (1856) became the textbook for courses in hygiene and calisthenics in the leading seminaries and in some women's colleges.[18] At Hartford students followed perhaps the most vigorous and sustained program of exercise available to women at the time. Calisthenics, riding, and sports also were taught at her Western Female Institute in Cincinnati, Ohio, between 1833 and 1837. Gardening and croquet were added for fresh air and social experience.

Mary Lyon employed Beecher's physical education program, including domestic chores—"daily exercise of the best kind"—at Mount Holyoke Seminary, which she founded in Massachusetts in 1837.[19] Formal physical exercises were practiced regularly at Mount Holyoke until 1862, when Beecher's system was adopted and modified by Diocletian Lewis to become the "new gymnastics."[20] Dr. Lewis, a fervent moralist and physiologist, and a great admirer of female moral reform societies, was influential in encouraging the further promotion of exercise for women. Through numerous writings he portrayed his anxiety about female ill health and his distaste for the selfish "Misses Languid" of fashionable society, commenting that "every acute observer knows that the feminine soul . . . utters its richest harmonies only through a perfect instrument, . . . Exercise is the great law of development [yet] . . . our girls have no adequate exercise."[21] Lewis attempted to introduce light gymnastics for girls into the public schools and popularized the use of wooden dumbbells, beanbags, and other types of light gymnastic equipment for school and home. His system of new gymnastics (which was essentially a form of rhythmics) laid considerable emphasis on proper dress and diet, and achieved widespread popularity during the 1850s, 1860s, and 1870s. His Normal Institute for Physical Education, established in 1861, represented the first attempt to prepare teachers of physical education in the United States, and he personally supervised the gymnastics training of 300 young women teachers through a series of 10-week sessions.[22]

It is important to place in perspective the drive for health reform and female exercise during the antebellum years. Catharine Beecher lived and worked in a rapidly expanding society that perceived that the fabric of the social order was being torn apart by industrial and economic changes. Developing industrialization spawned urbanization and a host of social problems for which traditional forms of social organization seemed inadequate. By midcentury almost one fifth of Americans were living in towns and cities, and many of them were recent migrants. People were constantly on the move, geographically and socially. Physical and moral deterioration seemed, to observers of antebellum society, to be an inevitable result of urban chaos that could be reversed only by a dramatic surge of idealism and institutional remedies.

The Cult of Domesticity

Beecher's analysis of the problem was that the careful subordination of women to men within the newly emerging middle-class family was necessary for the harmonious development of society. Citing the duty of American women to save their country, she emphasized the role of domesticity as an antidote to a world gone mad with change. As a daughter of a late 18th-century "Republican mother," she advocated the development of female intellect and physical energy, but only within a carefully defined female sphere of influence— the private world of home and children. Republican ideology had defined women's place in the new nation as mothers and moral guardians. The properly educated Republican woman would stay

in the home to nurture and shape the characters of her husband and children. Seen as a cultivator of morality, woman was held to be morally superior to man, even as she remained physically inferior. The clear distinction between female and male roles encouraged the social construction of separate realms of activity for men and women—an active, public role for men in society and a confined and domestic role for women in the privacy of the home.

Women were clearly different from men, Beecher insisted, and because they had disparate (though complementary) goals they needed a particular curriculum for health and exercise. Female goals naturally embraced the three departments of teaching, health, and domestic economy—as distinct and important as those of law, medicine, and theology for men.[23] The system of exercises Beecher devised was not meant to cultivate the muscle and brawn needed by men for their role in public affairs, but to correct the female form and provide appropriate physical discipline to fit women better for their work in the home. In using calisthenics as one part of her effort to interpret and shape the collective consciousness of American women, Catharine Beecher resourcefully insinuated strict gender definitions and capabilities into a gymnastics system that remained popular throughout the 19th century. Her exercise program was part of an education suited to the needs of mid-19th-century women as defined by the natural order. Her ideas about the female role and function were perpetuated by a steadily growing national obsession with motherhood and domestic matters during the 19th century. The cult of domesticity (alternatively called the cult of true womanhood), which prescribed specific behavior for women in domestic life, epitomized both the links and the tension that existed between 19th-century efforts to esteem female importance while at the same time limiting it.

Changing Status of Women

Some modern feminists note that an emphasis on women's obligations in the domestic sphere usually has been antithetical to the general progress of women. A biological conception of woman as a reproductive agent perpetuates an undue emphasis on only one aspect of the female role. This ideology in turn colors the content of health and physical education and delimits female aspirations and opportunities for success in sport and physical activities.

Yet it is one of history's ironies, says Clements, that while the cult of true womanhood, "a set of ideas ostensibly so traditional, was enjoining most women to devote themselves to housekeeping, it was propelling others into launching an assault on patriarchal traditions."[24] As the Civil War approached, although marriage, motherhood, and domesticity were still preached as the standards of achievement for American woman, alternative paths to fulfillment increasingly were being proposed—paths "sprinkled with examples of nonconformity and invitations to self discovery."[25] Many women became deeply involved in crusades to change the status of women. The first American feminist movement was born; women participated in Utopian communities, joined abolitionist groups, discussed dress reform and birth control, fought for better conditions for working women, demanded the vote, and sought entry into higher education and male-controlled professions such as medicine. Women's demands for sport and physical education were expressions of varied attempts at female liberation that would become increasingly evident as the century matured. In fact, says Park, improved health and greater freedom in the choice of physical activities were among the major demands of many of the American "feminists" of the middle decades of the 19th century.[26]

These impulses were not, of course, confined to the North American scene, for they were part of far-reaching economic and social forces at work generally within western Europe and North America. As industrialization fostered the move toward a more urban society, new opportunities and problems were created while developments in science and technological innovation reshaped the way many people thought and lived. Anxieties about health and exercise were common in the early stages of all Western industrializing societies, and gymnastic and exercise systems were linked to emergent nationalism and broad democratic impulses.

The Scandinavian countries, for example, were the nurseries of therapeutic gymnastics. Denmark and Sweden pioneered systems of gymnastics that benefited girls and women through school programs, teacher training, and folk high schools. Starting early in the 19th century as a form of therapy, gymnastics grew to be a means of systematic development and support for a variety of health and educational reforms.[27] Danish gymnastics, which were developed by Franz Nachtegall in the early 19th century and borrowed from the German system, focused initially on open-air exercises with little apparatus. Later at the folk high schools and rifle clubs the Swedish system of exercise was combined with the earlier German-based systems, adding new exercises on the horizontal and parallel bars, flying rings, and trapeze. Toward the end of the 19th century the Danish gymnastics system broadened to aim at improving the whole person through systematic exercise, organized games, dancing, and rhythmic gymnastics.

The Swedish gymnastics system of Pehr Henrick Ling was based on scientific principles derived from the study of anatomy and physiology. Suitable freestanding exercises were selected for their specific effect on each part of the body and then arranged in groups and sequences to make a "daily order" of calisthenics. Later, on Ling's insistence that medicine and physical education must be allies, three groups of therapeutic exercises were added: active, passive, and resisted movements. The school gymnasium was typically arranged so that large numbers of pupils could exercise together, with stall bars arranged around the walls, ropes and rope ladders, balance beams, long benches, and bucks for vaulting. The equipment was particularly suitable for quick and easy rearrangement, allowing a variety of activities and an efficient use of space and time. The whole system became enormously popular and was widely disseminated. Indeed, Ling's medically based Swedish gymnastics system was to attract wide attention and support in both England and the United States in the latter years of the 19th century, particularly in relation to the physical education of girls and in teacher training colleges.

In Germany, Frederick Ludwig Jahn's first *Turplatz* (open-air gymnasium) of 1811 grew into a vast *Turnverein* (popular gymnastic) movement with strong political and militaristic underpinnings. By midcentury, the idea of physical fitness and national welfare had become an integral part of the school systems in German states. After the 1848 revolution in Europe, the system of formal gymnastics was exported throughout the industrializing world by waves of political refugees and gained a particularly strong foothold in the United States.[28]

While the *Turnverein* was spreading throughout Germany and systems of therapeutic school gymnastics were being developed in Sweden, sport and organized games were taking root in English boys' public schools. North American concern for female health and physical development was echoed by medical personnel and health reformers in England, despite the fact that American reformers routinely acknowledged superior British thinking and practices in the domain of female health and sport. In the first half of the 19th century, English women of rank, wealth, and privilege continued to ride, hunt, fish, shoot, and practice archery, but they were only a very small minority. The complex forces associated with industrialization, urbanization, and the rising middle classes closeted the early and mid-Victorian lady within an increasingly indoor and sedentary world. "The arbiters of acceptable behavior," comments McCrone, "considered it undignified for the daughters of gentlemen to develop muscles or exhibit athletic prowess. . . . Not until the middle of the nineteenth century did even the most moderate advice about the advantages of exercise begin to be taken."[29]

Female Sport and Exercise After Midcentury

In the second half of the 19th century, two powerful cultural forces collided over the questions of female sport and exercise. The first was a complex amalgam of beliefs stemming from the cult of true womanhood, which stressed traditional social and physical limitations of women, and the dissemination of social Darwinist ideas concerning social efficiency and the "survival of the fittest." Those concerned about social progress underlined the crucial importance of motherhood to evolution and the need to gear female education to the reproductive rather than the intellectual development of women. Physicians and social theorists became convinced that intellectual education overtaxed women and robbed them of the energy required for physical development, thus diminishing their reproductive strength.

The laws of nature were advanced as reason to closely regulate the mental and physical efforts of women. Perceived as a discrete energy field, the body was believed to contain a specific amount of vital energy. If excess energy was used in one direction, less would be available for other needs. Energy had to be husbanded for the specific needs of mind and body, in the present as well as for the future. One's quota of energy for the life span had to be spent carefully, because overuse could well be billed to future generations, to their detriment. "Nature," warned Herbert Spencer, "is a strict accountant . . . and if you demand of her in one direction more than she is prepared to lay out, she balances the account by making a deduction elsewhere."[30]

Herbert Spencer was extremely influential in popularizing the supposed physical disabilities of women in this period. He was perhaps the supreme ideologue of the Victorian period, his prolific work reflecting dominant middle-class ideas and values.[31] His delineation of the relationship of women to both evolutionary theory and the social and physical energy scheme had a critical impact on the public debate concerning education for women and attitudes toward female physical activity. Men had always been stronger than women, he said. Referring to Lamarck's law of use and disuse, Spencer explained that what initial strength women had in primitive times they had lost over time as evolution had freed them from the necessity of hard physical work.[32] Although both girls and boys required energy for physical development, girls developed more rapidly and used up their energy more quickly. As a result, not only did women start with less strength and use it up more quickly, they were subsequently taxed with the special energy demands of menstruation and reproduction. This "reproductive sacrifice" necessarily limited individual development but was essential in preserving the fitness of the race. A woman, it seemed, could not do two things at the same time. Because she was required to spend her energy on the needs of reproduction, any extra effort used in intellectual endeavor or in vigorous physical activity resulted in weakness, disease, infertility, or damage to future generations.

Physicians focused particular attention on adolescent girls. They were concerned that the onset of menstruation was so physically taxing that special precautions and plentiful rest were required at this time of life. Yet, as influential medical authorities stressed, if the tenets of social Darwinism and "survival of the fittest" were to be followed, then girls also needed the healthful benefits of gentle games and moderate physical activity to become strong mothers. On the one hand, definitions of femininity and the menstrual disability theory encouraged girls to accept limits on their actions, including athletic limitations, as the price for having a female body. On the other hand, the development of physical strength and health was a necessary attribute of a robust, productive mother. Some resolution was required to support the training of strong and healthy girls for the demanding responsibilities of motherhood within the boundaries of social respectability and the domestic realm.

The second set of forces for change emerged as a natural corollary of the burgeoning demands for women's rights, higher education, and professional training. If work and sport were mutually reinforcing for men, then emancipating women could clearly see that they needed to take up sport. Feminist Frances Cobbe wrote in 1870 that women would never participate in sports and amusements until they began participating in meaningful work.[33] As a number of determined women pursued opportunities in the public domain, they also sought the right to use their own bodies as they wished, by choosing to marry or not, by pursuing professional careers, and by playing tennis or golf or riding a bicycle.

The result, suggests Holt, was paradoxical, for in spite of the liberating aspects of sport participation, in certain respects female sport subtly reinforced the orthodox view of woman's place in society. "A delicate balance was struck between new demands for physical emancipation and the continued, traditional constraints of social respectability."[34] By the end of the century, many women were certainly permitted a more physically active life. On the other hand, their sporting liberation remained carefully circumscribed by stereotyped notions of woman's nature, capacity, and role.

Popular Sport for Women

Popular female demands for sport began to appear shortly after the Civil War in the United States, and participation continued to increase throughout the rest of the century, especially but not only in athletic clubs and female educational institutions. Indeed, demands for women's inclusion in sport came mainly from the elite, for many lower-class women were too overwhelmed with physical labor inside and outside the home to have time or energy for sports.[35]

In 1866 a croquet craze swept the country, and the game became very popular as a female recreation. In local groups across the land, women joined with men in a popular and fashionable sporting pastime seen as perfectly appropriate for females.[36] Archery too became quite popular as an acceptable female sport, along with tennis. Archery was one of the first organized competitive sports for women, who were included as members of many archery clubs and were allowed to participate regularly in tournaments after the 1870s.[37]

⌈Lawn tennis, introduced to the United States at the Staten Island Cricket and Baseball Club by Mary Ewing Outerbridge in 1874, also suited prevailing views about appropriate female physical activity.[38] By the 1880s, socially advantaged women were playing the game at many private clubs, although the caliber of play was limited by restrictive dress and the danger of appearing "rompish." Henry Slocum worried that women would sacrifice grace by learning to smash, volley, and play the difficult strokes of lawn tennis.[39] More often the game was played with several partners on each side of a net, gently batting the ball to and fro without undue exertion or the displacement of long skirts and petticoats.⌋

As the century advanced, women could be found participating in horseback riding, bowling, rowing, canoeing, yachting, and ice and roller skating, although none of these activities achieved mass appeal across the country.

The sport that was to exert the greatest influence on women's physical emancipation, however, was bicycling— an activity introduced from England in the 1870s that became enormously popular in the late 1880s and early 1890s.[40] For women, bicycling offered the potential for physical mobility and the benefits of healthy, active recreation, as well as a new sense of liberty from restrictive dress and chaperonage. When American women took to the bicycle, dress reform became a necessity, demanding the loosening of corsets and the dividing of heavy skirts into knickerbockers or bloomers. Middle-class women who hitherto had lacked the time, wealth, and social status to participate in elite sport found a sporting activity to suit their needs and a new means of transportation to increase their freedom of movement.[41]

In the last decade of the century golf became increasingly popular as a sport considered "well paced" for women, and many athletic clubs began to build special facilities for women. These clubs played an important role in the development of women's sports; and although it is important to remember that they catered to the very rich, they played a significant role in making physical fitness and athletics respectable for the emerging "new woman."[42]

At the same time, considerable forces were ranged against the full participation of late-19th-century women in sports and recreation. Bicycling received strong criticism from a number of leading medical doctors who, initially having viewed the sport as an excellent means for women to gain health and strength, began to have doubts about its effects. Excessive activity was said to be the problem as too many women abandoned the law of moderation and exposed themselves to the dangers of heart overstrain, "bicycle-face" (a condition that included wild, staring eyes, a strained expression, and a protruding jaw), and damage to the spine and reproductive system.[43] Such attempts to involve the bicycle in the etiology of female disease illustrated the continued uneasiness of influential male physicians about the effects of physical exertion on middle- and upper-class women's health. It is difficult to avoid the conjecture that many of them were perhaps also nervous about the freedom, physical liberty, and new female ambitions that bicycling appeared to represent.

There did not seem to be a concomitant concern about working-class women. Physicians who worried about female exertion also believed that "Jane in the factory can work more steadily on the loom than Jane in college with the dictionary."[44] Historians have assumed that working-class women shared a belief in the cult of domesticity and thus embraced the same conditions and constraints as middle-class women when it came to sport. Such assumptions are beginning to be challenged as new evidence is uncovered about the

Figure 5.1   Ice boating on the Hudson River, circa 1880. Courtesy Sally Fox Collection.

Figure 5.2 Roller skating, circa 1885. Courtesy Sally Fox Collection.

recreational activities and zest for physical activity among working women.

Peiss, in *Cheap Amusements: Working Women and Leisure in Turn-of-the-Century New York*, has shown how many working women in New York ''carved out of daily life a sphere of pleasure that belied the harsh realities of the shop floor and tenement.''[45] Creating a working-class variant of the ''new woman'' in the late 19th century, young single working women danced in the tenement halls and social clubs and flocked to play ball and stroll in the city parks. As the new century dawned, the dance hall became a favorite arena for the physical pleasures of dancing as well as opportunities for social participation—opportunities sought just as avidly in England as ballroom dancing became universally popular.[46]

As was the case with concerns about female health and exercise, many of the female sporting activities that gained a following in North America were first popularized in England. Park has pointed out cogently that ''The vector arrow points westward from Great Britain to the United States.'' Indeed, she continues:

Figure 5.3 Women's bicycle race, London, circa 1890. Courtesy Sally Fox Collection.

the antecedents of American forms of sports—and the values associated with them, at least initially—came from Great Britain [and] nineteenth-century American concepts of proper gender role, particularly among the middle- and upper-classes were also derived substantially from English models.[47]

Archery, for example, had been popular among upper-class English women since the late 18th century, and participation and competition in this sport expanded rapidly after midcentury.

Croquet became the rage in fashionable English society after the 1850s, and although not a vigorous sport, it required a certain amount of skill to play well.[48] Tennis developed a strong appeal among the social set, and private clubs vied to provide facilities for ladies. Tennis was particularly useful in bridging the gap between the upper and middle classes, and it became enormously popular in gardens and at clubs in the spreading suburbs of English cities. By 1900 there were 300 clubs attached to the Lawn Tennis Association.[49] Championship competitions promoted excellent players such as Lottie Dod and Dorothea Lambert Chambers, who modeled high-level sporting performance to a society reluctant to believe that females could play hard and skillfully without losing grace and femininity. Tight corsets made it difficult to breathe, let alone lob, but 15-year-old Lottie Dod ''hiked up her skirt to calf length and got away with it on the grounds that she was still a girl.''[50]

Golf, too, became a very popular sport in England and, just as in the United States, was played at clubs for the affluent where women's play was restricted to the least popular times and least attractive parts of the golf course. In the clubhouse, areas were reserved for each sex, and women organized their own ''section,'' developing a strong social network of club women. Again it was the bicycle, however, that truly provided

Figure 5.4   Archery, 1885. Courtesy Sally Fox Collection.

English women a new sense of physical freedom. Although the same vituperative debate about the potential dangers of cycling that was taking place in America raged in England, by 1895 bicycling was established as a national pastime. It was seen as a revolutionary form of transportation providing new opportunities for many women to surmount social and geographical barriers. Above all, the symbolism of the bicycle as a means of flight to freedom worked to the advantage of emancipating women, coinciding with a range of demands for female entry into the professional domain and increased access of women to a variety of sports and recreational activities.

It was in schools and colleges on both sides of the Atlantic, however, that women made the greatest strides in sport participation, especially in team sports. In England, organized sport was cultivated in the Oxbridge women's colleges and at the elite girls' public day and boarding schools such as Roedean, Cheltenham Ladies College, and St. Leonard's in Scotland. In North America, the seeds of change were sown in the exclusive women's colleges of New York and New England. Indeed, the women who attended such colleges as Vassar, Smith, Wellesley, and Bryn Mawr from the late 1860s through the end of the century had a significant influence on sport as an important facet of the physical emancipation of women.

Physical Education and Sport in Women's Schools and Colleges

Though Oberlin College had opened its doors to women students in 1833, higher education was not generally accessible to American women in pre-Civil War years. In denying the privilege of higher education to women, the claim was repeatedly made that the female constitution was weakened by intellectual study and that a female presence in male colleges was detrimental to male academic progress.

In 1865 Vassar College was founded by Matthew Vassar to prove that women could engage in and profit from higher education in the same way as men without losing their health in the process. In the college's "General Scheme of Education," physical education came first. Students were required to engage in the Lewis system of gymnastics, and facilities were provided for bowling, horseback riding, swimming, skating, and gardening.[51] Smith (1875), Wellesley (1875), and Bryn Mawr (1884) all were opened within the next two decades, and each college similarly advertised close attention to the promotion of good health as a cornerstone of good scholarship.[52]

The strong focus on health and physical development in these colleges, as well as an increase in the number of coeducational institutions, was precipitated by an intensification of earlier medical concerns about the deleterious effect of brain work on female reproductive development.[53] The precise physiological disqualifications of young women were elaborated most clearly by a Harvard professor, Dr. Edward Clarke, in 1873. His treatise, *Sex and Education: Or a Fair Chance for the Girls* (which ran through 17 editions in 13 years), mounted a major attack on the educational and professional aspirations of American women during the 1870s and 1880s.

Dr. Clarke had the agreement of a number of eminent medical men that the reproductive development of girls between 12 and 20 could be permanently arrested should they expend scarce energy on study. "The results of female education," he said, "are monstrous brains and puny bodies; abnormally weak digestion; flowing thought and constipated bowels."[54] Those who encouraged female education were roundly criticized for valuing development of mind over body and contributing to the degeneration of the race.[55]

Not surprisingly, there were vociferous objections to the conservative and misogynist implications of Dr. Clarke's views. Women's rights advocates attacked the idea that higher education or professional training could be implicated in the health deficiencies of American women and placed the blame squarely on restrictive clothing and a lack of fresh air and exercise. Were educational institutions to provide opportunities for physical training and outdoor games, they claimed, then it could be proved that girls could maintain a healthy physique even as they improved their minds and entered professional work.[56]

Instruction in physiology, as well as calisthenics and a broad range of sports, rapidly became mandatory at colleges and in all institutions of higher learning in the United States to which women were allowed access. Well-organized physical education departments supervised, tested, and measured female students, providing a stream of anthropometric data to show that college women were healthier than their noncollege counterparts. In 1882 women's rights leader Elizabeth Cady Stanton was able to claim that "statistics show that girls taking a college course are more healthy than those who lead listless lives in society."[57]

In pursuit of the broad objectives of physical education, colleges such as Wellesley experimented with different exercise systems to facilitate group and individual development and introduced a variety of outdoor sports. Three main exercise systems competed for favor: Swedish gymnastics, which was based on a therapeutic model; German gymnastics, which used heavy apparatus and reflected military routines; and Sargent exercises, which consisted of a program of strength-development exercises designed by Dudley Allen Sargent, director of the Hemenway Gymnasium at Harvard University. At Wellesley the Sargent system initially found favor in the 1880s because of its attention to individual development and measurement, but by the 1890s Swedish gymnastics had become more prominent. In fact, "Swedish gymnastics became the most common type of physical training in women's colleges by the end of the nineteenth century."[58]

Athletic facilities grew alongside those for gymnastics. The two sports that became most popular at the women's colleges were tennis and basketball, the latter being the first team sport to be played by any significant number of women. Basketball, introduced to Smith College in 1892 by Senda Berenson (and quickly modified for women to minimize the roughness of play and exhaustion of players), signaled a change of direction in women's college athletics as women were introduced to competitive sports and intensive athletics. Basketball proved to be enormously popular among women students and was particularly useful in teaching women physical stamina and teamwork.[59] Notes Smith, "If croquet introduced women to sporting activity in the 1860s, and the bicycle made it fashionable for women to exercise by the 1890s, it was basketball, within a decade of its origin, that became the acclaimed game for women in colleges throughout America"—a new game for the new woman.[60]

Participation in college athletics offered women an acceptable way to compete in sports, especially in the coeducational colleges of the West, though intercollegiate competitions were frowned on by female physical educators in the elite colleges of the East who feared the effects of competition on the health and welfare of their female charges.[61] Such reasoning, of course, meant that no American woman was given the opportunity to compete in the newly established modern Olympic Games until after the turn of the century (and then only in sports such as tennis, golf, and archery).

Looking at a similar set of events in England, McCrone has described how the Victorian woman's entry into sport was directly related to the campaign for female higher education and the efforts of the founders of the first women's colleges at Oxford and Cambridge.[62] Just as in the United States, these early leaders had to cope with attacks against university-educated women by eminent physicians who claimed that young women could not study and mature physically at the same time. During the 1870s the influential Dr. Henry Maudsley of University College, London, added his voice to Dr. Edward Clarke's warnings that female education jeopardized the very future of the race.[63] Like their American counterparts, reforming educators in England realized that the threat of overstrain could be diminished only by proving that women could maintain health while studying. As a result, health-engendering gymnastics and sport became regular features of university life at Girton and Newnham in Cambridge and at Lady Margaret and Somerville Hall in Oxford. The graduates of these colleges then introduced games into the leading girls' public day and boarding schools.[64]

Early girls' public day schools such as the North London Collegiate School and Cheltenham Ladies' College, and boarding schools such as Roedean, initially embraced a "double conformity" where girls' education was concerned. On the one hand they emulated male academic student life, and on the other they attempted to maintain Victorian values of female decorum. Sports were seen as a valuable means of stimulating study and providing discipline, as well as improving the health and childbearing potential of girl students. At Roedean, for example, the first prospectus announced that "special pains will be taken to guard against overwork; and from two to three hours daily will be allotted to outdoor exercise and games."[65]

In the long run, a balanced system of physical education based partly on the Swedish gymnastic system was developed in conjunction with regular medical inspections and a wide range of organized games. Manliness and womanliness remained distinct concepts, however, and the products of 19th-century girls' public schools were well socialized to the limitations of their sex. In particular, the experience of serious sports competition was denied to them because of its perceived potential for stressful anxiety and loss of feminine decorum. Competitive play was not to be allowed to contaminate a proper feminine image, although games were encouraged for the lessons they taught in self-control, fortitude, and persistence. Girls learned the power of working together . . . to play up and do their best! Field hockey, netball, and lacrosse were deemed by female educators to be particularly useful. Not requiring physical contact or great strength, they were seen to be "less masculine" than other types of team sports and so more acceptable for girls to play.[66] Well beyond the turn of the 20th century, in the exclusive British girls' schools, the production of healthy women took precedence over the pursuit of high-level female athletic performance and the pleasures of competitive sport.

On the other hand, a new breed of collegiate sportswomen was already insisting that girls be allowed to learn those lessons on the playing fields that men had long claimed were essential to character building. Notwithstanding the warnings of ultraconservative medical doctors such as Arabella Kenealy who in 1899 claimed that too-active women were squandering the birthright of "the babies," and that "nature groaned for the muscle-energy wasted by excessive sport," a new climate of opinion was emerging that in the long run would redefine traditional concepts of the nature of appropriate female sport.[67]

The Professionalization of Physical Education: Female Physical Education Teachers

Staffing physical education departments in schools and colleges on both sides of the Atlantic was a new genre of professional woman—the female physical educator hired to teach gymnastics and games and to oversee student health, often joining or taking over from a female physician.[68]

Cheltenham Ladies College, for example, by the turn of the 20th century had six trained physical education teachers responsible for teaching a wide variety of games, gymnastics, and health classes. They were all products of an impressive British system of specialist women's physical education colleges, initiated when a graduate of the Royal Central Gymnastics Institute in Stockholm was appointed to the London post of superintendent of physical education in girls' schools in 1879. The appointment signaled the beginning of systematic physical education for girls in the country's elementary schools and the rise to dominance of the Swedish system of therapeutic gymnastics. When Martina Bergman, later to become Mme Bergman-Osterberg, arrived from Sweden in 1881 to take up this position, her interest shifted from grade school to the more influential girls' public schools, and she embarked on a successful strategy to train women physical educators exclusively for this role. (There was much greater hope, she surmised, in training middle-class girls for healthy motherhood than in squandering effort on the lower class.) Modeled on the Central Institute in Stockholm, Bergman-Osterberg developed a highly successful Physical Training College at Dartford that became a prototype for future training institutions for women "gym teachers." Swedish gymnastics supplemented with training in English games was, to Mme Osterberg and her supporters, "the basis of a perfect training system"; and Ling's system, with its emphasis on health and balance, permeated female physical education for over half of the 20th century.[69]

The Swedish influence was also apparent in women's training institutions in the United States. Like Dartford, the Boston Normal School of Gymnastics (BNSG), founded in 1889, modeled its programs on that of Stockholm's Royal Central Institute of Gymnastics, and its early graduates had a significant effect on physical education teaching in women's schools and colleges.[70]

The BNSG was part of the emerging professional apparatus of physical education in North America in the last decades of the 19th century. A number of training programs for physical education emerged. Dr. Dudley Sargent opened a 1-year course for physical training teachers at Cambridge in 1881, and William G. Anderson founded a training school in Brooklyn that later became the New Haven Normal School of Gymnastics.[71] Anderson also was responsible for founding the American Association for the Advancement of Physical Education in 1885, in which 6 of the 49 original members were women.

Four years later the association supported a physical training conference in Boston that introduced the Swedish system of gymnastics as a competitor to German gymnastics and the respected Sargent system of exercise and measurement. This "battle of the systems" occupied the profession for years to come, as did struggles over the relative importance of medicine and education to the training of physical educators.[72]

The BNSG, however, with its Swedish emphasis, became one of the most productive and respected physical training institutions in the country, merging with the department of hygiene and physical education at Wellesley College in 1909. Prominent female BNSG graduates such as Mabel Lee, Senda Berenson, and Ethel Perrin were "visible testimony," says Verbrugge, "against the myth of female invalidism."[73] The story of these women, and the influence many of them exerted over the development of the profession and women's sport, spills over into the 20th century. They were champions of female health and promoters of recreation, exercise, and sports for girls in schools and colleges, through the Young Women's Christian Association, in sports associations and athletic clubs, and in municipal parks and children's playgrounds.[74]

Summary and Conclusions

Despite the rising aspirations and the many real gains of 19th-century women in the realm of sport and physical activity, we must conclude with Guttmann that "any expectations that the female athlete was about to take her place next to the male were destined for disappointment."[75] The development of women's sport has remained closely tied to the fortunes of the more general movements for female emancipation. As these have waxed and waned, so too has the expansion of opportunities for women in sport. At the dawn of this century, sportswomen formed a minority among women on both sides of the Atlantic, and

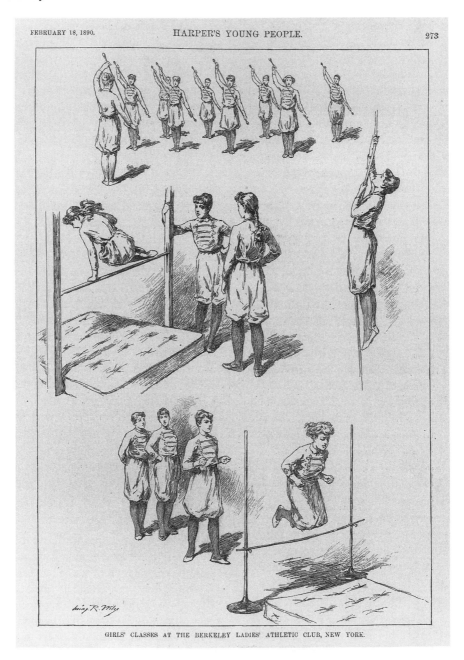

GIRLS' CLASSES AT THE BERKELEY LADIES' ATHLETIC CLUB, NEW YORK.

Figure 5.5   Girl's gym classes at the Berkeley Ladies Athletic Club, New York, 1890. Courtesy Sally Fox Collection.

relative to men they remained disadvantaged and experienced discrimination.[76]

Mass sport participation by girls and women was not a reality until the last third of the 20th century, when women's liberation helped make sport ''a respectable activity in a male dominated society.''[77] Yet negative interpretations of the consequences of sport for women persist. Elements of discriminatory practices against women in sport continue to be justified today by the claim that there are biological limits to women's capacity for high-level sport performance and that competitive sport is inherently problematic for women while beneficial to men. A reading of 19th-century history in the Western industrializing world can help us understand the salience of these ideas, but the resolution of the broad issues concerning equity and freedom of participation for women in sport lies in the future.

Notes

[1]Martha H. Verbrugge, *Able-Bodied Womanhood: Personal Health and Social Change in Nineteenth Century Boston* (Oxford: Oxford University Press, 1988), 196.

[2]Nancy L. Struna, ''Beyond Mapping Experience: The Need for Understanding History of American Women's Sport,'' *Journal of Sport History*, **11** (Spring 1984): 120-33.

[3]Allen Guttmann, *Women's Sports, A History* (New York: Columbia University, 1991).

[4]Harriet Martineau, *Society in America* (New York: Sanders & Otley, 1837).

[5]Jennie Holliman, *American Sports, 1785-1835* (Durham, NC: Seeman Press, 1931).

[6]''Riding on Horseback,'' *American Farmer*, **10** (June, 1928): 95.

[7]Margery A. Bulger, ''American Sportswomen in the Nineteenth Century,'' *Journal of Popular Culture*, **16** (Fall 1982): 2-3.

[8]C.F. Adams, ed. *Letters of Mrs. Adams, the Wife of John Adams* (Boston: Wilkins, Carter, 1848); Eleanor Flexner, *Century of Struggle: The Womens' Rights Movement in the United States* (Cambridge, MA: Harvard University Press, 1976).

[9]Verbrugge, *Able-Bodied Womanhood*, 13.

[10]Catharine Beecher, *Letters to the People on Health and Happiness* (New York: Harper & Bros., 1855; reprinted New York: Arno Press, 1972), 121.

[11]Patricia Vertinsky, ''Body Shapes: The Role of the Medical Establishment in Informing Female Exercise and Physical Education in Nineteenth-Century North America,'' in *From Fair Sex to Feminism: Sport and the Socialization of Women in the Industrial and Post-Industrial Eras*, ed. J.A. Mangan and R.J. Park (London: Frank Cass, 1987), 256-81.

[12]John Duffy, ''Mental Strain and Overpressure in the Schools: A Nineteenth-Century Viewpoint,'' *Journal of the History of Medicine and Allied Sciences*, **23** (January 1968): 63-79.

[13]William Bentley Fowle, in the *Medical Intelligencer*, quoted in *American Journal of Education* (1826): 698-99.

[14]*American Annals of Education*, **6** (1837): 100-105, quoted in Thomas Woody, *A History of Women's Education in the United States, Vol. II* (New York: Octagon Books, 1974), 99.

[15]W.A. Alcott, *Young Woman's Guide to Excellence* (New York: Harper & Bros., 1849); E.W. Duffin, *Influence of Modern Physical Education of Females in Producing and Confirming Deformity of the Spine* (New York: Chas. Frances, 1830); C. Caldwell, *Thoughts on Physical Education* (Boston: March, Capen & Lyon, 1834).

[16]Patricia Vertinsky, ''Sexual Equality and the Legacy of Catharine Beecher,'' *Journal of Sport History*, **6** (Spring 1979): 38-49.

[17]Almira Phelps, *Female Student: Or Lectures to Young Ladies—on Female Education* (New York: Leavitt & Lord, 1833), 49.

[18]Catharine Beecher, *Physiology and Calisthenics for Schools and Families* (New York: Harper & Bros., 1856).

[19]Edward Hitchcock, *The Power of Christian Benevolence Illustrated in the Life and Labor of Mary Lyon* (Northampton: Hopkins, Bridgman, 1852), 297.

[20]Woody, *History of Women's Education*, 114.

[21]Diocletian Lewis, *Our Girls* (New York: Harper & Bros., 1871), 67, 92.

[22]Fred E. Leonard and George B. Affleck, *A Guide to the History of Physical Education* (Philadelphia: Lea & Febiger, 1947), 261.

[23]Beecher, *Physiology and Calisthenics*, 72.

[24]Barbara Evans Clements, "Images of Women: Views from the Discipline of History," in *Foundations for a Feminist Restructuring of the Academic Disciplines*, ed. M.A. Paludi and G.A. Steuernagel (New York: Harrington Park Press, 1990), 116.

[25]Verbrugge, *Able-Bodied Womanhood*, 17.

[26]Roberta J. Park, "Embodied Selves: The Rise and Development of Concern for Physical Education, Active Games and Recreation for American Women, 1776-1860," *Journal of Sport History*, **5** (Summer 1978): 5-41.

[27]Peter C. McIntosh, "Therapeutic Exercise in Scandinavia," in *Landmarks in the History of Physical Education*, ed. J.G. Dixon, P.C. McIntosh, A.D. Munrow, and R.F. Willetts (London: Routledge & Kegan Paul, 1957), 81-107.

[28]Leonard and Affleck, *History of Physical Education*, 83-117.

[29]Kathleen E. McCrone, *Sport and the Physical Emancipation of English Women, 1870-1914* (London: Routledge & Kegan Paul, 1988), 7-11.

[30]Herbert Spencer, *Education: Intellectual, Moral and Physical* (London: Williams & Norgate, 1861), 179.

[31]For a discussion of Spencer's views on women and biological determinism, see Louise Michele Newman, ed. *Men's Ideas/Women's Realities: Popular Science 1870-1915* (New York: Pergamon Press, 1985), 1-11.

[32]The Lamarckian mechanism explained that the use of an organ resulted in its development, and disuse resulted in its degeneration over time. Because of prolonged disuse, women lacked a number of abilities that men had developed, especially abstract thought and reason. Woman, in short, was less completely evolved than man. George W. Stocking Jr., "Lamarckianism in American Social Science," *Journal of the History of Ideas*, **23** (1962): 239-59.

[33]Frances P. Cobbe, "Ladies' Amusements," *Every Saturday*, **9** (1870): 101.

[34]Richard Holt, *Sport and the British: A Modern History* (Oxford: Clarendon Press, 1989), 11.

[35]Allen Guttmann, *A Whole New Ball Game: An Interpretation of American Sports* (Chapel Hill: University of North Carolina Press, 1988), 139-58.

[36]"American Croquet," *Nation*, **3** (9 August 1866): 113-15.

[37]Maumee, "Modern Archery in America," *Outing*, **4** (June 1884): 35.

[38]Charles E. Clay, "The Staten Island Cricket and Baseball Club," *Outing*, **11** (November 1887): 104-5.

[39]Henry Slocum, "Lawn Tennis as a Game for Women," *Outing*, **14** (July 1889): 289.

[40]Robert A. Smith, *A Social History of the Bicycle: Its Early Life and Times in America* (New York: McGraw-Hill, 1972).

[41]Richard Harmond, "Progress and Flight: An Interpretation of the American Cycle Craze of the 1890s," *Journal of Sport History*, **5** (Winter 1971): 235-57.

[42]Bulger, "American Sportswomen," 11; Benjamin G. Rader, *American Sports* (New York: Prentice-Hall, 1983).

[43]James C. Whorton, "Hygiene of the Wheel," in *Crusaders for Fitness: The History of American Health Reformers* (Princeton, NJ: Princeton University Press, 1982), 304-30.

[44]Edward H. Clarke, *Sex in Education: Or a Fair Chance for the Girls* (Boston: Osgood, 1873), 131.

[45]Kathy Peiss, *Cheap Amusements: Working Women and Leisure in Turn-of-the-Century New York* (Philadelphia: Temple University Press, 1986), 3.

[46]Arthur H. Franks, *Social Dance: A Short History* (London: Macmillan 1963).

[47]Roberta J. Park, "Sport, Gender and Society in a Transatlantic Victorian Perspective," in *Fair Sex*, ed. Park and Mangan, 58.

[48]Duke of Beaufort and Alfred T. Watson, eds., *The Badminton Library of Sports and Pastimes*, 19 vols. (London, 1885-1902, vol. 12), quoted in McCrone, *Sport and Physical Emancipation*, 156.

[49]Holt, *Sport and the British*, 126.

[50]Adrianne Blue, *Grace Under Pressure: The Emergence of Women in Sport* (London: Sidgwick & Jackson, 1987), 10.

[51]Prospectus of the Vassar Female College (New York: Alford, 1865).

[52]Dorothy S. Ainsworth, *The History of Physical Education in Colleges for Women* (New York: A.S. Barnes, 1930); Betty Spears and Richard A. Swanson, *History of Sport and Physical Activity in the United States* (Dubuque, IA: Brown, 1983).

[53]Patricia Vertinsky, *The Eternally Wounded Woman: Women, Exercise and Doctors in the Late Nineteenth Century* (Manchester, England: Manchester University Press, 1990).

[54]Clarke, *Sex and Education*, 41.

[55]Thomas S. Clouston, *Female Education From a Medical Point of View* (London: Methuen, 1882).

[56]Julia Ward Howe, ed. *Sex and Education: A Reply to Dr. E.H. Clarke's "Sex in Education"* (Boston: Roberts Bros., 1874).

[57]Elizabeth Cady Stanton, "The Health of American Women," *North American Review*, **313** (1882): 510-17.

[58]Verbrugge, *Able-Bodied Womanhood*, 152.

[59]Senda Berenson, "Editorial," *Basketball for Women: Spalding's Athletic Library* (October 1901): 5-7.

[60]Ronald A. Smith, "The Rise of Basketball for Women in Colleges," in *The American Sporting Experience: A Historical Anthology of Sport in America*, ed. Steven A. Riess (New York: Leisure Press, 1984), 239; see also Joan S. Hult and Marianna Trekell eds. *A Century of Women's Basketball* (Reston, VA: AAPHERD, 1991).

[61]Cindy L. Himes, "The Female Athlete in American Society: 1860-1940" (PhD diss., University of Pennsylvania, 1986).

[62]McCrone, *Sport and the Physical Education of Women*.

[63]Henry Maudsley, "Sex in Mind and Education," *Fortnightly Review*, **14** (1874): 466-83.

[64]Kathleen E. McCrone, "The 'Lady Blue': Sport at the Oxbridge Women's Colleges From Their Foundation to 1914," *British Journal of Sports History*, **3** (1986): 191-215.

[65]Dorothy E. de Zouche, *Roedean School, 1885-1955* (Brighton, 1955), 27.

[66]Sheila Fletcher, "The Making and Breaking of a Female Tradition: Women's Physical Education in England, 1880-1980," in *Fair Sex*, ed. Mangan and Park, 145-60.

[67]Arabella Kenealy, "Woman as an Athlete," *Nineteenth Century*, **45** (1899): 642.

[68]"Female Physicians and their Views on Exercise," in Vertinsky, *The Eternally Wounded Woman*, Pt. 2.

[69]Dartford College Archives, M. Osterberg, "The Physical Education of Girls in England," 1913, 7; Sheila Fletcher, *Women First: The Female Tradition in English Physical Education, 1880-1980* (London: Athlone, 1984).

[70]Ainsworth, *The History of Physical Education in Colleges*.

[71]Verbrugge, *Able-Bodied Womanhood*.

[72]Mabel Lee and Bruce Bennett, "1885-1900. A Time of Gymnastics and Measurement," *Journal of Physical Education, Recreation and Dance*, **54** (April 1985): 19-26.

[73] Verbrugge, *Able-Bodied Womanhood*, 190.

[74] Leonard and Affleck, *History of Physical Education*, ch. 27; Paula D. Welch and Harold A. Lerch, *History of American Physical Education and Sport* (Springfield, IL: Charles C Thomas, 1981), 225-26.

[75] Guttmann, *A Whole New Ball Game*, 147.

[76] Donald J. Mrozek, *Sport and the American Mentality, 1880-1910* (Knoxville: University of Tennessee Press, 1983), 137.

[77] John A. Lucas and Ronald A. Smith, *Saga of American Sport* (Philadelphia: Lea & Febiger, 1978), 265.

Chapter 6

The Story of Women's Athletics: Manipulating a Dream 1890–1985

Joan S. Hult

Man for the field and woman for the hearth
Man for the sword and for the needle she
Man with the head and woman with the heart
Man to command and woman to obey
All else confusion.

ALFRED, LORD TENNYSON
"The Princess"

Tennyson clearly describes the gender division of the last three decades of the 19th century: Man to the marketplace, woman at home with her family; woman the mistress of domesticity, man the master of all else (war, diplomacy, economics, politics, education); man the rational thinker (needs an education), woman the guardian of morals (needs only religious convictions of the heart); man dominant, woman subordinate. Accordingly, if this "natural order of the universe" is disrupted, chaos results. Indeed, the injection of gender equality into secondary and higher education did introduce the potential for confusion, even chaos, for it challenged the very foundation of the social order. The mission of colleges and universities had been to graduate *men* to lead.

The ideology of separate spheres described by Tennyson illustrates why gender is a fundamental variable in our historical examination of women in education and sport. Gender, as distinguished from sex, denotes "cultural constructs"; or "the element of social relationships based on perceived differences between the sexes and gender is a primary way of signifying relationships of power."[1] The male and female sex difference, by contrast, can be defined as biological distinctiveness or a physiological phenomenon.

At the end of the 19th century came Theodore Roosevelt's declaration that males in our society had become too soft and effeminate because frontiers and battlefields no longer existed to test manly courage and perseverance. Only aggressive sports could create "the brawn, the spirit, the self-confidence and the quickness of men." The football field, Roosevelt contended, "is the only place where masculine supremacy is incontestable."[2]

A central theme affecting woman's freedom to engage in sport was found in Roosevelt's paradoxical belief that for men sport served as a "rite of passage" defining masculinity, whereas women's limitations were inherent in the "cult of true womanhood." In this chapter we examine women's experiences as they move from a separate female environment into a traditional masculine domain. This discussion of American higher education and sport probes gender constructs as they interact to influence the changing roles, bodily forms, functions, and meaning of sporting experiences for college women from 1870 through the 1980s. Recurring themes in the saga of women in higher education and sport that have significant influences are

- the medical profession's notions of the inherent weaknesses mandated by females' anatomy and physiology;
- marriage, motherhood, and service as the prevailing feminine occupations with accompanying assumptions of proper female behavior;
- changing concepts of health, beauty, and bodily form;
- separatist ideas and practices by physical educators acting in what Park has called "a

sheltered refuge in a competitive and male-dominated society"[3]; and
- power relations in athletic governance.

The wondrous story of athletic sports for women in American higher education starts in the 1870s. This was the first full decade of higher education for women, as well as the time during which women physical educators became prime movers in the manipulation of the athletic dream. In this chapter we concentrate on separatist practices in physical education and school athletics with particular consideration given to the nature of power relations in competitive athletics. The story of women's athletics differs significantly from that of men's athletics. Women's athletics emerged from programs of physical education. Women physical educators constantly sought to manipulate the dream of what ought to be the programs of athletics for girls and women. Knowledge of the prevailing cultural attitudes and behaviors, as well as women's separate spheres, is central to understanding women's experiences in higher education.[4]

Two separate case studies, 1920–1940 and 1960–1980, are presented to illustrate the struggle for governance and control of athletics in education. The 1920-1940 case study explores the formation and role of physical education and power relations surrounding educational athletics and the attempted control of athletics in the public sector. The 1960-1980 case study examines critical issues in physical education and governance in collegiate athletics with a major focus on the power relations between the Association for Intercollegiate Athletics for Women (AIAW) and the National Collegiate Athletic Association (NCAA).

The Age of Physical Education: 1870–1920

Medical opinion as discussed in chapter 5 illustrates the importance of the medical view in the actions taken by women physical educators to adjust girls' and women's programs. They focused on health objectives in higher education and for future physical education teachers.[5]

Physical Education

In the 1870s and 1880s colleges appointed female physical education instructors to teach gymnastics and calisthenics to the increasing numbers of female students. The women designed programs to inaugurate a hygiene that should lead to healthy and vigorous womanhood. By the mid-1880s physical education programs existed in all eastern women's colleges, and many midwestern colleges and universities had some type of sports and gymnastics for women. Western and southern college programs joined the others primarily in the 1890s.[6]

The vision of the ''new woman'' had emerged by the 1890s. The ''new woman'' was more independent than women of the previous generation. She moved outside the home to attend college and to work in professional occupations or with volunteer associations. However, the belief that the pressures of academic life could damage women's health, even the health of the ''new woman,'' continued to influence physical education practice well into the 20th century.[7]

During the 1890s, a shift was taking place in the popular view of the ideal female physical form and pursuit of beauty. Instrumental in this shift were the newly hired women physical educators, who by originating their programs during the 1880s and early 1890s had encouraged women to develop attributes in keeping with the Gibson Girl ideal and to experience greater freedom in active sports. (This ideal was named for fashion artist Charles Dana Gibson, who created the Gibson Girl look in *Life* magazine in the 1890s). The Gibson Girl was tall, vigorous, and commanding. She was, according to Banner in *American Beauty*, ''symbolic of the hopeful changes of the age: the new movement of women into the work force, the new freedom of behavior between men and women, the new vogue of athletics promising healthier bodies.''[8]

The sports available were in line with Catharine Beecher's nature-related prescription (e.g., croquet, archery, sailing, equestrianism, and tennis) mentioned in chapter 5. By 1900, basketball, cycling, baseball, swimming, golf, and field hockey were a part of the curricula in colleges; however, the mainstay was Swedish gymnastics and calisthenics, which incorporated medical, pedagogical, and aesthetic aspects. The classes used wands, Indian clubs, music, light apparatus, adaptive exercises, and ''Days Order'' (routine exercises). Many colleges hired women doctors to oversee the programs, and most programs emphasized recreational sport, fundamental gymnastics, posture, and anthropometric measurement, straying little from the medical opinion of the day.[9]

The female physical education instructors of the 19th and early 20th centuries accepted the medical profession's guidance, advice, and authority as truth. At the same time they saw themselves as the knowledgeable authority figures for their students. From the beginning they took control of a separate sphere of physical education programs in higher education. Their mission was to balance the rigors of intellectual life with healthful and ''appropriate'' sporting activities. This meant increasing strength and muscle to improve women's maternal function and to enhance beauty and feminine curves. Their goals included correct posture, facial and bodily beauty, health, recreation, and the democratic ideal of ''a sport for every girl and a girl for every sport,'' as opposed to pursuit of the Olympic laurel wreath.[10]

Women born between 1860 and 1900 who became physical educators included the first cohort of women to assume public vocations. Like other women who entered some type of public occupation, escape from the exclusively domestic female experience most often led them to the choice of remaining single. In this era and the next, nearly 90% of the most successful female physical education leaders subscribed to Victorian values, remained unmarried, and channeled their energies into teaching, relatively unburdened by domestic

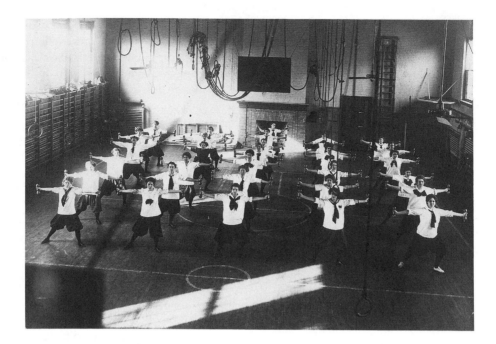

Figure 6.1 Gymnasium exercises at the University of Illinois, circa 1920. Courtesy University of Illinois Archives.

chores. Teaching physical education and determining appropriate sports, sport behaviors, and values for girls and young women, although not exactly in the mainstream of the domestic ideal, did share several features with that ideal. Exercise of control over their students, for example, was similar to a mother's control over her daughters. This quasi-maternalism is an important contributing factor to the women's sporting tradition.[11]

Athletics

Basketball may best exemplify the nature of the control and values of the female physical educators. In the 1890s basketball was the most popular team sport in educational programs and the country's fastest-growing sport for women, a dominance it retains to the present time. As early as 1892 Smith College women played basketball under the leadership of Senda Berenson. By 1896

coeds at the University of California and Stanford had engaged each other in the first officially recognized varsity game. Modification of the game ensued rapidly as a reaction to the masculine performance style of the female athletes. Berenson and her peers noted, ''Rough and vicious play seems worse in women than in men; . . . [and] the selfish display of a star by dribbling and playing the entire court, and rough-housing by snatching the ball could not be tolerated.''[12] In addition, physiological limitations demanded modification of rules. Consequently, women adopted the three-court game with no dribbles, snatching the ball, or touching an opponent. By 1899 physical education instructors had standardized these rules, declaring them to be the ''Official Women's Basketball Rules'' for *all* female players. Modifications of these occurred frequently after formation of the National Official Women's Basketball Committee, an antecedent

Figure 6.2   3-court basketball at Smith College, Northampton, MA, early 1890s. Courtesy of Naismith Memorial Basketball Hall of Fame.

organization of the present National Association for Girls and Women in Sport (NAGWS).[13]

Women physical education teachers from 1880 had a tightly knit structure and were an intensely dedicated group that persisted for decades. Thus they were able to retain an almost monopolistic hold over girls' and women's sports and athletics in higher education, and to a lesser degree in high schools and the public domain. The tradition of restricted competition, self-governance in athletic programs, and a feminine approach to individual and team sports prevailed.[14]

The mission of women's athletics, the philosophical approach and the nurturing motherly role of women physical educators, was different from the prevailing vision of men's athletics. Women's athletic tradition was built on the belief that *all* girls and women should experience the joy of sport, not just a few outstanding athletes as would occur if women were encouraged to train for and

compete in the Olympics. The cost of elite competition would have precluded financial support for sports for the masses and the diversification of sport and instead developed a few major "popular" sports.[15]

Women physical educators throughout the era 1890–1920 altered their perceptions and goals for athletics for girls and women. Physical education programs grew in number and in strength in colleges and larger high schools. Women's competitive athletics saw much growth with more and more varsity teams appearing in schools. The women leaders became alarmed at women's programs beginning to follow the male model of athletics. Thus they set out to achieve control of girls' and women's athletic programs. They began by seeing the whole world of female athletics as their domain and the setting of standards, policies, and rule modifications as all within their purview. They set out to accomplish this goal with sport by

Figure 6.3   Women's basketball team, University of Illinois, 1906. Courtesy University of Illinois Archives.

sport control instead of developing a governance structure. As a consequence, collegiate physical educators were successful in controlling primarily their own sports programs and student athletes, but were less successful in dominating high school and public recreation programs.

The Age of Recreational Athletics: 1920–1940

After World War I, America's growing economic and political power ushered in an era of prosperity and optimism that shaped many areas of American life in the 1920s. This prosperity had strong implications for the world of sport. The 1920s witnessed the growth and proliferation of a variety of women's sports in departments of physical education. The women leaders did indeed produce enclaves of strong women in a "sheltered refuge

from a competitive and male dominated society."[16] The women saw themselves as "captains of their ship and masters of their programs" and they controlled their students. The physical education programs of 1920–1940 reflected the women's own educational exposure to pragmatic and democratic methods and the ideals and experiences of philosophers like Dewey, Hall, and other progressive reformers. Other important influences came from their bold mentors, such as Senda Berenson, Amy Morris Homan, Delphine Hanna, Ethel Perrin, Frances A. Kellor, and Harriet Ballintine. Team sports, gymnastics, and individual "elite" sports dominated their programs, with scant attention paid to working-class women's sporting interests (track and field, bowling, and softball).

These were the circumstances surrounding the launching of an experimental female model of athletics. The manipulated men's athletic model would reflect the philosophical tenets underlying

Figure 6.4   Golfers, mid-1930s. Courtesy University of Illinois Archives.

the ideals of universal participation and recreational sport and would perpetuate democratic ideals for the new female athletic hero; that is, one who ought to be feminine, beautiful, strong, and self-confident yet always fully cognizant of her delicate reproductive system.

Alternative Models of Athletics: Play Days and Sport Days

To accomplish these idealized goals, the leaders' vision of intercollegiate athletics demanded manipulating the male model to an alternative version of intercollegiate competition, the Play Day. In a Play Day, three or more colleges (leagues, clubs, or schools) met for competition; but instead of playing under the school colors, athletes from each school (league or club) were divided up and played on a team of girls from all of the schools (all of the leagues or all of the clubs) at the event. (Play Days seldom mixed nonschool groups such as leagues with school groups.) As early as 1919 California high schools had such a program, and a Tri- College Play Day between Stanford University, the University of California at Berkeley, and Mills College (Oakland) may have been one of the first collegiate Play Days.[17]

This Play Day athletic model was far from universally accepted, although at the time the physical education literature represented it as such. It is now evident in historical research that varsity sport and competitive sport experiences for female athletes multiplied in the Roaring Twenties, and even during the Great Depression in the 1930s, despite the leaders' Play Day Model and rhetoric. Recent research on high school athletics, for example, reveals that in large sections of the country, varsity teams for girls flourished. Even in the "halls of ivy," many small colleges and some large institutions selected the competitive athletics route rather than the Play Day. Although large college physical education departments for the most part held to the women's athletic model with its democratic ideal of a "sport for every girl and every girl in a sport," restlessness grew among female athletes and some men who wished to promote women's competitive athletics.[18]

The Play Day concept lasted but a decade or so, yielding to the more competitive interschool Sports Days. In a Sports Day, three or more colleges met for competition, but the teams were made up of classmates playing under their school colors. A school would be declared a winner; however, the winning school was not honored for its success. In addition, there was mutual agreement that there should be no coaching during the game. Sports Days became a regular part of the alternative model of athletics. It was, however, the development of varsity programs that prompted the women to move toward an organizational structure that would obstruct the shift to highly competitive programs in colleges, high schools, and the public domain.

Organizational Actions

In the early 1920s women physical educators seemed unconcerned about women's presence in varsity sport programs or in Olympic competition in several gender-appropriate sports such as golf, tennis, swimming, and ice skating. However, these leaders saw the increasing prevalence of the exploitation of the Olympic-caliber athlete; the transfer of power from women leaders in physical education to men leaders in the Amateur Athletic Union (AAU) who were conducting athletic programs for female athletes; and the subsequent exposure of female athletes to the male model of athletics. Some top female athletes had begun to desire more competition, and AAU teams were formed in colleges in spite of the women's efforts to control the competitive programs. The physical educators and other women leaders, notably Lou

Henry Hoover, President Herbert Hoover's wife, became greatly alarmed.[19]

For many years the female physical education establishment, led by the Committee on Women's Athletics (CWA, an expansion of the Women's Basketball Committee) and a substructure of the American Physical Education Association (APEA), exercised considerable control over women's athletics in schools and colleges. In 1922 Blanche Trilling persuaded the APEA National Council to pass a resolution aimed at resisting affiliation with the Amateur Athletic Union (AAU) and vigorously protesting the inclusion of women's athletics in the First Women's International Track and Field Meet, to be held in Paris in August 1922. Women physical educators feared that women's collegiate athletics would adopt the elitism and exploitation observed in men's intercollegiate competition, the AAU, and the Olympics. By passing this resolution, the women intensified their efforts to fight the intruders of the AAU in women-controlled athletic programs.[20]

These second-generation physical educators saw themselves as having jurisdiction over women's physical education and athletics on all college campuses. They had a missionary zeal to control and direct women away from varsity and Olympic opportunities. Their philosophical orientation resulted in two major approaches: competitive restraints and female self-determination in athletic governance.

Members of the CWA and kindred organizations of the 1920s and 1930s would be quick to point out that the organizations were not anticompetition, but merely against the "wrong kind" of competition, that is, varsity or elite athletics at the expense of opportunities for the majority of girls and women.[21] They also argued that the financial drain on educational institutions and personnel would be excessive if they must provide athletics both for the masses and for the few expert players on varsity or Olympic teams. As CWA spokeswoman Agnes Wayman stated the issue: "It so happens we don't like the route the men have chosen. . . . We are setting forth under our sail with women at the helm and women manning the whole craft.''[22] Women stood firmly against having male coaches for girls' and women's teams on the grounds that only women could understand the psychological, motivational, and physiological needs of the female.[23]

Case Study: The Power Struggle 1920–1940

The 1920–1940 era witnessed a three-way contest among two women's organizations and one men's organization for control of girls' and women's athletics. The case study offers a vehicle for understanding the power struggle and conflicts in women's effort to develop an alternative model of athletics and to control women's athletics.

The first player was the Committee on Women's Athletics (CWA), an antecedent of the present National Association for Girls and Women in Sport (NAGWS). Although not a true governance structure, the CWA claimed legitimate jurisdiction over all females in educational sport and tried to control athletics in the public sector as well. Its control, however, was a reality only in physical education, where the separate departments permitted the CWA to control its own programs. One of the CWA's primary functions was to exercise authority over women's rules in team sports and some individual sports. The powerful rules committees developed and modified rules and published *Sport Guides*. This authority over women's basketball rules would give rise to a major conflict with the AAU.[24]

The second player was the Women's Division of the National Amateur Athletic Federation under the leadership of Lou Henry Hoover. (In 1922 the U.S. War and Navy secretaries established the National Amateur Athletic Federation [NAAF] to encourage sport and games for everyone and to address dissatisfaction with AAU and Olympic programs and standards.) The NAAF selected Lou Henry Hoover as a vice president. She advocated a separate Women's Division because she believed there was a different ideology of standards and purposes for women's sport. Having spearheaded a national conference in 1923 to develop the Women's Division of the NAAF, she became its first president.[25]

The mission of the NAAF Women's Division (WD) was to stand as a deliberating, investigating, legislating, promoting, advising, and controlling body on the special problems incident to the physical development of America's girls and women. Its actual major contribution was setting, promoting, and advertising standards for competitive athletics. The inadequacy of health training and physical development for girls and women in the public sector alarmed the Women's Division. They also were concerned about the potentially harmful and incorrect methods of physical training. As a result, they worked with and adopted the objectives of the women's physical education associations. The Women's Division became a strong influence on women's sport through political clout and financial resources. *The Platform* of the Women's Division, which set the standards for women's competition, also encouraged women's participation in both school and nonschool sports as well as wholeheartedly supporting the ideology of the Play Days. In addition, the WD mobilized with the Committee on Women's Athletics on behalf of women controlling women's athletics, published and distributed anti-varsity and anti-Olympic flyers, and promoted the alternative recreational model of athletics.[26]

By 1923 the third player was the Amateur Athletic Union (AAU), formed in 1888 to govern amateur sports. The AAU organization constantly struggled with the National Collegiate Athletic Association (NCAA) for control of amateur athletics. Although a men's organization, in the 1920s the AAU claimed jurisdiction over women's sports in swimming and track and field. Later the leadership added basketball, volleyball, and gymnastics to its women's offerings in local and national leagues, tournament competition, and

Figure 6.5   Track & Field, circa 1927. Courtesy University of Illinois Archives.

selection of Olympic teams. The United States Olympic Committee (USOC) recognized the AAU as the governing body of American amateur sport, so when the AAU determined to control women's amateur athletics as well as men's, a challenge from the women seemed futile. The AAU needed women members because the NCAA was challenging the AAU's authority, and the AAU's membership was faltering. For this reason it was prudent for the AAU to gain control of another source of income (from women members) and to broaden its control base by including women's programs.[27]

Open warfare between AAU and the two women's organizations began in earnest after the August 1922 Women's Olympic Games in Paris when the AAU announced that female athletes would be under its jurisdiction. The AAU was invading the women's separate spheres, and the women's power base teetered. After the an-

nounced AAU takeover, the women's associations quickly galvanized as a strong voice against varsity sports, against women's participation in the Olympics, against the AAU takeover, and against men coaching or officiating women's teams. The exploitation of the participants, commercialism, and overemphasis on winning gravely concerned the women. They feared that the factors that were characteristic of men's athletics would creep into the women's programs.[28]

The leaders of the Committee on Women's Athletics refused the AAU's request for affiliation and repeatedly resisted AAU overtures to gain CWA support in women's basketball and track and field. The AAU used the women's basketball rules but wanted more voice in the rule changes. The women withheld this approval too, until it was too late. The AAU decided to develop and publish its own women's basketball rules and to proceed with its own programs.[29]

Results of the Conflict

The women's physical education leadership lost most of its control over female athletes who had competed on AAU or other industrial teams away from college and high school campuses. When the conflict ended, women controlled large urban high school athletics and college women's athletic programs. In nonschool competitive sports, women controlled only women's rules for some team sports. The Women's Division and its *Platform* also failed. The AAU governed nonschool and Olympic competition with its own set of women's basketball rules and few women in decision-making positions. If women did serve beyond local levels, they served primarily on the Women's Basketball Rules Committee or the Women's Track and Field Committee. The lack of decision-making positions prevented women from influencing either the AAU's philosophical stance or its major policies. Although women lost much of their power base in the public domain, within the sacred walls of the school gymnasium the women physical educators reigned supreme. The rift between women physical educators and the AAU had the long-term effect of moving more of women's athletics out of education and into the public sector.

The Age of Transition: 1940–1950

In the years after World War II, attitudes concerning women in general and their participation in sports began to change. The decade of the 1940s was pivotal in changing the attitudes and behavior patterns of women. The war years demanded strong, healthy women workers in the labor market to replace the men at war. Competition became one means to develop fitness for war in programs sponsored or encouraged by the federal government. College coeds reacted favorably to such team sport competitive programs, as well as to

Figure 6.6   Basketball, early 1940s. Courtesy University of Illinois Archives.

the new emphasis on individual sports in physical education classes.[30]

The 1940s gave women physical educators experience in conducting highly competitive sport programs for the War Department and in leading elite-caliber athletics for the armed services. Young women recruits, who would later prepare for physical education careers, also competed in athletics in the armed services or in recreational settings. This experience led female athletes and young physical educators to question provincial attitudes. Finally, the separate interests of the physical educators, the amateur athletic establishment, and the popular culture merged to forge a supportive environment for highly competitive women's sports.[31]

The role and function of the old CWA, now called the National Section on Women's Athletics (NSWA), was in flux. The issue of endorsing and promoting women's athletic competition caused a split between established leaders and some of the younger members working their way up through the physical educators' mentorship system. The latter favored varsity and elite competition in a controlled environment, whereas the former were reluctant to sanction any athletics beyond Sports Days.[32]

The leaders of the NSWA, which became the Division for Girls and Women's Sports (DGWS) in 1952, began to readjust their concept of competition and to reconcile their practices and their rhetoric with the reality: The Play Day was buried, the Sports Day was in vogue, and many schools moved to interscholastic and intercollegiate competition. At the same time the leaders did maintain the fundamental goal of the earlier physical educators: to design sports programs for the good of the participant. The NSWA/DGWS acted as the central powerful force for the gradual transition to competitive athletics in education by (a) continuing to make and enforce playing rules in various sports; (b) demanding that women serve as coaches and officials (although over time men were increasingly visible in both capacities); and (c) enforcing standards of conduct in sports programs.[33]

On the other hand, with the political pressures of the younger physical educators, more opportunities for competition in the culture, and more demand for competition, the traditional philosophies concerning athletic competition were being swept aside. Even before passage of the federal Civil Rights Acts and Title IX, the women's physical education organizations had developed an embryonic governance structure to conduct intercollegiate athletics and would soon sanction tournament competition and national championships. At least two conferences sponsored by DGWS, the National Leadership Conference and the National Conference on Social Changes and Implications for Physical Education and Sports Programs, focused on the role of high-level competition in the development of sporting opportunities for girls and women.[34]

End of Transition

The protest against female participation in the Olympic Games became history for the new breed of women physical education leaders in secondary and collegiate institutions. By 1960 the positive attitudes toward women in sport had set in motion a women's sport revolution. Women physical educators, such as Katherine Ley and Phebe Scott, stepped boldly forward with a resolve to govern at least collegiate athletics. From a position of security in their separate spheres, and a separate national organization (DGWS), an increasing amount of local and regional varsity competition occurred. Women leaders openly revived and supported interscholastic and intercollegiate programs for women. As a result, a surprising number of underground secondary and collegiate programs surfaced throughout the country.[35]

The DGWS governed women's athletics in colleges and universities and controlled the rules of a few sports in the public domain. The control of competitive amateur sport had largely fallen into the hands of the Amateur Athletic Union (AAU). The AAU and the women's organizations, however, had more congenial relationships and soon would move into cooperative efforts in rule modifications and program development.

The transition to women's control of athletics resulted in part from the unwillingness of women physical educators to compromise with men (or perhaps forsake their principles). They believed men had a different set of political guidelines for and a different philosophical commitment to athletics.

The Age of Revolution in Athletics: 1960–1980

Federal legislation supporting equal pay and equal employment opportunity, Civil Rights acts, the proposed Equal Rights Amendment, the use of the 14th Amendment in lawsuits, and Title IX of the Education Amendments of 1972 all contributed to a strong movement toward equity in the sporting tradition. The women's liberation movement also engendered psychological support for women in sport by breaking down the Victorian "cult of true womanhood." A more flexible concept of what is feminine developed, and there was rejection of the myth that competitive athletics is masculine in nature. In turn, the influx of girls and women into the sports arena forced changes and redefinitions of the role and function of sport in our culture.

Self-Governance of Intercollegiate Athletics in the 1960s

A new liberal vanguard of athletic leaders from among women physical educators emerged early in the 1960s. These women had a dream of varsity sport with an alternative athletic model that emphasized the needs of students and rejected the commercialization of the men's mode. They led the DGWS, which evolved into the National Association for Girls and Women in Sport (NAGWS) to form a substructure of NAGWS, the Association for Intercollegiate Athletics for Women (AIAW).

The AIAW's first antecedent was the National Joint Committee for Extramural Sports for College Women (NJCESCW). It began its work at the end of the 1950s. The Joint Committee was comprised of members from three women's physical education organizations. Its function was to set guidelines and standards for women's intercollegiate athletic competition. As competitive athletics continued to grow, the Joint Committee dissolved so one organization, the DGWS, could take full responsibility for collegiate athletics. The consolidation eventually resulted in the DGWS forming the Commission on Intercollegiate Athletics for Women (CIAW) in 1967.[36]

The CIAW sanctioned tournaments and sponsored national championships. Almost before the CIAW was fully operational, however, the NCAA voiced concern about the legal necessity for conducting women's as well as men's championships.

The NCAA further began to discuss taking over women's athletics. The leaders of the CIAW believed the NCAA wanted to broaden the association's political clout in amateur athletics and on the international scene by increasing its membership to include control over female athletes.[37]

In response to the NCAA's rhetoric, the CIAW called a press conference to announce a new women's intercollegiate athletic plan. This action of the new commission seemed to forestall any NCAA action beyond taking the word *men* out of its constitution, thereby implying that women could compete on NCAA teams.[38]

Within a couple of years the leaders of the CIAW realized they were unable to manage the expanding problems and needs of collegiate athletics. They formed an association, with institutional memberships, devoted exclusively to intercollegiate athletics. In 1971–1972 the CIAW handed the torch to a newly organized AIAW. The association became a substructure of the DGWS and an affiliate of the American Association for Health, Physical Education and Recreation (AAHPER).

Title IX

Title IX, the Education Amendments of 1972, is a federal act that states: "No person in the United States shall, on the basis of sex, be excluded from participation in, be denied the benefits of, or be subjected to discrimination under any education program or activity receiving federal financial assistance."[39] This unusual government intervention in education and sport demanded full compliance for secondary schools and colleges by July 21, 1978. The Department of Health, Education and Welfare published guidelines and implementation regulations in June of 1975.

Title IX was the single most significant piece of legislation to affect the direction and philosophical tenets of women in sport. Much of the growth of girls' high school athletics and much of the growth and power struggle in collegiate athletics resulted from the act's implementation. The effect of Title

IX on female athletes was an incredible increase in competitive opportunities and support. However, although it brought millions of girls and women to the sports fields and arenas, it reduced thousands of women administrators to secondary positions of leadership and removed them from decision-making positions. As a consequence of the loss of women in decision-making positions, the governance of girls and women's athletics became the province of men and men's governance structures.

Passage of Title IX meant that physical education classes must be coeducational. In the class, if physical contact was part of the game, players could be separated by sex during the playing of the game. In varsity athletics, teams could be separate for men and women in both contact and non-contact sports when membership on the team depended on athletic ability. In separate athletic programs for women, Title IX not only requires that there be equal opportunity but also specifies that financial aid based on athletic ability must be awarded proportionate to the number of male and female athletes. For example, if there are 100 athletes (50 men and 50 women), then women must receive 50% of the aid. There must be parity in the overall program.[40]

Mergers

Title IX does not demand merged departments, nor are leadership issues addressed. Yet with Title IX came the merger of men's and women's physical education and athletic departments in practically all educational institutions. With each new merger, women administrators and directors of physical education and women's athletics were demoted to secondary positions. Both sport tradition and male sexist attitudes ensured that male rather than female athletic directors and heads of physical education departments were almost automatically appointed to direct the merged departments. Within the next decade, coaches for both men's and women's teams were increasingly male, a factor that not only affected women physical educators and coaches in thousands of school

systems but also caused the NAGWS to lose its authority over rules and officiating. Without women in positions of leadership who believed in the authority, control, rules, and officiating techniques of women, men moved to rules and officiating most like their own and selected men to officiate. The NAGWS thus lost most of its jurisdiction over women's athletics, and by the 1980s this previously strong organization had become primarily an advocacy organization. Its emphasis changed to networking, leadership development, mentoring, coaching, conducting workshops, and strategies for equity.[41]

Case Study: The Rise and Fall of AIAW

The 1960–1980 era witnessed at least a two-way struggle for the control of women's intercollegiate athletics. The two associations involved in this case study are the AIAW and the male-dominated NCAA. The NCAA was the far older, wealthier, and better established male counterpart of the AIAW. The NCAA conducts national championships in three competitive divisions. It is the most powerful organization in amateur athletics today.

The ramifications of Title IX were central to the rise and fall of the women's manipulated model of men's athletics. It represented a two-edged sword not only to female physical educators at individual institutions who lost their decision-making power through merged departments, but also to the AIAW. The male domination of nearly all programs eradicated the women's separate spheres of physical education and athletics. The situation in turn led to the demise of AIAW.

History of AIAW

In 1971–1972 the AIAW began with a clear vision of its mission and strategy and the role institutional members would play. The association was clear about what conflicts to avoid and what educational purposes to achieve. Its primary concern was the conflict of the educational versus the commercialized model of athletics. The difficulties experienced in the male model with its emphasis on winning, financial gain, and recruitment problems were ever present in the development of AIAW. Even with this heritage, however, the association continually had difficulty maintaining its focus and had to adjust to frequent rule changes.

The association started with a set of procedures for conducting national championships, eligibility rules for athletes, and plans for a legislative participatory approach to governance. The new governance association, in keeping with the experimental dream of the women physical educators, adopted a student-centered, education-oriented model with built-in safeguards designed to avoid abuses observed in the male athletic model. The 276 charter member institutions grew to 971 institutional members, and athlete membership increased from 10,000 to over 99,000. Each year the AIAW conducted 750 state, regional, and national championships under a unified membership plan. There were state and regional associations for the conduct of all preliminary tournaments leading to the national championships. In the 1981-1982 academic year the AIAW held 42 championships in 19 different sports. The AIAW had jurisdiction over all female athletes and the athletic program at each institution (unlike the NCAA, which was involved only in championships). An ethics and eligibility committee, based on self-policing policies, was the enforcement branch.[42]

The AIAW's annual budget was initially quite small and depended on membership dues and NAGWS funding. As the governing body grew in membership and prestige and acquired television contracts, the annual budget approached $1 million. Television revenues enabled the AIAW to pay partial reimbursement to teams that participated in national championships. Television funds from the 1980–1981 basketball championship, for example, enabled the association to pay over 50% of the cost of the 72 teams competing in the three

divisional national championships. In budgetary matters the association conducted its own business, but it did not have complete autonomy. The AAHPER had to be consulted about spending, and the Alliance had the power to accept or reject AIAW contracts. In July 1979, after much debate and argument between traditionalists (long-time leaders in DGWS/NAGWS) and modernists (athletic administrators and younger coaches), the AIAW became a separate legal entity with total autonomy. A close formal liaison was formed with the NAGWS. By 1980–1981 the AIAW had a 4-year, million-dollar television contract with NBC as well as other nonfixed television and sponsorship contracts.[43]

Title IX Conflicts

The most intense debate within the AIAW was prompted by its philosophical stance on basic policies of scholarship, eligibility, and methods of recruiting athletes. As the influence of Title IX implementation began to be felt, the AIAW had to adjust to major changes in policies that hampered the student-centered, education-oriented model. The specially designed women's model held to a vision of student first, athlete second and emphasized the sporting experience rather than the outcome on the scoreboard and the resulting commercialization. Maintaining the alternative vision became more difficult given the use of the male norm as the measure against which to judge equality.[44]

In 1973 the AIAW made its first momentous decision necessitated by the Title IX mandate for equality in financial aid. A tennis player from Florida filed suit in federal court against the National Education Association (NEA), AAHPER, NAGWS, AIAW, and other organizations on behalf of scholarship tennis players. The players wanted to compete in the United States Lawn Tennis Association's (USLTA) Women's Collegiate Championships conducted in cooperation with the AIAW. To forestall litigation, the AIAW's Delegate Assembly reluctantly voted to permit female athletes to receive financial aid and still have the right to participate in intercollegiate athletics. This was the first of many decisions that would move the AIAW's alternative model of student-centered athletics toward the NCAA model.[45]

Internal Conflicts

If the AIAW's first conflict was the direct result of Title IX, the second conflict was more indirect and internal. Traditionalists (long-time physical educators) and modernists (young, forceful physical educators) disagreed about new directions and how to restructure their eligibility, financial aid, and recruitment policies in light of Title IX. Modernists were more willing to make alterations that brought the AIAW dangerously close to the NCAA model. A small but vocal band of modernists led a movement toward a dialogue about merging with the NCAA. They sought an alliance with the NCAA and later negotiated for leadership roles within the NCAA. These internal conflicts undermined the solidarity of the AIAW and contributed to its subsequent demise. The AIAW's Waterloo, however, was its lifelong struggle with the NCAA for control of intercollegiate governance.[46]

AIAW and NCAA Approaches to Title IX

The philosophical conflict between the NCAA and the AIAW arose from their differences in basic policies, program commitments, enforcement practices, and administrative procedures. Their dissimilar stances on scholarship, eligibility, and methods of recruiting athletes prompted the greatest debate. The AIAW's alternative athletic model, with less funding, had posed no genuine threat to the NCAA's operation or to the budgets of membership schools before enforcement of Title IX. Enforcement of Title IX, however, meant that scholarships, money, facilities, personnel, and authority over collegiate athletics must be shared

equitably with women's programs. The challenge to the NCAA was simple: to govern women's athletics and force the demise of the AIAW.[47]

The NCAA feared that equality for women's athletics would drain needed resources from men's programs. Not surprisingly, the men's organization fought Title IX compliance guidelines in Congress. An independent group of NCAA members appealed to member institutions for funds to further resist Title IX implementation. The DeHart group (a group of about 75–100 universities that paid the DeHart law firm to campaign against final passage of the guidelines and to attempt to exempt football) and the NCAA leadership took their protest to the Office of Civil Rights, the courts, and Capitol Hill. But all their efforts were to no avail; Title IX's final guidelines became law July 21, 1978. The men's motivations for fighting Title IX were primarily commercial concerns long associated with men's athletics, that is, sharing funds, facilities, travel, coaches—and the spotlight—with women's teams. How could men's programs expand if women's programs were to be built? A less obvious territorialism emerged regarding the relationship between athletics and the myth of male superiority.[48]

Women in athletics saw a clear benefit in mandated parity. On the other hand, could equality be reconciled with the women's commitment to remain different and to preserve an educational emphasis? In large measure this was not possible. Despite recognizing the potential problem of being forced to duplicate the male norm, the AIAW nonetheless made a total commitment to Title IX. As a result, the AIAW poured enormous amounts of time, energy, and financial resources into Title IX compliance. The success of the NAGWS and the AIAW on the issues of Title IX led to phenomenal growth in collegiate athletics; ironically, that success was central to the AIAW's demise.[49]

At the same time, women physical educators formed a unified front with a network and a supportive educational coalition of women's organizations. The National Organization for Women

(NOW) and the Women's Equality Action League (WEAL) and later the Women's Sport Foundation (WSF) aggressively supported Title IX and athletic equality. Because of Title IX's assumption of the male model of athletics as the norm, the courts and many feminists also used the male model as the criterion for what parity meant. In the organization's total commitment to Title IX, the AIAW in part suspended the underlying philosophical commitments until victory in the war for equality could be won. The educational values of the women's alternative model seemed, in part, to be lost in the battle for equality.[50]

AIAW/NCAA Struggles

Throughout the 1970s the AIAW and the NCAA discussed the possibility of merging. The AIAW sought an equal merger; but, of course, the NCAA did not consider the AIAW an equal. With the enforcement of Title IX and the growth of women's sport, budgets, and television contracts, the NCAA wanted control. Growing representation of the AIAW on the United States Olympic Committee (USOC) and the National Sport Governing Bodies (NGBs) was a more subtle but equally important inducement for control: By taking over "women's" seats in the USOC and continuing to hold the men's seats, the NCAA had a greater influence over decision making regarding elite international competition, which, after all, had long been crucial to the NCAA rivalry with the old AAU and new NGBs.[51]

These motives, among others, stimulated the NCAA Council to bring the issue of initiating its own women's national championships to the voting representatives of NCAA, first in 1980 and again in 1981. The powerful Council strongly endorsed the championships, as did some women, particularly those coaching women's basketball. For several reasons many individual institutions also supported the takeover. First, the NCAA promised to subsidize team expenses for national championships. Second, the NCAA would not charge additional membership dues for the women's program. Third, women could use the same financial aid, eligibility, and recruitment rules as men, and administration of the program would be uncomplicated. Fourth, there would be more television coverage of the championships. The NCAA's far greater resources and capacity to deliver on these promises were appealing to the predominately male athletic directors and voting representatives, who cared little about the "different voice" of women's intercollegiate athletics. Thus would the alternative model of women's athletics be silenced with the subsequent folding of the highly successful AIAW.[52]

There was considerable political maneuvering by members of the NCAA Council during the introduction of and altercations about the proposal for women's national championships in Division I. This occurred both within the ranks of the NCAA and on college campuses. The result was a hotly contested vote and approval by a narrow margin for Division I institutions (collegiate programs with full scholarships) to initiate women's national championships under NCAA control. Just a week earlier the AIAW's Delegate Assembly had voted by a large majority to maintain the governance of women's athletics through the AIAW. In the AIAW vote, 75% of the voting delegates were women. In the NCAA's victory, over 95% of the voting representatives at the NCAA convention were men. Thus the NCAA, a male-dominated organization, voted to impose a men's decision on women's athletic programs.[53]

As a result of negotiations between the NCAA Women's Athletic Committee and the NCAA Council prior to the NCAA vote, a token number of women would enter the NCAA hierarchy. The women would enter the leadership in higher status positions than those afforded male members, who had to work their way up to Council and chairperson positions. As an inducement to gain their votes for women's national championships, women leaders from AIAW were assured 16% representation on the powerful NCAA Council and from 18% to 24% membership on other committees. Certainly the NCAA's willingness to place even a few women in leadership positions was a good-will gesture to gain membership support. This limited access to leadership positions did allow former AIAW leaders some decision-making roles. Although in no way a substitute for control of women's athletics, participation in the NCAA competitive structure ironically is part of the AIAW's legacy to women's athletics.[54]

In 1981–1982, the NCAA offered women's championships in all three divisions in most AIAW championship sports, women's championships for Divisions II and III having been approved the year before. A second male-dominated small-college governance organization, the National Association for Intercollegiate Athletics (NAIA), also had voted to conduct women's national championships for institutional members beginning in 1980–1981. A third male-dominated governance organization, the National Junior College Athletic Association (NJCAA), had offered women's national championships since the mid-1970s. This meant that all of the men's governing bodies for athletics were now offering women's championships.

For one confusing and disillusioning (for AIAW) academic year, the AIAW, the NAIA, and the NCAA all offered women's championships, forcing colleges to choose among the organizations' championships for each sport. Many larger institutions selected the NCAA championships. As a result, AIAW lost a large NBC-TV basketball contract. In fact, all three AIAW divisional basketball championships lost money in 1982, whereas they had made money in previous years. Recognizing that the NCAA inevitably would prevail, the AIAW suspended operations on June 30, 1982. It concentrated its remaining resources in a lawsuit against the NCAA for violation of the Sherman Anti-Trust Act that prohibits monopolies. The suit failed, leading to the AIAW's demise.[55]

Summary and Conclusions

Title IX proved to be a blessing and a curse. It led to the demise of separate spheres of women's

physical education and athletic departments, to the demise of AIAW, and to reduction in female leadership and coaching positions. However, it also furnished girls and women new opportunities in coeducational physical education classes and varsity competition. The AIAW's failure to survive as a separate organization ended women physical educators' dream of establishing a unique alternative model of athletics for women.

The National Association for Girls and Women in Sport for high schools and colleges became primarily an advocacy and service organization. The National Federation of State High School Associations controlled both boys' and girls' interscholastic athletics.

Although women physical education leaders lost the battle for control and reform in athletics, they have succeeded in their quest for competitive opportunity and more positive attitudes toward girls and women in athletics. The acceptance of girls' and women's right to participate in sport and the influx of large numbers of female athletes have revolutionized the sporting milieu. The acceptance of women in sport has encouraged female athletes both to seek out sport for individual expression and to feel more comfortable in the formerly "male-only" culture in the athletic tradition.

Acknowledgments

This chapter includes content and excerpts from the author's publications for which permission has been granted by the publishers. The articles include: Joan S. Hult, "The Governance of Athletics for Girls and Women: Leadership by Women Physical Educators, 1899-1949," *Research Quarterly for Exercise and Sport Centennial Issue* (April 1985): 64-77; idem, "Women's Struggle for Governance in U.S. Amateur Athletics," *International Review for the Sociology of Sport*, **24** (November 1989): 249-61; idem, "The Saga of Competition: Basketball Battles and Governance War," in *A Century of Women's Basketball From Frailty to Final Four*, ed. idem and Marianna

Trekell, 223-48; idem, "The Legacy of AIAW," in *A Century of Women's Basketball From Frailty to Final Four*, ed. Joan S. Hult and Marianna Trekell, 281-308.

The author made extensive use of the archives of the National Association for Girls and Women in Sport (NAGWS) housed at the American Alliance for Health, Physical Education, Recreation and Dance (AAHPERD) Archives, Reston, VA. The Association for Intercollegiate Athletics for Women (AIAW) Collection, housed in Special Collections, University of Maryland, College Park Libraries, was also a major resource.

A special thank-you and acknowledgment to Charles Walcott, Professor of Political Science at Virginia Tech University, for his insight and contribution to the AIAW section. Acknowledgment is gratefully given to Carol Jackson for her work as editorial consultant.

Thanks to Lauren Brown and his staff in Special Collections for their patience and assistance in uncovering essential documents. Thanks to Mike Everman and his assistant, Nancy Dosch, for archival assistance at AAHPERD.

Notes

[1] Joan Wallach Scott, *Gender and the Politics of History* (New York: Columbia University Press, 1988), 42.

[2] As quoted in Joe L. Dubbert, *A Man's Place: Masculinity in Transition* (Englewood Cliffs, NJ: Prentice-Hall, 1979), 116-17; Gerald F. Roberts, "The Strenuous Life: The Cult of Manliness in the Era of Theodore Roosevelt," (PhD diss., Michigan State University, 1970), 84-143; see also Theodore Roosevelt, *The Strenuous Life Essays and Addresses* (New York: Century, 1901).

[3] Roberta J. Park, "Sport, Gender and Society in a Translantic Victorian Perspective," in *From 'Fair Sex' to Feminism: Sport and the Socialization of Women in the Industrial and Post-Industrial Eras*, ed. J.A. Mangan and Roberta J. Park (Totowa, NJ: Frank Cass, 1987), 81.

[4] Park, "Sport, Gender and Society," 58-93; Patricia Vertinsky, "Body Shapes: The Role of the Medical Establishment in Informing Female Exercise and Physical Education in Nineteenth-Century North America," in *From Fair Sex to Feminism*, ed. Mangan and Park, 256-81.

[5] William Blaikie, "Is It Too Late for Women to Begin," in idem, *How to Get Strong and How to Stay So* (New York: Harper & Bros., 1879), 57-73; Dudley Allen Sargent, "The Physical Development of Women" *Scribner's Magazine*, **5** (February 1889): 172-85; Patricia Vertinsky, "Body Shapes: Medical Establishment," 256-81; Martha H. Verbrugge, *Able-Bodied Womanhood: Personal Health and Social Change in Nineteenth-Century Boston* (Oxford: Oxford University Press, 1988), 97-162.

[6] Midwest Association of College Teachers of Physical Education for Women, *A Century of Growth: The Historical Development of Physical Education for Women in Selected Colleges of Six Midwestern States* (Ann Arbor, MI: Edwards Bros., 1951); S.F. Richardson, "Tendencies in Athletics for Women in Colleges and Universities," *Popular Science*, **50** (February 1897): 517-26.

[7] Verbrugge, *Able-Bodied Womanhood*, 139-92; Park, "Sport, Gender and Society"; Roberta Frankfort, *Collegiate Women: Domesticity and Career in Turn-of-the-Century America* (New York: New York University Press, 1977); Delphine Hanna and Nellie A. Spore, "Effect of College Work Upon the Health of Women" in *Chronicle of American Physical Education*, ed. Spears and Lockhart, 190-92; Harriet I. Ballintine, "The Value of Athletics to College Girls," *American Physical Education Review*, **6** (June 1901): 151-53; Jessie H. Bancroft, "The Place of Automatism in Gymnastic Exercise," *American Physical Education Review*, **8** (December 1903): 218-31.

[8]Lois W. Banner, *American Beauty* (Chicago: University of Chicago Press, 1983), 169; idem, 154-201; Harriet Ballintine, "Out-of Door Sports for College Women," *American Physical Education Review*, 3 (March 1898): 38-43; Lucille E. Hill, ed. *Athletics and Outdoor Sports for Women* (New York: Macmillan, 1903), 1-15; Dorothy Ainsworth, *The History of Physical Education in Colleges for Women* (New York: Barnes, 1930), 1-12, 24-32.

[9]James C. Whorton, "Philosophy in the Gymnasium," in idem, *Crusaders for Fitness: The History of American Health Reformers* (Princeton: Princeton University Press, 1982), 270-303; Fred Leonard, "The New Gymnastics of Dio Lewis (1860-1868)," *American Physical Education Review*, 11 (1906): 83-95, 187-98; Betty Spears, *Leading the Way: Amy Morris Homans and the Beginnings of Professional Education for Women* (New York: Greenwood Press, 1986), 31-63, 106-17; Ellen W. Gerber, *Innovators and Institutions in Physical Education* (Philadelphia: Lea & Febiger, 1971), 283-92, 308-25, 357-70; Hill, *Athletics and Outdoor Sports*, 1-15.

[10]Spears, *Leading the Way*, 92-143; Elizabeth Halsey, *Women in Physical Education: Their Role in Work, Home, and History* (New York: Putnam, 1961) 1-42, 124-68; Agnes Wayman, ed. "Supplement to the Research Quarterly," *Research Quarterly*, 12 (October 1941): 615-703; Helen Lenskyj, "Common Sense and Physiology: North American Medical Views on Women and Sport, 1890-1930," *Canadian Journal of History of Sport*, 21 (May 1990): 49-64; Nancy Cole Dosch, "The Sacrifice of Maidens or Healthy Sportswomen? The Medical Debate Over Women's Basketball," in *A Century of Women's Basketball From Frailty to Final Four*, ed. Joan S. Hult and Marianna Trekell (Reston, VA: AAHPERD, 1991), 125-36.

[11]Ibid.; Joan S. Hult, "The Governance of Athletics for Girls and Women: Leadership by Women Physical Educators, 1899-1949," *Research Quarterly for Exercise and Sport Centennial Issue* (1985): 64-65; Julie Matthaei, *An Economic History of Women in America: Women's Work, the Sexual Division of Labor and the Development of Capitalism* (New York: Schocken Books, 1982), 203-5; Kate Gannett Wells, "The Transitional American Woman," *Atlantic Monthly* (December 1890): 819.

[12]Senda Berenson, "The Significance of Basketball for Women," in *Line Basket Ball or Basket Ball for Women 1901*, ed. Senda Berenson (New York: American Sporting, 1901), 20-27; Berenson, Editorial, *Basket Ball 1901*, 5-7; Alice Foster, "Basket Ball for Girls," *American Physical Education Review*, 2 (September 1897): 152-54.

[13]JoAnna Davenport, "Women's Basketball Rules: The Tides of Change," in *A Century of Women's Basketball*, ed. Hult and Trekell, 83-108; Hult, "Governance of Athletics," 64-68.

[14]Ibid., 67-73; Eline Von Borries, "Section V Education Outcomes Derived From Membership in Committees of the Section," Report of Policy and Finance Committee, National Section on Women's Athletics, 1 March 1937, NAGWS Papers, AAHPERD Archives. (Hereafter cited as AAHPERD Archives)

[15]Blanche M. Trilling, "The Playtime of a Million Girls or an Olympic Victory—Which?," *The Nation's Schools*, 6 (August 1929); Hult, "Governance of Athletics," 69-73.

[16]Park, "Sport, Gender and Society," 81; Gerber, *Innovators and Institutions*; Ainsworth, *History of Physical Education Women*; Mabel Lee, *Memories of a Bloomer Girl*, (Washington, DC: AAHPER, 1977), 273-378; idem, *Memories Beyond Bloomers* (Washington, DC: AAHPER, 1978), 74-138; Editorial,

"Intercollegiate Sport for Women," *APER*, **30** (April 1924): 517.

[17]Superintendent of Los Angeles School System Office, "Report on Play Days," 1919, Lou Henry Hoover's Papers, Hoover Library Archives, West Branch, IA (Hereafter cited as LHH, Hoover Archives); "A Southern California Sports Day," *The Sportswoman*, **2** (May 1926): 12; Helen Smith and Helen I. Coops, "What is a Play Day?," in *Women and Athletics*, ed. Ethel Perrin (New York: Child Health Association, 1928), 70-71.

[18]Ellen Gerber, "The Controlled Development of Collegiate Sport for Women, 1923-36," *Journal of Sport History*, **2** (Spring 1975): 1-28; Mabel Lee, "The Case For and Against Intercollegiate Athletics for Women and the Situation as It Stands Today," *American Physical Education Review*, **29** (January 1924): 13-19; idem, "The Case For and Against Intercollegiate Athletics for Women and the Situation Since 1923," *Research Quarterly*, **2** (May 1931), 93-127; see also "Section 3 High Level Competition," *A Century of Women's Basketball*, ed. Hult and Trekell, 137-206.

[19]Nancy Theriot, "Toward a New Sporting Ideal: The Women's Division of the National Amateur Athletic Federation," in *Frontier*, **3** (1978): 107; Joan S. Hult, "The Female American Runner: A Modern Quest for Visibility" in *Female Endurance Athlete*, ed. Barbara Drinkwater (Champaign, IL: Human Kinetics, 1986), 1-29.

[20]APEA, "Report of the Business Meeting, May, 1922," *American Physical Education Review*, **27** (September 1922): 332-25; Amateur Athletic Union (AAU), AAU Minutes of the Annual Meeting (1922 and 1923), AAU House, Indianapolis; Women's Division of National Amateur Athletic Federation, "Women's Division NAAF, Correspondence, Pamphlets and Newsletters, 1923-1939," AAHPERD Archives; Women's Division, NAAF "Newsletters," LHH, Hoover Archives.

[21]Agnes Wayman, "Women's Athletics: All Uses—No Abuses," *American Physical Education Review*, **29** (November 1924): 517; see also Perrin, *Women and Athletics*.

[22]Wayman, "Women's Athletic Abuse," 517.

[23]Dosch, "The Sacrifice of Maidens" 125-36; Steveda Chepko, "The Domestication of Basketball," in *A Century of Women's Basketball*, ed. Hult and Trekell, 109-24.

[24]Detailed discussion of the struggle is recorded in Hult, "Governance of Athletics"; idem, "Women US Amateur Athletics"; and idem, "The Female American Runner."

[25]Joan S. Hult, "Lou Henry Hoover: Champion of Recreational Sport." Paper presented at the Hoover Symposium, George Fox college, Newberg, Oregon, 11 March 1989; Lou Henry Hoover, "National Conference on Women's Athletics" Washington, DC: 6 April 1923 (transcript of the meeting), LHH, Hoover Archives; National Amateur Athletic Federation (NAAF) "Official Minutes of the Executive Board," December 1922 and December 1923, LHH, Hoover Archives.

[26]Hult, "Lou Henry Hoover, Champion"; Women's Division NAAF, "Conference Report" 200-246; Women's Division, NAAF *Platform*, (New York: NAAF Headquarters, 1923) LHH, Hoover Archives.

[27]As discussed in Hult, "Women US Amateur Athletics"; idem, "Go for the Gold"; idem, "The Female American Runner"; Virginia Evans, "The Status of the American Women in Sport, 1912-1932" (PhD diss., University of Massachusetts, 1982), 229-33.

[28]National Section on Women's Athletics (hereafter cited as NSWA), "Women's Basketball Committee Report to APEA Council," Cleveland, 1934 (a review of the basketball problems between AAU and NSWA from 1927 to 1934), AAHPERD Archives; Paula Welch, "The Emergence of American Women in the Summer Olympic Games: 1900-1972" (PhD diss., University of North Carolina at Greensboro, 1976), 40-97.

[29]NSWA, "Basketball Committee Report"; Olga Becker, "Ex-Champion, Now Chairman," *Amateur Athlete* (February 1934): 11-12; "Basketball Committee Report to APEA Council: Request to Rescind 1932 Ruling"; "The AAU Problem," Report to the Rules and Editorial Committee Meeting, December 1938, AAHPERD Archives.

[30]Hult, "Governance of Athletics," 69-71; NSWA "Minutes of the Legislative Board," April 1941 and 1-3 May 1941, AAHPERD Archives; Federal Security Agency, U.S. Office of Education, "Physical Fitness for Students in Colleges and Universities," (Washington, DC: Government Printing Office, 1943), 58-59; Rosalind Cassidy and Hilda Clute Kozman, *Physical Fitness for Girls* (New York: Barnes, 1943).

[31]NSWA, "Minutes Legislative Boards," April and May 1941; Lucia Ernst, "Women's Athletic Section News," *Journal of Health and Physical Education*, 14 (February 1943): 102-3; Gladys E. Palmer, "Presenting the Problem of Physical Fitness for Girls," *Journal of Health and Physical Education,* 14 (April 1943): 204-5, 233-34; Margaret H. Meyer and Marguerite M. Schwarz, *Technic of Team Sports for Women* (Philadelphia: Saunders, 1942), 1-2; Alice Schriver, "Competition: NSWA Faces the Issue," *Journal of Health and Physical Education*, 20 (September 1949): 451, 472.

[32]NSWA "Standards for Competition," AAHPERD Archives; Katherine Ley, "Standards for Girls and Women's Sports," Miami, FL, 1 December 1968, Katherine Ley's Papers, AAHPERD Archives; Katherine Ley and Sara Staff Jernigan, "The Roots and the Tree," *Journal of Health, Physical Education and Recreation*, 33 (September 1962): 34-36; National Section for Girls and Women in Sport, *Standards in Sports for Girls and Women* (Washington, DC: AAHPER, 1953).

[33]NSWA "Standards for Competition"; NSWA Folders of Standards, 1940-1949, and Folders of WNORC, 1941-49, AAHPERD Archives; see also the "Legislative Minutes of NSWA" for the years 1941-1949, AAHPERD Archives.

[34]National Section for Girls and Women in Sport, *The Story of the National Leadership Conference* (Washington, DC: AAHPER, 1955): 17-19; DGWS and National Association of Physical Education for College Women (NAPECW), *National Conference on Social Changes and Implications for Physical Education and Sports Program* (Washington, DC: AAHPER, 1958).

[35]Leyhe, "Attitudes of the Women Members"; Lucille Kyvallos, "Queens College: Success With No Frills," in *A Century of Women's Basketball*, ed. Hult and Trekell, 355-66.

[36]DGWS, "National Joint Committee on Extramural Sports for College Women, Joint Committee Report," June 1958, AAHPERD Archives; "Operation Code for the NJCESCW" (revised, n.d.), 1-2, AAHPERD Archives; Division for Girls and Women in Sport (DGWS), "DGWS Minutes of the Executive Council," Chicago: 18-22 March 1966, 5-6, AAHPERD Archives.

[37]Phebe M. Scott and Celeste Ulrich, "Commission on Intercollegiate Athletics for Women," in *Sports Programs for College Women*, DGWS National Conference, June 1969 (Washington, DC: AAHPER, 1970), 50-52; DGWS, "National Intercollegiate Athletic Championships for Women," *Journal of Health, Physical Education and Recreation*, 39 (February 1968): 24-27; Letter to Walter Byers from Rachel Bryant, 8 October 1971, AAHPERD Archives.

[38]DGWS, "National Intercollegiate Championship," 24-27; Scott and Ulrich, "Commission on Intercollegiate Athletics"; Virginia Hunt, "Governance of Women's Intercollegiate Athletics: An Historical Perspective,"

(Ed. D. diss., University of North Carolina at Greensboro, 1976), 186-207.

[39]Peter E. Holmes, "Memorandum for College and University Presidents, Chief State School Officers and Local School Superintendents," in *Final Title IX Regulation Implementing Education Amendments of 1972 Prohibiting Sex Discrimination in Education*, U.S. Department of Health, Education and Welfare (Washington, DC: U.S. Department of HEW, Office of Civil Rights, 1975).

[40]Holmes, *Final Title IX Regulation*, 2; "HEW Fact Sheet" in Holmes, *Final Title IX Regulation*, 1-11.

[41]C. Lehr, "Women in Sports Management: Fact or Fallacy Since Title IX?", poster presented at "The New Agenda," Washington, DC, 3-5 November 1983; Uhlir, "The Wolf is Our Shepherd," 172-76; R.V. Acosta and L.J. Carpenter, "Woman in Sport," in *Sport and Higher Education*, ed. J.O. Segrave and B.J. Becker (Champaign, IL: Human Kinetics, 1985), 313-25; D. Chu, "Benefits for Women," in *Sport and Higher Education*, ed. Segrave and Becker, 307-12; R.V. Acosta and L.J. Carpenter, "Women in Intercollegiate Sport, A Longitudinal Study—Thirteen Year Update 1977-1990," (Brooklyn, NY: Brooklyn College, 1990) (paper presented at the CCWAA Honor Award, Lexington, KY, October 1990).

[42]Christine H.B. Grant, "Facts You Should Know About a Very Special Governance Structure," *AIAW National Championship Newsletter*, 1980 AIAW Papers, Special Collections, University of Maryland, College Park Libraries Archives (hereafter cited as AIAW, [topic], CPL Archives); Hunt, "Governance of Women's Intercollegiate Athletics," 79-97; *AIAW Directory: Charter Member Institutions, 1971-72.* (Washington, DC: AAHPER, 1971); *AIAW Directory for Intercollegiate Athletics for Women Directory 1981-1982* (Washington, DC: AAHPERD, 1981), 10-55;

[43]Joan S. Hult, "The Legacy of AIAW," in *A Century of Women's Basketball*, ed. Hult and Trekell, 295-97; "AIAW Working Budget" 1975-1976, 1977-1978, 1978-1979, 1979-1980, AIAW, Executive Files, CPL Archives; Ann Uhlir, AIAW Executive Director, "1980-1981 Working Budget," AIAW, Executive Files, CPL Archives; "NBC Agreement of Understanding 1979-1981," AIAW, Legal Files, CPL Archives; "Memorandum of Understanding, AAHPER/NAGWS/AIAW Relationship," AAHPERD Archives.

[44]Joan S. Hult, "The Philosophical Conflicts in Men's And Women's Collegiate Athletics," *Quest*, **32** (1) (1980): 77-94; John Toner, "One Set of Rules for All Student Athletes," *Athletic Purchasing and Facilities*, **2** (November 1978): 6-11; Joan S. Hult, "Different AIAW/NCAA Eligibility Rules: Tip of the Iceberg?," *Purchasing and Facilities*, **3** (April 1979): 12-16.

[45]Carl Troester, "Kellmeyer, et al. v NEA, et al.," "Memorandum, 5 February 1973," AAHPERD Archives; "Bobbie Knowles' Court Case File," AAHPERD Archives; Carole Oglesby, "Court Suit Etc." Memo: AXB: 20 February 1973, AIAW, Legal Files, CPL Archives; Hunt, "Governance of Women's Athletics," 126-48.

[46]Hult, "Philosophical Conflicts," 77-94; Hult, "A Legacy of AIAW," 281-309; Hunt, "Governance of Women's Athletics," 184-223; NCAA, "Special Committee on Women's Athletics," 184-223; NCAA, "Special Committee on Women's Athletics," (1980-1982), AIAW, NCAA/AIAW Files, CPL Archives; AIAW, Committee on Men's Athletics Folder, AIAW, NCAA/AIAW Files, CPL Archives.

[47]"NCAA-AIAW Confrontation," Xerox, n.d., AAHPERD Archives; AIAW Joint Meeting of AIAW-NCAA, "Possible Alternatives for Future Governing Structures for Intercollegiate Athletics," n.d., AIAW, Executive

Files, CPL Archives; AIAW, "Association for Intercollegiate Athletics for Women AIAW-NCAA Fact Sheet," January 1975, AIAW, Legal Files, CPL Archives; John Toner, "How NCAA Can Accommodate, Fund Equal Women's Championships," *Athletic Purchasing and Facilities*, **2**, (December 1978): 8-14.

[48]NCAA, "NCAA Memorandum, HEW Draft Regulations," 21 February 1974, Xerox, 1974, 1-3, AIAW, Legal Files, CPL Archives; "DeHart List," AIAW, Title IX, CPL Archives; Donna A. Lopiano, "Affidavit," *AIAW (Plaintiff) v. NCAA (Defendant)* in the United States District Court for the District of Columbia, 48-236, AIAW, NCAA Suit Files, CPL Archives.

[49]For a more complete discussion see Joan S. Hult, "The Saga of Competition," 239-42; idem, "The Legacy of AIAW," 297-300; idem, "Philosophical Conflicts," 88-91.

[50]Alden, "Feminism and Women's Sports"; Hult, "Philosophical Conflicts," 88-91; United States Commission on Civil Rights, "The Current Status of Title IX Enforcement," in *More Hurdles to Clear, Women and Girls in Competitive Athletics*, idem. (Washington, DC: Clearinghouse Publication, July 1980), 33-44.

[51]Lopiano, "Affidavit *AIAW v NCAA*," 69-166, AIAW, Legal Files, CPL Archives; Fran Koenig to AIAW Executive Board, "Report on AIAW International Competition, September, 1975," AAHPERD Archives; Commission on Olympic Sports, *The Final Report of the President's Commission on Olympic Sports, 1975-77* vols. I and II (Washington, DC: Government Printing Office, 1977); Amateur Sports Act of 1978, "Report of the Senate Committee on Commerce, Science and Transportation," (Washington, DC: U.S. Government Printing Office, 1978).

[52]Lopiano, "Affidavit *AIAW v NCAA*," 130-264; NCAA, "Special Committee on NCAA Governance, Organization and Services,"

11-12 December 1979 and 28 December 1979, AIAW, Legal Files, CPL Archives; Christine H.B. Grant, "A 'State of the Union' Message," in *AIAW National Championship Newsletter*, 1980, 1-4; "Capsule Summary Analysis of NCAA Governance Proposal" (3 December 1980) and "Background Information on NCAA-AIAW Governance/Championships Issues" (January 1981), AIAW, CPL Archives.

[53]Lopiano, "Affidavit *AIAW v NCAA*," 138-44; "Affidavit AIAW-NCAA," 146-265; AIAW, "Official Minutes of the Executive Board and Delegate Assembly," Spokane, WA, 5-10 January 1982; Letter to AIAW Voting Representatives and Chief Executive Officers of AIAW Member Institutions from Donna A. Lopiano, President, Re: NCAA Convention Actions, 23 January 1981; Donna A. Lopiano, "A Comprehensive Look at the Complex Issues Concerning the Initiation of Women's Championships by the NCAA and NAIA," March 1980. All Items in this note in AIAW Papers, CPL Archives.

[54]Grant, "Capsule Summary Analysis NCAA Governance"; Lopiano, "The Impact on AIAW of NCAA," 265-96; AIAW, "Committee on Men's Athletics," AIAW, CPL Archives; Lopiano, "A Political Analysis," 168-76, AIAW, CPL Archives.

[55]AIAW, "Official Minutes of the Special Executive Board Meeting," Washington, DC, 4 March 1981; Donna A. Lopiano, "Impact on AIAW of NCAA Entry Into Women's Athletics," in Lopiano, "Affidavit *AIAW v NCAA*," 265-96; *AIAW (Plaintiff) v NCAA, (Defendant)*, Civil Action 81-2473, "Decision and Order," United States District Court for the District of Columbia, 11-12; Mimi Murray, "Affidavit" *AIAW v NCAA*, Case No. 81-2473," Memorandum of Points and Authorities in Support of Renewed Motion for Preliminary Injunction," filed in the United States District Court for the District of Columbia, 1-3. All items in this note in AIAW, Legal Files, CPL Archives.

Chapter 7

From Lowell Mills
to the Halls of Fame:
Industrial League Sport for Women

Lynne Emery

You have to understand that we'd rather play ball than eat.

PEPPER PAIRE
America's Working Women

What do Babe Didrikson, Bertha Tickey, Eckie Jordan, and Stella Walsh have in common? All of these women were sport stars and at some point in their careers competed under the sponsorship of industry.

For purposes of this chapter, industrial sport is defined as any sport activity initiated by industry that benefited both the employee and the company. One of employers' earliest concerns was the health of women workers; consequently, employers instituted physical activities to improve health and lower absence rates by the late 1800s. Sports activities were thought to increase loyalty to the company, thus decreasing employee turnover. Team sports were seen as activities that developed cooperation and team spirit, and employers hoped these qualities would carry over to the production line. At no time were these programs intended solely to benefit the worker; always implied was increased production for industry.

Sports programs for women increasingly were seen as good public relations tools for business and industry. Fielding a women's team was thought to demonstrate a company's progressive attitude and to enhance its public image.

Identifying a product with a women's team was excellent advertising and projected a clean, caring image in much the same way as companies today associate themselves with corporate sponsorship of the United States Olympic team or the Olympic Games. Also, although advertising and public image activities are conducted primarily to benefit business and industry, the fact that these groups sponsored women's sports certainly benefited the women involved.

Believing strongly in the benefits of sports programs, many companies created positions in their advertising, finance, or employee relations departments for the administration of these programs. From their inception, industrial sports programs for women were led primarily by men. Males were hired as activities directors or industrial recreators and charged with organizing company-sponsored activities. As the female work force expanded, a woman might be placed in the position of director of women or women's activities, but she usually worked under the leadership of a male. In companies with a large percentage of female employees, such as the telephone company or insurance companies, a woman might be designated as the activities director, but these appointments were rare. As teams were formed that required coaches and managers, these roles too were assumed by men, as demonstrated by perusal of basketball rules publications through the years.

Before looking at the actual sports, teams, and athletes involved in women's industrial leagues, we will present a brief history of women in the work force and the development of industrial sports.

Women Workers and Industrial Sports

One of the first industries to employ women in a factory setting was cotton mills in northeastern states. In the early 1800s, 80% of all cotton mill employees were women. By the late 1800s, women also were employed extensively in the shoe- and boot-making industry, as well as in cigar factories. Although women had always been teachers, it was not until the 1890s that their numbers were large enough to be counted. With the invention of the typewriter in the early 1900s, women entered the clerical professions and also began serving as saleswomen in stores.

In the early 19th century the number of women working outside the home in the United States was not very large. During World War II, however, women's participation in the work force jumped from 25% to 36% because of the employment of women in defense plants. After the war ended and heavy industries once again were closed to women, millions of women remained in the work force but returned to the traditional jobs they had formerly occupied.[1] Out of economic necessity, increasing numbers of women joined the labor force.

Among the first industries to sponsor activities for workers were the cotton mills of Lowell, Massachusetts, which in the early 1800s supervised the housing of employees to retain desirable workers. By the mid-1800s, some companies were providing meeting rooms and libraries for employees. In the late 1800s, companies such as Allis Chalmers began to sponsor sports teams for male workers. The Metropolitan Life Insurance Company of New York was especially noted for its sponsorship of athletics, albeit for males only.[2]

Corporate concern for female workers emerged just prior to the turn of the century when some companies began to sponsor calisthenics and posture-improving exercises. One of these was the National Cash Register Company (NCR), which provided daily 10-minute exercise breaks for office employees. These periods of calisthenics, which were first offered in 1894, were for the avowed purpose of improving health and efficiency. In 1905 NCR hired a physical training instructor, Minnie Rouland, for a 2-week training program for 20 calisthenics leaders in the various women' sections of the factory. In addition to their exercise breaks, female employees participated in calisthenics and dance immediately before lunch. The company also sponsored an evening exercise class for women workers.[3]

Another company concerned about employee health and recreation was the Kellogg Company of Battle Creek, Michigan. In the early 1900s, the company built a social hall so that dances could be held during the noon break. The company also sponsored an annual field day and picnic for employees and their families. Their second annual outing in 1911 included a wood-sawing competition for women. Always progressive, by 1912 the Kellogg Company employed 175 women out of a total of 743.[4]

Exactly when industry began to sponsor sports for women is unknown; however, it is clear that it was not until companies employed thousands of women with an interest in sports activities. U.S. Department of Labor surveys conducted in 1913 and 1918 showed that few companies sponsored activities for women, and the most common provisions for them were exercise classes and a rest or recreation area that contained couches and sometimes a phonograph or piano.[5]

A nationwide survey conducted in 1921 revealed the beginnings of women's involvement in industry-sponsored sports. Of the 51 companies that responded to the survey, only 15 reported offering no sports activities for women. Eight companies reported tennis teams, six had bowling teams, six had basketball teams, four had volleyball teams, two had baseball teams, and one had several hockey teams. One additional company reported golf for women employees, and one other reported indoor sports. The majority of respondents reported that team games were played outside of working hours, primarily in the evenings.[6]

In this same study, the author made an interesting point regarding class distinctions. In some companies there appeared to be a distinction between women who worked in the shop and those who performed office work, with neither group wishing to associate with the other.

The stenographers are the aristocrats and do not care to associate with the shop girls. The shop girls consider themselves far superior to the domestics, and with this feeling it is hard to make them forget their class distinction and forget themselves in the enjoyment of the game.[7]

Also to be considered is the fact that a large majority of the shop and domestic employees were recent immigrants, whereas the office workers were more likely to be native born and more highly educated.

The women's competitive sports teams sponsored by industry were composed primarily of blue-collar employees. Because newspapers and magazines most frequently report on items of interest to and about the middle and upper classes, there is a dearth of material on women's industrial sport. During the early years, very little was published about women's teams or leagues.

Although the 1921 study proclaimed bowling, basketball, and tennis to be the most popular women's activities, a 1926 survey conducted by the Department of Labor noted that baseball was becoming more widespread. This survey noted that ''diamond ball'' and ''kitten ball,'' both variations of baseball and forerunners of softball, were quite popular.[8]

A nationwide study of 639 companies, completed in 1940, found that of the companies that provided sports programs for women, 35% had bowling teams. Bowling was by far the most popular activity—so popular, in fact, that one company had as many as 600 teams. The study also found that bowling was more frequently a part of women's industrial programs than any other activity. Softball was in second place.[9] In the little written material on industrial sports for women, the three most frequently mentioned sports were bowling, basketball, and softball, and we will discuss each of these in greater detail.

Bowling

The majority of the companies that provided sports programs did not have their own facilities

Figure 7.1   The General Electric baseball team, 1925. Courtesy Sally Fox Collection.

but used either nearby YM/YWCA accommodations or those of commercial establishments. Bowling proved especially popular because of the large numbers of public lanes located in the large cities where many industries were based. Perhaps the fact that bowling had wide appeal to blue-collar workers helps explain its popularity in industry. The relative ease of learning the activity also may have been a factor; and because each team consisted of only five members, it was relatively simple to put a team and a league together. Finally, bowling appealed not only to young, gifted athletes but to women of all ages.

Bowling was especially popular in the ethnic neighborhoods of the large midwestern cities. German immigrants were particularly fond of the activity and frequently constructed an alley in the basement of the local clubhouse or saloon. Cincinnati, St. Louis, and Chicago, all areas with large German settlements, became centers for the sport.

Men's bowling was organized in 1895 with the founding of the American Bowling Congress, and thereafter national tournaments were organized annually. Women's bowling was not far behind; in fact, there is evidence of a tournament in Chicago as early as 1900.[10] A bowling league for women was organized in St. Louis in 1907, the same year the American Bowling Congress sponsored a national tournament for women in conjunction with its men's competition. In 1916 women formed their own governing body, the Women's National Bowling Association, which eventually became the Women's International Bowling Congress.[11] As early as 1920 the women's tourney offered $2,000 in prize money, and 84 teams were in contention.

Bowling quickly became the most popular, and frequently the only, sport for women in industry. Employers saw it as a morale booster that in turn developed company loyalty and reduced employee turnover. Teams in one factory not only

Figure 7.2   Schaper Products bowling team, 1934. Courtesy of The Women's International Bowling Congress.

bowled against each other but also competed against other factories' teams. For example, in 1925 the Los Angeles Department of Water and Power formed a girl's athletic committee under the auspices of the employees' association. The first competition was in bowling, and women from every department were invited to join. One of the first teams organized was called Lady Warehouse Mice, and these women challenged bowlers from any department to compete against them.[12]

Often women's bowling teams competed in city-wide leagues, such as the two-division league organized in Minneapolis in 1924. One division was for commercially sponsored teams from banks, stores, and factories; the other was for teams from churches, clubs, or any five women who wished to form a team.[13] A tournament sponsored by the *Chicago American* newspaper attracted hundreds of women bowlers from industry and elsewhere. So many entered the 1929 contest that the competition was divided into six classes based on each woman's average.[14] By the 1930s the *Chicago American* tourney consisted of more than 10,000 women bowlers from the city and surrounding areas.[15]

That bowling was a blue-collar or industrially based sport is borne out by a check of the national tournament winners in the 1910s and 1920s. Nearly all of the victorious teams had factory names: Alberti Jewelers, Page Dairy, Taylor Trunks. In addition, there is no indication that private athletic clubs entered teams in national competition.[16] Perhaps because of its connection with industry, women's bowling received little media coverage except when a newspaper sponsored a tournament.

Although companies added many sports for women workers during World War II, bowling remained the most popular, as evidenced by the 1,900 teams entered in the 1943 WIBC tournament. In 1946 the Allis Chalmers Company reported 800 women participants in its sports programs, and out of this number 500 were bowlers.[17] The greatest growth in the sport came during the postwar decades when the WIBC boasted a membership of 1 million in 1958 and more than 2 million by 1961.[18] Today, the Johnson Wax Company of Racine, Wisconsin, still maintains women's bowling leagues, and the Lockheed Corporation of Burbank, California, has at least five coed teams and between 20 and 30 women entered in special tournaments.[19] It is clear that bowling is still a popular industrial sport for women.

Basketball

It was in the sport of basketball that women's industrial teams achieved both visibility and fame.

Without industrial teams, the history of women's basketball in the United States would be far less illustrious, and the Amateur Athletic Union's national tournament might not have been established. Many of the people who made the game so exciting, as well as many Hall of Fame inductees, played with teams that were commercially sponsored.

Exactly when industry began sponsoring women's basketball teams is not known; it was perhaps as early as the mid- to late 1910s. Because at that time basketball was a popular sport in high schools and colleges, many working women knew the game and wished to continue playing. Many employers saw the public relations benefits of fielding teams in this all-American sport and quickly began to recruit women with basketball skills.

One of the most highly organized groups of girl and women basketball players was developed by textile mills in the South. Female employees and girls whose parents worked in the mills were given the same opportunities as males to play basketball and develop athletic skills. Many of the mills sponsored at least one team that competed against teams of other mills. As competition expanded, mills began to hire women with athletic skills. Mills also recruited women from other teams and paid them regular wages while they were on road trips.

A signal event for mill-sponsored teams was the founding of the Southern Textile Basketball Tournament in Greenville, South Carolina, in 1921. In the first tournament there were A and B divisions for men and a separate A division for women. By the late 1920s the tournament had grown from 8 to 150 teams representing five states. Later the tournament created a B division for women. With the exception of 1943–1945, the Southern Textile tourney has been played each year since its founding and continues today.[20]

Had industry not sponsored women's basketball, it is doubtful that the Amateur Athletic Union's (AAU) national basketball championship could have existed. The list of national tourney

Figure 7.3 Coca Cola Bottles basketball team, 1936. Courtesy Amateur Athletic Foundation of LA.

winners is a who's who of industrial teams. In the 1920s and 1930s, when colleges and high schools were eliminating varsity competition for women, industry expanded its offerings. Even the first AAU championship contained one industrial team, a harbinger of things to come.

The first women's national basketball championship was held in 1926 and sponsored by the AAU and the Pasadena Athletic and Country Club. Pasadena won the championship, the Anaheim Athletic Club was second, and in third place was the Wing Foot team sponsored by Goodyear Tire and Rubber Company.[21] Photos of the winning team show them clad in dark, sleeveless, V-necked shirts, dark shorts, and knee-length stockings with high-top gym shoes: a practical but not a very becoming uniform.

For some reason the AAU did not hold the tournament in 1927 or 1928.[22] When play resumed in 1929, industrial teams came to the fore. The 1929 nationals were won by the Schepps Aces of Dallas, Texas, who defeated the Dallas Golden Cyclones by one point, 28-27. The championships, which were held in Wichita, Kansas, included a few college teams; but the tournament was dominated by industrial teams such as the Wichita Coleman Lamps, the Oklahoma Gas and Electrics, the Thurston Garment Company, and Wallenstein-Raffman.[23] Although the scores in these early tournaments seem low, it must be remembered that until 1937 women were playing a two-division game in which the forwards played on one half of the court while the guards played on the other and only the forwards could score points.

Looking at photographs of teams, it is obvious that industry had discovered the publicity value of basketball and women's bodies. Players' uniforms had changed radically to brief shorts and tight shirts emblazoned with the sponsor's name. Frequently the uniforms were made of satin and included a waist-defining belt. The knee-length stockings of 1926 had disappeared, leaving legs bare to the ankle. When the Dallas Cyclones wore their new short shorts on the court in the late 1920s, the controversy over the uniforms raised by local newspapers increased attendance from 150 to 5,000 people per game.[24]

The 1930 championships, again held in Wichita, featured 28 teams and included the Sun Oilers (the former Schepps Aces)—who eventually won the tourney, the Dallas Cyclones, Wallenstein-Raffman, Lowe & Campbell, and the Yeagers from Denver. (See box on page 115.) For the second year the Cyclones lost by one point, this time in the semifinals to the Sun Oilers, 29-28. Three Sun Oiler players were named to the 1930 All-American first team, as were two from the Dallas Cyclones.[25] One of these, Mildred (Babe) Didrikson, became the top woman athlete of the first half of the 20th century.

The Golden Cyclones or the Dallas Cyclones, as they were commonly known, were sponsored by an insurance company, Employers Casualty Company. The man behind the team was Colonel Melvorne McCombs, who founded, coached, and recruited for the team using funds from the advertising department. He obviously believed that a nationally ranked women's team would publicize the company's excellence.[26] McCombs was said to have kept a file on all promising female athletes in Texas and surrounding states. With help from the personnel department, he eventually hired nearly 100 basketball players to work as filers, clerks, stenographers, or mailers.[27] Among the athletes he hired was Babe Didrikson.

According to Didrikson, McCombs came to see her play in 1930 when she was a junior in high school. She was released from school for 3 weeks so she could play with the Cyclones in the 1930

Figure 7.4 Babe Didrikson, shown here in the 1932 Olympics, began her athletic career in industrial league sport. Courtesy Amateur Athletic Foundation of LA.

nationals, and she was named All-American for the first time. After the tournament she returned to high school to finish the year and then went to Dallas in the summer for permanent employment with Employers Casualty. Didrikson played in two more national tournaments and was named to the All-American first team both years. In 1931 the Cyclones won the nationals by defeating the Wichita Thurstons 28-26, and in 1932 they lost to Oklahoma Presbyterian College by three points.[28]

In the 1930s, industrial women's basketball experienced tremendous growth throughout the

The "Legitimization" of Women's Basketball

In an attempt to legitimize women's basketball, the Wichita Elks Club included a sportsmanship trophy and pep, freethrow, and beauty contests as part of the 1930 AAU national championship. Beauty contest participants were the players in the tournament, a tradition that lasted for many years.

The chair of the Basketball Committee, J. Lyman Bingham, had such stereotypical remarks in his report that they warrant repeating to capture the true feeling of the era toward women's involvement in sports. In his discussion of the national tournament, Bingham wrote:

I will admit I too was sceptical and fully expected to see fainting girls carried away in ambulances, others laced in straight jackets after severe cases of hysteria and some in complete collapse after extreme cases of melancholia, the air permeated with smelling salts, etc., but I was agreeably pleased that none of these things happened. What I actually did see was a group of girls at the end of the game, rush to the center of the floor to cheer their opponents and then go arm in arm with them off the floor to appear later at a dance where a number of well behaved University of Wichita boys had been selected to dance with them.

Amateur Athletic Union, "Basketball Ball [sic] Committee Report," *Minutes of the Amateur Athletic Union 1930* (New York: Amateur Athletic Union, 1930), 196.

country. For example, female bank employees in Chicago formed the Chicago Bank Women's Athletic League for the primary purpose of playing basketball.[29] In the mid-1930s, when Memphis State University curtailed the women's varsity basketball program, several of the players formed an independent team sponsored by Coca Cola, a Memphis civic club. Others joined a team backed by Yellow Cab and continued to play.[30] Industrial women's basketball also was popular in Florida, and teams sponsored by the Alfar Creamery, the Baird Hardware Company, and Volk's Sport Shop played against each other in the state's AAU competition.[31]

One of the greatest women's industrial teams of the late 1940s and early 1950s was sponsored by Hanes Hosiery in the Southern Textile League. That Hanes won the AAU nationals in 1951, 1952, and 1953 was largely because of the efforts of mill employees Eunies Futch and Evelyn "Eckie" Jordan. Futch joined the Hanes team in 1947 and Jordan in 1948. At one point Hanes had a 102-game winning streak, and Jordan became a member of the Helms Basketball Hall of Fame after

being named to five All-American teams from 1950 to 1954.[32] Both Jordan and Futch also played softball for Hanes, and both were on the first U.S. women's basketball team to play in the Pan American Games in 1955.[33]

Basketball, particularly the type played in AAU tournaments, continued to be an important sport for working women throughout the 1960s and 1970s. Although many industrial teams still exist, they have declined in importance since the advent of national championships for college women, which began in 1972.

Softball

Business and industry also were major sponsors of women's softball teams. Even before the game was called softball (the title became official in 1932), industrial teams were playing the game on a grand scale. As early as 1931, Chicago's Western Electric Company had an eight-team women's baseball league. Also in Chicago, the Amalgamated Clothing Workers, a 16,000-member union, sponsored women's softball teams.[34]

In Los Angeles, many businesses backed women's softball. Among the teams was one for African-American women, the Eaglettes, sponsored by the *California Eagle*, a black newspaper. A team for women of Russian heritage was fielded by the A.B.C. Brewery. There also were Japanese, Chinese, and Mexican teams, but it has not been possible to determine whether they were sponsored by industry.[35] By 1938 there were close to 1,000 women's teams in southern California, with the majority having industrial backing. Some of these teams were the Bank of America Bankerettes, Columbia Pictures Starlettes, Payneheat Amazons, Balian Ice Cream Beauties, and Diamond Walnuts.[36]

With the onset of World War II and the huge influx of women into the defense industry, industrial women's softball expanded significantly. In Long Beach, California, in 1942 there was only one industrial team, the Calship Girls. The next year saw the addition of three industrial teams: Douglas, Vega, and Consolidated Vultee. Tremendous growth occurred in 1944 as 10 women's industrial teams joined the 17-team league. Among these teams were Calship, Douglas, Consolidated Vultee, Harvey Machine, Los Angeles Ship, Naval Dry Docks, Perry Forge Shop, Shell Oil, Torrance, and Western Pipe and Steel.[37] After the war there was no coverage of women's industrial softball in the Long Beach newspapers, but one or two teams were mentioned as being backed by businesses.

The influence of business and industry on women's softball is clear when one reads the list of Amateur Softball Association (ASA) national champions in women's fast-pitch softball. The second year the championship was held, 1934, the winner was Hart Motors of Chicago. The 1935 tourney was won by Cleveland's Bloomer Girls. This team was originally sponsored by Fleming Furniture, and as years passed, sponsorship changed and the team became known as the Blepp-Coombs Girls, the Individual Laundry Girls, the Favorite Knits, the Erin Brews, the Midvale Oils, and finally the Bloomer Girls.[38]

In the 1940s, the team to beat was the Jax Maids from New Orleans, sponsored by Jackson Brewery. They won the national title in 1942, 1943, 1945, 1946, and 1947. A major reason for the Jax team's success was its pitcher, Nina Korgan, who was inducted into the National Softball Hall of Fame in 1960. Born in Iowa, Korgan began her pitching career with a team in Syracuse, Nebraska, and then moved to the Pony Express team in Missouri. From there she led the Higgins Midgets of Tulsa, Oklahoma, to the 1941 national championship before signing with the Jax Maids. As in basketball, softball players were employed by their sponsoring company and were paid for their jobs, such as filing clerk or receptionist, and not for playing softball, because the ASA insisted that athletes be amateurs. Even so, a softball-playing typist could expect to earn her salary plus other incentives.[39]

Another astoundingly successful industrial team that is still active is the Raybestos Brakettes of Stratford, Connecticut. The Brakettes won their first nationals in 1958 and their most recent in the 1990s. Although there was a change of sponsors in 1985, the Brakettes recently signed an 8-year contract with the Raybestos Company and appear difficult to beat. Raybestos was led by Hall of Fame pitchers: Bertha Tickey, who was inducted in 1972, and Joan Joyce, inducted in 1983. Tickey, who also played for the Orange Lionettes, pitched three perfect games during national tournament play in 1950, 1954, and 1968 and had a lifetime record of 162 no-hit, no-run games. She also holds the record of 69 tournament wins earned by pitching in 19 national tournaments.[40]

Sex Appeal

Photographs of the Brakettes and other industrial teams such as the Phoenix A-1 Queens and the Phoenix Maids in the 1940s through the 1960s show the women attired in satin shorts and shirts.

The uniforms, impractical as they were for base sliding, certainly stressed the feminine qualities of the athletes, as did many of the articles written about the teams. (See box below.) One article stressed femininity by including inset photos of the players in action and also photos of them as mothers and wives and in typical female occupations. Photo captions included such descriptors as ''devoted housewife,'' ''peppery and pretty,'' and ''attractive.''[41]

In her dissertation on industrial sports, Hagen noted that ''industrial programs embraced the sexual stereotypes of femininity, and . . . administrators were keenly aware of the commercial value associated with flashy displays of the female body.''[42] Sex appeal for purposes of product promotion became part of the marketing strategy for many industries that sponsored women's sports teams. Although the sexier uniforms tended to increase attendance at games, Hagen concluded that a disservice was done to the athletes because recognition came from physical appearance rather that athletic prowess.

Some companies conducted highly publicized varsity programs specifically to capitalize upon women's feminity [sic] and sex appeal. In doing this, recreation directors were not only building upon an established approach toward advertising that used women's bodies to sell products, but they perpetuated the perception of women as sex objects. By promoting the sexy female athlete, these companies achieved their advertising objectives.[43]

The Phoenix Queens

In 1949 an article appeared in *Arizona Highways* that praised women's softball and contained every imaginable stereotype about the players. An excerpt of that article follows.

The [Phoenix] Queens, who annually have perhaps more people than any other softball team, have been labeled the most beautiful softball team in the world.

They were organized in 1936 when Larry Walker, . . . assembled a group of young girls anxious to swing a bat and don a glove for fielding practice. They had been playing with various other girls' teams, and he emerged with a club known as the Queens. To be more exact, they became the Arizona Brewing Company A-1 Queens, and the sponsor provides their equipment and some expense funds. Brewing company officials consider the attractive softballers one of their firm's finest advertisements.

When a national magazine, in an article on the sex appeal of women in sports, held that strenuous athletics are detrimental to femininity, Manager Walker strongly denied that feminine athletes tend to become masculine. Though admitting there are some masculine-type girls playing softball, Walker declared, referring to the Queens, ''We pass them up. . . . It is possible to be an athlete and still maintain feminine charm.'' He says newcomers to the Queens are screened on the basis of ''character first, feminine charm second and ability to play ball third.''

Walker, who believes girl softballers with outside interests have a better chance to remain feminine than those whose whole lives are devoted to sports, declares: ''Our team is based on good looking girls. Even though it is one of the top girls' teams in the world, it could draw well if it won very few games.''

Jerry McLain, ''Arizona's Larruping Lassies,'' *Arizona Highways*, August 1949, 25; 27.

Bill Plummer, publicity chair of the ASA, provided additional reasons for industrial sponsorship of women's softball teams. Plummer believed business and industry were attracted to the game because it had great spectator appeal, was highly visible to the public, drew well at the gate, and had a high caliber of play. Although sponsors received little in the way of tangible assets, the value of the publicity they garnered was immeasurable.[44]

Other Sports

From the earliest days of women's track and field competition, business and industry were sponsoring teams and meets. One of the first companies to field a women's track team was the Prudential Insurance Company of Newark, New Jersey, and Prudential athletes' names abound in the record books of the 1920s and early 1930s. In 1923 the Prudential team won the national AAU title, and two women emerged as stars. One was hurdler Hazel Kirk, and the other was Esther Behring, national basketball throw champion and winner of the shot put in the 1924 national championships.[45]

Other early industrial track teams were the Pennsylvania Railroad team based in Cleveland and the New York Central Railroad team, which at one time boasted 1932 Olympic gold medal winner Stella Walsh as a member.[46] Of course, the Employers Casualty Company of Dallas provided a track team to showcase the talents of Babe Didrikson in the 1930 and 1931 nationals, as well as the trials for the 1932 Olympic Games. Teams sponsored by Edison Lamp Works, City Bank, Metropolitan Life Insurance, Otis Elevator, Globe Indemnity Company, and Detroit Central were also prominent in the early days.

Besides track and field, business and industry at one time or another have sponsored tennis, golf, and swimming teams for women. Opportunities have been provided for participation in billiards, fencing, field hockey, gymnastics, volleyball, and many other sports. From participating for personal enjoyment to interdepartmental play, from contests between factories to competing at the national and international levels, women's industrial sport has run the gamut both in activities offered and levels of competition.

Summary and Conclusions

This brief overview of women's industrial sports leads to several conclusions. First, at a time when there was little opportunity for women to be involved in sports (the 1920s through the 1960s), industrial teams offered women a chance to compete. Whether a woman was a highly skilled athlete or a novice, opportunities existed.

Industrial sports programs were egalitarian, offering both blue-collar and white-collar workers opportunities for competition. As a result, women did not have to join a country club or athletic club to enjoy sports.

Although little appeared in the media about commercially sponsored women's sports, thousands of women workers were involved in many kinds of sports. Their actual numbers probably will never be known, but the information that does exist shows that the reach of women's industrial sports was extensive.

Through their sponsorship of sports for women, business and industry kept competition alive and booming. Although educational institutions were offering few opportunities for high-level competition, industry fortunately believed that women liked to compete and provided opportunities. Employers saw sponsorship of teams as a sound business practice that fostered increased employee loyalty, reduced turnover, and engendered camaraderie among participants. Although outwardly little appeared to be happening in women's sports, there were thousands of teams and competitions, all provided by industry. Industry was truly the savior of the women's sports movement.

Notes

1. Rosalyn Baxandall, Linda Gordon, and Susan Reverby, comps. and eds. *America's Working Women* (New York: Random House, 1976), 280-83.

2. Donald Hawkins, "The Formulation and Validation of Principles for Industrial Recreation in the United States" (PhD diss., New York University, 1966), 75.

3. John R. Schleppi, " 'It Pays': John H. Patterson and Industrial Recreation at the National Cash Register Company," *Journal of Sport History*, **6**, no. 3 (Winter 1979): 22-23.

4. Harold L. Ray, "Snap, Crackle, Pop for Fitness and Sport: The Kellogg Legacy" (paper presented at the North American Society for Sport History Conference, Clemson, SC, 1989), 3-4.

5. Ellen W. Gerber et al., *The American Woman in Sport* (Reading, MA: Addison-Wesley, 1974), 39.

6. Dorothy Schaper, "Industrial Recreation for Women," *American Physical Education Review*, **27** (March 1922): 106.

7. Ibid., 109.

8. Gerber et al., *American Woman*, 39.

9. Leonard J. Diehl and Floyd R. Eastwood. Industrial Recreation (Lafayette, IN: Purdue University, 1940), 2-3; 39.

10. Gerald Gems, "The Emergence and Development of a Woman's Sporting Culture: Chicago, 1880-1940" (paper presented at the North American Society for Sport History Conference, Banff, Canada, 1990), 13.

11. Gerber et al., *American Woman*, 95.

12. "Girls Roll Their Own" and "Sport Bulletins From the General Warehouse," *The Intake* (publication of the Los Angeles Department of Water and Power), May 1925, 35.

13. Virginia Lou Evans, "The Status of the American Woman in Sport, 1912-1932" (PhD diss., University of Massachusetts, 1982), 112.

14. Eli, "Caroline Curtis Rolls Into Class B Lead With 549," *Chicago American*, 1 March 1929, 49.

15. Steven Riess, *City Games* (Urbana: University of Illinois Press, 1989), 78.

16. Evans, "Status," 112.

17. Gerber et al., *American Woman*, 95.

18. Monys Ann Hagen, "Industrial Harmony Through Sports: The Industrial Recreation Movement and Women's Sports" (PhD diss., University of Wisconsin-Madison, 1990), 167.

19. Craig Wilsman (director of sports and fitness, Lockheed Corporation, Burbank, CA), telephone conversation, 26 February 1991.

20. Miriam F. Shelden, "Textile Leagues and Early Competition for Women" (paper presented at the North American Society for Sport History Conference, Columbus, OH, 1987), 5-6.

21. Amateur Athletic Union, *Minutes of the Amateur Athletic Union 1926* (New York: Amateur Athletic Union, 1926), 154.

22. Why there was a break in the AAU women's national basketball tournaments has never been satisfactorily explained. An article in the *Official A.A.U. Guide 1938-1939* (Carroll H. Smith, "Ten Years of A.A.U. Women's Basketball," p. 53) claimed that the sport was first sanctioned by the Amateur Athletic Union in 1929 and the first tournament held in Wichita, Kansas, in March of 1929. *The Official A.A.U. Basketball Handbook 1972-74*, however, gave a complete listing of the national women's champions and included the 1926 tournament won by the Pasadena Athletic and Country Club ("National A.A.U. Women's Champions," 124-26). In his book *The Cavalcade of Basketball* (New York: Macmillan, 1960, 209-10), Alexander Weyand mentioned the 1926 tourney as the first for women and then noted that there was a national tournament sponsored by the Wichita, Kansas, Elks Club in 1928. Because an ineligible team competed in this 16-team championship, the AAU refused to sanction

it and the results are therefore not included in the record books.

[23]Amateur Athletic Union, *Minutes of the Amateur Athletic Union 1929* (New York: Amateur Athletic Union, 1929), 106-7.

[24]Stephanie L. Twin, ed. *Out of the Bleachers: Writings on Women and Sport* (Old Westbury, NY: Feminist Press, 1979), xxxix.

[25]Amateur Athletic Union, "Basketball Ball [sic] Committee Report," *Minutes of the Amateur Athletic Union 1930* (New York: Amateur Athletic Union, 1930), 195-200.

[26]Roxanne M. Albertson, "Basketball Texas Style, 1910-1933: School to Industrial League Competition," in *A Century of Women's Basketball. From Frailty to Final Four*, ed. Joan S. Hult and Marianne Trekell (Reston, VA: AAHPERD, 1991), 160.

[27]Bill Cunningham, "The Colonel's Ladies," *Collier's*, 23 May 1936, 28; 61.

[28]Babe Didrikson Zaharias and Harry Paxton, *This Life I've Led* (New York: Barnes, 1955), 34-39. If Didrikson's account is accurate, she dropped out of school and became an industrial athlete at the age of 16, although she was ostensibly hired as a stenographer. In their book *Whatta-Gal* (Boston: Little, Brown, 1975, 64), Johnson and Williamson listed Didrikson's salary in 1930 as $900 and noted that an average typist earned $624 annually. Although Didrikson claimed she finished the 1930 school year, Johnson and Williamson wrote that she left school on February 17 and did not return. Was Didrikson a professional athlete without a high school diploma? Although neither Didrikson nor Johnson and Williamson mention it, she eventually earned her diploma through a correspondence course. As to her being a professional athlete, industrial team participants were considered amateurs even though they were paid for their athletic ability in much the same way as the "state amateurs" of the Eastern bloc countries in the 1950s through the 1980s.

Controversial though she was, Didrikson adopted the values of the era when it came to women's participation in sport. In her autobiography she stated:

> Nowadays the big sports for women are tennis, fancy diving, swimming and golf. And those are the best sports for women—some of the others are really too strenuous for girls. But back there in the 'thirties they made a big thing out of sports like women's basketball. (p. 36)

[29]Bernice A. Miller, "Growing Need of Physical Recreation Among Employed Women," *Journal of Health and Physical Education*, **1**, 10 (December 1930): 7.

[30]Jane Howles Hooker, "A History of the Women's Sports Program at Memphis State University, 1912-1938" (PhD diss., University of Mississippi, 1988), 264. Although Hooker's study is unclear on this point, it appears that the Memphis civic club Coca Cola had nothing to do with the soft drink of the same name.

[31]Paula Welch, "A Focus on Women's Sport in Florida During the Depression Decade" (paper presented at the North American Society for Sport History Conference, Banff, Canada, 1990), 7-8.

[32]Elva Bishop and Katherine Fulton, "Shooting Stars," *Southern Exposure*, **7**, 2 (Fall 1979): 50-51. It is interesting to note that during its heyday the Hanes team was coached by Virgil Yow, father of Kay Yow, who coached the 1988 U.S. Olympic women's basketball team.

[33]Angela Lumpkin, "North Carolina's Hall of Famers—From Golf to Bowling to Softball to Basketball" (paper presented to the North Carolina Alliance of Health, Physical Education, Recreation and Dance Conference, 1983), 6; 8.

[34]Gerald Gems, "Sport and the Americanization of Ethnic Women in Chicago" (unpublished paper, 1990), 25-26.

[35] Lynne Emery, "Sports of Southern California Black Women in the 1920's and 1930's" (paper presented at the North American Society for Sport History Conference, Clemson, SC, 1989), 9-10.

[36] F.J. Taylor, "Fast and Pretty," *Collier's*, 20 August 1938, 23; 38.

[37] Alison M. Wrynn, "Women's Industrial and Recreation League Softball in Southern California 1930-1950" (Master's thesis, California State University, Long Beach, 1989), 32-33.

[38] Hal Lebovitz, "A Boom in Women's Sports?," *Cleveland Plain Dealer*, 17 May 1981, Sec. B, 2.

[39] Robert M. Yoder, "Miss Casey at the Bat," *Saturday Evening Post*, 22 August 1942, 17; 48-49.

[40] Edward Claflin, *The Irresistible American Softball Book* (Garden City, NY: Dolphin Books, 1978), 69.

[41] Jerry McLain, "Arizona's Larruping Lassies," *Arizona Highways*, August 1949, n.p.

[42] Hagen, "Industrial Harmony Through Sports," 178.

[43] Ibid., 238.

[44] Bill Plummer (publicity chair for the Amateur Softball Association), telephone interview, September 1990.

[45] George H. Vreeland, "Track and Field Women Champions," *The National Athlete*, June 1924, 7-8.

[46] "Illinois Women's A.C. Team Wins U.S. Track Title," *Chicago Tribune*, 5 July 1930, 15. In the AAU national track meet in 1930, Stella Walsh set world records in winning the 100- and 220-yard dashes plus the long jump. Although Walsh was raised in the United States, because she was not a U.S. citizen she competed for Poland in the 1932 Olympic Games, where she won the 100-meter dash. Walsh's track career began in the 1920s and extended into the 1950s; many consider her the best track athlete of all time.

Chapter 8

A Century of Olympic Competition

Paula Welch
D. Margaret Costa

As most Olympians will tell you, . . . if you blow it, you're out. You can be a world record holder. You could have beautiful blond hair, gorgeous blue eyes. . . . Nothing matters but touching the end of the pool.

ANN CURTIS
(gold medalist, 400-meter freestyle, four × 100-meter freestyle relay;
silver medalist 100-meter freestyle, 1948 Summer Olympic Games)

Every 4 years, athletes from all over the world compete in the most prestigious of international sports competitions: the Olympic Games. As this competition among nation-states evolved from a feudal structure to an international forum for showcasing political ideals and athletic feats, the role of the woman athlete changed according to the social and political decrees of the day. Today's Olympic Games provide the dominant setting for the exhibition of physical prowess by women. Three main ideological factors have influenced the participation of women in the Olympic Games:

- Struggles over the admission of women to the early Games, as reflected in the controls of the organization of Olympic sport

- The use of women's performance to showcase political ideology
- The struggle for the admission of women to the more aggressive winter events

The Struggle for Admission

Baron Pierre de Coubertin, *renovateur* of the modern Olympic Games, envisioned them as sport festivals for the world's white, male upper-class youth. The ancient Greeks' exclusion of women from their festivals was acceptable to Coubertin, for he saw his modern version as a means of preparing French males for military service as well as for leadership roles in government and business. Such a posture rendered the participation of women irrelevant.

It is ironic, then, that the early slow and arduous evolution of women's participation in the first four Olympic Games can be indirectly credited to Coubertin. In the primary stages of its development, the International Olympic Committee (IOC) lacked sufficient organizational skills and cohesive structure to control the program of the Games. In 1900 and 1904, the selection of events for the Olympic programs was left to the Organizing Committees of Paris and St. Louis, respectively. As a result, a conglomeration of disorganized events was selected, among them the socially acceptable women's events of golf and lawn tennis in 1900 and the exhibition sport of women's archery in 1904.

The seven American women who entered the 1900 Paris Olympic Games matched the profile of late 19th-century scions of wealth. They belonged to social clubs; studied art, music, literature, and language; and, through their country club affiliations, entered sport from an acceptable realm. Robert Dunn, in "The Country Club: A National Expression, Where Woman Is Free," described country clubs as the primary channel for women to gain access to outdoor sports: "Her steps in politics have been infantile, in business quite subordinary. . . . But on the golf and tennis field, and as a huntswoman, she has leaped to equal place with man."[1]

The 1900 Olympic Games were overshadowed by the concurrent Exposition (world's fair), a showcase of world technology, culture, and progress. Consequently, the American women who participated were wealthy socialites who were drawn to Paris by the Exposition, participating in a little tennis and golf during the Paris "season"; they were not accorded team status, uniforms, fanfare, or recognition by the American Olympic Committee (AOC). Tennis player Marion Jones, credited by many historians with a third-place finish in ladies' singles and mixed doubles, was

the daughter of millionaire John Percival Jones and could easily afford to spend time in Europe.[2]

The inclusion of America's first generation of female Olympians in the golf competition was a coincidence rather than a calculated plan. The five women who entered the inaugural women's Olympic golf tournament lived in Europe or were on extended vacations. Margaret Abbott of the Chicago Golf Club, who finished first, and her mother, Mary, the seventh-place finisher,[3] were in Europe because Mrs. Abbott had arranged educational experiences for her daughter.[4] Polly

Figure 8.1 Margaret Abbott, winner of the first women's Olympic golf tournament held in 1900. Paula Welch Collection, Courtesy of Phillip Dunne.

Whittier, the runner-up, also was in Europe for educational purposes. Daria Pratt, who finished third, was in France planning her daughter's wedding to Count Alexandre Mercatti, a member of the 1896 Olympic Organizing Committee.[5] Ellen Ridgway, the fifth-place finisher, and her husband were long-time residents of Paris.[6]

The 1904 St. Louis Olympic Games were likewise overshadowed by the Louisiana Purchase Exposition World's Fair in the same city. Seven American women took part in archery competition that was declared by the AOC members to be an exhibition only.[7] Led by Coubertin's friend and confidant, James E. Sullivan, founder and a one-time powerful president of the AAU and an influential leader in the Olympic movement, the AOC opposed the participation of American women in the Olympic Games and any other competitions performed in the presence of men.[8] Determined to bring order to the chaos caused by the conflicting opinions on women's participation, the Olympic Committee for the 1908 games in London admitted the women's events of exhibition skating, tennis, and archery, as well as exhibition gymnastics and aquatics.

The initiative for the 1912 program content was primarily taken by the Swedish Olympic Committee. The Swedes admitted women into what was considered the first serious female competition, swimming. The only comment from the IOC on this occurrence came in the form of minutes for one of its meetings.

> The Swedes are opposed to specializations. They are feminists and women already admitted to the trials of lawn tennis and gymnastics exhibitions will be without a doubt in the swimming championships.[9]

In the U.S., however, Ida Schnall, captain of the New York Female Giants baseball club, was prevented from entering the diving events by the previously mentioned, James E. Sullivan, the dominant adversary of American women in the

Olympics.[10] Sullivan died in 1914, and the gateway to the Games appeared to open for American women.

Meanwhile, Coubertin continued his behind-the-scenes opposition to women's competitions through numerous pontifications in the monthly newsletter of the IOC. His opposition continued to be reinforced by three major factors:

- His wish to emulate as closely as possible the format of the ancient Greek Games
- The fact that the emancipation of French women had progressed more slowly than in other parts of Europe, so French women's involvement in sport was negligible
- His belief that women who engaged in strenuous activities were destroying their "feminine" charm

Coubertin used this last argument to appeal to the sensibilities of the male enthusiasts of sports in which women participated. For example, in reaction to a premiere match of women's fencing, he contended that coed competition would lead to the feminization of that noble sport.[11] Imagine Coubertin's horror when in 1917 the winner of the shot put at France's National Athletic Championship, Violette Gouirand-Morriss, had both breasts removed so she could better perform her event.[12]

Coubertin's authority did not reign supreme over Olympic competition, however. It was, as mentioned previously, because of the inability of Coubertin's own committee, the IOC, to implement a policy for the conduct of the Olympic Games, thereby relinquishing program selection to the respective organizing committees, that women's competition was permitted to develop against his will. World War I caused the cancellation of the 1916 Olympic Games, and American women did not reappear in the Games until 1920.

From European Struggle and Competition to U.S. Involvement

American women, with a few exceptions, entered the Olympic movement through a small number of private sports organizations and educational institutions. Six of the 15 members on the 1920 swimming and diving team were members of the Women's Swimming Association of New York (WSA). These six were from middle-class families who lived in New York City and joined the WSA to learn to swim.[13] The WSA was the first organization that provided women an opportunity to train for national and international competition.

America's first world-class swimmer, Ethelda Bleibtrey, a WSA protegée, set world records in various distances, often competing in adverse conditions when strong winds and cold water prompted other competitors to withdraw from races. Bleibtrey also made Olympic history when she won the 100-meter freestyle in the Olympic record time of 1 min 13.6 s on August 25, 1920.[14] Although the first American Olympic champion, Margaret Abbott, was awarded a porcelain bowl trimmed in gold at the 1900 Paris Olympic Games, Bleibtrey was the first American woman to receive a gold medal in Olympic competition. Paris officials had presented previous Olympians with art objects in commemoration of their victories. Bleibtrey collected her second gold medal in a world-record performance when she led all swimmers from start to finish in the 300-meter freestyle.[15] On August 29, 1920, Bleibtrey swam her final Olympic race when she anchored the 400-meter relay team.[16] Her unprecedented achievements in the Olympic Games reflected her ability, determination, and the preparation she received from the WSA.

Another group that deserves credit for the early Olympic participation of women was the International Federations. By 1912 the International Federations, which represented sports in which women could participate, were having a positive effect on the achievement of women in the Olympic Games. Particularly influential were the International Swimming Federation and the Gymnastics Federation. The influence of the federations prevented the intervention of Coubertin and led to the official acceptance of women in the Olympic

Games of 1924. The text of the annual IOC meeting minutes read:

> Women are admitted in certain competitions in the Olympic Games. The program will include contests which they can dispute among themselves.[17]

Between 1912 and 1928 the International Federations maintained a relatively positive attitude in support of women's competitions and were considered a major force influencing the IOC in this regard. The "gentleman amateur" composition of the IOC and its consequent lack of knowledge of the technical aspects of sport necessitated interactions with the International Federations. Such reliance on the federations and the local organizing committees led to the Committee's reserved acceptance of women as Olympians.

As sportswomen petitioned for acceptance into male sporting arenas, Coubertin's disapproving attitude toward women's Olympic competition became more evident. Nowhere was this attitude more pronounced than in Coubertin's own country, France. It was here that Mme Alice Miliat, leader of the newly founded Federation Sportive Feminine Internationale (FSFI), set about making plans for a Women's Olympic Games.[18] These Games were primarily to provide international competition in athletics for women and were to be held every four years beginning in 1922.

In response to Mme Miliat's "audacious" proposal, the IOC suggested that the International Federations take control of women's athletic activities. The International Amateur Athletic Federation (IAAF), the governing body of Olympic athletics, in turn permitted women to be members of its organization but denied them the right to compete in the 1924 Games.[19] In opposition to the IAAF's position, the women athletes, led by Mme Miliat, continued to conduct successful athletic competitions. In 1922 the first Women's Olympic Games attracted approximately 20,000 spectators for the 1-day event. Later the Women's International and British Games were attended by

5,000 spectators. Dismayed by the rapid expansion of the women's programs, the IAAF approached the FSFI for some agreement on the control of women's athletics, including the women's events in the Olympic Games.[20]

Throughout this controversy, the question of the effect of athletic competitions on women's health appeared and reappeared. Debates regarding the inclusion of women in Olympic competition raged in the newspapers. Finally the IAAF "agreed" to "organize" women's athletics and recommended five events for the 1928 Games. Mme Miliat was incensed because a full program was not recommended. The British, who had the strongest team, boycotted.[21]

Coubertin, absent from the Games in 1928, was not present to witness the women's athletic events to which he objected so fiercely. Adding

fuel to the fire of opposition to women's participation in endurance events was the incorrect report that some of the women in the 800-meter run appeared to stagger across the finish line, while others looked "pale" and "exhausted." The *New York Times* was quick to point to the "poor" health of the competitors as sufficient reason to bar women from athletic competition. Sport historian Lynne Emery, who reexamined the controversial 800-meter run, in which some of the finalists purportedly collapsed, determined that all nine finalists had completed the contest. As a result, she believed the Olympic officials were unjust in eliminating the event. The resulting controversy overshadowed the success of the first women's 100-meter dash gold medalist and anchor on the 400-meter relay team, Betty Robinson of Riverdale, Illinois. The women's

Figure 8.2 Betty Robinson winning the 100-meter gold medal in the 1928 Olympics. Courtesy Amateur Athletic Foundation of LA.

800-meter run was not to appear again in Olympic competition until 1960.

On the international scene, the world press used the incident to condemn athletics for women altogether. At its annual meeting in 1929 the IOC voted to eliminate the women's program in athletics. In reaction, Gustavius Kirby, president of the Amateur Athletic Union in the United States and a member of the IAAF, recommended that the IAAF adopt a resolution barring all male athletes from the 1932 games unless women were allowed to compete.[22] At its meeting in Berlin in 1930, the Olympic Congress voted in favor of admitting women.

With new confidence, Mme Miliat and the FSFI demanded that there be a full program of women's athletics in 1932. Added to that demand was the suggestion that if a full program was not added, no women's event should be staged at all.[23] Unfortunately, this ultimatum was the beginning of the end for the FSFI, as the IAAF succeeded in gaining complete control of the women's athletic competitions in future Olympic Games.

Interestingly, and in direct opposition to the desire of the FSFI, the Women's Division of the National Amateur Athletic Foundation in the United States continued its opposition to women's Olympic competition. At its convention in New York City, the theme was "Competition for Girls, More Rather Than Less but of the Right Kind." Further, most of the 360 attendees concurred with the objections of Ethel Perrin (chairman of the Women's Division, NAAF Executive Committee) to Olympic competition:

Figure 8.3   Lillian Copeland, gold medalist in the discus throw in the 1932 Olympics. Courtesy Amateur Athletic Foundation of LA.

- Specialized training for small numbers of participants
- Exploitation of athletes for the sake of winning
- Overemphasis on establishing records[24]

In addition, numerous articles that deplored highly organized sport for women were published in the *American Physical Education Review*. Women in the physical education profession did not succeed in eliminating women's sports from the Olympic Games, however. Babe Didrikson was very successful at the 1932 Los Angeles Olympic Games, winning gold medals in the javelin and 80-meter hurdles and a silver medal in the high jump.

An obscure debut occurred at the 1932 Los Angeles Olympic Games when Tidye Pickett of Chicago and Louise Stokes of Malden, Massachusetts, became the first black women to be selected for a United States Olympic team. Pickett and Stokes had previously competed for athletic clubs in AAU competition without interference. When they arrived in Los Angeles with the women's track squad as part of the relay team for the Games, however, they were denied the opportunity to compete. Tidye Pickett Phillips recalled in her genteel manner, "But times were different then. Some people just didn't want to admit that we were better runners." In 1936 Stokes did not compete, and Pickett was injured when she hit the second hurdle during the semifinal round of competition.[25]

By 1936, thanks to the FSFI and Mme Miliat, women's sports in general had proved a success. The stage was set to use women's Olympic events to further nationalistic and ideological objectives.

Much of the excitement of the 1936 Olympic Games, held in Berlin, was dampened by Adolph Hitler's nationalistic policy of Aryan supremacy. American opposition to the Berlin Olympic Games gathered momentum not long after 1932; however, influenced by the powerful Avery Brundage, the AAU and the AOC voted to send athletes to Berlin in 1936.[26] Brundage was president of the AAU and the AOC and was respected by sport leaders, who eventually were to elect him president of the IOC.

Politics and Ideology

Fundamental Principle No. 7 of the Olympic Code proudly states: "The Games are contests between individuals and not between countries." This idealistic claim has not been borne out in reality, because Olympic success is measured solely in terms of a national team's performance. Furthermore, much of the literature on the Olympic Games fails to distinguish between the contributions of women and men to each team's success.[27]

With the Games of 1948 and 1952 came the era of the Cold War Olympics, the era of the state amateur under IOC president Avery Brundage (1952–1972), and perhaps the era of women's participation for political purposes. In 1952 the Soviet Union reentered the Olympic arena with the sole intention of systematically counting medals, and consequently it applied pressure for the enlargement of the women's programs.

Meanwhile, on the other side of the globe, the staging of the first Pan American Games in Buenos Aires and Asian Games in New Delhi in 1951 brought the Third World into the Women's International sports arena. In 1964 in Tokyo, Japan, women athletes from Ghana, Nigeria, Uganda, Iran, Malaysia, Mongolia, Nicaragua, Peru, and Thailand also made their first appearance in the Olympic Games.[28]

Black Women Athletes: Tuskegee and Tennessee State Universities

On the American front, black women athletes became the first women to enter the Olympic movement through educational institutions. Athletes from the all-black Tuskegee Institute in Alabama were notable exceptions among the vast majority of women enrolled in American colleges and universities in the 1940s. Tuskegee, now Tuskegee

University, was dedicated to offering women educational and competitive opportunities, whereas the majority of white institutions emphasized intramural, interclass, Play Day and Sports Day competition. Tuskegee pioneered American women's entry into the Olympic movement by offering outstanding female athletes who otherwise could not afford an education work-study grants to pursue their education. Later another black school, Tennessee Agricultural and Industrial State College, created an athletic program for women based on the Tuskegee model.

The tutelage of Cleve Abbott, Tuskegee's coach, who was succeeded by Rose Owen and later Nell Jackson, set the standard for other black and white institutions of higher learning in developing female track and field athletes. During Tuskegee's "golden years" of track and field from 1937 to 1951, the Tigerettes unequivocally dominated AAU competition. Members of Tuskegee's track and field team won 14 of 15 outdoor titles and 5 of 6 indoor titles. Most teams entered national AAU championships with a goal of finishing no higher than second. One of the greatest margins of victory was scored in 1944 when Tuskegee amassed 107 1/2 points and the Philadelphia Moose Club, the runner-up team, posted 50 points.[29]

Three women from Tuskegee Institute, Mabel Walker, Theresa Manuel, and Nell Jackson, were named to the 1948 Olympic team.[30] Two other 1948 Olympians, Audrey Patterson and Emma Reed of Tennessee Agricultural and Industrial State College,[31] joined the Tuskegee athletes in inaugurating a new era in the preparation of female Olympians from the United States. The entry of women into the 1948 London Olympic Games as a result of elite sports preparation in institutions of higher education was indeed a prototype for the future. Because of the training she received in her first 3 years at Tuskegee, Alice Coachman (Albany State) was well prepared for the 1948 Games. Coachman became the first black woman Olympic champion when she won the high jump at the second postwar Games in 1952. Although

Tuskegee set the standard for athletic programs that refined female Olympic track and field talent, Tennessee State's Ed Temple began attracting some of America's best black talent. Temple eventually supplanted Tuskegee as the prime producer of track and field Olympians. Among Temple's athletes were such talented women as Wilma Rudolph and Wyomia Tyus.

Slow Removal of Obstacles to Admission

The United States was represented by U.S. Army equestrian teams in the Olympic Games from 1912 to 1948. The withdrawal of the Army as the controlling body of U.S. equestrian representation in the Games eliminated an obstacle for women who sought to enter the Olympic movement in equine events. In 1952 Marjorie Haines became the first woman to represent America in an Olympic equestrian event.[32]

During the 1950s Beth Kaufman, the indefatigable AAU swimming volunteer, nurtured Age-Group Swimming competition from its inception in 1951 until virtually every American, world, and Olympic record holder had graduated from the AAU's most successful swimming program (which divided swimmers by age to equalize competition). She persuaded the AAU's Women's Swimming Committee to allow her to test the program in the AAU's Pacific Association. The program immediately flourished and was adopted in 1952.[33] Christine Von Saltza was the first Age-Group Olympic champion, winning three gold medals and a silver medal at the 1960 Games.

Largely through the efforts of Harold Friermood of the YMCA, volleyball, the American sport and the first team sport for women, was admitted to the program and gained IOC approval for the 1964 Tokyo Olympic Games.[34] Women competed in 33 events in Tokyo, even though only 53 of 93 nations had women participants on their teams. In the 1968 Games, after an intermission of 40 years, an Asian athlete, Taiwan's Chi Cheng, won a bronze medal in the 80-meter

Figure 8.4 The first United States Olympic volley-ball team, 1964. Courtesy Amateur Athletic Foundation of LA.

hurdles. She was to become so popular in her country that she was elected a member of parliament.[35]

Sex Tests and Other Hurdles: Conquering New Heights

Despite their progress, female athletes still faced obstacles in the 1960s. In 1966, at the Bucharest championships, the IAAF ordered all female track and field contestants to undergo a nude parade in front of female gynecologists before they were allowed to compete. The association took this action in response to an accusation that pseudo-hermaphrodites were competing in the women's events. As Thomas Tutko noted, "It's a way of saying if you're this good in sports you can't be a real woman."[36] Sex tests that have been used in more recent decades, such as analyzing hair strands or cell tissue from inside the mouth, are far less degrading.

In 1972 the largest number of women ever to compete in an Olympic Games up until that time, approximately 1,300, represented only 61 of 121 participating nations.[37] Four years later in 1976,

basketball, rowing, and team handball were added to the women's program. The African boycott of the Games in Montreal had a very minor effect on the women's events, as approximately 24 women from 9 countries were involved. Not only had the number of women competing in 1976 changed little from 1972, with most of Africa not represented, but only 70% of the remaining participating countries had female representation.[38]

Under the patronage of Juan Antonio Samaranch (IOC president since 1980), who had an eye for sports with marketing appeal, Olympic athletes were finally allowed to be financially rewarded for their work through the use of trust accounts. This step opened the way not only for better performances but also for the inclusion of more challenging and aggressive sports for women and for the lengthening of women's athletic careers.

Before the Eastern bloc boycott occurred, feminist journalist Anita Verschoth called the Los Angeles Olympic Games of 1984 "the Olympiad for Women."[39] In hindsight, it may be more accurately called "The Olympiad of the American Woman," as many new firsts were established by the "home team." Darlene May made Olympic history on August 3 when she became the first woman to officiate an Olympic basketball game. In another historic event, Joan Benoit of Freeport, Maine, won the first women's Olympic marathon despite having had knee surgery before the Olympic trials.

The IOC had been slow to admit women's long-distance running events because there was still controversy surrounding the suitability of endurance events for women that had lingered since the 1928 Games. There was an unsuccessful attempt to add another distance race for women before the Los Angeles Games. Women in southern California wanted to add the 10,000-meter run in the women's track events at Los Angeles, but the deadline for adding events had passed and the event was not added until 1988. A women's 49-mile cycling road race and synchronized swimming were also among the firsts for women in

1984. Connie Carpenter-Phinney of Boulder, Colorado, who had competed in speed skating at the 1972 Olympic Games, won the first women's Olympic cycling race.[40]

In 1984, Valerie Brisco-Hooks became the first woman to win both the 200- and 400-meter running events. Her gold medal in the four × 400-meter relay made her the first American triple gold medalist since Wilma Rudolph in 1960. They were among the many outstanding Americans who had benefited from social changes and legislation such as the Civil Rights Act of 1964 and the Education Amendments of 1972 (Title IX).

Female Olympians enjoyed additional success—this time in a team sport that derived its members primarily from educational institutions—when the 1984 gold medal American basketball team coached by Pat Head Summitt of the University of Tennessee defeated its opponents by an average margin of 33 points and claimed the first gold medal in women's Olympic basketball competition. The 1988 gold medal team coached by Kay Yow of North Carolina State University proved to the world that American women were the dominant power in international basketball. Yow's team won the Olympic tournament by averaging a victory margin of 14 points.[41] American women claimed two more Olympic firsts in 1988 when they defeated the Soviet Union and scored over 100 points in their 101-74 triumph over Yugoslavia. In 1992 it was the bronze for the U.S. women, behind the unified team and China.[42]

In 1988 sprinter Florence Griffith-Joyner followed Valerie Brisco-Hooks's achievement by claiming three gold medals as well as a silver medal. Louise Ritter won the 1988 Olympic high jump championship, the first American to claim the gold medal since Mildred McDaniel of Tuskegee Institute won the event in 1956. In 1992 Jackie Joyner-Kersee, the ''wonder woman'' heptathlete, repeated her 1988 gold medal performance and won the Olympic title. Led by veteran Evelyn Ashford, who had first competed in 1976,

© ALLSPORT USA/Tony Duffy 1988

Figure 8.5   Jackie Joyner Kersee, 1988 Olympics.

the United States also pulled out the gold in the 400-meter relay.

Encouraged by the media attention given outstanding women Olympians, there has been much media discussion of the means by which such achievements were accomplished. Since the removal of the Berlin Wall, the Western media has highlighted the dehumanized lifestyles of former Eastern bloc athletes such as Nadia Comaneci and Olga Korbut. Western practices are not entirely pure, either. In the U.S., many young gymnasts, skaters, and swimmers are sent from their homes to live close to or with coaches of national reputation. Some parents have sold their homes, moved their businesses, or asked for job transfers to areas with better sport opportunities for their children.[43]

Overriding any thought of family togetherness, the goal of obtaining a gold medal for "the family" or "the country" has been a practice around the world. With the slow thaw of the Cold War, such practices may have decreased dramatically in the former Eastern bloc. However, the People's Republic of China and some Western countries' athletes still appear to be striving for Olympic gold without consideration of personal hardship.

The Olympic Winter Games

Figure skating was introduced as an exhibition event at the 1908 Summer Olympic Games. The sport was well received and opened the way for admission of winter sports competition in separate Olympic Games. In 1920, unofficial winter sports competitions consisting of figure skating and ice hockey were held in Antwerp, with the wealthy Bostonian and only American woman, Theresa Weld, finishing third in ladies' singles and fourth in doubles with her partner, Nathaniel Niles.[44] After observing the costumes worn by European skaters, the American skating delegation concluded that Theresa Weld's skirt was much too long and engaged a seamstress to make alterations. Expressing reservations about her elevated hemline, Weld recalled:

I insisted the result was far too immodest as it was only six inches below my knees and I knew the audience would see my bloomers when I jumped.[45]

Theresa Weld Blanchard continued to dominate the U.S. women's senior figure skating championships and represented America at the 1924 Chamonix competition, the first official Olympic Winter Games. Beatrice Loughran, runner-up in the 1923 American championships, also was named to the women's figure skating team, then the only event open to women.[46] Loughran was the silver medalist in ladies' singles,[47] the first American woman to win a medal in the Olympic Winter Games.

An AOC report credited the 1932 Lake Placid Olympic Winter Games with stimulating the popularity of figure skating in the United States. Prior to those Games, the sport had not garnered a widespread following. Aside from the fact that few communities had adequate facilities, only those who had the combined advantages of leisure and wealth were attracted to the skating rinks. Several factors linked to the Olympic Games can be attributed to the increased interest in figure skating. The 1930 world championships in New York City brought notoriety and captivated the attention of New Yorkers who marveled at renowned European skaters Sonja Henie and Karl Shafer.[48] Shortly before the 1932 Olympic Winter Games, skaters gathered in New York City for training and competition, which received widespread coverage by newspaper reporters and magazine writers. The print media carried predictions of Americans who were contenders for Olympic medals and generated more enthusiasm for the sport. Furthermore, for the first time, all the Olympic figure skating events were held in an indoor rink where spectators could view the events regardless of weather conditions. The electrified Olympic atmosphere created excitement as spectators crowded into the rink during practice sessions and others fought to see the actual events.[49]

Women's alpine skiing was added to the Olympic program in 1936. Ample skiing areas and numerous competitive events gave European skiers a distinct advantage over Americans. Alice Wolfe, manager of the American women's Olympic skiing team, credited Roland Ralmedo, president of the Amateur Ski Club of New York, with being a prime organizer of America's first women's Olympic ski team. Ralmedo raised some of the funds for the 1936 Olympic Winter Games in Garmisch-Partenkirchen, and the remainder of the expenses were assumed by the skiers. German athletes dominated the skiing events. Elizabeth Woolsey, top American finisher, was 19th among the 30 entries in the combined downhill and slalom races.[50] The austere post–World War II

1948 Olympic Games in St. Moritz did not include additions to the Olympic Games program.

Team members were chosen well in advance of the 1952 Oslo Olympic Winter Games, and this contributed to the successful performances of American women. Sixteen-year-old Tenley Albright placed second among 24 figure skaters representing 12 nations. Karol and Peter Kennedy finished second in the pairs event.[51] It had been two Olympic Winter Games since Americans had won medals in those events. Meanwhile, Andrea Mead Lawrence dominated the slalom events at Oslo. In the slalom, Lawrence competed against 43 skiers from 14 nations, and in the giant slalom she was the best of 47 skiers representing 17 countries.[52] She was the first American skier to win two gold medals in one Olympic Winter Games.

The 1956 Olympic Winter Games at Cortina, Italy, included figure skating, pairs skating, cross-country skiing, cross-country skiing relay, slalom, and downhill skiing for women. In addition, it marked the beginning of the U.S. women's push for the gold. In 1956, although American women did not enter the skiing relay or cross-country event because of their inexperience in international competition, four-time U.S. figure skating champion Tenley Albright made Olympic history by becoming the first American woman to win a gold medal in figure skating.[53]

Women's speed skating became an official event at the 1960 Olympic Winter Games in Squaw Valley. George O'Connell, a speed skating official at six Olympics, speculated that European women's minimal participation in competitive speed skating until the 1950s accounted for the IOC's delayed approval of the event. The conservative all-male IOC was slow to admit longer and more vigorous events for women athletes. When the IOC sanctioned women's speed skating, men were competing in four events of up to 10,000 meters, whereas women's events did not exceed 3,000 meters.[54] Obviously the IOC members were not aware that shorter distance competition requires power, immense speed, and endurance—

the three social barriers to Olympic admission of women's events because they were viewed by some as unfeminine.

Two firsts for American women occurred during the opening ceremonies at Squaw Valley. Skier Andrea Mead Lawrence became the first woman to carry the torch one segment of the distance before the torch-lighting ceremony. Figure skater Carol Heiss, who had won a silver medal in the 1956 Olympics and was the 1960 gold medalist, recited the Olympic oath on behalf of the athletes.

Three years before the 1964 Olympic Winter Games in Innsbruck, 18 members of the U.S. figure skating team were killed in an airplane crash en route to the world championships in Prague.[55] While the effects of the skating tragedy lingered, Olympic officials of the International Skating Union (ISU) debated into 1964 the value and suitability of cross-country skiing for women. The controversy centered on whether or not women should enter endurance events. In spite of divided opinion, 35 women from 12 nations entered the 10-kilometer cross-country event, and 32 women from 13 nations participated in the 5-kilometer cross-country race. Still, American women did not enter cross-country skiing because they lacked experience.[56] Luge was added to the women's program because of its popularity in Europe.

In 1968 at the Grenoble Olympic Winter Games, gold medalist Peggy Fleming became the first woman skater ever to be awarded a unanimous 5.9 out of 6.0. Another remarkable event occurred at Grenoble when Jennifer Fish, Dianne Holum, and Mary Myers tied for second place in the 500-meter speed skating event. It was the only triple tie among competitors from the same nation. Holum also finished third in the 1,000-meter race.[57] American women with little luge experience and no facility in the United States were no match for the veteran European lugers.

The town of Northbrook, Illinois, was well represented at the 1972 Sapporo Olympics as 5 of the 17-member speed skating team were from the affluent Chicago suburb. Three of the five were women.[58] Anne Henning and Dianne Holum won gold medals in the 500- and 1,000-meter races, respectively. Holum also won a silver medal in the 3,000-meter event, and Henning won a bronze medal in the 1,000-meter race.[59] In the 1976 Winter Games at Innsbruck, Austria, American women accounted for 7 of the 11 medals won by Americans. When the Winter Games returned to Lake Placid in 1980, speed skater Beth Heiden won a bronze medal in the 3,000-meter race and Linda Fratianne finished second in figure skating. Four years later at Sarajevo, Debbie Armstrong and teammate Christine Cooper led a one-two American sweep in the giant slalom. Silver medals went to Americans Rosalyn Sumners in figure skating and the adopted brother-sister pairs skaters, Kitty and Peter Carruthers.

American women have been most successful at the Olympic Games in singles figure skating and in speed skating. Debbie Thomas, the first black American figure skating medalist, won a bronze medal in Calgary in 1988 and became the first black medalist at an Olympic Winter Games. Kristi Yamaguchi took the gold medal in figure skating in 1992. In 1988 Bonnie Blair took the gold medal in 500-meter speed skating and the bronze in the 1,000-meter event. In 1992 she outdid herself by becoming the first U.S. double gold medalist in the Winter Games since Andrea Mead Lawrence (1952 and 1956). By adding two more gold medals in 1994 (for a total of five) Bonnie Blair became the all-time women's gold medal champion by surpassing Evelyn Ashford (track), Janet Evans (swimming), and Pat McCormick (diving), winners of four each.[60]

Summary and Conclusions

When one examines the performance of American women in the Olympic Games, five significant conclusions emerge.

First, women's success is governed by the admission of events to the Games. In the first half

© ALLSPORT USA/Shaun Botterill 1994

Figure 8.6 Bonnie Blair, 1994 Winter Olympics, Lillehammer, Norway.

of the 20th century, admission of events was influenced strongly by classist, racist, and sexist attitudes. In contrast, in the second half of the century, admission of women's events has been dictated by political ideology with emphasis on medal count. Although it has been reduced by the admission of long-distance events, the heptathlon, and some combative events, there continues to be resistance to women's participation, and equality has not yet been achieved.

Second, until women gain full representation in the organizations that create the policies and thereby control the competitions, little change can be expected.[61] As the Summer Olympic Games reach their centenary year, one might expect that half of each nation's medals would be earned by women athletes. Although there was a 130% increase in the number of women Olympians competing between the 1972 and 1992 Summer Games, women still constituted only 26% of the total participants.

Third, it appears that where there is strong European as well as strong upper-class participation, such as in winter sports, U.S. women have been more successful than men in the Olympic Games. Over the last 10 Winter Games, U.S. women have won 47 medals compared to 34 for men. Four were shared in pairs figure skating. An even brighter result was achieved in 1992. Of the 11 medals won by the United States in Albertville, women took home 9, including all 5 of the golds. In Lillehammer in 1994 women won 9 (4 gold, 3 silver, and 2 bronze) of the 13 medals awarded to the U.S. team.[60]

Fourth, with increased technological assistance, equal access to training and facilities, improved financial support, and the disintegration of the Soviet Union, American women Olympians will continue to dominate events in front of the television cameras of the world. The only challenge to this trend may be the desire of the powerful Chinese team to replace the former Soviet Union and Eastern bloc countries in the race for the gold.

Notes

[1]Robert Dunn, "The Country Club: A National Expression, Where Woman Is Really Free," *The Outing Magazine*, **42** (November 1905): 69.

[2]Dumas Malone, ed. *Dictionary of American Biography*, vol. 5, pt. 1 (New York: Scribner's Sons, 1960), 189.

[3]*The New York Times* (5 October 1900), 5.

[4]Elmer Ellis, *Mr. Dooley's America; A Life of Finley Peter Dunne* (New York: Knopf, 1941), 126.

[5]*The New York Times* (8 April 1900), 19.

[6]*The New York Times* (25 March 1900), 17.

[7]Asa S. Bushnell, ed. "All-Time U.S. Olympic Team Personnel," *United States 1956 Olympic Book* (New York: United States Olympic Association, 1957), 405.

[8]*The New York Times* (13 July 1913), IV, 2.

[9]"Minutes of the Annual Session of the IOC," *International Olympic Committee, 1911* (1911), 10.

[10]*The New York Times* (19 July 1913), 5.

[11]Pierre de Coubertin, "Les Femmes Aux Jeux Olympiques," *Revue Olympique* (January 1912).

[12]Mary Leigh and Therese Bonin, "The Pioneering Role of Madam Alice Miliat and the FSFI in Establishing International Track and Field Competition for Women," *Journal of Sport History* (Spring 1977): 72-83.

[13]Telephone interview between Paula Welch and Alice Lord Landon, 1920 Olympic diver, 4 September 1990.

[14]"Swimming (Women)," *Report on the American Olympic Committee Seventh Olympic Games Antwerp, Belgium* (Greenwich: Conde Nast Press, 1920), 320.

[15]*New York Tribune* (29 August 1920), 21.

[16]"Swimming (Women)," 321.

[17]"Minutes of the Annual Session of the IOC," *International Olympic Committee, 1923* (1923).

[18]Marie Therese Eyquem, *La Femme et Le Sport* (Paris: Éditions J. Susse, 1944), 942-43.

[19]"IAAF Minutes," *International Amateur Athletic Federation Congress* (1936).

[20]Leigh and Bonin.

[21]George Pallett, *Women's Athletics* (Dulwich, England: Normal Press, 1955); "Minutes of Annual Convention 1928," *Amateur Athletic Union* (1928).

[22]*New York Times* (1930).

[23]Ibid. Pallett.

[24]"Fifth Annual Meeting, Women's Division, National Amateur Athletic Federation," *American Physical Education Review*, **34** (April 1929): 241.

[25]"Berlin Olympics, 1936: Golden Memories," *Northern Illinois University Alumni News* (Summer 1984), 1.

[26]Moshe Gottlieb, "The American Controversy Over the Olympic Games," *American Jewish Historical Quarterly*, **61** (March 1972): 181-213.

[27]Uriel Simri, *Women at the Olympic Games* (Netanya, Israel: Wingate Institute), 1979.

[28]Ibid.

[29]Paula Welch, "Tuskegee Institute, Pioneer in Women's Olympic Track and Field," *The Foil*, **7** (Spring 1988): 10-13.

[30]"Women's Track and Field Team," *Report of the United States Olympic Committee 1948 Games XIV Olympiad London, England* (Greenwich, CT: Walker-Rackliff, 1948), 58. Alice Coachman, who had received most of her coaching from Cleve Abbott, transferred to Albany State her senior year because of financial difficulties and otherwise would have been the fourth athlete from Tuskegee on the 1948 team.

[31]Catherine D. Meyer, "Women's Track and Field Report of Committee Chairman," *Report of the United States Olympic Committee 1948 Games XIV Olympiad London, England* (New Haven, CT: Walker-Rackliff, 1948), 106-13.

[32]*The New York Times* (2 April 1951), 46.

[33]Dawson, Buck ed. "Beth Kaufman— Outstanding Contributor," *Swimming Hall of Fame Dedication Year 1968* (Fort Lauderdale, FL: International Swimming Hall of Fame, 1968), 45.

[34]*The New York Times* (7 May 1964), 48.

[35]Simri.

[36]Thomas Tutko. Quoted in Kaplan, J. *Women and Sports* (New York: Geoghegan, 1980).

[37]Uriel Simri, *A Concise World History of Women's Sports* (Netanya, Israel: Wingate Institute), 1983.

[38]Ibid.

[39]Anita Verschoth, "1984—An Olympiad for Women," *Olympic Message* (May 1982), **I**, 25-34.

[40]Dick Schaap, *The 1984 Olympic Games* (New York: Random House, 1984), 118.

[41]William A. Henry III, "Faster, Higher, Stronger," *Time* (20 August 1984): 60.

[42]"Olympic Medalist," *The Daily News* (10 August 1992), 5-8.

[43]D. Margaret Costa, personal communication with parents who wish to remain anonymous (July 1991).

[44]Theresa Weld, "The Figure Skating Team," *Report of the American Olympic Committee* (Greenwich, CT: Conde Nast Press, 1920), 104.

[45]Theresa Weld Blanchard, "The Olympics: 1920, 1924 and 1928," *Skating*, **25** (December 1947): 8.

[46]*The New York Times* (29 October 1923), 12.

[47]Niles, Nathanial W., "Report of Figure Skating Team," *United States Olympic Committee Official Report* (New York: Mehl-Roemer-Sullivan, 1924), 116.

[48]*The New York Times* (9 February 1936), VII, 14.

[49]George M. Lattimer, ed. "Figure Skating," *Official Report III Olympic Winter Games*. (New York: United States Olympic Committee, 1932), 213.

[50]Alice Damrosch Wolfe, "American Skiers at the Olympics," *Report of the American Olympic Committee* (New York: American Olympic Committee, 1936), 345-46.

[51]Harry E. Radix, "Figure Skating Report of Team Manager," *United States 1952 Olympic Book* (New Haven, CT: Walker-Rackliff, 1953), 301.

[52]Gretchen Fraser, "Women's Skiing Report of Women's Team Manager," *United States 1952 Olympic Book* (New Haven, CT: Walker-Rackliff, 1953), 315.

[53]*The New York Times* (3 February 1956), 26.

[54]Ibid.

[55]*The New York Times* (16 February 1961), 1.

[56]Harald Lechenperg, ed. "Women's Cross-Country Skiing," *Olympic Games 1964*, Innsbruck, Tokyo (New York: Barnes, 1964).

[57]Frederick Fleugner, ed. "Speed-Skating Women," *United States Olympic Book* (Stuttgart, West Germany: International Olympic Editions, 1969), 409.

[58]William Johnson, "Ice Cold Games and A Solid-Gold girl," *Sports Illustrated* (31 January 1972): 32, 36.

[59]*The New York Times* (15 February 1972), 1.

[60]"Recounting USA's 11 Gold, Silver, Bronze Medals," *USA Today* (24 February 1992), 10E; "Olympic Medals Count," *The Daily News* (28 February 1994), 9.

[61]For a discussion of women's membership in the IOC, see Lucas, John, *Future of the Olympic Games* (Champaign, IL: Human Kinetics, 1992).

Note. Portions of this chapter have previously appeared in "The Political Components Behind Women's Participation in the Modern Summer Olympic Games" by D. Margaret Toohey. In *Sports and Politics* by U. Simri (Ed.), 1984, Netanya, Israel: Wingate Institute Publishers. Adapted by permission.

Part II

Biomedical Considerations

T hroughout history, people have pon-
dered the biomedical workings of the
human body. The findings of the biological and medical sciences, often considered the
"natural" or "hard" sciences, rank high in reputation and prestige in the scientific hierarchy. A
major reason for this elevated ranking is the presumption of rationality, objectivity, and value
neutrality, which have long been considered major
characteristics of good science. Moreover, because the natural sciences are commonly believed
to be, at least in principle, less prone to subjectivity than the social sciences, they generally are
deemed more capable of producing universal and
immutable truths. Biological determinism—that
is, the notion that biological makeup fundamentally determines human nature—is one of these
presumed truths.

Feminists and other critics have shown, however, that values and biases enter all stages of the
research process from selection of the research
problem, hypotheses, and research design to collection and interpretation of the data. As a result,
the absolute objectivity in which most scientists

take such pride is largely an illusion. Moreover,
feminists have helped us see that even the natural
sciences are socially and historically structured;
for example, whoever gets a role in choosing what
questions are asked and which methods are employed also plays a powerful role in shaping
the picture of the world that scientific research
presents.

The fact that the natural sciences have received
such acclaim has led to the common belief that
not only do scientists "tell it like it is" but also
that they know what is best for our minds and
bodies. Feminists have criticized this dominant
model of science on numerous grounds, in particular its dualistic tendencies, which establish hierarchies that accord privilege to human over non-
human nature, the mind over the body and, in the
research process, the researcher over the infor-
mants. Moreover, as feminists have pointed out,
because men are more often linked with reason
and mental activity and women with nature and
the body, androcentric bias is inherent in such
scientific models.

Historically, biomedical and sport scientists
have claimed that women are less capable than

men of performing vigorous, aggressive, and long-endurance sports and that they are more likely to risk reproductive injury. Such claims were based largely on assumptions regarding the biological inferiority of women. Scientists rarely considered that sociopolitical factors may have caused such differences. They also seldom mentioned the advantages of the female body for some types of sporting activities (e.g., those requiring endurance and flexibility) or the possibility that sports participation might harm men's reproductive organs, which are less protected than women's. Although contemporary biomedical researchers may be less likely to assume female biological inferiority, concerns regarding the physical training of women are still prevalent. For example, warnings are still heard that women in contact sports risk serious injury and that strenuous exercise may lead to amenorrhea and thus infertility and osteoporosis.

It is important to note the striking similarity between current biomedical concerns regarding contemporary female athletes and the warnings of 19th century physicians. Admonitions regarding the amenorrheic possibilities associated with excessive physical training for women are undoubtedly grounded in valid health concerns and supported by a fair amount of research. In contrast, warnings regarding the vulnerability of the female body in contact sports are not well founded and rarely consider the social construction of such vulnerability. In earlier times, such concerns served as a powerful mechanism for controlling women's reproductive, sexual, and sport experiences and ultimately restricted our understanding of women's abilities. It behooves us today, therefore, to critically examine not only biomedical facts but also the social messages that they contain.

Our contributors in this section present current research findings that are relevant to female athletes, as well as those who are interested in physical fitness. Their writings represent both feminist and nonfeminist perspectives. In chapter 9 Jackie Hudson identifies the androcentric bias in bio-

mechanics, the science of human motion. She also charts the history of biomechanics and shows how the current biomechanical model contains both male and elitist biases. Hudson stresses the need for a feminist biomechanics. Such an alternative would emphasize a different approach to studying human movement, for example, one that explores the contextual nature of biomechanical skill.

In chapter 10 Patricia Freedson discusses the components of female body composition and desirable body weight for optimal health and sporting performance and explains the methods that are most often used to assess them. She also identifies the health risks associated with carrying too much fat, as well as those related to being too thin.

In chapter 11 Freedson discusses cardiovascular fitness, which has been linked with reduced incidence of coronary heart disease, hypertension, and diabetes. She points out that, although most of the research that indicates the health benefits associated with cardiovascular fitness has been conducted on men, there is now research that demonstrates the positive relationship between cardiovascular fitness and reduction in cardiovascular disease and cancer among women. Freedson also provides important information on how women can improve their fitness levels through exercise and how exercise can be structured to achieve maximal effects.

In chapter 12 Freedson discusses muscular strength and endurance as equally important components of fitness for women of all ages. It is commonly believed that men are stronger than women. Certainly, when comparisons are made using absolute measures, men generally are stronger than women, particularly in the upper body. Of significance, however, is the fact that when relative measures are used, that is, those measuring strength in relation to body mass and composition, gender differences in strength are significantly reduced. In fact, relative measures have shown the lower body strength of females to be slightly greater than that of males. Although testosterone, which results in muscle mass, has been found to account for most of the gender difference in strength, Freedson claims that greater gender differences in upper as opposed to lower body strength are largely the result of sociocultural factors.

Since the origins of medical science during the Middle Ages, medical scientists have expressed great concern about the negative effects of strenuous exercise on women's reproductive functions. This concern is very much alive today, perhaps to an even greater extent because amenorrhea and other menstrual irregularities have been observed among female athletes. In chapter 13 Mary Jane De Souza, Joan Arce, and Deborah Metzger discuss the growing body of research that associates extensive exercise training with changes in the menstrual cycle (e.g., menstrual irregularity and amenorrhea) and, more important, the possible health risks involved (e.g., osteoporosis, stress and vertebral fractures, cardiovascular disease).

In chapter 14 Mary Jane De Souza, Joan Arce, John Nulsen, and Jacqueline Puhl discuss a topic of great concern to physicians and researchers, as well as health-conscious women: bone health and its importance to overall health. We all experience bone loss as we age; however, as a group, women appear to be at greater risk for developing bone loss conditions such as osteoporosis, particularly women who are postmenopausal and no longer producing estrogen. The authors cite numerous factors associated with establishing and maintaining healthy bone mass: genetics, race, age, estrogen, a diet that contains an adequate supply of calcium, and exercise training. It is good news that exercise, particularly resistance training, can help women prevent bone loss and reduce the possibility of osteoporosis.

The contributors in this section give us much to contemplate as we plan for the 21st century and develop strategies to maximize women's health. Unquestionably, biomedical research has brought us closer to understanding and appreciating the tremendous importance of exercise and early physical training in optimizing female health and motor development. The fact that women are less likely than men to participate in such activities could be a factor in the higher incidence of certain health problems among women. For example, more females than males have osteoporosis and related bone density problems. If it is true that maximal bone mass is established during the first two decades of life and that mechanical overloading fosters this development, women begin their adult years at a distinct disadvantage.

Moreover, if weight, nutrition, and optimal hormonal milieu are factored into this equation, another problem arises. In a culture that equates thinness with female beauty, many girls, as well as grown women, attempt to lose weight by dieting stringently and engaging in intensive aerobic training. Some develop amenorrhea, which has been found to be associated with bone loss and porosity. Although the origins of amenorrhea are complex and not yet fully understood, research indicates that low body weight and intensive physical training are associated with the condition.

Perhaps medical treatments such as hormonal replacement deal with the symptoms and not the cause of the problem. The situation might be clarified by longitudinal studies of bone health among females who throughout their lives have engaged in sport and exercise, particularly resistance-type activities. However, although research advances help women understand the importance of physical activity and development in maximizing their quality of life, it is also important for each woman to become knowledgeable about the unique rhythms and functioning of her own body so that she may be the one who truly knows best what is good for her.

Chapter 9

It's Mostly a Matter of Metric

Jackie L. Hudson

Movement is used in some way, to some degree, in every task accomplished by human beings. The need of every individual is to understand human movement so that any task—light or heavy, fine or gross, fast or slow, of long or short duration, whether it involves everyday living skills, work skills, or recreation skills—can be approached effectively.

MARION BROER
Efficiency of Human Movement

Sports biomechanics is at the intersection of sports, biology, and mechanics. More specifically, the primary components of sports biomechanics are relatively vigorous physical activity, human anatomy and physiology, and matter and motion. The typical emphasis is on skillful and safe movement.

There are many perspectives or epistemological positions from which sports biomechanics can be approached. For example, a dualistic (either/or) perspective in sports biomechanics is likely to separate the biological from the mechanical and put a higher value on the mechanical. The result is that the body is replaced by a fragmented mechanical model and analyzed by reductionistic methods (described as using the narrow beam of a flashlight to illuminate one distinct object at a time [Starhawk, 1979]).

Another dualistic, or dichotomous, strategy is to separate sports biomechanics into so-called masculine and feminine aspects. Androcentric, or male-centered, scholarship focuses on such topics as men, mechanics, and Olympians. Gynocentric, or female-centered, scholarship focuses on such topics as women and children, biology or nature, and average and disabled movers.

Given that sports and science are viewed as "masculinity cults" (Hall, 1987), can there be a feminist sports biomechanics? Perhaps. At a minimum, a feminist sports biomechanics would not value the androcentric over the gynocentric approach. Better still, a feminist sports biomechanics would replace the either/or emphasis of dualism with continua, conjunctions, and context. For instance, the falsely dichotomous categories of mobility and stability could be seen in terms of a continuum rather than in either/or absolutes. In addition, disjunct categories such as biology/mechanics and body/mind could be conjoined such that presumably polar pairs could cooperate. Finally, the contextual character of physical activity would be acknowledged. Sports biomechanics conducted from this perspective (i.e., connected or constructed knowing [Belenky, Clinchy, Goldberger, & Tarule, 1986]) would explore problems of social concern such as the enhancement of health through safe and effective movement. Unfortunately, as Bleier (1988) cautions, such a science may remain "utterly and profoundly invisible, except to feminists" (p. 91).

History of Biomechanics

The foundation for sports biomechanics was laid more than two millennia ago when Aristotle (n.d.) recognized that "the animal that moves makes its change of position by pressing against that which is beneath it" (p. 489). This insight led him to observe (incorrectly) that "athletes jump farther if they have weights in their hands than if they have not" (p. 489). Nevertheless, our faith in Aristotle seems resolute: "Present-day physical education teachers . . . utilize some of the basic principles of Aristotle [including] the techniques of close observation as a means of evaluation" (Cooper & Glassow, 1963, p. 22).

Galen, in his capacity as trainer to the gladiators, was the first sports biologist. His knowledge of anatomy and physiology was developed as a result of "his opportunity to observe parts of the body laid open in mortal combat" (Cooper & Glassow, 1963, p. 23). This view held until da Vinci, with his interest in connecting science and art, learned (and redrew) anatomy by dissecting several cadavers. In addition, he analyzed movement by noting the relationship between the center of gravity and balance.

Galileo and Newton provided the impetus for sports mechanics with their ball-dropping experiments. These scientists and their cohorts at mid-millennium ushered in the era of active observation: "Their aim was to take things apart, analyze everything, be critical, and use logic ruthlessly" (Wolf, 1989, p. 25). As testimony to the popularity of this form of physics, treatises were written specifically for women (e.g., *Newtonianism for the Ladies* [Algarotti, 1737], *Sir Isaac Newton's Philosophy Explain'd for the Use of the Ladies* [Carter, 1739]).

Premodern Biomechanics: aka Kinesiology

Over the next two centuries a number of people made contributions to either sports anatomy/physiology or sports mechanics, but the first contemporary integration of sports, biology, and mechanics is attributed to Ruth Glassow. Dissatisfied with the curriculum of the time (1924), she "decided that the content of kinesiology should be something that could be applied to athletics, perhaps to all human movement" (Cooper, 1977, p. 10). She deemphasized the static anatomy of origins and insertions and instead conducted muscular analyses on moving bodies. In addition, Glassow and her students began to apply fundamental principles of mechanics to motor skills (Atwater, 1980). Her early work in kinesiology, published as *Fundamentals of Physical Education* (Glassow, 1932), underpinned decades of teaching, writing, and research on movement.

In addition to Glassow, Cooper (1977) identified seven other leaders of kinesiology at midcentury: Marion Broer, John Cooper, Thomas Cureton, Laura Heulster, Alice O'Connell, Gladys

Scott, and Katharine Wells. Most of these individuals were known for their teaching and textbooks. For example, Scott published *Analysis of Human Motion* (1942), Wells introduced *Kinesiology* (1950), Broer wrote *Efficiency of Human Movement* (1960), and Cooper and Glassow coauthored *Kinesiology* (1963). The following excerpts from Wells and Broer give a sense of the science:

> The function of kinesiology, therefore, is to contribute not only to successful participation in various physical activities, but also to the improvement of the human structure through the intelligent selection of activities and the efficient use of the body. . . . Finally, [the student] must remember that the skill itself is of less importance than the one who practices it. (Wells, 1950, pp. 1-3)

> This book does not give answers to those who seek definite description of *the correct form* for various movement situations. For example, the discussion of the golf drive does not in any way establish the "correct" length of backswing. It seeks to assist the reader in gaining an understanding of the *relationship* of the length of the backswing to the control of the clubhead and to the force which can be produced, so that the reader can choose intelligently that length of backswing which will be most efficient according to *his* strength and the *particular* purpose involved at any specific time. . . . It is my hope that the ideas that are expressed will stimulate the reader to question some of the traditional materials, to search for *basic* causes, to increase his own understanding, and to experience the thrill that comes with a new idea . . . (Broer, 1960, p. vi)

By the early 1960s there were inklings of a growth spurt in kinesiology. In 1963 the Kinesiology Section (later renamed Kinesiology Academy) of the American Association of Health, Physical Education and Recreation was formed to promote kinesiology and to provide professional outlets for kinesiologists (Atwater, 1980). Also, Cooper and Glassow (1963) addressed the previous technological limitations to research and heralded the new era of technology:

> If range and speed of joint action are to be measured from film, one frame must be viewed at a time. . . . Such measurement is a laborious and time-consuming task and explains in part the limited investigations which have used these devices. . . . With the devices now available, rapid advances should follow in determining the joint actions in man's inherent movement patterns and in his learned skills. (p. 17)

Modern Biomechanics

With the addition of digital computing to the technical arsenal in the late 1960s, reductionistic research was at last feasible, and specialized graduate programs, usually called biomechanics instead of kinesiology, were born. During the 1970s the growing cadre of researchers was absorbed with developing the tools of technology, attending conferences, and merging women's and men's physical education departments. The number of new and revised texts published in the 1970s virtually doubled the preexisting number. Most of the new books were written by men, and many adopted a mechanistic focus. For example, James Hay (1973) defined biomechanics as "the science that examines the internal and external forces acting on a human body and the effects produced by these forces" (p. 3). In a subsequent edition he added several deterministic models for assessing performance (Hay, 1985). The practical viewpoint of the older books was minimized or modified: "How can a [physical educator] determine which features of a champion's technique contribute to the high quality of his performance—and thus are possibly worth copying—and which are faults limiting that performance?" (Hay, 1973, p. 4).

The textbook-writing momentum of the 1970s was spent by 1981; the remainder of the 1980s saw no new texts in biomechanics. The emphasis on research that had been growing during the 1970s became all encompassing in the 1980s. The primary outlets were conference proceedings and eclectic journals such as the *Research Quarterly for Exercise and Sport* and *Medicine and Science in Sports and Exercise*. In 1985 the *International Journal of Sports Biomechanics* was launched to provide "scientists and scholars a unique opportunity to share their work through a publication concerned specifically with their scientific interests" (Nelson, 1985, p. 2). Six years and 24 issues later, the founding editor stated in his farewell, "I am especially pleased with [IJSB's] status as the primary international medium for communication and scientific exchange in this field" [Nelson, 1990, p. iii).

Insofar as a field can be judged through a content analysis of its "primary" journal, let us consider the following:

- The editorial board of *IJSB* was composed of 30 men and 2 women.
- These board members and their students and colleagues authored at least 112 of the 148 published articles.
- Elite and near-elite athletes were the subjects in most articles—only 25 of the 148 articles included data on nonelite subjects.
- Young adults were the modal population; the exceptions were three articles that focused on teenagers and one article that used an older adult cadaver.
- Women subjects appeared in 35 articles, but they were accompanied by men in 27 of these.
- Only six of the papers that included women subjects were not authored by insiders; of these papers, four tested elite athletes, one did not specify that the subjects were female, and in the other the subjects were not moving.
- Twelve articles were authored by women, including six by a board member (and protégée of the editor).

- Of the remaining six papers by women, three tested equipment, one tested horses, one tested a humanoid, and one tested men.
- No article was written by a woman about women.
- More than 50 articles by American men were published before one by an American woman.

Based on the foregoing statistics, one might assume that there are few women in sports biomechanics and that these few do not do feminist research. As to the former assumption, women comprise 51% of the total and 49% of the researchers in biomechanics who are affiliated with the Kinesiology Academy (the largest organization of biomechanists in the United States with about 2,000 members). As to the latter assumption, if feminist researchers exist, they are invisible in "primary" places.

The history of the last half century of sports biomechanics is summarized in Table 9.1. In general, the premodern period (also known as kinesiology) was characterized by a gynocentric perspective and a constructed epistemology. Interaction, holism, context, emotion, and cooperation were featured, but critical assessments of a gendered science and society were not. In addition, the premodernists advocated power-with (i.e., social power) and power-from-within (i.e., development of an individual's abilities [Starhawk, 1987]). With the introduction of computers and other technology and with the merger of women's and men's departments of physical education, modern biomechanics divorced itself from premodern biomechanics. The body was reduced to a computer model, and women were either patronized or eliminated. The aggressive exclusion of the "not-good-enough" (Painter, 1987, p. x) typified the power-over (i.e., domination and control [Starhawk]) orientation. In terms of assumptions, subjects, tasks, technologies, and profits, the premodernists and modernists were polarized at "allism" and elitism.

Table 9.1 Evolution of Biomechanics

	Premodern (aka kinesiology)	Modern
Date	ca. 1940-1965	ca. 1965-1990
Leaders	Mostly women	Mostly men
Perspective	Somewhat gyno-centric	Somewhat andro-centric
Epistemology	Constructed knowledge	Dualism
Emphasis	Teaching, developing skill	Research, describing Olympians
Foundations	Biology, mechanics	Mechanics
Focus	Holistic, process	Fragmentary, product
Subjects	All	Elite, computer models, equipment
Tasks	All	Specialized sport
Variables	Kinematics (e.g., range of motion)	Kinetics (e.g., force, power)
Technology	Low-moderate	High
Orientation	Power-with, power-from-within	Power-over
Profit	Mover	Researcher, corporations

Inferiority: Comparisons of Performance

If the reformation of biomechanics in the image of men and mechanics has an upside for women, it is this: Little emphasis has been placed on proving the biological inferiority of women. One explanation for this indifference is that men consider the inferiority to be obvious. After all, this point of view has been prominent for more than two thousand years (cf. Newman, 1985; Tuana, 1989);

and charges of "covering ancient prejudice with the palladium of scientific argument" (Morais, 1882, p. 70) continue to be ignored. (See box on page 148 for quotations.) Another explanation for this indifference is that *women* consider the inferiority to be obvious. For instance, Birke and Vines (1987) suggest that feminists have accepted the biologically deterministic view of women's inferiority in performance.

World Record Holders

Is the performance of women inferior to that of men? It depends on the terms of comparison: Who and what are being compared? First let us compare highly trained athletes who have approached the limits of their physical abilities. In addition, let us choose a holistic, product-based method, developed for use in comparing male weight lifters, that allows each athlete to be compared on his (or her) own terms. That is, we will compare pound for pound, or in the case of running and swimming, inch for inch. The key feature is the conversion of fixed race distances into units of competitor height. Then relative velocity is calculated by dividing distance in heights by elapsed time. (See box on page 148 for an example.)

Now we can answer the question: Who is the world's fastest human? Traditionally this title has gone to the world record holder of the men's 100-meter dash. Using our inch-for-inch method of comparison, we see that Carl Lewis, who stands 6'2" tall (*Seoul Olympian Entries*, 1988) and holds the men's world record of 9.92 seconds (Hoffman, 1990), has a relative velocity of 5.36 heights per second. But is he faster than the women's world record holder? Florence Griffith-Joyner, who stands 5'6-1/2" tall and runs the 100-meter dash in 10.49 seconds, has a relative velocity of 5.64 heights/second. In other words, the fastest woman is 5.3% faster than the fastest man!

While we acclaim "Flo Jo" as the world's fastest human, we should acknowledge that

Opinions on the Physical Inferiority of Women

Aristotle's axiom was that the "proper form" of human was male: "The female is, as it were, a mutilated male." (GA 737.a.27-28)

Galen argued that Aristotle overlooked one of the most obvious indications of women's inferiority: "Females must have smaller, less perfect testes." (14.II.301)

Darwin: "The male possesses certain organs of sense or locomotion, of which the female is quite destitute, [so] that he may readily find or reach her . . . and hold her securely." (p. 567)

What Is Your Velocity in Heights/Second?

Suppose you stand 1.67 meters (5'5-3/4'') tall and run the 10K in 50 minutes (3,000 seconds).

1. Convert the length of race to heights by dividing race length by height:

   10,000 meters/1.67 meters = 6,000 heights

2. Compute velocity by dividing heights by time:

   6,000 heights/3,000 seconds = 2 heights/second

women may have an inherent advantage in running events: Success in running depends on a strong lower body, and women are relatively strong in the hip and leg muscles (Wilmore, 1974). Part of this strength may result from the relative sturdiness of women. For example, women sprinters in the 1976 Olympics had 6% wider pelves than their male counterparts when width was expressed as a percentage of height (Carter, 1982).

Because men have relatively wider shoulders, perhaps they would fare better in an upper-body event such as swimming. Let us compare Janet Evans, the 5'5'' (*Seoul Olympian Entries*, 1988) world record holder with 15:52.1 min (Hoffman, 1990) in the 1,500-meter freestyle, with Vladimir Salnikov, the 5'11'' men's record holder with 14:54.76 min. Evans' velocity is .949 heights per

second and Salnikov's is .926 heights/sec, a difference of 2.5% in favor of Evans.

The preceding comparisons are based on strenuous individual events that test the limits of upper- and lower-body musculature as well as the limits of power and stamina. The comparators are talented and tirelessly trained world champions. When measurements are made in absolute, Brobdingnagian terms, the males are faster. However, when measurements are made from the context (i.e., size) of the individual, the physical abilities of females appear to be equal (if not superior) to those of males. Inferiority? It's mostly a matter of metric.

Olympians

What happens when the base of comparison is broadened? When the 57 women and 70 men who swam the 100-meter freestyle in the 1988 Olympics were compared inch for inch, the men were 2.1% faster (Kennedy, Brown, Chengalur, & Nelson, 1990). This difference appears to support the hypothesis that swimming, because it is an upper-body sport, favors men. However, other characteristics of the contestants deserve mention: Age was significantly related to velocity, and the men were 2.8 years older. Might the women reduce the velocity differential with 2.8 more years of training? Also, given that these swimmers represented a minimum of 29 countries, parity in preparation for women and men was unlikely. Although parity may be a fact in some of these countries, parity is not even a fiction in most. Otherwise, why did 10 different men from 7 countries of western Europe win medals in swimming while western European women won one? Moreover, this lack of parity is not unique to swimming. Consider the fact that Kenyan men won 17% of the track and field medals while Kenyan women won none (Siegman, 1989).

In sum, the abilities of elite women and men appear to be similar. However, there may be an interaction between gender and excellence. That is, when world champions are compared, the women are slightly faster, but when all Olympians are compared, the women are slightly slower. What could account for this interaction? What separates champions from challengers that might function differentially for women? If we assume that (a) champions have invested extreme effort, perhaps by training longer and/or harder than their competitors, and (b) the difference in effort between women champions and challengers is greater than the difference in effort between men champions and challengers, we have an explanation for the interaction: effort.

Young Adults

Does the similarity between elite women and men hold for nonelite women and men? No; there is once again a gender-excellence interaction: The difference between excellent and average women is larger than the difference between excellent and average men; and the difference between average women and men is larger than the difference between excellent women and men. For example, the average 18-year-old woman needs 10 min and 51 sec to run a mile (Ross, Dotson, Gilbert, & Katz, 1985), whereas the women's world record holder needs just 39% of that time (4:15) (Hoffman, 1990). By contrast, the male champion completes the mile in about half (49%) the time taken by the average 18-year-old man (7:35). Therefore, it appears that young adult women may be farther from their athletic potential than their male counterparts. Again, effort may be the explanation.

Children

If young adult women have relatively unactualized potential, one might ask at what age this develops. Based on an inch-for-inch comparison of fitness norms for 6- to 14-year-old children (Hoffman, 1990; Ross et al., 1985; Ross, Pate, Delpy, Gold, & Svilar, 1987), 6-year-old girls were 3.5% slower in distance running than 6-year-old boys. And the gap did not close: With astounding predictability the girls fell another 2.7% behind each subsequent year. Moreover, about half of the year-to-year change in performance was attributable to the boys improving; the other half resulted from the girls getting worse (see Figure 9.1).

By what mechanism did the boys get better: Was it a decrease in fat, an increase in cardiovascular fitness, an effective modification in technique? More important, by what mechanism did the girls get worse: increase in fat, decrease in cardiovascular fitness, ineffective modification in technique? Of course, these questions cannot be answered with cross-sectional fitness data, but the following point is worth noting: Although the girls had slightly thicker skinfolds than the boys at age 6, both groups gained fat at about the same rate between the ages of 6 and 12 (Ross et al., 1985; Ross et al., 1987). Thus the simple effect of fatness

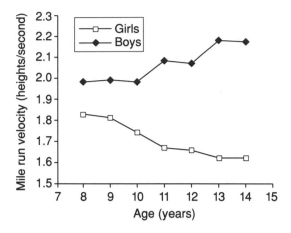

Figure 9.1 Divergence of fiftieth percentile girls and boys in running velocity between ages 8 and 14. The velocity-age correlation is −.964 for girls and .929 for boys.

does not appear to account for the differences in performance. And, inasmuch as fatness and cardiovascular fitness are correlated, fitness does not appear to account for the differences. Are boys learning effective modifications in technique while girls are "learning" ineffective modifications?

Although the preceding analysis of fitness data was based primarily on 50th-percentile scores, similar conclusions could have been drawn for scores at the 10th to 90th percentiles. However, in the most extreme deciles, difference was somewhat attenuated. In the lowest 10%, boys approached the trend for girls; and in the highest 10%, girls approached the trend for boys (Ross et al., 1985; Ross et al., 1987). That is, excellent girls were similar to (but slightly slower than) excellent boys.

Summary of Product-Based Comparisons

Combining inch-for-inch data from children, young adults, Olympians, and world record holders, it appears that there is a gender-

excellence interaction in performance with similarity associated with excellence (and effort). Also, from the fitness data in Figure 9.1, it appears that there is a gender-age interaction in performance with similarity associated with youth. In sum, similarity is connected with the young and the relentless.

If there were an inherent biological difference in performance due to sex, we would expect this difference to become exaggerated with effort (i.e., men have a greater capacity that can be developed into excellence; women have a lesser capacity that defies development). And we would expect this difference to become manifest at the time of puberty (i.e., when divergence of secondary sexual characteristics is thought to occur). However, similarity rather than difference is associated with excellence, and the great divide in performance has become entrenched several years before puberty. Thus observed differences in performance do not appear to be explainable in terms of inherent biological inferiority. Rather, these differences can be explained in terms of effort: People who expend meaningful effort improve and perhaps become excellent; people who do not expend meaningful effort can expect to deteriorate in performance and remain estranged from ability. If girls and women believe they do not have the capacity of boys and men, then they do not realize *mentally* their physical abilities. If girls and women do not expend meaningful effort to develop their capacity, then they do not realize *bodily* their physical abilities.

Analysis of Refined Biomechanical Measures

Positing that highly trained women and men are similar on holistic, product-based variables, are they similar or dissimilar on more "refined" biomechanical measures? One of the variables that has drawn recurrent attention in sports biomechanics is the use of stored elastic energy

(USEE). In simple terms, elastic energy is *stored* in a muscle when it contracts to stop a countermovement such as a backswing, and elastic energy is *used* in the same muscle when it contracts to cause a primary movement such as a forward swing. In other words, USEE is a temporarily available elastic recoil that can augment contractile force in a primary movement. Although there is much debate about the sites and mechanisms of USEE, there is agreement that USEE can alter performance in countermovement activities (e.g., jumping, running, striking, kicking, throwing).

Komi and Bosco (1978) compared women and men on USEE and concluded that the women were superior. However, they compared average women with elite men, made untenable assumptions in methodology, and provided no measures of variability or tests of significance. In contrast, when *equivalently* trained women and men were tested with more rigorous methods, there were no significant gender differences in USEE or other biomechanical variables (Hudson & Owen, 1985). Instead of intergender differences there were intragender differences: The ability to use elastic energy was quite variable in both women and men.

Another approach to analyzing jumping in women and men was provided by Nelson and Martin (1985). They tested college-based military trainees on the task of maximal vertical jumping while carrying a rifle and wearing an 80-pound backpack. (The authors claimed that this task had practical importance.) The women and men subjects differed significantly on three variables: The men jumped higher, took longer to jump, and created greater forces against the ground in preparing to jump. However, the force values were not significant when expressed in terms of body weight or body plus pack weight. From these results Nelson and Martin concluded that the men were "better performers" than the women. Yet the relative forces were insignificant, the jump scores probably would have been insignificant if expressed in relative (to height) terms, and taking longer to jump is a characteristic of poor performance (see later discussion). Although the authors

mentioned that performance declined when subjects were wearing the 80-pound pack as opposed to no pack, they neglected to point out that the decline in performance was similar for 135-pound women and 160-pound men.

More Abusive Biomechanics

If the foregoing study seems abusive to women, it is not alone. At the 1990 annual meeting of the American College of Sports Medicine (ACSM), three biomechanics papers with women subjects were selected for oral presentation. Snow and Williams (1990) compared the gait of women in 3/4''- and 3''-heel shoes. With the higher heels, the weight on the small bones in the forefoot increased by 46% as the line of gravity (which connects the center of gravity and the center of earth) moved forward 1 inch. Despite these changes as well as several other modifications around the ankle joint, the authors concluded that the differences were relatively small and unimportant. Hamill, Freedson, Clarkson, and Braun (1990) filmed women running on a treadmill 2 days before and 2 and 3 days after an experimental condition (30 min of downhill running at $-15°$) that resulted in "very sore" muscles. The subjects ran more stiff legged (i.e., had less knee flexion) when sore. Egbuonu, Cavanagh, and Miller (1990) wondered what would happen if trained women runners were tested in two experimental modes: (a) running with their hands behind their backs and (b) running with exaggerated bounciness. The result: inefficiency!

Efficient or Skillful Movement

But what if we wished to foster *efficiency* rather than inefficiency? One strategy is to conduct studies and construct theories about the differences between more and less efficient or skillful movement. For example, when novice, intermediate/advanced, and elite college women basketball players were compared on free-throw-shooting technique, the novice players were more likely to use a restricted range of motion and to veer off balance (Hudson, 1985b). In fact, because the regulation of balance was quite variable among novices, learning to regulate balance may be one of the challenges of the novice phase. Also, the limited range of motion may have been a function of the instability.

Among the intermediate/advanced players, missed shots were more likely to have reduced range of motion compared to made shots (Hudson, 1985a). Accordingly, learning to regulate range of motion may be part of the intermediate/advanced phase of skill development. In general, the elite players were well balanced and fully extended at release when shooting. They did not miss many shots, but when they did, the reasons seemed to be subtle and individual.

To explore the issues of subtlety and individuality, Walters conducted a case study of collegiate jump shooters. She found that the more successful women employed greater consistency in regulating ball and body velocity as they changed distance from the goal (Walters, Hudson, & Bird, 1990). In addition, the more advanced shooters may be making subtle adjustments in segmental coordination from shot to shot.

From these basketball studies, it appears that there may be different biomechanical challenges to meet at different levels of skill:

- Balance for the novice
- Range and speed of motion for the intermediate
- Segmental coordination for the advanced performer

Fortunately, balance, range of motion, speed of motion, and coordination are visual variables that can be monitored both qualitatively and quantitatively. (N.B. Other visual variables that may be useful in biomechanical analyses are: number of active segments, nature of segmental rotation [long axis or otherwise], extension at release, and sectional/somatic moment of inertia [Hudson, 1990].) An unexpected finding was that some apparently skilled athletes with years of practice were using relatively inefficient movement patterns (Hudson, 1985b).

The Mover and the Movement

A related strategy for fostering efficiency is to investigate the interactions between (a) the characteristics of the mover and (b) the process and product of movement. Bunn (1972) has suggested that stronger males crouch more deeply than weaker males when jumping. Does this apply for women? When we tested young women on leg strength and jumping technique, we found the opposite: The stronger women did not crouch as deeply (Hudson & Wilkerson, 1990b). Moreover, a deeper crouch was associated with right-left and/or anterior-posterior imbalances in strength. Are women who employ a deeper crouch more likely to become injured while jumping, or do women become injured through other means and then employ a deeper crouch?

Given that strength of the mover seems to be related to the *process* of movement (e.g., crouch depth), is strength of the mover related to the *product* of movement? From the previous study, there was a significant relationship between leg strength and velocity of jumping in a simple jump started from a crouch (Hudson & Wilkerson, 1990b). However, when a countermovement or an arm swing was added, the relationship between strength and performance was modest but insignificant. Thus it appears that as complexity of movement increases, the influence of strength diminishes in importance.

Presuming that practice (in jumping) is important to the development of skill (in jumping), does it matter what type of jumps are practiced? Apparently not. When volleyball players and dance majors were compared on several forms of jumping, there were obvious stylistic differences but no performance differences between the groups of women (Wilkerson & Hudson, 1987). Once again there were wide ranges of performance within the athletic and aesthetic groups.

From the previously cited fitness data, girls and boys appear to diverge in skinfold thickness, particularly on the extremities, around the age of 13 (Ross et al., 1985). What effect might this have on performance? In general, any increase in adiposity can be detrimental to performance in running (and other activities) because it must be lifted with each step. Moreover, fat on the extremities may be especially detrimental to performance because it must be rotated as well as lifted. To test the relationship between fat on a limb and rotary capacity of that limb, we measured 29 active young women on calf skinfold thickness and leg extension torque at slow and moderate speeds (Hudson & Wilkerson, 1990a). Thicker skinfold was negatively related to torque production at all speeds. In fact, it appears that a woman who can afford to lose 5% body fat might well expect to gain more than 10% in torque production at the speeds used in powerful and ballistic activities.

Stored Elastic Energy Revisited

Why were there such large intragender differences in the use of stored elastic energy (Hudson & Owen, 1985)? Perhaps the wide ranges in USEE were caused by an interaction between type of training and task. That is, half the subjects were track and field jumpers and half were distance runners; the task performed by all subjects was maximal vertical jumping. As expected, the jumpers were superior to the runners in height jumped, but there was no difference between jumpers and runners in USEE (Hudson & Owen, 1981). Again, there were wide ranges in USEE in both groups. Why is there so much difference among subjects in USEE, and is greater USEE beneficial to performance?

Answering the preceding questions required a redefinition of skillful movement. Rather than assuming that those who jumped highest (or had the greatest inch-for-inch velocity) were the most skillful, a within-subject paradigm was used to assess skillfulness. That is, 10 jumpers and 10

runners were tested in two maximal vertical jumping conditions: (a) from a stationary crouch (i.e., a simple upward thrust) and (b) from a standing start with a subject-selected crouch included (i.e., a downward countermovement followed immediately by an upward primary movement). Success in the first condition was significantly correlated with leg strength (Hudson & Wilkerson, 1990b). Success in the second condition relative to the first depended on an effective integration of the downward movement of the legs (while taking the crouch) with the upward movement of the legs (while making the thrust). Thus effective integration of the legs (EIL) was defined as the percent improvement in upward velocity in the second jump relative to the first. Because this is a within-subject improvement variable, the effects of strength, size, etc., are cancelled out.

On average the improvement was about 6%, but 3 of the 20 subjects did not improve at all, and 2 of the subjects improved by 16% (Hudson, in review). Only 4 of the 10 highest jumpers in absolute terms were included in the 10 most skilled jumpers in terms of EIL. In other words, many apparently skilled individuals may be using inefficient technique, and many apparently mediocre individuals may be using efficient technique. This fact may contribute to the wide range in scores on certain biomechanical variables. In addition, those with the highest EIL scores were also highest on USEE ($r = .845$), so it appears that USEE is beneficial to jumping performance.

Unfortunately, USEE, which is a summation of three forms of energy in several segments of the body over several intervals of time, is impractical to use outside the laboratory. There are, however, some visual variables that are correlated with USEE. For example, a quicker time of thrust was associated with USEE (Hudson & Owen, 1982), as was a simultaneous rather than sequential pattern of segmental coordination (Hudson, 1986). Also, those subjects who selected a deep crouch were less able to use SEE. Interestingly, a holistic measurement of crouch depth (i.e., the distance the center of gravity descended) was more explanatory than segmental measurements of crouch depth (i.e., hip, knee, and ankle positions at greatest flexion). Once again, range of motion and segmental coordination were indicators of skillful movement, and some apparently skilled athletes were using relatively inefficient movement patterns.

Summary of the Mover and Skillful Movement

There are some characteristics of the mover (e.g., strength, adiposity) that are both modifiable and associated with improvement in movement. Other characteristics (e.g., height) are less modifiable and relatively less important in efficient movement. Amount (and quality) of practice may be more important than mode of practice (i.e., dance jumps vs. volleyball jumps) for developing skill. In addition, personal attributes (e.g., strength) and practice are insufficient, without refined technique, for producing skillful performance in complex, vigorous movements.

Implications

Just as vigorous, refined practice is necessary for skillful movement, it is also necessary for assertive movement (Bennett, Whitaker, Smith, & Sablove, 1987). In fact, Bennett et al. (1987) argue that vigorous, refined practice is a precondition for "movement literacy—a well developed vocabulary of movement skills and [the ability to] choose among them freely" (p. 370). If, as they suggest, most girls are channelled into play activities that require little skill and limited use of space and force, one would expect results such as those in Figure 9.1. And one would expect most girls and women to have restricted and weak movements, if not illiteracy.

Implications for Girls

If girls and women have not spent hundreds (or thousands) of hours in vigorous practice and play, if they have not developed their strength and space, and if they have not learned skillful, assertive motor patterns, who is served by these omissions? Not the girls: Physical inactivity during the growth years is linked with poor health throughout the lifespan. In addition, physical inactivity during the growth years may compromise the amount of growth. For example, the shoulder widths of women controls, women swimmers, men controls, and men swimmers from Commonwealth countries in the 1976 Olympics were 21.42%, 22.22%, 22.40%, and 22.79% of height, respectively (Carter, 1982). Assuming that these Olympians were training during adolescence, if not sooner, there appears to be a gender-activity interaction in shoulder width.

Another influence of movement on young movers deserves mention: Mastery of fundamental movements during childhood is central to the development of power-from-within (Starhawk, 1987). If this opportunity is denied, a girl is likely to believe that she lacks control of her physical destiny (Bennett et al., 1987).

Implications for Young Women

As girls become young women, their restriction in movement and separation from self-control is reinforced: Constrictive clothing and "dignified" postures contribute to "shrinking" behavior in women. There is limited contact with the physical world when men open doors and move heavy furniture for women. Practically, the only movement that gets rewarded is seductive walking (Henley, 1977).

But if the walk is too seductive, it gets punished or pummeled. For example, a Danish woman was convicted for soliciting because a policeman testified that he determined her intention from her walk (Henley, 1977). According to Frye (1983, p. 31), "If one announces oneself female, one is presumed by potential assailants to be less rather than more likely to defend oneself or to evade the assault and, if the female-announcement is strong and unambiguous, to be a prime candidate for sexual assault.'' That is, because of their gender-coded movement, women are vulnerable (Bennett et al., 1987; Henley, 1977).

The connection between movement pattern and assault potential has been demonstrated by Grayson and Stein (1981). They videotaped a random assortment of adults who were walking along a city sidewalk. Qualities of movement were assessed with Labananalysis, and assault potential was rated by prison inmates who had been convicted of assaultive crimes. Compared to the ''nonvictims,'' the ''victims'' appeared to be signaling their vulnerability with spatially restricted and temporally disconnected movements. Evidently, inefficient movement is an invitation to injury. And avoiding injury by retreating from public is a form of immobility.

Assuming that assault is a statistical improbability, are most women likely to be affected by restricted movements and a lack of power-from-within? Yes, these movements and attitudes are signals that the mover is the subordinate in interpersonal interactions (Henley, 1977). And women who display these movements are dominated and precluded from access to power.

Implications for Older Women

Suppose a woman survives her reproductive years with a modicum of power and without assault. Are the senior years free of the problems accruing from restricted movement in girlhood? Probably not. Consider the following general scenario: The older woman is almost certain to have less strength than she once had. A person with less strength moves more slowly. And a person who moves more slowly must shift balance from side to side. (Hint: Imagine riding a bicycle slowly.) As forward movement becomes less mobile, lateral movement becomes less stable. Regulating lateral balance depends on muscles that are not used

during most tasks of daily living. (Climbing stairs is the exception.) If these muscles are not used, they become weak, and so do their bony attachments. Correcting a momentary loss of balance depends on a vigorous contraction in these unused and weakened muscles. Inability to correct the momentary loss of balance leads to a fall. Weak bones are fragile. The possibilities range from injury to disability to death.

Other Implications

If girls and women are not being served by restricted movements and lack of power-from-within, who is being served? Bennett's group (1987) suggests that disabling the bodies of girls and women and separating them from self-control are ploys of the patriarchy to gain control of women's bodies. That is, if women's bodies are not controlled by women themselves, then they are controlled by men.

A simple rationale for men to control the movement of women is given by Frye (1983) in the form of an analogy: In a play, the players (men) operate in the foreground against a background of props (women). Although the background is necessary for the play, any attention to the background is disconcerting and draws attention away from the play and players. In particular, the background is not permitted to have ''sudden or well-defined'' movement. An ''unchanging buzz of small, regular, and repetitive'' movement, however, is allowed.

How do girls and women get cast into the role of props instead of players? Bennett and cohorts (1987) detail specific treatments from silence to slander that discourage girls and women from being players. Rosser (1988) provides a thorough discussion of the escalating levels of disapproval of girls and women who wish to pursue science and math. From the prevalence of women who are elementary school teachers and who have minimal competency in science to the scarcity of women with advanced credentials in science, this discussion could be read with no loss of meaning by replacing "science and math" with "movement and exercise." In either case, the sanctions increase with age and excellence.

Henley (1977) speaks more generally of the increasing uses of power to produce conforming behavior in women. She suggests that the mildest effective form of force will be used. These forces range in intensity from internalized control to environmental structuring to nonverbal and verbal communication to physical sanctions. In other words, the easiest way to keep girls and women from being players is to have them cast themselves in the role of subordinate or prop.

> For subordination to be permanent and cost effective, it is necessary to create conditions such that the subordinated group acquiesces to some extent in the subordination. Probably one of the most efficient ways to secure acquiescence is to convince the people that their subordination is inevitable. . . . For efficient subordination, what's wanted is that the structure not appear to be a cultural artifact kept in place by human decision or custom, but that it appear *natural*—that it appear to be a quite direct consequence of facts about the beast which are beyond the scope of human manipulation or revision. . . . To make this seem natural, it will help if it seems to all concerned that members of the two groups are very different from each other, and this appearance is enhanced if it can be made to appear that within each group, the members are very like one another. (Frye, 1983, pp. 33-34)

When gender differences are explained in biological terms (Birke, 1986; Sayers, 1982) and women are portrayed as passive victims of a constraining biology (Newman, 1985), the conditions for subordination are in place. These conditions are legitimated and reinforced by an androcentric science that generates "false facts" about women and profits from the subordination of women (Hubbard, 1981; Rosser, 1990). To break this cycle of subordination, Hubbard (1981) suggests, "Not only must we not believe that biology is our destiny: we must reexamine whether it is even our biology" (p. 217). Despite the barrage of disabling information girls and women encounter daily, she believes that they must accept and appreciate their bodies and bodily functions (Hubbard, 1990). In fact, "We need to recognize our biological capabilities in order to value them and use them to benefit us" (Hubbard, 1990, p. 2).

A change in the *conception* of one's physical abilities could have a profound effect on the *achievement* of one's abilities. According to Lichtenstein (1987), the limiting factor in girls' and women's athletic achievement is the "negative internal voice." And even when the voice is positive—girls explain their athletic involvement as "I want to be the best I can be" or "[I want] to reach my potential" (Lichtenstein, 1987, p. 51)—it is still limited by individual perceptions of possibility. Well, what *is* possible?

Did you know that it is never too late to develop strength? Ninety-year-old women and men in a weight training program made astonishing improvements in strength (Fiatarone, Marks, Ryan, Meredith, Lipsitz, & Evans, 1990). And in lieu of weight lifting, stair climbing may be a convenient option for older women whose stability is not already compromised. Is it ever too late to develop efficient movement? What if people who had limited contractile force in their muscles could learn to use stored elastic energy? What else does biomechanics have to say to older women?

If girls became more skillful movers, if they fell down a few times, if they learned how to regulate balance, would they be less likely to fall when they were older? If women used the large, vigorous movements that are developed in most boys (and some girls), if they called on and maintained the platform of balance that is necessary for vigorous movements, would they be less likely to fall when they were older? How would the world be different if females achieved a higher degree of skill and safety in movement? What does biomechanics have to say?

Critique of Biomechanics

It should be clear that biomechanics has a lot to say about the mover and the movement that is not being said. Where are the biomechanical theories about skillful or safe movement? What is the connection between skillful and safe movement? What aspects of biomechanics can be most useful for the enhancement of skill and safety? How can a mover change the movement, and how can movement change the mover? How can we use qualities of movement to improve quantities of movement? How can we use quantities of movement to improve qualities of movement?

Will these answers come from modern biomechanics? In what developmental stage is the discipline of sports biomechanics? Let us use the McIntosh (1984) framework for critiquing biomechanics, as Rosser (1986; 1989) has done in charting biology.

According to McIntosh (1984), there are five phases of transformation in scholarship:

- **Phase I:** Womanless scholarship—This is the traditional view that excludes women and includes only great men and their events.
- **Phase II:** Women in scholarship—The field is enlarged to include a few exceptional or elite women who are seen to benefit the traditional culture.
- **Phase III:** Women as a problem or anomaly in scholarship—Using traditional categories of analysis, women are included as either victims or defective variants of men.
- **Phase IV:** Women as scholarship—The categories for analysis are enlarged and reconceptualized to become inclusive, multifaceted, and filled with variety. The experiences of normal women are valued and investigated.
- **Phase V:** Scholarship redefined and reconstructed to include us all—New constructs are created for examining the lives of all people. Women are seen as both part of and alien to the dominant version of scholarship.

Modern biomechanics appears to be moving from Phase I to Phase II: Most studies are based on the traditional, dualistic, androcentric perspective and feature great men and their events, such as the Olympics. A few studies have enlarged this field to include the exceptional women who compete in the Olympics. Perhaps it is encouraging that the trilogy of abusive studies appeared at ACSM; this is the first indication that we may be entering Phase III. So far, the gatekeepers of modern biomechanics have been averse to publishing and/or funding Phase IV studies. The stated reasons are typically traditional (e.g., she can't just define a new variable), dualistic (e.g., she said it could be both beneficial and detrimental—how can that be?), or androcentric (e.g., there is no valid reason why the older subjects in the falling study shouldn't be men).

As long as modern biomechanics is contained within the first three phases of scholarship, it will not produce a body of literature that is useful to girls and women who are neither exceptional nor defective. And as long as modern biomechanics "recognizes and rewards those who support and reinforce its ideologies and aims" (Bleier, 1986, p.16), there will be little stimulus for transformation beyond the first three phases of scholarship. What is needed is an emancipatory, postmodern biomechanics.

Postmodern Biomechanics

What would an emancipatory, postmodern biomechanics look like?

- It would be about expanding human potential (Longino, 1989); it would be about changing our possibilities (Bleier, 1986). We would understand ourselves and others as self-determining (Longino). We might "try to change that biology we so often criticize" (Birke, 1986, p. 1). We would create information and opportunities for girls and women to experience and increase their physical strength (Bennett et al., 1987). And we would redirect the forces that are misshaping our bodies into "the contours of the subordinate" (Frye, 1983, p. 38).

• It would include some tools of traditional science such as "refuting illogical and self-serving explanations, exposing unsubstantial claims, and disclaiming poorly conceived and inadequately controlled experiments" (Hubbard, 1981, p. 216).

• It might include research on the development of sex differences (Lambert, 1987). After all, "the overwhelming bulk of sex-differentiated behavior is learned and is developed to display otherwise unobtrusive differences" (Henley, 1977, p. 184). And, "difference *as* difference may teach us some things" (Heldke, 1989, p. 108). For example, such knowledge could aid in the design of social intervention measures to change the differences where that is desirable (Lambert, 1987).

• It would emphasize and value similarity as well as difference (Hubbard, 1981). This is problematic. "Which aspects are more important, the similar ones or the dissimilar ones?" (Potter, 1989, p. 142). "Where do I step over the line from denying difference to acknowledging it?" (Fausto-Sterling, 1985, p. 214). How are women and men *similar*? Given that biologically deterministic arguments disregard differences between women "as though women's experiences are everywhere and always the same" (Birke, 1986, p. 10), how are women *different* from each other? And, on the issue of exercise, how are various movements similar (Broer, 1960)?

• It would mean asking nicer questions (Birke, 1986)—not "How high can you jump with a rifle and a 60%-of-weight backpack?"

• It would require an expansion in the questions, models, subjects, designs, and interpretations we use (Rosser, 1986). It might redefine the way success is measured (Bennett et al., 1987). For example, if some people who are not world champions have more efficient movement than certain people who are world champions, then whom do we take for our paragons of performance? If overachieving one's personal attributes

is indicative of skillful movement, might not differently abled athletes be most worthy of study?

• It would include women's knowledge about women. This is far more difficult than it sounds. It challenges the opinion of men who represent women as "deficient," and it also confronts their authority (Spender, 1981). It requires us to take women's positive experiences as the norm and use those experiences to help women reclaim themselves (Bennett et al., 1987).

• It would be a science that seeks solutions to the problems facing the community (Birke, 1986) and provides explanations that women want and need (Harding, 1989b). For example, each year 12.5 million Americans are injured by falling. Of this number, 780,000 are hospitalized and 12,900 die. Among the survivors there may be a substantial loss in the quality of life, if not further complications that hasten death. The cost of these injuries is $37.3 billion per year (Russell, 1989). Do you know an older woman who has the risk factors for falling?

• It would involve both continuity with established science as well as dialectical evolution (Longino, 1989). In addition, it would illuminate ways that complex, dialectical science becomes transformed into monolithic rhetoric (Keller, 1989). And it would question the assumptions of both traditional and feminist inquiry (Harding, 1989a).

• It would discard many dualistic assumptions (Bleier, 1984); and it would erase the dichotomy and hierarchy between theory and practice. According to Dewey, the scope of practice can be expanded to include theory (Heldke, 1989). How could other dualistic concepts be expanded to incorporate continua and contexts?

• It would be a "process of living with, and utilizing, instability" (Heldke, 1989, p. 107). If the path to more skillful movement makes many passes through the realm of instability, we must learn more about it.

• It would recover some of the gynocentric traditions of our foresisters (Ginzberg, 1989); it would legitimate the "feminine" elements of scientific culture (Keller, 1989); and it would reintegrate values from the premodern world (Merchant, 1980). For example, we might resurrect some of the questions and viewpoints of premodern biomechanics. Why not reaffirm, as Wells (1950) does, that the mover is more important than the movement? Why not incorporate the constructed and contextual epistemologies and the power-with and power-from-within orientations of Broer (1960)? Why not develop our own styles of movement and our own understandings of movement (Broer)?

Summary and Conclusions

1. In contextual terms, the physical capability of females appears to be equal (if not superior) to that of males.
2. Compared to boys and men, most girls and women do not realize (either mentally or bodily) their physical abilities.
3. If the mover and her movements are underdeveloped, the result is immobility, instability, disability, or death.
4. Solutions for developing skillful movement in girls and women are unlikely to come from modern (dualistic, androcentric) biomechanics.
5. One possibility for empowering our bodies is to connect with our minds: We can believe in the capabilities of girls and women, and we can generate and disseminate solutions with a postmodern biomechanics.

References

Algarotti, F. (1737). *Il Newtonianismo per le dame*. Naples, Italy.

Aristotle (1984). *The generation of animals* (A. Platt, Trans.). In J. Barnes (Ed.), *The complete works of Aristotle*. (Vol. 8). Princeton, NJ: Princeton University Press.

Aristotle (n.d.). *Progression of animals* (E.S. Forster, Trans.). Cambridge, MA: Harvard University Press.

Atwater, A.E. (1980). Kinesiology/biomechanics: Perspectives and trends. *Research Quarterly for Exercise and Sport*, **51**, 193-218.

Belenky, M.F., Clinchy, B.M., Goldberger, N., & Tarule, J.M. (1986). *Women's ways of knowing: The development of self, body, and mind*. New York: Basic Books.

Bennett, R.S., Whitaker, K.G., Smith, N.J.W., & Sablove, A. (1987). Changing the rules of the game: Reflections toward a feminist analysis of sport. *Women's Studies International Forum*, **10**, 369-379.

Birke, L. (1986). *Women, feminism and biology: The feminist challenge*. New York: Methuen.

Birke, L.I.A., & Vines, G. (1987). A sporting chance: The anatomy of destiny? *Women's Studies International Forum*, **10**, 337-347.

Bleier, R. (1984). *Science and gender: A critique of biology and its theories on women*. New York: Pergamon Press.

Bleier, R. (1986). Introduction. In R. Bleier (Ed.), *Feminist approaches to science* (pp. 1-17). New York: Pergamon Press.

Bleier, R. (1988). Science and the construction of meanings in the neurosciences. In S.V. Rosser (Ed.), *Feminism within the science & health care professions: Overcoming resistance* (pp. 91-104). New York: Pergamon Press.

Broer, M.R. (1960). *Efficiency of human movement*. Philadelphia: Saunders.

Bunn, J.W. (1972). *Scientific principles of coaching* (2nd ed.). Englewood Cliffs, NJ: Prentice Hall.

Carter, E. (1739). *Sir Isaac Newton's philosophy explain'd for the use of the ladies. In six dialogues on light and colours. From the Italian of Sig. Algarotti*. London.

Carter, J.E.L. (Ed.) (1982). *Physical structure of Olympic athletes: The Montreal Olympic games anthropological project*. Basel: S. Karger AG.

Cooper, J.M. (1977). The historical development of kinesiology with emphasis on concepts and people. In C.J. Dillman & R.G. Sears (Eds.), *Proceedings. Kinesiology: A national conference on teaching* (pp. 3-15). Urbana-Champaign, IL: University of Illinois.

Cooper, J.M., & Glassow, R.B. (1963). *Kinesiology*. St. Louis: Mosby.

Darwin, C. (1871). *The descent of man and selection in relation to sex*. New York: D. Appleton.

Egbuonu, M.E., Cavanagh, P.R., & Miller, T.A. (1990). Degradation of running economy through changes in running mechanics. *Medicine and Science in Sports and Exercise*, **22**, S17.

Fausto-Sterling, A. (1985). *Myths of gender: Biological theories about women and men*. New York: Basic Books.

Fiatarone, M.A., Marks, E.C., Ryan, N.D., Meredith, C.N., Lipsitz, L.A., & Evans, W.J. (1990). High-intensity strength training in nonagenarians. *Journal of the American Medical Association*, **263**, 3029-3034.

Frye, M. (1983). *The politics of reality: Essays in feminist theory*. Freedom, CA: Crossing Press.

Galen (1968). *On the usefulness of the parts of the body* (M.T. May, Trans.). Ithaca, NY: Cornell University Press.

Ginzberg, R. (1989). Uncovering gynocentric science. In N. Tuana (Ed.), *Feminism and science* (pp. 69-84). Bloomington, IN: Indiana University Press.

Glassow, R.B. (1932). *Fundamentals of physical education*. Philadelphia: Lea & Febiger.

Grayson, B., & Stein, M.I. (1981). Attracting assault: Victims' nonverbal cues. *Journal of Communication* (Winter), 68-75.

Hall, M.A. (1987). Editorial. *Women's Studies International Forum*, **10**, 333-335.

Hamill, J., Freedson, P.S., Clarkson, P.M., & Braun, B. (1990). Effect of delayed onset muscle soreness on lower extremity function during running. *Medicine and Science in Sports and Exercise*, **22**, S1.

Harding, S. (1989a). Feminist justificatory strategies. In A. Garry & M. Pearsall (Eds.), *Women, knowledge, and reality: Explorations in feminist philosophy* (pp. 189-202). Boston: Unwin Hyman.

Harding, S. (1989b). Is there a feminist method? In N. Tuana (Ed.), *Feminism & science* (pp. 17-32). Bloomington, IN: Indiana University Press.

Hay, J.G. (1973). *The biomechanics of sports techniques*. Englewood Cliffs, NJ: Prentice Hall.

Hay, J.G. (1985). *The biomechanics of sports techniques* (3rd ed.). Englewood Cliffs, NJ: Prentice Hall.

Heldke, L. (1989). John Dewey and Evelyn Fox Keller: A shared epistemological tradition. In N. Tuana (Ed.), *Feminism & science* (pp. 104-115). Bloomington, IN: Indiana University Press.

Henley, N.M. (1977). *Body politics: Power, sex, and nonverbal communication*. New York: Simon & Schuster.

Hoffman, M.S. (Ed.) (1990). *The world almanac and book of facts 1991*. New York: Pharos Books.

Hubbard, R. (1981). The emperor doesn't wear any clothes: The impact of feminism on biology. In D. Spender (Ed.), *Men's studies modified: The impact of feminism on the academic disciplines* (pp. 213-235). New York: Pergamon Press.

Hubbard, R. (1990). *The politics of women's biology*. New Brunswick, NJ: Rutgers University Press.

Hudson, J.L. (1985a). Diagnosis of biomechanical errors using regression analysis. In J. Terauds & J.N. Barham (Eds.), *Biomechanics in Sports II* (pp. 339-345). Del Mar, CA: Academic Publishers.

Hudson, J.L. (1985b). Prediction of basketball skill using biomechanical variables. *Research Quarterly for Exercise and Sport*, **56**, 115-121.

Hudson, J.L. (1986). Coordination of segments in the vertical jump. *Medicine and Science in Sports and Exercise*, **18**, 242-251.

Hudson, J.L. (1990). The value of visual variables in biomechanical analysis. In E. Kreighbaum & A. MacNeill (Eds.), *Biomechanics in Sports VI* (pp. 499-509). Bozeman, MT: Montana State.

Hudson, J.L. (in review). Biomechanical identification of skill: Vertical jumping.

Hudson, J.L., & Owen, M.G. (1981). Utilization of stored elastic energy with respect to jumping ability and coordination. *Medicine and Science in Sports and Exercise*, **13**, 97.

Hudson, J.L., & Owen, M.G. (1982). Kinematic correlates of utilization of stored elastic energy. *Medicine and Science in Sports and Exercise*, **14**, 152.

Hudson, J.L., & Owen, M.G. (1985). Performance of females with respect to males: The use of stored elastic energy. In D.A. Winter, R.W. Norman, R.P. Wells, K.C. Hayes, & A.E. Patla (Eds.), *Biomechanics IX-A* (pp. 50-54). Champaign, IL: Human Kinetics.

Hudson, J.L., & Wilkerson, J.W. (1990a). Body segment parameters and isokinetic torque in women. In J. Clark (Ed.), *ABSTRACTS of Research Papers* (p. 141). Reston, VA: AAHPERD.

Hudson, J.L., & Wilkerson, J.W. (1990b). Relationship between strength and jumping performance. *Medicine and Science in Sports and Exercise*, **22**, S133.

Keller, E.F. (1989). Feminism and science. In A. Garry & M. Pearsall (Eds.), *Women, knowledge, and reality: Explorations in feminist philosophy* (pp. 175-188). Boston: Unwin Hyman.

Kennedy, P., Brown, P., Chengalur, S.N., & Nelson, R.C. (1990). Analysis of male and female Olympic swimmers in the 100-meter events. *International Journal of Sport Biomechanics*, **6**, 187-197.

Komi, P.V., & Bosco, C. (1978). Utilization of stored elastic energy in leg extensor muscles by men and women. *Medicine and Science in Sports and Exercise*, **10**, 261-265.

Lambert, H.H. (1987). Biology and equality: A perspective on sex differences. In S. Harding & J.F. O'Barr (Eds.), *Sex and scientific inquiry* (pp. 125-145). Chicago: University of Chicago Press.

Lichtenstein, G. (1987). Competition in women's athletics. In V. Miner & H.E. Longino (Eds.), *Competition: A feminist taboo?* (pp. 48-56). New York: Feminist Press.

Longino, H.E. (1989). Can there be a feminist science? In A. Garry & M. Pearsall (Eds.), *Women, knowledge, and reality: Explorations in feminist philosophy* (pp. 203-216). Boston: Unwin Hyman.

McIntosh, P. (1984). The study of women: Processes of personal and curricular revision. *The Forum for Liberal Education*, **6**(5), 2-4.

Merchant, C. (1980). *The death of nature: Women, ecology and the scientific revolution*. New York: Harper & Row.

Morais, N. (1882). A reply to Miss Hardaker on the woman question. *The Popular Science Monthly*, **21**, 70-78.

Nelson, R.C. (1985). The launching of IJSB. *International Journal of Sport Biomechanics*, **1**, 1-2.

Nelson, R.C. (1990). Farewell from the founding editor. *International Journal of Sport Biomechanics*, **6**, iii.

Nelson, R.C., & Martin, P.E. (1985). Effects of gender and load on vertical jump performance. In D.A. Winter, R.W. Norman, R.P. Wells, K.C. Hayes, & A.E. Patla (Eds.), *Biomechanics IX-B* (pp. 429-433). Champaign, IL: Human Kinetics.

Newman, L.M. (Ed.) (1985). *Men's ideas/women's realities: Popular Science, 1870-1915*. New York: Pergamon Press.

Painter, N.I. (1987). Foreword. In V. Miner & H.E. Longino (Eds.), *Competition: A feminist taboo?* (pp. ix-xi). New York: Feminist Press.

Potter, E. (1989). Modeling the gender politics in science. In N. Tuana (Ed.), *Feminism & science* (pp. 132-146). Bloomington, IN: Indiana University Press.

Ross, J.G., Dotson, C.O., Gilbert, G.G., & Katz, S.J. (1985). New standards for fitness measurement. *Journal of Physical Education, Recreation and Dance*, **56** (January), 62-66.

Ross, J.G., Pate, R.R., Delpy, L.A., Gold, R.S., & Svilar, M. (1987). New health-related fitness norms. *Journal of Physical Education, Recreation and Dance*, **58** (November-December), 66-70.

Rosser, S.V. (1986). *Teaching science and health from a feminist perspective: A practical guide*. New York: Pergamon Press.

Rosser, S.V. (1988). Women in science and health care: A gender at risk. In S.V. Rosser (Ed.), *Feminism within the science and health care professions: Overcoming resistance* (pp. 3-15). New York: Pergamon Press.

Rosser, S.V. (1989). Feminist scholarship in the sciences: Where are we now and when can we expect a theoretical breakthrough? In N. Tuana (Ed.), *Feminism & science* (pp. 1-14). Bloomington, IN: Indiana University Press.

Rosser, S.V. (1990). *Female friendly science: Applying women's studies methods and theories to attract students*. New York: Pergamon Press.

Russell, C. (1989, December). Accidents happen. *Greensboro (NC) News & Record*, pp. A9, A11.

Sayers, J. (1982). *Biological politics: Feminist and anti-feminist perspectives*. London: Tavistock Publications.

Scott, M.G. (1942). *Analysis of human motion: A textbook in kinesiology*. New York: F.C. Crofts.

Seoul Olympian Entrees. (1988, September). Published by Seoul Olympic Organizing Committee.

Siegman, G. (Ed.) (1989). *World of winners*. Detroit: Gale Research.

Snow, R.E., & Williams, K.R. (1990). Effects of gait, posture, and center of mass position in women wearing high heeled shoes. *Medicine and Science in Sports and Exercise*, **22**, S23.

Spender, D. (1981). Introduction. In D. Spender (Ed.), *Men's studies modified: The impact of feminism on the academic disciplines* (pp. 1-9). New York: Pergamon Press.

Starhawk (1979). *The spiral dance: A rebirth of the ancient religion of the great goddess*. San Francisco: Harper & Row.

Starhawk (1987). *Truth or dare: Encounters with power, authority, and mystery*. San Francisco: Harper & Row.

Tuana, N. (1989). The weaker seed: The sexist bias of reproductive theory. In N. Tuana (Ed.), *Feminism & science* (pp. 147-171). Bloomington, IN: Indiana University Press.

Walters, M., Hudson, J.L., & Bird, M. (1990). Kinematic adjustments in basketball shooting at three distances. In M. Nosek, D. Sojka, W.E. Morrison, & P. Susanka (Eds.), *Biomechanics in Sports VIII* (pp. 321-326). Prague: Conex.

Wells, K.F. (1950). *Kinesiology*. Philadelphia: Saunders.

Wilkerson, J.W., & Hudson, J.L. (1987). Artistic vs. athletic vertical jumping. In *Abstracts of XI International Congress of Biomechanics* (p. 326). Amsterdam, The Netherlands: Free University.

Wilmore, J.H. (1974). Alterations in strength, body composition and anthropometric measurements consequent to a 10-week weight training program. *Medicine and Science in Sports and Exercise*, **6**, 133-138.

Wolf, F.A. (1989). *Taking the quantum leap: The new physics for non-scientists* (rev. ed.). New York: Harper & Row.

Chapter 10

Body Composition

Patty Freedson

I think the one lesson I have learned is that there is no substitute for paying attention.

DIANE SAWYER
quoted in *The Quotable Woman*

What has been historically considered the ideal female physique can be described as slender, curvy, and voluptuous. In both entertainment and advertising today, the woman who is portrayed conforms to this so-called ideal woman with a "great figure." Beliefs and attitudes about the ideal female body have typically been perpetuated by men, who have identified what is visually appealing to them as being the right physique for the female. But appearance is not a sufficient criterion for evaluating physique. The concern with physique and body composition must be related to the implications for health.

Body weight for given heights, ages, and frame sizes has traditionally been used to classify people as being at, above, or below what is recommended for optimal health and performance. This method of evaluation assumes that body weight is a good predictor of body fatness, because it is the degree of fatness (too much or too little) that is associated with suboptimal health and performance. Simply using body weight as an index of body fatness, however, can misclassify individuals, particularly those with large muscle mass, who may fall into the overweight category because muscle mass weighs more than fat. More precise techniques are available to identify people who are underfat or overfat. In addition to giving more accurate evaluations of individuals, these procedures can be used to profile the body composition characteristics of groups of athletes. Such profiles can help determine the physique characteristics desirable for performance in particular sports and activities.

Composition of the Body

Behnke and Wilmore (1974) developed a model to describe the composition of the human body for the reference man and the reference woman. The three main components of the body are muscle, bone, and fat. The fat component can be further subdivided into essential and storage fat. Essential fat is the fat necessary for normal physiological function; it is found in the bone marrow, heart, lungs, liver, spleen, kidneys, intestines, muscles, and central nervous system. In the female, sex-specific fat is included in the essential fat component.

Storage fat accumulates in fat tissue and functions as a fuel source. It is the "extra" fat that is found under the skin (subcutaneous fat) as well as around the internal organs. Table 10.1 presents the absolute and relative proportions of fat, muscle, and bone in the reference woman and man. In this model, which represents the norms for college-age females and males, the average total percent body fat is 27% for the female and 15% for the male. The percentages of storage fat for the reference woman and man are 15 and 12, respectively. The gender difference in total body fat is in the relative proportion of essential fat, which is 12% for the female and 3% for the male. Approximately 12.5% of the female's sex-specific fat is in the breast tissue. The largest proportion

of sex-specific fat is found subcutaneously and in the thighs and hips. The precise function of the additional sex-specific fat in the female is not known, but it is thought to be related to childbearing factors and hormonal differences.

Although there is not yet any empirical evidence to support the Behnke and Wilmore model of essential fat, it seems intuitively logical that a certain amount of fat is necessary for health. However, it is not clear that the absolute amount of essential fat for women proposed by Behnke and Wilmore is correct. Their model implies that if percent body fat is below 12%, health is compromised. Although it is known that certain physiological functions, such as the menstrual cycle, are disrupted when body fat levels are low, a cause-and-effect link is lacking. More research is needed to clearly define the amount of body fat needed for normal function in women. No evidence is available that suggests a similar trend is present for men. The lower limits of acceptable body fat for women are likely to differ between individuals.

Percent body fat for prepubescent girls averages about 18% to 20%, which increases to 23% to 27% in adolescence. Further increases in percent body fat are observed in middle-aged and older women where percent fat averages about 28% to 32%. The average increase in percent fat seen with advancing years probably reflects a decrease in resting metabolic rate coupled with a decrease in physical activity and/or an increase in caloric intake.

Table 10.1 Composition of the Body for the Reference Male and Female

Variable	Reference male	Reference female
Age (yrs)	20-24	20-24
Height (in.)	68.5	64.5
Body mass (lb)	154	125
Fat mass (lb)	23.1 (15.0%)	33.8 (27.0%)
Storage fat (lb)	18.5 (12.0%)	18.8 (15.0%)
Essential fat (lb)	14.6 (3.0%)	15.0 (12.0%)
Muscle mass (lb)	69.0	45.0
Bone mass (lb)	23.0	15.0
Remainder (lb)	28.9	31.2

Note. Adapted from McArdle et al. (1991, p. 601).

Assessment Techniques

There are direct and indirect techniques to assess the composition of the body. Direct assessment on human cadavers and animal carcasses requires a chemical analysis of the different tissues of the body. This procedure was used to develop equations to estimate body composition from underwater weighing. Other indirect procedures include skinfolds, circumferences, bioelectrical impedance, and infrared technology. Commonly used indirect techniques include underwater weighing, skinfolds, and circumferences. Underwater weighing provides an estimate of percent fat. Body density is directly measured with underwater weighing, and percent fat is then estimated using an equation that assumes a constant density for lean (muscle and bone) and fat tissue. Underwater weighing is one of the more accurate indirect techniques, but there are significant errors in estimates of percent fat for young children and older women where bone density varies considerably.

Percent Fat in Female Athletes

Numerous investigations have obtained data on percent fat and lean body mass of different female athletes. Table 10.2 presents the results of some

of these studies. This is not a complete summary; it provides data from the broad spectrum of Caucasian female athletes. The lowest reported percent fat values were for pentathletes, gymnasts, middle-distance runners, and marathoners (11.0%, 15.5%, 16.9%, and 11.4%, respectively) to 27.0% for shot and discus throwers. The average percent fat range for a college-age female is approximately 23% to 27%.

Desirable Body Mass

A question that is often posed by athletes and nonathletes alike is: What is the target body weight at which a desirable body fat level will be attained? To answer this question, one must first define the optimal body fat level. This task is difficult because there are no data that define the optimal body fat levels. Average values for specific female populations are available, and if one

Table 10.2   Percent Body Fat of Selected Female Athletes

Sport	Age (yrs)	Height (cm)	Body mass (kg)	% Fat	References
Basketball	19.1	169.1	62.6	20.8	Sinning (1973)
Bodybuilders	27.0	160.8	53.8	13.2	Freedson et al. (1983)
Cyclists	—	167.7	61.3	15.4	Burke (1980)
Dancers					
Ballet	23.7	167.4	54.2	14.1	Chmelar et al. (1988)
Modern	30.4	161.8	53.3	12.2	Chmelar et al. (1988)
Distance runners	25.0	166.8	54.3	16.9	Wilmore et al. (1977)
Field event throwers	18.8	173.9	80.8	27.0	Wilmore et al. (1977)
Gymnastics	20.0	158.5	51.5	15.5	Sinning and Lindberg (1972)
Marathon	28.5	166.6	52.0	11.4	Wells et al. (1981)
Pentathalon	21.5	175.4	65.4	11.0	Krahenbuhl et al. (1979)
Rowing	23.0	173.0	68.0	14.0	Hagerman et al. (1979)
Sprint runners	20.1	164.9	56.7	19.3	Malina et al. (1971)
Swimming					
Sprint	—	165.1	57.1	14.6	Wilmore et al. (1977)
Distance	—	166.3	60.9	17.1	Wilmore et al. (1977)
Volleyball	21.6	178.3	70.5	17.9	Puhl et al. (1982)

assumes that the average for a given age and activity group is ideal, one can use the average percent fat values for a group.

Assume that a female marathon runner and her coach decide that 15% fat is optimal for performance. Underwater weighing reveals that the athlete, who weighs 125 lbs, is 20% fat. Her lean body mass is thus 100 lbs:

$$\begin{aligned} \text{lean body mass} &= \text{body weight} \\ &\quad - (\text{body weight} \times \% \text{ fat}) \\ &= 125 - (125 \times .20) \end{aligned}$$

Her desirable body weight at 15% fat is determined as follows:

$$\begin{aligned} \text{desirable body weight} &= \text{lean body mass/} \\ &\quad (1.0 - \text{desired body fat}) \\ &= 100 \text{ lbs}/(1.0 - .15) \\ &= 100 \text{ lbs}/.85 \\ &= 117.6 \text{ lbs} \end{aligned}$$

Body composition must be evaluated regularly during the course of an intervention so that adjustments to the desirable weight calculation can be made if lean body mass is modified.

Body Composition and Health

Women who are over 30% fat are in the overfat category, and fat loss is desirable from both a health and performance perspective. In the U.S. population, the average trend is for body fat to increase with age, and average percent fat values tend to increase by 2 to 4 points with each succeeding decade among American women. This increase reflects the decreasing basal metabolic rate, decreased activity, and/or increased energy consumption that typically accompany aging. Supporting this view are the data of Vaccaro, Dummer, and Clarke (1981), who reported a mean percent fat of 23.5 for two female masters swimmers (ages 70 and 71). This is considerably lower than the average of 40% fat typically seen for untrained 70-year-old women. If these data can

be extrapolated to the general population, women who remain active throughout life appear to have a good chance of maintaining body fat levels typical of active women in their 20s!

Another major health concern that confronts female athletes and coaches is the widely held belief that women can never be too thin. This conviction is especially strong among female gymnasts, middle- and long-distance runners, rowers, and ballet dancers.

Coaches of women athletes often warn them that they risk being cut from the team if they fail to meet a certain weight or body fat standard. This practice encourages unhealthy eating patterns and may lead to the development of eating disorders.

Summary and Conclusions

Unquestionably, the maintenance of optimal body fat is desirable, not only for maximizing performance in athletic events but also for reasons of health. The risk of chronic degenerative diseases such as heart disease, high blood pressure, stroke, diabetes, and even cancer is reduced dramatically if desirable body mass and, more important, body fat levels are maintained throughout life. There are also health risks associated with being too thin, and excessive emphasis has been placed on thinness as the ideal of female beauty. Some women athletes are overly concerned about thinness, which can lead to pathologic eating behaviors and practices that may compromise health and performance. Although performance in certain athletic events is associated with low body fat levels, attention should be focused on health and well-being.

There are laboratory and field techniques to assess body fat, and they should be employed whenever possible. From a health perspective, it is body fat and not simply body mass that is important.

As we approach the 21st century, the sporting woman is encouraged to maintain a high level of physical activity, with one purpose being to maintain desirable body fat levels for health and well-being. In addition, performance is affected by body composition; so if a high level of performance is the goal, it is necessary to maintain a desirable body fat level.

References

Behnke, A.R., & Wilmore, J.H. (1974). *Evaluation and regulation of body build and composition*. Englewood Cliffs, NJ: Prentice Hall.

Burke, E.R. (1980). Physiological characteristics of competitive cyclists. *The Physician and Sportsmedicine*, **8**, 78-86.

Chmelar, R.D., Schultz, B.B., Ruhling, R.O., Shepherd, T.A., Zupan, M.F., & Fitt, S.S. (1988). A physiologic profile comparing levels and styles of female dancers. *The Physician and Sportsmedicine*, **16**, 87-96.

Freedson, P.S., Mihevic, P.M., Loucks, A.B., & Girandola, R.N. (1983). Physique, body composition, and psychological characteristics of competitive female bodybuilders. *The Physician and Sportsmedicine*, **11**, 85-93.

Hagerman, F.C., Hagerman, G.R., & Nickelson, T.C. (1979). Physiological profiles of elite rowers. *The Physician and Sportsmedicine*, **7**, 74-83.

Krahenbuhl, G.S., Wells, C.L., Brown, C.H., & Ward, P.E. (1979). Characteristics of national and world class female pentathletes. *Medicine and Science in Sports*, **11**, 20-23.

Malina, R.M., Harper, A.B., Avent, H.H., & Campbell, D.E. (1971). Physique of female track and field athletes. *Medicine and Science in Sports*, **3**, 32-38.

McArdle, W.D., Katch, F.I., & Katch, V.L. (1991). *Exercise physiology: Energy, nutrition, and human performance*. Philadelphia: Lea & Febiger.

Puhl, J., Case, S., Fleck, S., & Van Handel, P. (1982). Physical and physiological characteristics of elite volleyball players. *Research Quarterly for Exercise and Sport*, **53**, 257-262.

Sinning, W.E. (1973). Body composition, cardiovascular function, and rule changes in women's basketball. *Research Quarterly*, **44**, 313-321.

Sinning, W.E., & Lindberg, G.D. (1972). Physical characteristics of college women gymnasts. *Research Quarterly*, **43**, 226-234.

Vaccaro, P., Dummer, G., & Clarke, D.H. (1981). Physiological characteristics of female masters swimmers. *The Physician and Sportsmedicine*, **9**, 105-108.

Wells, C.L., Hecht, L.H., & Krahenbuhl, G.S. (1981). Physical characteristics and oxygen utilization of male and female marathon runners. *Research Quarterly for Exercise and Sport*, **52**, 281-285.

Wilmore, J.H., Brown, C.H., & Davis, J.A. (1977). Body physique and composition of the female distance runner. *Annals of the New York Academy of Sciences*, **301**, 764-776.

Chapter 11

Cardiovascular Fitness

Patty Freedson

To be somebody, a woman does not have to be more like a man, but has to be more of a woman.

DR. SALLY SHAYWITZ
quoted in *The Quotable Woman*

Aerobic exercise is necessary to develop and maintain cardiovascular fitness. To enhance cardiovascular fitness, the exercise must satisfy specific frequency, intensity, and duration criteria and the activity must involve large-muscle groups. Regular physical activity and cardiovascular fitness have been shown to be related to a reduced incidence of several chronic degenerative diseases, including coronary heart disease, hypertension, and diabetes.

Most of the research supporting the positive effects of cardiovascular fitness on these diseases has been conducted on males. Recently, however, a landmark study was published that supports the association between cardiovascular fitness and reduced mortality from cardiovascular disease and cancer in women (Blair, Kohl, Paffenbarger, Clark, Cooper, & Gibbons, 1989).

Physiological Basis of Cardiovascular Fitness

The ability to transport and use oxygen is the factor that determines the capacity for aerobic energy transfer. In other words, the amount of oxygen that reaches and is used by the muscle cell to produce energy is closely related to cardiovascular fitness. The strength of the heart muscle determines the amount of oxygen that is transported to the working muscle. Specifically, the cardiac output, the product of heart rate and stroke volume (i.e., amount of blood pumped per beat), is the transport component described above. The higher the heart rate and/or stroke volume, the greater the cardiac output and oxygen transported to the tissue. The other critical factor for aerobic energy production is the ability of the working muscle to extract and use oxygen. The arteriovenous oxygen difference is the measure of oxygen extraction or how much of the transported oxygen is taken up by the muscle.

Humans can modify the capacity to transport and use oxygen through aerobic conditioning. With an appropriate regimen that considers frequency, intensity, duration, and mode of exercise, the heart and muscles will adapt to the training stimulus to increase cardiovascular fitness.

Measurement of Cardiovascular Fitness

Cardiovascular fitness is measured by either directly assessing or indirectly estimating maximum oxygen consumption ($\dot{V}O_2$max). $\dot{V}O_2$max is considered to be the best physiological indicator of aerobic capacity and aerobic fitness. The higher the $\dot{V}O_2$max, the greater the capacity for aerobic

energy production. $\dot{V}O_2$max is expressed either as absolute liters per minute ($l \cdot min^{-1}$) or relative to body mass ($ml \cdot kg\ BM \cdot min^{-1}$) or lean body mass ($ml \cdot kg\ LBM \cdot min^{-1}$). For 18- to 30-year-old women, $\dot{V}O_2$max ranges from approximately 40 $ml \cdot kg\ BM \cdot min^{-1}$ in untrained women to 65 to 70 $ml \cdot kg\ BM \cdot min^{-1}$ in world-class endurance athletes. For women between ages 30 and 50, the range is from 25 to 30 $ml \cdot kg\ BM \cdot min^{-1}$ for untrained women to 50 to 55 $ml \cdot kg\ BM \cdot min^{-1}$ for world-class masters endurance athletes.

Cardiovascular Fitness Levels in Women

Because $\dot{V}O_2$max is the best physiological measure of aerobic capacity and because aerobic capacity is related to cardiovascular fitness, average $\dot{V}O_2$max data for different female populations have been compiled. Table 11.1 presents mean $\dot{V}O_2$max ($l \cdot min^{-1}$, $ml \cdot kg\ BM \cdot min^{-1}$, and $ml \cdot$

Table 11.1 $\dot{V}O_2$max in Women

Group	$l \cdot min^{-1}$	$ml \cdot kg\ BM \cdot min^{-1}$	$ml \cdot kg\ LBM \cdot min^{-1}$	Study
Untrained	2.6	44.2		Bransford & Howley (1977)
Distance runners	2.6	48.8		Bransford & Howley (1977)
Untrained	2.4	41.6	53.1	Cureton et al. (1986)
Distance runners	2.8	55.7	68.9	Cureton & Sparling (1980)
Untrained	2.1	39.2		Kitagawa et al. (1977)
PE majors (untrained)	2.3	39.1	50.4	MacNab et al. (1969)
Marathon runners	3.0	51.6		Maughan & Leiper (1983)
Distance runners	3.0	55.8		Pate et al. (1985)
Alpine skiers	3.1	51.0		Saltin & Astrand (1967)
Cross-country skiers	3.8	64.0		Saltin & Astrand (1967)
Untrained	2.2	39.0		Saltin & Astrand (1967)
Alpine skiers	3.1	52.7	66.5	Sparling & Cureton (1983)
Cross-country skiers	3.4	61.5	75.4	Sparling & Cureton (1983)
Recreational runners	2.8	51.9	65.1	Sparling & Cureton (1983)
Untrained	2.3	38.1		Vogel & Patton (1978)
Marathon runners	3.1	59.2	66.8	Wells et al. (1981)

kg LBM · min^{-1}) values for a variety of female athletes, as well as sedentary younger and older females. It is not surprising that the highest $\dot{V}O_2$max values are seen in such endurance athletes as long-distance runners, marathon runners, and cross-country skiers.

With regard to the aging effect on $\dot{V}O_2$max, Drinkwater (1984) has postulated that as long as the level of conditioning remains stable, the rate of decline in $\dot{V}O_2$max with age is approximately 0.3 ml/kg BM/min/year beyond 30 years of age. Table 11.2 presents normative data for $\dot{V}O_2$max for women of different ages. The factors associated with the age-related decline in $\dot{V}O_2$max include a decrease in maximum heart rate, a decrease in maximum stroke volume, an increase in body fat, a decrease in active muscle mass (lean body mass), and a decrease in habitual level of physical activity.

Table 11.2   Normative Data for $\dot{V}O_2$max (ml · kg min^{-1}) in Women

| | Fitness category | | | | |
| | Low | | | | High |
Age	1	2	3	4	5
20-39	≤ 25	26-29	30-32	33-38	≥ 39
40-49	≤ 23	24-26	27-29	31-33	≥ 34
50-59	≤ 21	22-24	25-28	29-30	≥ 31
60-69	≤ 19	20-22	23-25	26-27	≥ 28

Note. Adapted from the American Heart Association (1972).

Gender Differences in $\dot{V}O_2$Max

There are significant gender differences in $\dot{V}O_2$max (Sparling, 1980; Wells, 1991). Females' $\dot{V}O_2$max is 56% of male values expressed as absolute l · min^{-1}, 28% of male values expressed relative to body mass (ml · kg BM · min^{-1}) , and 15%

of male values expessed relative to lean body mass (ml · kg LBM · min^{-1}) (Sparling, 1980). Thus sex differences are greatly influenced by differences in body size and composition. The percent difference between gender decreases as body size and composition are taken into account.

When men and women are equated for training status and competition level, the differences between the sexes are reduced to 51.5% (l · min^{-1}), 18.6% (ml · kg BM · min^{-1}), and 9% (ml · kg LBM · min^{-1}) (Sparling, 1980).

Effect of Body Composition

Gender differences in $\dot{V}O_2$max are attributable to percent body fat differences between females and males. Body fat is generally considered to be metabolically inactive but increases the energy cost, that is, oxygen consumption, of weight-bearing exercise. Bransford and Howley (1977) reported that on the average, the energy cost of treadmill running was 5% higher for trained and untrained Caucasian women than for their male counterparts. In another study of Caucasion male and female recreational runners, Sparling and Cureton (1983) reported that percent body fat accounted for 75% of the gender difference in 12-minute run performance. This research indicates that body fat accounts for a significant proportion of both $\dot{V}O_2$max and performance differences between the sexes. Although no studies have examined these gender differences among African Americans, it is likely that the same differences exist.

Effect of Hemoglobin Concentration

A physiological factor that in part determines the oxygen transport capacity of the circulatory system is hemoglobin concentration. Hemoglobin is a protein found in red blood cells that carries oxygen from the lungs to the working muscle. The average hemoglobin concentration in women is approximately 10% lower than that in men. This translates into 10% lower oxygen transport capacity for women. At maximum levels of exercise, in which the limits of oxygen transport become an important determinant of aerobic capacity, the lower hemoglobin concentration appears to be a true physiological difference that accounts for a portion of the 5% to 10% gender difference in $\dot{V}O_2$max. In a study designed to examine the influence of hemoglobin concentration on $\dot{V}O_2$max, Freedson (1981) reduced the hemoglobin concentration of men by 19%. This reduction in oxygen-carrying capacity was accompanied by a 6% decrease in $\dot{V}O_2$max. Freedson (1981) concluded that the reduction in hemoglobin concentration caused the decrease in $\dot{V}O_2$max.

Effect of Heart Size

Research has clearly established that heart size is smaller in women than in men. For example, Wells (1991) reported that the ratio of heart volume to total body mass is 10% to 15% lower in women than in men. Thus maximal stroke volume (the largest volume of blood pumped per beat) and maximal cardiac output (maximum volume of blood pumped from the heart per minute) are lower for females. Because maximal oxygen transport is highly dependent on maximal cardiac output, the lower maximal stroke volume that results from a smaller heart volume partially explains women's lower maximum aerobic capacity.

Effects of Cardiovascular Conditioning on Cardiovascular Fitness and $\dot{V}O_2$Max

With an appropriate training stimulus, $\dot{V}O_2$max increases approximately 15% to 25% for the average younger and older female. This relative change is similar to the cardiovascular training response observed for men. The principles governing cardiovascular conditioning therefore can be applied to young and old women and men. An excellent, detailed description of these principles can be found in Sharkey (1990). These principles are discussed briefly below.

Frequency of Training

The recommended number of times per week one should train depends in part on the level of conditioning. Significant improvements can be seen with as little as two aerobic workouts per week for the less fit person. For the more highly trained, it may be necessary to exercise five to six times a week to continue the increase in aerobic fitness. The average fitness-minded person can optimally enhance cardiovascular conditioning with three to four exercise sessions per week. In contrast, it is not unusual for world-class performers to engage in two training sessions a day during peak conditioning periods. Although the added benefits of this high training volume have not been documented in the research literature, most high-level endurance athletes believe that high training mileage is necessary for peak performance.

Intensity of Training

Intensity of training refers to how hard one exercises. Intensity can be measured as a percent of $\dot{V}O_2$max or as a percent of maximum heart rate. The validity of heart rate as an index of intensity is based on the linear positive relationship between heart rate and $\dot{V}O_2$ during aerobic exercise; that is, as $\dot{V}O_2$ increases, so does heart rate. When using heart rate to categorize intensity, one uses either a percent of actual or estimated maximum heart rate (estimated maximum heart rate = 220 − age) or a percent of actual or estimated maximum heart rate reserve. For example, 70% of estimated maximum heart rate for a 20-year-old is 140 beats per minute. With a resting heart rate of 60 beats per minute, 158 beats per minute would correspond to the training intensity using the percent of maximum heart rate reserve method. The

American College of Sports Medicine has recommended a training intensity ranging between 60% and 90% of maximum heart rate reserve, which corresponds to 50% to 80% of $\dot{V}O_2$max. The lower end of the range, 60% to 65% of maximum heart rate or maximum heart rate reserve, should be used in prescribing exercise for the less fit person; the upper end of the range, 85% to 90% of maximum heart rate or maximum heart rate reserve, should be used for the highly fit person.

Duration of Exercise

Exercise periods should range from 15 to 60 minutes. The lower end of the range (15 to 20 minutes) provides an attainable goal for the person who has just begun an aerobic exercise program. As one progresses, exercise time should increase so that one approaches and possibly exceeds 30 minutes of continuous exercise.

Type of Exercise

To adequately overload the cardiovascular system so that a training effect occurs, exercise must use large-muscle groups. Exercises such as walking, jogging, swimming, cycling, and cross-country skiing are examples of such activities. In the health club environment, various companies have developed high-tech machinery simulating stair climbing and rowing that are also considered to be large-muscle group activities.

Circuit training has been advocated as a form of exercise that can be done to promote a cardiovascular training effect. This activity is usually done on resistance machines in which exercises are completed in rapid succession over 10 to 20 minutes continuously. Heart rates during this kind of training are in the intensity range that is associated with an aerobic training effect. $\dot{V}O_2$max has been shown to increase with this kind of training; however, the magnitude of increase is approximately 50% to 70% of what is seen with the more traditional modes of aerobic exercise. Nevertheless, the advantage of circuit training is

that cardiovascular fitness and muscular strength and endurance are adapting simultaneously. This means that one can realize gains in both fitness areas with only one workout!

Progression of Overload

As one proceeds through an exercise program that conforms to the guidelines presented above, a cardiovascular training effect will occur. As the fitness level improves, it is necessary to increase the training stimulus. Thus to work at a given percent of maximum heart rate reserve, one must exercise at a faster pace. Exercise frequency, duration, and intensity also may be increased to stimulate further adaptations in cardiovascular fitness.

Cardiovascular Fitness for Older Women

As the average North American woman ages, she tends to decrease her level of physical activity. Consequently, $\dot{V}O_2$max and cardiovascular fitness decline. The average $\dot{V}O_2$max for 25-year-old women is approximately 39 ml · kg BM · min^{-1}; by age 65, it decreases to approximately 20 ml · kg BM · min^{-1}. Vaccaro et al. (1984) reported a mean $\dot{V}O_2$max of 32.1 ml · kg BM · min^{-1} for 11 female masters swimmers who were all over age 60.

A 10-week training study of 16 elderly women (ages 67 to 89) showed that low- and moderate-intensity training were associated with increases in $\dot{V}O_2$max of 12.7% (low-intensity training at 40% of maximum heart rate reserve) and 15.4% (moderate-intensity training at 60% of maximum heart rate reserve) (Foster, Hume, Byrnes, Dickenson, & Chatfield, 1989). In this study, maximum oxygen consumption increased from 12.6 to 14.2 ml · kg BM · min^{-1} for the low-intensity group and from 13.6 to 15.7 ml · kg BM · min^{-1} for the moderate-intensity group. Thus it appears that the older female has the capacity to adapt to a low- to moderate-intensity exercise training stimulus. Studies like the one by Foster et al. (1989) indicate that the training stimulus may not need to be at 60% to 90% of maximal heart rate reserve. In other words, a cardiovascular training effect will occur among sedentary elderly women who engage in minimal amounts of activity.

Cardiovascular Health Benefits of Cardiovascular Fitness

As mentioned at the beginning of the chapter, a recent study indicated that cardiovascular fitness had a positive impact on cardiovascular health in women (Blair et al., 1989). This study was the first large-scale epidemiological study of women, and the data agree with the numerous studies on men. In this study examining over 3,000 women, Blair et al. (1989) reported a significant favorable relationship between fitness (as measured by treadmill endurance time) and cardiovascular disease mortality. The age-adjusted death rates (from heart disease, cancer, and other diseases) were 39.5 (low fitness), 20.5, 12.2, 6.5, and 8.5 (high fitness) deaths per 10,000 person years for five fitness categories. In other words, death rates for cardiovascular disease, cancer, and other causes were over 4.5 times higher in the lowest fitness category than in the highest fitness category. In another analysis of these data, Blair et al. (1989) reported that if all the unfit women became fit, there would be a 15.3% decrease in death rate. The potential confounding effects of other risk factors such as age, smoking status, cholesterol, blood pressure, blood glucose, and family history were removed so they did not influence the effect of fitness described above. It should be noted that 99% of the women in this study were white, from the middle and upper socioeconomic groups, and worked in white-collar jobs. While there are no data on women of color, there is no reason to believe that the influence of fitness level on cardiovascular disease would be any different for these groups.

Summary and Conclusions

The potential to improve cardiovascular fitness is similar for women and men. Traditionally, improvements in cardiovascular fitness have been encouraged to improve endurance performance. As our society becomes increasingly concerned with health and well-being, more attention should be focused on the role of cardiovascular fitness in health maintenance and disease prevention for women.

References

Blair, S.N., Kohl, H.W., Paffenbarger, R.S., Clark, D.G., Cooper, K.H., & Gibbons, L.W. (1989). Physical fitness and all-cause mortality: A prospective study of healthy men and women. *Journal of the American Medical Association*, **262**, 2395-2401.

Bransford, D.R., & Howley, E.T. (1977). Oxygen cost of running in trained and untrained men and women. *Medicine and Science in Sports*, **9**, 41-44.

Cureton, K.J., Bishop, P., Hutchinson, P., Newland, H., Vickery, S., & Zwiren, L. (1986). Sex differences in maximal oxygen uptake: Effect of equating hemoglobin concentration. *European Journal of Applied Physiology*, **54**, 656-660.

Cureton, K.J., & Sparling, P.B. (1980). Distance running performance and metabolic responses to running in men and women with excess weight experimentally equated. *Medicine and Science in Sports and Exercise*, **12**, 288-294.

Drinkwater, B.L. (1984). Women and exercise: Physiological aspects. In R.L. Terjung (Ed.), *Exercise and sport science reviews*, **12**, 21-51.

Foster, V., Hume, G., Byrnes, W.C., Dickenson, A., & Chatfield, S. (1989). Endurance training for elderly women: Moderate versus low intensity. *Journal of Gerontology*, **44**, M184-M188.

Freedson, P. (1981). The influence of hemoglobin concentration on exercise cardiac output. *International Journal of Sports Medicine*, **2**, 81-86.

Kitagawa, K., Miyashita, M., & Yamamoto, K. (1977). Maximal oxygen uptake, body composition, and running performance in young Japanese adults of both sexes. *Japanese Journal of Physical Education*, **21**, 335-340.

MacNab, R.B.J., Conger, P.R., & Taylor, P.S. (1969). Differences in maximal and submaximal work capacity in men and women. *Journal of Applied Physiology*, **27**, 644-648.

Maughan, R.J., & Leiper, J.B. (1983). Aerobic capacity and fractional utilization of aerobic capacity in elite and non-elite male and female marathon runners. *European Journal of Applied Physiology*, **52**, 80-87.

Pate, R.R., Barnes, C., & Miller, W. (1985). A physiological comparison of performance-matched female and male distance runners. *Research Quarterly for Exercise and Sport*, **56**, 245-250.

Saltin, B., & Astrand, P. (1967). Maximal oxygen uptake in athletes. *Journal of Applied Physiology*, **32**, 353-358.

Sharkey, B. (1990). *Physiology of fitness*. Champaign, IL: Human Kinetics.

Sparling, P.B. (1980). A meta-analysis of studies comparing maximal oxygen uptake in men and women. *Research Quarterly for Exercise and Sport*, **51**, 542-552.

Sparling, P.B., & Cureton, K.T. (1983). Biological determinants of the sex differences in 12-min run performance. *Medicine and Science in Sports and Exercise*, **15**, 218-223.

Vaccaro, P., Ostrove, S.M., Vandervelden, L., Goldfarb, A.H., Clarke, D.H., & Dummer, G.M. (1984). Body composition and physiological responses of masters female swimmers 20 to 70 years of age. *The Physician and Sportsmedicine*, **55**, 278-284.

Vogel, J.A., & Patton, J.F. (1978). Evaluation of fitness in the U.S. Army. In *NATO proceedings of the symposium on physical fitness with special reference to military forces*. Toronto: Defense and Civil Institute of Environmental Medicine.

Wells, C.L. (1991). *Women, sport, & performance: A physiological perspective*. Champaign, IL: Human Kinetics.

Wells, C.L., Hecht, L.H., & Krahenbuhl, G.S. (1981). Physical characteristics and oxygen utilization of male and female marathon runners. *Research Quarterly for Exercise and Sport*, **52**, 281-285.

Chapter 12

Muscle Strength and Endurance

Patty Freedson

Power can be seen as power with rather than power over, and it can be used for competence and co-operation, rather than dominance and control.

ANNE L. BARSTOW
quoted in *The Quotable Woman*

Over the last few years, muscle strength and endurance have become important aspects of overall fitness. It is no longer acceptable simply to consider high levels of aerobic conditioning and cardiovascular capacity as the physiological characteristics of a fit individual.

A certain amount of muscle strength and endurance are necessary to carry on activities of daily living that require movement of one's body mass. With aging, there is a tendency to become less active; and muscle strength, endurance, and muscle mass tend to decrease. We must consider the role that muscle-strengthening exercises may play in decreasing the rate of decline in muscle strength and endurance typically seen with aging. Not much is known about muscle strength and endurance trainability of the elderly, but the principles underlying the acquisition of strength and endurance are the same for young and old alike, so the information that follows is applicable to all segments of the population.

Definitions

Muscular strength is defined as the ability of a muscle or group of muscles to exert a maximum force against a resistance. Muscular endurance is the ability of a muscle or group of muscles to maintain a submaximal force over an extended period of time. The three types of muscle contraction are *isometric*, *isotonic*, and *isokinetic*.

An *isometric* contraction is static: The joint surrounding the muscle or muscles does not move.

An *isotonic* contraction is dynamic: The muscle tension throughout the range of motion is variable, and the resistance being moved is constant. Isotonic contractions are either (a) concentric: The muscle shortens, the tension exerted by the muscle is more than the resistance, and the movement is against gravity (e.g., lifting a barbell); or (b) eccentric: The muscle lengthens and the movement is with gravity (e.g., lowering a barbell). An *isokinetic* contraction is dynamic: The muscle tension is maximal, and movement speed is constant throughout the range of motion. This type of contraction is also called variable resistance movement. The speed of the contraction is regulated mechanically and/or electronically, and the velocity remains constant at the preset speed (e.g., 180 degrees per second).

A maximal concentric isotonic contraction uses a resistance that can be moved through the weakest point in a range of motion. Thus the muscle or muscle group is not contracting maximally throughout the range of motion. It is maximal only at the weakest point in the range of motion. In contrast, an isokinetic contraction allows maximal tension at every point in the range of motion.

Measurement of Muscular Strength and Endurance

A variety of tests are available to assess and evaluate muscular strength and endurance. Such testing can be used to assess strength levels, to measure changes in strength and endurance consequent to a training program, and to determine strength levels during rehabilitation from musculoskeletal injury.

Gender Differences in Muscular Strength

When strength measures are expressed as absolute scores, that is, maximum weight lifted, males are considerably stronger than females in upper body strength measures. For example, Laubach (1976) reported that the upper body strength (using a composite strength score from numerous isometric and isotonic measures) for females was approximately 56% of male upper body strength. Similarly, Wilmore (1974) reported that the female bench press and arm curl strength were, respectively, 59% and 51% of those of males. In a more recent study of male and female swimmers and untrained controls, bench press strength of the female swimmers was 57% of that of the male swimmer. Although both groups trained for the same number of years and participated in similar resistance training programs, total training yardage was 25% greater for the males. The gender difference for the untrained controls was larger, with the females having 41% of the measured strength of the males (Bishop, Cureton, & Collins, 1987).

In contrast, gender differences in absolute strength for the lower body are smaller. Laubach (1976) reported that lower body strength for females was 69% of that of males. The percent difference for lower body strength measured by the leg press was 25% in the Wilmore (1974) study. In the study by Bishop et al. (1987), the female swimmers had 73% of the strength of the males in the leg press.

These regional differences raise an interesting question. Are there differences in males' and females' muscle physiology that explain why the differences in strength are less for the lower body than for the upper body? The answer to this question is an unequivocal "no." The explanation is probably related to sociocultural factors. Women traditionally have engaged in less upper body exercise than men. As a result, the amount of exercise overload to women's upper body is less, so, upper body strength is less than lower body strength. The lower extremities are naturally overloaded more than the upper body because of walking. This point is discussed by Wilmore (1974) and Singh and Karpovich (1968). Unquestionably, this gender gap in upper body strength will be reduced as women become involved in more regular upper body exercise.

Expression of strength relative to body mass and lean body mass greatly reduces the magnitude of the difference in strength between the sexes. Figure 12.1 illustrates the decreases in the differences in strength between males and females when the strength score is expressed relative to body mass and lean body mass (Wilmore, 1974). The strength ratio is female strength divided by male strength. At a ratio of 1.0, strength scores are equal between the sexes. When leg press strength is expressed relative to lean body mass, female strength is slightly greater than male strength. For upper body measures, however, female strength remains less than that of males.

A multiple regression analysis to examine the influence of muscle mass on gender differences in strength was completed by Bishop et al. (1987) and Hosler and Morrow (1982). The authors reported that gender accounted for no more than 3% of the variance in strength in similarly trained women and men; that is, muscle cross-sectional area and lean body mass accounted for at least 97% of the gender differences in strength in these similarly trained samples. The findings strongly suggest that if training status is similar for each sex, muscle mass differences account for nearly all of the gender differences in strength.

In summary, female upper body absolute strength is 40% to 50% lower than that of males, whereas female lower body absolute strength is only 20% to 35% lower than that of males. For lower body strength, the gender differences disappear when expressed relative to lean body mass.

Resistance Training Programs

A 3- to 4-day-per-week training program is recommended to elicit significant gains in muscle strength and endurance. The program should incorporate exercises for all the major muscle groups (four to five exercises each for upper and lower body muscle groups). In general, three sets of 10 repetitions per set are recommended. The number of repetitions should be maximal in every set. In other words, after 10 repetitions an 11th would not be possible. If maximizing strength is the primary objective, fewer repetitions at a higher resistance are desirable. If the emphasis is on endurance, a lower resistance of 12 to 15 repetitions should be completed.

Isometric Training

During the 1950s, isometric training was popular. Usually the training involved maintaining a 60% to 70% maximum voluntary contraction (60% to 70% of the maximum isometric strength) at a specific joint angle for 6 seconds. Isometric strength gains were realized; however, the gains were specific to the joint angle or angles used in training. Isometric training remains a popular muscle rehabilitation modality, primarily to counteract the effects of disuse atrophy (decrease in muscle size) commonly seen in immobilized limbs.

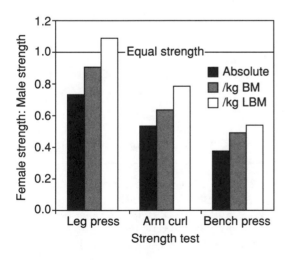

Figure 12.1 Ratio of female 1-RM strength to male 1-RM strength when strength is expressed as an absolute score relative to body mass (BM) and lean body mass (LBM). Adapted from Wilmore (1974).

Isotonic Training

This kind of training is done with either free weights or weight machines and involves both concentric and eccentric muscle contractions. Some manufacturers offer mechanically regulated variable resistance machines. Weight machines such as Universal and Nautilus are preferred for people who are just starting a resistance training program because minimal technique instruction is necessary.

Isokinetic Training

This kind of training uses accommodating resistance machines where the resistance changes based on the force exerted. The purported advantage of this kind of training is that it maximally overloads the muscle at every point in the range of motion where the resistance of the machine matches the force generated by the muscle. The speed of contraction is controlled, and training can be done at both slow (high force production by the muscle) or fast (low force production by the muscle) speeds of movement, depending on the individual's needs.

Resistance Training Effects

Three commonly held beliefs about resistance training are:

1. One kind of resistance training elicits greater strength gains than another.
2. Gains in muscular strength and endurance consequent to a resistance training program are less for females than those observed for males.
3. Resistance training causes large increases in muscle size in women.

This section will present scientific evidence that refutes such notions.

A study conducted at the University of Massachusetts compared the effects of isotonic (Universal Gym) resistance training with Hydra-Fitness hydraulic resistance training, a type of variable resistance exercise equipment. Thirty college-age women were assigned to one of these two circuit resistance training programs. The training program was 10 weeks long, three times a week, for 40 minutes per session. Each circuit consisted of three 20-second workout periods (separated by 55 seconds' rest) at each of five different exercise stations. The circuit was completed two times. The Universal Gym (UG) group completed the following exercises: bench press, biceps curl, latissimus dorsi pull, shoulder press, and leg press. The Hydra-Fitness (HYD) group exercises were: bench press, biceps curl, triceps extension, butterfly, shoulder press, and leg flexion/extension. The intensity of the workouts was increased over the course of the training program, as illustrated in Table 12.1.

The criterion measures of muscular strength and endurance were 1-RM free weight bench press, 1-RM UG lat pull, number of modified pushups, and peak arm power measured on the Hydra-Fitness Omnitron machine. In most cases

Table 12.1 Training Protocols for Universal Gym and Hydra-Fitness Training

Week	Universal Gym resistances[a]		Hydra-Fitness dial setting	
	Circuit 1	Circuit 2	Circuit 1	Circuit 2
1-2	60% 1-RM	60% 1-RM	2	2
3	+ 10 lbs	60% 1-RM	3	2
4-5	+ 10 lbs	+ 10 lbs	3	3
6	+ 20 lbs	+ 10 lbs	4	3
7-8	+ 20 lbs	+ 20 lbs	4	4
9	+ 30 lbs	+ 20 lbs	5	4
10	+ 30 lbs	+ 30 lbs	5	5

[a]Change in resistance relative to weeks 1 and 2.
Note. Data from Smurl (1987).

the increases for the controls, a group of nonexercising college women, were small and were significantly less than for the experimental groups. The results are illustrated in Figure 12.2.

The increases ranged from 7.1% (lat pull for HYD group) to 47% (number of modified push-ups). There were no significant differences in strength and endurance gains between the two training regimes. Table 12.2 presents a summary of women's 1-RM bench press strength increases observed in other resistance training studies. It is difficult to make direct comparisons across other studies because the mode, intensity, and duration of training varied; however, the range of increase was from 14.7% to 28.6%, and the reported changes were statistically significant.

The trainability of women is equal to that of men consequent to resistance exercise training. Wilmore (1974) reported gains of 10.6% to 29.5% for women and 5% to 26% for men after a 10-week, 2-day-per-week, 40-minute-per-session resistance training program. Thus the adaptability to a short-term resistance training program is similar for women and men.

Table 12.2   Changes in 1-RM Bench Press Following Resistance Training in Women

Study	1-RM bench press (kg)		% Increase
	Pre	Post	
Brown & Wilmore (1974)	49.5	56.8	14.7
Gettman et al. (1982)	30.0	36.0	20.0
Mayhew & Gross (1974)	22.2	28.1	26.5
Wilmore (1974)	54.1	69.6	28.6
Wilmore et al. (1978)	31.5	37.9	20.3
Smurl (1987)	30.8	36.5	18.4
Smurl (1987)	33.2	39.6	19.2

The only gender difference observed consequent to resistance training was in the amount of muscle hypertrophy. Even though the relative gains in strength are reportedly similar for the sexes, muscle mass gains are dramatically less for women. It has been hypothesized that this difference is caused by higher levels of testosterone in men that appear to stimulate muscle size increase. In the University of Massachusetts study described earlier, lean body mass changes for the women (measured using underwater weighing) were less than 3%. Flexed and relaxed biceps girth measures increased less than 5%. Table 12.3 presents a summary of the body mass and lean body mass changes observed in other resistance training programs.

Female bodybuilders are athletes who appear to have extremely large muscles. This may indicate that females do in fact have the potential to develop a large musculature. Wells (1991) has offered the following explanations for such muscle development:

- Genetic endowment
- Use of anabolic steroids
- Training regimes that focus on muscle shape development that makes the muscles appear large

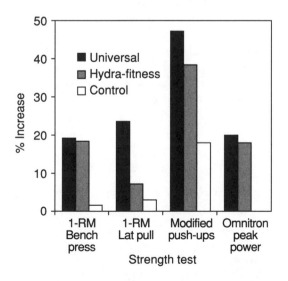

Figure 12.2   Changes in strength measures following a 10-week resistance training program in young women. Adapted from Smurl (1987).

Table 12.3   Changes in Body Mass and Lean Body Mass Following Resistance Training in Women

Study	Age	Duration (wk)	Frequency (times/wk)	Session length (min)	% Change BM	% Change LBM
Brown & Wilmore (1974)	20.7	12	3	60-90	−1.4	+0.7
Gettman, Ward, & Hagan (1982)	35.7	12	3	—	+0.2	+3.9
Katch & Drumm (1986)	—	10	3	40	−0.8	+1.6
Mayhew & Gross (1974)	20.9	9	3	40	+0.7	+3.7
Oyster (1979)	—	7	2	—	−0.2	—
Wilmore (1974)	20.3	10	2	40	−0.2	+2.4
Wilmore et al. (1978)	19.7	10	3	23	+0.2	+2.9
Smurl (1987)	21.9	10	3	40	+0.7	+1.3
Smurl (1987)	21.9	10	3	40	+1.8	+2.9

Note. BM = body mass, LBM = lean body mass.

- Minimal level subcutaneous fat
- Dehydration
- ''Pumping up'' that occurs just prior to a posing routine

Although these are all plausible explanations, more research is needed to quantify the maximum potential for muscle size increases in women.

Summary and Conclusions

There is no question that absolute strength levels are less for women than men. An interesting observation, however, is that the gender gap is much larger for upper body strength than for lower body strength. This regional difference appears to be related to social factors that cause women to engage in less upper body exercise. Women should be encouraged to incorporate more upper body exercise overload into their daily activity routines. The daily activities of pushing, pulling, and lifting require a certain amount of upper body strength. To be able to carry out these activities with ease, women must train the upper body musculature so they can attain their potential for upper body strength.

The effects of resistance training on muscle strength and endurance indicated that women and men have a similar training response to resistance training programs. The female appears to be as trainable as the male in terms of strength gains, but the degree of muscle hypertrophy is less for the female after resistance training.

Little is known about the strength and muscular development potential of women. Future study should include longitudinal investigation of women bodybuilders and powerlifters to identify the factors associated with muscle strength and muscle size development.

References

Bishop, P., Cureton, K., & Collins, M. (1987). Sex differences in muscular strength in equally-trained men and women. *Ergonomics*, **30**, 675-687.

Brown, C.H., & Wilmore, J.H. (1974). The effects of maximal resistance training on the strength and body composition of women athletes. *Medicine and Science in Sports*, **6**, 174-177.

Gettman, L.R., Ward, P., & Hagan, R.D. (1982). A comparison of combined running and weight training with circuit weight training. *Medicine and Science in Sports and Exercise*, **14**, 229-234.

Hosler, W.W., & Morrow, J.R. (1982). Arm and leg strength compared between young women and men after allowing for differences in body size and composition. *Ergonomics*, **25**, 309-313.

Katch, F.I., & Drumm, S.S. (1986). Effects of different modes of strength training on body composition and anthropometry. *Clinics in Sports Medicine*, **5**, 413-459.

Laubach, L.L. (1976). Comparative muscular strength of men and women: A review of the literature. *Aviation, Space and Environmental Medicine*, **47**, 534-542.

Mayhew, J.L., & Gross, P.M. (1974). Body composition changes in young women with high resistance weight training. *Research Quarterly*, **45**, 433-440.

Oyster, N. (1979). Effects of a heavy resistance weight training program on college women athletes. *Journal of Sports Medicine and Physical Fitness*, **19**, 79-83.

Singh, M., & Karpovich, P.V. (1968). Strength of forearm flexors and extensors in men and women. *Journal of Applied Physiology*, **25**, 177-180.

Smurl, L. (1987). *Changes in strength, power, and anthropometry following Universal Gym and Hydra-Fitness training in women.* Unpublished masters' thesis, University of Massachusetts, Amherst.

Wells, C.L. (1991). *Women, sport, & performance: A physiological perspective.* Champaign, IL: Human Kinetics.

Wilmore, J.H. (1974). Alterations in strength, body composition and anthorpometric measurements consequent to a 10 week weight training program. *Medicine and Science in Sports*, **6**, 133-138.

Wilmore, J.H., Parr, R.B., Girandola, R.N., Ward, P., Vodak, P.A., Barstow, T.V., et al. (1978). Physiological alterations consequent to circuit weight training. *Medicine and Science in Sports*, **10**, 79-84.

Chapter 13

Endocrine Basis of Exercise-Induced Amenorrhea

Mary Jane De Souza
Joan Carles Arce
Deborah A. Metzger

Most of the research completed to date has answered questions reflecting those parameters that do "NOT" cause exercise-induced amenorrhea, as opposed to answering the question: What causes exercise-induced amenorrhea?

ANNE B. LOUCKS
"Effects of Exercise Training on the Menstrual Cycle:
Existence and Mechanisms"

In an effort to optimize health, many women include physical activity and exercise as a part of their daily lifestyle. During the past three decades there has been explosive growth in the number of girls and women participating in sports, exercise, and recreational activity. Public health reports in the United States today estimate that 45% of women aged 20 to 40 participate in regular physical activity. This translates to approximately 8 million to 10 million young women, representing a significant sector of the female population.

A great deal of concern has arisen among participants, coaches, and physicians regarding the effects of strenuous exercise training on the menstrual cycle. There is an accumulating body of knowledge that associates intense exercise training with a broad spectrum of menstrual cycle alterations: luteal insufficiency in cycles of normal length, shortened luteal phases, menstrual irregularity, anovulation, and amenorrhea (De Souza & Metzger, 1991; Loucks & Horvath, 1985). Figure 13.1 displays the spectrum of

185

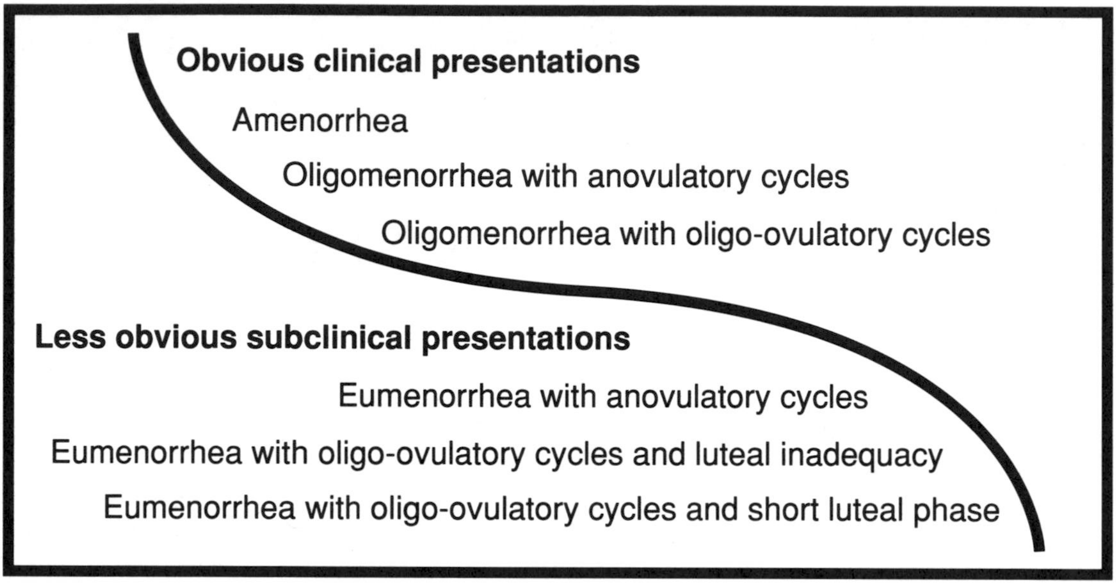

Obvious clinical presentations

Amenorrhea

Oligomenorrhea with anovulatory cycles

Oligomenorrhea with oligo-ovulatory cycles

Less obvious subclinical presentations

Eumenorrhea with anovulatory cycles

Eumenorrhea with oligo-ovulatory cycles and luteal inadequacy

Eumenorrhea with oligo-ovulatory cycles and short luteal phase

Figure 13.1   The spectrum of obvious clinical presentations and less obvious subclinical presentations of exercise-induced menstrual perturbations. Reprinted from De Souza, Arce, and Nulsen (1992).

clinical and subclinical exercise-induced menstrual perturbations observed in female athletes.

These issues raise several health-related questions concerning the long-term effects of menstrual dysfunction and amenorrhea in female athletes. Aside from the obvious clinical problems with fertility and reproductive potential during periods of oligomenorrhea and amenorrhea, exercise-induced menstrual alterations place athletic girls and women at risk for a serious health problem, osteoporosis (Drinkwater et al., 1984). This decrease in bone density is a direct consequence of their low levels of estradiol associated with menstrual cycle irregularities. Moreover, because of a diminished skeletal integrity, these young girls and women are at risk for developing stress and vertebral crush fractures similar to what is observed in postmenopausal women (Drinkwater et al., 1984). Persistent low estrogen levels also may compromise their potential to develop peak bone mass at maturity.

Other aspects of health may be affected by decreased estrogen status. Estrogens are known

to have a protective influence on the development of cardiovascular disease, an issue that has been studied primarily in postmenopausal women but is equally important among younger women with lower levels of estrogen (Lamon-Fava et al., 1989).

Understanding the etiology of exercise-induced amenorrhea is important to clarify the relationship between exercise training and perturbations of menstrual cycle function. Research investigations in this area extend well beyond an academic interest; clearly a spectrum of clinical health concerns are apparent for exercising women who experience menstrual cycle alterations (De Souza & Metzger, 1991; Loucks & Horvath, 1985).

Research on strenuous exercise training and the menstrual cycle has evolved through many levels and methods, including descriptive, survey, retrospective, prospective, and some epidemiological techniques, in attempts to understand the factors associated with exercise-induced amenorrhea. Through these associations, it was hoped that an understanding would develop of the potential physiological and endocrinological mechanisms involved in the etiology of exercise-induced amenorrhea; however, much of the initial research in this area is flawed with methodological problems that make interpretations difficult and unreliable (De Souza et al., 1992; Loucks & Horvath, 1985). The methodological concerns include poor subject selection criteria, inappropriate experimental designs, failure to accurately measure hormonal levels, failure to control confounding variables, and inaccurate measurement techniques. Thus, as Loucks (1990) has stated, most of the research completed to date has answered questions reflecting those parameters that do "NOT" cause exercise-induced amenorrhea, as opposed to answering the question: "What causes exercise-induced amenorrhea?"

In this chapter, we will address the following questions to facilitate a better understanding of exercise-induced menstrual irregularities:

1. Is a later age of puberty associated with exercise training?
2. What is the prevalence of amenorrhea in athletes?
3. What factors are associated with menstrual cycle irregularity?
4. What are the endocrine characteristics of the amenorrheic athlete?
5. What are some potential endocrine mechanisms that may be responsible for menstrual disorders in athletes?

To maximize our ability to answer these questions, we present a brief review of normal reproductive physiology associated with adolescence and adulthood.

Physiology of Puberty and the Menstrual Cycle

The initiation and maintenance of regular, cyclic menstruation depends on a complex system of negative and positive feedback interactions among the hypothalamus, pituitary, and ovary. The hypothalamus releases gonadotropin-releasing hormone (GnRH), which causes the release of follicle-stimulating hormone (FSH) and luteinizing hormone (LH) from the pituitary gland. FSH and LH in turn stimulate the ovary, ultimately resulting in follicular (egg) maturation, ovulation, and the production of the sex steroid hormones estradiol and progesterone. The production of estradiol and progesterone further modulates the secretion of GnRH, LH, and FSH. In addition, estradiol and progesterone initiate and maintain secondary sexual characteristics (i.e., breast development, female fat distribution), maintain bone mineral density, and prepare the uterus (endometrium) for implantation of the embryo. The interrelationships among the hypothalamus, pituitary, and ovary are such that suboptimal activity at any level in the feedback loop can result in disturbances that may lead to menstrual dysfunction, hypoestrogenism, and amenorrhea (Yen, 1986).

The Hypothalamus: The Pacemaker for the Reproductive System

The hypothalamus can be viewed as the pacemaker for the entire reproductive system. This master gland functions in that capacity by releasing pulses of GnRH at very precise intervals occurring every 60 to 120 minutes. The gonadotropins, LH and FSH, also are released in a pulsatile manner in response to stimulation by GnRH. Variations in pulse frequency or amplitude from the normal range can result in menstrual dysfunction such as shortened luteal phases, oligomenorrhea, anovulation, and amenorrhea (Speroff et al., 1983; Yen, 1986). Control of the pulsatile release of GnRH is poorly understood; however, it appears that neurons from "higher centers" may integrate external and internal data from a variety of sources and transmit this information to the hypothalamus by way of neurotransmitters and neuromodulators, such as endogenous opioids, dopamine, catecholamines, and catechol estrogens. Furthermore, the autonomic nervous system and other nonreproductive endocrine organs, such as the thyroid and adrenal, also modulate the hypothalamic pacemaker (Speroff et al., 1983). It is the summation of these inhibitory and stimulatory inputs that ultimately determines the functional activity of the hypothalamus.

The direct and indirect influences of the hypothalamic pacemaker on the entire reproductive system are seen most dramatically at the time of puberty. Prior to the onset of pubertal changes, the hypothalamus is relatively quiet, releasing very low levels of GnRH. A prominent stage of impending puberty is the progressive maturation in the operational level of the hypothalamic-pituitary-ovarian (H-P-O) axis that leads, over several years, to the development of regular ovulatory cycles (Apter, 1980; Ducharme et al., 1976). Figure 13.2 displays the change in sensitivity of

the H-P-O axis at puberty. Not only during puberty, but also during adulthood, the operational level of ovarian function corresponds directly with the degree of regularity of GnRH pulses from the hypothalamus (Styne & Grumbach, 1986). As the H-P-O axis matures and GnRH pulses become frequent and regular, ovarian function evolves from anovulation to oligo-ovulation, and finally ovulatory cycles result when GnRH pulses occur on a regular basis (see Figure 13.2). As will be shown later in this chapter, alterations in the menstrual function of adults correlate with the regularity of GnRH pulsatility, as they do during puberty.

Puberty

Puberty is a continuous process comprised of a series of endocrinological and physical events that occur in a successive and overlapping manner. Adrenarche is the first event of puberty, and the establishment of consistent and cyclic ovulatory

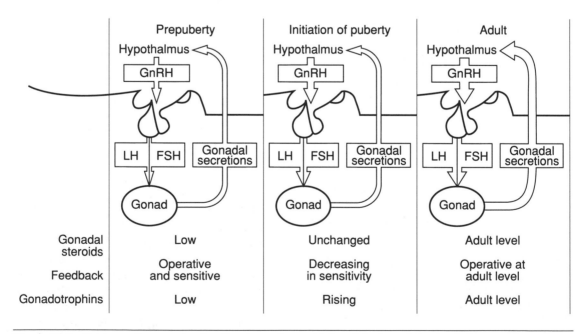

Figure 13.2 Summary diagram showing the change in sensitivity of the hypothalamic-pituitary-ovarian axis at puberty. Reprinted from Besser and Cudworth (1987).

cycles is the endpoint of puberty (Styne & Grumbach, 1986). Each hormonal change that occurs during the course of puberty produces a significant but separate transformation in the physical characteristics of the growing girl. A summary of the physical and endocrinological events of puberty is provided in Table 13.1.

Between the ages of 6 and 8 years, while the hypothalamic-pituitary-ovarian (H-P-O) axis is still working at a low level of activity, there is a gradual increase in production of the adrenal androgens (androstenedione, dehydroepiandrosterone, and dehydroepiandrosterone-sulfate) that continues until age 13 to 15 (Apter, 1980; Ducharme et al., 1976). This first event of puberty is referred to as adrenarche. Adrenarche results in the first physical sign of the ensuing chain of events leading to puberty: the development of pubic hair, axillary hair, and sebaceous glands. The second and predominant endocrine event of impending puberty is the progressive maturation in the operational level of the H-P-O axis that leads over several years to the development of gonadarche, thelarche, menarche, and eventually to regular ovulatory cycles.

It is not until the age of 8 to 10 years that the central nervous system (CNS) begins to mature

Table 13.1 Summary of Pubertal Events

Term	Type of event	Event monitored
Adrenarche	Endocrinological	Increased adrenal androgens
Pubarche	Physical	Tanner stages of pubic hair
Gonadarche	Endocrinological	Increased estrogens
Thelarche	Physical	Tanner stages of breast development
Menarche	Physical	First menstruation
Ovulation	Endocrinological	Midcycle LH surge

and the hypothalamic GnRH pulse generator becomes gradually less sensitive to gonadal steroids. Erratic bursts of GnRH release initially occur during sleep. Gradually, over a period of several years, the pulses become more regular at night and with time extend throughout the day (Apter, 1980; Ducharme et al., 1976). This diurnal GnRH activity corresponds to an increase in pituitary gonadotropin reserve and the pulsatile release of LH and FSH, which in turn stimulate the production of estrogens from the ovary. This pubertal event is referred to as gonadarche (Apter, 1980; Ducharme et al., 1976).

Also by the age of 8 to 10 years, the increasingly apparent estrogen levels coincident with gonadarche promote breast development. This pubertal event is termed thelarche. By the age of 12 to 14 years, the continued increase in ovarian estrogen concentration stimulates the endometrium, producing the first menstruation, called menarche (Apter, 1980). Menarche is a pubertal event that occurs largely because of genetic factors (Treolar & Martin, 1990) and is modified to a certain extent by environmental factors (Brooks-Gunn & Warren, 1988; Malina, 1983).

It should be noted that the appearance of menarche does not imply that the reproductive system is functionally mature. Anovulatory cycles, which lack the production of progesterone, are frequent in the years after menarche (Borsos et al., 1986). The hypothalamic GnRH pulse generator is still erratic at times; and unless the hypothalamus can maintain consistent pulses every 60 to 120 minutes, oligo-ovulatory or anovulatory cycles predominate (Styne & Grumbach, 1986). Moreover, the positive feedback of estrogens on hypothalamic GnRH and pituitary LH and FSH release requires several years of maturation before this feedback effect is present consistently during each cycle, resulting in regular and ovulatory menstrual cyclicity. When all of these physiological changes have taken place and the system has stabilized, we can assume that the transition of the reproductive system from childhood to adulthood has been completed. As will be demonstrated later in this chapter, however, the adult reproductive system is not static. Given the proper stimuli, such as high volumes of exercise or excessive weight loss, the H-P-O axis can exhibit a significant degree of plasticity with pubertal or prepubertal patterns of reproductive function reappearing.

The Menstrual Cycle

The menstrual cycle can be divided into two phases: the follicular phase and the luteal phase. The follicular phase, which begins with the first day of menstrual flow and ends with ovulation, is that portion of the cycle when follicular development occurs (approximately days 1-14). The luteal phase, which begins with ovulation and ends with the onset of menstrual flow, is that portion of the cycle when corpus luteum development occurs (approximately days 15-28). Figure 13.3 displays the hormonal events during the follicular and luteal phases.

The beginning of the follicular phase is initiated by an increase in FSH, which occurs in response to the decreased negative feedback of the diminishing concentrations of estradiol and progesterone during the preceeding luteal phase (Speroff et al., 1983; Yen, 1986). FSH induces the development and growth of follicles that secrete increasing amounts of estrogen. FSH and estradiol act synergistically to increase the number of FSH receptors present, thus progressively increasing the developing follicles' ability to respond to FSH. In addition, these two hormones increase the number of LH receptors present to prepare the follicle for ovulation. As the follicle reaches maturity in the late follicular phase, the ovarian secretion of estrogen reaches a peak level, resulting in a positive feedback effect on the pituitary (Speroff et al., 1983; Yen, 1986). The pituitary then releases a surge of LH that induces the final maturation and release of the oocyte (ovulation). During the luteal phase, progesterone and estrogen are synthesized by the corpus luteum of the ovary. The combined effect of these two hormones results

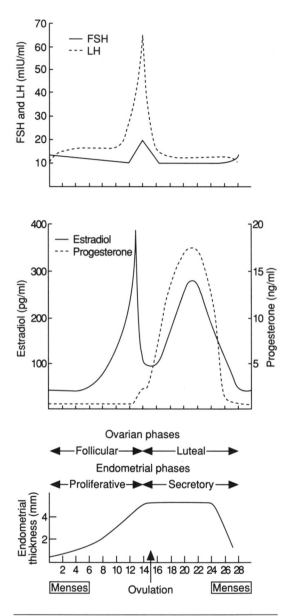

Figure 13.3 Diagram of reproductive hormone patterns during the menstrual cycle. Reprinted from Speroff, Glass, and Kase (1983).

in: (a) a direct negative feedback on the hypothalamus that inhibits the release of GnRH, and (b) a direct negative feedback on the anterior pituitary that inhibits the release of LH and FSH. Toward the end of the luteal phase, this inhibitory influence is released as the levels of estrogen and progesterone decline and another cycle is initiated (Speroff et al., 1983; Yen, 1986). The coordinated effects of these hormonal events are shown in Figure 13.4.

The effects of estrogen and progesterone are observed in many tissues and organs of the body. Estrogen, in particular, is responsible for breast development and maintenance of bone mineral density. Estrogen and progesterone also act sequentially on the uterus (endometrium) to prepare it for implantation. Estrogen induces proliferation of the endometrium, whereas progesterone promotes maturation of the endometrium. If pregnancy is not established, endometrial and blood vessel necrosis occurs, and menstrual flow begins as the secretion of estrogen and progesterone diminishes during the luteal phase (Speroff et al., 1983; Yen, 1986).

The occurrence of menstruation is not indicative of ovulation. Although the appearance of consistent and cyclic menstruation is generally considered an indication that all components of the female reproductive system are functioning optimally, significant alterations in hormonal secretion may occur without disturbing menstrual cyclicity.

Eumenorrhea refers to the status of a women with consistent and cyclic menstrual cycle lengths of 24 to 32 days; the key to this category is the term "consistent." Oligomenorrhea refers to the status of a woman with irregular or inconsistent menstrual cycles of 39 to 90 days; the key to this category is "inconsistent." Last, amenorrhea refers to the status of a woman with menstrual cycles that occur at intervals of greater than 90 days (Loucks & Horvath, 1985). There are two categories of amenorrhea: primary and secondary. Primary amenorrhea is the absence of menstruation by the age of 16, whereas secondary amenorrhea is the absence of menstruation in a woman who has had previous menstrual periods (Yen,

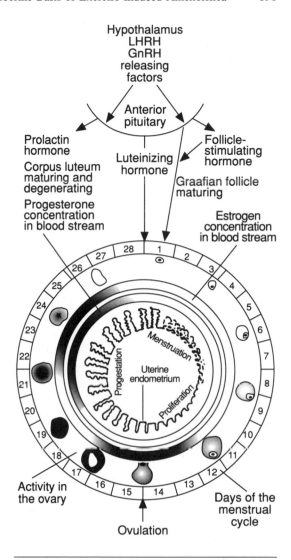

Figure 13.4 Summary diagram of the menstrual cycle with follicular and luteal events affecting egg and endometrial maturation. Reprinted from Barnes (1980).

1986). Most often when reference is made to athletes with amenorrhea, the reference is to secondary amenorrhea. The point should be made that these menstrual categories may be unrelated to ovulatory status. Many women with oligomenorrhea actually ovulate, although unpredictably. The accurate assessment of ovulatory status is important because anovulatory but menstruating women are at risk for health concerns that do not affect the oligomenorrheic, ovulatory woman.

Theories Related to Exercise-Induced Amenorrhea

Before the early 1970s women were discouraged from participating in strenuous physical training and elite athletic competition, particularly endurance events like marathon running and cross-country races. The fitness boom of the 1970s brought an increase in exercise and recreational sport participation for both women and men. Concern remained that women were not physiologically capable of engaging in some strenuous physical activities. It was not until 1984 that the International Olympic Committee finally allowed women to compete in the marathon. These and other historic events, including passage of Title IX, significantly increased the interest of women in physical exercise and initiated an intense pursuit of excellence in athletic performance. Not surprisingly, there has been a concomitant increase in the volume and intensity of exercise training among female athletes of all ages. Increasingly large numbers of females are participating in organized sport and exercise training at much earlier ages, which has raised numerous concerns about the effects of exercise training on pubertal maturation.

Effects of Exercise on Pubertal Development

Although several studies have provided evidence that a later age of menarche is associated with intensive exercise training, it is still unclear whether other specific events of puberty are affected. A primary issue to be addressed when reviewing the published investigations on this topic is the semantic difference between the expressions "delayed puberty" and "later age of puberty." Studies of exercising adolescents reported a later age of some pubertal events; however, these studies have not been able to clearly establish whether this difference represents a trend toward sports participation by "late"-maturing girls or whether exercise produces a "delay" in the appearance and progression of pubertal events (Malina, 1983; Peltenburg et al., 1984; Warren, 1980).

As previously described, the increase in adrenal androgens is the initial physiological change associated with puberty. In an attempt to determine whether adrenarche is affected by exercise training, investigators compared dehydroepiandrosterone-sulfate (DHEA-S) levels in female gymnasts and age-matched untrained girls and found that the physiological increase in DHEA-S levels was delayed about 1.5 years in the gymnasts (Brisson et al., 1983). Peltenburg et al. (1984) did not find any difference in DHEA-S levels between female gymnasts and swimmers and concluded that adrenarche occurs at a similar age in these two trained groups. In relation to pubarche, as assessed by the age of appearance and development of pubic hair, researchers found that exercising and nonexercising girls had parallel pubarcheal development (Warren, 1980; Plowman et al., 1991). In contrast, other investigators reported a lower pubic hair maturation stage in female gymnasts than in swimmers or controls (Peltenburg et al., 1984). Thus the onset of adrenarche in athletic girls may occur an average of 1 to 1.5 years later when compared to untrained girls, and these effects are independent of the mode of exercise training (Brisson et al., 1983; Peltenburg et al., 1984). However, the physical manifestation of adrenal androgen activity, pubarche, is unaltered in exercising girls (Warren, 1980; Plowman et al., 1991).

There are contradictory data regarding the timing of thelarche, breast development, in trained adolescent girls. Some investigators reported less maturity in breast development of female gymnasts and ballet dancers compared to swimmers and controls (Peltenburg et al., 1984; Warren, 1980). In contrast, other authors have found either no delay in breast development (Plowman et al., 1991) or a stimulatory effect of exercise training on breast development (Bar-Or, 1975).

Menarche, considered the culmination of events during the pubertal process and indicative of the advanced maturation state of the reproductive system, is the pubertal event most extensively studied in trained adolescents. Whereas early findings suggested that menarche in athletes occurs at the same age as or earlier than in sedentary girls, more recent data indicate that menarche occurs at a later age in exercising girls (Malina, 1983). Moreover, a later age of menarche has been reported in exercising girls of several different national origins participating in various sport activities (Malina et al., 1979; Malina, 1983; Mokha & Sidhu, 1989). Table 13.2 shows the age of menarche in adolescent girls from different exercising populations. Not only does exercise training appear to result in a later age of menarche in adolescents, but also it is interesting to note that the age of menarche seems to be directly related to the competitive level and years of intensive training prior to menarche (Malina et al., 1978; Mokha & Sidhu, 1989).

Table 13.2   Age of Menarche in Different Athletic Populations

Population	Age of menarche (years)
Sedentary controls	12.7
High school athletes	13.1
College athletes	13.0
Olympic athletes	13.7
Ballet dancers	15.4
Athletes trained before menarche	15.0
Athletes trained after menarche	12.6

Two models have been proposed to explain the later age of menarche in athletes. The first model is the theory proposed by Frisch and colleagues (discussed in detail later), who attempted to identify a minimal weight and body fat as critical requirements for the onset of menstruation (Frisch & McArthur, 1974; Frisch & Revelle, 1970, 1971a, 1971b). Applying this theoretical model to exercising adolescents, Frisch and McArthur (1974) suggested that intense exercise training delays menarche by decreasing body fat and the fat/lean ratio. Although it is clear that exercise training during adolescence results in changes in body composition and most likely in a later age of menarche, these two factors may be independent and unrelated. For this reason, the appearance of menarche associated with a specific or minimal percentage of body fat in these trained girls may be purely coincidental.

The second model is the two-part hypothesis proposed by Malina (1983) that excludes physical activity as a delaying factor for menarche. Malina (1983) proposed inherited "physique" as the first factor explaining the later age of menarche in exercise-trained girls. In other words, athletes are already genetically predisposed to be late maturers, which is a physical advantage for success in sports and athletic competition. The second factor is called the "socialization process," in which late maturers tend to be socially involved in sports because of their "biological lateness." Predisposition to a somatotype or physique appropriate for sports performance and a slower maturation process will direct these girls toward sports involvement. These two theories were helpful because they identified physiological and psychosocial data associated with the later age of menarche in athletes; however, both models appear incomplete in their approach to this issue.

There is little data on the occurrence of menstrual irregularities in adolescents during the years immediately after menarche. Märker (1981) studied the immediate postmenarcheal years in exercising adolescents and did not observe a menstrual dysfunction attributable to intensive prepubescent exercise training. Bonen et al. (1981), however, did find a higher incidence of anovulatory menstrual cycles in trained girls associated with a hormone profile that differed significantly from that of controls. The trained adolescents had lower FSH concentrations and lower FSH/LH ratios during the follicular phase than nonexercising adolescents, changes that result in inadequate follicular maturation and anovulatory cycles (Bonen et al., 1981). It is unknown whether these altered hormonal profiles and menstrual cycle characteristics of exercising adolescents early in the postmenarcheal years are related to a higher prevalence of shortened luteal phase lengths, anovulatory cycles, oligomenorrhea, exercise-induced amenorrhea, and infertility later in life.

Prevalence of Exercise-Induced Amenorrhea

Exercise-induced amenorrhea has been observed in a wide variety of activities, particularly long-distance running and ballet dancing (Abraham et al., 1982; Calabrese et al., 1983; Cohen et al., 1982; Dale et al., 1979; Sanborn et al., 1982;

Shangold & Levine, 1982; Wakat et al., 1982). Ballet dancers tend to display a consistently high prevalence rate (37% to 44%) of amenorrhea (Abraham et al., 1982; Calabrese et al., 1983; Cohen et al., 1982), whereas runners tend to display a more varied and lower prevalence rate (6% to 26%) (Dale et al., 1979; Sanborn et al., 1982; Shangold et al., 1982; Wakat et al., 1982). Table 13.3 displays the prevalence rate of exercise-induced amenorrhea in a wide variety of sports.

In general, the prevalence of exercise-induced amenorrhea varies from 1% to 44% depending on the definition of amenorrhea, the chronological and gynecological ages of the subjects, the sport and training history of the athlete, and the methods of data collection. It has been suggested that younger athletes who train very intensively and have an immature H-P-O axis experience exercise-induced amenorrhea more frequently than do older athletes with a more advanced gynecological age and a more mature H-P-O axis (Loucks & Horvath, 1985). Exercise-induced amenorrhea also tends to be most prevalent among athletes who have a history of menstrual irregularity prior to the initiation of a strenuous exercise training program (Frisch et al., 1981; Shangold &

Table 13.3   Prevalence of Athletic Amenorrhea

	N	% Amenorrheic	Criteria used for amenorrhea
Runners			
Dale et al. (1979)	90	46.0	Not defined
Feicht et al. (1978)	127	24.0	< 3 cycles/year
Sanborn et al. (1982)	237	25.7	< 3 cycles/year
Shangold et al. (1982)	393	6.0	< 1 cycle/10 months
Wakat et al. (1982)	41	5.0	> 6 months
Ballet dancers			
Abraham et al. (1982)	29	38.0	> 6 months
Calabrese et al. (1983)	34	44.0	> 3 months
Cohen et al. (1982)	32	37.0	> 3 months
Swimmers			
Sanborn et al. (1982)	197	12.3	< 3 cycles/year

Levine, 1982). There also appears to be an association between exercise-induced amenorrhea and exercise intensity. In fact, the incidence of exercise-induced amenorrhea tends to be highest among athletes who abruptly increase exercise volume and intensity during training (Bullen et al., 1985).

Factors Associated With Exercise-Induced Amenorrhea

Survey data have been helpful in assisting exercise scientists to identify possible factors associated with the occurrence of exercise-induced amenorrhea, the most extreme form of exercise-induced menstrual dysfunction. These factors include decreased body fat, weight loss, nutritional deficits in the diet, psychological stress, history of menstrual cycle irregularity, age of menarche, volume and intensity of training, and the rate at which exercise volume and intensity are increased. Figure 13.5 displays several intervening factors that may alter menstrual cycle regularity in female athletes.

Body Composition Factors— The "Critical Fat" Hypothesis

The most popular hypothesis proposed to explain exercise-induced menstrual irregularity is that the loss of body weight and, more precisely, body fat, causes amenorrhea in athletes (Frisch & McArthur, 1974; Frisch & Revelle, 1970, 1971a, 1971b). The major advocate of this theory is Frisch, who studied the relationships among body weight, body fat, and menstrual function (Frisch & McArthur, 1974). Frisch's work concluded that: (a) a female must weigh a minimum of 48 kg for menarche to occur, regardless of her height and age; (b) a minimum of 17% body fat is necessary for the onset of menarche; and (c) a minimum of 22% body fat is necessary for the maintenance of regular menstrual cycles (Frisch & McArthur, 1974; Frisch & Revelle, 1970, 1971a, 1971b).

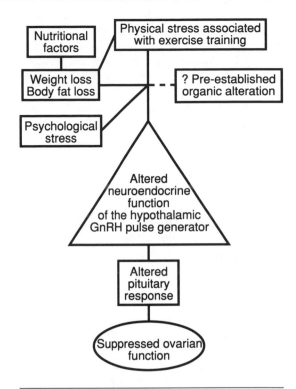

Figure 13.5 Factors thought to act synergistically to cause exercise-induced menstrual perturbations. Reprinted from De Souza, Arce, and Nulsen (1992).

Although these theories are conceptually attractive, many researchers have challenged them because they fail to hold true when applied to different populations. In addition, the equations that were used to develop these theories have statistical errors (Reeves, 1979; Trussell, 1980).

Frisch's conclusions regarding the critical fat hypothesis were extended to the assumption that a female will undergo menarche when 17% body fat is achieved and will experience amenorrhea if her body fat falls below 22%. Several researchers, however, have observed regular menstrual cycles in female athletes with less than 17% body fat (Carlberg et al., 1983; De Souza et al., 1987; McArthur et al., 1980; Sanborn et al., 1987). De Souza et al. (1987) observed that 56% of eumenorrheic runners had less than 22% body fat. In addition, Sanborn et al. (1982) found that amenorrheic and eumenorrheic runners had similar body fat percentages of 17%. Moreover, Warren (1980) observed that amenorrheic ballet dancers resumed menses when injured without any gain in body weight or body fat.

Aside from the above observations, there are intrinsic errors in the development of the critical fat hypothesis that make Frisch's conclusions somewhat tenuous. First, Frisch and colleagues did not perform direct measurements of body fat; rather, they made indirect estimates of body fat derived from height and weight equations that were used to predict total body water and percentiles of fatness (Mellits & Cheek, 1970). Second, the regression equation used was devised by Mellits and Cheek (1970) and has been invalidated as an estimate of fatness in athletic women because it grossly overestimates fatness in lean female athletes (Loucks et al., 1984). Third, Trussell (1980) has pointed out that many of the mathematical assumptions derived from the equations used were not statistically appropriate. For these reasons, factors in addition to body composition must be considered when studying exercise-induced amenorrhea.

Nutritional and Dietary Factors

Key factors that may contribute to altered menstrual status in athletes are inadequacies in diet and nutrition. Low caloric intake, inadequate supply of nutrients, and high energy expenditure may play a significant role in the alteration of menstrual cyclicity and may contribute to the development of exercise-induced amenorrhea (Calabrese et al., 1983; Carlberg et al., 1983; Drinkwater et al., 1984; Loosli et al., 1985; Marcus et al., 1985; Nelson et al., 1986; Wilmore et al., 1992). The "energy drain" concept introduced by Warren (1980) addresses a potential mechanism by which an imbalance between elevated energy expenditure and inadequate energy intake may modify the endocrine status of some athletes, resulting in menstrual dysfunction.

Anovulation and amenorrhea may occur in athletes with intense metabolic energy demands that are not adequately maintained by caloric intake. Several investigators have reported that amenorrheic athletes consume fewer calories than their energy utilization demands (Drinkwater et al. 1984; Deuster et al., 1986; Loosli et al., 1985; Marcus et al., 1985; Mulligan & Butterfield, 1990; Myerson et al., 1991; Nelson et al., 1986; Wilmore et al., 1992). Moreover, several groups have reported that amenorrheic athletes consume fewer calories than eumenorrheic athletes (Drinkwater et al., 1984; Deuster et al., 1986; Loosli et al., 1985; Marcus et al., 1985; Mulligan & Butterfield, 1990; Myerson et al., 1991; Nelson et al., 1986; Wilmore et al., 1992). Table 13.4 displays the results of several studies regarding caloric intake of amenorrheic and eumenorrheic athletes.

When considering other components of energy balance (i.e., resting metabolic rate, thermic effect of a meal, energy expenditure during exercise), Myerson et al. (1991) found that resting metabolic rate was significantly lower in amenorrheic athletes compared to eumenorrheic athletes and sedentary controls. No other differences in the energy balance equation were observed between amenorrheic and eumenorrheic athletes. These authors suggest that a lower resting metabolic rate is probably part of an adaptation process intended to maintain body weight and conserve energy in the face of high caloric expenditure that is not compensated for by caloric intake. Thus it is possible that amenorrheic runners adjust metabolically (decreased resting metabolic rate) to their exceptional energy demand in an effort to conserve energy stores (Mulligan & Butterfield, 1990; Wilmore et al., 1992).

This issue is further complicated by the high incidence of eating disorders observed among athletes (Crago et al., 1985; Wilmore, 1988; Yates et al., 1983). It has been well established that dieting (restrictive eating) and eating disorders, such as anorexia nervosa and bulimia, can have significant adverse effects on menstrual function, independent of exercise training. Eating disorders affect menstrual function by a hypothalamic mechanism somewhat similar to that which occurs

Table 13.4 Summary of Caloric Intakes (kcal/day) Among Amenorrheic Runners, Eumenorrheic Runners, and Eumenorrheic Controls

Reference	Amenorrheic or oligomenorrheic runners	Eumenorrheic runners	Eumenorrheic controls
Deuster et al. (1986)	2,151	2,489	
Drinkwater et al. (1984)	1,623	1,965	
Kaiserauer et al. (1989)	1,582	2,490	1,688
Marcus et al. (1985)	1,272	1,715	
Mulligan et al. (1990)		1,980	1,740
Myerson et al. (1991)	1,730	1,934	1,776
Nelson et al. (1986)	1,730	2,250	
Wilmore et al. (1992)	1,781	1,690	1,763

in exercise-induced amenorrhea (De Souza & Metzger, 1991). Coaches and teachers should note that any assessment of the amenorrheic athlete must include questions to help determine the presence of an eating disorder. This information will help in evaluating the relative contribution of these dietary factors and eating disorders to menstrual dysfunction.

In summary, most data at the present time point to several factors acting together or synergistically that lead to exercise-induced amenorrhea. One issue that is often overlooked but is essential to consider is that women may differ in their sensitivity to the precipitating events depicted in Figure 13.5. Some women may require the involvement of several factors to alter menstrual function, whereas other women may develop amenorrhea with a single stressor. The existence of individual variability makes the study of exercise-induced menstrual disorders difficult and demonstrates the need for strict and well-controlled techniques.

The H-P-O Axis in Exercise-Induced Amenorrhea

To determine the etiology of menstrual disorders in athletes, it is necessary to make a complete evaluation of the functional status of each gland of the H-P-O axis. Establishing the endocrine activity of the ovary, pituitary, and hypothalamus enables researchers to identify the locus of disturbance in exercise-induced menstrual disturbances. In this section we will review the reproductive hormone profile of amenorrheic athletes, beginning with a description of ovarian steroid levels, continuing with the characteristics of gonadotropin secretion, and concluding with an indirect evaluation of the activity of the hypothalamic GnRH pulse generator.

The Ovary

Initial interest in determining the etiology of exercise-induced amenorrhea was directed to the analysis of the functional status of the ovary. Estradiol and progesterone, the two major hormones produced by the ovary, are significantly decreased in amenorrheic athletes (De Souza et al., 1991, 1992; Loucks et al., 1989; Shangold et al., 1979). Similarly, the absence of menstrual cycle phase-related changes in ovarian steroid concentrations indicates that the ovary in amenorrheic athletes is functioning at a minimal activity level, similar to that observed prior to puberty (Loucks et al., 1989). To demonstrate this effect, Loucks et al.

(1989) collected daily samples of the urinary metabolites of estrogen and progesterone (estrone-glucuronide and pregnanediol-glucuronide) during one complete menstrual cycle and found that the urinary excretion of estrogen and progesterone in the amenorrheic athletes was much lower than in the eumenorrheic athletes and controls. The pattern of excretion was relatively flat and without any of the expected menstrual phase-related fluctuations in the amenorrheic athletes. Moreover, the mean level of ovarian steroid production was significantly lower than in sedentary controls. Figure 13.6 displays the levels of the urinary metabolites of estrogen and progesterone (estrone-glucuronide and pregnanediol-glucuronide) during one complete menstrual cycle (or 30 consecutive days) in amenorrheic athletes, eumenorrheic athletes, and controls. These data clearly show that the production of the ovarian steroids in amenorrheic athletes is minimal and is a direct indicator of inadequate follicular and luteal development.

The Pituitary

Now that it is established that ovarian function is suppressed, the next question to be addressed is: Why? Is it because of intrinsic ovarian failure to produce the steroids, or is it a direct consequence

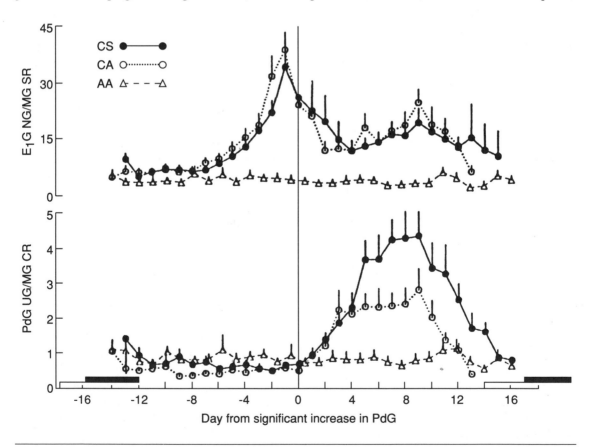

Figure 13.6   The monthly urinary pattern of estrone-glucuronide and pregnanediol-glucoronide in amenorrheic athletes (AA), eumenorrheic athletes (CA), and sedentary controls (CS). Reprinted from Loucks, Mortola, Girton, and Yen (1989).

of inadequate stimulation of the ovaries by the pituitary? To answer this question, it is necessary to evaluate the functional status of the pituitary, that is, the pulsatility characteristics (amplitude and frequency) of pituitary gonadotropin secretion. The accurate determination of gonadotropin (LH and FSH) pulsatility requires 24-hour serial sampling. Single serum samples are inadequate for determining the resting levels of gonadotropins, as well as the presence or absence of pulses that normally occur every 60 to 120 minutes. Twenty-four-hour serial sampling techniques have permitted scientists to accurately establish the resting levels of LH and FSH, as well as the pulsatility characteristics (amplitude and frequency of release) in amenorrheic athletes (Loucks et al., 1989; Veldhuis et al., 1985).

In amenorrheic athletes, the resting levels of LH and FSH are low or within the lower normal range. These low LH and FSH levels are comparable to those of eumenorrheic athletes during the early follicular phase and during puberty (Loucks et al., 1989; Veldhuis et al., 1985). The 24-hour LH secretory pattern in the amenorrheic athlete is erratic (Veldhuis et al., 1985; Loucks et al., 1989). In other words, LH pulse frequency is reduced and there is no distinct pattern to the timing of the few pulses that are observed in amenorrheic athletes (Loucks et al., 1989; Veldhuis et al., 1985). Moreover, some amenorrheic athletes have LH pulses in the waking hours, whereas other amenorrheic athletes have LH pulses in the evening or sleeping hours, a pattern that is very similar to the LH pulse pattern observed during puberty. Figure 13.7 displays the 24-hour pulsatility pattern of LH in two amenorrheic athletes, one eumenorrheic athlete, and one sedentary control.

The Hypothalamus

Because pituitary LH pulsatility is a direct expression of the hypothalamic GnRH pulse generator activity, the question remains whether decreased LH pulse frequency is attributable to a

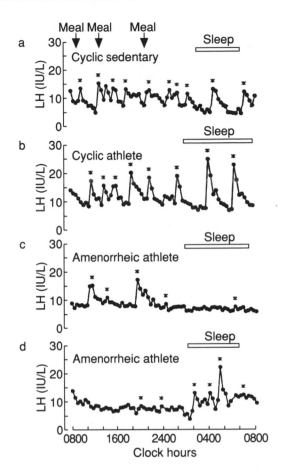

Figure 13.7   Different patterns of LH pulsatility (mean + SE) in (a) eumenorrheic controls, (b) eumenorrheic athletes, and (c and d) amenorrheic athletes. Plasma LH concentrations were obtained every 20 minutes for 24 hours. Reprinted from Loucks, Mortola, Girton, and Yen (1989).

defect in pituitary function or to a defect in hypothalamic function, that is, inadequate hypothalamic GnRH pulse stimulation to the pituitary. The studies by Veldhuis et al. (1985) and Loucks et al. (1989) addressed this issue by administering exogenous GnRH and measuring the subsequent release of LH. These studies demonstrated that pituitary responses to exogenous GnRH in amenorrheic athletes not only were adequate, but were exaggerated above the response observed for the eumenorrheic groups.

The reduced LH pulsatility in amenorrheic athletes thus is attributable to decreased activity of the hypothalamic GnRH pulse generator, rather than to decreased pituitary responsiveness to GnRH. These data suggest that the etiology of exercise-induced amenorrhea resides in the hypothalamus or in the higher brain centers that modulate hypothalamic activity.

Potential Mechanisms Involved in the Etiology of Exercise-Induced Amenorrhea

Several hypotheses have been proposed as contributing mechanisms in the etiology of exercise-induced amenorrhea. The proposed mechanisms are

1. a prolactin hypothesis,
2. an endogenous opioid hypothesis,
3. a neurotransmitter/neuromodulator hypothesis, and
4. an adrenal hypothesis.

The Prolactin Hypothesis

The prolactin hypothesis is based on the fact that prolactin produced in excessive amounts can cause amenorrhea. During acute exercise, elevated prolactin concentrations may result in transitory hyperprolactinemia that may cause amenorrhea (Boyden et al., 1982; Brisson et al., 1980).

Two primary findings in the literature prompted researchers to hypothesize that prolactin may be involved in the mechanism of exercise-induced amenorrhea. First, prolactin, produced by the lactotropic cells of the anterior pituitary, can cause amenorrhea when secreted in excessive amounts (Speroff et al., 1983). During acute exercise, increases in prolactin levels occur in a transitory fashion and may cause hyperprolactinemia that

results in amenorrhea (Boyden et al., 1982; Brisson et al., 1980). Second, elevated prolactin levels can be associated with inadequate secretion of progesterone during the luteal phase and, if prolactin levels are maintained high enough, can result in amenorrhea (Speroff et al., 1983).

Although the above observations form an attractive hypothesis, data fail to demonstrate an association between exercise-induced amenorrhea and the prolactin response to exercise. In fact, eumenorrheic runners demonstrate marked increases in prolactin after exercise (Boyden et al., 1982; Brisson et al., 1980; Shangold et al., 1979), whereas amenorrheic athletes have severely depressed prolactin levels both at rest and in response to exercise (De Souza et al., 1991; Loucks & Horvath, 1985).

The diminished prolactin levels in amenorrheic runners are attributed to the extreme ovarian suppression and hypoestrogenism associated with high-intensity endurance training. Because estrogen has been found to promote both the synthesis and release of prolactin by the pituitary (Yen et al., 1974), it is understandable that normal prolactin responses may be attenuated in the presence of a hypoestrogenic state, yet not be the cause of exercise-induced amenorrhea.

The Endogenous Opioid Hypothesis

Because the available data on exercise-induced amenorrhea indicate that the level of endocrine dysfunction resides in the hypothalamus and that exercise training may elevate the level of some endogenous opioid peptides, many investigations have focused on an opioid hypothesis to explain the etiology of exercise-induced amenorrhea.

Several findings suggest that the endogenous opioids have an inhibitory effect on GnRH release from the hypothalamus and consequently on LH pulsatility from the pituitary. The proposed opioid mechanism operational in exercise-induced amenorrhea is based on the inhibitory actions of the endogenous opioid peptides on the GnRH-releasing neurons, which result in decreased activity of the GnRH pulse generator and decreased LH pulsatility. The opioid hypothesis proposes that elevated levels of opioids that occur in response to exercise may modify the activity of the hypothalamic pulse generator by inhibiting LH pulsatility, thus resulting in amenorrhea.

To understand this hypothesis, it is necessary to review briefly the endogenous opioid peptides and, more specifically, β-endorphin, which is one of several components of the endogenous opioid peptide system (Facchinetti et al., 1987). Circulating or peripheral levels of β-endorphin are regulated independently from hypothalamic or central levels of β-endorphin. Peripheral β-endorphin is synthesized in the corticotropic cells of the anterior pituitary as part of a large precursor molecule called proopiomelanocortin, from which adrenocorticotropin (ACTH) is also synthesized. As a result, measurements of peripheral β-endorphin levels actually reflect corelease with ACTH in contrast to hypothalamic or central β-endorphin release that is associated with stressful events (Thoren et al., 1990). Furthermore, the reliability of the assays used to measure this peptide may be limited by the high cross-reactivity of β-endorphin assays with other opioid peptides, particularly β-lipotropin (McArthur, 1985). For more extensive reviews of opioid peptide physiology and exercise, refer to reviews by McArthur (1985) and Thoren et al. (1990).

Circulating levels of β-endorphins are increased as a result of acute exercise in both men and women (Farrell et al., 1982; Goldfarb et al., 1987). Moreover, Russell et al. (1984) were able to identify an elevation in the resting level of peripheral β-endorphin after 2 years of intensive exercise training in female competitive swimmers. These data provide preliminary evidence that long-term exercise training may result in elevated β-endorphin levels in some athletes.

The question that logically follows is: Do amenorrheic athletes have elevated resting levels of β-endorphin? To our knowledge, only two reports are available that identify higher resting levels of peripheral β-endorphin in amenorrheic athletes compared with eumenorrheic athletes and sedentary controls (Hothari et al., 1988; Laatikainen et al., 1986). Unfortunately, these results do not establish a cause-effect relationship between exercise-induced amenorrhea and endogenous opioids because of the inherent limitations of measurement techniques. As previously noted, peripheral levels of β-endorphin do not accurately reflect hypothalamic or central β-endorphin content associated with stressful stimuli (Thoren et al., 1990).

Infusion of an opioid antagonist increases the circulating LH levels in women with hypothalamic amenorrhea, thus demonstrating the inhibitory effects of opioids on the hypothalamic GnRH pulse generator. The administration of naloxone, an opioid antagonist, produces inconsistent alterations in LH pulsatility in amenorrheic athletes. Only 60% of these women exhibit an increase in LH pulse frequency after naloxone infusion (responders), whereas the other 40% of amenorrheic athletes exhibit no change in LH pulse frequency (nonresponders) (Dixon et al., 1984; McArthur et al., 1980; Russell et al., 1989; Szabo et al., 1987). Table 13.5 summarizes the LH responses to naloxone from several different studies of amenorrheic athletes.

If increased opioid activity was the sole mechanism responsible for the inhibition of GnRH activity in exercise-induced amenorrhea, a consistent increase in LH should be observed. Alternatively, the inconsistent response of LH release to naloxone in these studies may be attributable to the varying doses of naloxone administered, the different infusion times, and the subsequent length of the sampling period, all of which may or may not have been adequate.

Given the response of the majority of amenorrheic athletes to naloxone, it appears that opioid peptides may be a contributor to the mechanism of exercise-induced amenorrhea. The results of these studies are intriguing but at the same time emphasize the need for additional well-controlled studies.

Table 13.5 LH Responses to Naloxone Administration

Reference	Subjects	Dose	LH response
Dixon et al. (1980)	7 AR	1.6 mg/hr for 4 hr	7 nonresponders
McArthur et al. (1980)	3 AR	0.4 mg/hr for 8 hr	2 nonresponders
Russell et al. (1989)	4 OR	10 mg bolus	0 nonresponders
Szabo et al. (1987)	28 AA	2.8 mg bolus followed by 2.8 mg/hr for 4 hr	13 nonresponders

Note. AR = amenorrheic runners, OR = oligomenorrheic runners, AA = amenorrheic athletes.

The Neurotransmitter and Neuromodulator Hypothesis

Neurotransmitters, such as dopamine, norepinephrine, GABA, and catechol-estrogen, may participate in the pathophysiological mechanism of altered GnRH activity in exercise-induced amenorrhea. To date, however, few data are available on the involvement of these neurotransmitters in the hypothalamic dysfunction of amenorrheic athletes.

Dopamine antagonists, such as metoclopramide, increase circulating LH levels in some women with hypothalamic amenorrhea, thereby demonstrating the inhibitory effects of dopamine on the hypothalamic GnRH pulse generator (Quigley et al., 1980). Initial attempts to demonstrate a dopaminergic effect via metaclopramide infusion in amenorrheic athletes were unsuccessful, perhaps because of the relatively short infusion period used (4 hours) (Russell et al., 1989). However, after the 24-hour administration of metaclopramide in amenorrheic athletes, a significant increase in LH pulsatility was observed (Loucks, 1990). A dopaminergic mechanism thus appears to play a contributory role in the etiology of exercise-induced amenorrhea and certainly warrants further study.

Catechol-estrogens also have an inhibitory effect on hypothalamic GnRH release (Speroff et al., 1983). It has been suggested that catechol-estrogen formation is also increased in female athletes (Keizer et al., 1987). It is this elevation that is speculated to have a contributory role in the etiology of exercise-induced amenorrhea (Russell et al., 1984); however, the involvement of these and other neuromodulators in the pathogenesis of exercise-induced amenorrhea remains unclear.

The Adrenal Hypothesis

The adrenal hypothesis is based on the finding of mild hypercortisolism in amenorrheic athletes (De Souza et al., 1991; Loucks et al., 1989). Elevated cortisol levels and other adrenal factors can negatively affect reproductive function through inhibitory actions on the H-P-O axis. The mild hypercortisolism observed indicates that an alteration in the hypothalamic-pituitary-adrenal (H-P-A) axis is present that may participate in the reproductive alterations observed in female athletes.

In amenorrheic athletes, resting cortisol levels are elevated and are suggestive of mild hypercortisolism (De Souza et al., 1990; Ding et al., 1988; Loucks et al., 1989). This mild hypercortisolism is not as extreme as the hypercortisolism observed in Cushing's disease (Gold et al., 1986a) but is comparable to what is observed in women with functional hypothalamic amenorrhea (Shu et al., 1988) and anorexia nervosa (Gold et al., 1986b). The mild hypercortisolism is not attributed to a primary hyperfunctional defect of the adrenal cortex (De Souza et al., 1994; Loucks et al., 1989) or increased adrenal sensitivity to

ACTH (De Souza et al., 1994; De Souza et al., 1991).

The elevated cortisol levels in amenorrheic athletes also are not attributable to increased circulating levels of ACTH (De Souza et al., 1994; De Souza et al., 1990; Loucks et al., 1989). Moreover, the 24-hour ACTH pulse frequency and amplitude are also comparable in amenorrheic and eumenorrheic athletes and controls (Loucks et al., 1989). These data suggest that increased pituitary ACTH release is not the cause of the mild hypercortisolism observed; however, pituitary sensitivity may play a role in the etiology of mild hypercortisolism and therefore must be assessed.

Pituitary sensitivity is assessed by administering exogenous corticotropin-releasing hormone (CRH) and measuring the pituitary ACTH responses. In amenorrheic athletes pituitary responsiveness to exogenous CRH is actually decreased, suggestive of pituitary insensitivity to CRH (Loucks et al., 1989). This finding suggests that CRH release may be elevated in amenorrheic athletes and may desensitize the pituitary to stimulation by exogenous CRH (Gold et al., 1986a; Loucks et al., 1989). Within the framework of this proposed mechanism, even more CRH stimulation would be required to release an adequate amount of ACTH (Gold et al., 1986a; Loucks et al., 1989). More recent data, however, suggest that other extrapituitary modulators of adrenal responsiveness to ACTH may in fact be responsible for the mild hypercortisolism observed in amenorrheic athletes (De Souza et al., 1994).

The only study that reported CRH levels did not observe any significant difference in peripheral CRH levels between amenorrheic and eumenorrheic athletes (Hothari et al., 1988). It is prudent to note that the extent to which peripheral measurements of CRH accurately reflect central CRH activity remains unclear.

Prospective Studies

The survey and cross-sectional data presented in the previous sections indicated that (a) amenorrhea and menstrual dysfunction occur in athletes from several exercise modalities, particularly long-distance running and ballet dancing; (b) a relationship exists between the incidence of menstrual dysfunction and a high volume of intensive exercise training; and (c) amenorrheic athletes present with a characteristic reproductive endocrine profile. Thus, even though evidence of an association between exercise and amenorrhea has been shown, the cause-effect relationship between these two variables was not demonstrated until the publication of prospective experimental studies during the last decade by Bullen and co-workers (1985). Even with these data, however, few inferential conclusions can be made because of the abruptly increasing nature of the volume and intensity of the training protocol used by Bullen's group (1985).

Initial experimental studies using a low volume of exercise and a 1-year gradually progressive exercise training regimen in untrained women did not show significant changes in menstrual function (Boyden et al., 1982; Bullen et al., 1984). More intensive and rapidly increasing (over a 2-month period) training regimens, however, did indeed produce perturbations in menstrual function, including follicular and luteal phase deficiencies and anovulation (Bullen et al., 1985). Bullen and co-workers (1985) provide compelling evidence that participation in an intensive and rapidly increasing exercise training program may affect menstrual status. The point should be made that this finding can be applied only to younger athletes. A woman with a more advanced gynecological age and a more robust system may be less perturbed by exercise training, whereas a younger woman with a less mature gynecological age and a less robust system is significantly affected by exercise training.

Responsibility of Coaches Working With Female Athletes

The objective of coaches is to optimize athletes' performance. However, this goal must be accomplished without compromising the health status of female athletes. As we have pointed out, several menstrual alterations appear as a result of *intensive* exercise training, some clinically obvious (amenorrhea) and some less obvious subclinical alterations (luteal phase defects and anovulation). In fact, it has recently been demonstrated that even *recreational* joggers running only 10 to 20 miles per week show some evidence of disturbed folliculogenesis and luteal phase inadequacies (Broocks et al., 1990). Although this study was cross-sectional, it demonstrates that even low-mileage jogging performed in moderation may result in impaired menstrual function in some women. Thus, coaches must be aware of the health ramifications of exercise-induced menstrual disturbances. Two clinically important health consequences are associated with these menstrual abnormalities: infertility and osteoporosis.

As previously noted, exercise training disrupts the H-P-O axis in some female athletes whereby the endpoint is decreased ovarian steroid production and a dramatically increased risk for the development of osteoporosis. Menstrual alterations and anovulatory cycles are a physical manifestation of these decreases in estrogen and progesterone production associated with infertility and osteoporosis. Although infertility associated with exercise-induced menstrual disturbances may be temporary, the decreased bone mineral density associated with exercise-induced menstrual disturbances may be longer lasting. Decreased skeletal integrity may compromise the achievement of peak bone mass at maturity and may place these women at a higher risk for osteoporosis and fractures later in life.

As a result of the health consequences of exercise-induced menstrual disturbances, coaches should be concerned with the gynecological health and menstrual status of their athletes. Coaches must make their athletes aware of these facts and educate them on the importance of identifying menstrual alterations. Periodic evaluations of the female athlete by a physician will help identify both the clinical (amenorrhea) and subclinical (luteal phase defect and anovulatory cycles) pre-sentations of menstrual abnormalities and determine whether an athlete requires assessments of skeletal integrity and or hormone replacement therapy. It is the coaches' responsibility to understand exercise-induced menstrual disturbances, to understand the health consequences of these menstrual alterations, and to understand that these alterations require proper medical attention.

Summary and Conclusions

Exercise has become an important part of the lifestyle of many women and undoubtedly has contributed to improved health for most of these participants. Some highly trained athletes with exercise-induced amenorrhea may actually incur increased risk for decreased bone density and stress fractures. Because of the impact of the ensuing hypoestrogenic state on bone density and cardiovascular health, it is important to understand the etiology of amenorrhea in these women, particularly because not all women at risk are symptomatic.

Few data are available on the effects of exercise in pubertal development. Emphasis in this area has been directed toward menarche, a pubertal event that seems to occur at a later age in exercising girls (Malina, 1983). Scarce and controversial information, however, has been obtained regarding the effects of exercise on sexual maturation. In addition, few data are available on the endocrine profile of exercising girls in the premenarcheal and immediate postmenarcheal years. Future studies need to identify the nature of the relationship between exercise training and pubertal development.

Three major concerns arise when evaluating the literature on exercise training and puberty. First, although menarche is an important landmark and objective milestone in the pubertal development of the reproductive system, it does not guarantee a mature and functional reproductive system. More important, most of the studies assessing the effect of exercise training on puberty have focused on the age of menarche and omitted the other events that occur in the progression of puberty. A more complete description of the physical characteristics of subjects with respect to stage of adrenarche, thelarche, pubarche, menarche, as well as an assessment of skeletal maturity, would help to determine more clearly the effect of exercise training on puberty. Second, few data are available on the hypothalamic, pituitary, ovarian, and adrenal hormone changes in childhood and puberty associated with exercise training. Thus it is unclear whether there is any delay in the maturation of the adrenal and H-P-O axes. Third, controlled prospective experimental designs are necessary to determine the nature of the cause-effect relationship between exercise and pubertal development.

A summary of reproductive function in amenorrheic athletes includes the following points:

- Estradiol and progesterone levels are diminished and indicative of inadequate follicular and luteal development and anovulatory cycles.
- Gonadotropin pulsatility in amenorrheic athletes tends to be diminished with decreased pulse frequency and erratic episodic activity (Loucks et al., 1989); Veldhuis et al., 1985).
- The severity of the alteration in gonadotropin pulsatility is thought to reflect unobserved alterations in GnRH pulsatility.
- Pituitary responsiveness to exogenous GnRH is enhanced, suggesting that the locus of dysfunction in these athletes resides above the pituitary.
- Prolactin levels appear to be normal or low in amenorrheic athletes.

Table 13.6 provides a comparison summary of several hormonal levels in amenorrheic and eumenorrheic athletes.

Because we have an understanding of potential endocrine factors that can interfere with hypothalamic activity, it is interesting to note the apparent adrenal mechanism present. A mild degree of

Table 13.6   Comparative Hormonal Profile Between Amenorrheic and Eumenorrheic Athletes

Hormone	Amenorrheic athletes	Eumenorrheic athletes
Estradiol (luteal phase)	↓↓	=
Progesterone (luteal phase)	↓↓	=
LH (mean)	= or ↓	=
Pulse frequency	↓↓ or ↓ or =	↓ or =
Pulse amplitude	↓ or =	↑
FSH (mean)	= or ↓	=
Prolactin	↓	—
ACTH	=	=
Cortisol	↑↑↑	= or ↑
ß-endorphin	↑	?

hypercortisolism occurs in amenorrheic athletes that is independent of increased adrenal stimulation by ACTH. Another factor that should be considered in the occurrence of exercise-induced amenorrhea is β-endorphin. Endogenous opioids have been shown to inhibit LH activity, whereas opioid antagonists augment LH release in about 60% of amenorrheic athletes. The mechanism involved in altered LH activity in the remaining 40% of these women remains unclear but may still involve β-endorphin and other factors not yet defined. Dopamine also should be studied further to define the relative contribution, if any, this neurotransmitter makes to exercise-induced amenorrhea.

Although much has been done to elucidate the factors that can adversely affect menstrual function in athletes, a significant amount of work remains. Undoubtedly, controversy surrounding the etiology of amenorrhea in athletes will remain until controlled prospective studies are completed that use carefully characterized subjects, well-defined experimental protocols, and state-of-the-art exercise and endocrine techniques that can better define the neuroendocrine mechanism(s) involved in the endocrine basis of exercise-induced amenorrhea. Certainly, future research efforts should focus on the nutritional concerns and energy metabolism factors that may contribute to these exercise-induced menstrual perturbations.

References

Abraham, S.F., Beaumont, P.J.V., Fraser, I.S., & Llewellyn-Jones, D. (1982). Body weight, exercise and menstrual status among ballet dancers in training. *British Journal of Obstetrics and Gynecology*, **89**, 507-510.

Apter, D. (1980). Serum steroids and pituitary hormones in female puberty: A partly longitudinal study. *Clinical Endocrinology*, **12**, 107-120.

Barnes, J. (1980). *Lecture Notes on Gynaecology*. London: Blackwell.

Bar-Or, O. (1975). Predicting athletic performance. *Physician and Sportsmedicine*, **3**, 80-85.

Besser, G.M., & Cudworth, A.G. (1987). *Clinical Endocrinology*. London: Gower.

Bonen, A., Belcastro, A.N., Ling, W., & Simpson, A.A. (1981). Profiles of selected hormones during menstrual cycles of teenage athletes. *Journal of Applied Physiology*, **50**, 545-548.

Borsos, A., Lampe, L.G., Balogh, A., Csoknyay, J., & Ditroi, F. (1986). Ovarian function immediately after the menarche. *International Journal of Gynaecology and Obstetrics*, **24**, 239-242.

Boyden, T.W., Pamenter, R.W., Stanforth, P., Rotkis, T., & Wilmore, J.H. (1982). Sex steroids and endurance running in women. *Fertility & Sterility*, **39**, 629-632.

Boyden, T.W., Pamenter, R.W., Grosso, D., Stanforth, P., Rotkis, T., & Wilmore, J.H. (1982). Prolactin responses, menstrual cycles, and body composition of women runners. *Journal of Clinical Endocrinology and Metabolism*, **54**, 711-716.

Brisson, G.R., Ledoux, M., Dulac, S., & Peronnet, F. (1983). Dysadrenarche as a possible explanation for delayed onset of menarche in gymnasts. In H.G. Knutgen et al. (Eds.), *Biochemistry of Exercise* (pp. 631-636). Champaign, IL: Human Kinetics.

Brisson, G.R., Volle, M.A., DeCarufel, D., Desharnais, M., & Tanaka, M. (1980). Exercise-induced dissociation of the blood prolactin response in young women according to their sports habits. *Hormone Metabolism Research*, **12**, 201-205.

Broocks, A., Pirke, K.M., Schweiger, U., Tuschl, R.J., Laessle, R.G., Strowitzki, T., Horl, E., Horl, T., Haas, W., & Jeschke, D. (1990). Cyclic ovarian function in recreational athletes. *Journal of Applied Physiology*, **68**, 2083-2086.

Brooks-Gunn, J., & Warren, M.P. (1988). Mother-daughter differences in menarcheal age in adolescent girls attending national dance company schools and non-dancers. *Annals of Human Biology*, **15**, 35-44.

Bullen, B.A., Skrinar, G.S., Beitins, I.Z., Carr, D.B., Reppert, S.M., Dotson, C.O., Fencl, M.M., Gervino, E.V., & McArthur, J.W. (1984). Endurance training effects on plasma hormonal responsiveness and sex hormone excretion. *Journal of Applied Physiology: Respiratory Environmental and Exercise Physiology*, **56**, 1453-1463.

Bullen, B.A., Skrinar, G.S., Beitins, I.Z., Von Mering, G., Turnbull, B.A., & McArthur, J.W. (1985). Induction of menstrual disorders by strenuous exercise in untrained women. *New England Journal of Medicine*, **312**, 1349-1353.

Calabrese, L.H., Kirkendall, D.T., Floyd, M., Rapoport, S., Williams, G.W., Weiker, G.G., & Bergfeld, J.A. (1983). Menstrual abnormalities, nutritional patterns, and body composition in female classical ballet dancers. *Physician and Sportsmedicine*, **11**, 86-98.

Carlberg, K.A., Buckman, M.T., Peake, G.T., & Riedesel, M.L. (1983). Body composition of oligo/amenorrheic athletes. *Medicine and Science in Sports and Exercise*, **15**, 215-217.

Cohen, J.L., Kim, C.S., May, P.B., Jr., & Etrel, N.H. (1982). Exercise, body weight, and professional ballet dancers. *Physician and Sportsmedicine*, **10**, 92-101.

Crago, M., Yates, A., Beutler, L.E., & Arizmendi, T.G. (1985). Height-weight ratios among female athletes: Are collegiate athletics the precursors to an anorexic syndrome? *International Journal of Eating Disorders*, **4**, 79-87.

Cumming, D.C., Viekovic, M.M., Wall, S.R., & Fluker, M.R. (1985). Defects in pulsatile LH release in normally menstruating runners. *Journal of Clinical Endocrinology and Metabolism*, **60**, 810-812.

Dale, E., Gerlach, D.H., & Wilhite, A.L. (1979). Menstrual dysfunction in distance runners. *Obstetrics & Gynecology*, **54**, 47-53.

De Souza, M.J., Arce, J.C., & Nulsen, J.C. (1992). Effects of exercise training on sex steroids: Endocrine profile and clinical implications. *Infertility and Reproductive Medicine Clinics of North America*, **3**, 129-148.

De Souza, M.J., Luciano, A.A., Arce, J.C., Demers, L.J., & Loucks, A.B. (1994). Clinical tests explain blunted cortisol responsiveness but not mild hypercortisolism in amenorrheic runners. *Journal of Applied Physiology*, **76**(3), 1302-1309.

De Souza, M.J., Maguire, M.S., Maresh, C.M. Kraemer, W.J., Rubin, K.R., & Loucks, A.B. (1991). Adrenal activation mediates the prolactin response to exercise in eumenorrheic and amenorrheic runners. *Journal of Applied Physiology*, **70**, 2378-2387.

De Souza, M.J., Maresh, C.M., Abraham, A., & Camaione, D.N. (1987). Body compositions of eumenorrheic, oligomenorrheic, and amenorrheic runners. *Journal of Applied Sports Sciences Research*, **2**, 13-15.

De Souza, M.J., & Metzger, D.A. (1991). Reproductive dysfunction in amenorrheic athletes and anorexic patients. *Medicine and Science in Sports and Exercise*, **23**, 995-1007.

Deuster, P.A., Kyle, S.B., Moser, P.B., Vigersky, R.A., Singh, A., Schoomaker, E.B. (1986). Nutritional intakes and status of highly trained amenorrheic and eumenorrheic women runners. *Fertility and Sterility*, **46**, 636-643.

Ding, J.J., Sheckter, C.B., Drinkwater, B.L., Soules, M.R., & Bremmer, W.J. (1988). High serum cortisol levels in exercise-associated amenorrhea. *Annals of Internal Medicine*, **108**, 530-534.

Dixon, G., Eurman, P., Stern, B., Schwartz, B., & Rebar, R.W. (1984). Hypothalamic function in amenorrheic runners. *Fertility & Sterility*, **42**, 377-383.

Drinkwater, B.L., Nilson, K., Chestnut, C.H., III, Bremner, W.J., Shainholtz, S., & Southworth, M.D. (1984). Bone mineral content of amenorrheic and eumenorrheic athletes. *New England Journal of Medicine*, **311**, 277-281.

Ducharme, J.R., Forest, M., De Peretti, E., Sempe, M., Collu, R., & Bertrand, J. (1976). Plasma adrenal and gonadal steroids in human pubertal development. *Journal of Clinical Endocrinology and Metabolism*, **42**, 468-476.

Facchinetti, F., Petraglia, F., & Genazzani, A.R. (1987). Localization and expression of the three opioid systems. *Seminars in Reproductive Endocrinology*, **5**, 103-113.

Farrell, P.A., Gates, W.K., Maksud, M.G., & Morgan, W.P. (1982). Increase in plasma β-endorphin/β-lipotropin immunoreactivity after treadmill running in humans. *Journal of Applied Physiology: Respiratory, Environmental and Exercise Physiology*, **52**, 1245-1249.

Frisch, R.E., Gotz-Welbergen, A.B., McArthur, J.W., Albright, T., Witschi, J., Bullen, B.,

Birnholz, J., Reed, R.B., & Hermann, H. (1981). Delayed menarche and amenorrhea of college athletes in relation to age of onset of training. *Journal of the American Medical Association*, **246**, 1559-1563.

Frisch, R.E., & McArthur, J.W. (1974). Menstrual cycles: Fatness as a determinant of minimum weight for height necessary for their maintenance or onset. *Science*, **185**, 949-951.

Frisch, R.E., & Revelle, R. (1970). Height and weight at menarche and a hypothesis of critical body weights and adolescent events. *Science*, **169**, 397-399.

Frisch, R.E., & Revelle, R. (1971a). The height and weight of girls and boys at the time of initiation of the adolescent growth spurt in height and weight and the relationship to menarche. *Human Biology*, **43**, 140-159.

Frisch, R.E., & Revelle, R. (1971b). Height and weight at menarche and a hypothesis of menarche. *Archives of Disease in Childhood*, **46**, 695-701.

Frisch, R.E., Wyshak, G., & Vincent, L. (1980). Delayed menarche and amenorrhea in ballet dancers. *New England Journal of Medicine*, **307**, 17-19.

Gold, P.W., Loriaux, D.L., Ray, A., Kling, M.A., Calabrese, J.R., Kellner, C.H., Nieman, L.K., Post, R.M., Pickar, D., Gallucci, W., Avgerinos, P., Paul, S., Oldfield, E.H., Cutler, G.B., Jr., & Chrousos, G.P. (1986a). Responses to corticotropin-releasing hormone in the hypercortisolism of depression and Cushing's disease. *New England Journal of Medicine*, **314**, 1329-1335.

Gold, P.W., Gwirtswan, H., Avgerinos, P.C., Nieman, L.K., Gallucci, W.T., Kaye, W., Jimerson, D., Ebert, M., Rittmaster, R., Loriaux, D.L., & Chrousos, G.P. (1986b). Abnormal hypothalamic-pituitary-adrenal function in anorexia nervosa. *New England Journal of Medicine*, **314**, 1335-1342.

Goldfarb, A.H., Hatfield, B.D., Sforzo, G.A., & Flynn, M.G. (1987). Serum β-endorphin levels during a graded exercise test to exhaustion. *Medicine and Science in Sports and Exercise*, **19**, 78-82.

Hothari, H., Elovainio, R., Salminen, K., & Laatikainen, T. (1988). Plasma corticotropin-releasing hormone, corticotropin, and endorphins at rest and during exercise in eumenorrheic and amenorrheic athletes. *Fertility and Sterility*, **50**, 233-238.

Keizer, H.A., Kuipers, H., De Haan, J., Beckers, E., & Habets, L. (1987). Multiple hormonal responses to physical exercise in eumenorrheic trained and untrained women. *International Journal of Sports Medicine*, **8**, 139-150.

Laatikainen, T., Virtanen, T., & Apter, D. (1986). Plasma immunoreactive β-endorphin in exercise-associated amenorrhea. *American Journal of Obstetrics and Gynecology*, **154**, 94-97.

Lamon-Fava, S., Fisher, E.C., Nelson, M.E., Evans, W.J., Millar, J.S., Ordovas, J.M., Schaefer, E.J. (1989). Effect of exercise and menstrual cycle status on plasma lipids, low density lipoprotein particle size and apolipoproteins. *Journal of Clinical Endocrinology and Metabolism*, **68**, 17-21.

Loosli, A.R., Gillien, D.M., Benson, J., & Bourdet, K. (1985). Inadequate nutrition and chronic caloric restriction among ballet dancers. *Medicine and Science in Sports and Exercise*, **17**, 201.

Loucks, A.B. (1990). Effects of exercise training on the menstrual cycle: Existence and mechanisms. *Medicine and Science in Sports and Exercise*, **22**, 275-280.

Loucks, A.B., Girton, L., Mortola, J., & Yen, S.S.C. (1991). Effect of opioidergic and dopaminergic blockade on LH pulsatility in athletic women. *Medicine and Science in Sports and Exercise*, **23** (Suppl. 4), S123.

Loucks, A.B., & Horvath, S.M. (1985). Athletic amenorrhea: A review. *Medicine and Science in Sports and Exercise*, **17**, 56-72.

Loucks, A.B., Horvath, S.M., & Freedson, P.S. (1984). Menstrual status and validation of body fat prediction in athletes. *Human Biology*, **56**, 383-392.

Loucks, A.B., Mortola, J.F., Girton, L., & Yen, S.S.C. (1989). Alterations in the hypothalamic-pituitary-ovarian and the hypothalamic-pituitary-adrenal axes in athletic women. *Journal of Clinical Endocrinology and Metabolism*, **68**, 402-411.

Malina, R.M. (1983). Menarche in athletes: A synthesis and hypothesis. *Annals of Human Biology*, **10**, 1-24.

Malina, R.M., Bouchard, C., Shoup, R.F., Demirjian, A., & Lariviere, G. (1979). Age at menarche, family size, and birth order in athletes at the Montreal Olympic Games, 1976. *Medicine and Science in Sports and Exercise*, **11**, 354-358.

Malina, R.M., Spirduso, W.W., Tate, C., & Baylor, A.M. (1978). Age at menarche and selected menstrual characteristics in athletes at different competitive levels and in different sports. *Medicine and Science in Sports and Exercise*, **10**, 218-222.

Marcus, R., Cann, C., Madvig, P., Minkoff, J., Goddard, M., Bayer, M., Martin, M., Gaudiani, L., Haskell, W., & Genant, H. (1985). Menstrual function and bone mass in elite women distance runners: Endocrine and metabolic features. *Annals of Internal Medicine*, **102**, 158-163.

Märker, K. (1981). Influence of athletic training on the maturity process of girls. *Medicine Sport*, **15**, 117-126.

McArthur, J.W. (1985). Endorphins and exercise in females: Possible connection with reproductive dysfunction. *Medicine and Science in Sports and Exercise*, **17**, 82-88.

McArthur, J.W., Bullen, B.A., Beitins, I.Z., Pagano, M., Badger, M., & Klibanski, A. (1980). Hypothalamic amenorrhea in runners of normal body composition. *Endocrine Research Communications*, **7**, 13-25.

Mellits, E.D., & Cheek, D.B. (1970). The assessment of body water and fatness from infancy to adulthood. *Monogram of Social Research in Child Development*, **35**, 12-26.

Mokha, R., & Sidhu, L.S. (1989). Age of menarche in Indian female basketball and volleyball players at different competitive levels. *British Journal of Sports Medicine*, **23**, 237-238.

Mulligan, K., & Butterfield, G.E. (1990). Discrepancies between energy intake and expenditure in physically active women. *British Journal of Nutrition*, **64**, 23-26.

Myerson, M., Gutin, B., Warren, M.P., May, M.T., Contento, I., Lee, M., Pi-Sunyer, F.X., Pierson, R.N., Jr., & Brooks-Gunn, J. (1991). Resting metabolic rate and energy balance in amenorrheic and eumenorrheic runners. *Medicine and Science in Sports and Exercise*, **23**, 15-22.

Nelson, M.E., Fisher, E.C., Catsos, P.O., Meredith, C.N., Turksoy, R.N., Evans, W.J. (1986). Diet and bone status in amenorrheic runners. *American Journal of Clinical Nutrition*, **43**, 910-916.

Peltenburg, A.L., Erich, W.B.M., Bernink, M.J.E., Zonderland, M.L., & Huisveld, I.A. (1984). Biological maturation, body composition, and growth of female gymnasts and control group of school girls and girl swimmers, aged 8 to 14 years: A cross-sectional survey of 1064 girls. *International Journal of Sports Medicine*, **5**, 36-42.

Plowman, S.A., Liu, N.Y., & Wells, C.L. (1991). Body composition and sexual maturation in premenarcheal athletes and nonathletes. *Medicine and Science in Sports and Exercise*, **23**, 23-29.

Quigley, M.E., Sheehan, K.I., Casper, R.F., & Yen, S.S.C. (1980). Evidence for increased dopaminergic and opioid activity in patients with hypothalamic hypogonadotropic amenorrhea. *Journal of Clinical Endocrinology and Metabolism*, **50**, 949-954.

Reeves, J. (1979). Estimating fatness. *Science*, **204**, 881.

Russell, J.B., De Cherney, A.H., & Collins, D.C. (1989). The effect of naloxone and metoclopramide in the hypothalamic pituitary axis in oligomenorrheic and eumenorrheic swimmers. *Fertility & Sterility*, **52**, 583-588.

Russell, J.B., Musey, P.I., Mitchell, D., & Collins, D.C. (1984). β-endorphins and catechol estrogens in female athletes with amenorrhea. *Fertility & Sterility*, **41**, 1S-2S.

Sanborn, C.F., Martin, B.J., & Wagner, W.W. (1982). Is athletic amenorrhea specific to runners? *American Journal of Obstetrics and Gynecology*, **143**, 859-861.

Shangold, M.M., Freeman, R., Thyssen, B., & Mengold, G. (1979). The relationship between long distance running, plasma progesterone and luteal phase length. *Fertility & Sterility*, **31**, 130-133.

Shangold, M.M., & Levine, H.S. (1982). The effect of marathon training upon menstrual function. *American Journal of Obstetrics and Gynecology*, **143**, 862-869.

Shu, B.Y., Liu, J.H., Berga, S.L., Quigley, M.E., Laughlin, G.A., & Yen, S.S.C. (1988). Hypercortisolism in patients with functional hypothalamic amenorrhea. *Journal of Clinical Endocrinology and Metabolism*, **66**, 733-739.

Speroff, L., Glass, R.H., & Kase, N.G. (1983). *Clinical Gynecologic Endocrinology and Infertility*. Baltimore: Williams & Wilkins.

Styne, D.M., & Grumbach, M.M. (1986). Puberty in the male and female: Its physiology and disorders. In S.S.C. Yen and R.B. Jaffe (Eds.), *Reproductive Endocrinology* (pp. 313-384). Philadelphia: Saunders.

Szabo, E., Annus, J., Zalanyi, S., Jr., & Falkay, G. (1987). Disparate effects of naloxone in hypothalamic amenorrhea in athletes. *Functional Neurology*, **2**, 315-321.

Tanner, J.M. (1962). *Growth at Adolescence* (2d ed.). Oxford, UK: Blackwell Scientific.

Thoren, P., Floras, J.S., Hoffman, P., & Seals, D.R. (1990). Endorphins and exercise: Physiological mechanisms and clinical implications. *Medicine and Science in Sports and Exercise*, **22**, 417-428.

Treolar, S.A., & Martin, N.G. (1990). Age at menarche as a fitness trait: Nonadditive genetic variance detected in a large twin sample. *American Journal of Human Genetics*, **47**, 137-148.

Trussell, J. (1980). Statistical flaws in evidence for the Frisch hypothesis that fatness triggers menarche. *Human Biology*, **52**, 711-720.

Veldhuis, J.D., Evans, W.S., Demers, L.M., Thorner, M.A., Wakat, D., & Rogol, A. (1985). Altered neuroendocrine regulation of gonadotropin secretion in women distance runners. *Journal of Clinical Endocrinology and Metabolism*, **61**, 557-563.

Wakat, D.K., Sweeney, K.A., & Rogol, A.D. (1982). Reproductive system function in women cross-country runners. *Medicine and Science in Sports and Exercise*, **14**, 263-269.

Warren, M.P. (1980). The effects of exercise on pubertal progression and reproductive function in girls. *Journal of Clinical Endocrinology and Metabolism*, **5**, 1150-1157.

Wilmore, J.H. (1988). Disturbances in weight and eating problems in young athletes. *Tutorial Lecture, 35th American College of Sports Meeting*, Dallas.

Wilmore, J.H., Wambsgans, K.C., Brenner, M., Broeder, C.E., Paijmans, I., Volpe, J.A., & Wilmore, K.M. (1992). Is there energy conservation in amenorrheic compared with eumenorrheic distance runners? *Journal of Applied Physiology*, **72**, 15-22.

Yates, A., Leehey, K., & Shisslak, C.M. (1983). Running—an analog of anorexia. *New England Journal of Medicine*, **308**, 251-255.

Yen, S.S.C. (1986). Chronic anovulation due to CNS-hypothalamic-pituitary dysfunction. In S.S.C. Yen and R.B. Jaffe (Eds.), *Reproductive Endocrinology* (pp. 500-545). Philadelphia: Saunders.

Yen, S.S.C., Ehara, C.Y., & Siler, T.M. (1974). Augmentation of prolactin secretion by estrogen in hypogonadal women. *Journal of Clinical Investigation*, **53**, 652-657.

Chapter 14

Exercise and Bone Health Across the Life Span

Mary Jane De Souza
Joan Carles Arce
John C. Nulsen
Jacqueline L. Puhl

Any bone mass that is gained following a period of exercise training is quickly lost if the exercise training is not maintained.

BARBARA DRINKWATER
"It's Important, But Don't Bank on Exercise Alone
to Prevent Osteoporosis."

Regular physical activity plays an important role in bone health across the lifespan. In fact, the role of exercise in delaying bone loss is a topic of much discussion among researchers today. Continuous transformation of skeletal tissue takes place throughout the lifespan; and, in fact, it is noted that because the first three decades of life are dedicated to longitudinal bone growth and the achievement of peak bone mass, physical activity and exercise during this time may help minimize bone loss later in life.

Bone loss, a natural phenomenon associated with aging, rapidly accelerates during the immediate postmenopausal years (Snow-Harter & Marcus, 1991). Bone loss can lead to osteoporosis and may result in fractures associated with osteoporosis. The morbidity and mortality associated with osteoporotic fractures are inordinately high in the United States and represent a major public health concern (Mayo Clinic, 1984). Maintenance of optimal bone health across the lifespan can help reduce osteoporosis and the accompanying health hazards.

The primary factor affecting bone mass is the predetermined genetic component; however, other environmental factors modify the dynamic state of bone health, including physical activity and nutritional and hormonal factors. In the continuing quest to identify conditions that contribute to optimal bone health, much attention has been focused on the role of exercise as an osteogenic stimulus. Mechanical loading, in the form of exercise training, appears to aid the development and maintenance of bone mass. Moreover, in several populations with a compromised bone mass, exercise may even improve bone mineral density or at least minimize bone loss (Snow-Harter & Marcus, 1991). In this context, the use of exercise as a preventive and therapeutic tool to minimize bone loss and fractures is very promising.

In this chapter we will address several questions:

1. What are the effects of mechanical loading on the development of peak bone mass during adolescence and adulthood?
2. What are the effects of estrogen deficiency and menstrual status on bone loss and osteoporosis in female athletes and postmenopausal women?
3. What are the effects of exercise training on postmenopausal women?
4. What role does calcium play in the maintenance of bone mass?

Before discussing these issues, we present a brief overview of bone physiology and bone remodeling.

Bone Physiology and Bone Remodeling

In the human skeletal model, bone tissue functions primarily to provide the structural framework for the body and serves as the body's major mineral reservoir for calcium (Raisz & Rodan, 1990). Approximately 99% of body calcium is stored in the bones (and teeth). Besides calcium and other minerals, bone is also rich in collagen. Collagen is the fibrous support network that forms the organic matrix providing tensile strength to bone. In the human, there are two major forms of bone: cortical and trabecular. Approximately 80% of the skeletal mass is composed of cortical (compact) bone, and 20% is composed of trabecular (spongy) bone. Cortical bone is found primarily in the shafts of the long bones, whereas trabecular bone is found primarily in the ends of the long bones, in the flat bones, and in the vertebrae. Figure 14.1 displays the structure of bone: the trabecular layer and the cortical layer.

In spite of its rigid and stable appearance, bone is a dynamic skeletal tissue in continuous transformation and renewal. Clear indications of the characteristic plasticity of bone are depicted during the initial stages of fetal life when embryonic connective tissue is transformed into bone tissue (Martin, Ng, & Suda, 1989). Bones, except for the flat bones, grow by a process called endochondral ossification (the transformation of cartilage and

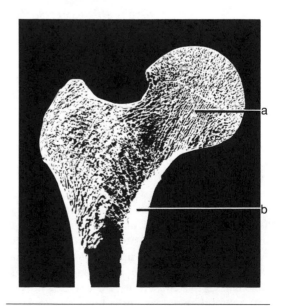

Figure 14.1   Bone structure: (a) trabecular core and (b) cortical layer. Adapted from Parsons (1980).

membranes from elastic tissue into hard bony tissue). The actual shape of bone is modulated by a process referred to as modeling, which occurs as skeletal growth takes place (Lanyon, 1987). Continuous growth, modeling, and development of bone are observed during the first two decades of life, are reflected by increased bone length and width, and are expressed by increased height (Martin et al., 1989). Nonetheless, changes in bone do not stop after cessation of tissue differentiation and longitudinal bone growth. Rather, bone remodeling, which is responsible for the functional integrity of bone, is an endless process that continues throughout the entire lifespan.

Bone Remodeling

Bone remodeling (or turnover) is possible through the precise coupling of the processes of bone formation (development of new bone cells) and bone resorption (removal by absorption). Ideally, skeletal homeostasis exists when bone formation and resorption are equal; when bone resorption is greater than bone formation, bone mass will decrease, resulting in pathologic problems such as

osteopenia (Sinaki, 1989). The mechanisms involved in the coupling of bone formation and resorption have not been completely identified; however, it has been established that these two processes are accomplished by different types of cells found in bone that form the basic multicellular unit. The cells of bone are *osteoclasts*, *osteoblasts*, and *osteocytes*, all of which are involved in the remodeling cycle.

The remodeling cycle consists of four steps: *activation*, *resorption*, *reversal*, and *formation* (shown in Figure 14.2; Raisz, 1988). *Activation* involves the changing of small surfaces on bones that are in a quiescent state to active bone remodeling surfaces. *Resorption* involves the breakdown of bone surfaces. *Reversal* occurs during the period of time in which the resorptive phase ends and the formation phase is initiated. Finally, *formation* involves bone matrix synthesis and mineralization (Raisz, 1988). The remodeling cycle of a basic multicellular unit, from activation to formation, requires approximately 100 days for the deposition of organic bone matrix; mineralization requires at least an additional 100 days (Parfitt,

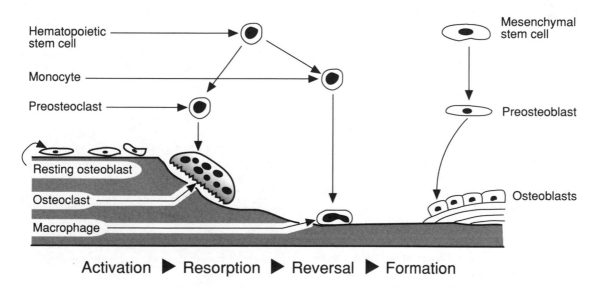

Figure 14.2 Summary diagram of the bone remodeling cycle. Reprinted from Raisz (1988).

1984). Any any given time, approximately 2 million basic multicellular units are active (Parfitt, 1984).

To further understand bone remodeling, it is important to note that bone formation essentially occurs in two phases: (a) the synthesis of the bone matrix and (b) the mineralization of bone (Raisz, 1988). Bone formation is accomplished by a specific group of mesenchymal-derived cells called *osteoblasts* (Raisz & Kream, 1983). Osteoblasts synthesize and secrete the organic components of the bone matrix. Derivative cells of the osteoblasts, the *osteocytes*, are very important in the bone mineralization process (Raisz & Rodan, 1990). Factors that influence bone formation include mechanical loading, circulating hormones, and local bone factors (Lanyon, 1987). Parathyroid hormone and calcitriol have a stimulating effect on bone formation; however, their anabolic effects are not well defined (Raisz & Rodan, 1990). Growth hormone, insulin, and epidermal growth factor are other circulating compounds that also may have a stimulating effect on bone formation (Martin et al., 1989). Local factors that positively affect bone formation include prostaglandins and transforming growth factors (Martin et al., 1989). Glucocorticoids may decrease osteoblast activity and thus decrease the rate of bone formation (Raisz & Rodan, 1990).

Bone resorption, on the other hand, is mediated by the multinucleated giant cells called *osteoclasts* (Raisz & Rodan, 1990). Regulation of bone resorption is achieved primarily by hormonal and local factors that activate and increase the number of osteoclast cells. Parathyroid hormone and calcitriol (1-25 dihydroxyvitamin D3) are the main circulating hormones that stimulate bone resorption (Raisz & Rodan, 1990). Other hormonal and local factors that increase bone resorption include thyroid hormones, prostaglandin E series, prostacyclin, vitamin A, epidermal growth factor, platelet-derived growth factor, and interleukin-1 (Martin et al., 1989). Bone resorption is inhibited by calcitonin, prostaglandin E-2,

and prostacyclin when they interact with the formation and activation of osteoclasts (Martin et al., 1989). Another hormonal factor, estrogen, has been suggested to slow down bone resorption by indirect actions on prostaglandin production (Raisz & Rodan, 1990).

In summary, several mechanical stressors, systemic hormones, and local factors affect the bone remodeling process by their specific actions on the bone cell populations. The coordination of the different mechanical, endocrine, and local factors that affect bone remodeling is not well understood; however, the interaction of these factors ultimately directs the bone remodeling process toward bone formation or bone resorption. Further studies in this area will help to better describe the specific roles and mechanisms of action for these factors.

Effects of Exercise on Bone Mass: Mechanical Loading

Mechanical forces applied to bone during physical activity are hypothesized to cause increased bone mineral density and retard the loss of bone. For example, data indicate that in conditions where minimal amounts of mechanical stress are applied to bone (such as during periods of immobility and inactivity associated with prolonged bed rest and the weightlessness associated with space flights), the result is a significant degree of bone loss (Snow-Harter & Marcus, 1991). However, the positive effects of mechanical loading (such as in athletes participating in weight-bearing and resistance exercise) result in increased bone mass compared with that observed in sedentary persons (Snow-Harter & Marcus, 1991; Smith et al., 1984).

The two primary mechanical forces applied to bone are (a) muscular contraction and (b) the force of gravity (Snow-Harter & Marcus, 1991; Smith, 1982). In fact, weight-bearing activity and muscle contraction that result from mechanical stress play a major role in skeletal integrity. Bone tissue responds to the mechanical loading of exercise and activity via actions of the force of gravity and muscular contraction by increasing the rate of bone formation above the rate of bone resorption and thus increasing bone mass (Lanyon, 1987). The increased mechanical loads (exercise) stimulate osteoblast activity, resulting in a higher rate of bone formation (Snow-Harter & Marcus, 1991). On the other hand, during periods of immobilization, prolonged bed rest, and the weightlessness of space flight, the degree of mechanical stress applied to bone is reduced. As a result, remodeling activity is triggered, culminating in a rate of bone resorption greater than the degree of bone formation and promoting a net loss of bone mass (Dalsky, 1990; Snow-Harter & Marcus, 1991).

The increase in mechanical loading as a result of participation in exercise training is responsible for the higher bone mass observed in young adult female athletes. This hypothesis is supported by the fact that the two forms of exercise with an increased volume of mechanical load acting on bone (weight-bearing and resistance exercise) significantly increase bone density. However, the overall response of bone tissue to mechanical loading is also modulated by the interaction of various other factors, including an optimal hormonal and nutritional environment.

Peak Bone Mass and Exercise

Longitudinal bone growth ceases late in the second decade of life in females, resulting in the attainment of peak height between the ages of 18 and 21 (Raisz & Rodan, 1990). However, it appears that skeletal mineralization still continues as trabecular bone mass increases in the 20s and attains its peak in the middle 30s (Rodin et al., 1990). Peak bone mass is the highest density of bone (value) that is achieved during a person's lifetime (Ott, 1990). Traditionally, it has been reported that peak bone mass is reached during the third decade of life (Snow-Harter & Marcus,

1991). However, very recent data suggest that peak bone mass may actually reach its maximal density in late adolescence (by age 20), which is much earlier than originally thought (Snow-Harter & Marcus, 1991). Snow-Harter and Marcus (1991) have reported preliminary data that show peak bone mass may be achieved by the age of 17. Similar results have been reported by other researchers (Gilsanz, Gibbens, Carlson, et al., 1988; Gilsanz, Gibbens, Roe, et al., 1988). Longitudinal research may help resolve the controversy regarding the age at which peak bone mass is achieved.

The attainment of a high peak bone mass during adolescence and young adulthood has been proposed to have a significant impact on the prevention of osteoporosis during the later stages of life (Chestnut, 1989). There are data to suggest that persons who attain a higher peak bone mass during early adolescence and young adulthood can lower their risk for fractures and osteopenia later in life. Matkovic et al. (1987) studied two groups, one with high and one with low bone mineral density, and found that the group with the lower peak bone mass at maturity had a higher incidence of fractures later in life than did the group with a higher peak bone mass at maturity. These findings suggest that the attainment of a high peak bone mass during the first two decades of life is important to minimize fracture risk later in life (Matkovic et al., 1987).

Attention has been directed toward various factors that promote the development of a high peak bone mass. Figure 14.3 displays several factors that affect peak bone mass. The most significant factor is the predetermined genetic component (Dequeker et al., 1987; Matkovic & Chestnut, 1987; Smith et al., 1973). Race also has a very strong effect on peak bone mass, and blacks tend to have a higher bone mass than Caucasians. Environmental factors, including nutrition (particularly calcium intake) and mechanical loading (exercise), also strongly affect peak bone mass (Chestnut, 1989).

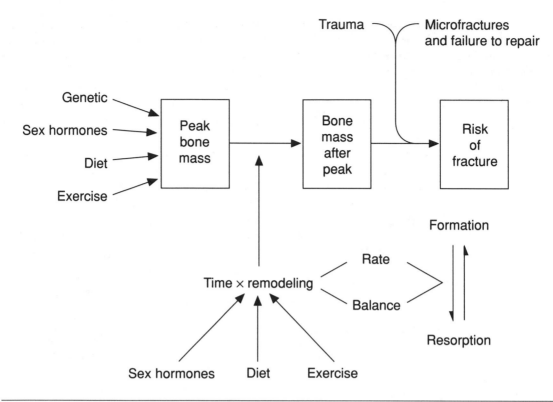

Figure 14.3   Summary diagram showing the determinants of bone mass. Reprinted from Woolf and Dixon (1988).

Adolescent Athletes

Whereas several investigators have observed a positive effect of regular physical activity and sport modality on bone mineral density in young adult females (22 to 30 years old), few data are available regarding the impact of physical activity on bone mass in adolescent premenarcheal and early postmenarcheal girls (13 to 20 years old). Jacobson et al. (1984) observed that young adolescent, female tennis players had a higher radial bone mineral density in the dominant arm compared to the nondominant arm, and concluded that exercise may increase bone density in adolescent females.

However, the positive effect of exercise (mechanical loading) on bone mineral density in young adolescent females may be modulated by several hormonal, anthropometric, and nutritional factors. Dhuper et al. (1990) reported a lower bone mineral density in adolescent female dancers who had a compromised estrogen status. They attributed the low bone mineral density in these young dancers to their relative hypoestrogenic state (less-established menstrual status). These data suggest that among adolescents who participate in a vigorous level of activity but have chronically low levels of estradiol, exercise is ineffective in maintaining bone mass. A low body weight may have contributed to the occurrence of the low bone mineral density found in these adolescent females (Dhuper et al., 1990). It is possible that the positive effects of exercise on bone mineral density are not expressed in the absence of an optimal milieu, part of which is hormonal (estrogen) and part of which is anthropometric (body weight).

In summary, the hypothesis that mechanical loading (exercise training) may have a positive effect on attainment of peak bone mass in adolescent girls is an issue with monumental impact on bone health across the lifespan that warrants further study. However, to date no longitudinal data are available that determine the effect of exercise training on peak bone mass during premenarcheal and early postmenarcheal years.

Young Adult Athletes

Physical activity has been proposed as an environmental factor that may increase peak bone mass in young adult women. Several cross-sectional studies have evaluated the effect of exercise on bone mineral density in young adult female athletes. Initial reports on the effect of physical activity on bone mineral density were provided by Jones et al. (1977) and Priest et al. (1977), who found a higher radial bone mineral density in the dominant arm of female tennis players. This point is depicted in Figure 14.4. These studies make the important point that hypertrophy is observed at the site where the mechanical load is applied: in these cases, the humerus. Several other reports have confirmed that other female athletes, like runners and weightlifters, have greater bone mineral density at the lumbar spine and femoral shaft than that observed in untrained sedentary women (Drinkwater et al., 1990; Heinrich et al., 1990; Howat et al., 1989; Jacobson et al., 1984; Marcus et al., 1985; Risser et al., 1990).

Interestingly, the magnitude of the effect of exercise training on bone density may vary between weight-bearing and non weight-bearing activities. Non weight-bearing activities, such as swimming, seem to have a less beneficial effect on axial or appendicular bone mineral density than do other weight-bearing sports, such as running, basketball, volleyball, and tennis (Drinkwater et al., 1984; Drinkwater et al., 1990; Jacobson et al., 1984; Risser et al., 1990). Table 14.1 displays the bone mineral density in eumenorrheic athletes participating in different sport modalities.

Several investigators have noted that resistance training may provide benefits for bone mass that

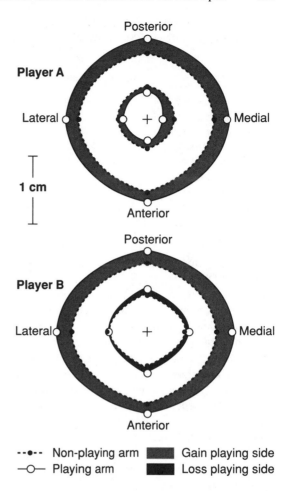

Figure 14.4 Cross sections of the humerus of the dominant and non-dominant arms in two tennis players derived by plotting the cortices of the humerus from the proximal to the distal end as measured from roentgenograms. Player A was a 24-year-old left-handed player; Player B was a 25-year-old right-handed player. Both had been playing for 18 years. Reprinted from Jones, Priest, and Hayes (1977).

are comparable to or possibly greater than the benefits derived from typical weight-bearing exercise (Howat et al., 1989). The amount of mechanical load applied to the bone as a result of high-resistance muscle contraction exceeds the load provided by weight-bearing activities and thus

Table 14.1 Spinal Bone Mineral Density (g/cm^2) in Eumenorrheic Women Participating in Different Sport Modalities

Reference	Running	Volleyball	Basketball	Swimming	Gymnastics	Weight-lifting	Sedentary
Drinkwater et al. (1984)	1.30						
Drinkwater et al. (1990)							
Fisher et al. (1986)							
Heinrich et al. (1990)	1.28			1.31		1.40	1.25
Howat et al. (1989)					1.37		1.20
Risser et al. (1990)		1.32	1.26	1.06			1.18
Nelson et al. (1986)							

constitutes a more powerful stimulus for bone formation (Snow-Harter & Marcus, 1991). Heinrich et al. (1990) reported a significantly higher bone mineral density in female bodybuilders compared to sedentary controls at several cortical and trabecular bony sites. Howat et al. (1989) also observed that female athletes participating in activities with a high component of resistance training present with a higher spinal bone mineral density than sedentary women. It appears that resistance-trained women have a slightly higher bone mass than female athletes participating in other activities, such as swimming and running (Davee et al., 1990; Heinrich et al., 1990; Howat et al., 1989).

It can be concluded that exercise training, especially weight-bearing and resistance activities, has a beneficial effect on bone mineral density. However, the observations are from female athletes with apparently normal menstrual cycles. Because menstrual history and menstrual status are clearly factors that determine trabecular bone mass in athletes, it is important to evaluate the effects of exercise training on bone in female athletes with menstrual disturbances (Cann et al., 1984; Drinkwater et al., 1984; Drinkwater et al., 1990).

Menstrual Disturbances and Bone Mass in Young Adult Athletes. Several investigators have observed a lower bone density in amenorrheic athletes compared to eumenorrheic athletes and eumenorrheic sedentary controls (Cann et al., 1984; Drinkwater et al., 1984; Drinkwater et al., 1990; Fisher et al., 1986; Jones et al., 1985; Lindberg et al., 1984; Marcus et al., 1985). Trabecular bone seems to be most affected in women with exercise-induced amenorrhea, whereas cortical bone is not as significantly altered (Jones et al., 1985; Marcus et al., 1985). It is alarming to note that the bone density at trabecular sites, such as the vertebral bodies of the lumbar spine, in female athletes with exercise-induced amenorrhea is comparable to the markedly decreased bone mass observed in postmenopausal women (Drinkwater et al., 1984). Figure 14.5 displays data that depict the bone mineral density of amenorrheic athletes in comparison to the bone mineral density of postmenopausal women.

The positive effect of exercise training on bone mineral density thus appears to be reduced when menstrual cyclicity is altered. The favorable action of physical activity on peak bone mass is attenuated in the face of menstrual cycle disturbances and decreased levels of estrogen. On the other hand, it is interesting that the bone density of women with exercise-induced amenorrhea is somewhat higher than that observed in untrained sedentary amenorrheic women (Marcus et al., 1985). This finding suggests that exercise may reduce the rate of bone loss in women with menstrual disturbances but certainly cannot substitute for an appropriate estrogen status (Marcus et al., 1985). Table 14.2 displays the bone mineral density in runners and sedentary untrained women categorized by menstrual status.

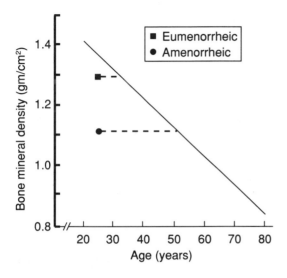

Figure 14.5 The bone mineral density of the lumbar vertebrae in amenorrheic and eumenorrheic athletes shown in relation to the regression of bone mineral density for age. Note that the amenorrheic athletes have decreased bone mineral density comparable to 50-year-old postmenopausal women. Reprinted from Riggs, Wahner, Dann, Mazees, Offord, and Melton (1981).

Interestingly, recent data indicate that subclinical forms of exercise-induced menstrual alterations, such as anovulatory cycles and luteal phase defects, also may negatively affect trabecular bone mass (Prior et al., 1990). For this reason, we must not overlook ovulatory status and luteal phase adequacy in our concern for optimal bone health among female athletes.

Several factors have been proposed to be involved in the decrease in spinal bone density among women with exercise-induced menstrual alterations, including: (a) hormonal factors, such as hypoestrogenism (Drinkwater et al., 1984; Fisher et al., 1986) and inadequate progesterone secretion (Prior et al., 1990); (b) anthropometric factors, such as low body weight (Drinkwater et al., 1990); and (c) nutritional components, such as "low energy intake" (Howat et al., 1989), calcium deficiency (Matkovic et al., 1987), and altered eating behaviors (Joyce et al., 1990; Nelson et al., 1986). Although most of these factors influence the loss of bone mass in women with exercise-induced menstrual alterations, hypoestrogenism contributes most significantly to their osteopenic state (Drinkwater et al., 1984; Snow-Harter & Marcus, 1991).

In summary, physical activity has a positive effect on the increase in bone mass during the early adult years among athletic women who

Table 14.2 Lumbar Bone Mineral Density (g/cm²) in Eumenorrheic Sedentary Women, Eumenorrheic Runners, Amenorrheic Sedentary Women, and Amenorrheic Runners

Reference	Eumenorrheic sedentary	Eumenorrheic runners	Amenorrheic sedentary	Amenorrheic runners
Drinkwater et al. (1984)		1.30		1.12
Drinkwater et al. (1990)		1.27		1.05
Fisher et al. (1986)		1.20		1.10
Bunt et al. (1990)		1.28		1.12
Jones et al. (1985)	0.73		0.67	0.74
Nelson et al. (1986)		1.20		1.10

maintain normal cyclic menstrual patterns (Hein-rich et al., 1990; Howat et al., 1989; Marcus et al., 1985). Women with exercise-induced menstrual disturbances may present with a decreased spinal bone mineral density (Cann et al., 1984; Drink-water et al., 1984; Drinkwater et al., 1990; Jones et al., 1985), which may be attributed primarily to their hormonal status but also is affected by their anthropometric and nutritional characteris-tics. Further research is necessary to clarify the effect of physical activity on peak bone mass in women and to better identify the best modality and volume of training to optimize peak bone mass and minimize bone loss under adverse hor-monal and nutritional conditions.

Bone Loss: Menopause, Osteoporosis, and Exercise

Bone loss is apparent with the advancement of age (Snow-Harter & Marcus, 1991). Although still controversial, a loss of 0.75% to 1% per year in bone mass occurs in the average woman with no endocrine or metabolic disorders between the middle 30s and the onset of menopause. Later, during the immediate postmenopausal years, a decrease in bone mineral density of approximately 2% to 3% is observed annually, and this may result in the development of osteoporosis and associated fractures (Smith, 1982).

Several researchers have reported a linear de-crease in lumbar bone mineral density with ad-vancing age (Buchanan et al., 1988; Hansson & Roos, 1986; Riggs et al., 1981); however, the majority of data support the notion that bone loss begins prior to menopause and is accelerated dur-ing the immediate postmenopausal years (Aloia et al., 1985; Krolner & Pors Nielson, 1982; Nilas et al., 1988). Figure 14.6 displays the changes in lumbar bone mineral density from ages 20 to 80. Clearly, bone loss is a product of both the aging process and the hormonal alterations associated with menopause.

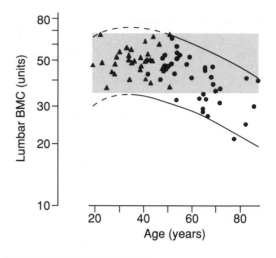

Figure 14.6   Bone mineral content in women from 20 to 80 years of age. Reprinted from Krølner and Pors Nielsen (1982).

Osteoporosis is a clinical condition character-ized by decreased bone mass and increased risk of fractures. It affects as many as 15 million to 20 million people in the United States today, par-ticularly postmenopausal women and the elderly (Mayo Clinic, 1984). In women aged 50 and older, as many as 1.3 million fractures occur every year as a direct result of osteoporosis. In fact, osteo-porosis is a major economic issue in the medical world because it results in costs upwards of $3.8 billion annually (Mayo Clinic, 1984).

Bones that are osteoporotic have enlarged inte-rior cavities that weaken the bone and thus make it more susceptible to fracture. Figure 14.7 illus-trates normal bone and osteoporotic bone. The largest bone loss occurs in the trabecular compart-ment (Snow-Harter & Marcus, 1991). The risk for the development of bone loss and osteoporosis is increased with advancing age, higher in women than men, higher in Caucasians than blacks, and increased in the presence of cigarette smoking, excessive alcohol consumption, calcium defi-ciency, and prolonged inactivity and immobility (Snow-Harter & Marcus, 1991).

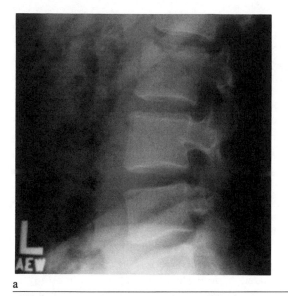 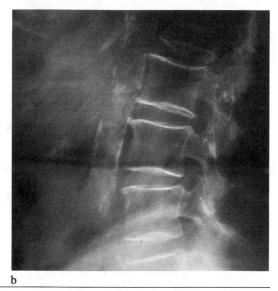

a   b

Figure 14.7   Comparison between (a) normal bone and (b) osteoporotic bone, which shows increased porosity (darkness) in (b).

Estrogen Deficiency During Menopause: Effects on Bone Mass

The decreasing estrogen levels during the aging process play a key role in the loss of bone mass in women. Estrogen deficiency is clearly associated with bone loss in both premenopausal and postmenopausal women, and places these women at risk for developing osteoporosis (Johansson et al., 1975; Lindsay et al., 1976). Other populations with hypoestrogenism, such as women with amenorrhea, including exercise-induced amenorrhea, hyperprolactinemia, and surgical menopause, are also at risk for the development of osteoporosis (Johansson et al., 1975; Parfitt, 1987; Raisz & Smith, 1989).

It is important to recognize that ovarian failure, characterized by irregular and anovulatory cycles and decreased ovarian steroid production, is initiated prior to the onset of menopause. In fact, these events occur approximately at the age of 35 and coincide with the apparent onset of loss in bone mass (Johnston et al., 1985). The decrease in ovarian production of estrogen is probably the single

most significant factor related to the decreased bone mass in women during the immediate postmenopausal years. It is during these immediate postmenopausal years (first 3 years) that bone loss occurs at an accelerated rate. In fact, Heaney et al. (1978) estimate that there is as great as a 20% increase in bone resorption but only a 15% increase in bone formation associated with the immediate postmenopausal period, which results in a net bone loss.

Bone loss during periods of estrogen deprivation and menopause is evident at all skeletal sites; however, trabecular bone is lost three to four times faster than cortical bone (Ettinger, 1987). Osteoporosis in postmenopausal women is most frequently characterized by decreased bone mineral density in the lumbar vertebrae and the proximal head of the femur (Parfitt, 1987; Raisz & Smith, 1989).

The pathogenesis of postmenopausal osteoporosis is not well understood, but the available data suggest that there is a relationship between increased bone loss in the presence of decreased estrogen production that allows the negative effects of parathyroid hormone to occur (Arnaud, 1987). The effects of estrogen on bone appear to occur through increased activation of remodeling sites and increased sensitivity to parathyroid hormone accompanied by a negative total body calcium balance (Arnauld, 1987; Dalsky, 1990). In addition, specific estrogen receptors have been identified in osteoblast cells, which suggests a direct effect of estrogen on bone (Eriksen et al., 1988). Estrogen deficiency is thought to be a very strong stimulus for increased bone turnover (Sinaki, 1989). As a result of the estrogen deficiency during the immediate postmenopausal years or after oophorectomy, bone resorption increases beyond the level of bone formation to cause a net increase in bone turnover and a net reduction in bone mass (Sinaki, 1989).

The single most effective strategy for postmenopausal bone loss is estrogen replacement therapy, provided the patient has no contraindications. Many investigators have clearly documented the positive effects of estrogen therapy at several different skeletal sites (Christiansen et al., 1980; Ettinger et al., 1987; Lindsay et al., 1984; Horsman et al., 1983). If estrogen therapy is initiated within the first 3 years of menopause, modest increases in bone mineral density can be observed in the area of 2% to 5% within a 2-year period (Ettinger, 1987). If estrogen therapy is delayed several years beyond menopause (more than 5 to 10), the degree of bone protection possible appears to be minimized.

For the prevention of bone loss, the minimum effective dose of estrogen (conjugated equine estrogen) is 0.625 mg (Lindsay et al., 1984). Ettinger (1987) states that estrogen therapy is effective in the prevention of osteoporosis provided it produces an adequate serum level of estradiol (40-60 pg/ml) and provided the patient complies with the therapy for a long period of time.

In a female with a uterus, the use of estrogen therapy necessitates the concomitant administration of a progestin to minimize the risk of endometrial hyperplasia that is apparent with unopposed estrogen therapy (Ettinger, 1987). The addition of a progestin to the therapeutic regimen does not appear to inhibit the positive effects of estrogen on bone (Gallager et al., 1991; Lindsay et al., 1978). In fact, there are data to suggest that progestins may stimulate bone formation and may act synergistically with estrogen to improve bone metabolism (Lindsay et al., 1978; Gallager et al., 1991; Prior, 1990).

Ettinger (1987) states that the ultimate documentation that estrogen replacement therapy has positive effects on bone mineral density is a systematic reduction in the incidence of fractures. Ettinger et al. (1985) have clearly documented that fractures of the wrist and vertebrae are reduced by 50% in women on estrogen therapy for an extended period. Data on fractures of the hip are not as readily available in postmenopausal women because hip fractures are typically observed in senile osteoporosis (women aged 75 or more); however, preliminary data suggest that fractures of the hip also may be reduced by at least 50% in postmenopausal women (Kreiger et al., 1982; Paganini-Hill et al., 1981; Weiss et al., 1980).

Menopause and Exercise: Effects on Bone Mass

The value of exercise as an osteogenic stimulus in estrogen-deficient women depends on the ability of the exercise (mechanical load) to decrease the rate of bone resorption and minimize bone loss (Dalsky, 1990). The mechanical stress of exercise may act as an osteogenic stimulus in postmenopausal women to increase bone mass by decreasing bone remodeling and the number of active remodeling sites. However, few researchers have tested this hypothesis prospectively.

To date, there are no concrete data to support the notion that an exercise program may serve as an adequate substitute for estrogen replacement therapy, especially during the immediate postmenopausal years when bone loss is accelerated (Snow-Harter & Marcus, 1991). Initial exercise intervention studies were not successful in using an exercise program as an osteogenic stimulus. Cavanaugh and Cann (1988) studied postmenopausal women using a 1-year intervention program consisting of brisk walking for 15 to 40 minutes a day, 3 days a week, at 60% to 85% of maximal heart rate. After the 1-year program the exercise group was unsuccessful in retarding spinal trabecular mineral density loss. The exercise group lost 5.6% compared to a 4% loss of trabecular bone in the sedentary control group. The frequency, intensity, and duration of this exercise program were not sufficient to elicit an increase in bone mass, nor was the program successful in retarding bone loss to a greater extent than that observed in sedentary women.

Dalsky et al. (1988), however, used a more aggressive exercise program in postmenopausal women that showed promising results. Sedentary postmenopausal women were enrolled in a 9-month weight-bearing exercise program involving walking, jogging, stair climbing, and upright rowing for 50 to 60 minutes a day, 3 times a week, at 70% to 90% of maximal oxygen uptake. After the 9-month intervention, the women experienced a 5% increase in lumbar bone mineral density compared to a loss of 1.4% in the controls. The frequency, intensity, and duration of this exercise regimen were effective as an osteogenic stimulus for the maintenance or improvement of lumbar bone density. However, after 12 months of additional training, no further increase in lumbar bone density was noted. Dalsky et al. (1988) attributed this phenomenon to the principle that bone adapts to the volume of mechanical loading applied and no further adaptation occurs unless the load applied is significantly increased. It should be noted that these women participated in an aggressive weight-bearing exercise program with a strength component (upright rowing) that specifically loaded the spine. Whether it is feasible or reasonable to increase the mechanical load beyond this level is not known.

It is interesting to note that the gains in lumbar bone density in Dalsky's patients were not maintained when the women ceased training for a 13-month period. The loss of bone density and return to pretraining values emphasize the principle that bone adapts dynamically to the mechanical load applied (Snow-Harter & Marcus, 1991). Thus, as Drinkwater states, we must be wary of the "principle of reversibility"; that is, any bone mass that is gained after a period of exercise training is quickly lost if the exercise training is not maintained (Skolnick, 1990).

Recently, resistance training has been the exercise of choice for researchers interested in improving bone density because of the ability of this form of training to load specific sites. Ayalon et al. (1987) tested the effectiveness of a 5-month dynamic loading program of the forearm and wrist in postmenopausal women and observed an increase in bone density of the distal radius. Sinaki and Mikkelsen (1984) also showed the effectiveness of loading a specific site via resistance training programs. They compared torso flexion and torso extension exercises in osteoporotic postmenopausal women. They found a decreased incidence of fractures in the group of women performing the torso extension exercises compared to the group performing flexion exercises. The authors concluded that the specificity of the exercise is important and that the mechanical loading exerted by torso extension exercise was more effective than torso flexion exercise in increasing back strength and loading the spine.

The type of exercise that is most successful in improving bone mineral density in postmenopausal women has not yet been determined. Table 14.3 reviews the results of several exercise intervention studies of bone density in postmenopausal women. Traditionally, it has been thought that weight-bearing exercise (e.g., jogging) may provide the greatest benefits to bone mineral density. However, more recently, resistance exercise has been suggested to provide an even greater osteogenic stimulus. Mechanical loading at specific sites may actively enhance bone formation, more so than the forces generated by gravity, as in weight-bearing exercise, and thus

Table 14.3   Studies Analyzing the Effect of an Exercise Intervention on Spinal Bone Mineral Density in Postmenopausal Women

Reference	Design	Exercise	Duration	Results on spine bone mineral density
Cavanaugh et al. (1988)	Prospective	Walking	12 months	Significant decrease in BMD in exercise and control groups
Chow et al. (1986)	Prospective	Aerobic classes only, or with addition of resistance training	12 months	Significant increase in bone mass in exercise group; no change in bone mass in control group
Dalsky et al. (1988)	Prospective	Walking, jogging, stair climbing, rowing	22 months	Significant increase in BMD in exercise group; no change in BMD in control group
Krølner et al. (1982)	Prospective	Walking, running, calisthenics	8 months	Significant increase in BMD in exercise group; significant decrease in BMD in control group
Sinaki et al. (1989)	Prospective (no weight-bearing)	Back strengthening	24 months	Significant decrease in BMD in exercise and control groups

may provide a better osteogenic stimulus (Snow-Harter & Marcus, 1991).

Drinkwater states that there is no consensus on an appropriate exercise prescription for optimal bone health, other than the agreement that women should remain physically active throughout their lives and that their regimen should include weight-bearing exercise (Skolnick, 1990). Drinkwater states that researchers recommend that, to have a positive effect on bone health, women should perform at least 30 to 45 minutes of weight-bearing activity a minimum of three times per week. The activities recommended include weight training, running, tennis, and low-impact aerobics (Skolnick, 1990).

Calcium: Effects on Bone Mass

Optimal nutritional status must be defined to incorporate calcium intake that is adequate to maximize bone health and to minimize the risk of developing osteopenia (Ettinger, 1987). Calcium intake, as recommended by the 1987 Consensus Conference on Osteoporosis, is 1,000 mg/day for premenopausal women and 1,500 mg/day for hypoestrogenic women, including postmenopausal women.

Although calcium intake is important to minimize bone loss, calcium supplementation cannot replace estrogen therapy in hypoestrogenic women (Ettinger, 1987). Postmenopausal women should not consider calcium supplementation a substitute for estrogen replacement therapy because calcium supplementation is not effective in retarding the accelerated rate of bone loss during the critical years immediately after the onset of menopause. Despite daily calcium supplementation, researchers have observed significant losses in bone density in women who did not also take estrogen compared to those observed in women taking estrogen without calcium supplements (Ettinger et al., 1986; Nilas et al., 1984; Riis et al., 1987).

There are some data, however, suggesting that inadequate calcium consumption may attenuate the osteogenic effects of physical activity. Lanyon et al. (1986) suggest that the osteogenic effects of physical activity in hypoestrogenic and calcium-deficient women may be improved if hormonal status (estrogen replacement) and nutritional status (calcium supplementation) are optimized. However, further research is needed to clarify the effects of calcium intake on bone metabolism and prevention of bone loss.

There are data to suggest that inadequate calcium intake during early adolescence and young adulthood can lower the peak bone mass achieved at maturity and place these persons at increased risk for fractures and osteopenia later in life. Matkovic et al. (1979) found that among two similar groups of Yugoslavians, the peak bone mass achieved was much higher in the group that had ingested more calcium throughout their lives. Both groups lost bone at similar rates with advancing age; however, the group with the lower peak bone mass had a higher incidence of fractures later in life. These findings suggest that calcium intake during the early years of life is important to maximize peak bone mass at maturity and minimize fracture risk later in life (Matkovic et al., 1979).

Summary and Conclusions

Bone is a dynamic tissue that is in continuous transformation throughout the lifespan. The first three decades of life are dedicated to longitudinal bone growth and to the achievement of peak bone mass. Peak bone mass and the maintenance of bone mass are affected by many factors, including hormonal milieu, nutritional status, and physical activity. The genetic component and race, however, are the major predetermined factors that affect bone mass.

Bone loss occurs as a natural phenomenon with aging (Snow-Harter & Marcus, 1991). Unfortunately, bone loss can lead to osteoporosis and associated fractures. The achievement of a high peak bone mass is important to minimize the bone loss associated with aging and to reduce the risk of fracture and the changing hormonal milieu at the time of menopause when bone loss is accelerated. Hormonal replacement therapy is effective in maintaining and minimizing bone loss in postmenopausal women.

Several studies have shown that bone density is increased in women who participate in exercise training compared to sedentary women. The effects of exercise training as an osteogenic stimulus depend largely on the ability of the mechanical load to stimulate bone formation activity above that of bone resorption. However, few data are available on longitudinal tests of this hypothesis. Some studies have shown a positive effect of vigorous weight-bearing exercise on bone mineral density; however, more recently, resistance training has been proposed to have a greater site-specific osteogenic stimulus than weight-bearing activities (Heinrich et al., 1990; Howat et al., 1989).

Physical activity seems to have a positive effect on bone mass during the early adult years in athletic women who maintain normal cyclic menstrual patterns (Heinrich et al., 1990; Howat et al., 1989; Marcus et al., 1985). Women with exercise-induced menstrual alterations demonstrate decreased spinal bone mineral density (Cann et al., 1984; Drinkwater et al., 1984; Drinkwater et al., 1990; Jones et al., 1985), which has been attributed primarily to their compromised hormonal (estrogen) status. The loss of spinal bone mineral density seems to be reduced by exercise training, especially resistance training; however, the exercise regimen must be maintained or the benefits gained will be quickly lost. Further research is necessary to clarify the role of physical activity to optimize peak bone mass and minimize the rate of bone loss in women.

References

Aloia, J.F., Vaswani, A., Ellis, K., Yeun, K., & Cohn, S.H. (1985). A model for involutional bone loss. *Journal of Laboratory of Clinical Medicine*, **106**, 630-637.

Arnaud, C.D. (1987). Calcium homeostasis and the pathogenesis of osteoporosis. In H.K. Genant (Ed.), *Osteoporosis Update 1987*. San Francisco: Radiology Research and Education Foundation.

Ayalon, J., Simkin, A., Leichter, I., & Raifman, S. (1987). Dynamic bone loading exercises for postmenopausal women: Effect on the density of the distal radius. *Archives of Physical Medicine and Rehabilitation*, **68**, 280-283.

Buchanan, J.R., Myers, C., Lloyd, T., & Greer, R.B., III. (1988). Early vertebral trabecular bone loss in normal premenopausal women. *Journal of Bone Mineral Research*, **3**, 583-587.

Bunt, J.C., Going, S.B., Lohman, T.G., Heinrich, C.H., Perry, C.D. & Pamenter, R.W. (1990). Variation in bone mineral content and estimated body fat in young adult females. *Medicine and Science in Sports and Exercise*, **22**(5), 564-569.

Cann, C.E., Martin, M.C., Genant, H.K., & Jaffe, R.B. (1984). Decreased spinal mineral content in amenorrheic women. *Journal of the American Medical Association*, **251**, 626-629.

Cavanaugh, D.J., & Cann, C.E. (1988). Brisk walking does not stop bone loss in postmenopausal women. *Bone*, **9**, 201-204.

Chestnut, C.H. (1989). Is osteoporosis a pediatric disease? Peak bone mass attainment in the adolescent female. *Public Health Reports*, **104** (Suppl.), 50-54.

Chow, R.K., Harrison, J.E., Brown, C.F., & Hajek, V. (1986). Physical fitness effect on bone mass in postmenopausal women. *Archives of Physical Medicine and Rehabilitation*, **67**, 231.

Christiansen, C., Christiansen, M.S., McNair, P., Hagen, C., & Stocklund, K.E. (1980). Prevention of early postmenopausal bone loss: Controlled 2-year study in 315 normal females. *European Journal of Clinical Investigation*, **10**, 273-279.

Dalsky, G.P. (1990). Effect of exercise on bone: Permissive influence of estrogen and calcium. *Medicine and Science in Sports and Exercise*, **22**(3), 281-285.

Dalsky, G.P., Stocke, K.S., Ehansi, A.A., Slatopolsky, E., Lee, W.C., & Birge, S.J. (1988). Weight-bearing exercise training and lumbar bone mineral content in postmenopausal women. *Annals of Internal Medicine*, **108**(6), 824-828.

Davee, A.M., Rosen, C., & Adler, R.A. (1990). Exercise patterns and trabecular bone density in women. *Journal of Bone Mineral Research*, **5**, 245-250.

Dempster, D.W., Shane, E., Horbert, W., & Lindsay, R. (1986). A simple method for correlate light and scanning electron microscopy of human iliac crest bone biopsies: Qualitative observations in normal and osteoporotic subjects. *Journal of Bone Mineral Research*, **1**, 15-21.

Dequeker, J., Nijs, J., Verstraeten, A., Geusens, P., & Gevers, G. (1987). Genetic determinants of bone mineral content at the spine and radius: A twin study. *Bone*, **8**(4), 207-209.

Dhuper, S., Warren, M.P., Brooks-Gunn, J., & Fox, R. (1990). Effects of hormonal status on bone density in adolescent girls. *Journal of Clinical Endocrinology and Metabolism*, **71**(5), 1083-1088.

Drinkwater, B.L., Bruemner, B., & Chestnut, C.H. (1990). Menstrual history as a determinant of current bone density in young athletes. *Journal of the American Medical Association*, **263**, 545-548.

Drinkwater, B.L., Nilson, K., Chestnut, C.H., Bremner, W.J., Shainholtz, S., & Southworth, M.B. (1984). Bone mineral content of amenorrheic and eumenorrheic athletes. *New England Journal of Medicine*, **311**(5), 277-281.

Eriksen, E.F., Colvard, D.S., Berg, N.J., Graham, M.L., Mann, K.G., Spelsberg, T.C., & Riggs, B.L. (1988). Evidence of estrogen receptors in normal human osteoblast-like cells. *Science*, **241**, 84-86.

Ettinger, B. (1987). Estrogen, progesterone, and calcium in treatment of postmenopausal women. In H.K. Genant (Ed.), *Osteoporosis Update 1987*. San Francisco: Radiology Research & Education Foundation.

Ettinger, B., Genant, H.K., & Cann, C.E. (1985). Long term estrogen replacement therapy prevents bone loss and fractures. *Annals of Internal Medicine*, **102**, 319-323.

Ettinger, B., Genant, H.K., & Cann, C.E. (1986). Low-dosage estrogen combined with calcium prevents postmenopausal bone loss: Results of a 3-year study. In *Proceedings of the Ninth International Conference on Calcium-Regulating Hormones, Current Strategies in the Treatment of Osteoporosis*. Nice, France: October 25-31.

Ettinger, B., Genant, H.K., & Cann, C.E. (1987). Postmenopausal bone loss is prevented by treatment with low-dosage estrogen with calcium. *Annals of Internal Medicine*, **106**, 40-45.

Fisher, E.C., Nelson, M.E., Frontera, W.R., Turksoy, R.N., & Evans, W.J. (1986). Bone mineral content and levels of gonadotropins and estrogens in amenorrheic running women. *Journal of Clinical Endocrinology and Metabolism*, **62**(6), 1232-1236.

Gallagher, J.C., Kable, W.T., & Goldgar, D. (1991). Effect of progestin therapy on cortical and trabecular bone: Comparison with estrogen. *American Journal of Medicine*, **90**, 171-178.

Gilsanz, V., Gibbens, D.T., Carlson, M., Boechat, M.I., Cann, C.E., Schultz, E.E. (1988). Peak vertebral density: A comparison of adolescent and adult females. *Calcified Tissue International*, **43**, 260-262.

Gilsanz, V., Gibbens, D.T., Roe, T.F., Carlson, M., Senac, M.O., Boechat, M.I., Huang, H.K., Schultz, E.E., Libanati, C.R., & Cann, C. (1988). Vertebral bone density in children: Effect of puberty. *Radiology*, **166**, 847-850.

Hansson, T., & Roos, B. (1986). Age changes in bone mineral of the lumbar spine in normal women. *Calcified Tissue International*, **38**, 249-251.

Heaney, R.P., Recker, R.R., & Saville, P.D. (1978). Menopauseal changes in bone remodeling. *Journal of Laboratory of Clinical Medicine*, **92**, 964-970.

Heinrich, C.H., Going, S.B., Pamenter, R.W., Perry, C.D., Boyden, T.W., & Lohman, T.G. (1990). Bone mineral content of resistance and endurance athletes. *Medicine and Science in Sports and Exercise*, **22**(5), 558-563.

Horsman, A., Jones, M., Francis, R., & Nordin, C. (1983). The effect of estrogen dose on postmenopausal bone loss. *New England Journal of Medicine*, **309**, 1405-1407.

Howat, P.M., Carbo, M.L., Mills, G.Q., & Wozniak, P. (1989). The influence of diet, body fat, menstrual cycling, and activity upon the bone density of females. *Journal of the American Dietetic Association*, **89**(9), 1035-1037.

Jacobson, P.C., Beaver, W., Grubb, S.A., Taft, T.N., & Talmage, R.V. (1984). Bone density in women: College athletes and older athletic women. *Journal of Orthopaedic Research*, **2**, 328-332.

Jacobson, P.C., Beaver, W., Janeway, D., Grubb, S.A., Taft, T.N., & Talmage, R. (1984). Single and dual photon densiometry: Comparison of intercollegiate swimmers, tennis players, athletic adult women, and age matched controls. *Transactions of the Orthopaedic Research Society*, 202.

Johansson, B.W., Kalj, L., Kullander, S., Lenner, H.C., Svanberg, L., & Astedt, B. (1975). On some late effects of bilateral oophorectomy in the age range 15-30 years. *Acta Obstetricia and Gynecologica Scandinavica*, **55**, 449-461.

Jones, H.H., Priest, J.D., & Hayes, W.C. (1977). Humeral hypertrophy in response to exercise. *Journal of Bone Joint Surgery*, **59**, 204-208.

Jones, K.P., Ravnikar, V.A., Tulchinsky, D., & Schiff, I. (1985). Comparison of bone density in amenorrheic women due to athletics, weight loss, and premature menopause. *Obstetrics and Gynecology*, **66**, 5-8.

Johnston, C.C., Jr., Hui, S.L., Witt, R.M., Appledorn, R., Baker, R.S., & Longcope, C. (1985). Early menopausal changes in bone mass and sex steroids. *Journal of Clinical Endocrinology and Metabolism*, **61**, 905-911.

Joyce, J.M., Warren, D.L., Humphries, L.L., Smith, A.J., & Coon, J.S. (1990). Osteoporosis in women with eating disorders: Comparison of physical parameters, exercise, menstrual status with SPA and DPA evaluation. *Journal of Nuclear Medicine*, **31**, 325-331.

Kreiger, N., Kelsey, J.L., Holford, T.R., & O'Connor, T. (1982). An epidemiologic study of hip fracture in postmenopausal women. *American Journal of Epidemiology*, **116**, 141.

Krølner, B., & Pors Nielsen, S. (1982). Bone mineral content of the lumbar spine in normal and osteoporotic women: Cross-sectional and longitudinal studies. *Clinical Science*, **62**, 329-336.

Lanyon, L.E. (1987). Functional strain in bone tissue as an objective, and controlling stimulus for adaptive bone remodeling. *Journal of Biomechanics*, **20**, 1083-1093.

Lanyon, L.E., Rubin, C.T., & Baust, G. (1986). Modulation of bone loss during calcium insufficiency by controlled dynamic loading. *Calcified Tissue International*, **38**, 209-216.

Lindberg, J.S., Fears, W.B., Hunt, M.M., Powell, M.R., Boll, D., & Wade, C.E. (1984). Exercise-induced amenorrhea and bone density. *Annals of Internal Medicine*, **101**, 647-648.

Lindsay, R., Aitken, J.M., Anderson, J.B., Hart, D.M., MacDonald, E.B., & Clarke, A.C. (1976). Long-term prevention of postmenopausal osteoporosis by estrogen. *Lancet*, **1**, 1038-1041.

Lindsay, R., Hart, D.M., Purdie, D., Ferguson, M.M., Clark, A.S., & Kraszewski, A. (1978). Comparative effects of oestrogen and a progestogen on bone loss in postmenopausal women. *Clinical Science and Molecular Medicine*, **54**, 193-195.

Lindsay, R., Hart, D.M., & Clark, D.M. (1984). The minimum effective dose of estrogen for prevention of postmenopausal bone loss. *Obstetrics and Gynecology*, **63**, 759-763.

Marcus, R., Cann, C., Medvig, P., Minkoff, J., Goddard, M., Bayer, M., Martin, M., Gaudiani, L., Haskell, W., Genant, H. (1985). Menstrual function and bone mass in elite women distance runners. *Annals of Internal Medicine*, **102**, 158-163.

Martin, T.J., Ng, K.W., & Suda, T. (1989). Bone cell physiology. *Endocrinology and Metabolism Clinics of North America*, **18**(4), 833-858.

Matkovic, V., & Chestnut, C.H. (1987). Genetic factors and acquisition of bone mass. *Journal of Bone Mineral Research*, **2**(Suppl.1), Abstract 329.

Matkovic, V., Fontana, D., & Chestnut, C.H. (1987). Influence of calcium on peak bone mass: A 10 month follow-up. *Journal of Bone Mineral Research*, **2**(Suppl.1), Abstract 339.

Mayo Clinic. (1984, August). Medical Essay: Osteoporosis: The silent epidemic in women. *Mayo Clinic Health Letter*, Rochester, MN.

Nelson, M.E., Fisher, E.C., Catsos, P.D., Meredith, C.N., Turksoy, R.N., & Evans, W.J. (1986). Diet and bone status in amenorrheic runners. *American Journal of Clinical Nutrition*, **43**, 910-916.

Nilas, L., Christiansen, C., & Rodbro, P. (1984). Calcium supplementation and postmenopausal bone loss. *British Medical Journal*, **289**, 1103.

Nilas, L., Gotfredsen, A., Hadberg, A., & Christiansen, C. (1988). Age-related bone loss in women evaluated by the single and dual photon technique. *Bone Mineral Research*, **4**, 95-103.

Ott, S. (1990). Editorial: Attainment of peak bone mass. *Journal of Clinical Endocrinology and Metabolism*, **71**(5), 1082A-1084A.

Paganini-Hill, A., Ross, R.K., Gerkins, V.R., Henderson, B.E., Arthur, M., & Mack, T.M. (1981). Menopausal estrogen therapy and hip fractures. *Annals of Internal Medicine*, **95**, 28-31.

Parfitt, A.M. (1984). The cellular basis of bone remodeling: The quantum concept re-examined in light of recent advances in the cell biology of bone. *Calcified Tissue International*, **36**, S37-S45.

Parfitt, A.M. (1987). Bone remodeling and bone loss: Understanding the pathophysiology of osteoporosis. *Clinical Obstetrics and Gynecology*, **30**, 789-811.

Priest, J.D., Jones, H.H., Tichnor, C.J.C., & Nagel, D.A. (1977). Arm and elbow changes in expert tennis players. *Minnesota Medicine*, **60**, 399-404.

Prior, J.C. (1990). Progesterone as a bone trophic hormone. *Endocrine Reviews*, **11**, 386-398.

Prior, J.C., Vigna, Y.M., Schechter, M.T., & Burgess, A.E. (1990). Spinal bone loss and ovulatory disturbances. *New England Journal of Medicine*, **323**, 1221-1227.

Raisz, L.G. (1988). Local and systemic factors in the pathogenesis of osteoporosis. *New England Journal of Medicine*, **318**, 818-828.

Raisz, L.G., & Kream, B.E. (1983). Regulation of bone formation. *New England Journal of Medicine*, **309**, 29-35.

Raisz, L.G., & Rodan, G.A. (1990). Cellular basis for bone turnover. In L.V. Avioli and S.M. Krane (Eds.), *Metabolic Bone Diseases and Clinically Related Disorders* (2d ed.). Philadelphia: Saunders.

Raisz, L.G., & Smith, J. (1989). Pathogenesis, prevention, and treatment of osteoporosis. *Annual Review of Medicine*, **40**, 251-267.

Riggs, B.L., Wahner, H.W., Dann, W.L., Mazees, R.B., Offord, K.P., & Melton, L.J., III. (1981). Differential changes in bone mineral density of the appendicular and axial skeleton with aging. *Journal of Clinical Investigation*, **67**, 328-335.

Riis, B., Thomsen, K., & Christiansen, C. (1987). Does calcium supplementation prevent postmenopausal bone loss? A double-blind controlled clinical study. *New England Journal of Medicine*, **316**, 173-177.

Risser, W.L., Lee, E.J., Leblanc, A., Poindexter, H.B., Risser, J.M.H., & Schneider, V. (1990). Bone density in eumenorrheic female college athletes. *Medicine and Science in Sports and Exercise*, **22**(5), 570-574.

Rodin, A., Murby, B., Smith, M.A., Caleffi, M., Fentiman, I., Chapman, M.G., & Fogelman, I. (1990). Premenopausal bone loss in the lumbar spine and neck of femur: A study of 225 Caucasian women. *Bone*, **211**, 1-5.

Sinaki, M. (1989). Exercise and osteoporosis. *Archives of Physical Medicine and Rehabilitation*, **70**, 220-229.

Sinaki, M., & Mikkelsen, B.A. (1984). Postmenopausal spinal osteoporosis: Flexion versus extension exercises. *Archives of Physical Medicine and Rehabilitation*, **65**, 593-596.

Skolnick, A. (1990). It's important, but don't bank on exercise alone to prevent osteoporosis, experts say. *Journal of the American Medical Society*, **263**(13), 1751-1752.

Smith, D.M., Nance, W.E., Won Kang, K., Christian, J.C., & Johnston, C.C., Jr. (1973). Genetic factors in determining bone mass. *Journal of Clinical Investigation*, **52**, 2800-2808.

Smith, E.L. (1982). Exercise for prevention of osteoporosis: A review. *Physician and Sportsmedicine*, **10**, 72-83.

Smith, E.L., Gilligan, C., McAdam, M., Ensign, C.P., & Smith, P.E. (1989). Deterring bone loss by exercise intervention in premenopausal and postmenopausal women. *Calcified Tissue International*, **44**, 312-321.

Smith, E.L., Reddan, W., & Smith, P.E. (1984). Physical activity and calcium modalities for bone mineral increase in aged women. *Medicine and Science in Sports and Exercise*, **13**, 60-64.

Snow-Harter, C., & Marcus, R. (1991). Exercise, bone mineral density, and osteoporosis. *Exercise and Sport Sciences Reviews*, **19**, 351-358.

Weiss, N.S., Ure, C.L., Ballard, J.H., et al. (1980). Decreased risk of fractures of the hip and lower forearm with postmenopausal use of estrogen. *New England Journal of Medicine*, **303**, 1195.

Woolf, A.D., & Dixon, A.S. (1988). *Osteoporosis: A clinical guide*. Philadelphia: Lippincott.

Part III

Psychological and Social Dimensions

P art III examines the major paradigms and debates that have shaped feminist theory and practice over the years. In Chapter 15, Margaret Costa and Sharon Guthrie emphasize the critical role feminist theory has played in understanding and furthering women's sporting experience. They also note the importance of such theorizing in mounting successful challenges to sexist oppression and in providing frameworks for social change.

Part III also provides contributions from the subdisciplines of sport psychology and sport sociology. Both fields of study emerged in the 1960s during an era of increased specialization in the sport sciences and are young in comparison to the biomedical specialties.

In their early efforts to build their subdisciplines and academic reputations, sport psychologists and sociologists adopted theories and research methods that were commonly accepted in the larger, earlier established disciplines of psychology and sociology. Similarly, psychologists and sociologists had modeled their disciplines after the earlier established natural sciences.

As we discussed in the biomedical section, feminists have criticized the natural science model that dominates the scientific enterprise. In fact, the feminist critique of science developed first in the social sciences. As each of the social sciences was examined for its own unique problems, it became clear to feminists that the critique of the social sciences could be applied to science in general.

Sport Psychology

Sport psychology is the study of human behavior in sport and exercise. Although the roots of the field may be traced back as early as 1913 when Baron Pierre de Coubertin organized the first International Congress on Sport Physiology and

Psychology in Lausanne, sport psychology developed as a distinct sport subdiscipline in the United States in the early 1960s. In the past three decades the field not only has experienced tremendous growth but also has emerged as a legitimate field of scientific inquiry.

Because interest in sport psychology arose from the explosive growth in elite sport, the primary emphasis in the field has been on the enhancement of elite athletic performance. Moreover, as is typical of most sport science specialties, primary interest has been in the study of males. Although interest in women has been stimulated in recent years because of increasing female participation, we still know very little about the female athlete from a psychological perspective. We know even less about the psychological processing of women of color, or of women in other ability groups and sporting environments (e.g., athletes with disabilities, recreational athletes).

In the early 1900s, female psychologists such as Helen Thompson Woolley, Leta Hollingworth, and Mary Calkins identified problems associated with sex bias in psychology, which at that time was a young discipline. During the 1970s, Naomi Weisstein and Carolyn Sherif furthered the critique. Weisstein claimed that psychology's androcentrism and essentialism prevented the gathering of accurate knowledge regarding women. Sherif identified *elementism* as another major factor perpetuating bias.

Elementism is the belief that one can determine the causes of an event by breaking it down into component parts, or elements, and studying those parts and their relationships to each other. According to Sherif, the problem with elementism was not the basic elements per se but rather the fact that physiological or biochemical parts were defined as more basic than environmental ones. Such bias reflected the higher value placed on the natural sciences and the belief that what can be quantified produces better (harder) data.

Since the 1960s, feminism has provided the context for the critical examination of such biased

theoretical assumptions and practices in psychology, particularly as they relate to women. Psychology's emphasis on individual solutions to problems, however, has been a major obstacle to incorporating feminist insights. Another obstacle has been psychology's hierarchy of methodologies, which originally was designed to reflect the high value placed on the natural sciences by the philosophers known as logical positivists. *Positivist empiricism* is founded on a false sense of objectivity, as well as a forced distinction between science and politics. The result is a science whose adherents have been resistant to challenging the status quo or attempting to transform oppressive relations in society. Although contemporary psychologists and sport psychologists are more likely to adopt interactional models that examine contextual circumstances in analyzing behavior, problems are still more often viewed as emanating from the individual (e.g., low self-esteem, internal motivations) rather than from the sociocultural environment.

The psychological contributions in Part III help us understand some of the problems that sport psychologists encounter, particularly those who move in feminists directions. In chapter 16 Diane Gill traces the development of psychological theory and research as they have been applied to understanding women, both inside and outside of sport. She also highlights problems in various research areas and offers suggestions for improvement.

Gill challenges sport psychologists to make more disciplined efforts to incorporate social context into their analyses of sport and exercise behavior. If sport psychology is to progress as a responsible science, Gill believes that a social psychological perspective must be adopted in understanding human behavior in sport and exercise. She further encourages sport and exercise psychologists to infuse their work with the insights derived from feminist scholarship. Such suggestions are critical in expanding our understanding of the psychological dimensions of women's sporting and exercise realities and potentials.

In chapter 17 Mary Duquin challenges further our traditional notions of sport psychology as she examines the feminist critique originating in psychology, as well as the insights gained from feminist psychoanalytic theory and poststructuralism. She shows us how feminist methodology, which accords privilege to women's subjective experience and knowledge, leads to alternative ways of practicing sport psychology and provides guidance in making sport healthier and fairer for all.

In chapter 18 Sharon Guthrie and Shirley Castelnuovo examine the relationship among sport, somatics, and women's empowerment. In particular, they explore liberatory possibilities as they relate to body image, self-concept, and the embodiment of feminist perspectives.

Although feminists have extensively criticized the mind-body dualism that is a prominent feature of Western science, many have failed to eliminate such dualism from their own proposals for women's liberation. Evidence is seen in strategies that have focused primarily on changes in mental constructs as the key to women's liberation, for example, feminist consciousness raising. In contrast, the authors view the mind and body as a unified entity and believe that strategies will be most effective in liberating women when they combine cognitive understandings drawn from feminist scholarship with somatic experiences that can strengthen women's body images and self-concepts. They explore how this aim can be accomplished in a physical education course designed to help women not only develop feminist perspectives, but also embody such ways of being.

Sport Sociology

Sociologists study human social life in numerous arenas. Those who call themselves sport sociologists focus their energies primarily on the social world of sport and somatic-related activities. Moreover, because sport sociologists generally consider sport an important social institution and cultural practice, they study its relationship to other social institutions such as the political economy, media, education, and religion. Not all sociologists or sport sociologists take the same approach to their subject matter, however. In fact, the history of sociology is marked by a tension between traditional and critical approaches, each characterizing a different way of thinking and of asking questions about human social life.

Traditional sport sociology, which originated in the 1960s primarily in physical education departments at universities in the United States, closely resembles the natural sciences in theory and methods. Moreover, like mainstream psychologists, traditional sport sociologists tend to view current social conditions as essentially nonproblematic; thus, although traditionalists may search for ways to improve sport practices (e.g., how to make the National Collegiate Athletic Association [NCAA] or U.S. Olympic Committee [USOC] run more efficiently), they are unlikely to question the injustice inherent in such practices or the ideology on which they are based. In contrast, sport sociologists who use critical approaches are more likely to view the social world of sport as problematic because it is grounded in systems of stratification (e.g., racism, sexism, classism, ageism) that fortify white male dominance. Consequently, their work often includes a critical questioning of the social order and proposals for changes in power relations. It is with this critical emphasis that feminist social theorists and cultural studies scholars would most often be aligned.

In the early 1970s, female sociologists (e.g., Dorothy Smith, Marcia Millman, Rosabeth Moss Kanter) and sport sociologists (e.g., Ann Hall) began writing about the problems of androcentric bias in their respective fields. More recent efforts by researchers, particularly those who have adopted critical feminist perspectives, represent an attempt to overcome such theoretical and methodological weaknesses. We find such an attempt in the work of Susan Birrell and Nancy Theberge.

Adopting what is called a feminist cultural studies approach, these authors introduce us to the social world of women in sport, documenting sociocultural and political-economic factors that have led to change for women in sport. They then elaborate on the areas that cultural studies scholars have chosen to examine, particularly those who adopt feminist approaches.

In chapter 19, Theberge and Birrell discuss how cultural studies differs from traditional approaches in sport sociology. Traditional models emphasize ''sport as a mirror of society'' and thus as passively reflecting the social relations that exist in the larger societal realm. In contrast, cultural studies analysts view sport as a dynamic cultural product that is actively created and recreated and thus can be changed by humans. More specifically, cultural studies analysts examine how play, games, and sports reproduce the dominant culture and in what ways they become transformed as persons and groups actively respond in the sporting context to the conditions of their social existence. Taking a feminist cultural studies approach—that is, one that more specifically follows women's responses to patriarchal dominance in sport—the authors convincingly show us the powerful role that sport plays in the cultural life of girls and women, regardless of whether or not they participate.

Exclusion of women in sport is achieved through structural and ideological means. In chapter 20 Theberge and Birrell discuss structural changes that have improved the status of women's sport, particularly in the United States. Although

the structural barriers to inclusion have weakened, they emphasize that women's sport is still a contested arena; that is, women continue to struggle for control of the institutions that regulate participation.

In chapter 21, Birrell and Theberge examine how the exclusion of women from sport is achieved today, particularly through ideological means such as the media. Using examples from the sports media, they show how mediated images of female athletes make gender difference and female inferiority appear natural and thus serve to bolster male privilege and patriarchal dominance.

In chapter 22 Birrell and Theberge further challenge us to think of sport as a powerful cultural and political institution. Indeed, as many of the contributors in this book have convincingly shown, sport is used for far more than recreation, diversion from the work world, and entertainment of the masses. Sport has been and continues to be a prime site for constructing oppressive gender relations, as well as other asymmetrical power relations. As such, sport also can serve as a site for resistance to and transformation of these relations.

The authors provide numerous examples that demonstrate how, throughout the history of sport, women (and men) have resisted oppressive conditions they have experienced in sport. Although they remind us that resistance does not always produce an equalitarian environment, Birrell and Theberge discuss what they believe to be important factors in maximizing the transformative effectiveness of resistance in sport as we approach the 21st century.

Chapter 15

Feminist Perspectives: Intersections With Women and Sport

D. Margaret Costa
Sharon R. Guthrie

We've chosen the path to equality; don't let them turn us around.

GERALDINE A. FERRARO
quoted in *Great "Quotes" from Great Women*

Women have a long history of sport participation, and today they receive far more sporting opportunities and encouragement to develop their athletic talents than at any time in the past. Most of this progress has been gained since the early 1970s and is the direct result of feminist activity. Therefore, to understand more fully the sporting experience of contemporary women, it is essential to examine feminism, in both theory and practice.

Understanding Feminism

Simply put, feminists seek to understand and eliminate the oppression of women through theoretical development and practices directed toward social change. According to Catherine MacKinnon (1989), a prominent feminist legal theorist:

A theory is feminist to the extent it is persuaded that women have been unjustly unequal to men because of the social meaning of their bodies. . . . Feminist theory is critical of gender as a determinant of life chances, finding that it is women who differentially suffer from the distinction of sex. Compared to men, women lack control over their social destinies, their contributions and accomplishments are restricted and undervalued, their dignity thwarted, and their physical security violated. (pp. 37-38)

As this quote illustrates, feminists view gender, that is, the social category that defines and distinguishes females from males, as a problem because it results in unequal relations between the sexes. Although critical of theories that minimize or deny the significance of differences such as race, class, age, and sexual orientation in shaping the social reality of women, feminists also view women as a group who share a common oppression. For this reason, in their efforts to understand and eliminate such oppression, feminists begin their analyses with women's experiences and perspectives.

Seventeenth-century England saw the emergence of the first widespread feminist movement involving organized struggle against the oppression of women. This movement later spread to France and the United States. The first large-scale feminist movement in the United States, called the "first wave," emerged in the mid-19th century. This first wave resulted in the establishment in 1837 of the first of the "Seven Sister" colleges, Mount Holyoke, as well as the suffragette movement in the 1850s, which culminated in women's right to vote in the 1920s. It is the "second wave," however, which began in the late 1960s after the beginning of the civil rights movement, that is most responsible for expanding women's current social and sporting opportunities.

Because feminism historically has accommodated multiple perspectives, it is comprehensive in nature rather than representative of one unified position. Moreover, feminists do not always identify themselves as belonging exclusively to one theoretical camp, although a particular approach may dominate their projects. With this caveat in mind, we will examine the major paradigms, issues, and debates that have helped shape feminism and will consider their impact on women's sporting experience.

The Liberal Model of Feminism

Liberal feminism is the major feminist paradigm in the United States, particularly outside of academic circles. The first wave of feminism was essentially a liberal feminist movement, although the liberal feminist tradition is firmly grounded in three centuries of liberal political thought. Throughout this long history, liberal feminists have challenged sexism and emphasized the importance of applying liberal principles equally to women and men.

Beliefs and Values

Liberal tradition presupposes a dualistic conception of human nature. *Dualism* is reflected in a belief in the separation of the mind and body, valuing the mind over the body and mental over physical capacities. Dualism also is expressed in the view that the human capacity to reason, which is considered primarily a mental quality, is what distinguishes humans from nonhumans. As a result, liberals often view the physical realm of the body as irrelevant to political theory (Jaggar, 1983).[1]

For liberals, a just society allows equal opportunities for all people to develop their rational powers, without interference from other people or the government. Indeed, the value placed on rationality and freedom from state intervention is expressed through liberals' demand for liberty, which guarantees individual autonomy and the right to establish one's own truth, morality, and goals. Moreover, within liberal theory a distinction is made between private and public domains, with legitimate state regulation generally being confined to the public domain.

Early liberal feminists opposed sexist discrimination by arguing that women are equal to men in their ability to reason and thus should be allowed the same freedoms. Contemporary liberal feminists in Western society continue to challenge sexism because it violates the liberal values of liberty, justice, and equality, which are generally understood as equal opportunity.

In contemporary American society, women suffer discrimination in a number of ways. According to liberal feminists, the most obvious form of injustice is that mandated by sex-biased legislation that assigns different rights, responsibilities, and opportunities to females and males. Although they focus on legal discrimination, liberal feminists are also aware that most sexist discrimination against women is informal or based on custom. In particular, they point to the sexual division of labor in both the private and public realms. Because the private domain generally is considered off limits for state intervention, however, liberal feminists direct most of their energy toward women's lack of equality in public life.

Goals and Strategies for Social Change

For liberal feminists, the just society is a fair meritocracy, that is, a society in which one's achievement in a competitive environment determines one's status and power. Consequently, their goals usually involve strategies for incorporating women into the mainstream of public life, which includes politics, the workplace, and sport.

According to Rosemary Tong (1989), liberal feminists claim that the goals of gender justice are, first, to make "the rules of the game fair and, second, to make certain that none of the runners in the race for society's goods and services is systematically disadvantaged" (p. 2). Although the rules are monitored for fairness, the game itself, which establishes the necessity of winners and losers, is rarely challenged. As a result, liberal feminist strategies for achieving a just society are typically characterized as attempts to reform socioeconomic and political structures rather than transform them.

Liberal feminists believe in the importance of public law in changing private attitudes; hence they seek to repeal all laws that provide differential rights, responsibilities, and opportunities to females and males. They also rely on the state to enforce "liberty and justice for all" so that women may have the opportunity for autonomy and self-fulfillment. Such is the case with Title IX of the Educational Amendments of 1972, the

law that prohibits sex discrimination in any institution receiving federal funds. Liberal feminists hailed the concept of equal opportunity for training, facilities, and practice as achieving the ultimate goal of gender equity in sport. Indeed, the success of American women in the 1984 Summer Olympic Games was the direct result of the implementation of Title IX. The appointment of an African-American woman, Anita DeFrantz, to the United States Olympic Committee as well as the International Olympic Committee is another indicator of the positive influence of Title IX in the sport realm.

The courts also have been used as a conduit for balancing the equation between women's and men's sports on both the international and local scenes. On the international level, for example, before the 1984 Summer Olympic Games in Los Angeles, liberal feminists filed a lawsuit to have the women's 10,000-meter track-and-field race added to the athletics schedule, arguing that women all over the world were already running such distances (Toohey, 1984). At the state level in California, liberal feminists also used their influence in gaining the enactment of laws such as California Education Code Section 41, which emphasizes equal opportunity for participation and calls for the redress of sex-biased inequities in sport (California Education Code, 1976). A pretrial settlement was reached in a case brought by the National Organization of Women against the 20 campus California State University system. Under the settlement, each campus was required to

- provide athletic opportunities for women proportional to the number of eligible female undergraduates on each campus, within 5%,
- provide grants-in-aid for women's sports in proportion to the number of eligible female undergraduates on campus, within 5%, and
- provide overall funding for women's sports in proportion to the number of eligible female undergraduates on campus, within 10% (DiGiovanna, 1993, p. C-1).

In response to suggestions that the University of California might be the next target, UCLA brought its programs closer to compliance with federal guidelines mandating gender equity by announcing that it would maintain its women's gymnastics program and add women's water polo as an intercollegiate sport. It also announced plans to add an additional, though unspecified, women's sport (Witherspoon, 1993).

Clearly, legal reform is a major part of the liberal feminist agenda. Another major goal is enhanced educational opportunity. One of the first results of the women's movement was the increase in the number of women obtaining law degrees and doctorates in philosophy, psychology, sociology, and political science, the fields that have had the greatest impact on feminist theory. Moreover, women began to use their education to study concerns that are of importance to women. For example, female lawyers revealed child abuse and wife battering, issues that had been overlooked and ignored by men. Women in the social and sport sciences began to examine their disciplines through women's eyes and realized that many theoretical assumptions on which their disciplines were founded were not valid when applied to women. They also began to realize the degree to which white heterosexual male experience is considered the human norm to which all others are compared.

Celebration and Critique

Liberal feminists have much to celebrate, for it has been primarily through their efforts that the legal status of women in the United States has improved considerably in the past two decades. Moreover, it is liberal feminists who are responsible for expanding sporting opportunities for women through Title IX and fostering an environment that is more supportive of women developing their physical selves (A guide to the equity laws, 1989). Indeed, we must pay tribute to those who have advanced the cause of women's rights, both in the United States and abroad, and are responsible for most of the major advancements for American women in sport.

It is also appropriate, however, to examine some of the problems that have been noted in the liberal feminist paradigm. For example, although Title IX resulted in a dramatic increase in the numbers of females participating in sport and exercise, it also drastically altered the governing structure of women's athletics, particularly at the college level. (See chapter 6.)

Twenty years ago it was assumed that laws preventing discrimination based on sex would allow women to participate in public life as the equals of men. Throughout the 1970s, however, it became apparent that the issues were far more complex. For example, although more women were taking advantage of increased educational opportunities, they were not necessarily able to translate their attainments into earnings equal to those of men working in the same fields and also were more likely to be unemployed (Adelman, 1991). In sport, although women gained more opportunities in general and more money on the professional level, they were quickly losing their positions of power in coaching and administration and still had restricted access to professional outlets in the United States (Acosta & Carpenter, 1992).

As a result, one of the central criticisms aimed at liberal feminists is their emphasis on reforming rather than transforming the existing structures of patriarchal capitalism. Women in sport and physical education, for example, while attempting to work within the current governing structures of sport (e.g., NCAA), have often adopted the patriarchal ideology and dualistic practices of the traditional male model of sport.

Dualistic thinking, which dates back as far as Plato but was crystallized in the work of Descartes in the 17th century, is responsible for the view that activities of the body (e.g., physical education, sport, physical work) are of lesser importance than activities of the mind. Dualistic thinking is responsible for fueling the stereotype of the "dumb jock," which implies that athletically gifted people lack intelligence. Additionally, because women are more often associated with their bodily functions (e.g., reproduction) than men, who are more often defined by mental characteristics, dualism also stimulates sexist ideology and women's oppression.

Although professionals in sport and physical education have nothing to gain from ideology that trivializes athletes and physical ability, their practices reflect other elements of dualism. Indeed, throughout the past 150 years, teaching and coaching in educational institutions have been structured to accommodate dualistic notions (Safrit, 1984; Wrynn, 1991). Take, for example, the separation of playing fields, gymnasia, and swimming pools from classrooms and laboratories in athletic and physical education departments throughout the Western world. Moreover, following the belief that rationality comes from mental reasoning, "chalk talks" and theoretical discussions are scheduled for the classroom, whereas athletic sessions are held in the movement areas. Dualism is also evident in the system by which success is determined; that is, statistical data accrued through physical contests are collected according to an objective schema whereas little credence is given to the sensuality or quality of the experience. The subjective experiencing of the moment is deemed secondary to objective measurements of faster, higher, stronger, because the latter are considered to be rationally developed characteristics of performance.

Further acceptance of dualism is found in practices that objectify the body. For example, athletes are appraised and tested in laboratories, according to preordered formulas and theories. Bodies are measured according to optimum height/weight charts, limb length, lung capacity, and narrowly defined aesthetic ideals of beauty. Individual body builds are also subordinated when they are forced to conform to norms that may be unnatural. To accommodate such norms, many athletes, particularly females, have subjected themselves to extreme forms of weight control such as anorexia nervosa and bulimia nervosa (Black, 1991). Although athletes of both sexes experience similar stressors and engage in unhealthy eating habits, eating disorders are often viewed as psychological abnormalities peculiar to female athletes rather than as a product of the capitalist excesses associated with the traditional male sport model.

Two additional examples serve to illustrate the problems women encounter when operating in the patriarchal-capitalist sport system. In particular, many liberal feminists have accepted the premise that women's sports must produce revenues if they are to compete with men's programs. As a result, success is judged largely by numbers of spectators, as well as by recognition through selection on all-star teams and placement in tournaments. A presumption is then made that if the community does not attend women's sporting events in the same numbers as they attend men's events, women's events are less exciting and thus not as "good" as men's. Such a practice, to quote Patricia Williams (1991), "reinforces the tyranny of the majority that has survived in liberal political theory as a justification of economic restraint" (p. 43). In other words, it gives sport boosters the power to determine what is "good" about sport.

Another example occurs in college sport in the United States. Scholarships for female athletes give them access to previously denied economic aid and place them on a more equal footing with men. This "fair share" system, however, is administered according to patriarchal NCAA or state high school regulations. As a result, male athletes generally receive more scholarships than females. Moreover, "equal" at the college level usually refers to the number of NCAA teams rather than the number of athletes sponsored by each institution or the amount of money spent per athlete.

Certainly the problems unresolved by liberal feminist strategies have led many to doubt liberal feminism's ability to end women's oppression. Despite such reservations, the actions of liberal feminists continue to move women forward, both within and outside of sport. We therefore have liberal feminists to thank for helping women in

20th century to achieve sporting goals
[?] of previous generations were capable
[?] imagining.

Critical Feminist Models

Marxist, radical, and socialist feminists are critical
of liberal feminist strategies because they believe
that women's liberation is unlikely within the context of patriarchal capitalism. What such feminists
have in common, and what distinguishes them
from liberals, is that they are more likely to follow
agendas that call for revolution and radical transformation of current structures and institutions,
as opposed to reform.

Marxist Feminism

Marxist theory, formulated by Karl Marx in the
mid-19th century, was a deliberate refutation of
liberal theory, which developed in close association with industrial capitalism. Marx observed that
in capitalist contexts, work was organized for
dominant class accumulation and resulted in class
distinctions and exploitation of workers. Marxists
criticize capitalism because it results in class
oppression, which they believe is the root of all
oppression.

Marxist feminists do not believe it is possible
for anyone, especially women, to achieve equal
opportunity in a class society in which the "rich
get richer while the poor get poorer." They argue
that equal opportunity cannot be actualized in a
meritocracy because those who occupy positions
of influence have the power to define criteria of
excellence in their own best interests. To actualize
a just society, class distinctions and oppression
must be eliminated.

Beliefs and Values

Marxists reject dualistic divisions between mind
and body, between mental and physical labor,
and between biological and social components of
human nature. Consequently, they believe that the
body has profound implications for social theory.
In fact, Marx claimed that praxis (i.e., physical
labor that transforms the material world to satisfy
human needs), not pure rational thought, is the
essential human activity, although he viewed the
two as fundamentally inseparable (Jaggar, 1983).

Marxists believe that a person's rational
thought, capacities, needs, and interests are determined by the dominant model of production that
characterizes the society in which one lives.
Human nature (of which rationality is a part) is
viewed as historically specific and changeable
rather than as universal and immutable. Moreover,
because Marxists view praxis as transforming not
only the material world but also human nature,
they believe it is necessary for the full and free
development of human potentiality.

Although freedom is a value for both Marxists
and liberals, their notions are different. For liberals, freedom involves autonomy, which is the
mental capacity of people to make their own moral
decisions or to fulfill their own interests without
interference from other individuals and the government. Moreover, freedom is not specifically
related to any type of work or activity, and thus
may be expressed in choosing not to work. In
contrast, Marxists view freedom in terms of conscious productive activity that includes both physical and mental components. Alison Jaggar (1983)
emphasizes this difference:

> Marx believes that the productive activity
> that characterizes freedom is typically de-
> manding and strenuous; a free individual
> would not choose to be idle . . . freedom,
> for the Marxist is a social achievement. One
> could not have freedom in the absence of
> society; nor while others lacked it. (p. 211)

Traditional Marxists believe that individual
freedom is possible only if two social pre-
conditions exist: extensive development of the
means of production and elimination of forced

labor that characterizes class society. They further believe that such freedom is possible only in a communist (socialist) system that provides collective ownership of the means of production.

Goals and Strategies for Social Change

The ultimate goal of Marxists is to achieve a socialist state through the revolution of those who are oppressed, which according to Marx would involve a revolution of the male proletariat. Feminists who rely on Marxist analysis have extended this concept to women. Because Marxist feminists view women's oppression in capitalist contexts as rooted in their exclusion from the public realm of economic production, they believe that liberation will come primarily from women's full entry into the work force. When women are wage laborers, they are no longer on the periphery of history; instead they are in a position to shape history, to realize their potentials for social action, and ultimately to transform the social world working in conjunction with men who are also wage laborers. To achieve this goal, housework and child rearing would be social services provided so that women could have full access to the world of production.

It is difficult to ascertain the implications of Marxist ideology for sporting practices primarily because Marxism is often considered synonymous with communism as practiced in countries such as the People's Republic of China, Cuba, and the former Soviet Union and eastern bloc countries. Both current and previous forms of communism are believed by many to be gross distortions of Marx's original political ideas and objectives because power and control have been structured along totalitarian lines. This is not, they argue, what Marx intended. Instead he envisioned a society in which world peace would reign and each person would receive compensation according to need.

With these caveats in mind it seems reasonable to suggest that according to Marxist feminism,

the right of women to participate in sport would be a natural carryover from the right of all persons to work. Certainly, in the schools, colleges, and institutions of many Marxist countries, some form of physical education program is provided for the workers. From military conditioning to gymnastics, everyone is given a chance for physical development. Hallmarks of present-day Marxism also are mass displays of physical activity by all persons, regardless of gender and age, as well as the training of sports instructors, provision of facilities, and extensive testing of both female and male athletes.

The close association between physical health and the quality of production also is recognized by Marxists. On-site physical training facilities are provided by industries in many communist countries, with resulting increases in productivity and decreases in sick leave. In addition, the subordination of individual choice to the needs of the society is an integral part of sport policy in many current and former communist countries (Knuttgen, Ma, & Wu, 1990).

For Marxists, the opportunity for all women to enter the sport realm brings about the production of physical achievements for the glorification of the socialist state. Consequently, Marxist feminists would point to the international stage for recognition of the achievements of women. In the Olympic Games and other international competitions, former eastern bloc women have dominated competition in numerous sports. Marxists have claimed that such achievements of women are the direct result of the elimination of class privilege and the consequent opportunity for all women to receive expert coaching and technological assistance. They further argue that because women athletes are government sponsored and are not dependent on corporate sponsorships or product endorsements for financial support, they have greater opportunities to train under "ideal" conditions. In addition, Marxist feminists undoubtedly would claim that notions of "ideal" body image and homophobic reactions to strong and powerful women, both of which are present in Western cultures, are less evident because they are considered irrelevant to sport production in socialist contexts.

Celebration and Critique

The politics of traditional Marxism have illuminated numerous problems inherent in the liberal feminist paradigm. Certainly the Marxist notion of human nature allows for more social change than does that of liberalism. Marxists also have explained why liberal feminist strategies of rational persuasion and piecemeal legal reform have not achieved full equality for women.

Despite the advantages of adopting Marxist perspectives, feminists have had reservations. Their major complaint has been that Marxists have not fully applied their theory and method to understanding female experience and generally consider women's oppression less important than that of workers. A deeper feminist criticism of the traditional Marxist strategies for revolution is that they are directed primarily toward the goal of democratizing production, which has been narrowly defined as work in the public realm, and thus omit the work of procreation. Responding to this critique, Marxist feminists have emphasized women's reproductive and sexual concerns as they relate to work (e.g., abortion, contraception, pornography, prostitution, sexual harassment, rape, battering); however, feminist critics of Marxist feminism still maintain that class rather than gender remains their primary concern.

Feminists are also critical of the ways in which the government-sponsored training of athletes has occurred in many communist and former communist countries. Although the use of sophisticated techniques and the provision of expert technological assistance may have produced superior athletic performance, the difficult training regime, which prevents the pursuit of other interests, and the use of life-endangering drugs to optimize performance undoubtedly have taken their toll on numerous athletes, regardless of gender. Moreover, the political and economic problems in the former eastern bloc countries and the disintegrated Soviet Union suggest an uncertain future for female athletes in these countries.

Radical Feminism

Radical feminism, a 20th-century movement that emerged in the late 1960s, is young in comparison to liberal and Marxist feminism, which are grounded in philosophical traditions that are centuries old. Use of the term *radical*, which literally means "growing or proceeding from a root," stems from the belief that all forms of oppression are rooted in women's oppression. Because patriarchy has existed in most societies and political-economic systems, radical feminists often view it as the primary form of domination. As a result, radical feminists place the subordination of women at the absolute center of analysis, which is different from the off-center position taken by liberals, who focus on legal, educational, and economic reform within a patriarchal-capitalist model. Radical feminism is also different from Marxism, which places class at the center of oppression analysis.

Beliefs and Values

Radical feminism reflects diverse theoretical insights. Early radical feminists believed that individual choice and freedom from sex roles were possible and desirable, and thus advocated the development of androgyny, (i.e., the expression of both feminine and masculine qualities and characteristics). Later, many recognized that the concept reinforced feminine and masculine stereotypes and did not help explain how sex roles were developed and maintained. Consequently, they shifted their focus to developing an alternative account of women's oppression that emphasized biological and psychological sex differences (Jaggar, 1983).

Radical feminists are diverse in their views on sex differences. Those who are "essentialists" emphasize fundamental biological differences between women and men; however, they celebrate women's nature as a source of special strength, knowledge, and creative power. They also give more credence to emotions, feelings, and nonverbal communication, and stress the importance of interpersonal relationships, which are more closely associated with women, as opposed to abstract notions of reason, which typically are constructed by men. In contrast, other radicals view gender as socially constructed. "Social constructionists" challenge women's nature as a biological given, and many even question the "naturalness" of childbearing, the female body, and sex difference itself.

Despite such differences in perspective, it is possible to discern a clear feminist challenge to androcentric conceptions of human nature. Moreover, like Marxist feminists, radicals generally reject dualistic notions of the body-mind and view the body as having major implications for social theory.

Goals and Strategies for Social Change

Radical feminists view contemporary society as a patriarchy, a system organized in ways that accord privilege to men as a group and allow them to have systematic coercive power over women. To legitimize domination, the dominant male culture constructs ideologies that define subordinate groups as inferior. Although myths and stereotypes are applied to subordinate groups, regardless of sex, patriarchal ideology defines women in a way specific to their sex, that is, as persons whose special function is to gratify male sexual desires and to bear and raise children (Jaggar, 1983). Such ideology defines the limits of what women may do and delegitimizes or trivializes them whenever they go beyond such definitional boundaries. The longstanding mythology surrounding the female athlete as less feminine and lesbian is a perfect example of an attempt to constrain women's physical potential.

To eliminate sexist oppression, radical feminists believe that patriarchy must be challenged and ultimately dismantled. They further believe that women suffer oppression as a result of the social meaning of their bodies, which includes being viewed as natural mothers and sex objects. Hence women's freedom must be grounded in their having full control over their bodies, which includes reproduction, motherhood, sexuality, and sporting activity.

Some radical feminists, most notably lesbians, view women's oppression as grounded in the heterosexual family unit and heterosexism (i.e., a belief that heterosexuality is the only normal and thus acceptable way of life), rather than in women's exclusion from full participation in the public realm. Such radical feminists most likely would adopt a nonheterosexual lifestyle and view lesbianism as providing one of the few refuges from patriarchal dominance. Regardless of sexual preference, however, a longer range goal for many radical feminists involves developing a woman-supporting culture; that is, developing communities or societies informed by female values, appreciation, and respect. Women engaged in such projects advocate separatism, or the creation of spaces for women that are free from male intrusion.

The radical feminist concept of separatism was truly embedded in the "Seven Sister" colleges. It was not by accident that Bryn Mawr, Wellesley, Smith, Mount Holyoke, Vassar, Barnard, and Radcliffe were called "hotbeds of radicalism" by prominent Americans, such as Calvin Coolidge. The naysayers knew that in such colleges, women were learning not only to master foreign languages and advanced mathematics, they also were learning to participate in sport in many vigorous and aggressive ways (Horowitz, 1989). According to Seelye (1874), the women's college had "its tradition, its sports, its esprit de corps, its intellectual and moral atmosphere, which mould and stimulate all who are connected with it" (p. 24).

Although the women who attended such colleges were from upper-class families, by the beginning of the 20th century they were playing physically demanding sports such as ice and field hockey, rowing, and lacrosse. In addition, within a month of its invention in 1891, basketball was accepted at Smith College, even though the men's game was altered to "suit feminine capabilities." Long- distance running, a popular weekend competition in New England in the 1960s and 1970s, also found dedicated participants in the women's colleges long before women were officially accepted as contestants in the New York and Boston marathons.

Throughout the first five decades of the 20th century, mainstream women physical educators practiced a form of separatism when they administered their own physical education programs, which were separate and vastly different from the men's. During this era, sport for women both in and outside of educational institutions took place in gynocentric settings. Moreover, experiencing the joy of movement, as opposed to elite athleticism and winning, was the primary objective; hence, opportunities to participate in sport were made available for all females, regardless of skill level. Many feminists have claimed that the early women physical educators' deemphasis on elite competition prevented college women from developing their full athletic potential. On the other hand, there are many who continue to advocate similar values and believe that women's potential can be best developed in gynocentric, female-only spaces.

Concurrently, and outside of mainstream educational settings, women of color also experienced the benefits of separatism. For example, both Margaret Costa and Lynne Emery have explored the importance of gynocentric settings to women of color. Through analyses of the sporting experiences of Nisei and African-American women, respectively, Costa and Emery demonstrate the importance of such separate establishments as the YWCA to the development of the full physical potential of women of color (Costa, 1993; Emery, 1992). Nisei are second generation Japanese-

Americans, "the first Americans of Japanese heritage to be born in the United States" (Costa, 1993, p. 37).

In the radical feminist reordering of society, the current sport structure would be changed dramatically. Because the dominant model of sport is structured to promote patriarchy, transformation would be required. Control of sports organizations, which are grounded in traditional models of male dominance, would be dismantled, as would the bodily objectification and exploitation of athletes. Moreover, governing bodies such as the International Olympic Committee (IOC) and the NCAA would self-destruct because their instrument of power, the patriarchal sport structure, would no longer exist. In addition, the use of sport to showcase political ideology would cease, as would commercial sponsorship, which relies heavily on elite competition.

Instead, physical activities that promote overall somatic awareness and skill would be instituted in all schools, from preschool through college, as well as in settings such as workplaces and convalescent homes. Emphasis would be placed on fitness and wellness across the lifespan. Competition would take on new meanings and be used to motivate and encourage excellence, but not at someone else's expense. Uniforms, designed by each team for purposes of identification, would reflect the culture of the participants, governance by consensus would take place in all sport settings, and sports emphasizing the advantages of the female body (e.g., those requiring endurance and flexibility) would be valued and encouraged for both girls and boys.

Radical feminists who advocate separatism, as either a long-term or transitional goal, no doubt would encourage women to develop their own all-women leagues such as the "feminist" softball leagues noted by Susan Birrell and Diana Richter (1987) and the lesbian leagues described by Yvonne Zipter (1988). Those who believe in "essential" sex differences and celebrate women's nature might encourage gynocentric sport models, that is, sporting practices grounded in values more

Figure 15.1   The Kalifans, a Los Angeles YWCA Basketball team. Southern California Japanese Women's Athletic Union Champions of 1941. Courtesy of Esther Fujimoto.

closely associated with women, such as those proposed by Carol Oglesby (1983, 1990).

Perhaps the major change in women's sport under radical feminism would be the emphasis on the exhilarating experience of physical accomplishment. Rigid notions of ''body beautiful,'' which are currently the focus of aerobics instruction and some sports (e.g., figure skating, gymnastics, synchronized swimming), would not be acceptable. Women athletes would be encouraged to write journals, diaries, and poetry that would be the subject of discussion in sports magazines and on the electronic media. Women of all races, abilities, sexual preferences, and generations would participate together in activities designed to encourage female bonding and respect for each other. It is also likely that if participation with effective instruction for all triumphed, women's movement disabilities would be diminished.

Celebration and Critique

Radical feminists have much to celebrate. Certainly their actions have helped raise our consciousness and illuminate the power of patriarchy in women's lives. Additionally, radical feminists have revealed an alternative explanation for women's oppression, one grounded in the social definition of their bodies and sexuality. They have helped us understand that women's oppression is intimately related to practices such as pornography, sexual harassment, wife battering, and incest.

They also have helped explicate the use of control of women's bodies by men and male institutions.

Despite these insights, not all feminists are convinced that radical feminism offers a feasible liberatory strategy. One of the major criticisms is that radical feminists often universalize women's oppression and patriarchy without considering the sociohistorical context. Women of color, working-class women, and lesbians are particularly critical of such "totalizing" theory because it oversimplifies and minimizes the complexity of women's experience of oppression.

Another criticism is aimed at separatist proposals. Critics grant that although a limited or transitional degree of separatism may be beneficial in developing in-group pride and understanding, continuous separatism minimizes possibilities for social transformation because it involves exclusion rather than inclusion.

Still another criticism centers on the way in which radical feminists conceive of women controlling their bodies. Although such a conception has revolutionary elements, its emphasis on women's control of their sexuality and fertility places it dangerously close to patriarchal definitions of women as procreative and sexual beings. In addressing this concern, feminist sport scholars have expanded the notion of women controlling their bodies to include increased participation in sport, exercise, and leisure activities. Empowerment of women through sport and transformation of the social world through somatic development may seem improbable for those entrenched in the liberal feminist world or in nonsport disciplines, however, we must acknowledge that women would move from the margins to the center of the sports arena if radical feminist notions were adopted.

Socialist Feminism

Socialist feminism developed in the 1970s as an attempt to merge the best of both radical feminism and the Marxist tradition while avoiding the problems associated with each, that is, the universalism of radical feminism and the "gender-blind" character of Marxist thought. What makes their analyses unique is that socialist feminists attempt to apply the historical materialist method of Marxism to the insights derived from radical feminism.

Beliefs and Values

Socialist feminists are committed to the Marxist notion that human nature is created and changed historically through interactions among human biology, society, and the physical environment, which in turn are mediated through human labor (praxis). Adopting essentially a Marxist conception of human nature, socialist feminists recognize that the differences between women and men are not biological givens; rather they are socially constructed and therefore changeable.

The socialist feminist concept of freedom is different from that of both liberal and Marxist feminists. For liberal feminists, freedom exists primarily in the private realm outside the confines of state regulation. In contrast, Marxists view freedom as existing primarily in the public domain. Socialist feminists do not make distinctions between private and public domains; instead, freedom emerges when one transcends the realm of necessity in all areas of human life, including sexuality and procreation. Moreover, socialist feminists believe that freedom cannot be achieved by isolated individual action without a complete reconstruction of society (Jaggar, 1983). In rejecting the private/public distinction, as well as viewing all aspects of human life as socially constructed processes, socialist feminist visions of a just society are closest to those of radical feminism.

Goals and Strategies for Social Change

Socialist feminists believe that women's oppression is rooted in both capitalism and male dominance. Because they have broadened the category of production to include activities that occur in both private (e.g., reproduction) and public spheres (e.g., goods and services), their proposals for social change include transforming the processes that govern sexuality and procreation. This does not include "reproductive rights" as ends in themselves, however. Instead, reproductive freedom for socialist feminists is a revolutionary demand and involves a complete reconstruction of the existing social order.

Sport is a perplexing realm for socialist feminists to conceptualize, particularly in light of the recent collapse of many socialist regimes. The political incorporation of socialist principles has been repudiated, and the centralization and special treatment of elite groups, including athletes, have been revealed. Even when these regimes existed, the participatory model of sport, which most socialist feminists would advocate, may never have existed.

Socialist feminists believe that for women to pursue sport in a freely creative manner they must be allowed to experience the joy of movement as well as the "zero sum" of competition, which requires at least one loser for every winner. The task for socialist feminists, then, is to create a sport environment in which women have equal access to the means of production and elite competition, while at the same time establishing a purely equalitarian sport society that would allow people free expression in both competitive and non-competitive settings.

Sport in both capitalist and socialist countries has been shown to be both hierarchical and male dominated. To eliminate male dominance and hierarchical structures, a new world order in sport would have to be created. This new world order would divide the means of production, training techniques, and facilities evenly among the peoples of the world. Given the fact that elite sport is closely related to political economy in both capitalist and socialist states, if a new world order were to be established, sport competition as we know it today would cease to exist.

Sport for women under socialist feminism would be structured according to the dictates of the psychological and health benefits accrued. In other words, women's experiences, needs, and interests would dictate the structure and function of their sporting and exercise experiences. Whenever possible, the exhilaration of physical activity would be incorporated, together with the positive self-image that results from achieving somatic control and efficiency of movement. Socializing agents such as female bonding and group cohesion also would be emphasized. Moreover, if women are to experience elite performance, then socialist feminists would acknowledge the importance of competition to that experience.

Socialist feminists recognize both patriarchy and capitalism as problems for women in sport, for example, how patriarchy promotes sexism and controls the sporting experience for women through formal organizational bodies (e.g., teams, athletic departments, NCAA, IOC) and informal practices (e.g., locker room activities) that are dependent on male bonding. Consequently, socialist feminists would strive to deconstruct these policies and practices so that women are brought from the margins to the center of sport. Perhaps socialist feminists would recommend the development of local sports clubs, established by those who participate. In addition, "women only" clubs would enhance women's control over their own bodies, as well as increase women's opportunities for self-definition.

Although many socialist feminists continue to support abolishing capitalism and replacing it with socialism, the establishment of a socialist state in the United States does not appear likely. For this reason, many feminist agendas include deemphasizing the negative aspects of capitalism, as well as support for enhanced government-sponsored social services (e.g., child care, health care). To this end, socialist feminists analyze the ways in which financial resources gained through capitalistic means (e.g., gate receipts, public donations, corporate sponsorships) can be distributed fairly to all members of society.

We have suggested that equal opportunity for women to experience sport also means equal access to the means of production—that is, training and technological assistance and facilities—and equal opportunity to participate at the elite level. For these changes to take place, socialist feminists would acknowledge the need for extensive financial support for female athletes. Whether financial support is derived from government or corporate sponsorship, women would participate equally with men in the distribution of such support. For example, at the college level, funds would be evenly distributed to athletes in direct proportion to the number of women and men in the campus population. In addition, female coaches, referees, journalists, and administrators would have control of sports equal to that of men.

Celebration and Critique

Although socialist feminism is younger than liberal, Marxist, and radical feminism, socialist feminists have made a disciplined effort to develop a theory that has comprehensive explanatory power, that is, one that attempts to weave into the analysis all the oppressive aspects of patriarchy and capitalism. In this respect socialist feminist theorizing is multidimensional, and its liberatory possibilities are limitless. Like all theories, however, socialist feminism is not flawless.

One of the central features of socialist feminism is its emphasis on organizational democracy. Proponents of this perspective have advocated democratic control of the economy and procreation, rather than private ownership. According to Jaggar (1983), a socialist feminist herself, the democratization of procreation may conflict with what is called "women's right to their own bodies." Socialist feminists have not yet explicated how this conflict may be resolved, nor have they suggested how to handle other conflicts involved in extending democracy to the more private concerns of the family (e.g., children's rights).

Socialist feminism also has been criticized for an undeveloped analysis of racism and its connections to other forms of oppression, particularly sexism and classism. As discussed previously, socialist feminists have blended aspects of both Marxism and radical feminism. Consequently, emphasis has been on understanding how gender and class operate to oppress women. Although socialist feminists have recognized the important linkages among class, gender, and race, they have not yet achieved their goal of developing a theory that fully explicates the interlocking nature of such variables. Nor have their attempts to synthesize Marxism and the insights gained from radical feminism been totally successful. Responding to this criticism, several socialist feminists have attempted to unify socialist feminism under one theoretical construct. (See the work of Alison Jaggar and Iris Young.) Although both attempts are ambitious, they and other feminists have expressed concern that such an action homogenizes the experiences of women and thus minimizes important differences and often renders them invisible.

Feminist Epistemology

We have examined four different versions of feminism that have emerged over the past three decades. Although such differences in theory and practice demonstrate the complexity of feminism, there are those who claim that more critical differences exist among feminists on the issue of epistemology, that is, the study of knowledge and its limits and validity. They argue that women's oppression is rooted in what we label as knowledge and the methods by which knowledge is generated.

As mentioned earlier, feminists place women's experiences and perspectives at the center of inquiry based on their view that both "hard" and social sciences have not adequately incorporated women's experiences in the production of knowledge. Sandra Harding (1987) notes the consequences of giving priority to women's lives and viewpoints:

> Once we undertake to use women's experiences to generate research problems, hypotheses, and evidence, to design research for women, and to place the researchers in the same critical plane as the research subject, traditional epistemological assumptions can no longer be made. (p. 181)

Challenging these traditional epistemological assumptions, Harding has delineated three distinct feminist approaches: feminist empiricism, feminist standpoint theory, and feminist postmodernism. Although advocates of each approach attempt to correct the androcentric bias existing within our current knowledge base, they go about it differently.

Feminist Empiricism

Feminist empiricists argue that sexist and androcentric biases enter into the research process at multiple points:

- When scientific problems are identified
- In the process of designing research
- In the collection and interpretation of data

Sexist methodology produces what Harding calls "bad" science, and ultimately limits our understanding not only of female experience but also human experience in general. For example, there has been a longstanding practice of assuming that female athletes can be understood using the findings derived from studies of male athletes.

Feminist empiricists claim that such sexist bias can be eliminated through studying women directly by adding them to the research sample, as well as by having more feminist women (and men) assume roles as researchers. They do not, however, challenge and undermine the grounding of what constitutes "good" scientific research, that is, the scientific notions of objectivism and universal truth. In this regard, feminist empiricism is remarkably similar to liberal feminism in that legal, political, economic, and scientific systems are not considered essentially antifeminist; rather, it is the sexist applications of the research process that are in need of correction.

Feminist Standpoint Theory

Feminist standpoint theorists argue that women's experiences informed by feminist theory provide a better grounding for more complete and less distorted knowledge claims than do men's experiences. It is through feminist struggles against male domination that women can produce a truer picture of social reality than can the ruling class of men. Standpoint theorists argue that men's vision of reality is incomplete because they are most often involved in only certain kinds of activities (e.g., the public world of work) and relegate activities they disdain to women (e.g., housework, childcare). As a result, men can know only a part of reality.

This economical and historical perspective of an oppressed class, a class whose vantage point can lead to revolutionary change, has its intellectual origins in Marxism. Marxist feminists, however, most notably Nancy Hartsock, have found Marx's male proletarian perspective to be biased. In response, they have developed a feminist standpoint theory to overcome this epistemological partiality. They believe that feminist standpoint epistemology can advance the objectivity of knowledge and become the basis for developing a more representative class than the proletariat; that is, women will lead the revolutionary struggle.

Feminist Postmodernism

Feminist postmodernists are skeptical about the universalizing claims of reason and science and do not believe that humans, female or male, have the capacity to generate absolute and universal knowledge. As a result, they criticize feminist theory that attempts to universalize women's experience of oppression and instead emphasize the many different stories women tell.

Working-class women, lesbians, and women of color also have criticized feminist theory that totalizes experience. For example, Bell Hooks (1984), an African-American feminist, argues that patriarchal oppression is experienced differently by women of color because of differences resulting from race and class. Consequently, there will be many feminist epistemologies involving multiple criticisms of various forms of male domination, rather than one universalizing perspective. Similar arguments have been made against efforts to develop unified theory in sport. Women of color have been particularly critical of these attempts.

We believe that the practice of assigning a universal prescription for all sporting women should be abandoned because socially constructed notions of gender, race, and class result in different experiences for different women. Not only do cultural heritage, belief systems, perceived ethnic body composition, religion, and political persuasion influence an athlete's disposition toward sport, but the preconceived attitudes of the observer, the teammate, and the coach often affect the athlete's perception of her embodied self. For example, writing from a black feminist position, Corbett and Johnson (1993) discuss how racist stereotypes have influenced societal expectations for African-American women:

> For the African-American woman, there was the presumption as a whole that because she represented an inferior status in society (not limited to, but featured as a tough, hardworking domestic or working-class individual), the roughness and toughness of the sporting world would only be natural and an acceptable activity at which she would be competent. (p. 182)

Racism influences not only the sporting expectations of women of color, it also influences their subsequent sporting experiences. When examining the importance of the Japanese YWCA in Los Angeles to Nisei female basketball players during the 1930s, for example, Costa (1993) found sport to be a highly significant avenue for expressing ethnic solidarity amid federally legislated racism. Basketball player Esther Fujimoto has remarked: "We had something. We all belonged to clubs and we played sports, regardless of skill . . . even though there was racial segregation" (Costa, 1993, p. 42).

Such cases reflect why women of color living in racist cultures may experience sport differently than others who do not suffer racial discrimination. Still, it is important to remember that differences among cultural groups also exist and will vary according to factors such as type of sport, body composition, presence of role models, physical capability, and even political perspective. For example, when illuminating the Chicana feminist position, Cherrie Moraga (1983) states:

> It is our tradition to conceive the bond between mother and daughter as paramount and essential in our lives . . . When we name this bond between the women of our race, from this Chicana feminism emerges. . . . This is what Chicana feminist means—making bold and political the love of the women of our race. . . . We must be the ones to define what it means to be female. (p. 139)

Projecting female bonding as described by Moraga to the sporting experience, we might conclude that the joy of shared physical experience would be of particular importance to Chicana athletes.

Likewise, Asian-American feminist consciousness is rooted in ethnic solidarity and fostered by the various exclusionary practices of the United States government and the forces of oppression (Costa, 1993). As Merle Woo suggests:

> Today I am satisfied to call myself either an Asian feminist or Yellow feminist. . . . This means I am working with others to realize pride in culture and women and heritage. (Moraga & Anzaldua, 1983, p. 142)

Such quotes reflect both the differences in expectations and the commonality of group cohesion present in the sporting experiences of various cultural groups. Whereas the African-American experience as expressed by Corbett and Johnson (1993) demonstrates an expectation of physical strength and mental toughness, the Chicana and Asian-American experiences tend to emphasize female bonding. We are quick to point out, however, that even within cultural groups the sporting experience will vary according to factors such as type of sport, body composition, physical capability, and presence of role models. In fact, the only universal sporting experiences found between and among women of color may be those that result from shared racial discrimination. Consequently, feminists would be wise to concentrate on the bodily experiences themselves, rather than superimpose a theoretical framework on those experiences. Moreover, when qualitative approaches that respect the diversity of human experience are more generally accepted and employed by dominant groups in sport research, we will likely gain a better understanding of sporting women and the significance of sport itself. A celebration of differences may also result.

Summary and Conclusions

Feminism is rich and diversified. Indeed, despite their differences, feminists have many beliefs and values in common. First and foremost, feminists believe that what exists now is not gender equality; that is, we still live in a patriarchal world that benefits men as a group far more often than it does women. Centrally related to this inequity is the social classification of gender, which has been used to construct unequal power relations between women and men. Feminists, regardless of perspective, strive to understand and change these patterns and believe that, to accomplish such goals, it is necessary to bring women's needs, values, and interests from the margins to the center.

Women who value sport participation in the late 20th century have feminists to thank for much of the freedom they now enjoy. In fact, we have come so far that there is a tendency to believe there is no longer a need for feminist action. As history has shown us, however, with every feminist step forward, a patriarchal backlash follows (see the work of Susan Faludi and Naomi Wolf). Sport is no exception. It behooves us to keep a critical eye on social change and to keep our feminist fires burning. Perhaps, then, women living in the late 21st century will achieve levels of accomplishment that we of the late 20th century can only imagine!

Note

[1]Alison Jaggar's (1983) work was used in developing theoretical discussion and categorization.

References

Acosta, V., & Carpenter, L.J. (1992). Title IX at twenty: The changing status of women in intercollegiate sport from 1972 to 1992. *Proceedings of the North American Society for Sport History* (p. 66).

Birrell, S., & Richter, D.M. (1987). Is a diamond forever? Feminist transformation of sport. *Women's Studies International Forum,* **10**(4), 395-409.

Black, D.R. (Ed.) (1991). *Eating disorders among athletes.* Reston, VA: AAHPERD.

California Education Code 41. (1976).

Corbett, D., & Johnson, W. (1993). The African-American female in collegiate sport: Sexism and racism. *Racism in college athletics,* Morgantown, WV: Fitness Information Technology.

Costa, D.M. (1993). Nisei women's sport in southern California in the 30s and 40s. *Perspectives: Journal of the Western Society for the*

Physical Education of College Women, **13**, 37-43.

DiGiovanna, M. (1993, October 22). College sports: Cal State system's plan to bring women's opportunities in line with men's could have nationwide ramifications. *The Los Angeles Times*, p. C-1.

Emery, L. (1992, November). *The southern California African American woman in sport.* Paper presented at the annual meeting of the Western Society for Physical Education of College Women, San Diego, CA.

A guide to the equity laws: Title IX of the Education Amendments, 1972. (1989, June 21). *Chronicle of Higher Education*, 25-27.

Harding, S. (1987). *Feminism and methodology.* Bloomington: Indiana University Press.

Hooks, B. (1984). *Feminist theory: From margin to center.* Boston: South End Press.

Horowitz, H.L. (1989). *Alma mater.* Boston: Beacon Press.

Jaggar, A.M. (1983). Feminist politics and human nature. Totowa, NJ: Rowman & Allanheld.

Jensen, J.M., & Lothrop, G.R. (1989). *California women: A history.* San Francisco: Boyd & Fraser.

Knuttgen, H.G., Ma, Q., & Wu, Z. (1990). *Sport in China.* Champaign, IL: Human Kinetics.

MacKinnon, C.A. (1989). *Toward a feminist theory of the state.* Cambridge, MA: Harvard University Press.

Moraga, C. (1983). Loving in the war years. New York: Women of Color Press.

Moraga, C., & Anzaldua, G. (1983). *This bridge called my back: The writings of women of color.* New York: Women of Color Press.

Oglesby, C. (1983). Interactions between gender identity and sport. In J.M. Silva & R.S. Weinberg (Eds.) *Psychological foundations of sport* (pp. 387-399). Champaign, IL: Human Kinetics.

Oglesby, C. (1990). Epilogue. In M. Messner & D. Sabo (Eds.), *Sport men and the gender order* (pp. 241-245). Champaign, IL: Human Kinetics.

Safrit, M.J. (1984). Women in research in physical education: A 1984 update. *Quest*, **36**, 104-114.

Seelye, L.C. (1874). *The need for a college education for women.* Unpublished manuscript, American Institute of Instruction.

Toohey, D.M. (1984). The political components behind women's participation in the modern Summer Olympic Games. In U. Simri (Ed.), *Sport and politics* (pp. 95-104). Netanya, Israel: Wingate Institute.

Tong, R. (1989). *Feminist thought: A comprehensive introduction.* Boulder, CO: Westview Press.

Williams, P.J. (1991). *The alchemy of race and rights.* Cambridge, MA: Harvard University Press.

Witherspoon, W. (1993, November 5). UCLA keeps gymnastics, adds women's water polo. *The Los Angeles Times*, p. C-8.

Wrynn, A. (1991). Look out for the ladies! Unpublished manuscript.

Zipter, Y. (1988). *Diamonds are a dyke's best friend: Reflections, reminiscences and reports from the field on the lesbian national pastime.* New York: Firebrand.

Chapter 16

Psychological Perspectives on Women in Sport and Exercise

Diane L. Gill

I had the sense of well-being which comes from regular, strenuous exercise. I developed an agility in my movements and a resistance to fatigue and stress. . . . I began to feel like a person to be reckoned with, strong and competent. I began to feel powerful, emotionally and physically.

LINDA PEARSON
"Learning to Be a Survivor: The Liberating Art of Tae Kwondo"

Women are everywhere in the world of sport and exercise, right? They take low-impact aerobics, pump iron at the exercise club, and jog through the neighborhood. Women throw baseballs in the back yard, swim at the Y, and win medals at the Olympics. They teach and coach, lead sport organizations, and conduct exercise and sport science research. Girls play in the youth soccer league and go to gymnastics camp.

Women do participate in diverse sport and exercise activities, but not quite "everywhere." As other chapters reveal, women's physical activity varies across historical and sociocultural contexts. Women's participation has not grown in parallel with men's, and even when women and men participate in similar activities, things are not as similar as they seem.

Gender has a profound, but often subtle, influence on sport and exercise participation and behavior. For example, everything is not the same for the starting centers of the women's and men's basketball teams at the state university, for the 10-year-old girl and the 10-year-old boy pitching in a youth baseball game, or for the middle-aged

253

woman and middle-aged man at the exercise club.

I examine in this chapter women's sport and exercise from a psychological perspective. *Psychology* typically is defined as the study of human behavior, and *sport and exercise psychology* may be defined as the study of human behavior in sport and exercise contexts. Certainly many questions might be raised (e.g., How does exercise affect women's self-image? Are men more competitive than women?), but most of those questions remain unanswered.

Although the research is not extensive, some scholars from the field of social psychology have examined gender in ways that help illuminate women's sporting attitudes and behavior. Still, psychological factors alone cannot fully explain women's sporting behavior. Such behavior takes place within a social and historical context, and individual differences and psychological processes operate within that context. Moreover, each woman brings to the sport setting a unique biological and psychological makeup. All of these factors interact in complex ways to influence sporting behavior, and we should keep the complexity and richness of human behavior in mind as we examine women's sport and exercise from a psychological perspective.

Sex Differences and Gender Influences

Sex difference refers to biologically based differences between females and males, whereas *gender* refers to social and psychological characteristics and behaviors associated with females and males. Early researchers studied sex differences and assumed that dichotomous psychological differences paralleled and resulted from biological female–male differences. Current scholars question these earlier interpretations and suggest that psychological characteristics and behaviors associated with females and males are neither dichotomous nor biologically based. In fact, most biological characteristcs are not dichotomous but rather

are normally distributed among both females and males.

Moreover, when females and males do differ, we find considerable overlap and similarity. For example, males generally are taller than females, but many women are taller than many men. For social psychological characteristics and behaviors, differences are elusive, no evidence supports a biological basis, and certainly no dichotomous sex-linked connections are evident. Thus, after a brief overview of the work on sex differences, I will refer to gender differences and gender influences.

The study of sex differences has a long and colorful history, with frequent social and political overtones. Studies of the brain during the 19th century, which often provided the justification for racist and sexist practices, serve as an example. The statement made by Le Bon, a brain scientist, in 1879 reflects the ideology of the period:

> In the most intelligent races, as among the Parisians, there are a large number of women whose brains are closer in size to those of gorillas than to the most developed male brains. This inferiority is so obvious that no one can contest it for a moment; only its degree is worth discussion. (Gould, 1981, pp. 104-105)

Although brain size is rarely used to explain race or sex differences today, biologically based justifications for continuing racist and sexist practices are still too common.

The history of psychological sex differences is similarly colorful. Maccoby and Jacklin's 1974 scholarship is the most notable work in this area. After compiling the available research, they suggested possible sex differences in four areas: math ability, visuo-spatial ability, verbal ability, and aggressive behavior. These "possible" sex differences quickly became accepted as common knowledge, even though Maccoby and Jacklin cautioned that the research provided little support for sex differences and that few conclusions could be drawn.

Unfortunately, many scholars have ignored Maccoby and Jacklin's caveats; instead they have accepted the tentative findings as facts and have directed their efforts toward finding the underlying biological basis of such sex differences. Fortunately, others have continued to question sex differences and to examine gender influences from different perspectives.

Despite many attempts to identify sex differences and their biological correlates, the bulk of the research casts doubt even on the four possible differences cited by Maccoby and Jacklin. Several reviews, most notably the meta-analyses by Eagley (1987) and Hyde and Linn (1986), have demonstrated that sex differences in these areas are minimal and not biologically based. Meta-analyses, which statistically combine the results of all studies reviewed, consistently indicate that less than 5% of the behavioral variance in these cognitive ability areas is accounted for by sex. Moreover, sex differences are inconsistent, and interactions are common. For example, sex differences might show up with one visuo–spatial task but not another, or boys might complete a timed math test faster than girls do but do no better on math accuracy with no time restriction. In general, overlaps and similarities are much more apparent than differences when males and females are compared on cognitive tasks and abilities.

In a review of the aggression research, Frodi, Macauley, and Thome (1977) concluded that the literature does not support the belief that males are more aggressive than females. Rather, gender differences are inconsistent and related to other factors such as justification, sex of the instigator, and situational cues. In a more recent meta-analysis, Eagley and Steffin (1986) concluded that males are somewhat more aggressive than females on average, but added that sex differences are inconsistent and related to methodological aspects of the studies, including type of aggressive behavior and perceived consequences. Most current explanations of aggressive behavior emphasize learning and social situational factors rather than biological sex differences. (See Gill, 1986b, for an overview of aggression and sport.)

Clearly aggressive behaviors are prevalent in sports and are reinforced in both direct and indirect ways (e.g., young players often are coached to engage in varied aggressive behaviors; top athletes display aggressive behaviors and serve as models). Moreover, it is just as clear that these reinforcements and inducements for aggressive behavior in sports are stronger for males than for females. Competitive sport situations encourage some aggressive behaviors for both males and females, but parents and coaches are more likely to encourage aggressive play among boys than girls. Thus any observed gender influences on aggressive behavior in sports likely are related to the immediate situation and previous social experiences of the participants rather than to underlying biologically based sex differences.

In more recent studies, investigators have reached similar conclusions about other cognitive skills and social behaviors, as well as those cited by Maccoby and Jacklin. Clear sex differences do not emerge with skills and behaviors such as conformity and nonverbal behavior any more than with verbal ability and aggressive behavior. Again, overlap and similarity are more apparent, and many interactions qualify observed differences (see Deaux, 1985, for an overview).

Perhaps the most telling statement about sex differences is that neither Maccoby nor Jacklin now advocates sex differences in cognitive skills and social behaviors. Instead, Jacklin (1989) contends that gender is *not* an important variable for explaining individual variation in intellectual abilities. She further emphasizes that although some biologically based gender differences may exist, their implications for behavioral development are currently unknown. Jacklin also notes that the rich literature on socialization processes yields so many contradictions and revisions that gender socialization may be a "moving target"; that is, gender changes as society changes, and final answers may not be possible.

Maccoby (1990) has placed even more emphasis on the social situation in her most recent writings. She notes that sex differences in behavior are minimal when children are tested or observed individually. She also reports that sex differences emerge mainly in social situations and vary with the gender composition of the group. For example, children tend to segregate into same-sex groups and develop distinctive interaction styles. Both Maccoby and Jacklin, then, have suggested that pursuing sex differences is not a viable research line. Such an approach assumes an underlying, unidimensional cause (i.e., biological sex) and ignores the rich and complex variations in gender-related behavior.

Psychologists like Maccoby and Jacklin are not the only ones to criticize research on sex differences. Bleier (1986), who trained as a physician and neuroanatomist, is particularly critical of the research on sex differences in brain structure and function. Bleier has argued that although we assume that such biological research is more objective and scientific than psychosocial research, this is not the case. Brain researchers are just as strongly influenced by sociopolitical factors and biases as are other researchers. Even if some sex-related differences exist in brain structure and function (and this is by no means established), and even if gender-related behavioral differences exist, we cannot assume that one causes the other or that they even have a common cause. Indeed, the differences may not be parallel or correlated at all. Notes Bleier (1986):

> The evidence that we have permits one important conceptualization of the development of cognition and behavior: biological and environmental factors are inextricable, in ways that make futile any efforts to separate them and measure *how much* of human behavior can be attributed to biology and *how much* to environment and learning. . . . It is because learning and environment are inextricable from the structure of neurons and because we have the property of mind, each mind the

unique product of our individual complex histories of development and experience, that I view as futile efforts to reduce human behaviors to biological parameters. Rather than biology, it is the cultures that our brains have created that most severely limit our visions and the potentialities for the fullest possible development of each individual. (pp. 161-163)

Like Bleier, I do not believe we can reduce women's sport and exercise behavior to biological parameters and find answers in brain research. Studies of brain lateralization typically include a small number of patients with brain injuries; lack control for type of impairment and background; yield weak gender relationships at best; and provide no demonstrated direct ties to behavior. Brain lateralization differences between right and left handers are clearer than gender differences, yet no one claims right and left handers behave differently in sports because of these differences; no one even examines the possibility. Studies relating gender differences to brain or biological factors therefore are not likely to help us understand sport and exercise behavior. Moreover, relying on a brain or biological explanation for gender differences diverts attention from investigating more viable possibilities.

Personality and Gender Roles in Sport and Exercise

Personality is one of the most prominent topics in sport and exercise psychology, as well as in psychology, so it is not surprising that much of the psychological literature on women's sport has emphasized personality. Many studies examine personality characteristics of athletes and nonathletes, successful and less successful athletes, athletes across sports, and the effects of sport or exercise participation on personality. Despite the many studies on sport personality, these studies are atheoretical and methodologically flawed; as a result, the findings are inconsistent and inconclusive. Generally, personality traits, as measured on most standard personality tests, are poor predictors of sport and exercise behavior. Situational factors (e.g., rules, coaching instructions, team norms, societal pressures) are far more powerful influences on sport behavior.

Moreover, most sport personality studies have used males, reflecting the long-standing male bias in both psychology and sport psychology, as well as the assumption that studies with females would yield results similar to those with males. The latter may be true, particularly for elite populations, but research using males exclusively does not permit such conclusions and has limited our understanding of women in sport.

Gender Role Orientation

Psychologists interested in gender-related behaviors have focused on *gender role orientation* (i.e., femininity, masculinity, adrogyny) as the relevant personality construct. The first prominent measure of masculinity and femininity was the Attitude Interest Analysis Survey (AIAS) developed by Terman and Miles (1936). Shortly thereafter Hathaway and McKinley (1940) developed the masculinity-femininity (MF) scale of the Minnesota Multiphasic Personality Inventory (MMPI), the most widely used psychological measure in existence. As Lewin (1984a, 1984b) notes, the MF (inversion) scale of the MMPI was intended as a measure of psychopathology, and the items confuse sexual orientation with personality. Moreover, the scale was never validated as a measure of masculinity and femininity, although it is commonly accepted as such. Hathaway and McKinley used 13 homosexual males as a criterion group to identify MMPI items that differentiated these 13 gay men from a group of 54 heterosexual male soldiers. As Lewin (1984b) asks, ''How did psychology end up in a situation where the distinctive responses of 13 male homosexuals came to define the nature of femininity?'' (p. 181). Although such

a validation procedure would be unthinkable today, many psychologists continue to use the MF scale. Moreover, the linking of masculine and feminine personality constructs with sexuality and sex role behaviors was the norm in psychology until Bem's work came to the forefront.

Bem's (1974, 1978) theoretical discussions and development of the Bem Sex Role Inventory (BSRI), which measures individual differences in gender role orientation, provided the major impetus for a large body of research. Spence and Helmreich (1978) also investigated gender role orientation and developed the Personality Attributes Questionnaire (PAQ) as a measure of femininity and masculinity (Spence, Helmreich, & Stapp, 1974). This research stimulated investigation of gender roles in sport psychology, as well as in psychology. In fact, most sport psychology research on gender used the constructs and measures developed by Bem or Spence and Helmreich.

In developing her perspective and measures, Bem dismissed the traditional, unidimensional models of gender roles and advocated a new approach, building on the work of earlier advocates of multidimensional approaches (Bakan, 1966; Constantinople, 1973), who suggested that masculinity and femininity should not be treated as opposite extremes of a single construct. Bem further suggested that the personality characteristics of masculinity and femininity are not necessarily linked to biological sex; that is, males are not inherently more masculine nor females more feminine in personality. Finally, Bem dismissed the notion that sexual orientation is linked to personality constructs (as the development of the MMPI MF scale had implied). Within Bem's conceptualization, femininity and masculinity are not opposite ends of the same personality dimension, but separate clusters of positive or desirable personality characteristics. Although feminine characteristics typically are seen as more desirable for women than for men, and masculine characteristics typically seen as more desirable for men than for women, Bem argued that there is no reason why females should possess only feminine characteristics or males only masculine characteristics. Indeed, Bem contended that people who are extremely sex typed (only masculine or only feminine) are inflexible with few behavioral options, whereas the most mentally healthy individuals are androgynous and possess both feminine and masculine characteristics.

Bem (1974) developed the BSRI to match her views. Specifically, the BSRI includes 20 stereotypically feminine items (e.g., affectionate, sensitive to the needs of others) to assess femininity, 20 stereotypically masculine items (e.g., independent, willing to take risks) to assess masculinity, and 20 filler items (e.g., truthful, happy). In her original work Bem emphasized the construct of androgyny, and the original scoring system for the BSRI included an androgyny score based on the difference between the feminine and masculine scores. Like the BSRI, the PAQ assesses separate clusters of positive or desirable feminine and masculine characteristics, although the authors (Helmreich, Spence, & Holohan, 1979; Spence & Helmreich, 1980) now suggest that the personality clusters are more appropriately labeled as expressive (feminine) and instrumental (masculine).

Although the construct of androgyny has remained popular, the original difference score calculation was quickly abandoned. With the difference scores, individuals who scored low on both scores, as well as individuals who scored high on both scores, were classified as androgynous. Investigators soon realized that this classification did not fit the spirit of the androgyny construct, and that only individuals who scored high on both feminine and masculine characteristics truly were androgynous. Current scoring procedures involve calculating the separate masculine and feminine scores and then using median splits to classify individuals into four categories, as shown in Table 16.1.

Persons who score high on both masculinity and femininity are classified as androgynous, those who score high on femininity and low on

Table 16.1 Four-Way Classification of Individuals on Masculinity and Femininity

	Masculinity	
Femininity	Above median	Below median
Above median	Androgynous	Feminine
Below median	Masculine	Undifferentiated

Note. From Bem (1978).

masculinity as feminine, those high on masculinity and low on femininity as masculine, and those low on both as undifferentiated.

Gender Role Orientations of Sports Participants

This work spurred considerable research not only within psychology, but also within sport and exercise psychology. Helmreich and Spence (1977) presented some of their early work to the North American Society for the Psychology of Sport and Physical Activity, and sport psychology researchers soon began to adopt the gender roles approach and measures for studies with athletes.

Helmreich and Spence sampled intercollegiate athletes in their early studies and reported that most female athletes were either androgynous or masculine. These athletes were similar to high-achieving female scientists in Helmreich and Spence's samples, but different from female college students, who were most often classified as feminine (see Table 16.2 for specific results).

Several subsequent studies with female athletes yielded similar findings. Harris and Jennings (1977) surveyed female distance runners and, like Helmreich and Spence, reported that most were androgynous or masculine. Both Del Rey and Sheppard (1981) and Colker and Widom (1980) used the PAQ with female intercollegiate athletes and found that most were classified as androgynous or masculine. Myers and Lips (1978) used

Table 16.2   Distribution of Male and Female Students, Male and Female Scientists, and Female Varsity Athletes on PAQ Classifications

	Undifferentiated	Feminine	Masculine	Androgynous
Male students	31	13	27	29
Female students	21	39	11	29
Male scientists	20	5	43	32
Female scientists	8	23	23	46
Female athletes	20	10	31	39

Note. From Helmreich & Spence (1977).

the BSRI with female and male racquet sports participants and reported that most females were androgynous, whereas most males were masculine. In a second study, players' reasons for entering a tournament were classified as competitive (e.g., to win, for competition) or noncompetitive (e.g., to have fun, to pass the weekend). All males were competitive and also androgynous or masculine. Competitive females also were androgynous or masculine, but noncompetitive females had lower masculinity scores and tended to be either feminine or undifferentiated. More recently, Wrisberg, Draper, and Everett (1988) used the BSRI with intercollegiate team and individual sport athletes. They reported that both female and male team sport athletes were mainly masculine or androgynous. Female and male individual sport athletes differed, however, in that most females were classified as feminine whereas males were distributed equally across the classifications.

Most of the studies of gender roles in sports involve athletes, but Henderson, Stalnaker, and Taylor (1988) extended the research to leisure settings by exploring the relationship between gender role orientation and perceived barriers to recreation. They reported that females who were classified as masculine perceived the fewest leisure constraints, followed by androgynous women, and finally feminine women, paralleling the findings with athletes.

Limitations of Gender Role Measures and Research

The BSRI and PAQ measures have been criticized on both psychometric and conceptual grounds (e.g., Locksley & Colten, 1979; Pedhazur & Tetenbaum, 1979). Both inventories were developed by incorporating items that were rated as more desirable for either females or males. This practice confuses stereotypes and attitudes with personality or individual differences. In addition, specific problems have been noted with the psychometric properties of items and of the clusters. For example, one could easily doubt that some of the presumably desirable feminine qualities are indeed desirable (e.g., childlike, gullible).

The androgyny construct is of little conceptual or empirical value in gender role research and not even Bem and Spence and Helmreich continue to advocate its use. The 2 × 2 classification is especially problematic. As Taylor and Hall (1982) concluded, there is no evidence that an androgyny construct adds anything to gender role research. Using the full range of feminine and masculine scores rather than arbitrary categories seems better suited to the questions and purposes of those interested in gender role orientation.

Most personality characteristics are not dichotomous categories or types, as some pop psychology literature suggests. Rather, people tend to be normally distributed across the range of scores, with few at the extremes of any characteristic. Moreover, the median split approach recalls the dichotomous classifications that plagued the early research on sex differences; we should move beyond that to new approaches in the effort to understand gender-related behavior.

Overall, the sport psychology research on gender role orientation suggests that female athletes possess more masculine or instrumental personality characteristics than do female nonathletes. Sport, particularly in highly competitive settings, requires instrumental, assertive behaviors. It is hardly surprising that participants have higher instrumentality scores than do nonparticipants. Both the BSRI and PAQ include ''competitive'' as one of the masculine/instrumental items. The higher masculine scores of female athletes probably reflect an overlap with competitiveness or sport achievement orientation rather than a connection to any other gender-related constructs or behaviors.

In one of my studies on competitive orientation (Gill & Dzewaltowski, 1988), we found that competitiveness (measured directly) clearly differentiated athletes and nonathletes and that this difference held for both females and males. We also administered the BSRI and PAQ. Consistent with other research findings, athletes scored higher than nonathletes on masculinity/instrumentality, but this difference was not nearly as strong as the difference between athletes and nonathletes on competitiveness. In fact, our analysis indicated that competitiveness was the only important discriminator; the BSRI and PAQ scores did not add any useful information. Sport participation is associated with instrumentality, but we can use direct measures of competitive sport orientation that do not invoke gender role connotations.

Perhaps more important, sport participation or athlete/nonathlete status is an indirect and nonspecific measure of behavior. If instrumental and expressive personality characteristics predict instrumental and expressive behaviors, we should examine instrumental and expressive behaviors.

Classifying sport as instrumental or masculine ignores the fact that many different instrumental *and* expressive behaviors occur in sport and exercise settings. Even within highly competitive sports, expressive behaviors may be advantageous. Creative, expressive actions may be the key to success for a gymnast; supportive behaviors of teammates may be critical on a soccer team; and sensitivity to others may help an Olympic coach communicate with each athlete.

I have just cited instrumental and expressive *behaviors*. We might assume that instrumental and expressive personality dispositions relate to these behaviors. As noted earlier, however, personality traits are not powerful predictors of behaviors. Situational factors typically exert greater influence, and many things moderate the influence of personality. Helmreich, Spence, and Holohan (1979) cautioned that gender role measures are only weakly related to gender role behaviors, and emphasized situational factors. For example, expressive behaviors are more appropriate in figure skating freestyle programs than when performing school figures. By considering the combined influence of instrumental and expressive personality characteristics along with situational constraints, incentives, and interaction processes, we move closer to understanding gender-related behaviors in sport and exercise.

Even if we recognize the limits of personality measures, research on gender role orientation raises concerns. Hall (1988, 1990), a sport sociology scholar and one of the first to take a feminist approach, charges that using gender role measures reifies masculine-feminine dichotomies that do not really exist in concrete terms. Focusing on gender role constructs leads us away from the wider range of characteristics and social psychological processes that influence sport and exercise behavior. Overall, the sport psychology research on gender role orientation has the drawbacks of early sport personality research along with gender stereotypes and biases.

Hall also notes that this early gender role research led to a focus on ''role conflict,'' assuming an incompatibility between the roles of woman and athlete. For example, some researchers (Del Rey, 1978; Harris, 1980, 1987) contended that female athletes experience role conflict because sport demands behaviors that conflict with the female gender role. Del Rey further suggested that women often resolve this conflict by adopting more extreme feminine behaviors (an "apologetic"). As both Hall (1990) and Allison (1991) have noted, the role conflict notion does not advance our research or practice, is not likely to guide future work, and should be abandoned. Instead, as Hall (1990) states, we should recognize that "femininity and masculinity are socially constructed, historically specific, and mediated by social class, race, and ethnicity" (p. 228).

Most researchers interested in gender and behavior now recognize the limits of these early sex differences and gender role approaches and look beyond the simple male-female and masculine-feminine dichotomies. Even Bem and Spence and Helmreich, moving beyond their earlier methods, now view gender constructs and behaviors in more complex ways.

Unfortunately, these limitations are not always recognized by some recent and popular discussions of gender issues. Gilligan's (1982) work on moral reasoning and moral development has stimulated debate and brought a needed consideration of women's experiences to that literature. Gilligan questioned the male biases inherent in Kohlberg's moral reasoning hierarchy and introduced alternative methods and analyses that highlighted women's perspectives. Her research was groundbreaking. However, if we contrast the "female" model of moral reasoning with a traditional "male" model, we are perpetuating a stereotypical dichotomy. We could easily end up arguing the merits of female and male moral reasoning and accepting the classification of people into extreme types without considering the complexities of gender influences with moral reasoning and behaviors.

Belenky, Clinchy, Goldberger, and Tarule's (1986) provocative work on women's ways of knowing introduced similar important women's perspectives, but also poses similar potential problems. Belenky et al.'s focus on women's experiences, as well as their nontraditional methods (e.g., interviews with women from diverse backgrounds), introduced important alternative ideas, methodologies, and indeed ways of knowing to our research.

Bredemeier has incorporated the work of both Gilligan and Belenky et al. in her work on moral development. Bredemeier and her colleagues (Bredemeier, 1984; Bredemeier & Shields, 1987; Weiss & Bredemeier, 1990) have advanced beyond Kohlberg's classic system by including Gilligan's emphasis on caring and responsibility in moral judgments. Bredemeier also incorporated Haan's interactive approach within the context of sport and physical education. The considerable work of Bredemeier and her colleagues suggests that sport can encourage moral development. In particular, Weiss and Bredemeier suggested that if we want to emphasize moral growth through sports and physical education, we should challenge young people by encouraging autonomous thinking about values, exposing them to alternative views, and providing opportunities for dialogue, negotiation, and balance of moral conflicts.

More recently, Bredemeier and her colleagues (1991) have adopted Belenky's approach to investigate women's epistemological perspectives or "ways of knowing" in physical activity settings. Specifically, Bredemeier et al. interviewed women in body building, mountain climbing, lesbian softball, intercollegiate field hockey, and noncompetitive individual activities. Following Belenky et al.'s framework, they noted that most women were subjective knowers (emphasize inner voice and experience, truth as intuition) or procedural knowers (emphasize reason and expertise, truth as observation and analyses). Also, participants' perspectives were related to their views of power, competition, and cooperation, and whether they tended to take the same perspective in physical activity and in their daily lives. Bredemeier's work is innovative and exploratory rather than conclusive; her most important contribution may be to encourage others to remain open to alternative approaches to understanding women's sport and physical activity.

Most important, sport psychologists should not blindly adopt Belenky et al.'s framework and approach. As was discussed in regard to Gilligan's work, classifying moral reasoning, ways of knowing, or anything else, into feminine and masculine forms (even if we acknowledge that both females and males could use either) focuses on a stereotypical dichotomy and reduces a complex phenomenon to a unidimensional explanation. Sport psychologists must move beyond simplistic models to consider gender as a complex construction within a sociocultural and historical context rather than a fixed characteristic of individuals.

Gender and Sport Achievement

Achievement, one of the most prominent topics in both psychology and sport psychology research on gender, has progressed from early research on sex differences and gender roles to more current models that include social cognitions and social context. Gender differences were recognized in the early research when McClelland, Atkinson, Clark, and Lowell (1953) noted that women did not respond to achievement instructions as men did. Gender differences were ignored at that point, and achievement researchers, like most other psychologists, took male behavior as the norm and conducted their work with men. The theories and findings on achievement motivation were theories and findings on men's achievement motivation.

It was not until the 1970s that women's achievement behavior and gender influences were considered. Early work emphasized gender differences in achievement motivation and focused specifically on the fear of success. More recently, researchers have turned to gender differences in achievement cognitions.

Gender and Achievement Orientation

Horner's (1972) doctoral work focused attention on the role of gender in achievement behavior. Horner adopted an individual differences approach and specifically proposed a "motive to avoid success" to explain gender differences in achievement behavior. Horner asserted that the motive to avoid success, more popularly termed "fear of success" (FOS), influences achievement behavior, just as the motives to approach success and avoid failure influence achievement behavior within the widely accepted Atkinson model. According to Horner, success has negative consequences for women because success requires competitive behaviors that conflict with the traditional feminine image. This conflict triggers the fear of success motive and leads to anxiety and avoidance. Men are less likely to exhibit fear of success because gender socialization does not lead to similar conflicts and negative consequences for them. Thus FOS is a negative or inhibitory motive that is more common in women than in men.

To test her ideas, Horner had female and male students respond to cues about Anne or John, a medical student at the top of the class. Horner coded these responses for FOS imagery and found that females wrote more fear of success imagery about Anne than males wrote about John. Horner further observed that females who scored high in FOS did not perform as well as females who scored low in FOS when later doing problems in a group competitive setting. Horner's original work was limited in many ways, and she did not follow up the original findings with more in-depth study. Nevertheless, her work was widely publicized in the popular media and inspired much debate and subsequent research.

Most subsequent work has cast doubt on Horner's FOS construct and measure (e.g., Condry & Dyer, 1976; Tresemer, 1977). Critics have noted that FOS imagery is prevalent among men as well as women. In addition, the FOS measure confuses stereotypical attitudes toward women's success with individual motives, and the research fails to link FOS directly to achievement behaviors. McElroy and Willis (1979), who specifically considered women's achievement conflicts in sport contexts, concluded that no evidence supports a FOS in female athletes and that achievement attitudes of female athletes are similar to those of male athletes.

Although Horner's FOS measure and motive have lost their initial appeal, gender is a prominent issue in the achievement literature. The earlier models emphasizing global achievement motives have been replaced with multidimensional constructs and an emphasis on cognitions as mediators of achievement behavior. For example, Helmreich and Spence (1978) developed a multidimensional Work and Family Orientation Questionnaire (WOFO) that assesses three separate dimensions—mastery, work, and competitiveness—and their research (Spence & Helmreich, 1983) indicates that gender differences vary across dimensions and across samples. Generally, males score higher than females do on mastery and competitiveness, and females score higher than males do on work. With high-achieving samples of scientists, businesspersons, and athletes, gender differences on mastery and work diminish, but males remain higher than females on competitiveness. Spence and Helmreich also reported that masculinity/instrumentality scores on the PAQ relate positively to all three achievement dimensions, whereas femininity/expressiveness scores relate slightly positively to work and negatively to competitiveness. In general, gender influence is strongest and most consistent for competitiveness.

My own work on sport achievement (Gill, 1988) suggests that gender influences vary across dimensions. Although we might assume that the gender difference in competitiveness reported by Spence and Helmreich carries over into sports, the research on sport achievement suggests a more complex picture. Following the lead of Martens (1977) and others who have developed sport-specific psychological measures, we developed a sport-specific measure of achievement orientation known as the Sport Orientation Questionnaire

(SOQ; Gill & Deeter, 1988). The SOQ is multidimensional, sport-specific, and yields scores for (a) competitiveness—an achievement orientation to enter and strive for success in competitive sport; (b) win orientation—a desire to win and avoid losing in competitive sport; and (c) goal orientation—an emphasis on achieving personal goals in competitive sports.

During the development of the SOQ we found consistent gender differences. Specifically, males scored higher than females did on competitiveness and win orientation, whereas females typically scored slightly higher than males did on goal orientation. Later, I (Gill, 1988) focused on gender and examined WOFO general achievement scores along with SOQ scores of females and males who participated in competitive sport, in noncompetitive sport, and in nonsport achievement activities. Overall, males consistently scored higher than females on sport competitiveness and win orientation, and males also reported more competitive sport activity and experience. Females were just as high as males, however, and sometimes higher, on sport goal orientation as well as on all general WOFO achievement scores except competitiveness. Females also were just as likely as males to participate in noncompetitive sport and to report nonsport achievement activities. Thus the gender differences in competitive orientation and sport participation do not seem to reflect either general achievement orientation or interest in physical activity. Instead, gender may influence a person's emphasis on social comparison and winning in sport.

Other researchers report similar gender influences on reactions to competitive sport. When McNally and Orlick (1975) introduced a cooperative broomball game to children in urban Canada and in the northern territories, they found girls were more receptive to the cooperative rules than were boys. Although they also noted cultural differences, in that northern children were more receptive to the cooperative rules, the gender influence held in both cultures. Similarly, Duda (1986) reported both gender and cultural influences on competitiveness with Anglo and Navajo children in the southwestern United States. Male Anglo children were the most win-oriented and placed the most emphasis on athletic ability. In an experimental study, Weinberg and Jackson (1979) found that males were more affected by success or failure than were females, who reacted more consistently. In a related study Weinberg and Ragan (1979) reported that males were more interested in a competitive activity, whereas females preferred a noncompetitive activity. Finally, Deci, Betley, Kahle, Abrams, and Porac (1981) suggested that competition and a focus on winning may act as an extrinsic motivator to decrease intrinsic motivation, and that the undermining of intrinsic motivation is especially likely for females.

Although several lines of research suggest gender influences on sport achievement, and particularly in competition, findings do not indicate any unique gender-related personality construct as an explanation. As a result most investigators are now examining socialization factors, societal influences, and a broader range of social cognitive constructs and models.

Gender and Achievement Cognitions

In contrast to the earlier emphasis on personality (e.g., need to achieve), current cognitive approaches emphasize the person's interpretations and perceptions as mediators of behavior. That is, what the person *thinks* is important *is* important. If you expect to do well at volleyball, you probably will. If you think about falling off the balance beam, you probably will.

Cognitive motivation theories vary in specific constructs (e.g., expectancies, confidence, self-efficacy, challenge, perceived competence) and proposed relationships, but nearly all highlight expectations. Regardless of the specific framework, research consistently indicates that expectations are good predictors of achievement behavior and performance (e.g., Bandura, 1977, 1986; Crandall, 1969; Eccles, Adler, Futterman, Goff, Kaczala, Meece, & Midgley, 1983; Feltz, 1988; Roberts, 1984).

In addition to expectations, cognitive approaches to achievement often incorporate attributions, which are explanations that people offer for events and outcomes. The most important attributional difference seems to be whether we see success and failure as the result of our inherent abilities (and therefore permanent and unchangeable) or as the result of effort (something we can change). High achievers tend to attribute success to abilities or effort, and thus take credit for success, whereas low achievers tend to take less credit for success. Low achievers also tend to attribute failure to lack of ability, and give up, whereas high achievers are much more likely to attribute failure to lack of effort, accept the challenge, persist, and put in extra effort to reach their goals.

Researchers (e.g., Deaux, 1984) also suggest that gender influences expectations and attributions. In general, females report lower expectations and make fewer achievement-oriented attributions than do males, and this certainly seems to hold for sport and exercise. One incident from my graduate school days made this particularly clear to me. I was testing fifth and sixth graders on a competitive motor maze task. I introduced each child to an elaborate computer competition setup, went through an experimental scenario to build up the competition, and asked, "Well, are you all set to really try hard to do well and win this competition?" Every boy (not one exception) responded eagerly, as did most of the girls. Then one girl responded meekly, "Well, I don't know; I'm not very good at games like this." As the study continued, I soon realized that she was not an isolated case; several other girls reacted the same way. I also noted the reactions of the children to winning and losing. A few of the children who lost became very upset and cried, and all of them were boys. Girls, presumably the emotional sex, never cried or appeared visibly upset at a loss. Many years later those unexpected and gender-related reactions remain as vivid images for me. Moreover, such gender influences on sport achievement expectations have not disappeared. More girls than boys expect to do poorly at sports and competition, and more women than men believe they cannot develop sport skills or maintain an exercise program. Indeed, this gender influence on expectations and confidence is one of the most important considerations for achievement, particularly in the realm of physical activity.

Although females generally report lower expectations and assume less responsibility for success than do males, gender differences in cognitive expectancy patterns are not completely consistent; rather, they vary with the situation. In her review of the self-confidence literature, Lenney (1977) concluded that gender differences in confidence are more likely to occur in achievement situations that (a) involve tasks perceived as masculine, (b) provide only ambiguous feedback or ability information, and (c) emphasize social comparison evaluation. As discussed in the earlier section on sex differences, task characteristics may mediate gender differences. Most of the earlier research used tasks traditionally seen as masculine. When tasks considered appropriate for females are used, gender differences typically disappear. For example, Deaux and Farris (1977) and Stein, Pohly, and Mueller (1971) reported that gender differences in achievement cognitions vary with the sex-linked nature of the task. With male-linked tasks, males are more likely than females to take credit for success and less likely to attribute failure to lack of ability: the typical achievement-oriented reactions. In contrast, if the task is not male-linked, females are just as likely as males to exhibit achievement-oriented cognitions. Lenney's research (Lenney, Browning, & Mitchell, 1980) confirmed that clear evaluation guidelines reduced gender differences in self-confidence.

Corbin and his colleagues (Corbin, 1981; Corbin, Landers, Feltz, & Senior, 1983; Corbin & Nix, 1979; Corbin, Stewart, & Blair, 1981; Petruzzello & Corbin, 1988; Stewart & Corbin, 1988) have conducted a series of experimental studies with motor tasks that confirm Lenney's propositions. Specifically, Corbin and his colleagues

demonstrated that females do not lack confidence with a gender-neutral, non-socially evaluative task, and that performance feedback can improve the confidence of low-confidence females. Petruzzello and Corbin also found that feedback-enhanced confidence did not generalize beyond the experimental task and suggested that lack of experience also affects females' self-confidence. In our lab (Gill, Gross, Huddleston, & Shifflett, 1984) we matched female and male competitors of similar ability on a pegboard task. Males were slightly more likely than females to predict a win, but specific performance expectations were similar. Moreover, females performed slightly better in competition than males did, and generally had more positive achievement cognitions (i.e., higher perceived ability, more effort attributions).

These studies suggest that females and males display similar levels of confidence when (a) tasks are appropriate for females; (b) females and males have similar experiences and capabilities; and (c) clear evaluation criteria and feedback are present. It is important to remember, however, that these are experimental studies in controlled settings. We cannot so easily equate task appropriateness, experience, and social influence in the real world of sport and exercise. Still, such studies indicate that we must consider socialization and social context to understand the influence of gender on achievement cognitions and behaviors.

Eccles's Model of Achievement

Several models of achievement orientation have been used in sport psychology, including Nicholls's (1984, 1989) task and ego orientation, Dweck's (1986) mastery and helpless orientations, and Harter's (1981) perceived competence (see Weiss & Chaumeton, 1992, for an excellent review of motivational orientation in sport). Eccles's (1985, 1987; Eccles et al., 1983) model of achievement, which incorporates sociocultural factors as well as achievement cognitions, is particularly promising. Recently, Eccles and Harold

(1991) have extended the model to sport achievement. Eccles includes expectations and values as key determinants of achievement behaviors, with a complex network of sociocultural factors, primary socializers, and individual needs, schemata, and experiences as determinants of these achievement cognitions. In addition, gender exerts an influence at all stages of the model. As discussed earlier, gender differences in expectations are common, and gender also influences the value or importance of sport achievement. Eccles has further emphasized that gender differences in expectations and value develop over time and are influenced by gender role socialization, stereotyped expectations of others, and sociocultural norms, as well as individual characteristics and experiences.

Recently, Eccles and Harold (1991) have provided evidence showing that Eccles's model holds for sport achievement, that gender influences children's sport achievement perceptions and behaviors at a very young age, and that these gender differences seem to be the product of gender role socialization. They report that adolescent boys see more value in sport and see themselves as more capable in sports than do adolescent girls, and that these gender differences are stronger than those for English and math expectations and values. Moreover, analyses revealed that the gender difference in free time spent playing sport (achievement choice) was mediated or explained entirely by these perceptions, supporting the model's links from expectations and value to achievement choice. In another study, younger elementary school children demonstrated similar gender differences on self-perceptions of sport value and ability. These children also completed a motor proficiency test in which boys scored slightly better than girls did. Gender accounted for only 2% of the variance in actual motor proficiency, but explained 14% of the variance in *perceived* sport ability.

Such gender differences in perceptions and values encouraged Eccles to examine the sociocultural and socialization components of the model for an explanation. Teachers rated boys' sport ability higher than girls' sport ability, suggesting a potential school socializing influence. When children rated gender stereotypes by indicating how important the abilities were for girls and boys, sport was rated much more sex-typed than math or reading. These ratings of sex-typing correlated with children's ratings of their own sport ability, suggesting that gender stereotypes influence sport confidence even at this young age. Finally, children rated how important it was to their parents that they did well in sports. Not surprisingly, boys gave higher ratings, suggesting a further parental influence on sport achievement.

Eccles's work takes a big step forward to help us understand gender and sport achievement. First, Eccles's research indicates that gender differences exist in sport achievement choices and behaviors. Second, gender apparently influences sport achievement through self-perceptions of value and expectations. Although physical characteristics and aptitude have some influence, the sociocultural context and socialization process seem to be the primary source of gender differences in self-perceptions. These sociocultural processes encompass many specific factors (e.g., parental influence, school influence, sociocultural stereotypes) that are interrelated in complex ways. Although we cannot pinpoint precise predictors and lines of influence, we must consider the socialization process to better understand gender and achievement in sport and exercise.

Physical Activity and Self-Perceptions

As well as looking at the influence of individual characteristics on sport behavior, we should consider the influence of sport and exercise on the individual. In particular, sport and exercise have the potential to influence self-perceptions, particularly self-esteem. Just as individual differences (e.g., gender role, achievement motivation) may affect sport participation and behavior, sport and exercise may influence psychological characteristics and perceptions. Potential benefits are not unique to women, but because we have been denied opportunities historically, we have a lot to gain. (See box below.)

Clearly, sport and exercise can enhance physical well-being; women can improve strength, power, physical skills, and cardiorespiratory fitness. Women also may derive important benefits from the psychological changes that accompany enhanced physical fitness and skill. As we noted previously, females tend to lack confidence in their abilities, particularly in sport and exercise. Many women who begin to participate in exercise and sport programs report such enhanced self-esteem, particularly a sense of physical competence that often carries over into other aspects of

their lives exemplified by Meg Christian's song *Gym II*:

> Now my days feel brighter, my loads feel lighter, and my t-shirts all feel tighter. I feel a little safer, walk a little stronger.

The sentiments expressed in Christian's lyrics are repeated in exercise settings when women report feeling more confident as they recognize gains in physical fitness and competence. Unfortunately, researchers have neglected the influence of exercise and sport on self-perceptions as they have focused on enhancing the performance of elite athletes. A few studies do add support to the testimonials. Specifically, Holloway, Beuter, and

---

Morning Athletes

for Gloria Nardin Watts

Most mornings we go running side by side
two women in mid-lives jogging, awkward
in our baggy improvisations, two
bundles of rejects from the thrift shop.
Men in their zippy outfits run in packs
on the road where we park, meet
like lovers on the wood's edge and walk
sedately around the corner out of sight
to our own hardened clay road, High Toss.

Slowly we shuffle, serious, panting
but talking as we trot, our old honorable
wounds in knee and back and ankle paining
us, short, fleshy, dark haired, Italian
and Jew, with our full breasts carefully
confined. We are rich earthy cooks
both of us and the flesh we are working
off was put on with grave pleasure. We
appreciate each other's cooking, each
other's art, photographer and poet, jogging
in the chill and wet and green, in the blaze
of young sun, talking over our work,

our plans, our men, our ideas, watching
each other like a pot that might boil dry
for that sign of too harsh fatigue.

It is not the running I love, thump
thump with my leaden feet that only
infrequently are winged and prancing,
but the light that glints off the cattails
as the wind furrows them, the rum cherries
reddening leaf and fruit, the way the pines
blacken the sunlight on their bristles,
the hawk flapping three times, then floating
low over beige grasses,
                              and your company
as we trot, two friendly dogs leaving
tracks in the sand. The geese call
on the river wandering lost in sedges
and we talk and pant, pant and talk
in the morning early and busy together.

Note. From *The Moon is Always Female* by M. Piercy, 1981, New York: Alfred A. Knopf.

Duda (1988), Brown and Harrison (1986), and Trujillo (1983) have reported that exercise programs, particularly weight and strength training, enhance the self-concepts of women participants.

In addition to developing feelings of physical strength and confidence, sports offer the opportunity to strive for excellence, the chance to accomplish a goal through effort and training, and the psychological challenge of testing oneself in competition. Diana Nyad (1978), the marathon swimmer, expressed the sense of physical capability and the satisfaction of testing and meeting challenges that can be gained in both competitive and noncompetitive programs:

> When asked why, I say that marathon swimming is the most difficult physical, intellectual, and emotional battleground I have encountered, and each time I win, each time I reach the other shore, I feel worthy of any other challenge life has to offer. (p. 152)

Too often we lose these benefits when we place too much emphasis on winning medals and trophies. Research (e.g., Deci & Ryan, 1985; Weiss & Chaumeton, 1992) clearly shows that a focus on such extrinsic rewards detracts from intrinsic interest, other psychological benefits, and even performance achievements. Internal, individual standards for both performance and nonperformance goals should be emphasized if women are to enhance their sense of physical competence and confidence, and achieve all the benefits of sports and exercise activities.

Gender Belief Systems

As Deaux (1984) reports, psychologists have shifted away from approaches that rely on sex differences and individual differences to emphasize gender as a social category. Gender belief systems extend beyond individual personality characteristics, cognitions, and behaviors to focus on social context, socialization, and socially developed cognitive frameworks. According to

Deaux (1984; Deaux & Kite, 1987) gender belief systems encompass diverse gender stereotypes and attitudes about appropriate characteristics, roles, and behaviors. Attempts to explain gender-related behaviors on the basis of sex differences or individual differences and immediate cognitions clearly are inadequate. Both Bem, who initiated much of the gender role personality research, and Deaux, who studied achievement attributions, have moved beyond individual differences to consider broader social belief systems.

Bem's Gender Schema Theory

Bem has shifted away from her early focus on personality to a broader, more social gender schema theory (Bem, 1981, 1983, 1985). Rather than classifying people as feminine, masculine, or androgynous, Bem now focuses on sex typing as an indicant of gender-schematic processing. Persons who are sex typed (i.e., high-masculine males and high-feminine females) are gender-schematic, whereas non-sex-typed persons, with more balanced feminine and masculine characteristics, are gender aschematic. Gender-schematic persons tend to see situations in gender terms, stereotype others, and restrict their own activities to conform to gender stereotypes.

Gender schema theory suggests that sex-typed persons are more likely than non-sex-typed persons to classify sports in gender terms. As a result, they restrict their participation to what they perceive as gender-appropriate sport and exercise activities. Matteo (1986, 1988) and Csizma, Wittig, and Schurr (1988) confirmed that sports are indeed sex typed as masculine or feminine (mostly masculine). Matteo further reported that sex-typed persons did not participate in what they considered gender-inappropriate sports.

Recently, Frable (1989) confirmed some predictions of gender schema theory and provided evidence that gender ideology may have subtle influences even with situational constraints on behavior. In Frable's study, sex-typed participants indicated that sex should *not* be a criterion, but sex typing predicted gender attitudes, rules, and discriminatory behaviors (e.g., devaluing female performance). The finding that sex-typed persons see the world in gendered terms and behave in line with those perceptions, even without intentional discrimination, has implications for sport and exercise. Gender-schematic processing by teachers, parents, coaches, and others in the world of sport and exercise may influence behavior just as does the participant's own gender schema. For example, a gender-schematic elementary physical education teacher might see vigorous, contact sports as more appropriate for boys and creative movement activities as more appropriate for girls. This teacher might establish different activities or standards for girls and boys or, more likely, attempt to be nonsexist, yet still engage in subtle gender-stereotyped behaviors. For example, the teacher might ask girls to demonstrate gymnastics moves, or tell a boy who just pushed a girl while going for the soccer ball to be more careful when playing with girls. Such behaviors may have a powerful influence, particularly on younger participants who are developing their own attitudes and behavior patterns.

Deaux's Work on Gender Belief Systems

In her most recent work on gender belief systems, Deaux (1984) has shifted from a focus on individual differences to social categories and social context. Deaux (1984, 1985; Deaux & Kite, 1987) emphasizes the social component and proposes that how people *think* males and females differ is more important than how they actually differ. As discussed earlier, actual differences between females and males are small and inconsistent. Nevertheless, most people maintain their beliefs in gender differences.

Deaux has proposed that gender stereotypes are pervasive and exert a major influence on social interactions. Considerable evidence confirms gender stereotypes. In their often cited research, Broverman, Rosenkrantz, and their colleagues

(Broverman, Vogel, Broverman, Clarkson, & Rosenkrantz, 1972; Rosenkrantz, Vogel, Bee, Broverman, & Broverman, 1968) found that people believe females and males differ on a large number of characteristics and behaviors (e.g., women are more emotional and sensitive whereas men are more forceful and independent). Broverman et al. identified clusters of personality traits associated with the typical man (competence, agency) and typical woman (warmth, expressiveness), and asked therapists to judge the healthy man, the healthy woman, and the healthy adult on several characteristics. As one might guess, the therapists' ratings of the healthy man and healthy adult were more similar than the ratings of the healthy woman and healthy adult. Apparently gender stereotypes are held even by those who study and practice psychology, and we all should be aware of such biases.

More recent work (Deaux & Kite, 1987; Deaux & Lewis, 1984; Eagley & Kite, 1987) has suggested that bipolar stereotypes continue to exist, and also that gender stereotypes have multiple components. As Deaux (1984; Deaux & Kite, 1987; Deaux & Lewis, 1984) has emphasized, we hold gender stereotypes about role behaviors, occupations, physical appearance, and sexuality, as well as about traits. For example, we tend to picture construction workers as men and secretaries as women; if women are construction workers or police officers we picture them as looking like men. Deaux has suggested that these multiple components are interrelated, and that the relationships and implications for gender-related behavior may vary with the social context. For example, Deaux and Lewis (1984) found that people weigh physical appearance heavily and infer other gender-related traits and behaviors (e.g., personality, sexuality) from physical characteristics.

Such multidimensional gender stereotypes certainly have counterparts in sports and exercise. We expect men with athletic body types to be athletes. Moreover, we expect such men to be aggressive, competitive, independent, and certainly heterosexual. Teachers and coaches seldom encourage a smaller young man, or one with artistic talents, to try out for football. We also tend to assume that women with athletic body builds or talents are aggressive, competitive, independent, and lesbian.

Although such gender stereotypes are of interest themselves, they are of even more interest because they influence a wide range of attitudes and behaviors. Considerable research suggests a gender bias in the evaluation of female and male performance and achievement. For example, in a provocative study, Goldberg (1968) reported a bias favoring male authors when women judged articles that were equivalent except for sex of author. Many similar studies followed Goldberg's initial work, and most confirmed a male bias in evaluations of females and males. However, findings are not completely consistent, and the bias varies with information and situational characteristics (Deaux & Taynor, 1973; Pheterson, Kiesler, & Goldberg, 1971; Wallston & O'Leary, 1981).

Gender Beliefs in Sport

Although sport psychologists have not examined multidimensional gender stereotypes and interrelationships, gender stereotypes and gender bias in evaluations certainly exist in sports. Deaux (1985) has described a shift toward more egalitarian attitudes in the general society, and sport attitudes seem to be moving in that direction. The Miller Lite Report (1983), for example, suggested that females and males hold similar attitudes and that parents are equally positive toward sport participation of daughters and sons.

Although such findings reflect positive trends, gender stereotypes persist; in fact, they seem more persistent in sport than in other social contexts. Metheny was one of the first scholars to identify gender stereotypes in sport. In her classic analysis of sporting activities that were socially acceptable for females (i.e., they fit the traditional feminine

image), Metheny (1965, pp. 51-52) listed a few general principles. (See box on page 271.)

According to Metheny, then, acceptable sports for women (e.g., gymnastics, swimming, tennis) emphasize aesthetic qualities and often are individual activities in contrast to those that emphasize direct competition and team sports. Although Metheny offered her analysis over 25 years ago, gender stereotypes have not faded away, and the analysis could serve as a model today. Moreover, Metheny injected some connections between class and sex bias in her analysis, connections that should be recognized in current analyses. More recently, Kane and Snyder (1989) confirmed gender stereotyping of sports, as suggested by Metheny, and more explicitly identified physicality as the central feature in gender stereotyping of sport.

Ostrow and colleagues (Ostrow, 1981; Ostrow, Jones, & Spiker, 1981) reported both gender and age biases in ratings of the appropriateness of various sport activities for females and males of different ages. Most activities were rated more appropriate for males (in line with Metheny's suggestions), and most activities were seen as less appropriate for older people. Griffin (1973) reported that undergraduates rated female athletes and female professors as furthest from the image of the ideal woman, whereas the roles of girlfriend and mother were rated much closer. Selby and Lewko (1976) found gender influences on children's attitudes toward women in sport. Girls were more positive than were boys; girls who participated in sport were more positive than nonparticipants; and boys who participated were more negative than were nonparticipants.

Brawley, Landers, Miller, and Kearns (1979) asked female and male observers to rate the performance of a female and a male on a muscular endurance task. Although the performances were identical, both female and male observers rated the male performer higher. In a subsequent study Brawley, Powers, and Phillips (1980) failed to replicate the male bias with an accuracy task,

Socially Acceptable Sports Competition for Women

1. It is *not appropriate* for women to engage in contests in which:

    the resistance of the *opponent* is overcome by bodily contact

    the resistance of a *heavy object* is overcome by direct application of bodily force

    the body is projected into or through space over long distances or for extended periods of time

2. It *may be appropriate* for women identified in the lower levels of socioeconomic status to engage in contests in which:

    the resistance of an *object of moderate weight* is overcome by direct application of force

    the body is projected into or through space over moderate distances or for relatively short periods of time.

3. It is *wholly appropriate* for women identified with the more favored levels of socioeconomic status to engage in contests in which:

    the resistance of a *light object* is overcome with a *light implement*

    the body is projected into or through space in aesthetically pleasing patterns

    the velocity and maneuverability of the body is increased by the use of some manufactured device

    a spatial barrier prevents bodily contact with the opponent in face-to-face forms of competition (Metheny, 1965, pp. 51-52)

suggesting (as we noted in earlier sections) that the task mediates gender influence.

Several studies have adopted the Goldberg approach to examine gender bias in evaluating sport performance. A series of studies on female and male attitudes toward hypothetical female and male coaches (Parkhouse & Williams, 1986; Williams & Parkhouse, 1988; Weinberg, Reveles, & Jackson, 1984) found a bias favoring male coaches. In contrast, Williams and Parkhouse (1988) reported that female basketball players coached by a successful female did not exhibit the male bias but actually exhibited a female bias, suggesting a more complex influence on the formation and consequences of gender stereotypes.

Not only do these studies reveal gender beliefs in sport and exercise, they also suggest that such gender beliefs are powerful, pervasive, and begin early in life (see Greendorfer, 1987). Gendered beliefs and behaviors are apparent even in infants. Furthermore, parents, teachers, the media, and other socializers convey gendered beliefs in many direct and indirect ways. Some of these influences are apparent in the Eccles work on achievement discussed earlier. Clearly, an understanding of gender socialization provides the basis for understanding individual gender-related behavior in sport and exercise.

Overall, gender belief systems seem to flourish in the world of sport and exercise. Sport activities are gender stereotyped, and the sex typing of sport activities seems linked with other gender beliefs (e.g., physicality). Gender beliefs influence social processes, particularly social evaluation, and the research on gender bias in evaluation of coaches suggests that influence is at least as likely in sport as in other social interactions. Overt discrimination is unlikely, in that participants may not recognize the influence of gender belief systems in themselves or others. For example, many sport administrators and participants fail to recognize gender beliefs operating when athletic programs developed by and for men, stressing male-linked values and characteristics, are opened to girls and women.

Sport psychologists can advance our understanding of gender by investigating gender belief systems in sport and exercise. There has been some work, but we have not yet begun to consider multiple components and interrelationships, and many questions remain unanswered. For example, how do gender beliefs about physical appearance or sexuality relate to beliefs about sport appropriateness? More important, how do gender belief systems in sport and exercise relate to evaluations of others, communication, and other social interactions and processes? Quite likely, many aspects of gender belief systems and their relationships to behavior are unique to sport and exercise. Nevertheless, Deaux's initial work and suggestions could provide a good starting point.

Gender and Social Context

Clearly we should consider gender beliefs to understand gender-related behavior but, as Deaux and Major (1987) have emphasized, we also must consider the immediate social context. Gender-related behaviors vary tremendously from situation to situation. Application of an interactive model that considers direct and subtle aspects of the immediate social context should permit greater insight into gender-related behaviors.

Deaux and Major's interactive model parallels the interactive models that have replaced early trait approaches to personality and sport behavior. In their model gender-linked behaviors are multiply determined, highly flexible, and context dependent. Individual characteristics and cognitions, as well as those of others, are important; however, the salience and influence of others' expectations, self-perceptions, and situational cues vary tremendously. Although this model seems similar to the typical personality × situation model, Deaux and Major clearly place more emphasis on the social

environment, that is, on socialization, social norms, and belief systems.

An emphasis on social context is critical for understanding gender-related behavior. In her book *The Female World*, sociologist Jessie Bernard (1981) has maintained that social experiences and contexts for females and males are quite different, even when they appear similar on the surface. Indeed, female and male worlds are different. In the early days of organized sport from the late 19th century to Title IX, separate sport worlds for females and males were the norm. Despite legal and organizational changes, the separate social sport worlds have not disappeared. For example, the social world differs for female and male members of a volleyball class, for male and female joggers, and for the girl and boy pitching a youth baseball game.

Sherif (1972, 1976, 1982) was a persistent advocate for social context in psychological research. She emphasized social context and process when considering gender influences and identified strategies for incorporating social context and gender into research on competition and sport behavior. Unfortunately, sport psychologists have not adopted Sherif's suggestions or other current *social* psychological approaches. Indeed, our research and practice seem narrower and more oblivious to social context and process than ever before. Overlooking social issues and processes cannot advance our understanding of gender as it relates to sport and exercise.

In sport and exercise science, sport sociologists have done the most to advance our understanding of gender, and to incorporate feminist frameworks and alternative approaches (e.g., critical theory, social construction). For example, Birrell (1988) traced gender and sport research from sex differences, through gender roles, to current considerations of gender relations in a dynamic, sociocultural context. As noted earlier, Hall (1988) criticized sport psychology's limited focus on femininity and masculinity and advocated a more thoughtful consideration of gender as a pervasive social influence. Lenskyj (1987), in her provocative analysis of sexuality and gender, emphasizes the historical and sociocultural pressures toward compulsory heterosexuality that influence women's sport and exercise. Dewar (1987) has extended feminist sport scholarship to a critical analysis of gender in physical education curricula and educational practice. Theberge (1987) also has written extensively on gender issues, and her discussion of the relationship of gender to power and empowerment in sport is particularly relevant.

Overall, these feminist sport scholars suggest that gender bias is pervasive in society, particularly in sport society, and that an understanding of the historical-cultural context and immediate social context is necessary to understand women's sport and exercise experiences. Sport and exercise psychologists can offer unique contributions and insights; nevertheless, any sport and exercise psychologist who seriously intends to pursue gender issues should be familiar with this feminist scholarship.

Promising Directions

Adopting a *social* psychological perspective is critical for sport psychology research on gender. Indeed, much sport and exercise behavior is interpretable only when social context is considered. As Deaux has suggested, components of social context vary tremendously, and such variations should be considered in our research on gender. Moreover, as Jacklin (1989) has noted, social context changes in a larger sense; that is, the norms and beliefs about sport and exercise vary over time.

Not only should we use more encompassing conceptual frameworks, but we should consider a wider range of issues and behaviors. Currently, psychological research on women in sport is remarkably limited in content, as well as in perspective. Researchers have focused most attention on individual characteristics related to participation in competitive athletics. Research efforts should

expand to youth and recreational sports, physical education classes, and exercise settings. Just as we should consider a wider range of sport and exercise activities, we should consider diverse participants. Most notably, as Duda and Allison (1990) note, research on racial, ethnic, and cultural influence is virtually nonexistent in sport and exercise psychology.

Most of the discussion on gender could be applied to race and ethnicity; that is, stereotypes and belief systems are pervasive and multifaceted; racial and ethnic socialization, self-perceptions, and social context influence sport and exercise behavior; and a grounding in sociocultural history would enhance our understanding of race and ethnicity in sport. (See box on page 274 for comments of one intercollegiate swimmer.)

In addition, gender belief systems and contexts probably interact with race and ethnicity systems in complex ways. For example, the experiences of an African-American female tennis player are not simply a combination of the experiences of white female and black male players. Althea Gibson (1979) highlights the complex interactions of race and gender, as well as influences of social history and the immediate social situation, in her development as a tennis player and person. Unfortunately, few scholars have considered race and ethnicity to enrich our understanding of women's sport and exercise experiences.

Not only should we consider diversity within gender, but to understand gender as a social category and process, we also should consider gender influences on both women and men.

There is little research on gender as it pertains to men in sport and exercise. Sabo and Runfola's (1980) anthology on sports and male identity is an important exception. Messner (1987) also has written on sport and male identity, offering analyses similar to those of the feminist sport scholars mentioned earlier. Other than the work of Sabo and Messner, who recently edited an important volume on sport, men, and gender (Messner & Sabo, 1990), gender issues in sport and exercise for men and boys have largely been ignored.

Race and Ethnicity in Sport

As a minority athlete participating in a non-traditional sport myself (swimming), I have seen and experienced the challenges that African-Americans are presented with when crossing over racial boundaries. I, too, have been underestimated, overlooked and in some cases been victimized because of my ethnic heritage. I was lucky enough to swim under a strong African-American coach who made me aware of the odds that were placed against African-American swimmers. I saw it in the USS (United States Swimming) swim meets that I went to when we were the only black swimmers there. I knew it when I applied for a life guard job and the employers were surprised by my race. And I experienced it when I was competing in a college meet at a local Boston area college. The response from a few girls on the opposing team to my "BLACK BY POPULAR DEMAND" tee-shirt was, "I didn't know that niggers could swim."

(Thomas, 1990, p. 5)

Finally, although I strongly endorse a social psychological perspective, sport and exercise psychologists should not dismiss biological influences. Sport and exercise are *physical* activities; that is our unique domain, and we cannot ignore biological influences. Instead we should incorporate physical characteristics and capabilities into our *social* psychological models to develop *biopsychosocial* models. We should not consider biological factors as unidirectional determinants of behavior, and we should not fall into the old trap of assuming that biological factors necessarily dominate or underlie social and behavioral influences. Rather we should consider biological influences as part of the social dynamic of sport and exercise. As Birke and Vines (1987) have suggested, biological factors are not static and absolute; instead they are dynamic processes that may interact with social psychological influences in varied complex ways.

Eccles' work, for example, suggested that physical capabilities had an influence (although a small one) on gender differences in sport achievement. By incorporating physical measures, Eccles more clearly illustrated social processes that lead to gender differences in sport achievement. Sport psychologists might well consider how we turn such minimal, and clearly nondichotomous, phys-ical differences into dichotomous gender influences. Consideration of physical characteristics and their relationship to social beliefs, self-perceptions, and social processes may add insight to research on body image, exercise behavior, youth sport, and health behavior, as well as competitive sport behavior.

Body Image and Physical Activity

Two specific topics that merit greater attention in future sport and exercise psychology research are body image and psychological skills for women. Both topics highlight gender, and we could advance our understanding of both body image and psychological skills by building from the work discussed in this chapter.

Melpomene Institute in Minnesota, in its recent book, *The Bodywise Woman* (Melpomene, 1990), has compiled research on women's physical activity and health. This information and the review of Rodin, Silberstein, and Striegel-Moore (1985) clearly point to sociocultural influences on body image. Images of the ideal body have changed through history and across sociocultural contexts, as Isadora Duncan related in Bas Hannah (1983):

When building a new world and creating new people, one must fight against the false conception of beauty. I am glad that I was young in a day when people were not so self-conscious as they are now . . . in those days too, thin was not equivalent to spirituality.

The slender and lean image of the female body today has not always been the ideal, as evidenced by the portrayals of larger and heavier women in earlier literature and artwork. We can document changes in current societal ideals by noting changes in Miss America contestants and *Playboy* centerfolds, who have lost 25 pounds over the last 20 years and are now 18% under the medical ideal or norm for their age and height. Certainly the ideal body in contemporary society is slender and lean. It is also clear that most women recognize and strive for this ideal, even though the ideal is far from ideal for optimal physical and mental health.

Even young children recognize and strive for the ideal. In a 1986 survey of school-age girls, 50% of the 9-year-olds and 80% of the 10- and 11-year-olds were dieting to lose weight. The numbers increase among young adults; and reports indicate that about 50% of all adult women are on a diet at any given time (Melpomene, 1990). Although boys and men also have concerns about body image, the literature indicates that girls and women are much more negative about their bodies. Moreover, the concerns are gender related; that is, girls are particularly concerned with physical beauty and maintaining the ideal thin shape, whereas boys are more concerned with size, strength, and power. Societal obsession with thinness and weight loss, particularly among women, has serious negative consequences for people who do not meet such standards. Among these consequences are eating disorders and the discrimination experienced by overweight individuals.

Clearly, then, society shapes body image. Societal pressure for a body image that is not attainable for most women has negative effects on self-esteem and psychological well-being as well as on physical health. Indeed, Mendleson and White (1985) report that overweight children have a lower opinion of their appearance and bodies than

nonoverweight children. Furthermore, these negative views carry over into self-esteem. Research indicates that most adult women perceive an underweight body as ideal, and also tend to see themselves as overweight even though most fall within the normal weight ranges. Older women surveyed in a Melpomene study on osteoporosis were more positive about their bodies than were younger women; perhaps older women feel less societal pressure about their bodies. Also, older women who were classified as high active were much more satisfied with the way they looked than were low-active women, suggesting that physical activity may have a positive influence on body image as well as on perceived health. In another Melpomene survey, mothers who were physically active were more likely to describe their children in terms of skill and personality, whereas most mothers (and most people) put more emphasis on size and shape. Perhaps physical activity not only benefits women participants, but those participants who are mothers may encourage the next generation to see themselves in relation to healthy standards rather than unrealistic, unhealthy societal images.

We also must note that biology plays an important role in body image and is particularly relevant in understanding weight management among women. Research (e.g., Kirschenbaum, 1992) has firmly established that biology is the strongest determinant of obesity and that obese people do not necessarily lack the willpower to lose weight if they "really" want to. Metabolic rates and processes vary greatly and are largely genetically determined. Most important, some of the assumed links between obesity and health may reflect psychological and social problems rather than medical problems; moreover, constant dieting, especially with a "yo-yo" pattern of weight gains and losses, may be more detrimental to health than remaining consistently overweight.

Most of these concerns about body image affect women in general, regardless of whether they participate in sport and exercise, but we should be mindful of how such bodily concerns influence women's physical activity. Body image may have particular relevance for women in exercise and recreational activities, especially those who have weight problems, lack physical skills, or do not have an "athletic" body. Ironically, exercise may be more important for obese persons than for persons of normal weight. Unfortunately, many obese persons have become disenchanted with available programs and as a result have avoided sports and exercise settings altogether. One encouraging trend over the past few years is the increased opportunities for larger women. We now see clothing stores devoted to fashions for large women, magazines, organizations, and even exercise programs that take a positive stance toward large women. The latest research efforts also offer promising directions.

Bain and her colleagues (Bain, Wilson, & Chaikind, 1989) conducted a unique and provocative study of overweight women in an exercise program. Their in-depth, qualitative analyses of participants' views and responses to the program are particularly enlightening. First, Bain et al. noted that these women varied in body size, background, interests, and most characteristics. The one experience shared by all, however, was social disapproval based on body size. They also reported that this experience affected their perceptions of exercise programs and decisions about participation. These women were especially critical of previous exercise programs and instructors who were not sensitive to some of their concerns, including safety, comfort, skill, and especially concerns about visibility, embarrassment, and judgments by others. Similar concerns were expressed by larger women at a 1989 Melpomene conference on body image, health, and fitness. In describing that conference, Lutter (1991) noted that many larger women encountered prejudice in exercise settings.

To provide a positive exercise environment, instructors and program organizers should avoid moralizing, and particularly avoid reinforcing social stereotypes and fat prejudice. Organizers of sport programs should not promote exercise as a way to lose weight. As noted earlier, the focus on weight loss outcomes is not desirable. In a supportive setting, larger women can gain the benefits of enhanced physical competence, strength, confidence, and control:

> Knowing you can do something is the best part. I always thought what a failure my body was, but when I exercise I know that's not true.

> The best part about physical activity is the sense of inner peace and gracefulness I attain after 45 minutes in the pool. It helps me reflect on my strengths, on who I am, and not that my body doesn't fit some rigid ideal. (Lutter, 1991, p. 17)

Anecdotal evidence, as well as the few available studies on body image and self-perceptions of women in physical activity, poses more questions than they answer about the relationships among body image, self-perceptions, and physical activity. Addressing some of these questions seems at least as important as answering questions about elite athletes. Certainly, more attention to the concerns and experiences of women with diverse physical and social psychological characteristics could make sport and exercise psychology work more relevant and beneficial to more women.

Psychological Skills for Women in Sport

Applied sport psychology and psychological skills training with athletes is the most rapidly expanding area in sport and exercise psychology. Many sport psychologists conduct psychological skills programs or consult with athletes, and many students are interested in this aspect of the field. Unfortunately, these sport psychologists have not incorporated information on gender to develop programs particularly suited to women or to diverse women. Typical programs are designed for highly competitive, elite athletes, but many sport participants are not elite, striving to become elite, or interested in competition. In fact, most participants are more concerned with personal health, fitness, and enjoyment than performance accomplishments. Psychological skills training designed for an Olympic skier is not particularly appropriate for a 10-year-old soccer player, a 30-year-old at the fitness center, or a 70-year-old in a walking group at the community recreation center. Yet these sport participants could use psychological skills to enhance their sport and exercise experience. In fact, their needs may be even greater than those of the Olympic skier.

Some sport psychologists have discussed applied sport psychology for women (e.g., Harris, 1987), but the discussions seldom go beyond suggesting that the existing programs designed for males could be used with women athletes. Generally, applied sport psychologists have yet to actually investigate specific psychological skills interventions, program goals, structures, and procedures that might be appropriate for women participants.

Currently we have little research on any sport psychology interventions. Instead we rely on reports of those who are developing programs that typically include such skills as anxiety management, concentration, imagery, and goal setting. As Vealey (1988) noted in her recent review of psychological skills training, we need to evaluate these programs and to expand the dimensions of psychological skills training. In particular, Vealey suggested expanding beyond elite athletes to coaches and youth. She also advocated a holistic approach based on a personal development model with more attention to communication and feedback, empathy and social support, lifestyle management, and personal arousal regulation. Although she did not explicitly call for attention to women's experiences and gender issues, her suggestions fit with feminist approaches.

Beyond Vealey's suggestions, we should pay more attention to women in noncompetitive exercise and physical activities. In *The Bodywise Woman*, the authors (Melpomene Institute, 1990)

included a brief discussion of sport psychology and suggested that women could use progressive relaxation, goal setting, self-talk, imagery, hypnosis, systematic desensitization, and attentional focus in their exercise activities. Unfortunately, they had few specific suggestions and no research evidence to provide guidance. This void in the sport and exercise psychology literature should be addressed. I hope future sport psychology researchers will address specific concerns of women in varied physical activities and provide information that will enhance sport and exercise experiences for all women. Perhaps, as Oglesby (1990) proposed in her epilogue to Messner and Sabo's book on men and gender, we should explicitly incorporate "feminine" qualities in sport and exercise. We might promote care, cooperation, and creative expression in our applied work to add empowerment and some flair to our sport and exercise activities.

Summary and Conclusions

We have many intriguing questions about gender and sport. Sound sport and exercise psychology research on gender could offer practical guidance and advance our knowledge of women in sport. At present our research is insufficient to make many important contributions. If we are to contribute to the emerging body of research and discourse on women's sport and exercise, we must expand our vision. Moreover, we must extend our research to a broader range of activities and settings. We should extend our research to encompass diverse women and men, and we should make a special effort to include racially and culturally diverse participants. Most important, we should be familiar with the feminist scholarship from historical, sociological, and biological perspectives. We could enhance sport and exercise experiences for all by incorporating such feminist values as tolerance for error, appreciation of diversity rather than elitism, relaxation rather than tension, an emphasis on process rather than outcome, and a sense of cooperation and sharing. We might then develop a feminist, biopsychosocial perspective on women's sport and exercise to guide research and serve participants.

References

Allison, M.T. (1991). Role conflict and the female athlete: Preoccupations with little grounding. *Journal of Applied Sport Psychology*, **3**, 49-60.

Bain, L.L., Wilson, T., & Chaikind, E. (1989). Participant perceptions of exercise programs for overweight women. *Research Quarterly for Exercise and Sport*, **60**, 134-143.

Bakan, D. (1966). *The duality of human existence*. Chicago: Rand McNally.

Bandura, A. (1977). Self-efficacy: Toward a unifying theory of behavior change. *Psychological Review*, **84**, 191-215.

Bandura, A. (1986). *Social foundations of thought and action*. Englewood Cliffs, NJ: Prentice-Hall.

Bas Hannah, S. (1983). Fat women as dancers. In L. Schoefielder & B. Wieser (Eds.), *Shadow on a tightrope* (pp. 102-105). Iowa City, IA: Aunt Lute.

Belenky, M., Clinchy, B., Goldberger, N., & Tarule, J. (1986). *Women's ways of knowing: The development of self, voice and mind*. New York: Basic Books.

Bem, S.L. (1974). The measurement of psychological androgyny. *Journal of Consulting and Clinical Psychology*, **42**, 155-162.

Bem, S.L. (1978). Beyond androgyny: Some presumptuous prescriptions for a liberated sexual identity. In J. Sherman & F. Denmark (Eds.), *Psychology of women: Future directions for research* (pp. 1-23). New York: Psychological Dimensions.

Bem, S.L. (1981). Gender schema theory: A cognitive account of sex typing. *Psychological Review*, **88**, 354-364.

Bem, S.L. (1983). Gender schema theory and its implications for child development: Raising gender-aschematic children in a gender-schematic society. *Signs: Journal of Women in Culture and Society*, **8**, 598-616.

Bem, S.L. (1985). Androgyny and gender schema theory: A conceptual and empirical integration. In T.B. Sonderegger (Ed.), *Nebraska symposium on motivation, 1984: Psychology and gender* (pp. 179-226). Lincoln: University of Nebraska Press.

Bernard, J. (1981). *The female world*. New York: Free Press.

Birke, L.I.A., & Vines, G. (1987). A sporting chance: The anatomy of destiny. *Women's Studies International Forum*, **10**, 337-347.

Birrell, S.J. (1988). Discourses on the gender/sport relationship: From women in sport to gender relations. In K. Pandolf (Ed.), *Exercise and Sport Science Reviews* (Vol. 16, pp. 459-502). New York: Macmillan.

Bleier, R. (1986). Sex differences research: Science or belief? In R. Bleier (Ed.), *Feminist approaches to science* (pp. 147-164). New York: Pergamon Press.

Brawley, L.R., Landers, D.M., Miller, L., & Kearns, K.M. (1979). Sex bias in evaluating motor performance. *Journal of Sport Psychology*, **1**, 15-24.

Brawley, L.R., Powers, R.C., & Phillips, K.A. (1980). Sex bias in evaluating motor performance: General or task-specific expectancy? *Journal of Sport Psychology*, **2**, 279-287.

Bredemeier, B.J. (1984). Sport, gender and moral growth. In J.M. Silva & R.S. Weinberg (Eds.), *Psychological foundations of sport* (pp. 400-413). Champaign, IL: Human Kinetics.

Bredemeier, B.J., Desertain, G.S., Fisher, L.A., Getty, D., Slocum, N.E., Stephens, D.E., & Warren, J.E. (1991). Epistemological perspectives among women who participate in physical activity. *Journal of Applied Sport Psychology*, **3**, 87-107.

Bredemeier, B.J., & Shields, D.L. (1987). Moral growth through physical activity: A structural/developmental approach. In D. Gould & M.R. Weiss (Eds.), *Advances in pediatric sport sciences* (Vol. 2, pp. 143-165). Champaign, IL: Human Kinetics.

Broverman, I.K., Vogel, S.R., Broverman, D.M., Clarkson, F.E., & Rosenkrantz, P.S. (1972). Sex role stereotypes: A current appraisal. *Journal of Social Issues*, **28**, 59-78.

Brown, R.D., & Harrison, J.M. (1986). The effects of a strength training program on the strength and self-concept of two female age groups. *Research Quarterly for Exercise and Sport*, **57**, 315-320.

Colker, R., & Widom, C.S. (1980). Correlates of female athletic participation. *Sex Roles*, **6**, 47-53.

Condry, J., & Dyer, S. (1976). Fear of success: Attribution of cause to the victim. *Journal of Social Issues*, **32**, 63-83.

Constantinople, A. (1973). Masculinity-femininity: An exception to a famous dictum? *Psychological Bulletin*, **80**, 389-407.

Corbin, C.B. (1981). Sex of subject, sex of opponent, and opponent ability as factors affecting self-confidence in a competitive situation. *Journal of Sport Psychology*, **3**, 265-270.

Corbin, C.B., Landers, D.M., Feltz, D.L., & Senior, K. (1983). Sex differences in performance estimates: Female lack of confidence vs. male boastfulness. *Research Quarterly for Exercise and Sport*, **54**, 407-410.

Corbin, C.B., & Nix, C. (1979). Sex-typing of physical activities and success predictions of children before and after cross-sex competition. *Journal of Sport Psychology*, **1**, 43-52.

Corbin, C.B., Stewart, M.J., & Blair, W.O. (1981). Self-confidence and motor performance of preadolescent boys and girls in different feedback situations. *Journal of Sport Psychology*, **3**, 30-34.

Crandall, V.C. (1969). Sex differences in expectancy of intellectual and academic reinforcement. In C.P. Smith (Ed.), *Achievement-*

related motives in children (pp. 11-45). New York: Russell Sage.

Csizma, K.A., Wittig, A.F., & Schurr, K.T. (1988). Sport stereotypes and gender. *Journal of Sport & Exercise Psychology*, **10**, 62-74.

Deaux, K. (1976). Sex: A perspective on the attribution process. In J.H. Harvey, W.J. Ickes, & R.F. Kidd (Eds.), *New directions in attribution research* (Vol. 1, pp. 335-352). Hillsdale, NJ: Erlbaum.

Deaux, K. (1984). From individual differences to social categories: Analysis of a decade's research on gender. *American Psychologist*, **39**, 105-116.

Deaux, K. (1985). Sex and gender. *Annual Review of Psychology*, **36**, 49-81.

Deaux, K., & Farris, E. (1977). Attributing causes for one's won performance: The effects of sex, norms, and outcome. *Journal of Research in Personality*, **11**, 59-72.

Deaux, K., & Kite, M.E. (1987). Thinking about gender. In B.B. Hess & M.M. Ferree (Eds.), *Analyzing gender* (pp. 92-117). Beverly Hills, CA: Sage.

Deaux, K., & Lewis, L.L. (1984). The structure of gender stereotypes: Interrelationships among components and gender labels. *Journal of Personality and Social Psychology*, **46**, 991-1004.

Deaux, K., & Major, B. (1987). Putting gender into context: An interactive model of gender-related behavior. *Psychological Review*, **94**, 369-389.

Deaux, K., & Taynor, J. (1973). Evaluation of male and female ability: Bias works in two ways. *Psychological Reports*, **32**, 261-262.

Deci, E.L., Betley, G., Kahle, J., Abrams, L., & Porac, J. (1981). When trying to win: Competition and intrinsic motivation. *Personality and Social Psychology Bulletin*, **7**, 79-83.

Deci, E.L., & Ryan, R.M. (1985). *Intrinsic motivation and self-determination in human behavior*. New York: Plenum.

Del Rey, P. (1978). The apologetic and women in sport. In C. Oglesby (Ed.), *Women and sport: From myth to reality* (pp. 107-111). Philadelphia: Lea & Febiger.

Del Rey, P., & Sheppard, S. (1981). Relationship of psychological androgyny in female athletes to self-esteem. *International Journal of Sport Psychology*, **12**, 165-175.

Dewar, A.M. (1987). The social construction of gender in physical education. *Women's Studies International Forum*, **10**, 453-465.

Duda, J.L. (1986). A cross-cultural analysis of achievement motivation in sport and the classroom. In L. VanderVelden & J. Humphrey (Eds.), *Current selected research in the psychology and sociology of sport* (pp. 115-132). New York: AMS Press.

Duda, J.L., & Allison, M.T. (1990). Cross-cultural analysis in exercise and sport psychology: A void in the field. *Journal of Sport & Exercise Psychology*, **12**, 114-131.

Duda, J.L., Olson, L.K., & Templin, T.J. (1991). The relationship of task and ego orientation to sportsmanship attitudes and the perceived legitimacy of injurious acts. *Research Quarterly for Exercise and Sport*, **62**, 79-87.

Dweck, C.S. (1986). Motivational processes affecting learning. *American Psychologist*, **41**, 1040-1048.

Eagley, A.H. (1987). *Sex differences in social behavior: A social-role interpretation.* Hillsdale, NJ: Erlbaum.

Eagley, A.H., & Kite, M.E. (1987). Are stereotypes of nationalities applied to both women and men? *Journal of Personality and Social Psychology*, **53**, 451-462.

Eagley, A.H., & Steffin, V.J. (1986). Gender and aggressive behavior: A meta-analytic review of the social psychological literature. *Psychological Bulletin*, **100**, 309-330.

Eccles, J.S. (1985). Sex differences in achievement patterns. In T. Sonderegger (Ed.), *Nebraska Symposium of Motivation, 1984: Psychology and Gender* (pp. 97-132). Lincoln: University of Nebraska Press.

Eccles, J.S. (1987). Gender roles and women's achievement-related decisions. *Psychology of Women Quarterly*, **11**, 135-172.

Eccles, J.S., Adler, T.F., Futterman, R., Goff, S.B., Kaczala, C.M., Meece, J.L., & Midgley, C. (1983). Expectations, values and academic behaviors. In J. Spence (Ed.), *Achievement and achievement motives* (pp. 75-146). San Francisco: Freeman.

Eccles, J.S., & Harold, R.D. (1991). Gender differences in sport involvement: Applying the Eccles expectancy-value model. *Journal of Applied Sport Psychology*, **3**, 7-35.

Feltz, D.L. (1988). Self-confidence and sports performance. In K. Pandolf (Ed.), *Exercise and Sport Sciences Reviews* (Vol. 16, pp. 423-457). New York: Macmillan.

Frable, D.E.S. (1989). Sex typing and gender ideology: Two facets of an individual's gender psychology that go together. *Journal of Personality and Social Psychology*, **56**, 95-108.

Frodi, A., Macauley, J., & Thome, P.R. (1977). Are women always less aggressive than men? A review of the experimental literature. *Psychological Bulletin*, **84**, 638-660.

Gibson, A. (1979). I always wanted to be somebody. In S.L. Twin (Ed.), *Out of the bleachers* (pp. 130-142). Old Westbury, NY: Feminist Press.

Gill, D.L. (1986a). Competitiveness among females and males in physical activity classes. *Sex Roles*, **15**, 233-247.

Gill, D.L. (1986b). *Psychological dynamics of sport.* Champaign, IL: Human Kinetics.

Gill, D.L. (1988). Gender differences in competitive orientation and sport participation. *International Journal of Sport Psychology*, **19**, 145-159.

Gill, D.L., & Deeter, T.E. (1988). Development of the Sport Orientation Questionnaire. *Research Quarterly for Exercise and Sport*, **59**, 191-202.

Gill, D.L., & Dzewaltowski, D.A. (1988). Competitive orientations among intercollegiate athletes: Is winning the only thing? *The Sport Psychologist*, **2**, 212-221.

Gill, D.L., Dzewaltowski, D.A., & Deeter, T.E. (1988). The relationship of competitiveness and achievement orientation to participation in sport and nonsport activities. *Journal of Sport & Exercise Psychology*, **10**, 139-150.

Gill, D.L., Gross, J.B., Huddleston, S., & Shifflett, B. (1984). Sex differences in achievement cognitions and performance in competition. *Research Quarterly for Exercise and Sport*, **55**, 340-346.

Gilligan, C. (1982). *In a different voice*. Cambridge, MA: Harvard University Press.

Goldberg, P. (1968). Are women prejudiced against women? *Transaction*, **5**, 28-30.

Gould, S.J. (1981). *The mismeasure of man*. New York: Norton.

Greendorfer, S.L. (1987). Gender bias in theoretical perspectives: The case of female socialization into sport. *Psychology of Women Quarterly*, **11**, 327-340.

Griffin, P.S. (1973). What's a nice girl like you doing in a profession like this? *Quest*, **19**, 96-101.

Hall, M.A. (1988). The discourse of gender and sport: From femininity to feminism. *Sociology of Sport Journal*, **5**, 330-340.

Hall, M.A. (1990). How should we theorize gender in the context of sport? In M.A. Messner & D.F. Sabo (Eds.), *Sport, men, and the gender order* (pp. 223-239). Champaign, IL: Human Kinetics.

Harris, D.V. (1980). Femininity and athleticism: Conflict or consonance? In D.F. Sabo & R. Runfola (Eds.), *Jock: Sports and male identity* (pp. 222-239). Englewood Cliffs, NJ: Prentice-Hall.

Harris, D.V. (1987). The female athlete. In J.R. May & M.J. Asken (Eds.), *Sport psychology: The psychological health of the athlete* (pp. 99-116). New York: PMA.

Harris, D.V., & Jennings, S.E. (1977). Self-perceptions of female distance runners. *Annals of the New York Academy of Sciences*, **301**, 808-815.

Harter, S. (1981). The development of competence motivation in the mastery of cognitive and physical skills: Is there still a place for joy? In G.C. Roberts & D.M. Landers (Eds.), *Psychology of motor behavior and sport—1989* (pp. 3-29). Champaign, IL: Human Kinetics.

Hathaway, S.R., & McKinley, J.C. (1940). A multiphasic personality schedule (Minnesota): Construction of the schedule. *Journal of Psychology*, **10**, 249-254.

Helmreich, R.L., & Spence, J.T. (1977). Sex roles and achievement. In R.W. Christina & D.M. Landers (Eds.), *Psychology of motor behavior and sport—1976* (Vol. 2, pp. 33-46). Champaign, IL: Human Kinetics.

Helmreich, R.L., & Spence, J.T. (1978). The Work and Family Orientation Questionnaire: An objective instrument to assess components of achievement motivation and attitudes toward family and career. *Catalog of Selected Documents in Psychology*, **8**, 35.

Helmreich, R.L., Spence, J.T., & Holohan, C.K. (1979). Psychological androgyny and sex role flexibility: A test of two hypotheses. *Journal of Personality and Social Psychology*, **37**, 1631-1644.

Henderson, K.A., Stalnaker, D., & Taylor, G. (1988). The relationship between barriers to recreation and gender-role personality traits for women. *Journal of Leisure Research*, **20**, 69-80.

Holloway, J.B., Beuter, A., & Duda, J.L. (1988). Self-efficacy and training for strength in adolescent girls. *Journal of Applied Social Psychology*, **18**, 699-719.

Horner, M.S. (1972). Toward an understanding of achievement-related coflicts in women. *Journal of Social Issues*, **28**, 157-176.

Hyde, J.S., & Linn, M.C. (Eds.). (1986). *The psychology of gender: Advances through meta-analysis*. Baltimore: Johns Hopkins University Press.

Jacklin, C.N. (1989). Female and male: Issues of gender. *American Psychologist*, **44**, 127-133.

Kane, M.J., & Snyder, E. (1989). Sport typing: The social "containment" of women. *Arena Review*, **13**, 77-96.

Kirschenbaum, D.S. (1992). Elements of effective weight control programs: Implications for exercise and sport psychology. *Journal of Applied Sport Psychology*, **4**, 77-93.

Lenney, E. (1977). Women's self-confidence in achievement settings. *Psychological Bulletin*, **84**, 1-13.

Lenney, E., Browning, C., & Mitchell, L. (1980). What you don't know *can* hurt you: The effects of performance criteria ambiguity on sex differences in self-confidence. *Journal of Personality*, **48**, 306-322.

Lenskyj, H. (1987). *Out of bounds: Women, sport and sexuality*. Toronto: Women's Press.

Lewin, M. (1984a). "Rather worse than folly?" Psychology measures femininity and masculinity, 1: From Terman and Miles to the Guilfords. In M. Lewin (Ed.), *In the shadow of the past: Psychology portrays the sexes* (pp. 155-178). New York: Columbia University Press.

Lewin, M. (1984b). Psychology measures femininity and masculinity, 2: From "13 gay men" to the instrumental-expressive distinction. In M. Lewin (Ed.), *In the shadow of the past: Psychology portrays the sexes* (pp. 179-204). New York: Columbia University Press.

Locksley, A., & Colten, M.E. (1979). Psychological androgyny: A case of mistaken identity? *Journal of Personality and Social Psychology*, **37**, 1017-1031.

Lutter, J.M. (March 1991). Does big mean bad? *Women's Sports & Fitness*, 16-17.

Maccoby, E.E. (1990). Gender and relationships. *American Psychologist*, **45**, 513-520.

Maccoby, E., & Jacklin, C. (1974). *The psychology of sex differences*. Stanford, CA: Stanford University Press.

Martens, R. (1977). *Sport competition anxiety test*. Champaign, IL: Human Kinetics.

Matteo, S. (1986). The effect of sex and gender-schematic processing on sport participation. *Sex Roles*, **15**, 417-432.

Matteo, S. (1988). The effect of gender-schematic processing on decisions about sex-inappropriate sport behavior. *Sex Roles*, **18**, 41-58.

McClelland, D.C., Atkinson, J.W., Clark, R.A., & Lowell, E.C. (1953). *The achievement motive*. New York: Appleton-Century-Crofts.

McElroy, M.A., & Willis, J.D. (1979). Women and the achievement conflict in sport: A preliminary study. *Journal of Sport Psychology*, **1**, 241-247.

McNally, J., & Orlick, T. (1975). Cooperative sport structures: A preliminary analysis. *Mouvement*, **7**, 267-271.

Melpomene Institute. (1990). *The bodywise woman*. New York: Prentice-Hall.

Mendleson, B., & White, D. (1985). Development of self-body-esteem in overweight youngsters. *Developmental Psychology*, **21**, 90-96.

Messner, M. (1987). The life of a man's seasons: Male identity in the life course of the jock. In M.S. Kimmel (Ed.), *Changing men: New directions in research on men and masculinity* (pp. 53-67). Newbury Park, CA: Sage.

Messner, M.A., & Sabo, D.F. (Eds.). (1990). *Sport, men and the gender order*. Champaign, IL: Human Kinetics.

Metheny, E. (1965). Symbolic forms of movement: The feminine image in sports. In E. Metheny, *Connotations of movement in sport and dance* (pp. 43-56). Dubuque, IA: Brown.

Miller Brewing Company. (1983). *The Miller Lite report on American attitudes toward sports*. Milwaukee: Author.

Myers, A.E., & Lips, H.M. (1978). Participation in competitive amateur sports as a function of psychological androgyny. *Sex Roles*, **4**, 571-578.

Nicholls, J.G. (1984). Achievement motivation: Conceptions of ability, subjective experiences, task choice, and performance. *Psychological Review*, **91**, 328-346.

Nicholls, J.G. (1989). *The competitive ethos and democratic education.* Cambridge, MA: Harvard University Press.

Nyad, D. (1978). *Other shores.* New York: Random House.

Oglesby, C. (1990). Epilogue. In M.A. Messner & D.F. Sabo (Eds.), *Sport, men and the gender order* (pp. 241-245). Champaign, IL: Human Kinetics.

Ostrow, A.C. (1981). Age grading: Implications for physical activity participation among older adults. *Quest,* **33**, 112-123.

Ostrow, A.C., Jones, D.C., & Spiker, D.A. (1981). Age role expectations and sex role expectations for selected sport activities. *Research Quarterly for Exercise and Sport,* **52**, 216-227.

Parkhouse, B.L., & Williams, J.M. (1986). Differential effects of sex and status on evaluation of coaching ability. *Research Quarterly for Exercise and Sport,* **57**, 53-59.

Pearson, L. (1979, summer). Learning to be a survivor: The liberating art of Tae Kwondo. *Canadian Women's Studies,* pp. 49-50.

Pedhazur, E.J., & Tetenbaum, T.J. (1979). BSRI: A theoretical and methodological critique. *Journal of Personality and Social Psychology,* **37**, 996-1016.

Petruzzello, S.J., & Corbin, C.B. (1988). The effects of performance feedback on female self-confidence. *Journal of Sport & Exercise Psychology,* **10**, 174-183.

Pheterson, G.I., Kiesler, S.B., & Goldberg, P.A. (1971). Evaluation of the performance of women as a function of their sex, achievement, and personal history. *Journal of Personality and Social Psychology,* **19**, 114-118.

Roberts, G.C. (1984). Toward a new theory of motivation in sport: The role of perceived ability. In J.M. Silva & R.S. Weinberg (Eds.), *Psychological foundations of sport* (pp. 214-228). Champaign, IL: Human Kinetics.

Rodin, J., Silberstein, L., & Striegel-Moore, R. (1985). Women and weight: A normative

discontent. In T.B. Sonderegger (Ed.), *Psychology and gender: Nebraska Symposium on Motivation, 1984* (Vol. 32, pp. 267-307).

Rosenkrantz, P., Vogel, S., Bee, H., Broverman, I., & Broverman, D.M. (1968). Sex-role stereotypes and self-concepts in college students. *Journal of Consulting and Clinical Psychology,* **32**, 286-295.

Sabo, D.F., & Runfola, R. (1980). *Jock: Sports and male identity.* Englewood Cliffs, NJ: Prentice-Hall.

Selby, R., & Lewko, J. (1976). Children's attitudes toward females' participation in sports. *Research Quarterly,* **47**, 453-463.

Sherif, C.W. (1972). Females and the competitive process. In D. Harris (Ed.), *Women and sport: A national research conference* (pp. 115-139). University Park: Pennsylvania State University.

Sherif, C.W. (1976). The social context of competition. In D. Landers (Ed.), *Social problems in athletics* (pp. 18-36). Champaign, IL: Human Kinetics.

Sherif, C.W. (1982). Needed concepts in the study of gender identity. *Psychology of Women Quarterly,* **6**, 375-398.

Spence, J.T., & Helmreich, R.L. (1978). *Masculinity and femininity.* Austin: University of Texas Press.

Spence, J.T., & Helmreich, R.L. (1980). Masculine instrumentality and feminine expressiveness: Their relationships with sex role attitudes and behaviors. *Psychology of Women Quarterly,* **5**, 147-163.

Spence, J.T., & Helmreich, R.L. (1983). Achievement-related motives and behaviors. In J.T. Spence (Ed.), *Achievement and achievement motives: Psychological and sociological approaches* (pp. 7-74). San Francisco: Freeman.

Spence, J.T., Helmreich, R.L., & Stapp, J. (1974). The Personality Attributes Questionnaire: A measure of sex role stereotypes and masculinity-femininity. *JSAS Catalog of Selected Documents in Psychology,* **4**, 127.

Spence, J.T., Helmreich, R.L., & Stapp, J. (1975). Ratings of self and personality on sex role attributes and their relation to self-esteem and conceptions of masculinity and femininity. *Journal of Personality and Social Psychology*, **32**, 29-39.

Stein, A.H., Pohly, S.R., & Mueller, E. (1971). The influence of masculine, feminine, and neutral tasks on children's achievement behavior, expectancies of success, and attainment values. *Child Development*, **42**, 195-207.

Stewart, M.J., & Corbin, C.B. (1988). Feedback dependence among low confidence preadolescent boys and girls. *Research Quarterly for Exercise and Sport*, **59**, 160-164.

Taylor, M.C., & Hall, J.A. (1982). Psychological androgyny: Theories, methods and conclusions. *Psychological Bulletin*, **92**, 347-366.

Terman, L., & Miles, C.C. (1936). *Sex and personality: Studies in masculinity and femininity*. New York: McGraw-Hill.

Theberge, N. (1987). Sport and women's empowerment. *Women's Studies International Forum*, **10**, 387-393.

Thomas, A. (1990, Fall). Getting black athletes in swim of things is a challenge that should be accepted. *CSSS Digest*, **2**(3), 5.

Tresemer, D.W. (1977). *Fear of success*. New York: Plenum.

Trujillo, C. (1983). The effect of weight training and running exercise intervention on the self-esteem of college women. *International Journal of Sport Psychology*, **14**, 162-173.

Vealey, R.S. (1988). Future directions in psychological skills training. *The Sport Psychologist*, **2**, 318-336.

Wallston, B.S., & O'Leary, V.E. (1981). Sex and gender make a difference: The differential perceptions of women and men. *Review of Personality and Social Psychology*, **2**, 9-41.

Weinberg, R.S., & Jackson, A. (1979). Competition and extrinsic rewards: Effect on intrinsic motivation. *Research Quarterly*, **50**, 494-502.

Weinberg, R.S., & Ragan, J. (1979). Effects of competition, success/failure, and sex on intrinsic motivation. *Research Quarterly*, **50**, 503-510.

Weinberg, R., Reveles, M., & Jackson, A. (1984). Attitudes of male and female athletes toward male and female coaches. *Journal of Sport Psychology*, **6**, 448-453.

Weiss, M.R., & Bredemeier, B.J. (1990). Moral development in sport. In K. Pandolf (Ed.), *Exercise and Sport Sciences Reviews* (Vol. 18, pp. 331-378). Baltimore: Williams & Wilkins.

Weiss, M.R., & Chaumeton, N. (1992). Motivational orientations in sport. In T.S. Horn (Ed.), *Advances in sport psychology* (pp. 61-99). Champaign, IL: Human Kinetics.

Williams, J.M. (1978). Personality characteristics of the successful female athlete. In W.F. Straub (Ed.), *Sport psychology: An analysis of athlete behavior* (2d ed., pp. 353-359). Ithaca, NY: Mouvement Publications.

Williams, J.M., & Parkhouse, B.L. (1988). Social learning theory as a foundation for examining sex bias in evaluation of coaches. *Journal of Sport & Exercise Psychology*, **10**, 322-333.

Wrisberg, C.A., Draper, M.V., & Everett, J.J. (1988). Sex role orientations of male and female collegiate athletes from selected individual and team sports. *Sex Roles*, **19**, 81-90.

Chapter 17

She Flies Through the Air With the Greatest of Ease: The Contributions of Feminist Psychology

Mary E. Duquin

The partnership model is a compassionate, egalitarian approach to sport in which athletes are motivated by love of themselves, of sports, and of each other. Power is understood not as power-over (power as dominance) but as power-to (power as competence) . . . partnership athletes maintain that sport should be inclusive; in balance with other aspects of life; cooperative and social in spirit; and safe.

MARIAH NELSON
Are We Winning Yet?

The stories we grow up with present to us many different versions of the world and of our place in it. They have an important influence on the psychological construction of our self-identities as women and men and as people who participate in sports. These stories come not only from family and friends, but also from the myriad social forms of culture, including schools, religion, art, science, and fashion. Culture continually evolves and reproduces normative descriptions of women and men, about who we are or should be. Under patriarchy, or male domination, these stories of gender and gender relations tend to favor or give status to the position of men in culture. The discipline of psychology, like other cultural institutions under patriarchy, engages in storytelling from a male perspective.

In modern society, psychology has the power not only to construct normative theories about gender relations but also to affect how children are raised to conform to these normative theories. Feminist psychology has exposed the male bias in normative views of gender and gender relations and has undertaken the reconstruction of gender relations to improve the material and social conditions of women in culture. In this chapter, I will explore three current influences on feminist psychology and explore how these influences inform sport psychology research and female experience in sports. These influences include subjective experience and knowledge from the standpoint of women, feminist psychoanalytic discourse on moral development, and poststructuralist ideas on the social construction of self-identity. In exploring each of these areas we will learn how some feminist versions of the world hope to revision and reshape women's relationships to each other, to men, and to sport.[1]

First, I examine the problem of integrating feminist criticism into the discipline of psychology and sport psychology. Feminists have challenged the ''sex differences'' approach psychology has taken toward understanding the psychology of gender. They also have criticized traditional psychology for according privilege to the values and behaviors exhibited by males over those exhibited by females. Such issues relate directly to women's experiences participating in sport structures historically designed by men, for men and administered by men. I outline feminist theory and practice as related to psychology from the perspective of how sport psychology research can be structured to fulfill feminist goals of dismantling gender inequalities and transforming the lives of women in relation to sport.

Second, I introduce and discuss the concepts of subjective experience and knowledge from the standpoint of women. Feminist psychology has given great importance to women's voice, to how women experience and interpret reality. Central to the discussion are the following questions: How do females experience sports, and what problems do they identify? What visions of a better sporting experience do they articulate? How can listening to women's subjective experiences in sports help develop better theories of gender relations?

Third, I discuss feminist psychoanalytic theory in relation to sports and moral development. A major tenet of psychoanalytic theory is that females and males develop different gender identities as a result of early female caregiving. Different gender identities may lead to different moral perspectives. According to this theory, females are more likely than males to experience their self-identity in relation to others and to employ a moral orientation reflecting an ethic of care. Males are more likely than females to separate their self-identity from others and to see morality in terms of a legal elaboration of rights. Given that sport often functions as a reproducer of masculine values and practices, does sport put at risk the psychological development of an ethic of care for both females and males?

In the last section I explore poststructuralist theory in relation to the development of self-identity. Poststructuralism focuses on how language and symbols are used in the social construction of reality and self-identity. Who we are or think we can be is constrained by the language we use and the symbol systems (e.g., TV, movies, books, art, sports) with which we interact. A major emphasis in this theory is power: the power to name, define, and give meaning to social reality and social identity. A primary tool in this theory is deconstruction. As applied to psychology, deconstruction involves an analysis of psychological texts, technologies, and forms of subjectivity produced by the discipline of psychology. Deconstruction uncovers the hidden contradictions and repressed meanings in psychological texts and reveals the forms of social control induced by psychological discourse. Poststructuralist analysis in sport psychology makes visible the social construction of athlete identity in Western culture.

Given the gendered nature of athlete identity in our culture, how can feminists use poststructural analysis in sports to test and subvert the meanings of gender identity and gender relations?

Feminist Critique in Psychology

The aim of feminist social science is both social understanding and social change. Social understanding serves people in helping them understand how social life is put together, how social relations and social structures affect their lives, and how they can begin to construct different realities. Feminist theory building and research take many conflicting forms, but feminist narratives and world views are significantly different from patriarchal ones, as Shotter and Logan (1988) explain:

> Patriarchy leads to a general, decontexted kind of theoretical knowledge that can be possessed by individuals of their external world. This knowledge is expressed in a hierarchically arranged, closed system of binary oppositions; it is concerned with achieving a unity of vision and thought, with everything in its proper place and all conflict eradicated, once and for all. Feminist thought can be seen as different in every respect: as a practical, particular, contexted, open, and nonsystematic knowledge of the social circumstances in which one has one's being, concerned with achieving a hierarchy of times and places for a plurality of otherwise conflicting voices. (pp. 75-76)

The dominant research paradigm of patriarchy in Western culture is positivist empiricism. This paradigm assumes the chimera of value free, objective, rational observation in identifying and solving "scientific" problems. Science, however, is never value free: It is political. Values and politics not only pose the important questions but also influence how they are phrased. Without values, all questions are equally interesting and

worthy of research. That all questions are equally important and interesting is a concept that few if any scientists would accept. Thus the positivist empiricism paradigm establishes a false separation of science and politics.

In contrast, values in feminist psychology openly guide theory, choice of topic, research questions, methodology, and interpretation of data. As Gergen (1988) states, "Feminist-inspired research would endeavor to recognize that scientists, subjects, and 'facts' are all interconnected, involved in reciprocal influences, and subject to interpretation and linguistic constraints" (p. 94). Feminist thought and research aim to be self-reflexive and guided by lived experience. It is theory developed through social relations and grounded in the multiplicity of people's cultural and historical contexts.

For at least two reasons, psychology may be the most intransigent of all the social sciences in addressing and incorporating feminist critique. First, unlike other social sciences the focus in psychology is on the individual; that is, the individual is psychology's most likely locus of explanation. As a result, problems are often located within a person's psyche rather than in the social relations or the material realities of the person's life (Holloway, 1991). Second, the positivist empiricist paradigm, through its false separation of science and politics, produces a kind of science that rarely questions the status quo or disturbs existing power relations within society (Wilkinson, 1991). Feminist psychology itself has come under criticism for its self-imposed adherence to disciplinary boundaries. Kitzinger (1991b) notes that most texts on the psychology of women avoid integrating insights from sociological and political theory in describing the psychological construction of women in society.

Psychology has also been criticized for producing theories that are androcentric, ethnocentric, and heterosexist. Most traditional psychological research has excluded women from its theories. It has distorted women's experience by imposing male norms. It has perpetuated stereotypes by regarding women as a unitary category, blurring class, race, and ethnic differences among women and exaggerating differences between females and males. Psychology has ignored the cultural and historical specificity of knowledge and the social/structural inequalities that create power differentials between and within groups. It has written into definitions of mental health and self-identity a Western liberal humanist bias that accords privilege to concepts of autonomy, independence, choice, freedom, and personal self-fulfillment. In addition, traditional psychological theory, with its heterosexist assumptions about development, has ignored and denigrated lesbians while promoting homophobic attitudes and behaviors (Burman, 1990; Worell, 1990).

Feminist Sport Psychology: Research and Reconstruction

Methodological as well as theoretical changes have been suggested to expand the feminist project in psychology. Meyer (1988) recommends that researchers take account of the material and normative context in which behavior occurs, pay attention to subjective experience, and be aware of the impact of the research on society. For example, psychological research on coach-athlete relations should take into account how resources like power, authority, time, and money are distributed differentially. How, for instance, does the coach's power to give or withhold scholarship money affect the honesty of an athlete in her communication about injuries? In female athlete–male coach relationships, the context of gender relations is embedded in the normative context of sport. Being aware of this double contextualization may be important for understanding shared as well as conflicting expectations for interpersonal behavior between female athletes and their male coach (Blinde, 1989b; Duquin, 1984a). Recording subjective experiences of the relationship between the athletes and the coach provides insight into

the meanings of these relations for the coach, the athletes, and the researcher. Subjective experiences of related personnel such as athletic trainers, assistant coaches, and team managers can provide still a different perspective on the athlete-coach relationship. Giving voice to the subjective experiences of women has the potential for restructuring existing social relations within the particular teams studied. In addition, research on sport relationships, if more broadly understood, has the potential to influence normative change on a wider social scale. For example, Dewar (1991) states that coming out as a lesbian in sport "is not just a declaration of a particular sexual affiliation—it can be a powerful way of making challenges to oppression visible and clear" (p. 8).

Further proposals for feminist research in psychology are offered by Fine and Gordon (1991). They suggest that

> by examining what women do traditionally
> . . . to sustain relationships and to maintain
> social secrets; and by studying what women
> do subversively . . . to generate feminist politics and to imagine possibilities; we incite
> a project of psychological research which
> would empower as it exposes, which would
> offer social critique as it reveals what could
> be. (p. 22)

Part of the feminist project in psychology involves studying female relationships by examining women's connections and relations to friends, lovers, and kin over time. In the realm of sport we might ask how play and sport build, reinforce, and/or threaten female friendship bonds with others, both female and male (Meyer, 1990). For example, girls' play groups are often noted for according privilege to player relationships over the rules of the game. If a dispute in a game threatens to disrupt the affective bonds between friends, girls are more likely than boys to stop the game and switch to another activity (Lever, 1976). This behavior has often been interpreted negatively from a male point of view in that it shows how females let emotions and personal relationships get in the way of accomplishing goals. An alternate interpretation of this situation might be that the ''goal'' from the male point of view is to play by the rules and determine the winner of the game, whereas the ''goal'' from the female point of view is to affirm that friendship is more important than the game or the rules. The ties between female friendship and how sport challenges and enhances those friendships appear to be a rich area for research in sport psychology (Booth-Butterfield & Booth-Butterfield, 1988; Mathes & Battista, 1985).

A second aspect of the feminist research project in psychology is to tell female secrets and de-silence the female underground. This involves publicizing aspects of women's experience that are kept hidden. In competitive sport, desilencing might include making explicit the costs of having to hide one's sexual identity, of the pain in hearing the sexual jokes of homophobic athletes and coaches, and of putting up with sexual harassment so as not to risk one's place in the lineup (Duquin, 1983; Griffin, 1991; Lenskyj, 1987). Desilencing also might include talking about aggression, steroid drug use in sport, and images of physical and psychological gender normality. Desilencing means recording the extent and quality of the sporting life of women in prisons, mental hospitals, nursing homes, senior citizen centers, girls in preschool, lesbian separatist softball teams, working-class women in local health clubs, and black women in community recreation centers (Cole, 1989; Redican & Hadley, 1988; Zechet-mayr, 1991).

An important aspect of desilencing is making visible the histories of female participation in physical activities both in the past and cross-culturally. Historical and anthropological research on play and sport provides a much broader racial, ethnic, and national diversity of women's voices than is usually heard in sport psychology. This information is needed if sport psychology is to broaden its ethnocentric perspective on what is

considered psychologically ''normative'' (Allison, 1981; Berlage, 1990; Boutilier & SanGiovanni, 1983; Hult, 1985).

Political self-reflective critique is another goal of feminist research. How do we reproduce within our own feminist groups status differentials based on age, sexual orientation, class, race, ability, or theoretical perspective? How much has our own personal vision of feminism separated us from developing relationships with other women who don't share our theoretical perspective on truth or reality? How much of our research is aimed at understanding and improving the performance of a relatively small group of primarily white, presumably heterosexual, middle-class, collegiate, female athletes? A feminist agenda in sport psychology would broaden the settings in which sport is studied, seek out those women whose voices have yet to be heard, and maintain a dialogue between researchers as to the strengths and weaknesses of each theoretical perspective.

Finally, a feminist research project in psychology requires studying the damage of not changing social conditions. Psychologists need to expose the conditions under which women suppress their rage and rebellion and the conditions under which oppression is met with resistance (Spelman, 1989). Research must be transformative, creating images of what is not yet imaginable. Feminists in sport psychology must document the human costs of not changing sport structures and gender ideology. We need to measure the psychological costs to women of being afraid to walk or run in their neighborhoods after dark. We need to publicize the psychological role sport plays in teaching boys and young men misogynistic attitudes and behaviors. We need to make known the psychological interrelationships among sport, war, and violence against women (Birrell, 1991; Edelson, 1991; Minton, 1991; Sabo & Panepinto, 1990). We need to document the physical and psychological damage done to young athletes as they pursue a normalized and valorized vision of competition and domination. We need to focus on the conditions under which females will define sport situations as oppressive, exploitive, racist, or sexist and resist either individually or collectively. We need to record the desire and trend toward more cooperative forms of sportive leisure: activities that do not separate us by age, gender, race, and ability. Research in sport psychology must work to envision and realize sport and sporting conditions that enhance the health and well-being of women, men, and society at large (Duquin, 1993a; Kohn, 1986; Montgomery & Duquin, 1991).

Sport, Women, and Subjective Experience

The importance of subjective experience has a strong foundation in feminist psychological theory and methodology (Young-Eisendrath, 1988). The issue of subjective experience brings up questions about who has the right to talk about how things ought to be, about how things "really are," and about how things might be changed. We live in a society where power relations are reproduced by maintaining the legitimacy of scientific knowledge (to the exclusion of other forms of knowledge) and by vesting material power and institutional authority in small groups of primarily white males who claim expertise. In this milieu, the subjective experiences of women are generally not voiced and when given voice tend to hold little authority.

In contrast to this view, some theorists have claimed an epistemological privilege for the standpoint of oppressed peoples. Jaggar (1989) suggests that women's perspectives are less distorting of reality and more likely to generate visions of a culture in which all could thrive. Feminists have argued that the women viewpoint offers a corrective vision of relations of dominance and that for gender and power relations in society to change, women's subjective experience must be given legitimacy. From this perspective secretaries possess valuable information

about how offices should be run, and athletes possess a special knowledge of how sport should be structured.

The model we use for most of our sporting experiences today replicates the reliance on the voice of the expert and on the scientific management of the body. Physical recreation is guided by instruction from tennis, golf, and karate experts. Exercise workouts are measured and monitored for improvement. Dance experiences are guided by experts who require, of 5-year-olds, serious preparation for "professional" recitals. Competitive sports rely almost solely on the expertise of coaches, referees, trainers, and sport scientists, including psychologists. In these examples, females need never voice, indeed are not expected to voice, an account of their physical and emotional experience as subjects in sport. (See box on page 291.) As Olympic gymnast Kathy Rigby recalled: "I was not able to grow up, because my coach did it for me. He talked for me, he thought for me" (Flatow, 1991, p. 5). Thus Kathy kept silent for a long time about her 12-year battle with anorexia and bulimia. The story of a female athlete's sporting life is often a progressive delegitimation of her personal physical and psychological experiences.

First-person narratives help shape and reshape theory and ground it in lived experience (Probyn, 1993). According to Code (1989), theoretical structures that emerge from personal stories and from responsible reflection of experience "will more likely be piecemeal, comprised of interpretations of stories, and interpretations of interpretations" (p. 169). Including personal experiences in theory building helps avoid the trap of positing the truth of any one, single, unified theoretical perspective. As Smith (1991) notes:

> There are a multiplicity of sites of experience and activity and in exploring a world from any one of these we can discover the relations organizing the different sites of experience and generating precisely the differences in how people are situated in the world. (p. 16)

Women's Subjective Experiences

As the following quotes show, when women talk about sport they often reveal not only their feelings and cognitions about their sport experiences but beliefs and values about who they are, who women are (both as distinct from one another and in relation to men), and who coaches are (or should be).

Women are very sensitive. They react strongly to minor comments from the coach. It seems we need more positive strokes than the guys.

Women are as emotional as men athletes but simply express it more openly. We keep less pain inside, that's why we cry. Women athletes are not too receptive to aggressive commands from coaches.

Female coaches seem to have greater insight into the feeling of players than male coaches. I think the word is empathy. Some women have a stronger need to compete than others. It's important to me to beat a certain school and especially beat a higher-ranked opponent.

Joking around is important for me. Competing has its pressures, so I need to unwind and have fun sometimes. Coaches should always have a sense of humor.

Menstruation changes my attitude. Sometimes I feel depressed and this affects my ability to play my best. Also my weight goes up, which upsets my coach. He needs to understand a woman's chemistry.

The worst thing a coach can do to motivate me is yell and scream. I absolutely "freak out." I need to be respected. Straightforward, honest talk is all I ask.

Before he left the school, my coach tended to flirt with his favorite players. That wasn't right. (Anshel, 1990, pp. 385-386)

Communicating subjective experience has been integral to clinical and therapeutic forms of feminist psychology. Speaking from and listening to subjective experience helps people reformulate their understanding of themselves, their social circumstances, and their relations to one another. Relating subjective experience can create a sense of solidarity with other women and can act as a catalyst for changing circumstances and social relationships (Varpalotai, 1987).

Feminist Critiques of Subjective Experience

Psychology's use and interpretation of women's subjective experience has been criticized by some feminists for its tendency toward essentialism and reductionism. Essentialism is viewing the subjective experiences of women as a reflection of their biology or feminine essence. As such, when a female reports fear, excess competitive pressure, or negative feelings about aggression in a sport context, a psychological interpretation will often focus on the category of gender with references to the tendency of women toward timidity, noncompetitiveness, and passivity.

Reductionism reduces a woman's subjective experiences to simple reflections of her psychological identity or personality. Reductionism tends to make a woman's negative experience "her problem." When the focus is on subjective experience, psychologists often locate the problem in the individual. For example, when female (or male) athletes reveal high levels of anxiety caused by the pressures and stresses of sport, psychologists suggest individual "coping strategies." Youth sport coaches and parents are told to be on the lookout for children who can't handle the stresses of sport. This advice tends to locate the problem of stress in a person's ability to cope, rather than in the conditions of sport that produce unmanageable levels of stress for many athletes. The emphasis on individual adaptation to the system, as it exists, tends to normalize the competitive situations that produce inordinate amounts of stress (Al-Saka, 1990).

Feminists also note that a psychological emphasis on women's subjective experience risks reproducing stereotypical images of women and gendered categories of thought. In addition, it tends to ignore or leave out of the analysis the more material and structural aspects of women's relations to men. Keeping these limitations in mind, let us turn to some examples of women's subjective experiences in sport.

Voices of Women in Sport

Women's subjective experiences in sport are not unmediated. Athletes interpret their subjective experience through the "lens" of cultural beliefs that they have come to accept. Yet subjective experiences do provide a point from which to view the various realities of sport practice. Anshel (1990) in his book *Sport Psychology: From Theory to Practice* has one chapter on the female athlete. In this chapter he reports on interviews he had with collegiate female athletes. His questions concerned emotions, leadership, attributions for performance, and what it means to be a woman sports competitor. Anshel concludes that, based on the comments he received, female athletes have certain needs that are not really very different from those of male athletes. He notes that female athletes "need" physical activity, competition, respect, communication, and close relationships with teammates. This text reflects a strong cultural

tendency to *psychologize* experience into a reflection of intrapsychic needs. Positive and negative relations and experiences in sport are thus made to appear dependent on individual abilities of people to mesh needs, rather than on the social structures that create patterns for normative social behavior in sport between women and men, athletes and coaches, and children and adults. Rather than a description of personal needs, women's accounts of their sport experiences also may be read as a call for change in power relations or the structure of sport itself (Duquin, 1978, 1991; Postow, 1980).

Indications of the importance of material relations do sometimes slip through the psychological veil. In explicating the reasons why women do not respond productively to a coach's anger, Anshel (1990) notes that "Relatively few women receive scholarship funding, and thus, they do not feel obligated to take abusive treatment from the coach. They are not dependent on college funding for living expenses as are most (male) athletes on scholarship" (p. 383). It is worth noting here that the male athlete's assumed willingness to take abuse from the coach is attributed to conditions of material reality (need for money) and not to some general male pathology like masochism.

When Anshel later tries to explain why coaches often fail to meet athletes' needs, however, his reasons are again psychological. Coaches, he says, are more concerned with giving than receiving information, are selective in soliciting feedback, tend not to view athletes' feelings as valid, are not comfortable allowing athletes' input, don't feel obligated to meet certain needs of players, and often don't have a personality conducive to healthy relationships with athletes! Whether we view this as a description of unhealthy leaders, an unhealthy sport system, or both, it appears that the well-being of a substantial number of athletes is at risk in today's sport structures.

Further evidence of the potentially abusive conditions in sport is presented by Blinde (1989a). Interviews with college athletes revealed that females experience various forms of academic, physical, social, and psychological exploitation. The following quote from Blinde (1989a) reflects the anger women sometimes feel when the hierarchy of gender relations is compounded by the hierarchy of athlete-coach relations:

> Our coach likes to play with words and he is very emotionally manipulative, specifically with women. He talks down to them, he puts his hand on your shoulder and you know, 'Oh, Mary, how are you feeling, today?' And you just want to belt him across the face. I had the gull (sic) to tell him that this is incredibly demeaning and that I don't mind him asking how I am, but that I am an adult and that I don't need to be coddled. His bottom line is that he is going to revert to behaviors that he is safest with and that's coddling and intimidating women . . . another instance of being used by yet another male hierarchy. (p. 118)

As this perspective demonstrates, writing about sport from the standpoint of women can increase our understanding of how sport is experienced and can be used to create alternate visions of sport. (See box on page 294.)

Recording women's subjective experience is just the beginning of a process that has transformation as its goal. Sport psychology has focused on changing the attitudes, skills, and mindset of the athlete to improve performance and to conform to the structures and values of sport as it exists. Many athletes have internalized this focus on self-change. Feminists suggest an approach to sport psychology that would focus on the material realities of sport structures and the social relationships in sport and how these affect the subjective experiences of athletes. Shotter and Logan (1988) contend that "a feminist practice would allow a conversation within which the creative, formative power of talk could be put to use in reformulating, redistributing, and redeveloping both people's knowledge of themselves and their immediate circumstances, and the nature of their practical-historical relations to one another" (p. 82). This

is one hope and goal of a feminist approach to sport psychology.

Feminist Psychoanalytic Theory: Sport in a Different Voice?

Feminist psychoanalytic theorists have tried to account for male domination and gender differences in moral perspective by focusing on the dynamics of early childrearing. Psychoanalytic theory postulates that females and males develop differently because women are the primary caregivers during the early years when gender identity is learned. Men are generally absent from important nurturing responsibilities during these years.

When women are the primary early caregivers, both sexes experience a primary identification, a symbiotic union, with the mother (or mother-figure) and eventually undergo a separation from the mother to establish self-identity. Because our earliest needs are satisfied through close and nurturant contact with the body of the mother, our identification with the body of the mother forms the basis for our identity as an embodied self. This early female mothering and subsequent separation has different effects for girls than for boys.

Girls have in their mothers a same-sex model for their gender behavior and identity. Although the female child eventually develops a separate identity from the mother, separation is not total and there remains a connection to the mother that is basic to the girl's self-identity. The mutually reinforcing identification between mothers and daughters develops in females a sense of self that is *relational* in nature, that sees relations with others not as a threat to self-identity but as necessary for the realization of one's own identity. Chodorow (1978) states that female identity is connected to the world of others and that females "emerge with a strong . . . basis for experiencing another's needs . . . as one's own" (p. 167). Girls, as a result of female mothering, incorporate into

Female Athletes Suggest Change

Given an opportunity, many athletes are willing to make suggestions, based on their personal experience, on how sport might be improved. In a study by Bohan and Duquin (1991), female athletes from various colleges and various sports were asked the question: If given the opportunity, what changes would athletes on this team make to improve the quality of their athletic experience in this sport? Areas in need of improvement included better off-season conditioning, better team spirit, and better communication with the coach:

> There are so many things that I would change, especially concerning the athletes. I would hold practices differently and pay closer attention to the way the athletes feel, after all athletes make up athletics. This team has no spirit and motivation. There are too many careless injuries that could easily be avoided if the coach would just listen. I'm not saying that the coach should do everything to make the athlete happy, but when an athlete is happy and likes his

(sic) coach, he enjoys doing all that he can for him and his team. I don't believe that we also eat right (especially on days of meets) or sometimes even train right. Many things can be changed to enhance the performance of this supposedly Div. I team [track].

I would improve the individual communication between the coach and players. Too infrequently does the coach project a caring demeanor towards the physical-emotional welfare of a player who truly is hurting. It seems that there is no time available to devote attention to this aspect [basketball].

Given the opportunity athletes should work harder in the off season and get ready for the season. This will allow a more prosperous and injury free season. Also athletes should try to build up coach-athlete and athlete-athlete relationships. If there are any difficulties both parties should try to work them out [softball]. (Bohan & Duquin, 1991)

their gender identity values of caregiving, nurturance, and empathy.

Boys' development of gender identity takes a different route. The absence of men in early nurturance and caregiving denies boys same-sex models for developing their self-identity. In defining who they are, males separate their identity from their mother and define themselves in opposition to the mother figure. Masculinity is associated with separation. To be male is to be unlike mother; to be not-female. This often leads to a denigration and disavowal of what is considered feminine. Females are seen a threat to masculine identity. This perceived threat forms the basis for the male's desire to have power and control over females.

Males thus develop a gender identity that is oppositional in nature rather than relational. This creates a self-identity that is less empathetic with others and that tends to separate from others, establishing an invulnerability by achieving distance from and control over others. According to feminist psychoanalytic theory, men's rejection of the mother and of what are considered feminine characteristics are foundational to understanding masculine tendencies toward the domination of nature, a dispassionate or disembodied rationalism, a repudiation of the body and emotions, and the perception of self-other relations as threatening or conflictual.

Sport has long served as an area of male identity and bonding. As Young (1983) states, "to secure his masculine identity, the boy rejects the mother and joins with other boys and men in a positive, exclusive sphere without the attributes of nurturance and dependence associated with the feminine'' (p. 132). Whether one chooses to believe part, all, or none of the psychoanalytic account of gender identity formation, males do form, and attempt to maintain, exclusive spheres of male activity. The description of all-male sports as a psychologically needed space to support male identity and male bonding has been in the literature for a number of years. Proponents of sex segregation in sport reveal the male fear of feminization. As Fisher (1972) notes:

> At a time in our society when much attention is being given to Women's Liberation, one should also realize that . . . young males are undergoing a considerable degree of feminization. It is *imperative* that the masculine concepts of certain sports be retained. (p. 98)

All-male sports are spheres for male identity creation, and children of both sexes learn at very early ages to associate athleticism with male identity (Oglesby, 1989). In addition, sport structures and norms often mitigate against affiliative motives and the development of caring relations associated with feminine values (Crown & Heatherington, 1989).

Feminist researchers are beginning to investigate the effects of male bonding based on an opposition to feminization, violence against the body, or a repudiation of feminine values. There is little information on what effects such male bonding practices have on female-male relations. However, Curry's (1991) study of fraternal bonding in the locker room reveals how jock talk denigrates females, objectifies women's bodies, and sets the foundation for attitudes that promote a rape culture. Data collected on the connection between sport and domestic violence suggest that wife battering increases on days of violent sport events like the Super Bowl (Lurie, 1991). Systematic study is just the beginning of the processes by which male sport socialization and certain sport environments promote violent, misogynistic, and homophobic attitudes and behaviors (Messner & Sabo, 1990). Documenting the negative psychological and social effects of all-male sport groups covertly or overtly dedicated to purging the feminine is an important area for feminist research in sport psychology. As Balbus (1987) points out:

> If boys . . . are obliged in order to become "men" to suppress the mother within them, this can only mean that they will be obliged to suppress their bodies as well. Only when the male child internalizes the body of a nurturer of his own gender—only under coparenting—will the mortifying repudiation of the body no longer be associated with masculinity. (p. 126)

Thus another fertile area for sport psychology research is the investigation of the effect of early coparenting on the sport socialization and psychological development of young children. One way for males to become more relationally oriented is to join women in early caregiving responsibilities. Through coparenting, the male child can form a primary identification with someone of his own gender and will no longer need to take an oppositional stance toward the mother in defining his self-identity. As more fathers become early nurturers of their children there may be a corresponding change in both the social structure and the social psychology of sport experience. Investigating the relationship between the psychological effects of coparenting and the potential changes in sport practice and values provides a rich area of interdisciplinary research for sport psychologists, sociologists, and philosophers.

Sport and the Psychology of Moral Development

Psychoanalytic theory has been criticized for its dualistic and essentialistic characterizations of gender.[2] Although dualistic and oppositional thinking, in relation both to women and men and to social life in general, creates stereotypes and can lead to rigid categories of thought, it also has been used to expose contradictions, clarify alternate value systems, and provide the basis for creative dialectical analysis (Sanday, 1988).

Carol Gilligan's (1982) seminal work in the psychology of moral development, *In a Different Voice*, uses feminist psychoanalytic thought to explore the psychological differences between women and men in empathetic response and moral perspective. She argues that women have a different moral perspective than men in making moral decisions. Women, she claims, are more likely than men to emphasize the importance of maintaining relationships, contextual understanding of moral situations, and empathetic response. Men are more likely to emphasize abstract, universal principles, conformity to rules, and the legal elaboration of rights. Recent contributions by feminists to the psychology of moral behavior have differed from traditional male-centered theory by shifting moral discourse from a dispassionate rational ethics approach to a more relationally centered moral position that accords privilege to the concrete over the abstract, interconnectedness over individuation, and the valued integrity of the lived body over a disembodied attachment to principle. This approach to the psychology of moral behavior incorporates the importance of needs and emotions, social relationships and responsibilities, and sensitivity to context-specific circumstance. This feminist challenge to the traditional rationalist approach to morality is related to maternal practice and is known variously as the ethic of care, nurturance, inseparability, contextuality, and attentive or preservative love (Noddings, 1984; Ruddick, 1983a; 1983b).

Research in sport psychology has found that females are often more sensitive than males to moral issues in sport. Bredemeier (1984) has conducted research on the relationship between sport and the moral development of athletes. She found that nonathletes and female athletes tend to have higher moral reasoning about issues in sport than male athletes. She also found that athletes' moral reasoning about everyday life events is higher than reasoning about morality in sport. Bredemeier (1984) concluded that "to the extent that competition is allowed to dominate interpersonal relations in sport, sport's potential for facilitating moral development is diminished" (p. 411).

In a series of studies on the perception of injustice in sport settings, Duquin (1984a; 1984b; 1989a) found that females (athletes, coaches, and nonathletes in high school and college) were significantly more likely than males to employ an ethic of care orientation when making moral judgments in sport. Females were more likely than males to perceive injustice to athletes and more likely to rate the injustice as serious. Males were more likely than females to take a "self-interest" orientation toward perceiving injustice, blaming athletes for not watching out for themselves. Males also were more likely than females to accept the norm of "expected inequity," normalizing self-interested behavior on the part of coaches and other athletic personnel.

Sport that is constructed or conducted to eliminate all that is perceived as feminine psychologically undermines the development of caring relations and the ethic of care. Sport practices often violate the integrity of embodiment, which is the foundation of care for self and others. Sport internalizes habits of self-objectification. Bodily objectification builds on dualistic notions that accord privilege to mind over body and that hold the body morally suspect, legitimizing bodily mortification and denigration. In sport, athletes are taught to subdue and control the corporeal. Socialization toward self-abnegation in sport is evidenced not only in training and dieting regimens but also in the valorization of athletes' willingness to sacrifice bodily health and well-being for victory. Bodily sacrifice involves the process of disembodiment, of separating self from body (Scarry, 1985). Socialization toward disembodiment has contributed to an increasing incidence of sport injuries among youth: annually over 1 million in basketball; 900,000 in baseball; 600,000 in football; and over 100,000 each in gymnastics and soccer. Statistics also show more fatalities and serious injuries ending in permanent disability, higher surgery rates, greater incidence of anorexia and diet-related illnesses, more chronic injuries related to overuse, higher rates of drug abuse, and increased stress-related psychological and emotional problems (Arnheim, 1985; Knoppers, 1990).

The valued integrity of the body and of embodiment is a consistent theme in feminist psychological analysis. Preserving and protecting life, fostering growth, and promoting health and welfare are ethical ideals derived from maternal practice. According to Kuykendall (1983), critical to assessing what is moral "is that an ethical mode of action must be life-affirming and that in our bodies or in our speech we manifest these life-affirming values" (p. 267). Thus practices that objectify the athlete, that require her to engage in deconstructive pain, mortification of the flesh, or life-denying violence to her body, inhibit the psychological development of the ethical self.

Along with according privilege to the body as a source of moral import, recent feminist theorists have resurrected the importance of emotions in moral discourse and behavior (Pellauer, 1985; Whitbeck, 1983; Young, 1987). Rationalistic ethical theories fail to recognize the role of emotions, sympathy, and compassion in motivating moral behavior. According to Noddings (1984), caring behavior springs from our childhood, from a felt remembrance of loving and being loved. To become skilled in the ethic of care requires the cultivation of the caring response, of empathy, engrossment, and of a willingness to extend to others. This development of emotional receptivity becomes crucial to the development of the ethical ideal and the moral self. Consequently, environments that desensitize athletes to their own feelings and to the feelings of others sabotage the ethic of care. Although sport undoubtedly is a place for the expression of strong emotions, there is at the same time a structural and systematic harnessing of certain kinds of emotions. Emotions that might negatively affect competitive performance, be they fear, pain, or empathetic identification with an opponent, are actively discouraged.

The most morally dangerous aspect of the socialization of emotions is the legitimacy sport gives to the infliction of pain on others and the sado-ascetic identities developed in the practice of some sports (Duquin, 1988a, 1988b). As Noddings (1984) notes, "the desire to prevent or relieve pain is a natural element of caring, and we betray our ethical selves when we ignore it or concoct rationalizations to act in defiance of it" (p. 150). Yet much of sport practice not only condones the infliction of pain on self and others but also suppresses emotional responses to this pain. Sport suppresses emotional sensitivity and receptivity by the process of distancing or disassociation. Athletes are taught to block pain by disassociation, that is, by separating themselves from their body and ignoring the feelings of their body. Similarly, emotional receptivity to others is blocked in sport by the social distancing of competing athletes and lack of communication between athletes and coaches. In these ways sport can diminish emotional receptivity, which is the basis for an empathetic response.

To develop the psychological skills associated with an ethic of care, people need to engage in caring practices in all aspects of their lives, including sport. When sport is used to devalue or to disassociate from what is perceived as feminine, both the ethic of care and the moral development of participants are put at risk (Duquin, 1993c).

Poststructuralist Theory: The Social Construction of Identity

Poststructuralist ideas focus on the ways social forms and institutions, through language and symbol systems, construct social reality and self-identity. Poststructuralism explores how a culture's language and symbol systems (e.g., the social sciences, religion, media, written texts, art, sport) define and legitimize what is to be taken as true or untrue, normal or abnormal, and good or bad in society. A major emphasis in poststructuralist theory is power: the power to name, define, and give meaning to reality. Analysis of language and symbols reveals that everything of symbolic value communicates a perspective or position. Language not only defines legitimate categories of thought but also communicates hierarchies of status. As a result, some people, ideas, and things have more worth in society than others. Words often connote value. For example, in sports, adjectives like fast, hard, and male have more status than slow, soft, and female. Thus hardball has more status than softball, fast pitch more status than slow pitch, and male athletes more status than female athletes. Those who create or control symbol systems in society can use these systems to maintain relations of power that favor their position in society. The power referred to in this theory is not only the overt power of coercion, but the more subtle powers of definition, normalization, and legitimization (Derrida, 1982; Foucault, 1979; McLaren, 1991). As Morawski (1988) notes, the struggle over definitions is a struggle over what is to "count as reality, truth, and progress and, consequently, what counts as experience, identity, desire, and "the good" (p. 189).[3]

A primary tool in poststructuralist theory is deconstruction. Deconstruction examines the historical and cultural variability in the construction of social identity. Deconstruction also involves an analysis and subversion of psychological texts, technologies, and forms of subjectivity (identity) produced by the discipline of psychology. Deconstruction uncovers the hidden contradictions and repressed meanings in psychological texts and reveals the forms of social control induced by psychological discourse. Through such analysis of psychological texts we can begin to understand how our knowledge of ourselves as females and males is shaped by what psychological theories historically establish as normal.

Poststructuralism and Feminist Psychology

One of the strengths of poststructuralist theory for feminist psychology is the recognition of the socially constructed nature of knowledge (Haraway, 1991; Jacobus, Keller, & Shuttleworth, 1990). As Burman (1992) writes, "Rather than knowledge being seen as universal, eternal and value-free, we can now show it to be provisional, culturally and historically specific, and both arising from and contributing to social interests" (p. 46). Recognizing the relative nature of psychological knowledge is especially important for feminists studying gender and athlete identity.

Analysis of texts and practices in psychology and sport psychology show how these disciplines have conflated notions of male gender identity and athlete identity. Athlete identity is embedded in a male-gendered body. Thus most of sport psychology is the psychology of males. In many sport psychology texts, athletes are addressed and discussed as male and few references are made to female athletes. Females reading sport psychology texts can make a number of interpretations. One interpretation is that the author is indeed discussing and describing (solely) males and that the information given by the author may or may not apply to females. Another is to feel that the author is describing a generic athlete and that gender does not matter in the psychological information being discussed. In this case, although the pronouns used to describe the athlete are he and his, the female reader generalizes the psychological information to herself. Identification with the generic (male) athlete may work well until the female reader finds a special section or chapter in the book devoted to female athletes. Now the question arises as to whether all the information she was generalizing to herself as an athlete really did apply only to males and everything important for her to know about herself as an athlete is contained in this small section devoted to females. For females, finding themselves in sport psychology texts is not the only problem. Psychology has helped create, and continues to maintain, an overlap between male identity and athlete identity that can make it difficult for some females who want to incorporate sportive competence into their sense of self.

Poststructuralist theory focuses attention on both what is dominant and what is left out or marginalized in psychological constructions of the body and identity. Certain psychological themes dominate research in sport psychology. These themes include arousal, competition, motivation, achievement, aggression, leadership, and cognitive strategies for improving performance. Left out or less emphasized areas of research in sport psychology include affiliation, emotion, socialization, communication, power relations, kinesthetic pleasure, moral orientation, and aesthetics. Who the athlete is and what she/he is concerned about are both created and reflected in the production of psychological research. The psychological identity of athletes created by the discipline of sport psychology has focused coach and athlete attention on the productive/performance aspects of self and has marginalized all other aspects of athlete self-identity.

Poststructuralist ideas also draw attention to the social and historical development of psychology as a discipline of social control, especially in the area of gender identity and gender relations. Poststructural analysis shows how psychological definitions and labels affect individuals via the classification and segregation of people through the use of personality tests. For example, in one research study young boys were labeled feminine based on what psychology deemed abnormal male play behavior. Sport retraining programs were conducted to masculinize these boys into proper male play patterns (Marlowe, Algozzine, Lerch, & Welch, 1978). In another study, young girls who played games competitively to win were labeled aggressive, hyperactive, and masculine (Sutton-Smith & Roberts, 1970). As can be seen from these examples, the ability to decide normal behavior and label people as deviant is a powerful

tool in the discipline of psychology. This technology of social control not only creates in society a fear of difference, but also can produce hostility toward nonconforming groups and individuals (Carse, 1986). If people believe what psychologists pronounce as reality, then when psychology gives negative meaning to certain behaviors (e.g., competitiveness in females, sensitivity in males), these judgments can have a life-altering affect on a person's self-identity or self-esteem. Not unlike religion's power to label someone a sinner, the power psychology uses to label someone abnormal serves to control social behavior. The association of aggression and dominance with "normal" male behavior acts as a strong social control mechanism that reinforces gender power relations in society. Furthermore, psychology's creation of gender pathologies related to appropriate gender play and personality characteristics continues to restrict the sport and recreational choices of females and males.

The social construction of female athletic identities is produced through many symbol systems. How females come to understand what it means to be an athlete and what they come to value about the sporting experience is an important and complex phenomenon. Earliest words and images of athletes come from family and friends, children's books, television, and other media, all of which are influenced by psychological theories of gender (Duquin, 1977, 1993b; Kunesh, Hasbrook, & Lewthwaite, 1990). One aim of the feminist agenda in psychology is directed at women's greater participation in self-definition, in negotiating self-identity within various power relations. Messner (1988) notes, however, that while "the current wave of women's athleticism expresses a genuine quest by women for equality, control of their own bodies, and self-definitions . . . [this project is being undertaken] within historical limits and constraints imposed by a consumption-oriented corporate capitalism and men's continued attempts to retain power and privilege over women" (p. 207). Thus research on the social construction of athletic identities via psychological texts must assess the influence of patriarchy, racism, and capitalism in normalizing specific psychological characteristics and identities. This area of research should prove to be a fruitful source of collaboration among sport psychologists, anthropologists, and sociologists.

Feminist Critique of Poststructuralism

Feminists have criticized poststructuralism's focus on language and symbols for directing attention away from the more material aspects of women's oppression under patriarchy. Women's experience of male violence and their lower economic status are two material manifestations of patriarcal ideology. Kitzinger (1991b) observes: ''We cannot stop rape, murder, sexual abuse and oppressive legislation simply by changing symbolic representations of them. Some writers, inspired by poststructuralism's focus on discourse and subjectivity, seem not to realize this. . . .'' (p. 126). Similarly, language analysis does not change the violence permitted under sport rules and structures. In most sport structures weakness is exploited and physical dominance is paramount. In some sports the body is used as a weapon to express the self and to silence others. For males, sport is often used as a training ground for the reproduction and legitimization of male violence.

Feminists also criticize poststructuralism for its tendency toward the moral leveling of all ideology. In poststructuralist theory all social construction is ideology. No single ideology is accorded privilege over any other for its greater truth value or its higher moral worth. According to poststructuralism, there is no way to stand outside of ideology to make such a judgment of superiority. So while feminists may use poststructuralist theory to deconstruct patriarchal language and symbol systems, they are aware that the theory itself considers feminism to be as much an ideological mythmaker as patriarchy, capitalism, or Marxism. The poststructuralist moral leveling of all ideology is contrary to the feminist goal of creating more morally responsive environments in which all people thrive (Burman, 1992).

Despite its drawbacks, feminist psychology uses poststructuralist theory to make visible the multiple interpretations of reality, to reveal the power in creating definitions, and to clarify the processes involved in the social construction of gender. In sport psychology, feminists use poststructuralism to help athletes understand how patriarchal images are used to define and delimit women and sportswomen alike. Sport psychologists also use poststructuralism to test and subvert traditional meanings of gender and athlete identity and to assist athletes in creating new images and definitions of themselves and of sport (Davis, 1989; Duquin, 1989b).

Summary and Conclusions

One of the most subversive, liberating, and risky activities people can engage in is to question authority (Stenstad, 1989). Feminists challenge the authority of traditional constructs of gender and emphasize the importance of women's participation in self-definition. Feminists in psychology dispute the authority of past theories of gender, the authority of patriarchal world views, and the authority of men's voices over those of women. Morawski (1988) reminds us that we cannot dream our way out of political realities:

> This is where active resistance, political strategies, and even cunning refusal come in. We need to use the skill and strategies that enable us to pass through points of greatest resistance, to arrive at places where our refusal to participate in traditions and our visions of new worlds can be elaborated (p. 191).

In most cases, especially in sport, people are expected to accept the rules given them and accept the authorities already in place. Rarely do athletes believe they have the power to question the structure or rules under which they play. Yet the institutions with which we interact are crucial in shaping both our bodies and our identities. Sexist legislation and institutions deform female and male identities just as abusive sport deforms bodies. Because we come to know ourselves through our relations with others, oppressive and exploitive human relations warp our moral sense of self. To become self-reflexive and morally responsible requires that we question the authorities who set boundaries on our behaviors, feelings, and values. We also must question the legitimacy of many sport structures. Nelson (1991) gives a good example of the establishment of female authority with regard to pain and violence in sport:

We seem to have come full circle, from the days when men said, "Our games are too dangerous for you," and women argued, "No, they're not," to an era in which some women are saying, "We've tried your games, and you know what? They are too dangerous. From the looks of your mutilated bodies, they're too dangerous for you too. We're going to make up our own games, or alter your games so we can take care of ourselves." (p. 185)

Questioning authority, withdrawing support from traditional authorities, becoming our own authority, and investing in other women's authority are all strategies for changing sporting experiences and gender relationships.

Feminists recognize the power of female bonding, of women talking with, listening to, and supporting each other in the process of making changes in a patriarchal society (Lugones, 1989). The value of female bonding and relationships has led many athletes into alternate models of play. Many women realize that it is not enough to say, "Let women be all they are capable of being," because women, like men, are capable of being very dangerous people both on and off the playing field. For feminist athletes, feeling joy,

pride, and confidence in one's body and in sport becomes problematic if those emotions are achieved through the denigration, injury, or humiliation of another.

Feminist psychology reminds us of the importance of social relations and social narratives in the formation of psychological identities. We need sport structures that allow females to have experiences that are joyful in spirit, physically sensual, playful in relations, and skillfully exciting. The many visions of feminist psychology may help us realize that in changing sport and gender relations we must include a wide diversity of women's voices and experiences. We must recognize the importance of early development in establishing categories of thought and value about sport and identity. We must recognize the contributions of history, culture, traditions, social institutions, and dominant groups in constructing our sports and sport identities. Finally, we must recognize our own contribution and responsibility in creating meaning for ourselves in sport.

Notes

[1]There are many different approaches to feminist thought and practice. These include liberal feminism, black feminism, radical feminism, socialist feminism, and lesbian feminism. The feminist approach to psychology referred to in this paper respects the diversity among women and acknowledges the similarities and differences between various social inequalities (e.g., race, class, sexuality, ability) as well as gender. Feminist psychology aims at supporting the social and political change needed to improve the social and material conditions of women's lives (Wilkinson, 1991).

[2]Psychoanalytic theories have been criticized from many directions. Opposition to psychoanalytic theory has focused on its ethnocentrism, its assumption of fixed identity, its assumed opposition of self and other, and its blindness to gendered power relations that have

relegated women to the private sphere. Morawski (1988) points out that "adopting psychoanalytic models obscures even further the power relations that determine both psychological experience and theorizing about that experience" (p. 189). Ferguson (1989) criticizes the theory for reproducing fictions about a fixed and singular identity rather than seeing the self as capable of many identities in a process that is ongoing throughout one's life. Kitzinger (1991a) criticizes psychoanalysis for its ethnocentrism, its tendency to "explain the 'nature' of women with reference to Western individualistic models of personhood, which assume the biological nuclear family, and stereotypical notions about the experiences of infants and their caretakers" (p. 53). She notes that the generic woman in most psychological theory, including psychoanalytic theory, is Western, middle class, white, heterosexual, and able bodied.

[3]A classic example of the power to define reality in sport occurred when the men's NCAA (National Collegiate Athletic Association) took over women's collegiate sports in the early 1980s, putting the AIAW (Association for Intercollegiate Athletics for Women) out of business. The NCAA established itself as the primary definer of both women's and men's collegiate sport. Women lost a significant amount of legitimate power to define what it meant to be a female athlete, to make rules, to define relationships, and to honor values different from those of men's sports. After a long legal battle, the courts ruled in favor of the NCAA over the AIAW. The men's model of sport was deemed to be the "good" model, the most progressive model for women. The NCAA's power to define the female collegiate athlete was thus given moral sanction and was backed by the power of law.

References

Allison, M.T. (1981). Competition and cooperation: A sociocultural perspective. In A. Cheska (Ed.), *Play as context* (pp. 92-100). West Point, NY: Leisure Press.

Al-Saka, S. (1990). *Predictors of post-game anxiety for girls and boys in sports.* Unpublished master's thesis, University of Pittsburgh.

Anshel, M. (1990). *Sport psychology: From theory to practice.* Scottsdale, AZ: Gorsuch Scarisbrick.

Arnheim, D. (1985). *Modern principles of athletic training.* St. Louis: Times Mirror/Mosby.

Balbus, I. (1987). Disciplining women. In S. Benhabib & D. Cornell (Eds.), *Feminism as critique* (pp. 110-127). Minneapolis: University of Minnesota Press.

Berlage, G.I. (1990, November). The All American girls' professional baseball league. Paper presented at the annual conference of the North American Society for the Sociology of Sport, Denver.

Birrell, S. (1991). *Feminist resistance and transformation in sport in a time of war.* Paper presented at the Symposium on Girls and Women in Sports. Slippery Rock University, Slippery Rock, PA.

Blinde, E. (1989a). Unequal exchange and exploitation in college sport: The care of the female athlete. *Arena Review*, **2**, 111-123.

Blinde, E. (1989b). Participation in a male sport model and the value orientation of female intercollegiate athletes. *Sociology of Sport Journal*, **6**, 36-49.

Bohan, D., & Duquin, M. (1991). *Quality of relations questionnaire: Self-assessment of women's sports team.* Unpublished manuscript, University of Pittsburgh.

Booth-Butterfield, M., & Booth-Butterfield, S. (1988). Jock talk: Cooperation and competition within a university women's basketball team. In B. Bates & A. Taylor (Eds.), *Women Communicating.* Norwood, NJ: Abbex.

Boutilier, M.A., & SanGiovanni, L. (1983). *The sporting woman.* Champaign, IL: Human Kinetics.

Bredemeier, B. (1984). Sport, gender, and moral growth. In J. Silva & R. Weinberg (Eds.),

Psychological foundations of sport (pp. 400-413). Champaign, IL: Human Kinetics.

Burman, E. (1990). Differing with deconstruction: A feminist critique. In I. Parker & J. Shotter (Eds.), *Deconstructing social psychology*. London: Routledge.

Burman, E. (1992). Feminism and discourse in developmental psychology: Power, subjectivity and interpretation. *Feminism & Psychology*, **2**, 45-59.

Carse, J.P. (1986). Finite and infinite games. New York: Free Press.

Chodorow, N. (1978). *The reproduction of mothering*. Berkeley: University of California Press.

Code, L. (1989). Experience, knowledge, and responsibility. In A. Garry & M. Pearsall (Eds.), *Women, knowledge, and reality: Explorations in feminist philosophy* (pp. 157-172). Boston: Unwin Hyman.

Cole, C.L. (1989). *Sport and its discontents: The ongoing processes of sexual politics and sport*. Paper presented at the meeting of the North American Society for the Sociology of Sport.

Crown, J., & Heatherington, L. (1989). The costs of winning? The role of gender in moral reasoning and judgments about competitive athletic encounters. *Journal of Sport & Exercise Psychology*, **11**, 281-289.

Curry, T.J. (1991). Fraternal bonding in the locker room: A profeminist analysis of talk about competition and women. *Sociology of Sport Journal*, **8**(2), 119-135.

Davis, L. (1989). A postmodern paradox? Cheerleaders at women's sporting events. *Arena Review*, **2**, 124-133.

Derrida, J. (1982). *Positions*. London: Athlone Press.

Dewar, A. (1991). *Working against oppression in sport: Towards an inclusive critical sport sociology*. Paper presented at the meeting of the North American Society for the Sociology of Sport.

Duquin, M. (1977). Differential sex role socialization toward amplitude appropriation. *Research Quarterly*, **48**, 288-292.

Duquin, M. (1978). The androgynous advantage. In C. Oglesby (Ed.), *Women and sport: From myth to reality* (pp. 89-106). Philadelphia: Lea & Febiger.

Duquin, M. (1983). Feminism and patriarchy in physical education. In A. Dunleavy, A. Miracle, and R. Rees (Eds.), *Studies in the sociology of sport* (pp. 167-179). Fort Worth: Texas Christian University Press.

Duquin, M. (1984a). Social justice in sport: The norm of expected inequity. In N. Theberge & P. Donnelly (Eds.), *Sport and the sociological imagination* (pp. 177-189). Fort Worth: Texas Christian University Press.

Duquin, M. (1984b). Power and authority: Moral consensus and conformity in sport. *International Review of Sport Sociology*, **19**, 295-304.

Duquin, M. (1988a). *Sportive play: Pain as discourse*. Paper presented at the meeting of the North Central Sociological Association, Pittsburgh.

Duquin, M. (1988b). Gender and youth sport: Reflections on old and new fiction. In R. Magill, M. Ash, & F. Smoll (Eds.), *Children in sport* (pp. 31-41). Champaign, IL: Human Kinetics.

Duquin, M. (1989a). *Perceptions and rationalizations on social justice in sport*. Paper presented at the North Central Sociological Association Conference, Akron.

Duquin, M. (1989b). Fashion and fitness: Images in women's magazine advertisements. *Arena Review*, **13**(2), 97-109.

Duquin, M. (1991). Sport, women and the ethic of care. *Journal of Applied Recreational Research*, **16**(4), 262-280.

Duquin, M. (1993a). One future for sport: Moving toward an ethic of care. In G. Cohen (Ed.), *Women in Sport: Issues and Controversies*. Newbury Park, CA: Sage.

Duquin, M. (1993b, November). *Of bodies, books, and bicycles: An interactive critical pedagogy of the body*. Presidential address presented at the North American Society for the Sociology of Sport Conference, Ottawa, ON.

Duquin, M. (1993c). *The body snatchers and Dr. Frankenstein revisited: The social construction and deconstruction of bodies in postmodern times*. Manuscript submitted for publication.

Edelson, P. (1991, May). Sports during wartime. *Z Magazine*, **4**(5), 85-87.

Ferguson, A. (1989). A feminist aspect theory of the self. In A. Garry & M. Pearsall (Eds.), *Women, knowledge, and reality: Explorations in feminist philosophy* (pp. 93-108). Boston: Unwin Hyman.

Fine, M., & Gordon, S.M. (1991). Effacing the center and the margins: Life at the intersection of psychology and feminism. *Feminism and Psychology*, **1**, 19-27.

Fisher, A.C. (1972). Sports as an agent of masculine orientation. *The Physical Educator*, **28**, 96-98.

Flatow, S. (1991, May). It's okay to grow up. *Parade* (pp. 4-5).

Foucault, M. (1979). *The history of sexuality: Vol. I. An introduction*. London: Allen Lane.

Gergen, M.M. (1988). Toward a feminist metatheory and methodology in the social sciences. In M.M. Gergen (Ed.), *Feminist thought and the structure of knowledge* (pp. 87-104). New York: New York University Press.

Gilligan, C. (1982). *In a different voice*. Cambridge, MA: Harvard University Press.

Griffin, P. (1991). *Changing the game: Homophobia in women's sport*. Paper presented at the Symposium on Girls and Women in Sports. Slippery Rock University, Slippery Rock, PA.

Haraway, D.J. (1991). *Simians, cyborgs, and women: The reinvention of nature*. New York: Routledge.

Holloway, W. (1991). The psychologization of feminism or the feminization of psychology? *Feminism & Psychology*, **1**, 29-38.

Hult, J.S. (1985). The governance of athletics for girls and women: Leadership by women physical educators, 1899-1949. *Research Quarterly for Exercise and Sport, Centennial Issue*, 64-77.

Jacobus, M., Keller, E., & Shuttleworth, S. (1990). *Body/Politics: Women and the discourses of science*. New York: Routledge.

Jaggar, A.M. (1989). Love and knowledge: Emotion in feminist epistemology. In A. Garry & M. Pearsall (Eds.), *Women, knowledge, and reality: Explorations in feminist philosophy* (pp. 129-156). Boston: Unwin Hyman.

Kitzinger, C. (1991a). Politicizing psychology. *Feminism & Psychology*, **1**, 49-54.

Kitzinger, C. (1991b). Feminism, psychology and the paradox of power. *Feminism & Psychology*, **1**, 111-130.

Knoppers, A. (1990, November). *Always too fat, never too thin*. Paper presented at the annual conference of the North American Society for the Sociology of Sport, Denver.

Kohn, A. (1986). *No contest: The case against competition*. Boston: Houghton Mifflin.

Kunesh, M.A., Hasbrook, C.A., & Lewthwaite, R. (1990, November). *Physical activity socialization: Peer interactions and affective responses among a sample of sixth grade girls*. Paper presented at the annual conference of the North American Society for the Sociology of Sport, Denver.

Kuykendall, E. (1983). Toward an ethic of nurturance: Luce Irigaray on mothering and power. In J. Trebilcot (Ed.), *Mothering: Essays on feminist theory* (pp. 263-274). Totowa, NJ: Rowman & Allanheld.

Lenskyj, H. (1987). Female sexuality and women's sport. *Women's International Forum*, **10**(4), 381-386.

Lever, J. (1976). Sex differences in the games children play. *Social Problems*, **23**, 479-488.

Lugones, M. (1989). Playfulness, "world"-traveling, and loving perception. In A. Garry & M. Pearsall (Eds.), *Women, knowledge, and reality: Explorations in feminist philosophy* (pp. 275-290). Boston: Unwin Hyman.

Lurie, R. (1991, January). Unnecessary roughness. *The Village Voice*, p. 132.

Marlowe, M., Algozzine, B., Lerch, H.A., & Welch, P.D. (1978). The games analysis intervention as a method of decreasing feminine play patterns of emotionally disturbed boys. *Research Quarterly*, **49**(4), 484-490.

Mathes, S., & Battista, R. (1985). College men's and women's motives for participation in physical activity. *Perceptual Motor Skills*, **43**, 15-18.

McLaren, P.L. (1991). Schooling the postmodern body: Critical pedagogy and the politics of enfleshment. In H.A. Giroux (Ed.), *Postmodernism, feminism, and cultural politics* (pp. 144-173). Albany: State University of New York Press.

Messner, M. (1988). Sports and male domination: The female athlete as contested ideological terrain. *Sociology of Sport Journal*, **5**, 197-211.

Messner, M., & Sabo, D. (1990). *Sport, men and the gender order*. Champaign, IL: Human Kinetics.

Meyer, B.B. (1990, November). *The perceptions and experiences of female student-athletes revisited: A longitudinal approach*. Paper presented at the North American Society for the Sociology of Sport Conference, Denver.

Meyer, J. (1988). Feminist thought and social psychology. In M.M. Gergen (Ed.), *Feminist thought and the structure of knowledge* (pp. 105-123). New York: New York University Press.

Minton, L. (1991, April). How did you overcome your greatest fear? *Parade*, pp. 22-23.

Montgomery, K.L., & Duquin, M.E. (1991, April). *Saving face and body: Structuring differences in educational gymnastics*. Paper

presented at North Central Sociological Association meetings, Dearborn, MI.

Morawski, J.G. (1988). Impasse in feminist thought? In M.M. Gergen (Ed.), *Feminist thought and the structure of knowledge* (pp. 182-194). New York: New York University Press.

Nelson, M. (1991). *Are we winning yet?* New York: Random House.

Noddings, N. (1984). *Caring: A feminine approach to ethics and moral education*. Berkeley: University of California Press.

Oglesby, C. (1989). *Gender commandments*. Unpublished presentation, Association for the Advancement of Applied Sports Psychology, annual conference, University of North Carolina at Chapel Hill.

Pellauer, M. (1985). Moral callousness and moral sensitivity: Violence against women. In B. Andolsen, C. Gudorf, & M. Pellauer (Eds.), *Women's consciousness, women's conscience*. New York: Winston Press.

Postow, B.C. (1980). Women and masculine sports. *Journal of Philosophy of Sport*, **7**, 51-58.

Probyn, E. (1993). *Sexing the self: Gendered positions in cultural studies*. New York: Routledge.

Redican, B., & Hadley, B. (1988). A field studies project in a city health leisure club. *Sociology of Sport Journal*, **5**, 50-62.

Ruddick, S. (1983a). Maternal thinking. In J. Trebilcot (Ed.), *Mothering: Essays on feminist theory* (pp. 213-230). Totowa, NJ: Rowman & Allanheld.

Ruddick, S. (1983b). Preservative love and military destructiveness. In J. Trebilcot (Ed.), *Mothering: Essays on feminist theory* (pp. 231-262). Totowa, NJ: Rowman & Allanheld.

Sabo, D.F., & Panepinto, J. (1990). Football ritual and the social reproduction of masculinity. In M.A. Messner & D.F. Sabo (Eds.), *Sport, men, and the gender order* (pp. 115-126). Champaign, IL: Human Kinetics.

Sanday, P. (1988). The reproduction of patriarchy in feminist anthropology. In M.M. Gergen (Ed.), *Feminist thought and the structure of knowledge* (pp. 49-68). New York: New York University Press.

Scarry, R. (1985). *The body in pain: The making and unmaking of the world.* New York: Oxford University Press.

Shotter, J., & Logan, J. (1988). The pervasiveness of patriarchy: On finding a different voice. In M.M. Gergen (Ed.), *Feminist thought and the structure of knowledge* (pp. 69-86). New York: New York University Press.

Smith, D.E. (1991). Writing women's experience into social science. *Feminism & Psychology*, **1**, 155-169.

Spelman, E.V. (1989). Anger and insubordination. In A. Garry & M. Pearsall (Eds.), *Women, knowledge, and reality: Explorations in feminist philosophy* (pp. 263-274). Boston: Unwin Hyman.

Stenstad, G. (1989). Anarchic thinking: Breaking the hold of monotheistic ideology on feminist philosophy. In A. Garry & M. Pearsall (Eds.), *Women, knowledge, and reality: Explorations in feminist philosophy* (pp. 331-339). Boston: Unwin Hyman.

Sutton-Smith, B., & Roberts, J. (1970). The cross-cultural and psychological study of games. In G. Luschen (Ed.), *The cross-cultural analysis of sport and games.* Champaign, IL: Stipes.

Varpalotai, A. (1987). The hidden curriculum in leisure: An analysis of a girls' sport sub-culture. *Women's Studies International Forum*, **10**(4), 411-422.

Whitbeck, C. (1983). The maternal instinct. In J. Trebilcot (Ed.), *Mothering: Essays on feminist theory* (pp. 185-191). Totowa, NJ: Rowman & Allanheld.

Wilkinson, S. (1991). Feminism and Psychology: From critique to reconstruction. *Feminism & Psychology*, **1**, 5-18.

Worell, J. (1990). Images of women in psychology. In M. Paludi & G.A. Steuernagel (Eds.), *Foundations for a Feminist Restructuring of the Academic Disciplines* (pp. 185-224). New York: Harrington Park Press.

Young, I.M. (1983). Is male gender identity the cause of male domination? In J. Trebilcot (Ed.), *Mothering: Essays in feminist theory* (pp. 129-146). Totowa, NJ: Rowman & Allanheld.

Young, I.M. (1987). Impartiality and the civic public. In S. Benhabib & D. Cornell (Eds.), *Feminism as critique* (pp. 56-76). Minneapolis: University of Minnesota Press.

Young-Eisendrath, P. (1988). The female person and how we talk about her. In M.M. Gergen (Ed.), *Feminist thought and the structure of knowledge* (pp. 152-172). New York: New York University Press.

Zechetmayr, M. (1991, April). *Physical activities and sports in nursing homes.* Paper presented at North Central Sociological Association meetings, Dearborn, MI.

Chapter 18

The Significance of Body Image in Psychosocial Development and in Embodying Feminist Perspectives

Sharon R. Guthrie
Shirley Castelnuovo

Not to have confidence in one's body is to lose confidence in oneself. . . . It is precisely the female athletes, who being positively interested in their own game, feel themselves least handicapped in comparison with the male. . . . Let her swim, climb mountain peaks, pilot an airplane, battle against the elements, take risks, go out for adventure, and she will not feel before the world that timidity.

SIMONE DE BEAUVOIR
The Second Sex

Most theoretical and empirical scholarship generated in sport psychology has been directed at maximizing the quantitative performance of elite athletes, that is, those who compete for external rewards such as governmental acclaim, money, prestige, and education. Certainly, as high-performance sport has become increasingly scientized and commercialized over the years, sport psychologists have become heavily invested in understanding the psychological bases of such performance. Moreover, as is typical of most sport sciences, there has been a long-standing male bias. Consider the fact that until recently it was not uncommon for sport psychologists to study only male athletes, yet generalize their findings to females, without questioning whether or not differences existed or were relevant. Of course, as increasing numbers of women have become involved in elite sports, researchers now examine the psychology of female athletes more often than they did in the past; however, the emphasis on elite populations and quantitative efficiency in athletic performance is still clearly evident.

Although such elite, male, and quantitative biases may not be difficult to comprehend, such a narrow focus has resulted in a number of gaps in our knowledge base. For example, we know far less about how women psychologically process their sporting and movement experiences than we know about men. We also know relatively little about the psychosocial consequences and qualitative experiences of sporting participation for diverse groups of people (e.g., people of color, athletes with a disability).

In this chapter we move beyond these biases as we explore the transformational possibilities in sport and other somatic activities for women, particularly those that relate to body image, self-concept, and the embodiment of feminist perspectives. Such exploration is based on our belief that the oppression of women is intimately connected to their bodily experience in the world, which for many is rooted in a sense of inferiority, helplessness, and vulnerability. We also believe that although women's body images are profoundly shaped by socioeconomic, political, racial, age, and sexual/gender constructs, individual choices can provide a basis for resistance and change, particularly when they are nurtured in settings that foster female bonding.

A feminist analysis of Western female embodiment reveals a patriarchically imposed movement vocabulary that physically disables and thus oppresses women. Ideology regarding the female body, which is deeply embedded in Western societies, reinforces this practice. Consider, for example, the following notions, all of which have been used to construct and therefore control women's bodies and sporting practices:

- Women's bodies are inferior to men's because they are more embedded in their physical lives (e.g., menstruation, pregnancy, childbirth).
- Women's bodies are softer, weaker, and more vulnerable to injury than men's and hence need to be protected.
- Movement activities are useful for females only when they help produce healthy, potentially procreative bodies.
- Women's bodies are not suitable for sports that require physical contact, particularly those that emphasize the use of one's bodily powers to overcome an opponent.
- Women who participate and excel in such sports are masculine or are not "real" women.

Historically, these notions, which were converted into scientific findings and incorporated into the biomedical and psychosocial disciplines, have regulated sporting practices for women. Indeed, the idea of women's biological inferiority has been used extensively to justify sport and movement restrictions. There also has been a

Figure 18.1 Ideology regarding the female body reinforces the idea that sports requiring physical contact are inappropriate for women.

long-standing belief that certain sports masculin-ize the female participant or promote lesbianism. In particular, sports emphasizing physical contact and aggression toward others (e.g., football, rugby, wrestling), high levels of muscularity, physical strength, and power (e.g., track and field events, weightlifting), and female bonding (e.g., most team sports) have been considered problem-atic in this regard. On the other hand, individual sports, particularly those that emphasize the aes-thetic and erotic elements of the body either through costume or movement, have been encour-aged for women (e.g., gymnastics, swimming, tennis, figure skating). It is clear that such beliefs and practices have constricted the sporting experi-ence of female athletes; they also have resulted in a restricted and oppressive movement vocabu-lary for most women.

Feminist social analysis has been directed to-ward understanding women's oppression, as well as proposing strategies of resistance and em-powerment. Such oppression is often attributed to the dominance of masculinist paradigms that focus on the rational and diminish the feminine, which has been identified with the body and emo-tions. Although feminists have been critical of the mind-body dualism inherent in such masculinist mental constructs, many have failed to eliminate a mind-body dichotomy in their own liberation proposals. This is evidenced in the emphasis given to feminist consciousness as the key to liberation. The recent work of Frigga Haug et al. (1987), for example, poses the liberatory possibilities when groups of women collectively reconstruct the sex-ualization of their own bodies through techniques involving memory and writing. We believe that feminist liberatory strategies emphasizing mental processes alone are insufficient. In contrast, we will argue that the mind and body must be con-ceived of as a unity in understanding the social

Figure 18.2 Many individual sports, such as tennis, have historically been deemed acceptable for women. Courtesy of Sharon R. Guthrie.

construction of gender, as well as in embodying a feminist perspective.

Such a perspective can be fostered in a physical education course that combines both theory and praxis; that is, one that helps women cognitively understand the social construction of their bodies, yet also provides them with somatic experiences that strengthen their body images and self-concepts. Moreover, while incorporating the diversity of socially constructed experiences of women and thus avoiding universal or essentialist claims, such an environment would also yield concrete strategies for self-directed social change. The purpose of such a course, then, is to provide experiences, both verbal and nonverbal, that empower women and ultimately may foster not only the adoption of a feminist consciousness but also the embodiment of such a way of being. Although this is an academic course intended for women who have poor body images and little confidence in their motor skills, similar strategies can be adopted by women in alternative settings and of varying motor abilities.

Our chapter is divided into five sections. Section I briefly reviews the research findings on body image. Section II focuses on Nancy Hartsock's essentialist feminist critique of the male-constructed female body and male-biased body image research. Section III offers an alternative perspective to Hartsock's female essentialist approach, that is, Michel Foucault's research supporting the social construction of the human body. Although Foucault's position is closely aligned with our own beliefs regarding the social construction of human bodies, his analysis does not include the possibility of individuals autonomously evaluating the socialization process and directing social change. For this reason, in Section IV we examine the work of Maurice Merleau-Ponty, a theorist who conceptualizes human subjectivity as the capacity of persons to make evaluative choices and defines the change process as a unity of mind and body. In Section V we demonstrate how theory, namely genderized versions of Foucault and Merleau-Ponty, can be used to inform practice,

in this case a physical education course designed to foster the embodiment of feminist perspectives.

The Body and Body Image as a Theoretical Construct in Western Science

Theoretical interest in the connection between the mind and body, as well as the body and self, has an extensive history in Western society. Unfortunately, mind-body dualism, that is, the notion that the mind and body are separate entities and the body is the lesser of the two, has been a dominant part of this history. Identifying women primarily in terms of their bodies and thus as inferior to men, who more often have been defined by mental characteristics, has been an equally common practice.

The notion of body image, which is generally considered a psychological construct, also has a long history, particularly among philosophers, neurologists, sociologists, and psychiatrists, as well as psychologists. Among the voluminous data that have been collected, several themes emerge:

- Body images are multidimensional and multifaceted; that is, they include perceptions, attitudes, and behaviors that involve components as diverse as physical appearance, size, sensations, spatial position, boundaries, and sexual identity.
- Body images are personalized and subjective experiences; thus the images we have of our own bodies may be quite different from the way others see us.
- Body images are dynamic and changeable rather than static and absolute.
- Body images are socially constructed rather than genetically determined.
- Body images influence information processing and behavior; that is, how we feel and think about our bodies influences the way we perceive and act in the world.

- Body images are intimately related to self-concept (Pruzinsky & Cash, 1990).

Indeed, as Seymour Fisher (1990), a premier body image theoretician and researcher, has said: "Human identity cannot be separated from its somatic headquarters in the world" (p. 18).

Despite a vast array of research, body image and related subjects have received relatively little emphasis in sport psychology and other sport sciences. This may seem surprising, considering the somatic nature of sport and physical education; however, let's examine why this might be. The multidimensional nature of body image, which creates problems of definition and measurement, likely has motivated researchers to explore phenomena that they consider more accessible. The paucity of body image research likely stems also from the emphasis on psychological determinants of elite performance, rather than the consequences of participating in diverse settings. Researchers may even have assumed that because elite athletes perform physically at supernormal levels, they possess healthy body images and consequently have chosen to investigate other areas.

Research, however, clearly indicates that sport and exercise psychologists have much to gain from a thorough study of body image. Of particular relevance are findings suggesting deep connections between body image and the processes of self-perception, information processing, and behavior. For example, recent research has indicated a growing epidemic of eating disorders, particularly among women. The problem has grown so extensive that currently there are more deaths from anorexia than from most other mental health disorders, and even more deaths than those resulting from AIDS (Wolf, 1991). Researchers also have found athletes, regardless of gender, to be a high-risk group, particularly those who participate in sports in which small body size, low body weight, and thinness are deemed important to success (Black & Burckes-Miller, 1988; Burckes-Miller & Black, 1988, 1991; Guthrie, 1991). Most important, research indicates not only that eating disorders and negative body image are significantly related, but that negative body image is a key factor in both the development of eating pathology and the prediction of treatment failure (Rosen, 1990). These kinds of findings firmly indicate the need to examine body image phenomena more carefully, particularly if we are to understand what role somatic experience, whether it be sport or exercise, plays in the development of body image and self-concept. However, the way we conceptualize body image and the way we go about our inquiry are important.

Twenty-two years ago, Dorothy Allen (1972), a sport scholar, asked:

Who is this sportswoman? What is it that she experiences? If she is much less than what she is, then what is it that she can be? I am suggesting that we develop new techniques for studying the psychological experience of the self concept of the woman participant, that we develop an experiential-behavioral approach to our study. (p. 46)

Allen's call went unheeded until recently when feminist theorists began to challenge the gender blindness and insensitivity of body image research. Although researchers have identified consistent gender differences (e.g., women are far more likely than men to have eating disorders, undergo cosmetic surgery, experience their bodies negatively, and suffer job discrimination based on appearance), they often have failed to question the structural forces and ideological patterns that foster and sustain such differences. Moreover, as we will see in the next section, the ways in which researchers generally have defined body image have emerged in accordance with perceived norms of male development, for example, the belief that a firm body image boundary, which clearly differentiates self from others, indicates superior psychological adjustment. It has been feminist scholars who have brought to light the theoretical and methodological weaknesses of such research, particularly as it has been applied to women.

The Significance of the Body: A Feminist Perspective

Nancy Hartsock (1984) provides a feminist critique of the male-constructed notions of body experience and body image, which she claims are grounded in Western patriarchal dualistic thinking. In contrast, her work is an example of essentialist feminist ''standpoint'' theory. Standpoint theory is founded on the notion that all women share similar experiences of oppression because of their biological and reproductive capacities (e.g., menstruation, pregnancy, childbirth, lactation). Hartsock claims that such essentially female experiences can become fertile ground from which to create a liberatory body image. Most important, she believes that empowering women's body images and self-concepts is one of the important steps that can lead to economic, political, and social change.

Hartsock identifies herself as a materialist feminist. Material feminists apply Karl Marx's method of historical materialism, which examines the economic, political, and social conditions of particular societies to gain understanding of the impact of patriarchal capitalism on the lives and bodies of women. Although Hartsock accepts Marx's conclusion that the liberation of women and men requires radical system change, she, like most materialist feminists who have been influenced by Marxist theory, finds Marxism deficient. Such feminists grant that Marx provided a powerful critique of modern capitalism and developed a complex analysis of domination and oppression, particularly that involving the working class (proletariat) and the owners of the means of production (bourgeoisie). They fault, however, his lack of gender analysis, particularly his dismissal of the labor contributions of women in reproduction, child rearing, and household maintenance.

According to Hartsock, women are more immersed in the material world than are men because of their ongoing and continuous involvement in the devalued sphere of household, reproductive, and child-rearing activities. Even women who work outside the home, many of whom have jobs involving household maintenance and child rearing for others, typically are responsible for such activities within their own homes. In contrast, the involvement of men's bodies in the exploited materialist world of capitalism generally ends when they leave their commodity-producing activities and enter the private world of family and household. Unfortunately, women's bodily involvement in reproduction, child rearing, and housework is regarded by the capitalist and patriarch as noncommodity-producing labor and hence not worthy of wages. According to Hartsock, this experience of oppression is more likely to lead women to develop a deeper criticism of patriarchal capitalism than that of the male workers (proletariat), which was predicted by Marx. Thus in Hartsock's schema, women replace Marx's male workers as the revolutionary class.

Hartsock's examination of the body image research on boundary experiences provides an illuminating example of the profound differences that distinguish feminist historical materialists from liberal feminists on the notion of the body. According to Hartsock, female bodily experiences, in particular, menstruation, coitus, pregnancy, lactation, and childbirth, make rigid separation from the object world impossible to maintain because they represent challenges to bodily boundaries. Consider the following remarks in which Hartsock (1984) displays her reasoning:

> Women and men, then, grow up with personalities affected by different boundary experiences, differently constructed and experienced inner and outer worlds, and preoccupations with different relational issues. This early experience forms an important ground for the feminine sense of self as connected to the world and the masculine sense of self as separate, distinct, and even disconnected . . . girls come to define and experience themselves as continuous with

others. In sum, girls enter adulthood with a more complex layering of affective ties and a rich, ongoing inner set of object relations. Boys . . . have repressed ties to another. As a result, women define and experience themselves relationally, and men do not. (p. 239)

Now compare Hartsock's remarks with the conclusions of Dorothy Harris (1973), an early sport psychologist, who drew on the research findings of Fisher and Cleveland. Fisher and Cleveland (1968) developed the body image barrier concept and related their findings to levels of activity and aspiration; that is, high-barrier subjects, more often males, showed evidence of higher needs for achievement and assumed an active muscular approach to the world, whereas low-barrier subjects, more often females, had a flaccid approach that devalued activity and physical assertiveness. Harris speculates about the potential of various athletic activities in helping an individual strengthen her or his body boundary and concludes, with regard to improving body image, that all human beings, female and male, should experience physically enhancing activities to strengthen body boundaries.

Such a perspective, which has been used frequently by researchers of body image, both in sport and other disciplines, emphasizes individual perceptions of body image and body boundary. For example, although Harris concluded that women's negative body images and permeable body boundaries could be positively enhanced through movement and sport activities, an analysis of the socioeconomic and political structures of Western capitalist systems did not enter into her conclusions[1]. Instead her strategy for change assumes that more extensive, positive sport and movement experiences for women (i.e., through an enforced Title IX) could transform their negative body images. Although Harris warns that problems exist in the body image research, her comments indicate that she has accepted the valuation of a strong body boundary as a positive

criterion for individual development applicable to both women and men. Such a perspective, which resembles the reasoning of liberal feminists, implies that if women become more like men, or are given legal equality within the present socioeconomic and political structures, their achievement potentials can equal those of men.

Hartsock, on the other hand, is critical of the application of male standards that are portrayed as universal norms. She believes that women have their own unique, more permeable boundary images that reflect a superior relational style. It is this style related to their household, childbearing, and child-rearing activities that offers women the possibility of developing a "feminist standpoint." Moreover, what is evident from Hartsock's work is the presence of a different set of assumptions regarding women's bodies and women's sexuality. According to Hartsock, women's sexuality, as constructed by men, relates to the resolution of the Oedipal crisis as it occurs in patriarchal capitalist societies. Within this particular psychosexual drama, masculine ego formation requires both repressing the mother and painfully separating from her. Hartsock claims that these psychological processes result in men's negative imagery of women (e.g., forced submission, hostility, physical mutilation), which is a central feature in their erotic lives, as well as in boys' developing strong body boundaries. She reminds us, however, that these are not universal norms of self-development. Instead they represent processes that males experience in the context of patriarchal capitalism.

Hartsock shares with radical feminists the view that women's bodies are the locus of male power and the site at which male supremacy is expressed. Practices that emerge from this power imbalance include rape, incest, pornography, sexual harassment, prostitution, lower wages for women's jobs, as well as no wages for household services and child rearing. Because women are subjected to such practices, Hartsock believes they can develop, through intellectual and political struggle, a "standpoint" that reveals the oppressive nature of gender relations. She further believes that this "standpoint" can form the basis for transcending all oppressive relationships and thereby dismantle patriarchal capitalism.

Although Hartsock's perspective emphasizes the positive potential of women's bodily experiences, it is not without problems; in particular, she narrowly defines and universalizes such experiences in terms of procreation. As a result, women's bodily experiences in sport and physical activities, as well as work, are not recognized. Women of color, non-Western women, and lesbians have been particularly critical of this type of feminist exclusionary theory. Ironically, such an essentialist position aligns the feminist "left" with the "new right" and its emphasis on women's "natural" role within the family. Alison Jaggar (1983) notes the revolutionary, as well as reactionary, dimensions of essentialism:

> It is revolutionary insofar as it asserts that women's bodies can no longer be viewed as territory to be colonized by male culture. In its emphasis on women's control of their sexuality and their fertility, however, (it) comes close to accepting the patriarchal definition of women as primarily procreative and sexual beings. (p. 293)

Jaggar (1983) argues that

> women's bodies have other parts as well . . . women's bodies are involved in tending dangerous machines, eating contaminated food or breathing polluted air. (p. 293)

We would add to her list women's involvement in sport and exercise. Although Jaggar's omission of such somatic activities is typical of feminists in nonsport disciplines, her point is well taken. Feminists who view the body as the root of oppression, most notably radical feminists, would be wise to expand their strategies for liberation (i.e., women's control over their own bodies) to include a fuller range of bodily sites and possibilities.

Although we recognize the importance of validating women's experiences, which often have been disdained and diminished, it is a problematic basis for developing feminist perspectives. In contrast to Hartsock's universal female experiences, our own position is based on the diverse social constructions of the female body. We therefore turn to Michel Foucault, a theorist whose interdisciplinary work strongly supports a social constructionist perspective of human bodies. He substantiates his perspective through an historical developmental account of the bodily disciplinary practices, which he also calls power/knowledge discourses, that characterize post-17th century Western societies. Because Foucault does not consider the particular disciplines (discourses) that produce feminine embodiment and body image, however, we have genderized his analysis of body disciplinary practices to better understand the socialization of female bodies. We refer to these feminizing body practices as the "feminine body beauty discourse," a discourse aimed at shaping a feminine body of a particular size and shape with a set of gestures and movements that are restrictive, deferential, and seductive. It is this feminizing body beauty discourse that provides the social component of women's body image.

The Body as Socially Constructed

Michel Foucault is a theorist who places the body and sexuality at the center of social analysis. Foucault argues that in the contemporary Western world, bodily desires are directed and controlled by scientific discourses associated with the body; that is, experts in fields such as medicine, biology, and psychiatry provide us with knowledge that we use to shape our bodies and desires in particular ways. According to Foucault (1990), during the 18th century, knowledge and power began to center on positive, rather than punitive, ways to control and socially construct the body. He identified two poles of development around which the organization of power over life was deployed. One pole emphasized the "body as a machine" in which disciplinary procedures were used to optimize the economic usefulness of the body. Such a move was critical to the development of capitalism, which required the controlled insertion of bodies into the new machinery of economic production. The second pole, which he called the "species body," emphasized propagation, birth, mortality, and health. This pole was equally important to the growth of capitalism because it resulted in knowledge and practices that optimized the conditions of existence and the control of bodies so that social space could be used in an optimal manner.

Foucault claims that the notion of sexual identity, which combined anatomical and biological elements with sensations and pleasures in an artificial unity, became the critical nexus of these two poles and the juncture around which the management of social life was organized. Although he notes that all societies organize sexual activity and desire, self-identity often has been defined more broadly than it was in post 17th-century Western society. Foucault (1988) claims, for example, that the ancient Greeks did not define themselves primarily in terms of sexual identity. Instead they constituted themselves through what he calls a "care of the self ethic," which involved practices aimed at self-mastery and becoming a virtuous human being. In contrast, post 17th-century Western society emphasized femininity and masculinity as the critical elements of self-identity. As a result, one's "true" sexual identity, that is, feminine or masculine, became the primary and restricted way that individuals defined themselves. As we can see, Foucault does not believe that sexual identity is an unmediated reality; rather it is the creation of social constructs and classifications. For this reason his discussion of sexual socialization, which we have genderized and refer to as the feminine body beauty discourse, is useful in understanding the social dimensions of feminine body images and body concepts.

Although Foucault offers us a compelling version of the way in which discourses shape our lives, his work is not without problems. As mentioned previously, the lack of gender analysis in his work results in a genealogy of modern Western disciplinary practices that treats the bodily experiences of women and men as if they were the same. Moreover, throughout Foucault's sociohistorical analysis of the body, the individual body as the center of action is nowhere to be found. Unfortunately, this absence of an evaluative subject implies that the social sexualization of our bodies is controlled by the intertwining discourses related to the body. It also implies that the body images and self-concepts of contemporary Western women are simply a mirroring of the feminine body beauty discourse.

Foucault does discuss the possibility of resistance within dominant discourses; however, he does not include a subject who evaluates a power/knowledge discourse, decides to resist such a discourse because it undermines equality, and thus develops a new personal code. As a result, he does not provide an analytic framework for understanding social change. Because we believe in the possibilities of self-directed social change, we searched for a theoretical model that allows for women breaking out of the feminine body beauty discourse and thereby enhancing their body images and self-concepts.

We found in the work of Maurice Merleau-Ponty a theory of the body and body image as dynamic and changing constructs. The additional strengths of his analysis are his views of human subjectivity, located not in the mind or consciousness, but in the body, as well as his notion of intersubjectivity and its relationship to social change. Unfortunately, Merleau-Ponty's presumably neutral human subject is implicitly male; for this reason we genderized his work, as we did with Foucault's, to understand the bodily movements, gestures, and physical engagement specifically associated with female embodiment and body images. In the following section we provide a brief summary of Merleau-Ponty's conclusions about the body that when genderized have particular theoretical relevance for women who seek not only to develop a feminist consciousness but also to embody such a perspective more completely.

The Body as Subject

Merleau-Ponty (1962) offers an analysis in which the defining feature of human existence is the movement of human bodies in the world. His theoretical analysis of the body combines the physical and the conscious dimensions of the body into a single unified entity. With the exception of sport philosophers, Merleau-Ponty's work has largely been ignored in sport-related disciplines, despite its obvious relevance to somatic theory. No doubt his critique of the traditional scientific method, which is grounded in bodily objectification, as well as the increased adoption of such an approach by physical educators and sport scientists, has led to this lack of recognition.

We explore the work of Merleau-Ponty as a way of introducing subjectivity, agency, and bonding as the bases for women developing and embodying feminist perspectives. For Merleau-Ponty, there is a dynamic relationship between body subject and the world; that is, the external world is not the objective reality of science or the world as I think about it; rather, the world is what I live. As a result, according to Merleau-Ponty, the body is never merely a physical object but always an embodiment of consciousness.

Movement, or what Merleau-Ponty refers to as *motility*, is the critical experience in which the meaning of human life develops. For human beings to think about and experience space, they must project their bodies into that space. Motility thus involves moving one's body toward an object and interacting with that object in a way that always produces a new embodied reality. It is through this process of movement that the body builds its identity and body image develops. For women, movement is also likely to involve the inner body experiences of menstruation, pregnancy, childbirth, and lactation. Unfortunately, the restrictions on women's involvement in the public world of sport, work, and politics have been constructed primarily from traditional notions of the female procreative body, as we noted in our critique of Hartsock's "standpoint" theory. Although acknowledging the reproductive sphere, we think it is equally important to emphasize the external spatial dimensions of movement; for this reason, we apply Merleau-Ponty's understanding of motility as a way of engaging the outer world. We believe this is a necessary liberatory strategy for women as they build their body images and self-concepts.

As you can see, Merleau-Ponty's (1962) notion of body image is not a static representation but rather a dynamic, ever-changing process in which the body perceives itself "not only as a system of present positions but . . . as an open number of equivalent positions directed to other ends" (p. 141). Although continuing individual choices influence our body images, they also are shaped by particular socioeconomic and historical circumstances. Moreover, because our experiences link us up with others in similar circumstances, there is meaning beyond that which is constituted by each individual body. According to Merleau-Ponty, each body is an "intersubjective field"; that is, each person lives in a particular historical period and interacts with other subjectivities (persons) living through and developing a shared understanding of these historical conditions. Intersubjectivity thus is a process that involves the embodiment of a shared commitment to a set of values. Indeed, it is because we are profoundly influenced by such contextual relations that Merleau-Ponty believes a social revolution is possible only at certain moments in history.

Merleau-Ponty's analysis of becoming politically conscious, which incorporates his notions of intersubjectivity and embodiment, is evidenced in his discussion of the proletariat. According to Merleau-Ponty, a worker in a factory, which was the unique creation of the industrial revolution, perceives in a concrete way that his working conditions, wages, and living conditions are synchronized with those of other workers and that they share a common lot. As a result of this shared experience, "social space begins to acquire a magnetic field and a region of exploitation is experienced" (p. 445). To be a worker or a bourgeois is to identify oneself as a worker or bourgeois and take a stand through an existential project that "merges into our way of patterning the world and coexisting with other people" (p. 447). If we apply Merleau-Ponty's analysis of historical embodiment to contemporary feminist projects, we recognize that our proposed physical education course is a product of 20th-century America. Women in the 1990s move in economic, political, and educational settings that did not exist in previous societies and that provide unique potential sites for bonding, resistance, and social change. As a result, equalizing the status of women and men is possible in contemporary America because of unique economic, social, and political conditions.

Although Merleau-Ponty's phenomenological perspective did not directly address the female experience, his work is relevant to the process of women embodying feminist perspectives. One of the central features of Merleau-Ponty's phenomenology is the description of bodily experiences in terms of one's own subjective observations and feelings. Iris Young (1990) provides one such feminist phenomenological analysis of female bodily experience, particularly as it relates to motor skills. She describes this in the following:

Women often approach a physical engagement with things with timidity, uncertainty, and hesitancy. . . . Women tend not to put their whole bodies into engagement in a physical task with the same ease and naturalness as men . . . the whole body is not put into fluid and directed motion, but rather, . . . the motion is concentrated in one body part. . . . The woman's motion tends not to reach, extend, lean, stretch, and follow

through in the direction of her intention. (p. 146). . . . We often experience our bodies as fragile encumbrances, rather than the media for the enactment of our aims. We feel as though we must have our attention directed upon our body to make sure it is doing what we wish it to do, rather than paying attention to what we want to do through our bodies. (p. 147)

Young also observes that although most men do not possess superior athletic skills, they nevertheless tend to play sport with more free motion and open reach than do women. She argues that these movement differences cannot be attributed to innate biological factors; instead women's movement patterns are learned through social practices designed to construct disability.

Although we agree with Young's conclusion regarding the social construction of bodies, she does not provide an analysis of how the lived experience of movement disability and bodily oppression can generate the momentum for social change. Instead her focus is on individual consciousness as the vehicle of change. In contrast, Merleau-Ponty's notion of social change is both an intellectual and physical process that requires bonding with others who have shared a similar experience. His remark, "I am never a thing and never bare consciousness," suggests the necessity of exchange between the person and the surrounding environment. Moreover, what seals one's commitment is not a consciously adopted intellectual decision but rather the bodily experience of identifying with comrades under whose gaze one lives. According to Merleau-Ponty, it is this particular conjunction of historical circumstances, as well as the expectations of comrades, that encourages a person to become part of a political movement. Our own research with elite women bodybuilders suggests the significance of bonding with those of "like minds and bodies" in validating a physical appearance that deviates from the dominant discourse of feminine body beauty (Guthrie & Castelnuovo, 1992).

As we can see from this analysis of Merleau-Ponty's phenomenology, he restores individual agency to social analysis and provides a theoretical basis for challenging the determinism of Foucault's socially constructed body. Moreover, his individual account of embodiment, when genderized in conjunction with a Foucaultian analysis of the discourse of feminine body beauty, brings together a way of thinking about the impact of patriarchal views in shaping women's bodies and movement. He also reminds us that women are far more likely to challenge such discourses and develop alternative practices when their own embodiment of oppression is shared with other women. We believe that when this occurs in a context in which they can analyze their own socialization through the feminine body beauty discourse, as well as create an alternative liberatory discourse that involves both mind and body, there is even greater potential for developing and sustaining feminist theory and praxis.

Using Theory to Inform Our Practices

In this section we use both Foucaultian discourse analysis and Merleau-Ponty's phenomenological notions of human subjectivity, agency, and bonding to inform our design of a concrete setting, for example, a physical education course in which women may come to embody feminist perspectives. Both theorists dissolve mind-body dualism and view the body as the critical source of social analysis. Because they do not include gender in their analyses, however, they have not taken into account the fact that women's oppression in Western societies is rooted in the social construction of their bodies. In an effort to overcome this theoretical weakness, we interpret their works through a feminist lens.

This course is primarily based on phenomenological principles because they are closely aligned with those of feminism on issues of the body in three critical areas. The first shared agreement is nondualism, emphasizing the unity of the body and mind. Dualistic thinking has fostered the objectification of women's bodies and a socially constructed movement vocabulary closely connected to the biological functions of pregnancy and child rearing. The second shared agreement is that personal bodily experience and subjectivity are basic sources of reality. Women have come to realize the importance of their subjective experiences in naming the source of their oppression and in validating an alternative view to male-constructed reality. The third shared agreement is the rejection of scientific paradigms that rely on the assumption of an objective reality and as such provide only a partial understanding of bodies and somatic experience. From a feminist perspective, such a paradigm does not accurately and fully render women's movement experiences; it also encourages the sexual objectification of women's bodies. These phenomenological feminist assumptions, together with our understanding of the feminine body beauty discourse and the need to develop alternatives to this discourse, constitute the foundations for our proposed physical education course for women.

Body-mind experiences will characterize this course. The theoretical, consciousness-raising foundation is developed through the activity of analyzing literature that focuses on the female body and body image from both masculinist and feminist perspectives. The liberatory possibilities of this component can be heightened further within the context of collectively sharing and reconstructing personal memories of critical life events and sequences that have contributed to the social construction of the participants' body/self concepts. The praxis component builds on this consciousness-raising experience through women engaging in shared somatic experiences that are designed to enhance bodily awareness and movement competency.

Feminist readings, as well as our genderized accounts of Foucault and Merleau-Ponty, can provide course participants with an analysis of the feminine body beauty discourse within which to understand their own movement abilities and disabilities. We also recommend that participants read, write, and analyze phenomenological (experiential) descriptions of the somatic lives of women, both in sport and nonsport activities. Keeping journals or diaries of body and movement experiences, as well as sharing critical events and insights with others through art, poetry, and photography, can facilitate understanding of both the common and diverse aspects of female socialization. (See boxes below and on page 320.)

Frigga Haug et al. (1987) have employed a similar approach in which women's individual memories of female sexualization are collectively mobilized and then submitted to readings and critique. They contend this is a necessary clearing ground that precedes women rewriting the stories of their bodies. What they have omitted from their liberating strategy is a component that physically reconstructs female somatic experience.

Although the activities suggested by Haug et al. are critical components of our proposed course, we believe that somatic activities are equally important. From our perspective, however, developing a course based only on somatic enhancement is also grounded in dualism and is therefore incomplete. Bennett, Whitaker, Smith, and Sablove

(1987) offered such emphasis in a class called Physical Education Without Fear. Bennett et al. agree with Young's conclusion that women in sexist, patriarchal society are assigned a movement vocabulary that physically inhibits, confines, and objectifies them. They believe that such physical handicapping occurs in most movement activities, particularly in play, games, and sport. As a result, the vast majority of girls and women do not develop skillful movement patterns, nor are they often encouraged to gain these skills.

According to Bennett et al., all women should have the possibility of developing an extensive movement vocabulary, that is, one that allows them to experience self-control and instrumentality. Throwing, catching, and jumping, which are the bases of game and sport forms, are among the movement-enhancing activities that Bennett et al. (1987) included in their ''Physical Education Without Fear'' course. Although these activities are critical components in our course, we also would include body strengthening and self-defense (e.g., martial arts) skills as significant sources of movement and bodily empowerment. Such activities would help women experience their bodies as physically skillful and powerful rather than as sources of vulnerability and awkwardness. Movement empowerment, however,

Feminist Reading

I am in junior high school now and no longer ''one of the guys.'' I was always in this category due to my participation on male sports teams as a kid. I competed with boys as their equal and they accepted and respected me as their equal. But now I am in junior high and am no longer allowed to be in this category, you see it is no longer ''cool'' to be as athletically strong and talented as a male. I am lost for I know no other way. Now, instead of competing with the boys, I am supposed to compete with the girls, *for the*

boys I used to compete with in sport. I am further lost because I cannot understand why girls flirt with guys I used to physically challenge and find it tough to shift competitive gears. The idea is ''weird'' to me.

Needless to say, I didn't have a boyfriend until late in high school. I honestly did not know how that kind of competition worked; it was nothing like the playing field.

Alison Kuhi

For Boys Only

Robbed of my fun
Lost oppportunity
Stole my pride
Forced suppression
On a little girl
You took my world
Locked it away
For the little boys to play
While I fell prey to submission

Sally Kidd

must be joined together with feminist theory and consciousness raising, components that were omitted from the Bennett et al. model.

Shared games and sports, which include elements of both competition and interdependency, also can contribute significantly to the reinforcement of movement skills as well as female bonding. Such activities need not reproduce the male norms of competition, which often require disembodiment and viewing the "other" as enemy. Instead, feminist critiques of traditional male sport could provide the basis for emphasizing subjective interpretations of excellence and success that do not rely on male measuring sticks. They also might encourage an alternative notion of competition, for example, one that views the "other" as a partner in developing movement competency, which is closer to the true meaning of the term "competition" (i.e., to seek together)[2] and is more consistent with the views of the early female physical educators. According to Merleau-Ponty, these deeply embodied and interdependent activities can provide the intersubjective experiences that lead to the development of an individual commitment to a political movement. If this is true, such shared somatic experiences, in conjunction with shared feminist consciousness raising, may encourage women to develop and embody feminist

perspectives that may become integrated into other aspects of their lives.

R.W. Connell (1987) has described the embodiment of males and offers an analysis that can be applied to women:

> So the concern with force and skill becomes a statement embedded in the body, embedded through years of participation in social practices like organized sport. . . . The social definition of men as holders of power is translated not only into mental body-images and fantasies, but into muscle tensions, posture, the feel and texture of the body. (pp. 84-85)

According to Connell, men's ability to physically dominate women is one of the primary ways in which patriarchy not only is established and sustained, but also becomes perceived and experienced as part of the natural order. We agree with Connell and believe that the ability to self-defend, as well as other somatic skills, are of critical importance to girls and women; however, in attempting to help women develop and sustain the embodiment of feminist perspectives, we must rely on more than improving their motor skills or athletic prowess. Although movement expertise, particularly self-defense, may help women minimize, if not completely overcome, differentials in size, strength, and physical power, we believe that somatic experience must be informed by feminist consciousness raising to effectively challenge male hegemony. What makes our course different from the Bennett et al. and Haug models is its synthesis of mind and body, a process that we believe will allow women not only to develop feminist ways of thinking but also to embody such ways of being.

Summary and Conclusions

In this chapter we have raised a number of issues that feminist theorists and researchers in sport and exercise psychology as well as the sport sciences should continue to investigate. Among them are the further exploration of feminist epistemology in which researchers and study participants work together to describe and understand women's somatic experiences and their connection to mental processes. This involves the development of a methodology for translating a woman's body, self, and movement conceptions, available only to the woman herself, into representations available to the researcher. Phenomenology points to the complexity of the subjective self. Consider, for example, that your own notion of self is comprised of aspects as varied as your authentic, perceived, and ideal selves, as well as how you think others perceive you and the way they actually do. Body image is equally complex. The multidimensionality of both self-concept and body image is further compounded by the heterogeneity that results from such factors as race, ethnicity, age, class, and sexual orientation; for this reason we need to be sensitive to such complexity when operationally defining our terms and selecting methods of assessment.

Researchers and practitioners also should continue to explore how increased movement competency "within feminist settings" empowers the lives of women in sport, career, and family contexts, as well as provides them with perspectives that challenge the confines of the feminine body beauty discourse and other oppressive discourses. Research that not only identifies sites of resistance but also helps us gain insight into the processes of such resistance is particularly important because of the long-standing hegemonic control men have had over women's bodies and somatic experiencing.

Notes

[1]Dorothy Harris's conclusions were drawn in the early 1970s. As a result, she did not have the advantage of an extensive and popularized feminist literature to inform her research perspectives.

[2]Competition has long been a feminist "taboo" because it is viewed as limiting human development and interaction. Feminists often identify competition with male centers of power and have abandoned spheres such as sport, in both theory and practice. Unfortunately, this attitude leaves the centers of power and privilege uncontested. Moreover, the potential benefits of competition in stimulating self-growth and interdependency are overlooked or denied.

References

Allen, D.J. (1972). Self concept and the female participant. In D.V. Harris (Ed.), *Women and sport: A national research conference*. Penn State HPER Research Series No. 2.

Bennett, R.S., Whitaker, K.G., Wooley Smith, N.J., & Sablove, A. (1987). Changing the rules of the game: Reflections toward a feminist analysis of sport. *Women's Studies International Forum*, **10**(4), 369-379.

Black, D.R., & Burckes-Miller, M.E. (1988). Male and female college athletes: Use of anorexia nervosa and bulimia nervosa weight loss methods. *Research Quarterly for Exercise and Sport*, **59**, 252-256.

Burckes-Miller, M.E., & Black, D.R. (1988). Behaviors and attitudes associated with eating disorders: Perceptions of college athletes about food and weight. *Health Education Research: Theory & Practice*, **3**, 203-208.

Burckes-Miller, M.E., & Black, D.R. (1991). College athletes and eating disorders: A theoretical context. In D.R. Black (Ed.), *Eating disorders among athletes: Theory, issues, and research* (pp. 11-41). Reston, VA: AAHPERD.

Connell, R.W. (1987). *Gender and power: Society, the person and sexual politics*. Stanford, CA: Stanford University Press.

Fisher, S. (1990). The evolution of psychological concepts about the body. In T.F. Cash & T. Pruzinsky (Eds.), *Body images: Development, deviance, and change* (pp. 3-20). New York: Guilford Press.

Fisher, S., & Cleveland, S.E. (1968). *Body image and personality* (rev. ed). New York: Dover Press.

Foucault, M. (1988). Technologies of the self: A seminar with Michel Foucault. In L. Martin, H. Gutman, & P. Hutton (Eds.), *Technologies of the self: A seminar with Michel Foucault* (pp. 16-49). Amherst: University of Massachusetts Press.

Foucault, M. (1990). *The history of sexuality: An introduction* (Vol. 1). New York: Vintage Books.

Guthrie, S.R. (1991). Prevalence of eating disorders among intercollegiate athletes: Contributing factors and preventative measures. In D.R. Black (Ed.), *Eating disorders among athletes: Theory, issues, and research* (pp. 43-66). Reston, VA: AAHPERD.

Guthrie, S.R., & Castelnuovo, S. (1992). Elite women bodybuilders: Models of resistance of compliance? *Play and Culture, 5*(4).

Harris, D.V. (1973). *Involvement in sport: A somatopsychic rationale for physical activity*. Philadelphia: Lea & Febiger.

Hartsock, N.C.M. (1984). *Money, sex, and power: Toward a feminist historical materialism*. Boston: Northeastern University Press.

Haug, F., et al. (1987). *Female sexualization: A collective work of memory*. London: Verso.

Jaggar, A.M. (1983). *Feminist politics and human nature*. Totowa, NJ: Rowman & Allanheld.

Marx, K. (1964). *The economic and philosophic manuscripts of 1844*. New York: International Publishing Co.

Merleau-Ponty, M. (1962). *Phenomenology of Perception*. London: Routledge & Kegan Paul.

Pruzinsky, T., & Cash, T.F. (1990). Integrative themes in body-image development, deviance, and change. In T.F. Cash & T. Pruzinsky (Eds.), *Body images: Development, deviance, and change* (pp. 337-349). New York: Guilford Press.

Rosen, J.C. (1990). Body-image disturbances in eating disorders. In T.F. Cash & T. Pruzinsky (Eds.), *Body images: Development, deviance, and change* (pp. 190-214). New York: Guilford Press.

Wolf, N. (1991). *The beauty myth: How images of beauty are used against women*. New York: Morrow.

Young, I.M. (1990). Throwing like a girl: A phenomenology of feminine body comportment, motility, and spatiality. In I.M. Young (Ed.), *Throwing like a girl and other essays in feminist philosophy and social theory* (pp. 141-159). Bloomington: Indiana University Press.

Chapter 19

The Sociological Study of Women and Sport

Nancy Theberge
Susan Birrell

We haven't come a long way, we've come a short way. If we hadn't come a short way, no one would be calling us "baby."

ELIZABETH JANEWAY
quoted in *Words on Women*

In this chapter we present the progression of issues and insights that have marked the sociological study of women and sport as a basis for the analysis offered in chapters 21, 22, and 23.

A Heritage of Exclusion

The sociological study of women in sport has developed against a backdrop of two related themes. The first is the history of women's exclusion, which was supported and reinforced by the second, a set of beliefs about women's frailty and inferiority that, it was argued, rendered

them unsuited for vigorous physical activity (Theberge, 1989).

With few exceptions the exclusion of women from sport and the ideology of female frailty existed without formal recognition until the mid-1960s. It was in this decade that women physical educators began to write about their awareness of these conditions. Among these early voices were Elizabeth Halsey (1961) and Margaret Coffey (1965), who began their "musings on the state of women's sport programs" (Birrell, 1988, p. 463). Although the differential experiences and conditions of women athletes were identified, no analysis was offered.

323

The classic statement of the period was Eleanor Metheny's (1962) *Connotations of Movement in Sport and Dance*, a work that critically appraised the ideology that kept women from full, meaningful participation in sport (see chapter 16). Her focus on these larger social issues, and her reliance on her own ability to read the meanings in social practices, make her work more contemporaneous with the work of the 1980s than of the 1960s. Even today, after dramatic increases in the number of girls and women involved in sport programs, Metheny's framework provides an insightful analysis into the cultural pressures on women athletes.

The decade of the 1970s saw the first major effort to analyze the condition of women in sport. The developments in the field in this decade occurred in the context of a number of important political and social developments. One of these was the growing strength of the women's movement. Challenges to restrictive gender prescriptions and the unequal participation of women in society gradually come to form the basis for a developing consciousness of the condition of women in sport.

Other developments in sport also contributed to this growing interest. Two events were especially critical. One was the establishment of the Association for Intercollegiate Athletics for Women (AIAW) in 1972. The circumstances surrounding the formation of the AIAW and its growth and eventual demise are chronicled in chapter 6. It is sufficient to note here that the AIAW provided a focus of activity and interest in women's sport. More important, it provided a setting for the development and nurturance of a feminist vision of sport. The leaders of the AIAW strove to build an organization that would serve the interests of women athletes. The vision of women's sport espoused by the leaders of the AIAW came to be a basis for feminist critiques of the organization of sport that followed some years later.

The second major event of the 1970s in the United States was the passage of Title IX of the Educational Amendments Act in 1972. Interest prompted by the bill led to concern with identifying and rectifying the enormous differences in support for men's and women's programs that have existed since the rise of organized sport in North America in the previous century. In addition, the legislation itself led to tremendous increases in the participation of women in sport. These developments provided a major push for women in sport to move onto the agenda of sport sociologists.

Although the 1970s saw a number of social and political developments that would dramatically affect the condition of girls and women in sport, the first wave of scholarly research on women and sport took a different tack in a focus on psychological issues. Researchers conducted studies on attitudes toward female athletes, personality traits of female athletes, and motivation for involvement. Despite a virtual mini-industry of research on these topics, the results were inconclusive and "no clear personality or motivational pattern can be found for female athletes, for team or individual athletes, or for athletes in specific sports" (Birrell, 1988, p. 465).

The topics of research on women that exerted the most influence on the sociology of sport at this time were related to sex roles. Particularly prominent was the research on role conflict, a theory proposed by Dorothy Harris. Harris (1971, 1980) argued that the contradictions between athleticism and femininity were so extreme that many women chose not to participate in sport, and those who did take part often experienced debilitating conflict between their roles as athletes and women.

Related to role conflict theory was research on the apologetic (Del Rey, 1978; Felshin 1974; Griffin, 1973). Researchers reasoned that one important way for women athletes to resolve their conflict and "reduce cognitive dissonance" was to apologize for their involvement by overemphasizing their feminine side, for example, by wearing makeup, jewelry, and pastel colors; by discussing their boyfriends at every opportunity; and by giving every indication that sport was not important to them. A further effort in this tradition was the research on masculinity, femininity, and androgyny (Colker & Widom, 1980; Del Rey, 1977; Myers & Lips, 1978).

These early traditions grew out of attempts to make sense of the patterns of women's sport involvement. They offered psychological rather than social explanations for those patterns, and they conceived of women as not fitting into sport. By subtly assuming that the problem behind women's low involvement lay within women themselves, they tended to blame women for their own lack of participation. The social context in which sport and women have been defined was dealt with in only the vaguest manner; the real focus was on the responses of the person to a social world whose ideology and structure were taken for granted. These approaches do not question the organization of sport, nor do they see sport as an institution that is produced through human agency and thus subject to social change.

The Sociology of Women in Sport

The first truly sociological analyses of women in sport began in the late 1970s. Here we saw for the first time discussions that take account of social and cultural conditions that structure, constrain, and give meaning to women's sport experiences. One topic that received considerable attention was socialization *into* sport (Greendorfer, 1978, 1983; Greendorfer & Ewing, 1981; Snyder & Spreitzer, 1976, 1978). Another prominent topic was socialization *through* sport, which looked at the effects of sport participation on the development of attitudes, values, and orientations. These included analyses of the relationship between athletic participation and academic achievement (Hanks, 1979; Landers et al., 1978; Snyder & Spreitzer, 1977) and the effects of sport participation on the "professionalization" of attitudes toward play (Webb, 1969; Loy, Birrell &

Rose, 1976; Theberge, Curtis, & Brown, 1982). The extensive research on socialization into and through sport was by no means confined to the study of girls and women. Then as now, most research was concerned with boys and men. Nonetheless, some researchers began turning their interest to girls and women; and it is significant that they began to examine females' experiences in sport in light of wider social and cultural factors.

The late 1970s and early 1980s saw some significant changes in the study of women in sport. Again, these changes were affected by ongoing developments in sport and in the sociology of sport. In sport, the effects of Title IX were now becoming evident and were greeted with mixed reviews. On one hand, the tremendous growth in women's school sport programs was welcomed and applauded. On the other hand, some further outcomes of this process were now apparent. In particular, this growth was accompanied by a decline in women's representation in leadership positions. As women's programs grew and in many cases merged with men's programs, women coaches and administrators lost their jobs to men (Theberge, 1989).

Research during this period was marked by a developing awareness of the political dimensions of gender in sport and, for the first time, attempts to theorize the condition of women in sport. Politically informed research was concerned with women's loss of leadership positions (Acosta & Carpenter, 1985 a,b,c; Holmen & Parkhouse, 1981) and with the conflict between the AIAW and NCAA for control of women's sports (Grant, 1984; Lopiano, 1984; Slatton, 1982).

Efforts to theorize the condition of women in sport marked the beginnings of an explicitly feminist analysis. Researchers identified both the inadequacies of traditional approaches in the social sciences for the analysis of women's experience and the need for a feminist alternative. The dominant assumptions of this new approach were summarized by Boutilier and SanGiovanni in their book, *The Sporting Woman* (1983), which provided the first feminist and sociological analysis of the relations between women, sport, and other social institutions. Their observations and assumptions form an agenda for further analysis that underlies much of the work of the 1980s:

- Sport is a patriarchal institution.
- Sexist ideology pervades sport.
- If women change, men and sport don't have to.
- There is a liberal bias in the study of women and sport.
- Sport sociology is dominated by sexist research.
- Women are not men (pp. 17-19).

These principles formed the basis for feminist analysis that became increasingly sophisticated. It provided an understanding of the dynamics of gender and sport using feminist theory to explore such dynamics.

For the most part, the research of this period was grounded in assumptions of liberal and radical feminism in which sport was conceptualized as being dominated by men, and that women should form their own organizations (see chapter 15). The work that emerged in the 1980s drew on a number of more critical intellectual traditions. One focus was on feminist and Marxist theories and the connections between gender oppression and class oppression (Theberge, 1984, Beamish, 1984; Bray, 1983, 1984). This perspective allows us to see, for example, the connections between the commercialization of sport and the continuing exclusion of women. More recently, a particularly fruitful alliance has been forged between feminist analysis and cultural studies.

Gender Relations and Cultural Studies

The project of cultural studies is similar to the project of more traditional social sciences: to produce and present an interpretation of how culture works and what it means. Cultural studies evolved out of critiques of traditional sociological perspectives as oversimplified and flawed by the emphasis on producing quasi-scientific models of social life. In contrast, analyses in the cultural studies tradition emphasize the complexity of social life. In addition, the perspective is grounded in the assumption that cultural practices, including sport, are arenas in which values, meanings, and ideologies are contested (Donnelly, 1988).

For example, cultural studies offers a needed corrective to somewhat oversimplified models of gender roles. The classical socialization tradition is replaced by theories that conceptualize gender relations as more diffuse and complex. In this perspective, it is more appropriate to look for the sources of young girls' behavior and attitudes toward sport not only in the discrete set of circumstances in the family and school environment but also in the diffuse patterns of gender representations and ideologies of gender available throughout our culture.

In sport, the cultural studies approach focuses on sport as a cultural form that is embedded in and constituent of sociopolitical forces of culture. Thus sport is not seen in the traditional way as simply ''a mirror of society.'' Such a conceptualization underplays the significance of sport to actively serve as a site for the creation and maintenance of societal forces and institutional forms. Such an approach also moves us beyond the false assumption of sport as separate from and outside the concerns of everyday life.

The power relations that capture the attention of cultural studies scholars are the systematic hierarchical structures of wealth, privilege, jurisdiction, and dignity. In our culture such structures are organized along lines of gender, race, ethnicity, class, age, sexual preference, and the physically and mentally challenged. Relations of dominance are maintained through many interlocking and reinforcing forces ranging from violence and coercion at one extreme to subtle forms of socialization, ideological indoctrination, and apparent consent at the other.

These forms have both a structural and an ideological dimension. *Structure* is the framework of roles, statuses, rules, and norms that form the backdrop of our everyday life. *Ideology* is a set of ideas that serve the interests of dominant groups but come to be understood and taken up as the societal common sense about the way things naturally are and thus should remain. When even the groups that are decentered, ill served, and in fact subordinated by these ideas accept them as logical, we can speak about the hegemonic power of that system.

Hegemony is a fairly complete system of ideological dominance that works through the apparent complicity of those disenfranchised by it. Ideology and hegemony work to legitimate the status quo in many different and mutually reinforcing ways. For example, we can talk about the masculinist ideology of sport in North America. In this ideology, our cultural understanding of the meaning of sport includes assumptions about sport as a male preserve where women's sport experience is termed derivative and thus inauthentic. To the extent that we are thankful for the relatively few opportunities we do enjoy in sport, we may talk about the hegemonic control of sport by patriarchal forces.

Hegemony and ideology work through the construction of common sense and the conflation of cultural constructs with natural forces. In other words, those who are not well served by a particular system or practice are less likely to challenge their inferior status and deprivation if they can be made to think and feel that (a) their inferiority is the result of their own individual failings and not some systematic discrimination; and (b) the patterns of such inequity are really a natural condition of life. For example, we may reason that someone must work on the assembly line for low wages, believing, "It's too bad it has to be me." Such acceptance of the status quo fails to challenge the fundamental assumptions associated with the class system of, for example, capitalism and accepts the existing economic relations as "natural" or outside the control and creativity of human agents.

Ideology also works through ahistoricity (historical inauthenticity) and the provision of pleasure. When we obscure the cultural origins of something, we ignore the part that human agency plays in cultural processes. We ascribe to humanly contrived conditions a natural essence, thus making that arrangement unassailable. Ideology also is reproduced to the disadvantage of those who lose their critical edge because of their own desire for pleasure. This is the bread and circuses phenomenon of the Roman Empire, and the practice Marx deplored when he critically attacked organized religion as "the opiate of the masses."

Hegemony is never complete. In many different ways—overt and covert, conscious and unconscious, public and private—subordinated groups protest, rebel, resist, and otherwise work to undermine the power relations that seek to control

Figure 19.1 Sport is a site of contest that encompasses patterns of gender relations in wider society. Photo courtesy Keith Ian Polakoff.

them. Power relations are constantly contested, and hegemony is often "leaky" and must be constantly reviewed, recreated, and maintained at structural and ideological levels.

Summary and Conclusions

In this chapter we have reviewed the history of sociological study of women in sport, ending with a discussion of the cultural studies approach and how such an approach helps us to analyze the sporting experiences of women. The insights and perspectives from the cultural studies tradition provide the basis for our own analysis in the chapters that follow. Specifically, we examine sport as a site of struggle or contest. The contest is wide ranging and encompasses patterns of gender relations both in sport and in the wider society.

Some of the most important recent work concerns the ideology of gender and sport, for example, the way in which sport is a setting for the construction of ideas about gender and gender differences. Analyses of media representations have offered fascinating insights into the construction of the ideology of gender and sport. As we shall see, media representations are far from a neutral rendering of the world around us, and the images they represent have important implications for the way we think about sport, gender, and gender relations.

References

Acosta, R., & Carpenter, L. Women in athletics—A status report. (1985a). *Journal of Health, Physical Education, Recreation and Dance*, **56**, 30-34.

Acosta, R., & Carpenter, L. (1985b). Status of women in athletics: Changes and causes. *Journal of Health, Physical Education, Recreation and Dance*, **56**, 35-37.

Acosta, R., & Carpenter, L. (1985c). Women in sport. In D. Chu, J.O. Segrave, & B.J. Becker (Eds.), *Sport and higher education*. Champaign, IL: Human Kinetics.

Beamish, R. (1984). Materialism and the comprehension of gender-related issues in sport. In N. Theberge & P. Donnelly (Eds.), *Sport and the sociological imagination* (pp. 60-81). Fort Worth: Texas Christian University Press.

Birrell, S. (1984). Separatism as an issue in women's sport. *Arena Review*, **8**, 49-61.

Birrell, S. (1988). Discourses on the gender/sport relationship: From women in sport to gender relations. *Exercise and Sport Science Reviews*, **16**, 459-502.

Boutilier, M., & SanGiovanni, L. (1983). *The sporting woman*. Champaign, IL: Human Kinetics.

Bray, C. (1983). Sport, capitalism and patriarchy. *Canadian Woman Studies*, **4**, 11-13.

Bray, C. (1984). Gender and the political economy of Canadian sport. In N. Theberge & P. Donnelly (Eds.), *Sport and the sociological imagination* (pp. 104-124). Fort Worth: Texas Christian University Press.

Cochrane, J., Hoffman, A., & Kincaid, P. (1977). *Women in Canadian life: Sports*. Toronto: Fitzhenry & Whiteside.

Coffey, M. (1965). The sportwoman then and now. *Journal of Health and Physical Education*, **36**, 38-41, 50.

Colker, R., and Widom, C. (1980). Correlates of female athletic participation. *Sex Roles*, **6**, 47-58.

Del Rey, P. (1977). Apologetics and androgyny: The past and the future. *Frontiers*, **3**, 8-10.

Del Rey, P. (1978). The apologetic and women in sport. In C. Oglesby (Ed.), *Women and sport: From myth to reality* (pp. 107-111). Philadelphia: Lea & Febiger.

Donnelly, P. (1988). Sport as a site for popular resistance. In R. Gruneau (Ed.), *Popular cultures and political practices* (pp. 69-82). Toronto: Garamond.

Duquin, M. (1981). Creating social reality: The case of women and sport. In S. Greendorfer & A. Yiannakis (Eds.), *Sociology of Sport: Diverse perspectives* (pp. 77-82). West Point, NY: Leisure Press.

Felshin, J. (1974). The triple option . . . for women in sport. *Quest*, **21**, 36-40.

Grant, C. (1984). The gender gap in sport: From Olympic to intercollegiate level. *Arena Review*, **8**, 31-48.

Greendorfer, S. (1978). Socialization into sport. In C. Oglesby, (Ed.), *Women in sport: From myth to reality* (pp. 115-140). Philadelphia: Lea & Febiger.

Greendorfer, S. (1983). Shaping the female athlete: The impact of the family. In M. Boutilier and L. SanGiovanni, *The sporting woman* (pp. 135-155). Champaign, IL: Human Kinetics.

Greendorfer, S., & Ewing, M. (1981). Race and gender differences in children's socialization into sport. *Research Quarterly for Exercise and Sport*, **52**, 301-310.

Griffin, P. (1973). What's a nice girl like you doing in a profession like this? *Quest*, **19**, 96-101.

Halsey, E. (1961). *Women in physical education.* New York: Putnam.

Hanks, M. (1979). Race, sex, athletics and education achievement. *Social Science Quarterly*, **60**, 482-496.

Harris, D. (1971). *The social self and the competitive self of the female athlete.* Paper presented at the Third International Symposium on the Sociology of Sport, Waterloo, ON.

Harris, D. (1980). Femininity and athleticism: Conflict or consonance. In D. Sabo and R. Runfola (Eds.), *Jock: Sports and Male Identity* (pp. 222-239). Englewood Cliffs, NJ: Prentice-Hall.

Hoffman, A. (1976). *About face: Towards a positive image of women in sport.* Toronto: Ontario Status of Women Council, Ontario Secretariat for Social Development, and Ontario Ministry of Culture and Recreation.

Holmen, M., & Parkhouse, B. (1981). Trends in the selection of coaches for female athletes:

A demographic inquiry. *Research Quarterly for Exercise and Sport*, **52**, 9-18.

Landers, D., Feltz, G., Obermeier, G.E., & Brouse, T. (1978). Socialization via interscholastic athletics: Its effects on educational attainment. *Research Quarterly for Exercise and Sport*, **49**, 475-483.

Lenskyj, H. (1986). *Out of Bounds: Women, Sport and Sexuality.* Toronto: Women's Press.

Lopiano, D. (1984). A political analysis of the possibility of impact alternatives for the accomplishment of feminist objectives within American intercollegiate sport. *Arena Review*, **8**, 49-61.

Loy, J., Birrell, S., & Rose, D. (1976). Attitudes held toward agonic activities as a function of selected social identities. *Quest*, **26**, 81-93.

Metheny, E. (1962). *Connotations of movement in sport and dance.* Dubuque, IA: Brown.

Myers, A., & Lips, H. (1978). Participation in competitive amateur sport as a function of psychological androgyny. *Sex Roles*, **4**, 571-578.

Slatton, B. (1982). The greening of American athletes. In J. Frey (Ed.), *The governance of intercollegiate athletics.* West Point, NY: Leisure Press.

Snyder, E., & Spreitzer, E. (1976). Correlates of sport participation among adolescent girls. *Research Quarterly for Exercise and Sport*, **47**, 804-809.

Snyder, E., & Spreitzer, E. (1977). Participation in sport as related to educational expectations among high school girls. *Sociology of Education*, **50**, 47-55.

Snyder, E., & Spreitzer, E. (1978). Socialization comparisons of adolescent female athletes and musicians. *Research Quarterly for Exercise and Sport*, **49**, 342-350.

Theberge, N. (1984). Joining social theory to social action: Some Marxist principles. *Arena Review*, **8**, 21-30.

Theberge, N. (1989). Women's athletics and the myth of the female frailty. In J. Freeman (Ed.), *Women: A feminist perspective* (4th ed.) (pp. 507-522). Mountain View, CA: Mayfield.

Theberge, N., Curtis, J., & Brown, B. (1982). Sex differences in orientations toward games: Tests of the sport involvement hypothesis. In A. Dunleavey, A. Miracle, & R. Rees (Eds.), *Studies in the Sociology of Sport*. Fort Worth: Texas Christian University Press.

Webb, H. (1969). Professionalization of attitudes toward play among adolescents. In G. Kenyon (Ed.), *Aspects of Contemporary Sport Sociology: Proceedings of the CIC Sport Symposium* (pp. 161-178).

Chapter 20

Structural Constraints Facing Women in Sport

Nancy Theberge
Susan Birrell

You don't know anything about a woman until you meet her in court.
NORMAN MAILER
quoted in *Words on Women*

Recent years have seen tremendous changes in women's social position and in gender relations in the wider society. Significant change also has occurred in women's sport and women's experiences of sport. These changes are intimately and dialectically connected: Developments in sport are inseparable from conditions in the wider society, so that changes in women's relationship to sport may signal or even influence transformations in women's position in society at large. In this chapter we review the status of women's participation in recreation and leisure settings, as well as collegiate and professional sport.

In this chapter we will examine sport as a *contested arena*. Sport historically has been a setting marked by struggles structured along lines of class, race, and gender. In recent years, barriers to women's participation have weakened, and cultural views of women athletes have been revised. Women's sport continues to be marked, however, by struggle for control of both the institutions that regulate women's participation and the meanings of our sporting experiences. Struggle for institutional control is evident in efforts to increase the opportunities for participation and the representation of women in administrative and coaching positions. Ideological struggle is evident in campaigns to increase and improve the coverage of women's sport in the media and to transform cultural images and ideas about women and physical activity.

Most information available on women and sport has focused on the needs and experiences of relatively young, middle- and upper-class, heterosexual, white women. Wherever possible, we attempt to broaden this homogeneous and undifferentiated concept of women to suggest the limits of the current status of our knowledge.

Background to the Developments in Women's Sport

The changes that have occurred in women's sport in the United States in recent years can be understood against a background of broader social developments. In this section we consider the effects of legislative and political initiatives, the feminist movement, and the health and fitness movement. In quite different ways, each has had a significant impact on women and sport.

Legal and Political Initiatives

Some of the most important influences on women's sport have come from government efforts in the area of gender equity. The United States government has played a particularly active role in the transformation of school and university sport programs. Probably the single most important event affecting women's sport in the United States in the last 30 years was the passage of Title IX of the Educational Amendments Act of 1972. Title IX prohibits sex discrimination in educational institutions that receive federal funding, which includes virtually all institutions in the United States. Although Title IX did not single out sport as a target area, its obvious significance for sport was immediately apparent, because virtually all educational institutions had vastly unequal sport programs for females and males. Title IX prompted enormous change in girls' and women's sport. (See box on page 334 for a discussion of Title IX.)

The Feminist Movement

Until the late 1970s it appeared that the women's movement had few connections to sport, and it was not unusual to hear the lament that there were no feminists in sport. It would have been more accurate to say that those working on behalf of women in sport and in particular women athletic administrators had little or no visibility outside sport and few formal connections to the wider feminist movement. Since then there has been a growing feminist consciousness and movement in sport. A number of conferences have been held, and The Women's Sport Foundation in the United States has grown in size and influence. These activities have been complemented by a flourishing feminist scholarship and research. All of these developments have been part of the increasing impact of feminism on women's sport.

The Health and Fitness Movement

The "fitness boom" of the past two decades has had an undeniable impact on the expansion of women's physical activity and sport in North America. Not all of this influence, however, has been positive. Rader (1991) argues that North American preoccupation with "strenuous living" entails the "presentation of a particular self": The "new strenuousity" emphasizes style and appearance and often is explicitly sexualized (p. 255). The most glaring instances of the sexualization of women's physical activity are exercise classes and videos that concentrate on body image and heterosexual attraction. Moreover, the fitness boom appeals particularly to members of the middle and upper classes, who have the means to purchase fitness club memberships, expensive equipment, and the fashionable leisure clothing that is now a signature of the "good life." The commodification and sexualization of women's physical activity seen in the health and fitness movement are alarming

Figure 20.1 The "fitness boom" of the late 20th century often emphasizes style and appearance.

aspects of the expansion of this activity in recent years.

Women's Participation in Sport Today

The recent increases in girls' and women's physical activity have occurred at most levels and in most types of participation. The main exception is professional sport, where there continue to be few opportunities and there has been little change. Although opportunities and involvement by women have increased greatly, as we will see there remain significant differences in the participation of women and men. Moreover, these differences are exacerbated by racial and class barriers, and they become more pronounced at higher levels of involvement.

Recreational Sport and Physical Activity

One of the settings that has witnessed impressive changes in girls' and women's physical activity is recreational sport. Much of this activity is not well documented, and we have little reliable information on involvement in community and recreational sport leagues and programs. Data on patterns of unorganized physical activity, however, provide a picture of gender differences in activity, as well as details of women's involvement.

The annual surveys of the National Sporting Goods Association (NSGA) (1990, 1990a, 1990b) of 10,000 U.S. households show that females 7 years of age and older are more active in fitness activities than males: 62% of girls and women compared to 52% of boys and men regularly participated in fitness activities in 1989. These differences remain, but are less pronounced, when *frequency* of involvement is taken into consideration. According to the NSGA definition of a "frequent participant" as one who has participated in an activity at least twice a week, 22.5% of all women and 18.1% of all men fit that profile (NSGA, 1990a). These data also show, however, that men and boys are more likely than women and girls to participate in competitive sports, a pattern that no doubt reflects a history of greater opportunities for men in sport.

Information from the NSGA (1990a) does not provide analyses that take into account race, class, or age distinctions among women. The NSGA does report that for men and women together, household income is positively related and age is negatively related to involvement in fitness activities (NSGA, 1990a).

Women's Leisure Activities

Just how powerful women's domestic responsibilities are as barriers to leisure activity, including sport activity, is vividly described in research by the British sociologist Rosemary Deem (1987) in her study in Milton Keynes, a town in England.

Challenges to Title IX: Grove City and the Restoration Act

Title IX was resisted by male sport administrators and school and university officials. A particularly strong attack was mounted by the NCAA, which correctly saw that the growth of women's sport would cost money and feared that this money would come from men's programs. It fought the application of Title IX to athletics both in the courts and by a vigorous lobbying effort of government officials and the department of Health, Education and Welfare (Carpenter, 1985).

Resistance from university administrators also concerned the scope of the bill's application. Under the original guidelines issued by HEW, all programs and departments in an institution were subject to Title IX if any program or department received federal funds. Several court challenges were filed in which school districts and colleges argued that only specific programs and departments that received federal funds should come under the bill's jurisdiction.

In a 1984 ruling in *Grove City College v. Bell*, the Supreme Court upheld the program-specific interpretation of Title IX. This revised interpretation effectively eliminated athletics from the bill's coverage, because few athletic departments receive federal funds directly (Carpenter, 1985).

The effects of *Grove City* were felt immediately. Soon after the decision, the Department of Education's Office of Civil Rights dropped its investigation of 64 Title IX complaints, including several complaints against university athletic departments (Carpenter, 1985). In addition, many of the gains achieved under Title IX were eroded as schools and universities began to cut back on women's programs. The effects of *Grove City* were reversed when Congress passed the Civil Rights Restoration Act in 1988. This bill restored the original scope of Title IX and once again provided strong legislative support for equality in school sport programs.

Two of the women Deem interviewed commented on the place of leisure in their lives:

> "Leisure—that's a good one, alright—wouldn't know what it looked like—*if* and it is *if*, I ever get any time at the end of the day I generally fall asleep...." "Sport—no, definitely not—wouldn't catch me running nowhere or wearing one of them leotards—sport's what me husband does on Saturdays ... a lot of silly men chasing a ball around—mind, I get asked to wash the kit." (p. 423)

As Deem indicates, for many women the difficulty in separating out periods in the day when uninterrupted leisure is possible is a major barrier to their participation in sport and physical activity.

The accounts provided by the women Deem interviewed capture graphically some of the conditions that continue to restrict women's experiences of sport and physical activity. Another important consideration is the types of activities in which women are participating. Although data on rising rates of involvement among women are encouraging, optimism should be tempered by a consideration of the feminization of physical activity present in some types of fitness activities. Exercise and training programs that emphasize weight control, appearance, and sex appeal are contemporary incarnations of the myth of female frailty in women's athletics. By emphasizing the connections between physical activity and sexuality, they maintain the image of feminine athleticism that was the foundation of an ideology that restricted women's sport involvement earlier in the century.

Governance of U.S. Collegiate Sport

The passage of Title IX was perhaps the most important event affecting women's sport participation in the United States (see chapter 6). Because of Title IX and subsequent occurrences, most women's athletic programs are now governed by the NCAA, where control is largely in the hands of men. In 1991–92, women were 9% of the President's Commission, 32% of Council members (including the president of the Council), and 33% of the Executive Committee (National Collegiate Athletic Association, 1993).

Loss of control also took place in individual institutions. As women's sport grew and drew a larger share of resources, many institutions merged men's and women's programs under one administrator, who almost always was a man. The visibility and importance attributed to men's sport virtually ensured that the person judged to be the most ''qualified'' to head a newly combined program would be the head of the men's program. The wealth of experience that heads of women's programs possessed went largely unrecognized and unrewarded. As a result, since the passage of Title IX the proportion of women athletic administrators and coaches declined in both high schools and universities. In 1972, 90% of head athletic directors of women's collegiate programs were women; in 1990, 15.9% of women's programs were directed by women (Acosta & Carpenter, 1990).

Professional Sport

Professional sport remains largely a male preserve. Career opportunities for women athletes remain concentrated in a few sports, notably golf

© ALLSPORT USA/Bob Martin

Figure 20.2   Career opportunities for women are concentrated in sports such as tennis and golf.

and tennis, which are nurtured in the private country clubs of the white upper classes. Although there has been some expansion of the professional tours in these sports, there has been little change overall in the gender imbalance at this level. Most opportunities in professional sport are still in men's sports.

Disparities are evident in comparisons of the earnings of individual men and women athletes. Of the 20 highest paid athletes in 1992, only three were women. One is Monica Seles, whose earnings from her winnings and bonuses totaled $3 million; however, Seles's endorsement income is estimated to be $6 million, putting her well below male athletes such as Evander Holyfield and Michael Jordan, whose incomes for 1992 are estimated to be more than $25 million each. Steffi Graf's income of $2.2 million from winnings and bonuses and $5.5 million from endorsements placed her number 15 on the list (Kiersh & Buchholz, 1993).

Further indications of the second-class status of women in professional sport are the problems encountered in efforts to establish women's sports leagues in North America. Both the Women's Professional Softball League (WPSL) and the Women's Professional Basketball League (WBL), which were organized in the 1970s, were plagued by inadequate financing and poor attendance. In the WBL, games were played in high-rent arenas and expensive promotions were directed toward the general sports audience rather than a narrower segment of sports fans who are followers of women's sport, particularly basketball. Coakley (1990) suggests the problems with the approach taken by the league:

> They did not tap into the potential interest among people with personal connections to girls' basketball all over the United States. If two or three regional leagues had been organized, if teams had had lower budgets for coaches and less demand for returns on investment, if games had been played in smaller gyms, if marketing had been localized and directed at girls and their families

connected with community and interscholastic leagues, the fate of women's professional basketball might have been different. (p. 241)

The failure of these leagues also may be attributed to lingering cutural biases that associate team sports and their potential for contact and physical aggression with racial, class, and heterosexist stereotypes. Perhaps for that reason, promotions for the Women's Professional Basketball League emphasized the coaches more than the athletes. All but one of these coaches were men, and many of these were former professional players or coaches. As well, the familiar pattern of trivialization of women's sport was evident in some of the team names, such as the California Dreams, Minnesota Fillies, Philadelphia Fox, and Milwaukee Does ("Scouting Reports: WBL," 1979).

Diversity in Women's Sport

Perhaps the most important issue facing feminist analysis and the women's movement today is the need to give voice to and better represent the interests of women who historically have been marginalized or excluded from dominant cultural forms. Cultural constraints on women's involvement in sport have been particularly pronounced for women of color, poor and working-class women, lesbians, older women, and physically challenged women. In this section we will consider two particularly overlooked issues of diversity in women's sport: sport for the physically challenged and homophobia.

Sport and Physically Challenged Women

One of the most important changes in thinking about the place of sport and physical activity in women's lives in recent years is increased recognition of the needs and rights of physically challenged women. For too long, physical activity was viewed as an interest of only the able bodied and often was thought to be exclusively the prerogative of the skilled and talented. Not only

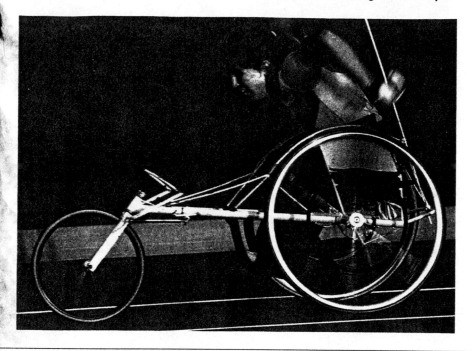

ure 20.3   Jean Driscoll. Courtesy of The Daily Illini, University of Illinois.

re those with disabilities excluded from sport,
ut their exclusion contributed to an ideology of
ble bodiedness that further disadvantaged them
n their struggle for dignity.

The physically challenged constitute a significant segment of our population. A 1986 survey
by Harris & Associates estimated that 14% of all
Americans 16 years of age or older are disabled,
nd of these 56% are women (cited in Grimes &
rench, 1987). The definition of *disabled* used in
e survey is "an individual who has an impair-
ent that significantly impairs them (sic) in one
r more daily life activities, or are considered to
ave or have had such a condition" (Funk, 1986,
cited in Grimes & French, 1987, p. 24).

Heterosexism, Homophobia, and Women Athletes

Women's full participation in sport also is restricted by homophobia, that is, "the irrational

fear or intolerance of homosexuality, gay men or
lesbians, and even behavior that is perceived to
be outside the boundaries of traditional gender
role expectations" (Griffin & Genasci, 1990,
p. 211). Homophobia is at the heart of the long-
standing concern with the supposed masculinizing
effects of sport that underlies research on sex
role conflict among women athletes. As Lenskyj
(1991b) indicates, "Since the stereotype of
'female-athlete' and 'lesbian' share so-called
masculine traits such as aggression and independence, the association between sport and lesbianism has frequently been made" (p. 49). Elsewhere
Lenskyj (1986) notes that the popular association
between sport and lesbianism is fundamentally an
issue of male power:

(R)egardless of sexual preference, women
who reject the traditional feminine role in
their careers as athletes, coaches, or sport
administrators, as in any other nontraditional

pursuit, pose a threat to existing power relations between the sexes. For this reason, these women are the frequent targets of labels intended to devalue or dismiss their successes by calling their sexuality into question. (p. 383)

Homophobia directed against women in sport has produced numerous damaging consequences. In its most overt form, homophobia is the basis for discrimination in decisions about hiring and firing women in coaching and administrative positions. One study of college coaches found that the majority of both male and female coaches believe that "fear of a lesbian influence is a real consideration of administrators during the hiring process in women's programs" (Sweet & Malec, reported in Knoppers, 1988, p. 76). Lenskyj (1991a) cites additional evidence that sexual orientation is a key factor in administrators' decisions concerning women's employment in sport.

Homophobia operates in other ways to prevent women's full participation in sport. One of these is the denial of athletic opportunities to known or suspected lesbians. Another is through campaigns to discredit all women in sport through accusations about their sexual orientation, which is a form of sexual harassment. Yet another is the lack of support for team sports thought to be closely associated with masculine or lesbian images (e.g., rugby, football, softball).

Because of homophobia, all women face pressures to conform to a dominant image of feminine athleticism. Of course, not all women experience and deal with the pressure in the same ways; that is, some actively resist it, whereas others internalize the homophobia and conform quite closely by practicing "apologetic" behavior, such as devoting excessive attention to feminizing their appearance. Regardless of one's sexual preference or one's responses to homophobia, the power of these dominant images and expectations constitutes a form of oppression that all women face.

Perhaps the most insidious way that homophobia has harmed the cause of women in sport

is by challenging the solidarity among them. As Boutilier and SanGiovanni (1983) note, "Lesbians are present in every type, level and degree of sport participation. While this point may be laughingly obvious to some, it is apparently vigorously denied by others" (p. 120). The denial of a lesbian presence in sport has resulted in barriers of ignorance and isolation that hurt heterosexual women as well as lesbians. In the decade since Boutilier and SanGiovanni's observations have been published, some discussion has begun (see in particular Kidd, 1983; Griffin, 1989; Griffin & Genasci, 1990; Lenskyj, 1991a); however, homophobia directed against women in sport continues to be inadequately addressed by athletes, coaches, administrators, and scholars. The result of this silence is a separation between lesbian and heterosexual women, which is often experienced as antagonism and divisiveness and which retards the progress of all women in sport.

It is critical to see heterosexism and homophobia as dynamics that are defined by wider patriarchal interests and that work to consolidate heterosexist male privilege. Homophobia acts as a means of social control, which not only keeps women out of the male preserve of sport but also invokes a fear of association that separates women from one another, effectively undercutting the potential for female solidarity and empowerment. To the extent that it manages to divide women, it further oppresses all of us.

Summary and Conclusions

The preceding discussion indicates that developments in women's sport in recent years are marked by a number of tendencies. On the one hand, the increasing involvement of girls and women in an expanding range of activities is cause for optimism. Other aspects of women's involvement, however, are less encouraging. Women continue to be excluded from most positions of power and influence in both the educational and amateur sport systems. In addition, the opportunities for

Figure 21.1   Women's involvement in sport disturbs the logic of male supremacy. © Ann Meredith, from Gay Games II.

rooms of major league baseball teams. On behalf of women reporters, Ludke won the right to equal access to the locker room; however, the struggle was far from over.

In September 1990, Lisa Olson, a sports reporter for the *Boston Herald* whose regular beat was football, was sexually harassed in the New England Patriots locker room. Supported by many of her reporter colleagues, she publicly protested such treatment. Victor Kiam, owner of the Patriots, dismissed the incident until considerable media attention and threatened feminist boycotts of the Remington shaver company, which he also owns, convinced him that the incident was being taken seriously by the public. Kiam sent Lisa Olson an official apology. In private, however, some players and officials continued to treat the incident as a joke. Four months later Kiam apologized again for a blatantly sexist joke about Olson, which he told at a Patriots banquet.

Olson's ordeal was not yet over. She then began receiving threatening and harassing phone calls and letters; vendors sold inflatable "Lisa dolls" outside Foxboro Stadium, and fans amused themselves by subjecting the dolls to lewd and suggestive acts. In addition, other female reporters experienced renewed antagonism in other locker rooms. Sam Wyche, coach of the Cincinnati Bengals, barred women from the Bengals locker room in direct contravention of NFL policy and was fined $27,500. Despite an NFL investigation, which concluded that Olson had been sexually harassed, a fine of $50,000 to the Patriots, and $27,500 in fines to the three players directly implicated, Olson found it impossible to continue her job as sports reporter. By April 1991 she had moved to Australia to begin a new life. The male preserve of sport had been successfully defended.

The Lisa Olson case shows us how close to the surface those sexist defenses of traditional male spaces and practices are. But it is not only the "boorish sport fan" who displays such deep-seated fears: As recently as 1986, John Carroll argued in a highly respected academic journal that

women must be excluded from sport to preserve sport as a place for the display of masculine "virtue and grace." Carroll's argument exemplifies the patriarchal fear that women will colonize sport and spoil one of the few male preserves where men work symbolically to create an ideology of masculine superiority:

> . . . Women should once again be prohibited from sport: they are the true defenders of the humanist values that emanate from the household, the values of tenderness, nurture, and compassion, and this most important role must not be confused by the military and political values inherent in sport. Likewise sport should not be muzzled by humanist values: it is the living arena for the great virtue of manliness. (p. 3)

What is being contested in sport is the construction and meaning of gender relations. Paul Willis (1982) argues that sport provides particularly dramatic evidence of the construction of gender relations because sport appears to be "autonomous," outside the bounds of "real life" and thus real social relations; that is, we continue to believe that "Sport is just itself and part of the ideologically important area of the 'natural' " (p.130). Sport offers a further "bonus" for those served by the preservation of traditional gender relations because it focuses on the apparently incontrovertible physical and biological differences between women and men. Willis (1982) reports the logic this way:

> The fact that no one can deny female difference becomes the fact of female sports inferiority, becomes the fact that females are innately different from men, becomes the fact that women who stray across the defining boundary are in a parlous state. An ideological view comes to be deposited in our culture as a common sense assumption—of course women are different and inferior. (p. 130)

It is in this sense that we talk about the naturalization of gender relations through sport. The relationship of power between the sexes, which has cultural origins and is maintained through social processes such as gender role stereotyping, is misunderstood as having a biological or "natural" basis. As a result, the cultural origins are obscured. In this way sport serves to construct and legitimize gender difference and to naturalize women's social inferiority through reference to women's traditional physical inferiority.

Lois Bryson (1987) discusses the "inferiorisation of women's activities" (p. 424) by noting that certain sports provide ritual support for male dominance through "linking maleness with highly valued and visible skills and linking maleness with the positively sanctioned use of aggression, force, and violence" (p. 421). The result of such social processes is the reproduction of an ideology of dominance based on the representation of males as naturally superior to females.

Jennifer Hargreaves (1986) also views sport as a site of production of an ideology of male superiority. She focuses on muscles as an apparently "natural" sign of sex difference and argues that the ideology of masculinity is rooted in images of male muscularity. She notes the irony of muscularity as an image of man's "natural" superiority, because muscles "are produced by much 'pumping of iron' and ingesting of drugs" (p. 113) to meet the increasing standards of our particular historical time. Hargreaves's points demonstrate that a good deal of cultural work must go on to create the illusion that sex differences based in physicality are natural and inevitable. The social consequence is the reproduction of relations of power that privilege one gender over the other.

Gender, Physicality, and Power

The discussion above indicates that to a great extent the gendered power relations in sport are closely related to issues of women's embodiment

and physicality. In a patriarchal culture, one of the primary mechanisms of power is the control of women through the control of their bodies. Such control is accomplished through an ensemble of cultural practices that includes rape, domestic violence, sexual harassment, pornography, male-defined standards of female beauty, unattainable media images, and compulsory heterosexuality. As a physical activity, sport is also a site where the struggle over control of women through control of women's bodies can be publicly observed.

Increasingly in the past 20 years, with the demise of the AIAW and the consolidation of women's and men's athletic programs under the NCAA, men have been accepted as legitimate organizers of women's sport experiences, telling us how to play, when to play, where to play, and how to train our bodies. Supplementing and legitimating that structural control of women in sport are subtle ideological forms of control such as media representations. One thus may argue that women are controlled in patriarchal cultures not just through direct control of their bodies, but also through the control of images of their bodies. These processes can be clearly observed in sport in the trivialization of women's sporting accomplishments and the denial of women as real athletes.

Feminist scholars, both within and outside the field of sport studies (Martin, 1987; MacKinnon, 1987), increasingly are turning their attention to the theoretical connections between sport as a physical activity and physicality as the key to women's oppression. This approach has historical resonance as well, because fears that a woman's involvement in sport could compromise her health, her beauty, her reproductive capacity, and her femininity were the earliest rationales for women's exclusion from sport. Helen Lenskyj (1986) shows how the impact of the medical profession and cultural standards of femininity worked together to dampen the enthusiasm and thwart the ambitions of most North American women for sport. Myths about women's frailty appear to have lost some of their power, but Lenskyj shows how the same argument resurfaces today in concern over amenorrhea in women athletes. Fears that women may lose their reproductive abilities through athletic injuries or strenuous activity account for both explicit and implicit restrictions on female involvement.

Theories of Textual Analysis

In this review of media representations of women athletes we will follow a cultural studies approach as we consider the media as a site of ideological power (Gitlin, 1978, 1987; Jhally, 1989). A complete analysis of this sort would investigate all three parts of the classical media model: the producer, the mediated message (the text), and the audience.

Traditional Theories

Over the years scholars have revised their theoretical understandings of the relationship between the media and the audience. Early theories conceptualized the text or message as having enormous power to influence an audience, which was conceptualized as a homogeneous mass undifferentiated by gender, class, race, or other identities or experiences. This "hypodermic" model overemphasized the power of the media to "inject" its message directly into the consciousness of a passive audience. Later, the dominant model in the United States focused on the ways that individual members of the audience used media messages for their own gratification. According to such theories, audience members were conceptualized as individual agents who made conscious choices about their own use of the media and their own interpretations of the messages. Research during those years took a consumer behavior approach that continues to underlie advertising research today; that is, attempts were made to understand media consumption so as to control the message and thus predict the behavior of the consumer.

This theory granted more power to the audience (Gitlin, 1978).

Contemporary Perspectives

Critical theories such as cultural studies reject these alternatives as too simplistic. They favor more complex conceptualizations of the relationship that take into account the control of the production process by special interests (the rich, whites, men), the manipulation of representations within the text, and, most subtly, the hidden cultural context within which "decoding" or reading of the text occurs. This reading context is structured along lines that favor dominant interests. Thus, although scholars no longer endorse the simplistic theories that granted total power to the media to manipulate our perceptions, they also no longer credit the "overromanticized" counter-theory that argues that the audience is capable of fully conscious readings of media messages. As a result cultural studies focuses on a complex dynamic among the producer of the text, the structural qualities of the text, and the context in which the text is consumed (Gitlin, 1987; Jhally, 1989).

We can talk then about the ways that dominant ideologies are encoded into texts by dominant groups and how texts are decoded by readers who may or may not make the preferred reading that dominant forces would like them to make. It is also possible to talk about reading against the text or finding and celebrating subversive messages in a text. With this approach in mind, we would focus upon the ways in which readers make use of texts, but we would not assume that the reader always reads the text in a way that serves his or her best interest.

Readers are always located within particular cultural relations, and those contexts will restrict the interpretations available to them. A major question in media studies today is: To what extent, and under what conditions, can a person in a sexist, heterosexist, racist, classist, ageist, lookist culture exercise some interpersonal control of the texts available to him or her?

Most researchers in sport have presumed that the significance of such images is self-evident. Only recently have studies taken the more critical step of problematizing the relationship between reader and text. Our review of the research on women in sport in the media makes use of both theoretical traditions.

Media Representations of Women in Sport

The representations of female athletes available to us through the media restrict our imagination about what women athletes can accomplish and what their performances mean in a cultural sense. The underrepresentation and misrepresentation of female athletes thus harm women's chances for equal opportunities in sport. But the impact of these representations is even farther reaching: They also produce an image of women as physically inferior to men.

This relative "inferiority" of women in sport is one of the most frequently cited reasons for restructuring women's involvement. As Willis (1982) points out, however, the gender comparison that sport constantly dramatizes is used far more subtly as a rationale for the social inferiority of women. To move one step further, the artificial separation of the sport world into two spheres delineated by sex clearly marks gender difference as significant and worth maintaining. Consequently, sex difference is constructed as a logical and necessary part of our cultural world. Once the logic of difference is established, it is only a short step to the valuation of these two different entities, an ensuing difference that provides the grounding for the establishment of a hierarchy of worth that becomes the basis for political relations.

A survey of the representations of women athletes constructed by the media demonstrates the following themes:

- The underrepresentation of women athletes in the media and thus their "symbolic annihilation"
- The trivialization and marginalization of women athletes
- The objectification and sexualization or, more properly, the heterosexualization of women athletes
- The hidden discourse of homophobia in sport
- The depiction of women's involvement in sport as tragic
- The construction of women as unnatural athletes and of female athletes as unnatural women

Underrepresentation

One of the long-standing criticisms of media accounts of women's sport concerns the amount of coverage, which remains far below that of men's sport. Media researcher George Gerbner (1978) has labeled this general pattern of underrepresentation of women in the media "symbolic annihilation," because erasing women from our view effectively tells us that women are not an important presence in our culture. The underrepresentation of female athletes in the media conveys or confirms the impression that women are not an important part of the sport world and their accomplishments do not deserve our attention.

Women athletes are underrepresented as subjects of media coverage in newspaper accounts, sports magazines, television broadcasts, sports novels, and feature films. Some evidence of the symbolic annihilation of women in sport in the print media was provided in a recent review of coverage of women's and men's sports in 13 major daily newspapers from across Canada on one day, Saturday, September 23, 1989 (Gelinas & Theberge, 1989). The results of this analysis showed that only a small percentage of coverage was concerned with women's sports. The message conveyed to the reader is that on a typical day in Canada, women's sports for the most part don't happen. We know of course that

this isn't true; what is true is that in the judgment of newspaper editors and managers, women's sports in universities, colleges, schools, and communities across the country are not of interest. In the United States, comparable patterns exist. A survey of four daily newspapers indicated that sports stories focused on women comprised only 3.5% of all stories; only 7% of all photographs were of women athletes (Duncan et al., 1991).

Television coverage of sports also relegates women to the sidelines. A recent study of television coverage of women's sports found that 92% of all coverage was allocated to men, whereas only 5% was allocated to women (Duncan et al., 1990). This general pattern holds even when the sporting event being reported is relatively open to female involvement, such as the Olympic Games. Television coverage of the 1976 Olympic Games (McCollum & McCollum, 1980) allocated 21% of the time to women's events. By 1984, attention had increased to 29% (Brown & Fraser, 1985). In print media, *Sports Illustrated* devoted 23% of its articles to men and 77% to articles on both men and women; no articles covered women athletes only. Although one might argue that ABC Sports coverage is "statistically fair" (Rintala & Birrell, 1984) because women comprised 22% of the athletes in the Games, *Sports Illustrated*'s lack of coverage can hardly be excused in that light. Moreover, although the number of items might represent "fair" coverage, further examination shows that stories about male athletes were featured more often on covers and in other prominent places.

The pattern of underrepresentation is repeated in sports magazines. As the most popular sports magazine in North America, *Sports Illustrated* helps define and legitimate what counts as sport and who count as athletes. It is also well known that *Sports Illustrated* habitually ignores women's sports. The swimsuit issue, a tradition for 25 years, in which women are posed in revealing bathing suits and provocative poses, is sometimes the only issue of the magazine to feature a woman on the cover in a given year (Finch, 1991). In his analysis of all *Sports Illustrated* covers featuring human subjects, Finch reports that only 6% of all covers feature women: 4% feature legitimate women athletes, whereas 2% feature the swimsuit models. The proportion of women on the covers, although never high, has even decreased in recent years. Moreover, a woman was not honored as "Sports-(wo)man of the Year" until 1972, when Billie Jean King shared the honor with John Wooden. Three other women have earned that honor since: Chris Evert, Mary Decker, and Mary Lou Retton, who shared the cover with Edwin Moses. In contrast, men who are named as "Sportsman of the Year" rarely share the cover with other men.

In her study of feature articles in *Sports Illustrated*, Mary Jo Kane (1988) reported that the pattern of exclusion of women athletes has not changed significantly since the passage of Title IX, although the amount of coverage of "serious" women athletes (as opposed to swimsuit models) has increased slightly. Angela Lumpkin and Linda Williams (1991) reported that only 8% of all feature articles in *Sports Illustrated* focus on women. They also reported on the magazine's coverage by race: Seventy-six percent of all articles focus on white athletes (male and female), and 22% focus on black athletes. Comparing the number of column inches allotted to coverage of these different groups, Lumpkin and Williams reported that stories of white men average 68.5 inches, stories on black men average 61 inches, stories on white women average 56 inches, and stories on black women average 42 inches.

Some special-interest sports magazines, such as *Runner's World* and *World Tennis*, provide more coverage of women's sports than do the general-interest magazines, such as *Sports Illustrated* and *Sport* (Bryant, 1980). In her study of 50 years of *Racquet/World Tennis* magazine, Kathy Romme (1990) found that the number and size of photographs of women players had increased over time, but photographs of men still outnumbered photos of women by a 2 to 1 ratio.

It could be argued that sports magazines aimed at children, such as *Young Athletes* and *Sports Illustrated for Kids*, have a special obligation to represent the sports world responsibly because the reading tastes of their young readers are less critical than those of adult readers. Yet despite the fact that a large proportion of their readership is girls, both those magazines underrepresent women athletes. Rintala and Birrell (1984) showed that only one third of the photographs in *Young Athletes* feature female athletes; prominent photos such as cover photos and centerfolds are even more likely to feature men. Moreover, *Young Athlete* underrepresents girls' involvement in team sports, even sports that girls in fact dominate such as field hockey, softball, and volleyball. Duncan and Sayaovong (1989) found much the same pattern in the pages of *Sports Illustrated for Kids*. Taken together, these patterns of underrepresentation convey the cultural message that women are not a significant presence in sports.

The Trivialization and Marginalization of Female Athletes

When women athletes are represented in the media, they are often portrayed as inferior athletes incapable of competing on the same ground with "real" athletes, that is, men. Their involvement and accomplishments also are often marginalized and trivialized.

Lois Bryson (1987) discussed trivialization as a major process through which the masculine hegemony of sport is maintained. She cites several examples from the Australian press in which patronizing tones and sexual innuendos create an atmosphere of dismissal of serious athletic efforts on the part of women. Willis (1982) noted the same dynamic in Britain:

There is a very important thread in popular consciousness which sees the very presence of women in sport as bizarre. Frequently, reporting of women's sport takes its fundamental bearings, not on sport, but on humour, or the unusual. The tone is easy to recognise, it's a version of the irony, the humour, the superiority, of the sophisticated towards the cranks. (p. 121)

Such situations are common in American broadcasting as well, as Duncan et al. (1990) have documented. One of their major conclusions about the coverage of basketball was that "Significant differences in the quality of technical production tend to trivialize the women's games, while framing men's games as dramatic spectacles of historic significance" (p. 2). The use of techniques such as slow motion, instant replays, and on-screen graphics, and the provision of verbal statistics were far more pronounced in the coverage of men's games than women's games. They also noted an "infantilization" of women athletes in the television broadcasts they studied. Women were referred to as "girls" and "young ladies," whereas men were referred to as "men," "young men," and "young fellas." Women athletes were also far more likely to be called by their first names, whereas men rarely were. In basketball broadcasts, the only men referred to by first name were men of color, an interesting pattern that substantiates the pattern of infantilization across oppressed groups.

Stanley Eitzen and Maxine Baca Zinn (1989) investigated the naming of women's athletic teams. Names, they argue, "reinforce a basic element of social structure—that of gender division. Team names reflect this division as well as the asymmetry that is associated with it" (p. 364). The sexist practices they report include using the male as a false generic (the Cowboys), modifying the men's team name by adding the prefix Lady (the Lady Buckeyes), adding a feminine suffix to the men's team name (the Tigerettes), creating male/female paired polarity (the Panthers and the Pink Panthers), and using the male name with a feminine modifier, a practice which results in the often hilarious invention of team names such as the Lady Rams and the Gamecocks. Eitzen and Baca Zinn report that over half of all colleges trivialize women's teams and women athletes in either their names or their logos. They refer to

this process as "the deathleticization of women," because they see such naming practices as publicly diminishing women as athletes by representing them as diminutive forms of "real" (male) athletes.

Margaret Duncan and Cynthia Hasbrook (1988) have noted the ways that women's athleticism is also denied by television commentaries. Women's strength, speed, and athletic ability are undercut with objectifying comments about their physical attractiveness and private lives. In their analysis of broadcasts of men's and women's basketball, surfing, and marathon running, they found ambivalence, contradiction, and conflicting messages between the visual and spoken narratives, between the commentators, and even within the comments of the same commentator. They conclude that the ambivalence of television coverage symbolically denies power to women by its exclusionary and denigrating tactics: "It excludes women by its brute neglect of women's sport . . . it denigrates them by conjoining images of female strength with images of female weakness" (Duncan & Hasbrook, 1988, p. 19).

The Sexualization and Heterosexualization of Women Athletes

Women and men in our culture are generally understood as essentially and irrevocably embodied. Given the physical aspects of sport, it is not particularly surprising that women athletes are often represented in terms of their physicality. In sport, however, women's physicality is portrayed quite differently that men's physicality.

Women athletes who are presented in the media are often sexualized or, more specifically, heterosexualized; that is, they are seen and constructed as objects of heterosexual desire (Birrell & Theberge, 1989; Duncan, 1990). The most obvious example of this tendency is the swimsuit issue of *Sports Illustrated* magazine. The issue is immensely popular and is by far the best-selling issue each year. In 1989, 5.5 million copies of

Figure 21.2   The Lady Techsters.

the swimsuit issue were printed—almost double the regular printing of 3 million for other issues (Davis, 1992). Laurel Davis notes that the annual protests that follow the publication of the swimsuit issue began as outrage at images of soft-core pornography being made accessible to young boys. More recently, that response has been joined by angry feminists outraged by the mockery the issue makes of women's serious involvement in sport.

But the *Sports Illustrated* swimsuit issue is not an aberration. It is merely the most blatant example of our culture's tendency to regard women as sexual objects. Televised sports consistently present women as a form of "sexualized comic relief" (Duncan et al., 1990, p.8). The continuing association of women's sport and sexuality is graphically documented further in Duncan's (1990) analysis of photographs that accompanied sports stories concerning the 1988 Winter and Summer Olympic Games and the 1984 Summer Games in five North American magazines. Duncan's examination of photographic features as conveyors of meaning revealed that the photographs emphasized sexual difference through a variety of methods:

- Emphasizing physical appearance
- Poses resembling those of soft-core pornography
- Submissive body positions
- Emotional displays
- Camera angles that look down on women, signaling their inferior position

Women's sexuality was explicitly referenced in these photographs from the expected highlighting of women athletes thought to be glamorous, such as Florence Griffith-Joyner and Katarina Witt, to the positioning of women in sexually suggestive fashion. Often the photos and their accompanying text conveyed mixed messages about women athletes, once again undercutting women's athletic ability with references to their appearance. Florence Griffith-Joyner is a favorite subject of these trivializing practices. Photographs and written texts celebrate her speed and skill while constantly referencing her appearance as well (Duncan, 1990).

Even magazines produced for predominantly female audiences often disappoint their readers by undercutting women's serious involvement in sport with sexualized images. When *WomenSports* magazine began publication in 1974, it was defined as a consciously activist magazine aimed at increasing girls' and women's involvement in and enjoyment of competitive sport (Endel, 1991). To that end, early covers conferred a sense of power and competence on women athletes through camera angles and posturing. However, with its

Figure 21.3   Katarina Witt, 1987.

© VANDYSTADT/ALLSPORT

reorganization and subsequent restyling as *Women's Sport and Fitness*, the magazine lost is activist stance and feminist sensibility. It now promotes fitness and physical activity in primarily heterosexualized terms of attractiveness and physicality. As Barbara Endel (1991) sees it, the magazine's focus has moved its readers "from political activity to personal improvement" (p.130). Even when *WomenSports* featured portraits of strong women athletes on its covers, the magazine contradicted those strong portrayals with written accounts that emphasized sexuality. For example, in a 1976 feature on Virginia Wade, the cover depicts Wade's intensity as she waits to return a shot. The story inside is titled "The Power and Passion of Virginia Wade," and the text constructs her as both a powerful athlete and sensuous woman:

> She is the most feline of tennis players— sleek, strutting, self-conscious, a lioness of the courts. On court she is sensuous. She plays tennis, and passions ooze from her. When she slashes a volley, we can feel a tingle. When frustrations mount we can see her being consumed. (Endel, 1991, p. 162)

Aerobic exercise and other aspects of the fitness boom directed to women also have been criticized as practices that can promote objectification, fragmentation, and heterosexualization of women's bodies. The technology of the fitness boom with its muscle-isolating machines and focus on parts of the body produces the body as an object of increasingly isolated and fragmented parts. It also encourages an idea of the body as an object to be worked on and managed.

The fitness industry relies heavily on conventions of soft-core pornography to promote and sustain the boom and to represent to female consumers the true feminine ideal they must strive to approach through fitness regimes. That ideal— thin, beautiful, sexually attractive, white, young, and clearly heterosexual—is, of course, virtually unattainable. Yet these images are prominent in advertisements for fitness products and in televised aerobic workout shows. Margaret MacNeill (1988) shows how techniques such as camera angle and visual framing "create sexual images rather than images of physical activity" (p. 199).

A final effect of the sexualization of images of the fitness boom is the reconstruction of women's motives for involvement; that is, desires to become strong or fit are reworked by the media and replaced by women's desire to please the men in their lives by becoming more sexually attractive. By undercutting more empowering meanings, the media constrain the possibilities of physical activity as a liberating activity for women.

The Hidden Discourse on Sexuality: Homophobia

Homophobia, or the irrational fear of people who love those of the same sex (Griffin & Genasci, 1990), underlies the media discourse on women in sport. Homophobia is manifested in sport in many different ways, and it reflects not only a fear of women's sexuality but also a fear of the loss of male control of that sexuality. When women no longer need men for emotional or sexual fulfillment, the balance of power in gender relations is endangered.

Homophobia is pervasive, insidious, and divisive. Women athletes particularly have been endangered by homophobia; and until recently, those in athletics and physical education have maintained a silence about the topic that has furthered its power. Coming out as lesbian in sport, as Linn ni Cobhan argued in 1982, results in the confirmation of "an ancient male fantasy": All women in sport are lesbians. Remaining silent, however, can have more devastating effects, for it undermines the sense of pride that precedes unity and action, and it sends a message to those who would abuse the power of heterosexual privilege that lesbians—and women—are unlikely to protest their oppressive treatment.

The power of homophobia and internalized homophobia, or self-hatred by lesbians and gay men, is startling, for it works in a number of ways. By "discrediting" all women in sport as lesbians, men can rest assured that their territory is not being invaded by "real" women after all; by mobilizing social prejudices against homosexuality, they may be able to keep the number of women involved in sport to a safe minimum; by creating an atmosphere of danger, they can, through innuendo, effectively prevent individual women from wanting to be involved in sport; and by keeping women from sport, they keep women from discovering the joy and power of their own physicality, as well as remove a potential arena for the development of female solidarity. As Bobbie Bennett (1982) astutely observes, "Calling one a lesbian is . . . not primarily a way to control lesbians. It is a way to control women" (p. 41).

Lesbianism was not an issue in the field until the 1930s when, among other factors, the popularization of Freudian theories led to a conflation of gender behavior and sexual preference. Female athletes' "mannishness," accepted as a form of gender diversity until that time, came to be understood as a sign of lesbianism and was no longer tolerated in physical education and sport (Cahn, 1994). That legacy remains with us today. Our more recent obsession with psychological masculinity and femininity may be a subtle substitute for homophobic responses to women athletes (Lenskyj, 1986). Whatever its source, it is clear that sexual labeling is a potent weapon in the social control of women in sport.

Mediated responses to this hidden discourse can be seen in the representation of women athletes as either highly attractive by heterosexual standards, or overly masculine. An example here is a Miller Lite beer advertisement in which Joe Piscopo appears with several large, muscular, and hairy male athletes, attired in dresses and women's wigs, and smoking cigars. The ad copy asks: "Why does Helga Piscopo drink Miller Lite?" and the response is: "To keep the girlish figure." The ad makes full use of stereotypes of women athletes as unnatural and unfeminine. It accomplishes this message by invoking questions about "Helga's"

sexuality. The ad also plays on nationalism and ethnocentrism by implying that eastern European women athletes are of questionable femininity.

Women's Involvement as Tragic

A less obvious but equally intriguing message in the representation of female athletes in the media is the construction of women's involvement as tragic. This "tragedy" is constructed on both the individual and cultural levels.

At the cultural level the tragedy centers around women's loss of womanhood. Historically, this has been reflected in fears about the loss of women's reproductive capacities. Explicit warnings that urged middle-class white women not to participate in strenuous activity were common during the Victorian era when damage to the vital and reproductive organs was a taken-for-granted result of women's strenuous and competitive sport activity. Such warnings bear the appearance of protectionism. But as Ehrenreich and English (1979) demonstrate in their critique of medical treatment of women, and Lenskyj (1986) takes up more specifically in the case of women's sport, these patronizing attitudes work to protect not women but a patriarchal structure of privilege. Moreover, they do it subtly, by obtaining women's consent.

Even more fascinating are the themes of individual tragedy that are exploited by the media. The exemplar of this practice can be found in contemporary accounts of the women's 800-meter run in the 1928 Olympic Games discussed in chapter 8. More recent examples can be drawn from the 1984 Olympic Games, where the dominant mediated images of women athletes were of Mary Decker tripping in the 3,000-meter final and Gabriela Andersen-Schiess staggering toward the finish line of the marathon. The match-up between Decker and Zola Budd was a much-heralded event in the 1984 Olympics. As Budd moved to pass Decker at the 1,600-meter mark, the two tangled. Budd was thrown off stride; Decker fell into the

Robert Hagedohm AAF/LPI 1984

Figure 21.4 Gabriela Andersen-Schiess finishing the 1984 Olympic Marathon.

infield where she lay writhing in pain and frustration. It was a horrible moment for Decker. She had missed the 1972, 1976, and 1980 Games, and now she saw her final opportunity disappear. *Sports Illustrated*'s coverage of the incident is indicative of the focus taken by the media. No fewer than 12 photographs of the incident accompany the article titled ''Triumph and Tragedy in Los Angeles'' (Moore, 1984). The ''triumph'' belonged to Carl Lewis.

Andersen-Schiess was struggling to finish the first women's marathon ever held in the Olympic Games. She stumbled the last meters around the track surrounded by officials who honored her request not to assist her. Had they touched her, she would have automatically been disqualified. Marty Liquori, the television analyst, was not

impressed with her courage, repeatedly saying, ''Someone should take charge and stop her. . . . Someone should walk out there and take responsibility and grab her . . . there's nothing to be accomplished'' (reported in Halpert, 1988, p. 39).

Scott Ostler of the *Los Angeles Times* had a different opinion:

> Nothing to be accomplished? How about finishing? . . . If a woman wants to push herself beyond sanity and reality, isn't that in the Olympic tradition? . . . Why is it that women have to cross the finish line with their hair neatly combed and their makeup fresh? Why can't they gasp and sweat and stagger, just like the guys do? Amid all the pixies and sweethearts comes a Swiss marathoner who stumbles and staggers and somehow finishes. If she were a man, they would salute her courage. But she is a woman and the TV people wonder why the officials don't grab this poor girl and help her. (quoted in Halpert, 1988, p. 39)

Another dimension of this incident is that it overshadowed the winning performance of Joan Benoit, an exceptional female athlete whose triumph was accorded less attention in the print media the next day than the ''tragedy'' of Andersen-Schiess. Andersen-Schiess, incidentally, recovered within 2 hours of the race.

These incidents do not occur often, but their sensationalization by the media reinforces an antiquated but still extant notion that women are not suited to the rigors of sport. Although ''tragedies'' in men's sport receive similar attention, for example, Dan Jansen's fall in the 1988 Olympic speed-skating event, the sheer volume of coverage of male triumphs places these moments of tragedy in perspective. For women, they often appear to be the whole story.

Athletes as Unnatural: Gender, Sport, and the Construction of Difference

Media coverage of sport today does not simply exclude and ignore women, trivialize or marginalize women, deathleticize or deny power to women; it constructs women and men and the difference between the two in such a way as to present gender differences as an important and natural feature of social life. Moreover, it constructs women who transgress the boundaries as "unnatural" and thus "denatures" them as athletes and women.

Televised images, advertisements, cartoons, and sports photographs show convincingly the continuing emphasis on the distinctions between female and male athletes. Photographs have a particularly powerful capacity to contribute to the construction of ideology because they "do not simply create images of women or girls, men or boys; they construct differences between female and males and address viewers as though the differences are natural and real" (Duncan, 1990, pp. 24-25). This is accomplished by an array of media practices. Camera angles often depict women athletes from above, which suggests a position of inferiority; they present male athletes in an elevated position, suggesting superiority. The positioning of photos also often presents men in dominant positions and women in supportive, subservient, or subsidiary positions. Duncan concludes that "Focusing on female difference is a political strategy that places women in a position of weakness" (p. 40).

Written media texts naturalize gender divisions in sport so that they too appear to be the outcome of biological differences. This occurs through the sexualization of imagery discussed above, the presentation of a "psychological modality" of the female athlete that is rooted in traditional descriptions of female hysteria (i.e., references to athletes' nerves, dispositions, emotions, and tears), and the use of male standards and norms to evaluate and interpret women's performances (Klein, 1988).

Personal portrayals of athletes in feature articles, "up close and personal," and in sports magazines also report on the emotional side of female athletes, particularly their tearful responses to victory or defeat. Dan Hilliard's (1984) study of magazine articles about female and male professional tennis players notes this theme. The articles often followed a "debunking motif" as they focused on the "imperfections and character flaws" of their subjects. These flaws follow predictable gender stereotypes. The men are seen as one dimensional, unfriendly, or ill tempered, whereas the women are portrayed as overly dependent on others, particularly men; prone to anxiety and depression; having doubts about their sexual identity; and unable to fulfill their athletic potential. The articles tend to forgive the men their flaws because they also had positive attributes: their superb athleticism, determination to succeed, aggressiveness, toughness, and honesty. In contrast, the women's flaws are not balanced by redeeming positive attributes. The articles suggest that their emotional states undercut their athletic abilities. In sports photographs, Duncan (1990) observed the same tendency to depict women as emotional: "Tears, displayed in photographs and underscored in captions, may be another external indicator of difference—women cry often, displaying their weakness for all to see; real men hardly ever cry, reaffirming their strength" (p. 38).

Michael Messner (1988) suggests that there has been a shift in media strategies in portraying female athletes. The recent advances of women athletes have rendered the formerly common media practices of marginalization and trivialization too obviously unfair and inappropriate. They have been replaced by another strategy that applies a standard of apparent "equality" in sports reporting. As Messner describes it, "They want to be treated equally with men? Well, let's see what they can do" (p. 206). The coverage goes on to compare women's performances with men's. But as he indicates, given current physiological differences between women and men and the organization of sport around definitions that favor male performance, this strategy is likely once again to reproduce and solidify masculine hegemony. Ironically then, an apparent ideology of equality becomes a means to explain and justify apparently "natural" differences between women and men.

Messner argues that although accounts of women's sport appear to be somewhat liberated from the degradations of earlier times, the media nonetheless maintain practices that reinforce ideas about women's physical inferiority. Because these accounts appear to be fair and equitable, they are a particularly powerful support for hegemonic practices.

A final, dramatic example of the ways in which the media produce and enforce notions of gender difference can be found in Susan Birrell and Cheryl Cole's (1990) analysis of the entrance of constructed-female transsexual Renee Richards into the women's professional tennis tour. Renee Richards's story was newsworthy not necessarily because of his/her transsexuality but because he/she wanted to enter sport. As a transsexual in a world divided into two and only two apparently natural sexes, and in a sport system that is still accepted as legitimately and legally divided by sex, Renee Richards had no place to play. This dilemma reveals that sport is not just focused on, but structured around, the apparently incontrovertible physical and biological differences between the sexes.

Media accounts of the ensuing legal battle to determine Richards's correct sex status and their representations of the controversy Richards evoked on the tennis tour reveal some interesting cultural assumptions about sex, gender, and difference. The controversy over whether Richards should be allowed to play on the women's tour was framed by the media as an issue of "competitive equality." Richards asserted that s/he had given up the advantages of male embodiment and thus had no unfair advantage over the women on the tour. Many of the women felt differently.

These debates were translated by the media into issues related to the body and power. Through their descriptions of Richards's physical body as an attractive female-seeming body and the apparent demasculinizing effects of the transsexual surgery and drug treatments, the media ultimately constructed Richards as "less than male" and

thus an acceptable challenge for women players. As Birrell and Cole (1990) conclude:

> The discourse on bodies within the Richards controversy demonstrates the cultural significance of constructing women's bodies as different from and representing them as physically inferior to men's bodies. The challenge of Richards' presence in women's sport works to naturalize women as physically inferior. (p. 16)

Summary and Conclusions

In this chapter we have reviewed some of the ideological constraints encountered by women in sport: in particular, media representations that help construct an image of female athletes as inferior and vulnerable. Media representations of women in sport thus can be seen as ideological sites for the production and reproduction of relations of gender that undermine women and privilege men through reference to the "natural" differences between them. Because sport is a physical activity that features apparently unassailable biological and physiological differences between the sexes, it works as a natural site for the production of such relations.

But the process of control is never complete. Subordinated groups do not merely step aside and allow dominant groups to work their will on them. Rather these relations are actively challenged, contested, and sometimes transformed. We close these chapters with a discussion of the possibilities of such action in sport. We have argued that an increasingly clear focus of current theories of women's oppression is on physicality and the control of women through the control of women's bodies. In chapter 22 we argue that as a central issue in gender relations, the body can be seen as political territory—the central site for the struggle over gender relations.

References

Angell, R. (1982). *Late Innings: A baseball companion*. New York: Simon & Schuster.

Bennett, R.S. (1982). Sexual labelling as social control. *Perspectives: Western Society for Physical Education of College Women*, **4**, 40-50.

Birrell, S. (1987, November). *Women and the myth of sport*. Paper presented at the meeting of the North American Society for the Sociology for Sport, Edmonton, AB.

Birrell, S. (1988). Discourses on the gender/sport relationship: From women in sport to gender relations. In K.B. Pandolf (Ed.), *Exercise and Sport Sciences Reviews*, **16**, 459-502.

Birrell, S., & Cole, C.L. (1990). Double fault: Renee Richards and the construction and naturalization of difference. *Sociology of Sport Journal*, **7**, 1-21.

Birrell, S., & Theberge, N. (1989, November). *Packaging fitness: Women and the fitness boom*. Paper presented at the meeting of the North American Society for the Sociology of Sport, Washington, DC.

Brown, B., & Fraser, F. (1985, October). *Fair play: Media coverage of women at the 1984 Olympic Games*. Paper presented at the meeting of the North American Society for the Sociology of Sport, Boston (revised version).

Bryant, J. (1980). A two-year selective investigation of the female in sport as reported in the paper media. *Arena Review*, **4**(2), 32-40.

Bryson, L. (1987). Sport and the maintenance of masculine hegemony. *Women's Studies International Forum*, **10**, 349-360.

Cahn, S. (1994). Crushes, competition and closets: The emergence of homophobia in women's physical education. In S. Birrell & C.L. Cole (Eds.), *Women, Sport and Culture* (pp. 327-339). Champaign, IL: Human Kinetics.

Carroll, J. (1986). Sport: Virtue and grace. *Theory, Culture and Society*, **3**, 91-98.

Cobhan, L. (1982). Lesbians in physical education and sport. In M. Cruikshank (Ed.), *Lesbian studies: Present and future* (pp. 179-186). Old Westbury, NY: Feminist Press.

Connell, R.W. (1987). *Gender and power: Society, the person, and sexual politics*. Stanford, CA: Stanford University Press.

Davis, L.R. (1992). Sports Illustrated's swimsuit issue: A critical media analysis. Unpublished doctoral dissertation, University of Iowa.

Duncan, M.C. (1990). Sport photographs and sexual difference: Images of women and men in the 1984 and 1988 Olympic Games. *Sociology of Sport Journal* **7**, 22-43.

Duncan, M.C., & Hasbrook, C.A. (1988). Denial of power in televised women's sports. *Sociology of Sport Journal*, **5**(1), 1-21.

Duncan, M.C., Messner, M., Williams, L., & Jensen, K. (1990). Gender stereotyping in televised sports. Los Angeles: Amateur Athletic Foundation.

Duncan, M.C., Messner, M., & Williams, L. (1991). Coverage of women's sports in four daily newspapers. Los Angeles: Amateur Athletic Foundation.

Duncan, M.C., & Sayaovong, A. (1989). *Visual images and gender in Sports Illustrated for Kids*. Paper presented at the North American Society for Sociology of Sport annual meeting, Washington, DC.

Dunning, E. (1994). Sport as a male preserve: Notes on the social sources of masculine identity and its transformations. In S. Birrell and C.L. Cole (Eds.), *Women, Sport, and Culture* (pp. 163-179). Champaign, IL: Human Kinetics.

Ehrenreich, B., & English, D. (1979). *For her own good*. Garden City, NY: Anchor.

Eitzen, D.S., & Baca Zinn, M. (1989). The de-athleticization of women: The naming and gender making of collegiate sport teams. *Sociology of Sport Journal*, **6**(4), 362-370.

Endel, B. (1991). *Working out: The dialectic of strength and sexuality in Women's Sports and Fitness magazine*. Unpublished doctoral dissertation, University of Iowa, Iowa City.

Finch, G. (1991). *A content analysis of Sports Illustrated magazine: The cover story.* Unpublished paper, University of Iowa.

Gelinas, M., & Theberge, N. (1989). A content analysis of the coverage of physical activity in two Canadian newspapers. *International Review of Sociology of Sport, 21*, 141-149.

Gerbner, G. (1978). The dynamics of cultural resistance. In G. Tuchman, A.K. Daniels, & J. Benet (Eds.), *Hearth and home: Images of women in mass media.* New York: Oxford University Press.

Gitlin, T. (1978). Media sociology: The dominant paradigm. *Theory and Society, 6*, 205-253.

Gitlin, T. (1987). Prime time ideology: The hegemonic process in television entertainment. In H. Newcomb (Ed.), *Television: The critical view* (pp. 507- 532). New York: Oxford University Press.

Griffin, P., & Genasci, J. (1990). Addressing homophobia in physical education: Responsibilities for teachers and researchers. In M. Messner & D. Sabo (Eds.), *Sport, men and the gender order* (pp. 211-221). Champaign, IL: Human Kinetics.

Halpert, F.E. (1988). You call this adorable? An open letter to the producer of NBC Sports. *Ms., 17*(4), 36-39.

Hargreaves, J. (1985). 'Playing like gentlemen while behaving like ladies': Contradictory features of the formative years of women's sports. *The British Journal of Sport History, 2*, 40-52.

Hargreaves, J. (1986). Where's the virtue? Where's the grace?: A discussion of the social production of gender relations in and through sport. *Theory, Culture and Society, 3*, 109-119.

Hilliard, D.C. (1984). Media images of male and female professional athletes: An interpretive analysis of magazine articles. *Sociology of Sport Journal, 1*(3), 251-262.

Jhally, S. (1989). Cultural studies and the sports/media complex. In L. Wenner (Ed.), *Media,* sports and society (pp. 70-93). Newbury Park, CA: Sage.

Kane, M.J. (1988). Media coverage of the female athlete before, during and after Title IX: Sports Illustrated revisited. *Journal of Sport Management, 2*, 87-99.

Klein, M. (1988). Women in the discourse of sport reports. *International Review of Sociology of Sport, 23*(2), 139-152.

Lenskyj, H. (1986). *Out of bounds: Women, sport and sexuality.* Toronto: Women's Press.

Lorge, B. (1976, September). The power and passion of Virginia Wade. *WomenSports, 3*, 6-9, 20.

Lumpkin, A., & Williams, L.D. (1991). An analysis of Sports Illustrated feature articles, 1954-1987. *Sociology of Sport Journal, 8*(1), 16-32.

MacKinnon, K. (1987). *Feminism unmodified: Discourses on life and law.* Cambridge, MA: Harvard University Press.

MacNeill, M. (1988). Active women, media representations, and ideology. In. J. Harvey & H. Cantelon (Eds.), *Not just a game: Essays in Canadian sport sociology* (pp. 195-211). Ottawa, ON: University of Ottawa Press.

Martin, E. (1987). *The woman in the body.* Boston: Beacon Press.

McCollum, R.H., & McCollum, D.F. (1980, February). *Analysis of ABC-TV coverage of the 21st Olympiad games, Montreal.* Paper presented at the Olympic Games Symposium, Saratoga Springs, NY.

Messner, M. (1988). Sports and male domination: The female athlete as contested ideological terrain. *Sociology of Sport Journal, 5*(3), 197-211.

Moore, K. (1984, August 20). Triumph and tragedy in Los Angeles. *Sports Illustrated,* pp. 22ff.

Peiss, K. (1986). *Cheap amusements: Working women and leisure in turn of the century New York.* Philadelphia: Temple University Press.

Rintala, J., & Birrell, S. (1984). Fair treatment for the active female: A content analysis of

Young Athlete magazine. *Sociology of Sport Journal*, **1**(3), 213-250.

Romme, K. (1990). *The portrayal of women in World Tennis magazine from 1934-1984.* Unpublished master's thesis, University of Iowa.

Sheard, K., & Dunning, E. (1973). The rugby football club as a type of male preserve: Some sociological notes. *International Review of Sociology of Sport*, **5**, 5-24.

Theberge, N. (1989). Women's athletics and the myth of female frailty. In J. Freeman (Ed.), *Women: A feminist perspective* (4th ed.) (pp. 507-522). Mountain View, CA: Mayfield.

Willis, P. (1982). Women in sport and ideology. In J.A. Hargreaves (Ed.), *Sport, culture and ideology* (pp. 117-135). London: Routledge & Kegan Paul.

Chapter 22

Feminist Resistance and Transformation in Sport

Susan Birrell
Nancy Theberge

Remember, no one can make you feel inferior without your consent.
ELEANOR ROOSEVELT
quoted in *Women on Men*

In this chapter we discuss sport as a site for fighting gender oppression by contesting gender relations. We will argue that, as a culture, we underestimate the cultural significance and political importance of sport. We also will argue that this oversight keeps us from intervening in the processes and institutions of sport that serve political ends, that is, that serve to reproduce asymmetrical power relations structured along lines of gender, class, race, age, and sexuality.

If sport is a site for the reproduction of relations of dominance and subordination, as we have argued in chapters 20 and 21, then it also may serve as a site for resistance and transformation of those relations. A significant debate in the study of such power relations focuses on the problem of recognizing and theorizing resistance, transformation, and reproduction. In this chapter we enter that debate with reference to the practices of resistance and transformation as they can be and are enacted by feminists in sport.

Sport as a Site for Cultural Struggle

Our understanding of the cultural meaning of sport has undergone some important shifts in the last two decades. Dominant images of sport in the early days viewed sport as apolitical and neutral, a separate reality outside the concerns of everyday life where social relations are suspended while we take pleasure in physical activity. In this view the athlete is depicted as a childlike, happy player who experiences a spiritual freedom that transcends the problems of everyday life, and who acts with total agency (i.e., personal control over the situation). Michael Novak's (1976) *The Joy of Sports* is often cited as the exemplar of this tradition. This approach romanticizes sport and tends to obstruct critical analyses of the role sport plays in reproducing social inequities.

Later conceptualizations of the social nature of sport, particularly those grounded in Marxist traditions, offered harsh critiques of sport as a form of totalizing social control. Those involved in sport were portrayed as passive and unreflective, as cultural dupes and falsely conscious cultural players who were subject to the total constraint of dominant forces and could not act in their own best interests. Paul Hoch's (1972) *Rip off the Big Game* and Jean Marie Brohm's (1978) *Sport: A Prison of Measured Time* are classic examples of this scenario.

More recent theorizations of the relationship between agency and constraint are exemplified in Richard Gruneau's (1983) book *Class, Sports and Social Development*. In Gruneau's view, individual choices involve a dialectical relationship between freedom and constraint. Following Marx, Gruneau argues that "While human agents certainly make their own history, they do not make it completely under conditions of their choosing" (p. 55). Constraints such as the systemic relations of power structured along lines of sex, race, and class create a social context that makes it difficult to act with total freedom on our own behalf.

Girls who wish to be involved in sport, for example, cannot "just do it," that is, cannot just act in their own best interests and try out for a team. Structural constraints, such as rules that prohibit girls from playing on boys' teams, and ideological constraints, such as the unspoken "common sense" that sport is for boys, form a context of constraint that makes it difficult for girls to act as free agents or even apparently choose to act. Yet rules can be changed, and ideologies can be uncovered and challenged. Indeed, the last 20 years have been marked by visible changes in the quantity and quality of opportunities for girls and women in sport.

The belief that we can make our own history, that we can work to control our own futures, must underlie a belief in the possibilities of cultural transformation or social change. The issue of agency and constraint concerns the relative power of persons vis-à-vis cultural forces. The cultural studies perspective, which underlies our analysis in this chapter, focuses on the struggle between agency and constraint, and the associated struggles between dominant forces and subordinated forces and between the cultural reproduction and the cultural transformation of power relations. As we discuss below, transformation and resistance are best understood in relation to conceptualizations of consciousness and praxis. Consciousness is politically reflexive knowledge, and praxis is the social action that follows from it. Praxis is social action undertaken by politically conscious agents. Thus praxis is practical political work because it is focused on the transformation of power relations.

Sport is an important, though often overlooked or underestimated, site for these struggles:

- For patriarchal privilege
- For unrestricted capital accumulation
- For white skin privilege
- For compulsory heterosexuality
- For the reproduction of privilege

We cannot understand the meaning of women's presence in and absence from sport without clear reference to the context of relations of dominance and subordination, which in our culture are structured along the lines of gender, race, class, sexual preference, and age.

Moreover, we cannot transform that complex, diffuse, and self-interested set of relations with simple interventions. We have tried in the past to increase women's involvement in sport with research and social action focused on role models, mentors, and socialization models. In this chapter we choose not to discuss women's involvement in sport in those terms because we believe that they reference a different theoretical era. Although increasing our presence as role models and taking responsibility to act as mentors and to intervene in the socialization process are useful personal commitments, these actions alone will never be enough to effect the level of cultural change necessary to transform gender relations in sport or in society at large. To meet the challenge of transformation on its own terms, we must respect the complex interrelationship among sport, culture, and gender. In this chapter we wish to explore the potential for human agency in sport. The cultural constraints, particularly structural and ideological constraints that help produce gender inequity, also are considered. We begin by offering a framework for understanding the dynamics of resistance and transformation of gender relations in sport.

Varieties of Resistance and Transformation

Transformation, or social change, can be understood as a fundamental change in the structure of relations of power and the ideologies that hold those structures in place. Resistance is the process by which disempowered groups or persons refuse to submit fully to their disempowerment. Both resistance and transformation may be enacted at the structural and the ideological level, but transformation always must be realized at the level of material practice. A change in a person's or group's understanding of its relationship to power and its attempts to contest that positioning may be recognized as resistant, but those acts are not transformative unless there is a change in the structure of power manifested in real lived experiences. Resistance alone thus is not transformative,

and change at the ideological level is not sufficiently profound to count as transformative work.

Although it is important to distinguish between resistant and transformative acts so that we do not falsely celebrate rebellion as salvation, speaking of resistance and transformation as two distinct categories of social action misrepresents the connections between the two. We might more properly think of transformation as the goal and resistance as the path. To increase the chances that they will lead to transformation, resistant acts should share certain characteristics; that is, they should be conscious, collective, political, and public.

To lead to transformation, resistance should be a conscious act. Consciousness is the recognition of the social relations that constrain us. To enable social change, a subordinated group or person must recognize its misfortune not as a private tragedy but as one instance of systematic oppression structured along certain lines such as class, gender, and race.

Resistance for transformation also must be a collective process that moves the actor beyond the personal in both analysis and action. Transformative action must move us beyond the limits of personalized resistant actions, that is, those that serve only the individual and do not provide a basis for more profound and fundamental change. Transformation must be accomplished in a larger sphere of human relations. In addition, transformative resistant acts must be overtly political, which implies an analysis of power relations and a demonstrable attempt to undermine them.

Finally, to maximize the possibilities for transformation, resistance must be public and announced. Transformative action must enter the consciousness of dominant groups so that it works as active ideological work. The tools of dominance can be subtle, for they are pervasive and they need work only to reinforce and reproduce commonsense assumptions already in place. For example, former President Bush's conscious mispronunciation of Saddam Hussein's name during the Persian Gulf War worked at a subtle level to draw parallels with Saddam and Satan or sadism and reinforce support for the war through demonization of the enemy.

Because they do not speak from a dominant position, the voices of resistance and protest must be clearly, loudly, and publicly articulated. For example, our personal boycott of products whose manufacturers' politics or productive practices offend us is a thoughtful act of resistance; however, that boycott is far more powerful if the base of activism is expanded and the company is made aware of the reasons for the boycott.

Acts of resistance may be enacted either consciously or unconsciously. They may be crafty and surreptitious or openly rebellious, and they may be successful or unsuccessful; that is, they may directly or indirectly produce some form of social change or transformation, or they may leave social relations unaffected. We often recognize only the most overt acts of resistance and rebellion: what Peter Donnelly (1988) calls "self-conscious political protest." Examples of such popular resistance in sport include the boycotts of South Africa in the Olympic Games beginning in 1960 and the subsequent boycotting of teams not boycotting South Africa in international sport in general; and the black power salute of John Carlos and Tommie Smith at the awards ceremony at the Mexico City Olympics of 1968. Insistence by Olympic officials, most notably the late Avery Brundage, that this use of sport is illegitimate is evidence of the resistance to resistance that characterizes the efforts of dominant groups to remain in position. Their concern verifies sport as an important arena for symbolic political work.

Many acts of resistance are less public and spectacular; however, in *Weapons of the Weak*, anthropologist James Scott (1985) reminds us that "Most subordinate classes throughout most of history have rarely been afforded the luxury of open, organized, political activity" (p. xv). Open and collective resistance risks brutal retaliation. Scott prefers to focus on the less spectacular "everyday forms of resistance" that "make no

headlines" (p.36) because he sees them as significant elements in cultural struggle. Resistance that operates from underground, although seldom recognized as heroic, may be highly effective. Individual private acts of resistance mount up, causing inconvenience and disruption to the system and those it serves. A critical mass of resistance can lay the groundwork for more global, systemic change.

Scott (1985) offers several examples of the forms of resistance available to the disempowered:

Ordinary weapons of relatively powerless groups: foot dragging, dissimilation, desertion, false compliance, pilfering, feigned ignorance, slander, arson, sabotage and so on. . . . They require little or no coordination or planning; they make use of implicit understandings and informal networks; they often represent a form of individual self help; they typically avoid any direct, symbolic confrontation with authority. (p. xvi)

Examples include the original meaning of the term *sabotage*, which meant to throw one's sabot, or shoe, into the machinery and disrupt production; the resistance of the Luddites to industrialization and mechanization; and the pilfering, malingering, and desertion of African-American slaves.

Resistant behavior can be so subtle that it is unrecognized as such by dominant groups, with unforeseen results. For example, the resistance of African-American slaves was misunderstood by whites as lazy and shiftless behavior. Today's negative stereotype, taken up as the "natural" behavior of blacks, is actually grounded in a resistant folk style. A similar example can be taken from gender relations at the turn of the century, when inadequate means of birth control and the assumption of husbands' rights to intercourse on demand forced women to feign sickness and frailty. "Not tonight, dear, I have a headache" became the only acceptable means of birth control. But this resistive practice too was misunderstood and taken up by the dominant culture as a sign of women's physical and emotional infirmity and social inferiority.

In sport, subtle resistant practices sometimes take the form of what Donnelly (1988) calls "opposition to colonial rule." Resistance to ideological colonization, that is, the eradication of a group's identity, customs, language, sensibilities, values, and sense of community, can be seen in a group's stubborn insistence on preserving its indigenous cultural forms. The persistence of banned sporting practices is one form that such resistant work takes. Clifford Geertz (1973) has eloquently described the persistence of cockfighting in Bali, despite governmental interdiction. He reads this persistence as a deeply significant sign of the Balinesian character. Shirley Prendergast (1978) offers a similar example when she discusses the playing of stoolball by rural women as a willful symbol of the persistence of female bonding and community building in Kent and Sussex.

Resistance also can be seen in the appropriation of activities offered by colonizing forces but reshaped and claimed by native culture as something uniquely their own. Donnelly (1988) offers the example of Trobriand cricket, in which the proper British game is imbued with tribal meanings and comes to take on a ritual rather than competitive meaning within Trobriand culture. Fox (1961) recorded the same processes at work in Pueblo baseball in the southwestern United States.

Thus we can think of the cultural struggle for power in terms of a vocabulary of resistance and resilience. The processes of production, reproduction, and colonization work to secure the interests of those enfranchised with power. Against such domination, subordinated groups resist through protest, opposition, rebellion, empowerment, resilience, persistence, subversion, sabotage, and disruption. To fully recognize and represent the dialectical nature of this struggle for power, our vocabulary also must include terms that signal the power of dominant forces to "resist resistance" and recapture, recuperate, co-opt, buy out, and incorporate the forces of rebellion and opposition.

As we explore the cultural struggles enacted through sport, we will focus on these dialectic processes of ideological reproduction, resistance, transformation, incorporation, and renewed resistance of relations of dominance and subordination.

Sport as a Site for Feminist Resistance and Transformation

As we have shown in chapter 21, current theories of women's oppression and the reproduction of inequitable gender relations increasingly emphasize physicality and the control of women through the control of their bodies. As a central issue in gender relations, the body can be seen as political territory and as the central site in the struggle over gender relations. The prescription for change is for women to take conscious control of their own bodies so that the site of oppression becomes a site of resistance, transformation, and liberation.

Sport can be a significant element in that liberating process. If gender relations are ever to be transformed, that transformation may first have to be realized on the symbolic or ideological level, and it is on that level that sport works. Sport is an excellent site for examining how patriarchal relations are played out, for it is in sport that dominant notions of masculine superiority are produced as commonsense. It is in sport, too, that such commonsense can be directly challenged and resisted by the appearance of girls and women who are capable athletes. With the recognition of sport as a political site, we can reexamine our motives for increasing the presence of girls and women in sport. From a traditional liberal perspective, of course, we would argue that sport is an attractive and personally enriching human activity that ought to be available to all people regardless of sex, race, age, class, sexual preference, or other discriminatory criteria. But if that is our only reason for promoting sport for women, we are underestimating the true power of sport and women: the possibility of using sport to transform social relations.

At the most basic level, women can use physical activity in sport to experience a sense of personal empowerment. On both a symbolic and a real level, reclaiming physicality is a way for women to repossess themselves and intervene in their own behalf to counter restrictive patriarchal practices. Thus physical empowerment through sport can serve as a metaphor for personal empowerment.

In a broader context, feminist involvement and intervention in sport might serve as a springboard for the transformation of gender relations by dislodging the gender hierarchy that sport helps preserve. By compromising the sanctity of sport as a male preserve and a site for the celebration of male physical superiority and difference, sport might serve instead as a site for the construction of alternative visions of gender relations.

Feminist intervention in sport also might accomplish a transformation of sport, not just for women, but for the mass of people that dominant sport forms do not serve in this culture. Sport might be transformed by the provision of alternative sport forms, and feminist revision and resistance might provide a significant proportion of that challenge.

Finally, feminist-inspired transformations in sport might have even broader repercussions: They might serve as a means to challenge and transform other power relations, such as class relations and racial relations, by using as a model the deconstruction of dominant and naturalized notions of gender relations. All of these relations of power are consolidated through a logic of difference that is reproduced as logical and natural through sport. Disturbing that logic may have profound transformative effects.

Sport and Feminist Resistance: Women Athletes as Resistant Figures

Women's involvement in sport is a history of stubborn resistance. According to Cheryl Cole and Susan Birrell, "The very presence of women in the male preserve of sport is evidence of 'leaky hegemony' " (1986, p. 24) or the inability of dominant groups to exercise total control over subordinates. Cole and Birrell note that "The persistent presence of women in sport can be understood as the result of tension between attempts of a dominant group to establish and maintain sport as a male preserve and the active resistance of a subordinate group to their own subordination" (p. 24).

Jan Felshin (1991) has provided some wonderful historical examples of women's refusal to give up sport. Forbidden by charter, by law, or by cultural stereotypes to participate in highly competitive sports, women at the eastern schools during the "playday period" from 1923 to 1972 often adopted resistant practices. They organized games in local church basements, and they sneaked out of their dorm rooms at night to play organized games in the gyms. They were following an old tradition. In another example, Ellen Gerber quotes a Vassar graduate's recollections about playing baseball in 1870: ' "The public, so far as it knew of our playing, was shocked, but in our retired grounds, and protected from observation even in these grounds by sheltering trees, we continued to play in spite of a censorious public' " (Richardson, 1897, quoted in Gerber, 1974, p. 10).

In more recent times, the recomposition of the structure of girls' and women's athletics has posed a new challenge to women who wish to remain in leadership positions in sport. As more and more coaching and administrative positions go to men, those women who persevere should be acknowledged as resistant figures.

The embodiment of "leaky hegemony" also may be found in that familiar cultural type, the tomboy: the preadolescent girl more interested in activities traditionally assigned to boys than the passive pursuits of girls. The term often has been used in a pejorative sense to dismiss, trivialize, and contain generations of budding feminists. It is no coincidence that the tomboy lost her acceptability—her license— during adolescence, that period of time when girls become sexualized in our

Figure 22.1   The presence of women in sport can be understood as an act of resistance.

culture. In fact, much of the disapproval of the tomboy is homophobia disguised as sexism.

Like tomboys, women in the male preserve of sport are generally viewed as intruders. Marcia Anderson (1991) has documented the experiences of the first female athletic trainers in physical education and the heavy price they paid as pioneers. Because she was the only woman in an all-male class, the woman trainer was usually isolated from her potential colleagues. Moreover, because most training rooms were in the men's locker rooms (women athletes have only recently been allowed the luxury of training facilities), she was often barred physically from gaining access to the education she needed. One woman told of practicing her taping in the hall outside the training room because she was not allowed inside; the instructor came outside and checked her progress from time to time. Instructors questioned women's intentions and doubted their capabilities,

and they were often subjected to harassment and sexual innuendos.

Nancy Theberge (1993) shows how elite women coaches struggle to gain respect and acceptance within a profession heavily populated by and defined by men. Although their presence in this male preserve signals an impressive level of ability and perseverance—indeed a level of resistance to their total exclusion from these positions of leadership—women coaches struggle to be regarded as more than just token women within a male establishment. Unfortunately in coaching, as in athletic performance itself, an ideology of male superiority prevails, grounded on assumptions of the physical superiority of men in terms of strength and size. Women coaches must work overtime to challenge the misconceptions.

Another familiar example of women's struggles in the male preserve of sport is that of the women sports reporters who have had to fight to be admitted to men's locker rooms to do their jobs as reporters. Melissa Ludke was successful in 1979 in making major league baseball admit women reporters to the locker room (Angell, 1982). Lisa Olson's experience, discussed in chapter 21, demonstrates that Ludke's was an incomplete victory. These exclusionary practices have taken their toll on many women trainers, coaches, and reporters, but those who persevere serve as the role models for a new generation of women in sport.

The history of women in sport is replete with examples of the women who pioneered new roles for women in sport. Some women, such as Babe Didrikson Zaharias, have reached heroic proportions. Others, such as Eleanora Sears, achieve the less public status of folk legend. It is an indictment of our culture that many of these pioneering moments are still fresh in our minds, and most of us can still recall hearing about "the first" woman jockey, the first woman race car driver, the first woman umpire. Jean Balukas, "the best female billiards player in the world since 1972" (Nelson, 1991, pp. 18-19), did not begin playing in men's tournaments until 1987. Janet Guthrie first drove in the Indianapolis 500 in 1977. Barred from official participation in the Boston Marathon in 1967, Kathrine Switzer ran anyway. Women were not officially admitted until 1972.

Bernice Gera and Pam Postema were the first women to apply to umpire professional baseball. Gera was driven out of the game in 1972. In 1988 Postema had a tryout in the major leagues before being sent down; she subsequently filed suit charging sex discrimination. These women and many like them remain far too long as tokens of exemplary effort to transform the male preserve of sport. They serve as symbols of resistance and

Indianapolis Motor Speedway Corporation

Figure 22.2   Janet Guthrie, the first woman to drive in the Indianapolis 500.

perhaps reluctant accommodation by the dominant sporting establishment, but they are also reminders that real transformation is still a distant goal.

Legal Challenges

Legal remedies have represented the most public challenges to women's exclusion from sport. Many girls and women have had to resort to litigation to gain entry. In 1972, with the help of the National Organization for Women, 12-year-old Maria Pepe sued for the right to play Little League baseball in Hoboken, New Jersey; the next year she and her parents successfully petitioned Congress to open Little League for girls. Still, much indignity remains. Nancy Winnard, one of the first girls to play Little League baseball, was kicked out of a game for not wearing the required protective cup (Nelson, 1991), and Natasha Dennis, a 10-year-old soccer player from Texas, was subjected to the embarrassment of having two grown men claim she wasn't a girl and demand a strip search because her soccer skill was so impressive ("Dads want proof," 1990).

In 1969 Phyllis Graber earned the right to compete on the boys' tennis team in New York state, and in 1972 the Indiana Supreme Court ruled that the state high school athletic association could not bar girls from participating in noncontact sports on boys' teams (Nelson, 1991; Weber, 1974; Boutilier & SanGiovanni, 1983). Although still rare enough to be remarkable, girls now play on their high school football, baseball, and ice hockey teams and wrestle on the boys' team as well (Nelson, 1991).

Title IX of the Education Acts of 1972 and the Civil Rights Restoration Act of 1988 provide the legal grounding for many cases of gender equity in sport. In 1972 a group of college women in Florida filed suit against the AIAW's ban on scholarships for women; the result was a major change in the structure of athletic resources for women's intercollegiate athletics. Among the more famous class action suits is *Haffner v.*

Temple University (Wong, 1988). Filed in 1980 and delayed in court until it was finally decided in Haffner's favor in 1988, the case is important because it is an example of unselfish protest. By the time the court ruled that Temple had in fact discriminated against its female athletes, Rollin Haffner had graduated and could not personally benefit from the ruling. Legal remedies such as these are formal acts of resistance to dominant structures of sport. One may question, however, the extent to which these remedies work toward transformation rather than accommodation within existing structures and value systems.

Self-Conscious Protests

Another public form of resistance in sport is self-conscious political protest. In the sphere of women's sport, the most dramatic example is the confrontation between the women tennis players led by Billie Jean King, and Jack Kramer and the United States Lawn Tennis Association. The women's dissatisfaction with the gross inequity of prize money finally reached a critical level in 1970 when Kramer refused to restructure the purses for the Pacific Southwestern Championship. The women, who were to receive only one twelfth as much money as the men, boycotted the tournament. With King's support, Gladys Heldman organized an alternative tournament in Houston that went on to become the first event in the Virginia Slims Tour. This move changed the economic structure of women's professional tennis (King, 1974; Lichtenstein, 1974).

At the University of Iowa women's athletic director Christine Grant refuses to buy athletic shoes for her teams from companies that use conventions of soft-core pornography in their ads (and there are a disappointing number that do). Realizing that a silent boycott by one school has little effect, Grant also makes sure to write the companies a letter that clearly states her opinion of their advertising strategies.

A particularly notable example of public challenge is the women's resistance to the 1981 New

Zealand tour of the South African rugby team. As Shona Thompson (1988) recounts, women organized the massive campaign of protest against the South African team as a protest against that country's apartheid policy. Thompson argues that women's resentment of their own exclusion from the mainstream of male sport in New Zealand, particularly the male preserve of rugby, produced a consciousness of the politics of exclusion. Seeing a parallel in the exclusion of native Africans from the privileges and rights of their native land, the New Zealand women also recognized the usefulness of boycott as a political statement and tool.

Alternative Sport Forms

Another form that resistance to mainstream sport has historically taken is the creation of alternative cultural forms. In protest of the International Olympic Committee's untenable position that the Games are above politics, several groups have organized alternative celebrations of sport. These include the Women's Olympic Games (or Women's International Games), which were held from 1922 through 1934; the Workers' Olympiads "organized (in 1921) as a counter to the chauvinistic tendencies of the more well known modern Olympic Games and as an expression of international working-class solidarity" (Wheeler, 1978, p. 200); and the Gay Olympics organized in 1982, enjoined by court order from using the title Olympics in January 1986, which are now highly successful as the Gay Games.

The invention of the "playday" in the 1920s, though highly criticized in the decades that followed by girls who believed it stifled their competitive spirits, was a self-conscious effort to provide a model of sport for women that avoided the pitfalls of men's sport. The women who met with Lou Henry Hoover at the White House in 1923 and came up with the famous platform for the conduct of girls' and women's sport and the famous saying, "A sport for every girl and every

girl in a sport," were working to replace the overcommercialized, elite sporting practices endorsed by the predominantly male athletics establishment. That they replaced that corrupt (male) form with a form that repressed the women they sought to serve does not undermine the act as an act of resistance. Indeed, to the dismay of many women who came after, they did succeed in transforming girls' and women's sport. Today's criticism of their actions lies in the fact that although their blueprint for change was properly grounded in a critique of the male practice of sport, the remedy they endorsed was grounded in some rather questionable essentialistic assumptions about the nature of women.

Fifty years later, women physical educators' commitment to finding alternative sport forms that did not mimic the dominant model practiced by men resulted in the founding of the Association for Intercollegiate Athletics for Women (AIAW). According to Bonnie Slatton (1982), the AIAW represented the greening, i.e., revitalization, of American sport. Slatton and other AIAW leaders saw that organization as an agent for change in intercollegiate athletics. Kristin Burns (1987) documented how that change was manifested in the leadership styles that emerged from this alternative sporting structure. She found that the presidents of the AIAW were characterized by qualities not generally discussed in mainstream leadership theory: a commitment to fairness, even at the expense of self-interest; an extraordinary sense of mission to the organization; an open and trusting style; and a commitment to shared leadership. This last quality is particularly interesting. These women were uncomfortable with traditional ideas of power, preferring to see power as a resource to be shared with others.

With the demise of the AIAW, the possibility of alternative models for women's sport at the institutional level looks considerably dimmer. Moreover, although the historical examples of the playday era and the AIAW provide important instances of distinctly different visions of women's sport, they offer little guidance for the practices that women bring to the contemporary situation where women's sport is not a separate sphere but is controlled by men and subjected to increasing pressures to adopt the values and orientations of mainstream sport. Women in leadership positions today face an even greater challenge to resist the dominant model and effect an alternative model and vision of sport.

Nancy Theberge (1987, 1990) explored this challenge in a study of the careers of 49 women coaches in Canada. Theberge found that these coaches, like the AIAW presidents Burns (1987) studied, had a vision of leadership that rejected a conception of power as dominance in favor of a vision of coaching as empowering. The differences between the two groups are quite instructive. The AIAW presidents were guided by a clearly articulated feminist critique of traditional leadership roles and mainstream models of sport. Because they governed women's athletics in a sphere separate from direct male interference, they enjoyed greater freedom to realize alternative values and forms. In contrast, the coaches in Theberge's study were not in a position to enact alternative models. Their dilemma lay in their attempts to realize an alternative practice of power while accepting the legitimacy of the institution that sanctions traditional sport practices.

Perhaps sporting opportunities outside the mainstream of institutionalized sport hold greater promise for the realization of alternative and resistant sport forms. Libby Wheatley (1994) has explored women's rugby clubs as sites where women consciously rebel against cultural definitions of appropriate sporting practices for women. In their appropriation of the exaggeratedly masculine rituals of men's rugby, particularly the singing of outrageously lewd lyrics of male drinking songs, female rugby players deliver a strong message of rebellion: Women can penetrate even the "malest" of male preserves. Their intrusion into the rugby subculture deconstructs that space and those practices as quintessential male practices. Moreover, by changing the lyrics to express and celebrate lesbian sexuality, women rugby players

go even further to disturb the alliance between masculine hegemony and heterosexual privilege.

Finally, Susan Birrell and Diana Richter (1987) show how feminists reappropriated a previously alienating sport form and, through conscious intervention, transformed it into an experience that had meaning in their own lives. These feminists enacted a form of softball that was suffused with the following counterhegemonic practices: an emphasis on the process of play that rejects sport as a rational practice; an inclusiveness that insists on providing opportunities for women of all sizes, ages, classes, and races, and a safe space for those who have not had an opportunity to develop their skills; collective coaching practices that deconstruct the hierarchical relationship between player and coach; and a refusal to see the opponent as other.

The examples above are meant to document, albeit somewhat anecdotally, a range of resistant practices in sport. We argue that although it may be useful to celebrate the spirit of such actions, it is important not to romanticize them, for resistance is not transformation. Premature or naive celebrations of resistance may undermine the motivation for transformation. Moreover, although resistance produces its own positive outcomes, partial victories are ultimately not satisfying. Resistance, in and of itself, is not change, and change is the goal of political action. Rather than indulging in "the romance of resistance," as Abu-Lughod (1989) aptly calls it, we must tackle the more difficult theoretical and practical tasks of exploring the relationship of resistance to power.

Contesting Resistance

Resistance is never wholly successful, nor does it always, or even often, result in transformation. Just as hegemony and dominance are always contested and in need of maintenance, so resistance is hard won and must constantly be shored up and maintained. The greatest danger to transformation is reincorporation: the pull of dominant forces to recapture dissidents, rebels, and resisters. As a result of these struggles for reproduction, resistance, transformation, and recapture, a major theoretical and practical debate revolves around the recognition of resistance or transformation; that is, when has a disenfranchised group or person triumphed, and when is it only contained within the illusion of triumph?

Florence Griffith-Joyner's engaging and dramatic flair for style is a good example of this shifting dynamic, as Alison Dewar (1991) also has argued. Griffith-Joyner creates, produces, and even markets an image of herself as a self-conscious agent; yet she does so within the dominant discourses on gender, race, sexuality, class, age, and ableism. Like Griffith-Joyner, no matter

Figure 22.3   Florence Griffith-Joyner.

how flashy and apparently original our self-styling, we never get outside these discourses. But we can be conscious of them and attempt to modify and use them to our own advantage, as Griffith-Joyner does.

The fitness movement offers another example of the struggle for dominance, resistance and incorporation. Since the mid-1970s the fitness boom has offered women an opportunity to build their bodily strength and feel more comfortable with and more powerful in their bodies. But as many analyses have demonstrated (Birrell & Theberge, 1989; Endel, 1991; Duncan, 1990; Duncan & Hasbrook, 1988), the early images of strength and control have been replaced with images of women as objects of heterosexual desire, produced with the advertising techniques of soft-core pornography. How are we to understand our involvement in such an activity?

Doubts over the "reality" of resistance or the possibilities of transformation can work to undercut our motivation for change. We should not discount the gains and triumphs of women, even when those achievements have later suffered serious setbacks. At the same time, we should be aware that apparently liberatory actions and activities can contain us in ideological moments that oppress us. Why do we work so hard to become fit? Is it ever really for ourselves as women and people? How can we ever be sure that we are freely acting agents, acting in our own best interests? Like Florence Griffith-Joyner, we cannot control the circumstances of our actions. We always take action within cultural constraints; our actions are always understood by ourselves and others within the meanings that dominant discourses of sex, gender, sexuality, class, race, etc., make available for us. We are in that sense always culturally contained, but we are not completely imprisoned.

Discussing the "everyday forms of Bedouin women's resistance" and trying to work through the difficult issues of resistance and power, Abu-Lughod (1989) asks:

© ALLSPORT USA/B. Spurlock

How might we develop theories that give these women credit for resisting in a variety of creative ways the power of those who control so much of their lives, without either misattributing to them forms of consciousness or politics that are not part of their experience—something like a feminist consciousness or feminist politics—or devaluing their practices as prepolitical, primitive, or even misguided? (p. 47)

This difficult issue requires careful examination.

Resistance as Discourse

The relative strength of dominant and resistant forces, and how to recognize the differences, is presently a major debate in cultural studies. The problem, as Abu-Lughod (1989) sees it, is caused by "the popularity of resistance." Scholars have responded to a tradition of analysis grounded in models of oppression by reconceptualizing relations of power and recasting cultural dupes as crafty agents of resistance. Recently the pendulum of theory has begun to moderate, and the uncritical celebration of resistance is being examined more closely (Gruneau, 1988a; Abu-Lughod, 1989; Budd, Entman, & Steinman, 1990).

For the most part these debates have focused on questions about the nature of resistant acts. Can an act be immediately recognized and known as resistant? Are some acts resistant by their very nature? Or are all human acts, however motivated, regardless of intention and consciousness, texts open to the interpretation and labeling of the reader? Such questions reflect wider debates in cultural studies with regard to the meaning and interpretation of written text. Where one analysis (McRobbie, 1982) focuses on the containment of adolescent girls by teenage magazines that on the surface appear to reproduce dominant notions of patriarchy, other analyses (Frazer, 1987; Winship, 1985) of the same texts and interactions are more

willing to view the readers as agents with some ability to use the texts in their own interests.

Are the preferred readings that are supposedly encoded in the text the same messages the reader decodes? Where does the power to make meaning reside: with the producer, the text, or the reader? What is at stake is the ontological status of the text and the relative power of the consumer to act as an agent. When human action is the text the situation is further confused, for the producer and the text are merged.

These debates require careful attention, for they have theoretical and practical consequences. They shift the focus from whether an act is resistant or transformative to how an act counts as resistant or transformative. Recognizing, acknowledging, and labeling resistance is an exercise of authority, dominance, and struggle. What cultural criteria surround those judgments? What is the dominant cultural discourse on the nature of resistance and transformation, and whose ends are served by finding or denying resistance? In short, what are the political stakes?

Anthropologist Emily Martin (1990) is skeptical about the resistance to resistance movement in her field. She argues that such smug certainty that change is always recuperated is politically immobilizing and self-defeating. But we need equally to guard against premature celebrations of resistance, particularly in a culture of advanced hegemonic sophistication in which social changes, when they occur, are gradual and liberal, rather than sweeping, radical, and revolutionary.

When a woman athlete, mercilessly harassed by the men on the opposing team, throws down her mitt, leaves the field in tears, and refuses to play again, what are we to make of her actions? Is this an act of resistance, cowardice, or desperation? She confronts a particularly obnoxious taunter, is thrown out of the game, and her team—short handed—loses by forfeit. Is this an act of resistance or desperation? Is she a victim, a martyr, a hero, or a fool? Where can we go for answers to these questions? Does the athlete herself have the answers? Although she may have produced the act, she is not the only owner of the act's meaning. Will future events help reveal the "meaning" of these events? What does it mean if she goes home and never comes back? What does it mean if she becomes a spokesperson for the rights of women to play in men's leagues? What does it mean if, against her will or even without her knowledge, she becomes the symbol for a movement against such harassment in sport? The meaning of an act, the definition, the judgment of an act as resistant or transformative are never closed, never complete, never finished. Behavior and its products are like a text open to diverse readings.

This line of reasoning moves us dangerously close to the postmodern romance with the impossibility of certainty, completion, and closure. To move to one postmodern conclusion, there is no real resistance. How an act (of resistance) is read, in what context, and toward what end are more culturally important than the actor's intention. The act itself and the intention of its producer fade into the background because the act's publicness, its openness to spectation and speculation, render it not an act but the subject of a discourse. The contest over the meaning of that act is in every way a political event. The issue then becomes not whether an act is resistant, but which vested interests claim the act as resistant and which demand that it be understood as hopeless capitulation. The struggle then is over what counts as resistance and who has the power to decide.

In the end, we can never know if we truly are acting in our own best interests or if the subtle tools of pleasure and deception are enfolding us even more deeply into relationships that favor the dominant group. Realizing that the knowledge of our conditions has been incomplete or in error could lead us to despair; however, it is more useful if we choose instead to renew our commitment to social action and to a thoughtful analysis of the political outcomes of our actions.

Summary and Conclusions

In this chapter we have discussed sport as an important site for fighting gender oppression and contesting gender relations. We also have emphasized some of the theoretical debates that have emerged in discussions regarding what constitutes resistance and transformation in sport and society at large. Although we need to be aware of such debates, we should not be disempowered by them. Although troubling, they are ultimately empowering because they address and enlighten a more subtle level of power and hegemony. If we worry about whether our actions will truly matter, we will censure ourselves and take no risks, and inimical power relationships will be reproduced without the dominant group having to lift a finger to maintain its control over us. This is one manifestation of hegemonic control. Instead we might take a lesson from the women discussed in this chapter and find our own way to protest, oppose, rebel, empower, persist, subvert, sabotage, disrupt, and transform patriarchial sport forms and the gender relations they reproduce.

References

Abu-Lughod, L. (1989). The romance of resistance: Tracing transformations of power through Bedouin women. *American Ethnologist*, 41-45.

Anderson, M. (1991). *Pioneer women athletic trainers*. Unpublished dissertation, University of Iowa.

Angell, R. (1982). Sharing the beat. *Late innings: A baseball companion*. New York: Simon & Schuster.

Birrell, S., & Richter, D. (1987). Is a diamond forever: Feminist transformations of sport. *Women's Studies International Forum*, **10**, 395-409.

Birrell, S., & Theberge, N. (1989, November). *Packaging fitness: Women and the fitness boom*. Paper presented at the meeting of the North American Society for the Sociology of Sport, Washington, DC.

Boutilier, M. & SanGiovanni, L. (1983). *The sporting woman*. Champaign, IL: Human Kinetics.

Brohm, J.M. (1978). *Sport: A prison of measured time*. London: Ink Links.

Budd, M., Entman, R., & Steinman, C. (1990). The affirmative character of U.S. cultural studies. *Critical studies in mass communication*, **7**, 169-184.

Burns, K. (1987). *Reconstructing leadership experiences: Toward a feminist theory of leadership*. Unpublished doctoral dissertation, University of Iowa.

Cole, C. & Birrell, S. (1986, November). *Resisting the canon: Feminist cultural studies*. Paper presented at the meeting of the North American Society for the Sociology of Sport, Edmonton, AB.

Dads want proof soccer star is a girl. (1990, October 20). *Des Moines Register*, p. 1S.

Dewar, A. (1991). Incorporation or resistance? Towards an analysis of women's response to sexual oppression in sport. *International Review of Sociology of Sport*, **26**, 15-23.

Donnelly, P. (1988). Sport as a site for "popular" resistance. In R. Gruneau (Ed.), *Popular cultures and political practices*, pp. 69-82. Toronto: Garamond Press.

Duncan, M. C. (1990). Sport photographs and sexual difference: Images of women and men in the 1984 and 1988 Olympic Games. *Sociology of Sport Journal*, **7**, 22-43.

Duncan, M. C., & Hasbrook, C. A. (1988). Denial of power in televised women's sports. *Sociology of Sport Journal*, **5**(1), 1-21.

Endel, B. (1991). *Working out: The dialectic of strength and sexuality in Women's Sports and Fitness magazine*. Unpublished doctoral dissertation, University of Iowa.

Felshin, J. (1991, February). *Historical notes on women's participation*. Paper presented at the Girls and Women in Sport Symposium. Slippery Rock University, Slippery Rock, PA.

Fox, J.R. (1961). Pueblo baseball: A new use for old witchcraft. *Journal of American Folklore*, **74**, 9-16.

Frazer, E. (1987). Teenage girls reading Jackie. *Media, culture and society*, **9**, 407-425.

Geertz, C. (1973). *The interpretation of cultures*. New York: Basic Books.

Gerber. E. (1974). *Chronicle of participation*. In E. Gerber, J. Felshin, P. Berlin, & W. Wyrick (Eds.), *The American woman in sport* (pp. 3-176). Reading, MA: Addison-Wesley.

Gruneau, R. (1983). *Class, sports and social development*. Amherst: University of Massachusetts Press.

Gruneau, R. (1988a). Introduction: Notes on popular culture and political practice. In R. Gruneau (Ed.), *Popular cultures and political practices* (pp. 11-32). Toronto: Garamond Press.

Gruneau, R. (1988b). Modernization or hegemony: Two views on sport and social development. In J. Harvey & R. Gruneau (Eds.), *Not just a game* (pp. 9-32). Ottawa, ON: University of Ottawa Press.

Hargreaves, J. (1986). *Sport, power and culture*. New York: St. Martin's Press.

Hoch, P. (1972). *Rip off the big game*. New York: Anchor Books.

King, B.J., with Chapin, K.. (1974). *Billie Jean*. New York: Pocket Books.

Lichtenstein, G. (1974). *A long way, baby*. Greenwich, CT: Fawcett.

Martin, E. (1990, September 17). *Medical metaphors of conception*. Unpublished lecture presented during the Women's Studies Program lecture series, Theorizing the Body, University of Iowa.

McRobbie, A. (1982). *Jackie: An ideology of adolescent femininity*. In B. Waites, T. Bennett, & G. Martin (Eds.), *Popular culture: Past and present* (pp. 263-283). London: Croom Helm.

Messner, M. (1988). Sports and male domination: The female athlete as contested ideological terrain. *Sociology of Sport Journal*, **5**, 3.

Nelson, M.B., (1991). *Are we winning yet? How women are changing sport and sport is changing women*. New York: Random House.

Novak, M. (1976). *The Joy of Sports*. New York: Basic Books.

Oberlander, S. (1989, June). Advocates for women's sports say 1988 Civil-Rights Act has not brought hoped-for equity with men. *Chronicle of Higher Education*, **21**, A23-A24.

Prendergrast, S. (1978). Stoolball: The pursuit of vertigo? *Women's Studies International Quarterly*, **1**, 15-26.

Scott, J.C. (1985). *Weapons of the weak: Everyday forms of peasant resistance*. New Haven, CT: Yale University Press.

Slatton, B. (1982). AIAW: The greening of American athletics. In J. Frey (Ed.), *The governance of intercollegiate athletics* (pp. 144-154). West Point, NY: Leisure Press.

Theberge, N. (1987, November). *Feminist change and the mobility of women to leadership positions in sport: The case of coaching*. Paper presented at the meeting of the North American Society for the Sociology of Sport, Edmonton, AB.

Theberge, N. (1990). Gender work and power: The case of women in coaching. *Canadian Journal of Sociology*, **15**, 59-75.

Theberge, N. (1993). The construction of gender in sport: Women, coaching, and the naturalization of difference. *Social Problems*, **40**(3), 301-313.

Thompson, S. (1988). Challenging the hegemony: New Zealand women's opposition to rugby and the reproduction of a capitalist patriarchy. *International Review of Sociology of Sport*, **23**, 205-212.

Weber, Ellen. (1974, September). Revolution in women's sports. *WomenSport*, 33-56.

Wheatley, E. (1994). Stylish ensembles on a different pitch. In S. Birrell & C. Cole (Eds.), *Women, sport, and culture*. Champaign, IL: Human Kinetics.

Wheeler, R. (1978). Organized sport and organized labour. *Journal of contemporary history*, **13**, 191-210.

Winship, J. (1985). A girl needs to get streetwise: Magazines for the 1980's. *Feminist Review*, **21**, 27-46.

Wong, G. (1988, June). Congress puts bite back in Title IX. *Athletic Business*, 16-17.

Index

About the Editors

D. Margaret Costa

Sharon R. Guthrie

D. Margaret Costa, PhD, is the director of Interdisciplinary Studies at California State University–Long Beach. A professor of Physical Education and Women's Studies, Dr. Costa has taught courses on women in sport at CSULB for more than 10 years and has long been involved in promoting the women's sport experience as a serious area of study in sport history.

Dr. Costa is the author of numerous scholarly articles on women in sport and has made presentations on the subject before members of more than a dozen professional associations in the United States and abroad. Her co-authored article comparing women's sports competition in the 1980s in southern California, the USSR, and Jordan led the way for many cross-national studies of women's sports throughout the world. Dr. Costa's most recent research focused on the sporting experiences of Japanese-American women in the 1930s and 1940s. In her leisure time Dr. Costa enjoys running and playing golf.

Sharon R. Guthrie, PhD, has been an assistant professor in the Physical Education Department at California State University–Long Beach since 1990. Her teaching specialties include sport psychology and sociology, as well as courses related to women in sport.

A native of southern California, Dr. Guthrie received her doctorate in 1985 from The Ohio State University and taught at DePaul University in Chicago from 1986-1990. She wrote the first master's thesis on the impact of homophobia on women in sport and physical education (1982) and the first doctoral dissertation examining eating disorders among collegiate athletes (1985). Since then, she has published several articles and book chapters on issues related to women in sport. A former member of the UCLA varsity tennis team and a competitive racquetball player, Dr. Guthrie is an avid yet noncompetitive bodybuilder.

About the Authors

Joan Carles Arce is a clinical scientist. He is currently working in the International Clinical Development Department of LIPHA in Lyon, France.

Susan Birrell is a professor in the Department of Sport, Health, Leisure and Physical Studies at the University of Iowa. She also is the chair of the school's Women's Studies Program. Birrell holds a PhD in human movement with a concentration in sociology of sport from the University of Massachusetts at Amherst. She is co-editor of the book *Sport in the Sociocultural Process* and a former editorial board member for the *Sociology of Sport Journal*.

John Marshall Carter received a PhD in history from the University of Illinois at Urbana-Champaign. He has taught both in public secondary schools and in universities. He has published numerous books and articles on sports history and recently was invited to be listed in *Contemporary Authors*. His latest book is *Medieval Games*.

Shirley Castelnuovo is a professor of political science at Northeastern Illinois University, where she teaches courses in political and legal theory with a particular focus on feminism and racism. Her articles have appeared in *Play and Culture*, *The Oral History Review*, *Jewish Political Studies Review*; and in *Japanese Americans: From Relocation to Redress* (ed. Daniels, Taylor, & Kitano) and *Research in Law and Sociology* (ed. Spitzer). She is currently collaborating on a book, *Liberating the Amazon: Feminism and the Reconstruction of Female Embodiment* with Sharon Guthrie (Lynne Reinner Publishers, 1995).

Mary Jane De Souza is an assistant professor in the Division of Reproductive Endocrinology and Infertility at the University of Connecticut Health Center, Farmington, Connecticut. Dr. De Souza is Director of the Women's Health, Exercise and Reproduction Center at the University, which focuses on health concerns of women of all ages. Her main area of research is in the effects of exercise training on reproductive function in female and male athletes. Dr. De Souza has published widely in this area in several peer-reviewed journals and books. She is also a Fellow of the American College of Sports Medicine.

Mary E. Duquin is an associate professor at the University of Pittsburgh. She received her PhD from Stanford University in 1975, specializing in the psychosocial aspects of sport. She has served as President of the North American Society for the Sociology of Sport and Chairperson of the Sport Sociology Academy. Her writings and research have blended psychological, sociological, and philosophical perspectives on gender issues in sport. Her most recent work has focused on advocating and implementing an ethic of care in sport.

Lynne Emery is a professor in the Department of Kinesiology and Health Promotion at California State Polytechnic University, Pomona, where she teaches sport history. She graduated from Bowling Green State University and earned an MS in physical education/dance at the University of Southern California. Her major research area is the history of women in sport. She is the author of *Black Dance in the United States from 1619 to Today* (1971; 2d ed., 1988).

Patty Freedson is an exercise physiologist in the Department of Exercise Science at the University of Massachusetts-Amherst. She holds an adjunct associate professor position in the Department of Medicine at the University of Massachusetts Medical Center-Worcester. She has published over 70 papers and given over 100 presentations on a variety of topics in exercise physiology, including women in sport and children and exercise. She is a fellow of both the American College of Sports Medicine and the Research Consortium of the American Alliance of Health, Physical Education, Recreation, and Dance.

Diane L. Gill is a professor in the Department of Exercise and Sport Science and Associate Dean of the School of Health and Human Performance at the University of North Carolina at Greensboro. She has published over 50 research articles, several book chapters, and the book, *Psychological Dynamics of Sport*. Her teaching and research focus on the social psychological aspects of sport and exercise. She is a former Editor of the *Journal of Sport & Exercise Psychology*, Past-President of NASPSPA, and a fellow in AAASP, American Academy of Kinesiology and Physical Education, and Division 47 of APA.

Jackie L. Hudson is a movement analyst and feminist. As a pre-teen in Gruver, Texas, she taught herself the fall-away jump shot by observing and imitating older players, and she was denied the opportunity to compete in youth-league baseball because she was female. Decades and degrees later, she is still absorbed with the mechanical forces that enable skillful movement and the social forces that inhibit it. Jackie teaches biomechanics at California State University-Chico.

Joan S. Hult is Professor of Kinesiology and Affiliate Professor of Women's Studies at the University of Maryland, College Park. She was a national officer and executive board member of the AIAW, a national basketball and volleyball official, coach of five different varsity sports over

20 years, and a semi-professional basketball and softball player. She has received the Educationalist Award from the USOA, and has been a member of the USOC, an honor fellow of the NAGWS, a Hoover Scholar, and a Research Fellow of AAHPERD. She has written extensively and presented over 100 papers on women Olympians, sport governance, women's athletics, and physical education, including being co-editor of *A Century of Women's Basketball from Frailty to Final Four*.

June Kennard is an associate professor of Physical Education at Towson State University in Baltimore, Maryland. She has written in and teaches courses in history, sociology, and philosophy of sport. She has been involved in women's studies for more than 20 years. She has a deep affection for the ancient world as well as gardening, traveling, and dancing.

Deborah A. Metzger, PhD, MD, is an associate professor of Obstetrics and Gynecology at the University of Connecticut Health Center in Farmington, Connecticut. Her specialty is Reproductive Endocrinology and Infertility.

John C. Nulsen, MD, is an associate professor of Obstetrics and Gynecology at the University of Connecticut Health Center. His specialty is Reproductive Endocrinology and Infertility.

Roberta J. Park is a professor and former Chair of the Department of Human Biodynamics at the University of California, Berkeley. She has been President of the American Academy of Kinesiology and Physical Education, Vice President of the International Society for the History of Physical Education and Sport, and an officer in numerous other organizations. Her research focuses upon the history of the biological sciences as these pertain to exercise, physical education, and health—and the history of sport in the United States and Europe. *Sport and Exercise Science: Essays in the History of Sports Medicine* (with Jack W. Berryman) and *Play, Games, and Sports in Cultural Contexts* (with Janet C. Harris) are among Professor Park's many publications. She served for sixteen years as the women's field hockey coach at the University of California and has competed in that sport in Australia, New Zealand, and Mexico.

Catriona M. Parratt received a Master's degree in Human Kinetics from the University of Windsor, Ontario, in 1985 and a PhD from The Ohio State University in 1994. A U.K. native, her doctoral dissertation focuses on the topic of gender and working class sport and leisure in late Victorian and Edwardian England. She is a visiting lecturer in sport history in the Department of Physical Education and Sports Studies at the University of Iowa, where she teaches undergraduate and graduate courses in sport history. Her research interests are the British working class and women's culture, sport, and leisure.

Jacqueline L. Puhl is an exercise scientist. She is currently in the Division of General Internal Medicine at Rhode Island Hospital, Providence, Rhode Island.

Nancy L. Struna is an associate professor in the Department of Kinesiology and an affiliate faculty member in the Department of History at the University of Maryland, College Park. She teaches both the social history of sport and colonial history, and most of her research and writing has focused on colonial and early national America and early modern Britain. She is currently completing a book on sport and recreations in the context of the changing relationships between labor and leisure in early America. Nancy is involved in numerous historical organizations, including the North American Society for Sport History, of which she is president-elect.

Nancy Theberge is a professor at the University of Waterloo, where she holds a joint appointment in the Department of Kinesiology and Sociology and is Chair of the Advisory Board of the Women's Studies Program. She holds a PhD in sociology from the University of Massachusetts at Amherst. Her main areas of research are gender relations and the sociology of the body.

Patricia Vertinsky is a professor in the School of Human Kinetics at the University of British Columbia in Vancouver, Canada. She has published widely in books and journals on gender relations and the history of science and medicine related to embodiment, health, sport, and physical activity. She is the author of *The Eternally Wounded Woman: Women, Doctors, and Exercise in the Late Nineteenth Century* (University of Manchester Press, 1990) and is on the editorial board of numerous sport history, sport sociology, and physical education journals.

Paula Welch is a professor of Exercise and Sport Sciences at the University of Florida. She completed degrees at the Florida State University, George Peabody College for Teachers, and the University of North Carolina at Greensboro. Her post-doctoral work has included the Institute for Irish Studies at Trinity College in Dublin, Ireland and the History Department at the University of Florida. In addition to numerous articles and research presentations, she serves as Vice-Chair of the Education Committee of the United States Olympic Committee.